MY COUNTRY

Stories, Essays & Speeches

DAVID MARR

MY COUNTRY

*Stories,
Essays &
Speeches*

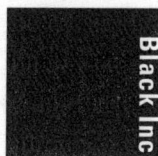

Black Inc.

Published by Black Inc.,
an imprint of Schwartz Books Pty Ltd
Wurundjeri Country
22–24 Northumberland Street
Collingwood VIC 3066, Australia
enquiries@blackincbooks.com
www.blackincbooks.com

9781760645281 (paperback)
9781743820674 (ebook)

NATIONAL LIBRARY OF AUSTRALIA   A catalogue record for this book is available from the National Library of Australia

Book design by Tristan Main
Typesetting by Beau Lowenstern
"Harry Seidler Retirement Park" (p. 126) by Patrick Cook, reproduced with permission
of the artist

Printed in Australia by McPherson's Printing Group.

MIX
Paper | Supporting responsible forestry
FSC® C001695

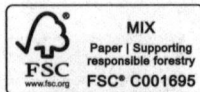

Contents

Arts and Artists

Skin in the Game

Australia Under Howard

Pink Pages

Table for Two

Back in Safe Hands

To my editors, brutes and angels for fifty years. Thank you.

MY COUNTRY IS THE SUBJECT THAT interests me most, and I have spent my career trying to untangle its mysteries. I studied law but couldn't imagine being a lawyer. Curiosity, mischief and exasperation made me a journalist. At a difficult point in my twenties I accepted I was gay. That made me, in those days, a criminal. Wanting to understand my country came, right from the start, with wanting it to change. I had a naive notion that change would come simply by setting out the facts with clarity and goodwill. I had a lot to learn.

As a rookie on *The Bulletin* I watched Gough Whitlam crash and burn. The lessons I learnt then have never left me. First, the true radicals in Australia are those who call themselves conservative. Conventions mean nothing to them if they stand in the way of power. They'll bet the house for power. Second, Australians are a practical people: we lived with the discomfort of great principles violated to see Whitlam gone. Down the track another complicated truth about this country became clear: we fight change hard here – often brutally hard – but the leaders we come to admire most are reformers.

I wrote a life of Garfield Barwick, chief justice and key conspirator in the scandal of 1975. By that time, I'd been a few years on *The National Times* writing about law, the arts and politics. I was the paper's editor at thirty-three. It ended unhappily. Writing once more for the paper, I saw out the Fraser years before making a leap in the dark: I began writing the life and editing the letters of Patrick White. He looked this country in the eye. To keep body and soul together in that decade, I worked on and off as a reporter for *Four Corners* and sometimes wrote the Clancy column in *The National Times*.

I was never going back to newspapers. But after a couple of years presenting *Arts Today* on Radio National I was lured to *The Sydney Morning Herald* just as John Howard came to power. There was work to do. The dark angels of this country were being roused once more by a politician of consummate skill. Stopping the *Tampa* was the signature act of this prime minister – Marian Wilkinson and I wrote about his battle with the boats in the book *Dark Victory* – but right from the start Howard played on this country's unease with race. He brought a dirty game back to Canberra and Australia rewarded him.

I presented *Media Watch* for three years from 2002. This plunged me into the culture wars, that faux conflict fought on American lines to prove the evils of progress. I returned to the *Herald* more determined than before to explore the true obstacles to progress in my country. I wrote a good deal about the Tory press, political censorship, the enemies of rights, and campaigns still being waged by the faiths against sex. Why, I wonder, is a secular, educated, prosperous and decent country so prey to fear and capable of such cruelty? Why are we ruled from the edges?

I was given a seat from time to time on the *Insiders* couch. I began writing Quarterly Essays: brief lives of Howard, Rudd, Abbott, Shorten, Hanson and George Pell. More than ever I was convinced that character is the great neglected subject in politics. I wrote occasionally for *The Monthly*. In the dying days of the Gillard government, I left *The Sydney Morning Herald* for *The Guardian*.

Labor crashed. Abbott came and went. So did Turnbull and Morrison. Albanese is there now, decent enough but timid. Over the last decade or so, faith in our political parties collapsed. Voters need to be in their forties to remember the last time Canberra addressed and solved any of the country's big problems. Yet I still have this unshakeable faith that in the end Australia gets so much right. The pity is that the way is hard and it takes so long.

I've written hundreds of thousands of words. I can't claim they've had much impact on the country I once thought I knew but find I am still getting to know. This is a collection of a few pieces written over fifty years that I hope make sense of the place.

AUGUST 2024

Personal Details

Shame and forgiveness

I WAS FOURTEEN, STANDING ON THE DECK of the ferry wearing a snazzy pair of white pants as it chugged across Port Hacking towards Camp Howard. What I couldn't admit to myself then is what I most vividly remember now: the erotic charge in the air. It was frightening and compelling. That week of messing about in the bush, swimming in deserted bays, sleeping out and listening to the Word was suffused with the promise of sex. Nothing happened but a lot happened. Some of it was ludicrous. One night in the dining hall we were given a sex education lecture. The slides weren't of men and women but chooks. I still remember a cross-section of tubes and eggs, and awkward talk of reproduction as that hen glowed on the screen.

Afterwards, over cocoa – here's the point – a serious, handsome young man spoke intimately to a dozen or so of us about committing ourselves to Christ. I was deeply drawn to the idea of a man who could love me knowing all my faults, indeed who could love me for my faults, even for the worst of them. One day I would need to be saved, but Judgement Day seemed a long way off in 1961. On that night and at that moment I needed to fall in love, and here was this counsellor – a radio sports commentator in later life – telling me there was a man available: Christ. By a miracle that seemed obvious then, Christ would satisfy me and cure me and protect me from the worst fears I held for myself. I didn't have the courage to come forward over cocoa. Two did. I piked. But as I walked back to the tent I shared with half a dozen other boys on the edge of the bush, it struck me that I had committed myself at that moment to Christ. The future would be different now, pure, thrilling and safe.

The school chaplain had already been pursuing my soul for years, hammering on about sin and salvation. Three times a week we assembled in the chapel to be taught the only lesson Anglican schools in Sydney teach thoroughly: the need for all us awful human beings to be Forgiven. I wasn't convinced. There didn't seem anything worth forgiving, until sex came along. Uneasiness at thirteen was turning to shame at fourteen. This was the raw material I took across the water to Camp Howard. I couldn't have been the only one. We were there to be recruited and the counsellors knew what they were doing, setting us free in that stretch of bush and talking sin at the same time. They challenged us to take Christ into our hearts, but that first required deep acknowledgement of shame. First shame and then forgiveness. That's their business.

You don't have to be a young queer for this to work. There's a trace of self-disgust in most of us that can be worked up into shame, especially in those most difficult, precious years when we are on the threshold of sex. But a young homosexual is particularly easy pickings, fearful of himself, his family and the disapproval of his world. Christ offers a gay kid consummation of a kind, strength to resist sin, the minor heroics of teenage self-sacrifice, and a chance – important for children living day-to-day with an undertow of shame – to do good. That was the Christ I took into my life at the age of fourteen. It was a kind of falling in love, tepid compared with the real thing when that came along, but it was love nevertheless. What followed were a dozen wasted and painful years. I wasn't very brave. My circumstances weren't desperate and I got out the other side with most of myself intact. But it's left me unable to forgive those Christians who are still at work, inflicting misery on kids.

Where does shame come from? I look back to my childhood and can't remember anything being said. My parents had no idea what was happening. Children like me were bred in other suburbs to other families. Homosexuality was a vice too dark for the Anglican Church to condemn. All I heard from the pulpit were grim hints. I vaguely knew the Crimes Act promised a decade or so in the slammer and once in a while the afternoon papers had appalling stories of citizens caught in lavatories. The only instruction my school ever gave me came when I was seventeen and the senior year was in the assembly hall for a talk by the school doctor. It wasn't much of an advance on cross-sections of chooks. "You can tell a homosexual," Dr Day said, and by my calculation about a dozen boys must, like me, have frozen with curiosity and terror. "You can tell them by the décor of their flats."

Though this advice has not been entirely useless ...

Silence was the most potent source of shame in my childhood. Preachers like Fred Nile claim Christians have the right to keep their children "wrapped in cotton wool" and campaign for the state to collaborate in that. For years I used to scoff at the pointlessness of trying to keep the young innocent in this way. My answer to the Fred Niles was that, try as they might, our subversive bodies will always tell us the truth. But I was missing the point. What censorship is really designed to achieve is the sort of silence that turns what our bodies tell us into shame. This calls for more than censorship of books and films. It also needs the censorship of learning. Those many Christians who still oppose sex education use the rhetoric of intimacy, innocence and faith. What they're fundamentally about is cultivating shame.

If the clergy I met while I was a keen young Christian had been a more inspiring lot, I might have joined them. I was a shame-driven kid hungry for a spiritual life, but all I heard were Sydney Anglicans hammering out their formula for salvation. Even so, I thought a lot about joining the church in the year or so after Camp Howard. My reasons were muddled, but strong in the confusion was a sense that the church might be somewhere to shelter while I set myself right. It would be a respected response to my troubles. A cover and a cure. But I knew so little of what service to a church might mean; all I saw was the prospect of Anglican boredom for the rest of my life. My vocation was stillborn.

Talking to priests and ex-priests, trying to puzzle out why men commit their lives to religion, I heard over and again the familiar note of gay shame. Often it was deeply hidden or entirely disguised at the time it was doing its work. At first glance it seems an incongruous way of dealing with vilification to join the church of the vilifiers. But that's the beauty of shame. It drives you inwards towards the pain because somewhere in there is also the promise of relief. The churches offer pain and shame, but provide the mechanism of forgiveness and relief. Catholicism differs from other churches only in offering guilty young men the supreme reassurance of celibacy. For those who fear their sexuality, that vow of abstinence for life looms like a bulwark against temptation.

At some point after Camp Howard I made a solemn pact that by the time I left school for university I would stop feeling this way. I devised a number of spiritual exercises to make certain. These included prayer, daily Bible reading, eating, staying clear of the beach and not letting thoughts of men come into my mind when I wanked. Keeping a blank mind while masturbating seemed a significant moral achievement. There was one image I had trouble keeping out: Johnny M. diving into a creek at cadet camp. His body hung in the air for a moment, naked and beautiful, before it hit the water. That split-second has lasted forever, of course, but back then I thought I could lock it away with all my other troubles and contradictions, each in their separate cell. I suppose the idea was to turn myself into a prison, a sort of Pentridge for inappropriate emotions, then throw away the key and walk into university a free man.

I invested a decade of my life in the pursuit of a profound, sincere, determined and hopeless ambition not to be homosexual. It's an ordinary story with an ordinary ending. Christ failed me. So did alcohol. So did marriage. Whatever damage I did to myself along the way, I did worse to others I loved. Eventually the price of heaven proved too high and in my late twenties, with all these wasted years on my conscience, I set about doing what I might have done in my teens but for that problematic encounter with Christ over hot cocoa – I began to try to live as myself.

From *The High Price of Heaven*, 1999

Holes in the road

I'D RUN OUT OF MONEY BETWEEN SCHOOL and university. This was ridiculously easy to do. My father was reluctant to help. My brother – who never ran short – suggested I dig up roads for the Sydney Water Board and dropped me at the depot just up from the gasometer early one morning. I had boots and a cut lunch. At the last minute I decided against taking a book.

To say I *worked* for the Sydney Water Board is overstating the case. I didn't have to prove I could dig ditches when I signed on in the summer of 1964. Ditch-diggers must have been in short supply.

A truck dropped half a dozen of us at a corrugated-iron shed parked in Stanhope Road, Killara. The shed was stacked with picks, spades, tin dishes and kerosene safety lamps. I was given a shovel. The new ones on the team were all given shovels. The demeaning suggestion was that we didn't have the life skills to wield a pick.

After a bit of shovelling, we had a cup of tea.

The work was no harder than a forced day's home gardening. But it was boring. At that point in my sheltered life, I'd thought the most boring thing in the world was Singleton cadet camp in summer: the hills, the heat, the flies. But that was nothing compared to shovelling rubble out of a ditch over and over and over and over again. I took it too seriously. I concentrated. The blokes who knew how to survive the work let their minds wander. I couldn't think of anything else. For this amateur, the ditch was everything.

Self-pity is the great vice of writers. At a time of gross self-pity after working on a book for nearly seven years I declared I would rather do any work, "even on the roads in the Northern Territory", than write books. Then

I remembered the utter tedium of my time with the Water Board twenty-five years earlier and shut up.

Most of the crew were waiting to be somewhere else. Some were waiting for university. One or two were on the way up to Queensland or down to Victoria. The only guy I remember at all clearly – a shy man who liked wiping the sweat off us with his towel – was waiting to take the fire brigade entrance exam. He'd failed twice.

The bloke who boiled water for tea seemed to be called "the wassal". To this day I don't know if I misheard that. The Macquarie Dictionary people have been no help. Did the Middle English *wassail* – to celebrate with drinking, or drink to someone's health – survive on Water Board gangs on the Sydney North Shore?

We never seemed to finish a job before moving to the next. After the sewer pipes in Killara there was a water main in the bush at the back of St Ives and broken pipes on Rosedale Road, Gordon. I still think of those points on the map with an affection born of utter boredom.

I wasn't dedicated. I came and went. The board was flexible. When you turned up you were paid. But no one seemed to worry when you didn't show. The message was: it's your loss. Bad habits began here that I've never shaken off. There were other life lessons.

Work is easier if you keep going.

Time passes faster when you don't look at your watch.

Finding work you enjoy changes your life.

Far more ditch is dug when the foreman stops giving orders and works with his crew.

The financial crises continued all through my university years. But I never went back to digging ditches because I discovered the money was twice as good serving booze at twenty-first birthday parties. It was another lesson: the work society doesn't need at all pays best.

The Sydney Morning Herald, 9 January 2012

Send down the rain

I CAN REMEMBER WAKING IN SUMMER to the sound of rain and feeling not disappointment but relief. I wouldn't be forced to the beach. I liked surfing well enough once I'd dragged myself down to the water. But hot days had their inflexible routine: up, breakfast and beach. A wet day meant freedom.

One of the lies we tell ourselves about summer is how we love the sun. Can't get enough of it, etc. But even back in the 1960s the sun spelled danger. In our house there was a rule against moping around on "good" days – you had to be outside – but another rule not to spend all day in the sun. We were all fair.

This meant time under the umbrella. Society in those little patches of shade was tedious. At no other point in those years did you spend so many hours so close to your parents. It is another of the odd contradictions of summer we tend to forget. The freedom of the beach was hard-won.

So wet days were a wonderful release. Heavy rain was dramatic but soft rain was best: it lasted longer. Slow grey, damp days left you free to laze about, dream and read. Above all read. One wet summer when I was about ten I discovered *The Count of Monte Cristo*. I can still remember that book, and the memory comes with the sound of rain.

Another of the lies we tell is that the beach is a wonderful place to read. If we were honest with ourselves we'd admit books and hot sun are a tricky combination at best. Try to read sitting up and the glare from the sea puts the page into black shadow. Try to read lying down and your back breaks. No one in their right mind sits in the full glare to read a novel, not on the page and not on the screen. Reading is an activity naturally pursued in the shade.

Every December the lists appear of best summer books. I applaud them: I want bookshops to prosper and writers to survive. Christmas is still the great bonanza for the book trade. But the best hope those books have of being read is a long, wet January.

The bad habits parents drum into children are largely to blame. Mine loved us reading and boasted how hard it was to get us to turn off the light and go to sleep. But during the day they had other imperatives: sunlight and chores. Whole generations like mine were left with the dysfunctional notion that reading has to wait until everything that must be done is done. While the sun is up, reading is a last resort.

I taught myself to type one wet summer when I was about fourteen in a house we'd rented on the cliff at Avalon. I still pass the old place with a sense of gratitude. I'd been given – at my request – an old typewriter for Christmas. I bought the *Teach Yourself to Type* manual and spent long days plunking the keys, staring at a chart on the wall with my hands hidden under a bib. Tragic really: the most useful thing I learnt on those long summer holidays of my childhood was not how to stand on a surfboard, or fish (my father's passion) or drink or have sex, but to type. I've been at it ever since.

Every nation tells reassuring lies about itself. Another of the many we tell is that Australians flourish in the heat. Not endure, but flourish. We see ourselves as a people who come into our own when the mercury climbs above thirty-five degrees. We think of our history as one long, blazing summer.

The reality is a little different. Summer is disaster time on this continent. It is the time of fires, floods, cyclones and plagues of locusts. Holiday news bulletins are an unending national tally of death on the roads, in the surf, over waterfalls, by snake and spider, from balconies (a new development) and by stupidity in the wilderness. It's not just personal but national. When did the first bombs drop on Darwin? Summer, 1942. Whitlam sacked? Summer, 1975. Newcastle hit by earthquake? Summer, 1989. Jørn Utzon dismissed? Summer, 1966. Bogle and Chandler murdered? Summer, 1963. Pauline Hanson elected? Summer, 1996. The Duke of Edinburgh shot at Clontarf? Summer, 1868.

You get the picture?

The truth is this nation does its best work in winter. We think better when we're cool. Somebody somewhere has probably done the PhD I need to quote at this point tracing the impact of air-conditioning on the national IQ, on political sanity and the spread of rational ideas in the bush. The last of these matters enormously. The sense of entitlement that came from sitting on a tractor for long hours in furnace heat has, for a century or more, shaped the politics of the nation. A lot of poor thinking was done bringing in the wheat. But now that work is carried out in air-conditioned ease by farmers listening to Radio National.

But for this being such a conservative, traditional country it might be possible to predict the extinction of the National Party for this reason alone: cool heads west of the divide and north of the border. Keeping summer at bay carries a huge carbon cost, but the benefits for the politics of the nation over the decades ahead are, frankly, inestimable.

Summers seemed to last forever when we were kids. There was one summer before Christmas and another after. We were back at school well before summer was done. Algebra and French made less sense than ever in those final weeks of a season that seemed to last every year from late October to early April. It was as good as forever. Adults have a different calendar, of course. Time isn't our own. Summers have shrunk from months to weeks, from a season to a break.

Much of this is inevitable, but we've connived in the contraction. Who of us, after a run of sweltering days, doesn't secretly look forward to autumn? Much as we dream (and lie) about summer, autumn is the season that most reconciles us to living down here on this difficult continent. The sun is friendly and the air sparkling. Energy returns. Our brains slip into gear. We start thinking again. The future is bright.

But before then, before we find ourselves back in winter, let there be a few more hot days.

The Sydney Morning Herald, 13 January 2010

The image of man

WHEN WE'RE KIDS, WE FIND SEX where we can. I found it in Roseville, in a dark corner of my grandfather's house that was called, for some reason, the sunroom. It was very hot and very quiet. My parents were a few rooms away, watching the Davis Cup on television. I can still hear the electric fan and the distant pock, pock of Rosewall and Hoad whipping the Americans.

There I was in the gloom, leafing through an old *National Geographic,* magazine when I turned the page and – without any warning – found myself staring at an artist's impression of the building of the pyramids: a panorama of thousands of near naked bodies heaving blocks of stone up ramps, the sun beating down, the sweat, the chests, the loincloths. Dear God, I was only nine or ten, and sex hit me like a bolt of lightning. Life was never the same after that.

It's time I thanked the *National Geographic,* and I do so now. Maybe the editors – like Charlton Heston filming *Ben Hur* – didn't really know what was going on. But those artists did, and so did the photographers who took their cameras on my behalf into the darkest jungles to bring out illustrated stories of hunting in Borneo with snaps of black buttocks and thighs. Never white buttocks – which may explain the passion Australian males have for black Americans: it all goes back to those innocent years of our childhood, when a white body was lewd, but black was anthropology.

They were the years of pretending, and the exhibition *The Image of Man: Photography & Masculinity 1920–1950* celebrates, in an odd sort of way, the pretences of the trade that once signalled nudes were art photography. To establish that beyond any doubt photographs of naked bodies were often published with poetry on the facing page. Or interspersed with snaps of driftwood or of the body *as* driftwood. I think all the major pretences are on show in this exhibition.

First, of course, there are classical nudes. It's art to show a naked man so long as somewhere in the frame there's a discus or an olive wreath. Leni Riefenstahl knew that. It's a very German thing: who of us can forget, much as we might try, the depressing experience of seeing Baron von Gloeden's studies of naked Sicilian youths as figures from Greek mythology – perhaps the saddest holiday photos of all time. If only von Gloeden had put those boys to work building something!

Men at work is the other honoured device for turning males – as naked as possible – into art. And there's a lot of that upstairs. For the first time in something like fifty years, all on show together, we have the men at work of the Australian photographer Keast Burke. Here is major pretence! Yet it's not to be sneered at. Timid as it is, this is of its time. All those blokes doing something with their shirts off, resolutely not quite looking us in the eye so we can't see if they know that we know that all this is really about sex.

It makes them so Australian – of the Australia, anyway, that more of us than would care to confess it, grew up in – where a man at ease with his body was damned, and probably damned forever, for "loving himself". So Keast Burke's blokes are awkward, and a bit shy, and hide what *The Guide to Virile Manhood* – the only manual of sex instruction I was given as a kid – called "the tube outside your body". Keeping the cock out of sight is a major preoccupation of the art photography of this time. Again, let's not sneer, for it became an art of almost infinite resource.

Shadow is the photographer's great ally. How true it was in this era to say "only the shadow knows". But hiding the cock also means that most naked men in *exhibited* photographs in these years turn away from the camera in a pose that always looks a little like shame – even in Keast Burke's sunlight there's a sense somewhere of sadness and shame.

I said *exhibited* photographs because all the time other photographs were being taken, photographs never intended for publication, photographs that make nonsense of scholarly studies of sexuality based only on images that were allowed out into the market of books and magazines. There's one upstairs: a tiny 1940 photograph by Minor White – no sadness, no shame, just sex. I mean to praise it highly when I say it could almost be a William Yang.

By the way, there is, I think, a very simple test of the difference between porn and art in male photography – and this test could become useful when Brian Harradine's Senate Committee on Community Standards really gets down to work. It is this: art works more than once. Porn is one sharp shock and it's over. Art lets you come back for more.

But I digress – what I'm really getting to with all this folderol is a warning. We can laugh at the pretence of a lot of the photographs upstairs and think we live now at a time when there is no need to pretend anymore. But can we be sure? Isn't even Mapplethorpe enmeshed in pretences of his own, pretences we will one day look back and laugh at? I think this exhibition poses the same challenge that Mardi Gras poses to this city: to face and celebrate the truth, to stop pretending.

I had one of those blinding moments of truth at my first Mardi Gras party. I was nearly forty and I walked into the Royal Hall of Industries and saw a panorama of men, thousands of nearly naked men, pumping, sweating, and I realised this was not dancing. Good Christ, these men were building the pyramids.

Opening *The Image of Man: Photography & Masculinity 1920–1950*, a Mardi Gras exhibition at the Art Gallery of New South Wales, 6 February 1997

Hanging onto the facts

BY THE TIME I SAT IN THE GREAT HALL where you are sitting, I knew I wasn't going to be a lawyer. I think I might hold some kind of record in New South Wales: I practiced as a solicitor for one day between being admitted to the profession on Thursday and leaving for Europe on Monday, never to return to a lawyer's office. But I've never thought I wasted the six years of not very hard work spent getting the degree I then abandoned. University offers us dead ends to explore, to discover what we are, certainly, but also to find what we are not.

By the time I left this place I knew I was not a Christian. The philosophy department destroyed my faith one day in 1966 by asking us to try to reconcile – with reference to the state of the world – the propositions that God is all powerful and all good. That finished my faith. By that time I had already discovered I was not a smoker and that I should stop playing the fiddle. (I should make it clear, they were separate discoveries.) I found I was not a writer of fiction, having abandoned after only three instalments a serial in *Honi Soit*. The best thing about it and all I can remember was the title: 'Cockroach Weather'.

I found I was not a conservative, not as my parents were. The Vietnam War did that for me. But I also found I was not much of an agitator. Flour bombs were distributed one year at a huge anti-war demonstration outside the American consulate in Barrack Street. The idea was to chuck them at the cops. I was not arrested. I let mine drop in the gutter. I like to think of this not as an act of abject cowardice but an early commitment to working for change by other means – by persuasion rather than violence.

And I found I wasn't a lawyer.

But what I *did* find here at this university – a discovery I believe we share because it's the deepest purpose of this place – is trust in facts. This is not a small thing. In the world beyond the gates the authority of fact is under constant attack. The arts of spin and deception have never been more subtle. So much rides these days for so many interests on persuading us all to overlook the facts.

I became a journalist. I work in a world awash with commentary – at times colourful and offensive commentary, commentary that's often untethered from fact. This goes beyond making mistakes. Even the best of us make mistakes. You may have made one or two in your time. I certainly have in the forty years I've been a journalist. What I'm talking about are habits of thinking and ways of working where facts aren't thought to matter. For the most part this untethered commentary is designed to stoke our fears – fears of crime and disorder, of drugs and terrorists, of great big taxes and dusky people in little boats; of governments and of oppositions and, worst of all, of one another and even of ourselves.

How can facts have so little traction nowadays? The answer lies deeper, I think, than the bad habits of the press and the old capacity of power and money to warp public debate. I fear that our trust in fact is ebbing away. We've come to place too much faith in spin merchants who can turn facts on their heads. We've come almost to admire their magic. After all, we are human: we love facts that support our values and views and we don't necessarily warm to facts that undermine our beliefs. I remember my chemistry master one day coming into the classroom ashen-faced with news just in from Europe. Despite what he had taught us almost on day one, it had been discovered that inert elements *could* form compounds. He was facing a new fact. His world was shifting.

So you doctors of philosophy – the real thing – you masters of art curatorship and digital communications culture and all the degrees I've never heard of, and you bachelors of arts – my people down the back – keep doing for life what's brought you to this absurd and wonderful room today: face facts and keep on facing facts.

And be prepared: one or two things might happen in the next thirty or forty years that will make you change your mind. I hope so. I even hope I've got one or two somersaults left in me.

The University of Sydney, 11 October 2013

My marriage was a house of cards

FIVE HUNDRED RUINED MY MARRIAGE. You might think there were more fundamental problems in play. But I knew then and know now that they were manageable. We could have gone on despite me being ... not really made for marriage. But cards brought us undone.

Forgive me for taking tonight's theme so literally. But after a lifetime at Fairfax I can't come at any subject in any original way. Fairfax employed skilled teams of subeditors to beat originality out of us, and they did their work well. So when I was told that tonight I had to "tell a true story on the theme of 'A House of Cards'", I knew I had to tackle the subject head-on and tell the truth about the destruction of my marriage – how a union meant for life was brought undone by my wife's passion for five hundred.

Young people today grow up in a world where they expect gay men to pair off, dance once or twice at Mardi Gras, then get a dog and save for a house on Scotland Island. It seems the natural order of things. But there was a time when being married – to a woman – was a perfectly respectable way for gay men to live. Even quite admirable. Their families loved it. The community applauded. Role models were everywhere back then and aren't too hard to find even now – in Hollywood and federal politics. The truth overlooked in these impatient times is that ambitious gay men make splendid husbands. They have careers, children, rather stocky wives and the occasional lifesaver on the side. But splendid husbands.

I was determined to be one of those.

First I needed to have sex. Like so many young Australian men at that time, I waited till I got to London. What followed was a tale of two suburbs: Notting Hill, first time with a man; Willesden Green, first time with a woman. I like to think my own sweet fumbling affair with Gavin in 1972 is part of the erotic substrata that made Notting Hill a natural setting for the films of Hugh Grant in the 1990s.

Perhaps I should have stuck with Notting Hill instead of switching to the Jubilee line – two changes as it happens: Edgware Road and Baker Street – to make a risky appointment with fate in Willesden Green.

I know this sort of audience at this sort of event craves grubby detail. I am going to be relatively discreet and merely report that on an unstable night-and-day sofa bed in a second-floor flat in that plain suburb, I proved I could do it.

And I was terribly pleased with myself.

What a high-minded coupling it was. Having done it once or twice and a few times more, I felt – we felt – we must hurry home and take our part in building a new Australia under Gough Whitlam.

I can see now that the rickety structure of my marriage was built on optimism, patriotism, blind faith in the Labor Party, naive masculine pride and an affection for Jennie which has survived everything to this day. I left Australia a terrified proto-poofter and returned a man. We were a couple and we settled in the bosom of the heterosexual Left: Balmain.

So determined was I that our marriage was going to work, I ignored all the omens. The collapse of the Whitlam government should have been a warning. Foolishly I took it to have only national repercussions.

From time to time I was ambushed by erotic delirium, like the night at the Nimrod when Andrew Sharp kissed Tony Sheldon in Peter Kenna's very personal melodrama *A Hard God*. Let me tell you, in 1974 that kiss was quite something.

I drank that away. Drink was frankly helpful. If you were scared to go to bed, a few drinks made anything possible – usually sleep.

Keeping busy seemed to be the key to the marriage. We were both busy: busy, busy, busy. Lots of friends. Lots of cooking. And weekends at guesthouses in the Blue Mountains. The '70s was the era of chic guesthouses: great food, icy bedrooms and a dunny down the hall. We couldn't get enough of the discomfort.

We were happy. Sex was ... OK. The future looked bright but something began to come between us. My wife had a passion I couldn't share: cards. She wanted to play more and more. Soon she wasn't happy unless she'd had a few hands of five hundred two or three times a week. When I claimed to be too busy, too tired, a bit down in the dumps tonight, she insisted I play.

I never approached a game with enthusiasm. I never picked up the cards with pleasure. And I never won.

I rang Jennie yesterday. After all this time I wanted to have something out with her again: how come she was so good at the game? "Don't you remember?" she said a little tartly. "They made me repeat the matric at Firbank because I was too young for university and I spent most of the second year playing five hundred."

I did remember once she reminded me. But I've put so much detail out of my mind. Even thinking about all this after all these years gives me a flush of humiliation. Some failures you never live down.

Do you know the game? It's bridge with training wheels. You're dealt a heap of cards and there's all this coded talk back and forth and then you take turns throwing a card into the middle of the table and someone wins the trick. I went on the internet yesterday to look at the rules – those fiddly rules and that fucking jargon: "no-ies" and "misère" and "slams" and "going out backwards".

What brought me up with a jolt was the heading: "Play of the joker. If there is a trump suit, the joker counts as the highest trump ..." And so on. Nothing provoked my wife's growing exasperation with me in those years more than my failure to grasp the role of the joker. My instinct was always to play the damn thing. Why hold back? Put it out there. Show them what you've got. Win early. Win often. Get it over and done with. The sooner we're done, the sooner we're gone.

I grasped *intellectually* that this was wrong. Yes, cards are about hiding and waiting and biding your time. But I was a man in the grip of his instincts – and those instincts were all wrong.

The marriage unravelled fast once we couldn't face each other over the card table. There was never so much drinking, never so much reading in bed. The image I have of those last months is a dark bedroom with two people, two books and two little pools of light – as far apart as possible in a double bed.

There was misery everywhere and I was responsible. This was my mistake, my fault. We broke up. I found men. I rediscovered the erotic charge of kissing stubble. I found sex. And I found my partner.

He won't remember this, but I do. One day early on he suggested we have a game of cards. I said, "I don't play." And, thank God, he took me at my word. It's our anniversary next Sunday. We've been together eighteen years. I know why, and I plan to keep it that way.

Story Club, 3 November 2014

Life and death

THEIR DEATHS WERE AWFUL. Dad was a fair-skinned surfer. Mum was a smoker. A young GP gave my father his death sentence. The melanomas cut out years before were back, and nothing could be done. As we drove home he said, perfectly seriously: "This is going to kill your mother." But she carried on, a game old woman with no flesh on her bones, determined to live as she had for as long as she could. We heard things we had never heard before: "When we were courting, your father handed me a Turf and said 'You might like one of these' and I did." She didn't blame him at all. Smoking was one of the loves of her life. Her brand was Du Maurier but she later switched to Benson & Hedges. British was best with her: British clothes, British accents, British books, British cigarettes. We fetched them for her. We bought them. We lit them and took a puff when she was driving. We emptied the ashtrays. Dad gave up but she ploughed on. By my rough calculation she had smoked 350,000 cigarettes by the time a bad heart forced her to go cold turkey at the age of sixty-nine. Twelve years later she couldn't shake off a dry cough.

Because there was no hope for either of them, we wanted it over quickly. We didn't want them dead but we wanted them to die. Yet as cancer ate away, they seemed indestructible. "I'm not enjoying this," my father remarked when he emerged from a morphine stupor one afternoon. Days later I heard him say: "Give up, heart. Give up." His dying was like a long sleepless night. The hours passed very slowly. He often asked the time and it was never late enough. He was tormented by hallucinations. "Son, tell me, are rats running around the mirror?" He kept his eye on two clocks: the little electric one by his bed and the old clock ticking all our lives in the hall. He rang me once or twice to come to the house and fiddle with the pendulum to keep the two in synch. Accuracy was his lifelong passion. He was an engineer, a mathematician. "All that's left," he said quietly one afternoon, "is to work towards zero."

I had no unfinished business with him. All the great disputes we had when I was young had been resolved. I risked everything in my twenties telling him who I was. That was absolutely fine. My career was a mystery to him but he accepted that too. He faced facts and taught us to do the same. I loved him profoundly. We all did. I have an older brother, Andrew, and two younger sisters, Annabel, who lives in the city and Jane, a doctor in the bush. Not until we came within sight of the finishing line did I see how difficult her position became as the doctor-daughter. We were all taking our cues from her: the family, the nurses and his GP. She was not his doctor but she was in charge. I took notes.

Wednesday

He was back at work, worried about an order for Pyrmont. Transverse sections. The bishop came in the afternoon. We had tea and discussed texts. Mum wanted the funeral to be right. No false sentiment, no intrusion into the family's privacy, some brake on religiosity. Her old friend the bishop was her guarantee. She'd baked coconut biscuits and put out the silver. He asked if he could go in to Dad and pray. Mum agreed. I watched him go into the bedroom and Dad said "Don" and shook his hand. I went into the kitchen but my niece appeared a few moments later and said we were all wanted in the bedroom. We stood round Dad's bed with the bishop bowing over him. It was a good prayer. We were all in tears. Dad said a breathy amen and there was a fusillade of weeping in the room. The bishop left.

A guy called Alex arrived with an oxygen machine and gave complicated instructions. But as the thing was being set up in the study – with a long green tube to the bed delivering air into Dad's nose via two prongs – Jane was already on the phone, first to the doctor, then the hospital and then the ambulance. She'd decided he had gone too far down hill to be at home that night. We were all relieved, even Dad, that the decision had been made. Jane told him it may only be for a night, just to get him stabilised. Mum packed his overnight bag: razor, brush, a change of pyjamas. His boxes and bottles of pills were put in a plastic bag.

The ambulance arrived about six. Two quiet, direct guys wearing rubber gloves wheeled their trolley into the bedroom. We shifted furniture. They slid him onto the trolley and out to the ambulance. He lay very high under the neon light in the back. Jane rode with him. She said one of the men apologised to Dad for having to take his blood pressure. Dad said, very clearly, he was to do it and not to worry. I brought Mum in the car. We arrived a few minutes after the ambulance and were sent to a television room while they got Dad ready. We made tea, ate dry biscuits and watched the seven o'clock ABC news. Then they called us.

Dad was in a five-bed ward, calm, with oxygen up his nose. He was polite to the last. A nurse asked if he would like sandwiches for tea. Yes. And a cup of tea? Yes. We must have looked amazed. She asked us, "Would he like coffee instead?" We laughed and explained he hadn't eaten solids for a week or so, nor had tea for weeks. She left and returned with a little vanilla milkshake with Sustagen. Dad drank some. Mum said, "It's Sustagen." Dad said bluntly, "It's not Sustagen." Across the ward an old man with a plaintive English accent begged to be let out of bed. I started to give him a hand before I realised he couldn't move. He was tied to his bed with a catheter up his dick. I swung his legs back in. He moaned and protested through the night. The nurses dealt with him patiently, like a child. The only other sound in the ward during the night was a soft but urgent voice somewhere calling, "Ex-cuss-a-me, ex-cuss-a-me."

Dad was out of it. We left to have dinner. "See you in the morning," Drew said and Dad replied, "Right, see you in the morning." Back at the house, Jane called me out of the dining room and asked if I would go back and sit with him. She was worried. Being distressed is a sign of life but Dad was now so calm. "I think he might die tonight."

When I got back at about 10.15 he was breathing loudly. I sat in the dark holding his hand. He had a strong grip on mine. A couple of times he pulled the oxygen line out to rub his nose with his knuckles – he's always scratched his nose that way – and I put the prongs back in, telling him it was me. He was quite agitated. I called a nurse. They put a "butterfly" into the skin of his chest to inject him. As she opened his pyjamas she said, "No hair." I thought she was giving him a breakthrough dose of morphine but it was a sedative. She checked with her torch the dilation of his pupils. He quietened down.

I asked for a torch to read by. They gave me one but a little later brought a reading light. I settled down with a new novel, *The Dark Palace* by Amitav Ghosh. I was only half reading. My eyes slid all over the pages. I never finished it and never want to. I held Dad's hand through the bars of the bed. His breathing was company. I was scared of him dying on my watch. Doubted he would. Wished he would. Afraid he might. My fear was cold and gentle.

Thursday

About 1.30 am the nurse looked in through the curtains and said, "Oh, I forgot. A couple of hours ago your sister rang to say to ring her if you need to be relieved." She couldn't remember the name. Did she sound city or country? She couldn't say. "She sounded normal." I thought, there is going to be trouble here if I don't ring, but I can't wake everyone to find out who it was.

The oxygen was annoying Dad and he very precisely removed the tubes from his face. The nurse put a peg of some kind on his finger and decided the level of oxygen was OK, so the tank was turned off. He started counting: "Thirty-eight, thirty-nine, forty, forty-one"; sometimes only a couple of numbers, sometimes out of order. Only afterwards I thought these may have been the war years. He grew agitated again and they sedated him again.

Somewhere between two and three he started to gurgle, breathing heavily. He was also twitching. I called the nurse. She thought the twitching was dreams but said they could give him something to dry out the gurgling, though it might dry out his mouth too much at the same time. After hesitating a little they gave him a shot, again through the "butterfly". Her torch wasn't working well so I held the reading light for her to check his pupils. They offered me a bed, reassured me he was OK and I said, still believing it, "He's got a few days left in him." I was crying in bursts. At some point I said to him, "You can go. You can go."

About 4.30 he was agitated again and this time they rang the hospital doctor and the nurse gave a third, stronger dose of sedatives through the butterfly. Again, he calmed down quickly. His hands were crossed over his chest. The gurgling was very loud. Sometime after five there was a sudden change in the rhythm of his breathing. He wasn't digging down deep with each breath. I called the nurse. She checked his pulse. She knew what was on my mind: I could ring people, she said, but his pulse was strong. "It's too early."

I decided I would ring the house either at six or when I finished the book, whichever was sooner. I was telling the time all night by Dad's watch. But at six I was afraid to move. There was a public phone in the hall – I'd used it the night before – but I hadn't yet taken in the obvious fact that there was also a little phone on his bedside table. At 6.10 he stopped breathing. I pressed the buzzer. Luckily the nurses thought this was the troublesome English guy and ignored the call. So I was alone for this. Dad was lying straight in his bed with his hands crossed over his chest. I had my hands on his. Often during the last week he had not breathed for a stretch. This was a very long stretch. His face was absolutely still with his mouth hanging open. Then there was a little breath and a long silence. By his watch it was 6.10.

I found the phone. Rang Jane and said come. Dad gave a soft, long fart. That was it. I rang Annabel and couldn't say he was dead, just come to the hospital. Couldn't remember Drew's number and had to ring directory assistance. Didn't have a pen. A nurse appeared. She asked if I was alright. I was and said so. She asked if she should close Dad's mouth with a towel rolled under his chin. I said no. She left. I found his brush in the drawer beside the bed and brushed his hair. I kissed him on the forehead when it was done. He looked milky pale. I don't think I cried. Outside there was a burst of noise from birds – lorikeets, I think – and then it was quiet again. The nurse brought me a mug of tea.

I sat with him. At 6.30 Mum's and Jane's feet appeared under the curtain. Mum sat on the far side of the bed. I said, "He just stopped breathing." Mum asked, "Is he breathing now?" Jane said, "No, Mum." I made tea for them. I went out and walked up and down the road for a bit. It was a beautiful early autumn morning. There was a woman rushing down the hill to the station. I wanted to yell: It doesn't matter!

Drew arrived and went inside to say his goodbyes and do what had to be done. We sat in the sun waiting for Annabel. An hour passed. We wanted to be away. The nurses knocked off from their shift. They were surprised how quickly he had gone. His pulse had been strong. The twitching had not been dreams, it seems, but a sign he was dying. Annabel arrived. Mum had packed Dad's things. I went to pick up a pair of green viyella pyjamas from the bedside table. Mum said, "Leave those. They always wonder what to dress people in." We should have had his old overalls for the job.

I went back to the television/tea room for a few moments and came back to find him alone. Mum had left. A nurse with rubber gloves was about to start work on the body. She shook my hand then evaporated. I kissed Dad again on the forehead and said goodbye. Mum was in the vestibule. I hugged her and she flinched. She looked terrible but was holding herself upright. A nurse appeared and slipped Dad's watch into her hand. She had trouble finding somewhere for it in her handbag. It disappeared. We left.

The days that followed had their horrors. We righted ourselves. My brother, a born older son, did everything well. The bishop held to his side of the unspoken bargain: my father was buried not as a Christian but as a decent man. Men from the works came to the wake to talk affectionately about the old days and Mr George. We threw his ashes off the rocks where he used to fish at Whale Beach, and as we climbed back up the cliff a pod of dolphin swam by, paying their respects.

My mother's pretence that little had changed served us all well. But her life was broken. My parents had adored each other. Even in old age they still thought themselves lucky to have met. He protected her. "Don't upset your mother," was one of his tougher commands. She was the centre of attention but he had the authority. At the age of seventy-eight she was batting on without much of the reason for her life. Something shifted in her. This deeply conventional woman – an authority on doing the right thing – seemed not to care so much about the verdict of the golf club. It was a relief to her. She was funny and unexpected. "What you want to know," she announced combatively one afternoon, "is whether I went to the altar a virgin." We did. She had. Her days were long. She kept saying as she had all our lives, "We must keep an eye on the time." But there was less and less reason to do so. She had the housework done by 9 am and cooked us the same ghost meals we'd laughed about for years: great recipes reduced ingredient by "unnecessary" ingredient to shadows of themselves. She kept a stern watch on the upbringing of her grandchildren.

No one mentioned the little cough. A bad shoulder drove her from the court. After playing tennis for something like seventy-five years, she wasn't going to suffer the indignity of serving underarm. The pain grew worse. X-rays showed a mass in her left lung. She knew what it was. "I could operate," said the young man who had given my father his death sentence only a couple of years before. "I don't think so," she replied. He offered chemotherapy. "No. We won't do anything about this." She knew she was going the same hard way my father had gone. She stuck to all the old routines. Suddenly breathless one afternoon, she was taken to hospital and never came out. She shrank. When she could no longer swallow she was sent to see a surgeon. The driver lost his way navigating the suburbs where she had lived all her life. This was my mother's territory. At death's door, her last triumph was to show the driver the back way from Wahroonga to Hornsby.

Annabel kept smoking. "This," she told me in the hospital garden, "is no time to give up cigarettes." Later she did. One day she brought good news that had to be kept absolutely secret for a week. My mother, a gossip absurdly sure of her discretion, made all the right promises but the first nurse into the room was told: "My grandson is going to be a Wallaby." The nurse had no idea what she was talking about. That young man and his brother came to say a final goodbye. As they made for the door, crumpled with grief, she issued a last command: "Boys, stand up straight. Now off you go."

Beneath her Anglican exterior lurked a Presbyterian belief that the day and the hour of all our deaths is set. She had always kept a meticulous diary, a little book that once ruled our lives. No obligation pencilled there – however remote – could ever be shifted. Her notion that death had the same perfect manners seemed to comfort her. They had an appointment. "When?" she asked as if she wanted to put it in the book. "When will it happen?" He came at 3 am. We had been asked to leave her room while she was washed. By the time we returned, the fight had entirely gone out of her. I hope some skerrick of consciousness was there at the end to welcome death's arrival on the dot, at this conventional hour.

The second funeral was subtly different from the first. People spoke more freely now they were both gone. Nothing remarkable came to light – no scandals, no other families – but we began to learn things we had never known before. What began at the wakes has continued ever since: telling stories about the dead. Fresh facts are welcome as they come along and so are people who have never heard the stories before. But really we tell them because we love telling them. While they are being told, the dead are with us again. And they still have things to tell us about ourselves. "Pam could never resist showing her hand," a formidable aunt remarked out of the blue one afternoon. "We laughed about it for years. She always played the ace too soon." I'd never heard this killer detail before, absolutely true of her and all of us.

We were never a close family, affectionate but not entangled. Finding ourselves orphans in our forties and fifties meant reordering our ties to one another on a basis not defined by our parents: us without them. We ditched the last traces of the roles assigned in childhood. They hadn't been a good fit for a long time yet we had kept playing them while there was still someone left to applaud. That was over. My mother was no longer the clearing house for family news. We had to deal direct. That was a revelation. And we rediscovered each other in the practical business of dismantling our parents' lives and taking responsibility for their property. It was sobering work. Wills make adults of us all. We sent to auction the last bits and pieces no grandchild could be persuaded to take. My mother's uncomfortable chaise lounge, her fiercely protected pride and joy, disappeared without attracting a bid. We raised a guilty cheer.

Once both parents are dead their children are supposed to feel in the firing line. I didn't and don't. An older brother's last duty is surely to block the way. What the second death brought was something odd I hadn't expected: a feeling of having grown up at last. Despite the encouragement of many people over many years, I'd thought whatever was possible in that department had happened long ago. Not so. In my mid-fifties, with both parents gone, I felt more adult than I ever had. It's about getting on without them. Of course I'd been doing that for a long time. But the backstops were gone. The lines were cut. We were left with whatever they had given us. As I was puzzling this through, I was struck by something quite unexpected: a sense of growing into them. It's not that I felt any less myself, but who they were was bedding down in me. They haven't taken over. Far from it. But as each year goes by since they died I find I am more them than I ever was. It's a reassuring surprise. I'm easy in their company.

They died in character. Death is only a transfiguring experience in fiction. We go the way we came. I'll make a noisy exit clamouring for attention. I hope it's not too embarrassing. A good last line would be welcome, some quip to be remembered by, and not a terrible death like theirs. Something swift and a long way off. Until then I'll tell their grandchildren the old stories, hoping I don't bore them talking about the past, hoping to give them a few clues to themselves and, I suppose, hoping to keep this sweet man and forceful woman alive.

From *My Mother, My Father*, edited by Susan Wyndham, 2013

Whitlam

1975 dismissal diary

LORD DE L'ISLE SPOKE TO our people in London this week about facing constitutional crises: "I nearly had the experience of having to make a constitutional decision in 1961 when the federal election looked like finishing in a tie. If it had been a tie there was the question of the election of a Speaker. This could have led to the question of whether there should be a dissolution. But God is merciful and Queensland saved the day for me by electing a man called Killen."

How, we wondered, would he have solved the problem if it had come up? "I would have consulted the chief justice and having heard his opinion I would then have made up my mind about what I would do. It is a lonely situation but that is what you are appointed for."

Other holders of the office have not been so free to talk to the press during the crisis. Sir William McKell (1947 to 1953) was not available and we couldn't raise Sir Paul Hasluck (1969 to 1974). But we did get through to Edrington, the Caseys' house in Berwick, and spoke to what sounded like a resolute Maie Casey. "No, no. Lord Casey won't come at that. Keep your mouth shut I think – everyone."

The Bulletin, 1 November 1975

Where were you when the news flashed around the nation? The traditional two minutes' silence of Armistice Day came after instead of before lunch, as people took it in: "Kerr's sacked Gough." Then, after a fashion, life went on. We asked a random selection of people what they were doing at that moment in history.

Sydney interior decorator Leslie Walford recalled: "I was where I nearly always am, on the phone surrounded by paper, doing my thing, decorating. Someone said, he's been fired. I said, brilliant; I'll think about it later."

Actress Kate Fitzpatrick said: "I was in a restaurant and the owner came and told us. All I could think of was the night in December 1972 when he was elected. I was doing a TV program, *Boney*, then and we told the owner of the motel that if he won we'd have a champagne party in the pool at midnight. And we did. All the cast got into the pool, drinking champagne until four in the morning. There were so many of us in such a tiny pool. It was in a little town outside Orange. That's all I could think of."

Writer Frank Hardy was revising a play on Henry Lawson in his Manly flat when he switched on the radio and heard the news. "I wasn't surprised," he said. "I've been saying for two months that Fraser would force the issue, win the election, and be utterly unable to rule."

The Bulletin columnist Ross Campbell was having a cheery lunch at the Four Seasons restaurant in Sydney (a great haunt of the Labor Party) with, among others, Robert Close, who has recently returned to Australia after many years and who remains the only writer ever jailed here for indecency (over his novel *Love Me Sailor*).

Someone had just told a story about a friend, now dead, who once turned up at his brother's wedding anniversary dinner somewhat drunk, behaved badly and was sent home in a taxi. Campbell laughed heartily at this, and, as is his wont, made a note, against possible future use. At that moment a waiter came back with the message, "Kerr's sacked Whitlam." The table laughed heartily at this joke. Campbell made another note on his pad.

Angus Lloyd, a teacher, said: "I was supervising an exam when I heard. The librarian monitors ABC radio and TV all day in case tapes have to be made and she picked it up. She sent a child in the library off with the news but could only think of the history master to pass it on to. The history master came down to me. We agreed she'd made a mistake, that she's carelessly heard a program about Jack Lang."

The Bulletin, 22 November 1975

When the High Court rose for lunch, Barwick climbed the stairs to his chambers. A blanket was spread on the carpet and an easel stood there holding his unfinished portrait. He was not very happy with the picture: he had expected something bigger and more dramatic.

His tipstaff brought him lunch. He ate quickly and then changed into Windsor rig, tying ruffles of lace at his throat and wrists. The tipstaff took out his tray and the artist entered. Barwick took up his position, turned slightly away from the painter, glancing back, his head turned to throw into prominence the side of his face and one gnarled ear. The black robes were sharply silhouetted against the ochre walls, the light from the windows falling on his forehead and deeply furrowed cheeks. His wig lay behind him on a low bookcase. He carried his glasses folded in his left hand, the fingers of each hand lightly clasped. The artist painted the skin of the fingers in impasto. They were blunt, strong hands on the canvas. He painted the lips shut, the nose jagged and the eyes gazing out sharply under circumflex eyebrows.

It might have been an intimidating picture, but the artist had worked in soft browns and greys, which gave the face a weather-beaten quality. The lace, the pugnacious stance, the sharp old face suggested a preacher, some veteran of the circuit in whom the fire might have died a little but was yet capable of flaring.

Barwick seemed cheerful that day, but subdued. At earlier sittings there had been a flow of anecdotes about his childhood. The days living down behind the courts in Paddington, about yachting and grandchildren, the Dobell case, and political figures he had known and tussled with. That day, the flow of anecdote had slowed. The sitting lasted a little more than an hour. Barwick took off the lace, put back on his tapes and wig, and began to walk down to court. A young woman from the court registry came running along the corridor. She stopped Barwick for a moment on the stairs and then ran into the anteroom. She was shocked. "Kerr's just sacked Whitlam and put Fraser in and I told the Chief and he just smiled at me and nodded."

From *Barwick*, 1980

It is lunchtime in a factory car park in Marrickville. Tony Whitlam has forty or fifty workers to address. "After three years, three very hard years, Labor was making progress, and that is why the Fraser clique had to strike.

Medibank was becoming a fact of life and this was their last chance to Chipp, Chipp, Chipp it away. They tell you they'll keep Medibank (gesture with upraised hand), but is that what they say to their friends the doctors at fundraising functions held in much more lavish surroundings than these?"

It's a smooth job. The crowd (mostly migrant women) hangs back, leaving the candidate in the middle of the yard looking even more huge than he is. He flicks off the flies. Planes come in overhead, punching holes in his rhetoric. For a minute or two he loses them with a line about Hayden's tax proposals vs concessional deductions, but he gets them back with education, Medibank and Kerr.

"That's Whitlam's son," said a man at the back peeling an orange.

"Naaarrr."

"I tell y' it is. Look at the nose." He traces it out with his finger.

Whitlam hands over to an Italian girl for a blast of *liberta, democrazia, il senato* etc., and a British lady with a very British name follows on in Yugo-slav – and that is it. A neat twenty minutes, all tied up and $16 collected. "It's impossible to get a meeting normally," says the man from the AMWU as he packs his microphone away. "This was a ninety-five per cent turnout."

The Bulletin, 6 December 1975

The little people fight back against the caretakers: Andrew Peacock was leaving the squat, Stalinesque building that houses Foreign Affairs in Canberra when the guard asked to see his pass. The minister smiled. "I'm Andrew Peacock." The guard, with his "Shame Fraser, Shame" badge shining on his lapel, pointed out that routine demanded everybody leaving the building had to show a pass and sign the book. "I'm Andrew Peacock." This went on for some time, but when a queue of office girls forming behind him broke into giggles, Peacock signed and left. The guard completed the job column beside the signature: Janitor.

The Bulletin, 13 December 1975

In Ash Street, Sydney, back-lane headquarters of the Liberal Party, everything was done up in red, white and blue – pictures of Malcolm Fraser, pictures of Churchill, even the colour television. The workers, fresh-faced youngsters from the suburbs, some of them wearing their first t-shirts, were gathered round watching the tally-room broadcast on the ABC.

"Don't look so downhearted, Richard Carleton."

A party worker with an enamel Australian flag in her lapel stood by the phone taking the calls. Most of them were cranks. There were lots of (photocopied) Malcolm Mackerras pendulums about being amended, annotated, as the news came in. Out the back you heard corks popping from time to time.

"Enderby's gone in Canberra."

"Oh, isn't that lovely."

There was no arrogance in the audience. Their victory was huge, but success was not so much theirs as the leader's and the people of Australia's. They sat around drinking, relaxing, just a happy group come indoors from a barbeque. The biggest barbeque in Australian political history.

At the Marseille – one of Sydney's best, most serious, most expensive restaurants – we thought Liberals would be thick on the ground and celebration unrestrained. But everyone in the place was wearing a "Shame Fraser, Shame" badge. It was solid Labor. And there were no radios. Yesterday's ruling class was munching away at the exquisite food as power slipped from them, not even listening as the count came in.

"What's the use," said a waitress. "You know who's going to win."

About 9.30, the well-bred silence was getting beyond a joke. At five to ten I went to the car. Backlit in the doorway opposite, two tarts hung about for trade. The ABC was broadcasting *Siegfried* from Bayreuth. News time. The portentous dreary fanfare. "And in the tally room the Liberal–Country Party Coalition led by Mr Malcolm Fraser has won and will lead the government with a handsome majority …"

Of course there had been a radio hidden away at the Marseille. Hubert Arriat (prop.) appeared with it in his hand. The news didn't cause much of a stir among the Labor eaters.

ARRIAT: "They were no good for me. I voted for Labor last time but [shrug] they were no good for me. Some came here one night and were terribly drunk. That's okay, you get drunk at home but don't perform here. You don't turn against a party for that, but …"

WAITRESS: "They're gloating in the kitchen."

ARRIAT: "The chef – he change colour."

Back at Ash Street the party wound up about midnight. The fall of Gorton, Morrison, Gordon Scholes brought happy applause from the crowded room.

The Bulletin, 20 December 1975

The women in
John Kerr's life

IN THE MIDST OF HIS EXTRAORDINARY performance at the National Press
Club last week, Gough Whitlam was taken to task for writing about Elizabeth Reid and the governor-general in *The Truth of the Matter*. It was, the
questioner said, below the navel. Bad taste. Whitlam replied that it was
essential to show Kerr's state of mind at that critical time – it was the time
when Kerr signed the first loans minute, from which (in his memoirs) he
dates his profound suspicion of Whitlam and the Whitlam government. Far
from standing aloof and distrustful, Whitlam told the Press Club: "Kerr was
fraternising with me, my ministers and my staff."

But the Reid story is also important because it illuminates key aspects
of Kerr's character that are central to his dismissal of Whitlam. It fills in
the picture of a man deeply influenced by the women in his life. While still
a senator, Jim McClelland would tell colleagues: "The basic traits of Kerr's
character are fairly unchangeable. They have been restrained or set loose
by the women in his life."

Whitlam's relations with Kerr were also profoundly affected by the
governor-general's two wives. Kerr and Lady Alison (Peggy) had been married thirty-six years when she died shortly after he took office. After her
death he presented the picture of a floundering man. This was the time of
his greatest intimacy with the Whitlam administration, of the start of the
loans affair, of his courting Elizabeth Reid. It was also the time his grandiose notions of his office became exaggerated. Then came the marriage with

Nancy Robson, changes to the court at Yarralumla, doubts about Whitlam, regrets about the loans affair, and the dissembling towards his prime minister that led in late 1975 to the sacking.

That makes three women in Kerr's career. But Whitlam told the Press Club of a fourth. Kerr had always claimed to be the protégé of Bert Evatt, who supported this boy from Balmain at the law school of Sydney University. But Whitlam told the Press Club the real source of the support was Evatt's wife, Mary Alice.

*

Kerr was an attractive candidate. He met all of Whitlam's key requirements. He was on Sir Paul Hasluck's list of possible successors, an Australian, not washed-up at the end of his career, and not an ex-politician. His position as chief justice of New South Wales would both blunt any jobs-for-the-boys accusations and set at rest that peculiar Australian anxiety that a Labor man wouldn't know how to behave with the Queen. In *The Truth of the Matter* Whitlam confirms that he first approached Ken Myer for the job, but Myer turned him down. "I then thought of chief justice Kerr, who was also on Sir Paul Hasluck's list. His wife Peggy and my wife had studied together for the Diploma of Social Studies at the University of Sydney in 1942 and 1943." He writes later: "She and my wife had been loyal friends for over thirty-two years."

It wasn't that Whitlam was giving the job as a favour to his wife's friend – they were never in any case as close as that – but that being married to a woman like Peggy seemed to vouch for Kerr. Peggy Kerr was a determined and sensible woman. One of Kerr's oldest friends told *The National Times* last week: "She was a considerable character and kept him in one piece for years. He was always a boozer. He'd been carried to bed for years – I'd done it myself a couple of times – but she was a restraining influence."

Kerr always said his wife gave him "direction". They married in 1938 when Kerr had been only nine months at the Bar. When he went to war she worked to help support him and their daughter. When he got mixed up with the Alf Conlon push and was tempted by a diplomatic career, she urged him to get back to what he was best at: the Bar.

Kerr was tempted by politics in 1953. He'd had an immediate success at the turbulent postwar industrial Bar and there was loose talk of him as a future Labor prime minister. Richard Hall wrote in his book *The Real John Kerr*: "There was, however, one barrier and a formidable one: Peggy Kerr did not like politics or politicians. It was, in part, a matter of disliking the role of a politician's wife. A friend summed it up: 'She found it distasteful and a threat to the family.'"

Kerr had always displayed an odd insecurity about his future. He seemed to think that, vast though his practice was, he would one day run out of clients. He became oddly fixated on the question of pensions, a fixation that he was never to lose. When his wife became ill in 1965 Kerr began to worry about their future if anything should happen to him. Kerr had lived well. Whitlam writes that Kerr told him that: "While he had enjoyed a good income at the Bar he had spent freely ..." A judicial post would mean a secure income and tenure. He decided to take the first good offer of a place on the Bench, which turned out to be the ACT Supreme Court.

Peggy Kerr was, in Kerr's words, "substantially out of action for a couple of years. It took her two years of hard work with physiotherapy to get back to reasonable wellbeing. She did not achieve full freedom of movement. Thereafter she had a minor limp and minor weakness of the left hand but in due course she returned to all her activities: she began marriage counselling again and lived a full social life."

Kerr was six years in Canberra and then two in the post of chief justice of New South Wales before Whitlam approached him with the offer of Yarralumla. It was not, as Kerr suggested in *Matters for Judgement*, an offer quickly accepted. It was a teasing process over many months. There were negotiations over pensions and tenure, which Whitlam describes in *The Truth of the Matter* as "perfectly proper". But he was disturbed by the stress Kerr placed on the advantages of having Yarralumla servants. "There would be a staff available to assist him as governor-general in a way there would not be as chief justice. And I have to say, however offensive to him it might be to recall it, he did indeed put this very point to me."

Kerr put it more vividly to his friends. Richard Hall wrote: "At the first approach, Kerr held back. Peggy was ill again and she told friends that she begged him not to accept. Kerr later explained that Peggy's illness had been a decisive reason for going. The servants would be of great help to her and the valet might sew on his buttons, which Peggy was no longer able to do. At this time, the reference to the valet was treated as a half-joke on Kerr's part."

Whitlam put considerable effort into convincing Kerr that the governor-general was not a figurehead. He explained that the governor-general saw cabinet documents and minutes, important cables and had an up-to-date picture of what the government was doing. He arranged for Kerr to see Hasluck and Sir John Bunting. He sent him material on the role of the office. Whitlam wanted Kerr to "show the flag" overseas and expected him to travel.

The Persepolis Principle (as Whitlam now calls it) was a vital part in talking Kerr into the job. In *The Truth of the Matter* Whitlam says he explained how Sir Paul Hasluck had, in the absence of the Queen, been treated as a fully-fledged head of State at the celebrations to mark the "2500th anniversary" of the Shah dynasty. The principle was to continue. Kerr found it attractive. If Kerr was to suffer later from an exaggerated sense of position, some of the seeds were planted by Whitlam himself.

Peggy Kerr became seriously ill again between the announcement of her husband's appointment in February 1974 and the move to Yarralumla in July. She persuaded him to give Whitlam a chance to reconsider the appointment. Whitlam asked them to carry on if they thought they could. "Had the decision been otherwise," Kerr commented, "I should have been without any office at all and without any pension."

It seemed a good omen that Kerr was to abolish the curtsy. It was not the atmosphere in which to ask arcane questions about the man's views of "reserve" powers. Had it ever been thought necessary to ask such questions of an Australian governor-general before? Whitlam should have – after all, he had been forced by the Senate once to an election. He appears to regret in *The Truth of the Matter* that he didn't, but it seemed, he writes, like asking if the guns at Singapore could be turned around: wholly unnecessary.

But a bad omen followed. Whitlam writes: "The following day Sir John arrived for his installation, to my surprise shared by many others, in morning dress of ample proportions and a top hat a size too small. This uniform was to be a cartoonists' delight until he went into exile." It should also have alerted Whitlam to the man's pretensions. *The Truth of the Matter* must have been a painful book for him and Freudenberg to write: every piece of evidence of the man's unsuitability for the job now late revealed must count against the judgement that placed him there.

But the appointment was a public success: it seemed rather a coup for Whitlam. Both sides of politics applauded the decision: Whitlam had rung

Snedden once the Queen had agreed to the appointment and Snedden guaranteed Kerr a second term should government change hands. Snedden, in fact, made the first announcement to the press in his room at the time Whitlam rang to discuss his viceroy's tenure.

Shortly after the move to Yarralumla, Peggy Kerr became seriously ill once more, entered hospital and died there on 9 September 1974. Whitlam has told many colleagues since: "What followed would never have happened if Peggy had lived."

Kerr withdrew from Yarralumla to Admiralty House, the beautiful villa overlooking Sydney Harbour. He was a lonely figure in those months, giving the impression of a man casting about for a new source of the reassurance and direction Peggy Kerr had given him. He was drinking heavily, and brooding on the importance of his office. At the other end of his garden was the prime minister's residence, Kirribilli House. Kerr and Whitlam came closer then than at any time in the seventeen months they shared in power.

Whitlam claims it was shortly after Peggy Kerr's death that he and Kerr discussed what would happen in the event of a dispute between the Senate and the House of Representatives over supply. Kerr put the argument to Whitlam that if the Senate couldn't alter or originate money bills, then it couldn't reject them either. The bills could go straight from the Representatives to the governor-general for signature. Whitlam rejected the argument as likely to invite a challenge in the High Court, a possible rebuff and certain delay. However, Whitlam took away from the conversation a strong feeling (which he says Kerr never corrected before November 1975) that in any dispute between the Houses, Kerr would be on the side of the Representatives and the government formed in the Representatives.

Also at that time Kerr renewed contacts with old friends. One was John Atwill (now Sir John), who became president of the Liberal Party and an important figure in holding the troops together in the supply crisis of 1975. Kerr visited Rupert Murdoch. Whitlam gives a long account of a day Kerr turned up on the verandah at Cavan, Murdoch's property near Canberra. "He wouldn't have come out to the property if he wasn't a friend," Jim Hall told *The National Times*. Hall was then editor of *The Australian* and one of the Murdoch senior staff having afternoon tea at the property that day.

*

From Admiralty House Kerr would often travel to the Opera House. Once or twice he made the journey by barge from the landing steps in his garden. On the night of 13 December 1974 he went to the ballet (*Romeo and Juliet*) while down in Canberra. Whitlam took the (at least) unusual step of holding an Executive Council meeting without first informing Kerr. The meeting formalised the decision to raise a petro-dollar loan of US$4 billion for temporary purposes. The necessary minute was brought to Kerr next morning and he signed it – signing, in effect, the death warrant of the Labor government.

A great deal of Kerr's memoirs are devoted to the profound worries he had about this loan-raising exercise but in *The Truth of the Matter* Whitlam presents a very convincing picture of a man untroubled – at this time – by what was going on. "Except in a telephone call to Mr Byers (Solicitor-General), Sir John Kerr never raised the matter of the loan minute with any minister, departmental head or legal adviser before a public controversy arose in June or July," Whitlam writes. Whitlam cites occasions when Kerr showed enthusiasm for the project. At one Executive Council meeting Kep Enderby (who was not at that time attorney-general) "had never seen Sir John so excited."

For some weeks Kerr had been inviting Elizabeth Reid for dinner and drinks at Yarralumla and Admiralty House. At one of these dinners, Kerr asked Reid if she would help him with material for some of his speeches, notably his speech opening the meeting of the Associated Country Women of the World. Reid gave the governor-general material for this speech and for several others. She got to know Kerr quite well. The governor-general began ringing her frequently, asking her to drinks or dinner. Her visits to Government House were never shown in the vice-regal notes. The discussions between them covered a wide range of political and personal issues.

Reid used this situation in her job as the Labor government's special adviser on women's affairs. She told *The National Times* last week: "In December when Whitlam was overseas, I asked the governor-general if he would appear on television with me to inaugurate International Women's Year. We appeared together on New Year's Eve 1974 in a national television broadcast." The arrangements for this broadcast had been sorted out before the incident at Kirribilli House described in *The Truth of the Matter*, when Kerr walked through the garden that evening and tapped on the French windows.

Whitlam was expected back any minute from Europe (via the disaster in Darwin). It would have been an easy opportunity for Kerr to get off his chest the worries he catalogues in his memoirs about the loans minute. Elizabeth Reid and Patti Warn, another Whitlam staffer waiting for the return of the prime minister, didn't find Kerr in any way concerned. The three sat on the verandah at Kirribilli House from 8.30 until a little after eleven. Kerr drank whisky. They discussed Darwin, International Women's Year and Junie Morosi's appointment to Jim Cairns' staff. The women present confirm that Kerr rang an aide to get hold of Sir Alan Cooley, chairman of the Public Service Board, to see what could be done to block the appointment.

When it was clear Whitlam would arrive too late to do any work that night, Warn decided to return to a party being held at her flat a few streets away. They issued an invitation to Kerr to join them. He was not going to take a raincheck. He asked them for the address and Patti Warn wrote it out on a piece of paper and handed it to him. Kerr wandered back through the garden, and as Warn and Reid were leaving, the housekeeper told them Kerr might turn up at the party and asked if there was any whisky at the flat as that was his drink. Patti Warn said there wasn't, and the housekeeper gave them a bottle. They lightheartedly promised to return it the next day if Kerr did not appear. The bottle was never returned.

The balcony of Patti Warn's flat was about five storeys above the water at Kirribilli. It was just "a couple of corners away" from Whitlam's house. When she and Elizabeth Reid got back there, about six people were left at the party. It was a beautiful, balmy Sydney summer night. There were buckets of prawns to eat.

Kerr's aide rang the buzzer a bit after midnight. "I made a hasty and flimsy attempt to tidy the place up," recalled Warn. Kerr arrived and "it was really quite amicable after people got over the initial shock". The aide-de-camp, Chris Stephens, seemed worried by the strange company and the informality of the occasion. He asked whether the guests had been cleared by security. The party went out onto the balcony. They talked mainly of Darwin and the women's problems in Darwin. Patti Warn recalled Kerr's discomfort when they discussed getting supplies of tampons and Modess to the flattened city.

"It wasn't a very big balcony," one of the guests, Shirley Castley, told *The National Times* last week. "Kerr took Liz to a corner and pushed tables and chairs between them and the others and told us to talk among ourselves."

At one stage Reid said to Warn: "For Christ's sake don't leave me alone with him."

Conversation became more general. Castley: "Someone asked him what it's like to be governor-general and he brightened at that and said one of the things he liked was that he had access to both the Opposition and the Government which meant that, if any situation arose, then he was the one who knew more about it than anyone else, and, therefore, he could arbitrate, and that it made him more powerful than the prime minister."

When another guest, Adrian Lynch, asked him how citizens get into contact with the Queen – the incident reported in *The Truth of the Matter* – Kerr became rather boring. Castley said: "He got very stiff and pompous. We found it very boring and so we got a little irritable. People more or less told him to come off it: why shouldn't we, loyal citizens, get in contact with the Queen without going through him?" Castley said: "It must have dawned on him that here he was, Her Majesty's representative in Australia, stuck on a private balcony five floors up from the water, and it was after 3 am and maybe he'd had enough and ought to leave." The party broke up.

Elizabeth Reid describes her impression of Kerr at this time: "The overwhelming impression I had was of his growing megalomania. He was very conscious of, and often referred to, the fact that he was the first man in Australia. He told me he wanted to go down in history as Australia's greatest twentieth-century governor-general. He didn't want his appointment by a Labor government to work against this. He wanted to be above politics: he saw himself as a man in a unique position straddling two political parties, who was able to talk to and cooperate with both of them. He wanted to do this with the Liberals as well as with a Labor government. He seemed to think in this way he would become apolitical and rid himself of his Labor Party label. He was particularly keen to be the longest-serving governor-general."

Elizabeth Reid never told Whitlam about Kerr's advances or the degree of confidence the governor-general gave her. "But before I left Whitlam's office in October 1975, I told Whitlam not to trust the governor-general: that he would work against us. Apparently this advice didn't hit home."

*

On 14 March 1975 Nancy Robson, the wife of a Sydney judge, petitioned for divorce. Under the old laws then still in force, it would normally have taken about fifteen months for Mrs Robson to be free to remarry. The hearing was unlisted and after hours. Six weeks and a day later, she married the governor-general in Sydney. She was known as Lady Anne.

At the time of the marriage, Whitlam was at the Commonwealth Heads of Government meeting in Jamaica. Late one afternoon all the Australian party – press, staff and officials – were called to the main office in the Sheraton Hotel, Kingston. It was obvious something special was going on, but no one among the press knew what it was. "We arrived, had drinks, and after a while Whitlam arrived looking extremely pleased with himself," Paul Kelly recalls. "He then called the room to attention and made a brief announcement: 'I am delighted to tell you all before the news is released in Australia that the governor-general has just married.'"

Lady Kerr has never enjoyed a warm press. Her aloofness is apparent on sight. She brought a formality to bear on her position that politicians and those familiar with the Yarralumla round found faintly ridiculous. As we reported some time ago in the Clancy column (and the item is passed on in *The Truth of the Matter*), she took Mrs Fraser aside one afternoon to say that in private she might call her Anne.

An old friend of Kerr said: "She encouraged and thrived on the worst in him; the whole panoply of power that went on out there – coats of arms, the curtsying – obviously appealed to her as much as him. She was not a restraining influence." Around Lady Anne Kerr a new court grew up at Yarralumla. It was she who encouraged the National Gallery push, and young gallery assistants like Richard Cobden became familiars of Government House very much for her amusement. In *The Truth of the Matter*, Whitlam lists the works of art purchased by the National Gallery that were ordered to be hung at Yarralumla in the time of the second Lady Kerr. Many appear to have gone direct from salesroom to Government House. The Kerrs made a bit of a meal of it.

Jim Hall wrote: "The newly married couple began to entertain on a larger scale, at a time when the loans affair was coincidentally coming into the limelight. In May, June and July their guests noticed how obsessively Kerr brought up this subject." This dates Kerr's worries over the loans some five months later than he himself claims in his memoirs. Whitlam writes: "In July and August he told me that he was being embarrassed in the clubs by snide questions whether he had been approving any billion-dollar loans recently."

The Truth of the Matter presents a devastating rebuttal of Kerr's account of his relations with the prime minister in 1975. Kerr claimed four occasions when Whitlam seemed to make it clear that the "reserve" powers might be used against him. In Kerr's *Matters for Judgement* these are written up at length with details of often witty exchanges between himself and his prime minister.

Whitlam says one of those occasions did not take place since he was in fact in Sydney opening the Gymea Lily Festival. On another two, Whitlam claims the conversations did not occur: one was in Port Moresby at the Independence Day celebrations, the other in the anteroom of Government House, Melbourne, where the Whitlams and various vice-regals were waiting to go into a Melbourne Cup ball: "It was not the time nor the place for political pronouncements or confidences." The fourth was a crack he made to Kerr the night supply was blocked. It was before a dinner for Tun Abdul Razak at Yarralumla. Whitlam said: "It could be a question of whether I get to the Queen first for your recall or you get in first with my dismissal."

Whitlam writes that his old friend Razak had raised the matter of the crisis, but he had no wish to discuss it and made that "flippant remark" to move the conversation on to some other topic. "If Sir John had regarded the remark as sinister, why did he not take it up with me afterwards?"

Whitlam claims Lady Kerr influenced the governor-general's decision not to raise the dismissal issue with him. He writes: "Sir John related how he had told his wife that he intended to discuss with me proposals to dismiss my government and order an election, but she had told him not to do that because I would have the Queen sack him." The conversation had happened at the house of the poet James McAuley. Later there was an ambiguous denial by McAuley, but Whitlam holds his ground: "He did not deny the conversation I have recounted: he knew my informant and could not deny it."

Much of the dismissal controversy has centred on the question of whether Whitlam would have sacked Kerr had he known what was planned. To an extent Whitlam avoids the question in *The Truth of the Matter*: he did not know what was planned so he didn't give it a moment's thought. In any case it was a practical impossibility by November 11 itself. At the Press Club last week, Whitlam was asked: what would you have done if you'd learnt a week beforehand? Whitlam replied: "I'm not saying that if a governor-general is acting in a wrong way you don't take corrective action. Of course you do."

One of the great puzzles about the sacking is why Whitlam wanted to ease off the pressure by making alternative arrangements for paying public servants. The prospect of chaos brought on by the senators' refusal to pass supply was the only thing focusing the minds of the Opposition. The alternative financial arrangements injected a fresh controversy into the crisis, allowed Fraser to claim Whitlam was trying to stay in office illegally and were politically counterproductive to the government's "tough it out" strategy. Whitlam merely says: "My government was arranging for advances to be made by the banks to public servants ..." His assertion that the private banks would have joined the scheme "for fear of alienating" their customers is highly dubious.

In *The Truth of the Matter* Whitlam asserts that Fraser and Lynch knew what was to happen on November 11. He relies on the evidence of a Commonwealth car driver, Eric Kennedy, who overheard Lynch and Fraser in his car late on the night of November 10: "He doesn't seem to know anything about it. All we have to do now is hope the press doesn't get hold of it, because it could all blow up in our faces." This is interesting but falls far short of proof. Whitlam has still not the information that will establish a conspiracy between the Liberal Party and the governor-general.

The Truth of the Matter demonstrates that, above all, Kerr was lucky in the endgame. Kerr's luck held all afternoon. Even after the government had been sacked, Labor allowed the supply bills to go through the Senate. Whitlam makes a virtue of this terrible mistake. The failure of the Labor Party to inform its Senate leadership of the sacking and to deny supply to Prime Minister Fraser – one of the conditions of his commission – is excused by saying that Labor stuck to the rules to the bitter end.

But the great tactical error was to send the passed supply bills out to Yarralumla by messenger. Once they were in Kerr's hands he could dismiss parliament. On this, Whitlam, in *The Truth of the Matter*, comes as close as he ever does to an admission of misjudgement: "With the wisdom of hindsight we can all see that it would have been wiser if Mr Scholes [the Speaker] had taken the appropriation bills together with the resolution of the house to his appointment with the governor-general, instead of sending the bills ahead with the usual written message. This would have been a legitimate and, even against Sir John Kerr, an effective tactic."

For Kerr it all went like a dream.

The shedding of John Kerr was a painful business for Australia. It took two years. According to the same source that had Lady Kerr dissuading her husband from warning Whitlam of dismissal, she also dissuaded him from resigning after the election. A trip had been planned for the Kerrs at the end of 1975. They left, but the itinerary had vastly changed. It was not to be the exercise of the Persepolis Principle that Whitlam had planned. Whitlam writes: "None of his intended hosts were now willing to entertain him."

That was perhaps sweeping. He spent some time at Sandringham.

The National Times, 17 February 1979

The wreckage left behind

THEY WERE REMARKABLE DAYS. Concorde was flying its first passengers. Brett Whiteley, smacked off his brain, was at his peak. A team from the Australian embassy in Jakarta was in Balibo to see if four bodies might be dead Australian reporters. Of course, they were.

The federal government was entangled with that tar-baby fraud Tirath Khemlani but Gough Whitlam and his adversary, Malcolm Fraser, did the right thing by Princess Margaret, turning out on the tarmac to greet her when she arrived in Canberra. All three were all smiles.

This paper was demanding the overthrow of the government. "It is in the plainest interest of national self-preservation to get rid of a management which has reduced a rich and fortunate country to the verge of economic and social disintegration," *The Sydney Morning Herald* thundered on page one. It was not alone.

All the papers, in the end, were baying for Whitlam's blood. There was inflation, the loans affair, even a latent threat of communism. The Senate must cut off Labor's money and drive the government to the polls. If irregularities happen along the way, they could be washed clean at the ballot box.

To read their yellowing pages twenty-five years later is to stare media bias in the face.

The Liberals moved hesitantly towards November 11, urged on by the press, reassured for a while by opinion polls, buoyed by a sharemarket boom and blessed by Tory lawyers. They had a great run in the *Herald*. The initials "QC" had probably never appeared so often in the columns of the paper to such effect. Their advice was all the one way: combine the literal powers of the constitution (to block supply) with the historical powers of the Crown (to dismiss ministers) and Whitlam could be thrown out of office just about any time.

Labor lawyers were writing, too, of course, and some of their ideas were just as far-fetched, especially when it came to defending Whitlam's wild ideas for funding government if supply ran out. But the lawyer letter-writers defending the old understanding of how government worked in Australia didn't get much of a run in the papers. When eight of the most distinguished constitutional authorities in Australia – Stone, Sawer, Castles, Nettheim, Sackville, Zines and Howard – wrote urging the Liberals and the Senate to stop in the interests of the nation, they were sidelined by the press and their opinions dismissed by the Bar.

The year 1975 is not tucked away in a little historical cocoon. We keep discovering its impact on this country. Apart from everything else, 1975 has pride of place in the continuing history of whacky constitutional debate in Australia. Debate is good. Differences over the constitution are real. But whenever there's a big constitutional issue in the air, and every time we have a referendum, we find ourselves in a debate where no silly possibility is ever knocked out. Over the years the public impression has been that this damn document can be made to mean anything we like. No wonder it's all but impossible to change.

The silliest theories are always about the monarchy. Perhaps that's what monarchies are for: injecting mystery and romance into what should be the plain operation of a national constitution. Monarchy is a permanent source of uncertainty in the workings of government. Last year we heard what has to be the oddest constitutional notion ever seriously advanced in Australia: that the Queen is not the head of state.

Back in 1975, these same monarchists claimed the Crown had never lost the right to sack a ministry, even if it still has the confidence of the House of Representatives. Pat Lane, the feisty professor of law at Sydney University and one of the pro-sacking commentators used extensively by the press during the crisis, urged readers to forget humbug about conventions limiting the power of the governor-general: "He can seek his own advice, make his own decision."

Not in a democracy.

Those who reckon 1975 has no real meaning in Australia today might take another look at the republic debate. It's the afterlife of 1975. Still going. Still unresolved. The players then have been players for decades. Lloyd Waddy QC, now on the sidelines as a judge of the Family Court laid out the fantasies of the ultra-monarchists in the pages of this paper during the crisis of 1975 and went on to be the founding chair of Australians for a Constitutional Monarchy. Back in the crisis, Waddy sifted through the sordid local history of legislative councils busting state governments. He concluded that this showed "ample authority" for vice-regal intervention. Hardly. All that's absolutely clear from this history is that upper houses only ever bust Labor governments.

Commentators who dismiss November 11 as a tired cause of the Left would no doubt like this underlying rule forgotten. But Tories are always the busters and Labor is always the busted; 1975 still matters today because it brought that game to Canberra.

Very sensibly the Senate hadn't gone in for this sort of thing before Malcolm Fraser because, unlike the once Tory-dominated legislative councils, the Senate changes hands. Any party in the Senate busting a government in the Reps invites a return of the compliment. So even though the power to block supply is there in black and white in the constitution, it wasn't used. Prudent politics and democratic restraint produced the convention broken in 1975.

Constitutional chaos more or less forever was predicted by Whitlam's supporters. The fact that it hasn't turned out that way shouldn't be taken as proof that we can forget 1975. The aftermath has been calm because no government since Whitlam's has been so catastrophically vulnerable. 1975 broke the taboo. Now any Senate controlled by the Opposition can bust a government if it's certain it can win the election that would follow.

Early intervention by Sir John Kerr in 1975 was a godsend for Malcolm Fraser, but it isn't crucial to the way these exercises work. All the Opposition had to do was sit it out until supply was truly exhausted, in early December in Whitlam's case, and then no one could sensibly complain if the governor-general directed the prime minister to take the government to the people. At the end of the day, but only at the end of the day, Kerr had the power to resolve the dispute.

Newspapers of the time fudged the crucial issue of the clock superbly. As October turned to November and Whitlam showed no sign of capitulating, Laurie Gruzman QC, in the letters columns of this paper, called this "an illegal de facto exercise of power". The press was lapping up any bizarre scheme from Phillip Street to excuse an early intervention by Kerr. The problem was not constitutional but political, of course. There were real doubts whether Fraser's troops could take the punishment much longer.

Sir Garfield Barwick invented the excuse: the idea that governments can be sacked if they refuse to resign once they lose the "confidence of Parliament". When the old man died in 1997, I rang around the law schools of Australia and spoke to fifteen leading constitutional authorities. None backed Barwick's idea about the "confidence of Parliament". Not a single one. Neither before nor after 1975 has it ever been doubted that the only "confidence" a government needs is the "confidence" of the House of Representatives. The Senate has no say whatsoever in John Howard being prime minister of Australia. But in the overheated atmosphere of 1975, Barwick's idea did the trick.

Curiously we have to live less with the aftermath of Kerr and Barwick than we do with Fraser and the Senate. Political division keeps the public debate on 1975 unresolved, but there is a strong professional consensus that what Kerr and Barwick did was wrong in law. Any future governor-general who tried to intervene early in a brawl between the Senate and the Reps would immediately be challenged in the High Court.

Some of us will live to see the fiftieth anniversary of this shameful little incident. The question then will be whether the deepest inheritance of that day has been dealt with: the fact that we don't really know where power ultimately lies in our constitution. We look at the Queen, the governor-general and the Senate and see a line of question marks, endless debate with pages of footnotes. It's not going to change by calling the governor-general Mr President.

Sometime or other we're going to have to do what most nations do: sit down and list the powers of our head of state on a piece of paper. The press will have a fabulous time. Open season for the heirs of today's QCs. Mad theories everywhere. Only then will we be able to forget 1975. What a relief.

The Sydney Morning Herald, 11 November 2000

Fraser's first
cabinet meeting

AFTER THE DRAMA OF NOVEMBER 11, Malcolm Fraser found himself the next day holding his first cabinet meeting. The ministers were stunned and excited, recalled John Menadue, who was present in the cabinet room of the Old Parliament House in his role as head of the Department of Prime Minister and Cabinet. "They had never really thought they would pull it off, and they had."

It was a long afternoon. The documents released yesterday record the nuts and bolts: a briefing on the economic situation from Treasury; permission given to TAA to buy an aircraft; notice given to the staffs of Labor ministers; and the rescinding of the Whitlam cabinet's penny-pinching measures to save money as supply dwindled. Bills and superannuation contributions would now be paid; ministerial and departmental hospitality would resume; season's greeting would be sent. Paragraph 3 (c) of decision No. 8 of the first Fraser cabinet reads: "The Cabinet agreed to remove the special restrictions introduced by the previous government in respect of Christmas cards."

But the great drama of the afternoon is unrecorded in that spare list. To Menadue's amazement, the Liberal grandee Sir John Carrick raised at that first meeting accusations that Australian non-government organisations and the World Council of Churches were supporting liberation movements in southern Africa. Menadue recalled: "There was speculation that money from these organisations had been used not just for humanitarian purposes in Rhodesia and South Africa but had been used in fact to support terrorist activity." Carrick's intervention was met by mutterings of support around the cabinet table.

The response was a ferocious rebuke. "Malcolm Fraser took this opportunity to tear into Ian Smith – that he wasn't just politically mad, he was clinically mad, and that he, Malcolm, wouldn't have a bar [of] him and people around the cabinet table should forget all these stories about World Council of Churches money being diverted to terrorist activities and that he could understand this opposition to those white regimes in Southern Africa. I just shook my head – first that it was considered so urgent that it was raised at that first cabinet meeting, and second at Malcolm's response, which had me amazed. He pinned his flag to the mast on that one very early."

Many political issues were canvassed that afternoon, but Menadue recalls no discussion about the possibility of civil violence in the aftermath of the sacking of Whitlam. "It says something about the passivity of the Australians. If they wouldn't go on riots or strikes over something like that, what would upset them?"

Cabinet had to deal with the limits Sir John Kerr set on the government he installed: no appointments, no new policies, and customary restraint on exploiting the records of the outgoing government. Menadue had the "general impression" that Fraser and the cabinet complied with the spirit of Kerr's original directives on appointments and policy. Yet new policies were put in place in these weeks. Menadue explains these decisions as a tactical response to hostile leaks from within the public service. "There was certainly a fair bit of leaking going on out of the departments of material that had been prepared for the government in anticipation of the elections, and I know that was leaked because it cropped up in the press and it was probably used by Labor candidates."

Fraser held two cabinet meetings before the elections, on November 12 and 19. After his sweeping victory on December 13 cabinet met only once more in 1975. Discussion about rebadging the country "The Commonwealth of Australia" once more began but was postponed. With that whimper, the most extraordinary year in Australia political history ended.

The Sydney Morning Herald, 2 January 2006

Edward Gough Whitlam shuffles off his mortal coil

IN THE END, DESPITE THE ORATORY and anthems in Sydney's immense town hall, this was a sad occasion. Gough Whitlam lived forever but his time in power was so short. The more speakers eulogised his achievements, the more pressing the question: what might he have done if he had been allowed more time?

Even on a great state occasion, crowds can be brutal. Julia Gillard was given an immense ovation. They stood for her, shouting, whistling and stamping. She was kissed. Flowers were pressed into her hands. Kevin Rudd walked the aisle in stony silence. The Labor faithful sat as if stuck to their seats.

Though Whitlam spent years finessing the details of this event, the Sydney Town Hall was not the site he wanted. "His first choice was to have a funeral pyre in the Senate," claimed Kerry O'Brien, the ABC television journalist who once served on Whitlam's staff. "He rather liked the idea of taking the Senate with him."

His old nemesis Malcolm Fraser was there. The two men had long reconciled. He was received politely. So was Tony Abbott. None of the speakers said so directly – they didn't have to – but in mourning Whitlam they were also mourning that power was back in the hands of his old opponents, those who had done so little for so long.

Two men brought Whitlam most alive at the microphone: his old speechwriter and collaborator Graham Freudenberg, and his old friend and confidant Senator John Faulkner. Faulkner even dropped into The Voice as he told Gough jokes. But in his own voice Faulkner declared: "Whitlam made the Labor Party electable. More importantly, he made the Labor Party worth electing."

Yet Noel Pearson raised the roof. He is beyond contest the greatest Lutheran preacher in the country. He barely mentioned Whitlam's name, as if he were honouring the dead in his own people's way. He called him "This old man". He said: "This old man was one of those rare people who never suffered discrimination but understood the importance of protection against its malice." Pearson was not the only speaker to acknowledge Whitlam's great mistakes. But to a roar of applause he declared the government of 1972 to 1975 "the textbook case of reform trumping management".

So many in the Town Hall had invested such hope in Whitlam. The word tolled through the speeches: hope. And bursts of applause offered surprising evidence of old causes that have never died. Who would have thought mention of Whitlam abolishing conscription would electrify a crowd in 2014?

He loved a long meeting. This was as long as the grandest requiem mass. Margaret Whitlam was not there to do as she did for years: bang her stick on the floor and suggest we wind things up. No one shifted in their seats. No one drifted out as the clock ticked over into a third hour.

The great William Barton played the didgeridoo. Whitlam had left instructions for the Sydney Symphony and the Sydney Philharmonia Choirs to perform Bach and Verdi. It would seem his strategy was to remind us of the Crucifixion with one and the liberation of Italy with the other – a couple of events against which he seemed to think now was the time to measure himself.

Tony Whitlam, a big, elegant man, did all the right things: he thanked those who had worked for his father in and out of power through all those years and "endured his occasional changes in temperament". He reminded us that stamina is crucial in politics and that until a couple of months ago his father, at the age of ninety-eight, was still turning up to the office a few days a week. He spoke of the "grace and serenity with which he accepted the decline of his health".

And then the orchestra played the only possible recessional for any Labor leader, even an old atheist like Whitlam: "Jerusalem", William Blake's great hymn to the coming of civilisation to the satanic mills of industrial England.

You suspect Whitlam sees it as a work in progress.

The Guardian, 5 November 2014

Political History

Franz Ferdinand and the guns of Narromine

IN ABSOLUTE SILENCE, TWO MEN stood beside the Wollondilly River. It was barely light. The grazier touched his distinguished guest's shoulder and pointed. "On the surface of the murky water I saw only a narrow, black, moving line," wrote Archduke Franz Ferdinand. With the "greatest joy" he then fulfilled his "burning desire" to shoot a platypus.

West of Moss Vale, New South Wales, with killing on his mind was the man whose assassination was to provoke World War I. Since leaving home in a mighty warship to tour the globe in late 1892, the heir to the throne of Austria-Hungary had shot his way across India, Ceylon and Java before turning the attention of his guns on New South Wales. Among the cavalcade of royal tours in the late nineteenth century, this one is forgotten: a ten-day visit by the man who had unexpectedly become heir to an empire on the suicide of his cousin at Mayerling. He was a hunter and collector. As he waited for his one big moment in history, he was living by the gun.

"With an utter absence of all ostentatious display," reported *The Daily Telegraph*, "and with the unassuming quietness of a simple gentleman, his Imperial and Royal Highness Franz Ferdinand Charles Louis Joseph Marie d'Este, Archduke of Austria" – there followed a string of titles, ranks, regiments – "landed in Sydney yesterday." Not quite without display. His ship had come up the harbour with guns blazing in a ceremonial salute. The lieutenant-governor and the lord mayor had quickly come on board to grovel. But as no one had a clue what the thirty-year-old archduke looked like – dead eyes, upturned moustache – he was later able to get ashore unrecognised and tootle round the town with friends in a couple of hansom cabs. He spoke no English.

After a visit to the Australian Museum to inspect the marsupials he was about to slaughter, the archduke left by special train for Narromine. The killing began early. "Immediately after breakfast the party set out with twenty horsemen to drive the game," *The Sydney Morning Herald* reported. "At the first drive his Imperial Highness succeeded in shooting, with great rapidity, five kangaroos, so that he very soon established himself in the estimation of those present as being a first-class marksman."

The carnage over the next few days in Narromine and Mullengudgery was terrible: more kangaroo, wallaby, duck, pelican, ibis, crane, eagle, bush turkey – plentiful but shy – emu and several "lovely" parrots. The archduke was "absolutely delighted" to bag a pair of black swans. Travelling with the party was the royal taxidermist and photographer. "Specimen skins of all the animals and birds shot are preserved," noted this paper, "with a view to their being ultimately stuffed."

Franz Ferdinand was planning to publish his diary. The Australian chapters of *My Journey Round the World* record many pleasures and a few disappointments. Not all the horses were up to scratch. The habit of ring-barking trees was producing "desolate vistas". His host at Narromine, Frank Mack, scared away the pelicans. He deplored the hunting time wasted by the British habit of stopping for lunch. It wasn't as bad as in India. "There was no Champagne or silver cutlery, nor a set table, but only an open fire on a grate and roasted mutton half raw, half burnt to eat. I used the time these culinary preparations required to shoot some examples of bird species new to me."

After a touching homage from a poorly dressed young Austrian who appeared out of the crowd at Narromine station, the archduke returned to Sydney, endured a two-and-a-half-hour mass at St Mary's, inspected a meat works at Auburn – and found the product delicious – then headed to Moss Vale for more sport.

Newspapers were complaining. "The archduke is giving Sydney the cold shoulder," wrote the *Illustrated Sydney News*. "He seems to prefer the country and the kangaroos to the metropolis and the maids." Along the new front, casualties were high: "About 300 head including bears, rock walla-bies, kangaroos, hares, duck, pademelons and platypus etc," the *Herald*'s correspondent telegraphed to Sydney. "His Highness is an excellent shot, having with a bullet potted a magpie at about a hundred yards distance whilst standing in his carriage."

Unreported was the koala shot on the way down to the river on that dawn platypus hunt. Koalas disappointed the archduke. He thought them like sloths: pathetic and lazy. They didn't flee. He shot several. The shooting went on before breakfast and after dinner. Following a "sumptuous" banquet in the bush to celebrate Queen Victoria's birthday, the archduke led a party to hunt possums for three hours by moonlight.

The killing had to end. After inspecting the Art Gallery of New South Wales, shopping for skins and specimens, watching demonstrations of shearing and boomerang throwing, holding a most successful afternoon dance on his warship and attending the Randwick races and FitzGerald's circus, the royal visitor steamed out of the harbour and the memory of New South Wales.

Franz Ferdinand had a long wait for destiny to strike. Twenty years after his trip around the world, he was still doing the things heirs do when they're waiting for their mother or father or uncle to die. Shooting and touring. That took him on a goodwill visit to the Bosnian capital of Sarajevo on 28 June 1914.

Seven Serbian suicide terrorists were waiting. But only a single bomb was thrown at the archduke's motorcade, injuring one military aide. After an uneasy reception at the town hall, Franz Ferdinand decided to visit the injured man in hospital. What followed was the most crucial accident in modern European history. No one had briefed the chauffeurs. After taking a wrong turn into the old city, they were ordered to stop. Standing by chance on the narrow footpath beside the open car was one of the terrorists who had lost his nerve earlier that morning. Gavrilo Princip leant forward and shot the royal couple with a Browning pistol.

A month later the world was at war. On memorials in Narromine and Moss Vale are recorded those districts' contribution to the fifteen million slaughtered in the bloodiest and most pointless conflict in history. Nothing for the animals.

The Sydney Morning Herald, 25 April 2009

The night Ben Chifley died

THE HEART RESERVES ONE OF its best tricks for last. As it's about to fail, it gives a stray, deceptive hint of trouble: a pain in the left arm, sometimes a toothache. Perhaps both. On the last afternoon of his life, Ben Chifley opened the door of his office and said, "I've got to go to the dentist now. I'll see you tomorrow."

About 4 pm, he sauntered out of the parliament, leaving behind a building in the last stages of preparations for that night's state ball. Palms had sprouted in the unheated corridors. The party rooms were now bars, with temporary sinks and plumbing. Scrubbed to vice-regal standards were the senators' lavatories. Huge bowls of red, white and blue flowers – poinsettias, gladioli, carnations and delphiniums – were in place in King's Hall. A platform was there for the band. Parliament's red carpet was ready to be rolled down the steps and out into the winter murk. But Chifley was passing on the party. "You can go and trip the bloody light fantastic," he told young Fred Daly. "I'm going home to read a couple of westerns."

One of the many myths of this night is that Ben Chifley stayed away from the ball because he didn't have the "Evening Dress or Dinner Jacket with Decorations" demanded by the invitation. It's true he always refused to dress up, but he was never deterred by protocol. On these matters he always got his way. Even the King had worn a plain suit at the palace one night so Mr Chifley would come to dinner. It was just that balls were not for him, not even a ball to mark the fiftieth anniversary of the first sitting of federal parliament.

He didn't dance. He was not a drinker. He had no partner. His wife lived in Bathurst in deliberate and permanent exile from his political world.

Frail and timid, an invalid most of her life, Elizabeth Chifley spent her days in their cottage playing cards and doing needlework with her companion, Mrs Clarke. Chifley drove home every fortnight, but spent most of those eighteen-hour visits on electoral business. He never stopped working; his wife never took part.

And perhaps Chifley felt there was nothing much to celebrate. By June 1951 he had lost office as prime minister and led Labor to two election defeats in eighteen months, the latter having occurred only weeks previously. Indeed, the jubilee celebrations had been postponed for a month so the new prime minister, Bob Menzies, could call elections to inflict that second terrible defeat on Chifley. Now Labor had lost even control of the Senate. The party's dreams of a reconstructed Australia were slipping away.

Late in the afternoon Chifley arrived at the Hotel Kurrajong, where he always lived when in Canberra. Even when he was prime minister, Chifley preferred the domestic buzz of the Kurra to the lonely comforts of The Lodge. He had a plain room on the first floor – supposedly never locked – with a bed, a phone, a cupboard and a bathroom down the hall. Until the last couple of elections, the Kurra had been a Labor stronghold. Now things were changing even here: Menzies had brought a new generation of Liberal politicians to town who couldn't afford to live with party grandees at the Hotel Canberra.

Chifley always ate with the Calwells. At some point in this day he told Elizabeth Calwell he was not going to the ball. "I'm doing something I like very much. I'm going to bed and reading." Mrs Calwell replied: "I too am doing something I like very much. I'm looking after the Beazley children." Merrilyn was one and Kim was four.

Chifley was in his room in time to listen to the ABC news, made his daily call to his wife and settled down with a pipe to listen to Nation's Forum of the Air. Two of his own men were on a panel of parliamentarians addressing the question, "Are we happier than we were fifty years ago?"

Later in the evening, a few Labor couples looked in on the way to the ball. With Chifley was Phyllis Donnelly. The outside world knew nothing of her before this night but she had been with Chifley all his political career. Her formal position was personal typist, and next day the press would explain her presence in the room by reporting that she had taken her boss "some newspapers" (*The Herald*) or "a cup of tea" (*The Telegraph*). They would lie that she had "found" Chifley – but she was there.

Such discretion was of its time. But it says a great deal for the man that, fifty years later, pains are still being taken to preserve the image of his bedrock respectability. Diane Langmore was coy in *Prime Ministers' Wives*: "The closeness and intimacy of his relationship with Phyllis Donnelly, who devoted her life to him, must have been a great comfort." Even *True Believers,* the official Labor history published only the other day, baulks at saying the word. But when Labor men and women discuss the history of their party they take for granted what has only once – in David Day's *John Curtin: A Life* – been put bluntly in print: this tall Bathurst woman with a marked sense of fun and strong public reserve was Chifley's mistress. The great man was a human being.

All this happened fifty years ago: 13 June 1951. In King's Hall, at nine pm, Jim Gussey's twenty-two-piece ABC Dance Band began to play the 'Jubilee Waltz'. Menzies was at the top of the steps waiting for the governors and the governor-general, Bill McKell. They were late. Beside him stood Mrs Menzies "in a gown of misty grey chiffon embroidered all over with leaves of gold thread and mounted on sunset pink satin". *The Age* also reported "a diamond tiara glittered in her hair".

Balls are curious political events. All through history they've marked the return of monarchs and the restoration of old ways. After austere political years, dancing returns. Something of that spirit was in the air in Australia's bush capital. This was to be the grandest bash Canberra had ever seen, and the political message of the event – despite butter shortages, inflation, war in Korea and the communist menace at home – was that, under Menzies, Australia was heading for a new, prosperous version of the old days. Months of manoeuvring had gone into this night. Menzies had even had to placate the cantankerous, teetotal, Catholic-convert speaker of the House of Representatives, Archie Cameron, before the event could go ahead. "I do not object to the use of the Parliament House for the functions proposed to be held in it," Cameron wrote to Menzies. "Nor do I object to either dignity nor hospitality. My observations have taught me they seldom go hand in hand."

Dignity was very much on the prime minister's mind. His people had produced a rigorously official invitation list: Australia's governors, privy councillors, knights, premiers, service chiefs, permanent heads of Commonwealth departments – many of whom still lived and worked in Melbourne – plus justices of the High Court, church leaders, all high commissioners and ambassadors, and every member of the national parliament.

This last category included irascible Billy Hughes, the only parliamentarian to have sat there all those fifty years. The postponement of the ball from May to June had dashed Menzies' hopes that a squad of Commonwealth prime ministers would lead the list of overseas guests. New Zealand's Sidney Holland had made the trip across the Tasman, but otherwise the British nations were represented only by statesmen politicians. From across the Pacific came two Democrats and two Republicans from the United States Congress.

The arrival of these visitors by air gave particular glamour to the celebrations. Canberra was hard-pressed to accommodate them. The embassies were full. All hotel and hostel accommodation had been requisitioned by the Prime Minister's Department. The McKells had been persuaded to take all the governors at Yarralumla. At The Lodge, Menzies had two house guests of his own, the graziers Roy McCaughey of Darling Point and Otway Falkiner of Boonoke. These were, after all, the wool boom years, and while they lasted the doomed aristocracy of the bush had never seemed so splendid.

Considered and rejected for the ball were a number of importuning political widows, but Lady Isaacs, widow of the first Australian-born governor-general, was issued an invitation. Not so lucky were academics newly arrived at the National University and Canberra College. A long list was considered and all but a couple of names rejected. Among those not coming to the ball were the Manning Clarks, the A.D. Hopes, the Marcus Oliphants, the Geoffrey Sawers, the C.P. Fitzgeralds and the Ernest Tittertons. Dancing, not intelligent conversation, was the business of the night.

Here the organisers faced a problem familiar to readers of Tolstoy and Austen: there are never enough young men at balls. The daughters of all members of Parliament were coming; so were the daughters of the governors and important citizens. Suitable dancing partners had to be found. In April an official of the Prime Minister's Department rang Duntroon, Point Cook and the Royal Naval College, asking each for the names of a dozen cadets who would be marching at the ceremonial opening of parliament the week of the ball. War, age and accident have taken their toll on these thirty-six eligible young men, but the survivors have talked about this night all their lives. They arrived by bus, were dumped at the door, then farmed out by vice-regal aides-de-camp.

Another military detachment had arrived some hours before. These were orderlies from Duntroon brought in to reinforce the parliament's staff

and waiters bussed from Sydney for the occasion. Archie Cameron's decision to pay them partly in undrunk beer – 140 dozen of the 244 dozen bottles
on ice for the ball – was to lead to a nasty brawl, with Cameron complaining to the prime minister of the "rank impertinence" of his department for
tampering with parliament's prerogatives. But that was still some unhappy
months away. All afternoon the staff had worked with sober, military precision and the buffet was ready before the first of the 834 guests arrived.

Everything was cold: roast suckling pigs in party hats; whole snapper
in aspic; corned silverside; roasts of mutton, duck and turkey; oysters and
prawns; fowl cooked seven ways – according to the menu, "*a l'escarlate*;
Dampierre; *Chaud. Froid Rossini*" – soused herring; pressed tongue; lobster
prepared eight different ways – "Grammont; Belle Vue; Mousse; Archangel
Cutlets; In Aspic" – plus hams, salads, savouries, puddings, fruit pies and
two novelty cakes: one of a tropical island with a hula girl and one of a Tu-
dor cottage.

Malcolm Baird, now a pastoralist in Tasmania, was then a seventeen-
year-old naval cadet: "It was a magic evening. I remember us being in our
naval uniforms, which we thought frightfully flash, and talking to people
whose names I'd only ever read in the newspapers, like Arthur Fadden and
his daughter. I couldn't believe my eyes – the splendour of people, music,
the portraits on the walls, the jewels. I thought to myself, crikey, fancy this
for a boy from the bush."

As the governor-general's car was pulling up outside the floodlit parliament about 9.30, Ben Chifley sat up in bed complaining of chest pains.
On the wireless was the voice of the ABC compere: "Your excellencies,
my lords, ladies and gentlemen, His Excellency the Governor-General and
Mrs McKell are now entering King's Hall." At the Kurra, Chifley made light
of what was happening and refused to let Phyllis Donnelly call his doctor.

These days, anyone who smoked as much as Chifley would be marked
as a walking corpse. But in 1951 a pipe was still the sign of a man you could
trust. He had spent his days lighting, puffing and sucking them. Chifley's
rooms were full of smoke, ash and spluttering matches. He was an addict
and pipes were his trademark. But tobacco didn't worry his friends nearly
as much as the toll politics was taking on Chifley. He was sixty-five. After a
decade as wartime treasurer and peacetime prime minister he was trying
to hold his party together as radical Catholics fought their anti-Left crusade through its ranks. "You can't give in to a few fanatics within your own

party," Chifley had said. "You know, the religious fanatic is worse than the political fanatic." But he was made to give way. Nothing so aged Chifley as the humiliations of 1950 when his party forced him to allow anti-communist and conscription legislation through parliament in violation of fundamental Labor principles. Then as now, Labor was in one of its gutless moods.

A few weeks before Christmas 1950, while at the wheel of the powerful Buick he kept garaged in Bathurst, Chifley had had a first heart attack. He lay in the District Hospital for a month making a recovery the press called "remarkable", "marvellous" and "splendid". The *Mirror* also reported: "He was admitted very limited use of his pipe." Chifley was back in Canberra after only two months, promising to stick to a new regimen: naps in his office in the afternoons. But to Fred Daly and young Clyde Cameron, he confessed he was only hanging onto office in the hope of finding someone other than Bert (Doc) Evatt to succeed him. "You look tired. Why don't you get out?" Cameron asked him one day. "Bert is my deputy," Chifley replied. "I honestly don't think he could do it."

Any chance of shifting the course of Australian history ended on the night of the Jubilee Ball. Chifley was still protesting he didn't need a doctor, but at about 9.45 Phyllis Donnelly rang John Holt, medico to prime ministers, who lived near the Kurrajong and arrived in time to find Chifley still arguing against doctors and hospitals as he slipped into a coma. Holt called the ambulance.

Someone roused Bill O'Connor in his room at the Kurra. The Labor member for Martin was not a dancing man. "He walked with a stick," Kim Beazley Snr remembers. "And his legs were curiously close together." O'Connor was also a devout Catholic and knew that in the eyes of his church, Chifley had some reckoning to do. The Chifleys had married in a Protestant ceremony and for nearly forty years Chif had been "a back-pew Catholic" – a regular attender but never taking mass. At St Christopher's in Bathurst a little chair was kept up the back for Mr Chifley. O'Connor rang a priest. Perhaps it was O'Connor who got a message through to Evatt at the ball. Evatt then found Daly. "Fred, come into the library immediately, Chifley's dying." They alerted the Labor leader in the Senate, Nick McKenna, and the three left for the hospital. Chifley's loyal press secretary, Don Rodgers, was at the ball and remained behind waiting for news. Menzies was told of Chifley's collapse. He sent instructions, "If he needs one heart specialist or half a dozen, get them."

O'Connor travelled in the ambulance that brought Chifley to the Canberra Community Hospital at 10.30. An hour had passed since the attack. The medical superintendent directed the patient be placed in an oxygen tent. Dr Lloyd Olver later admitted this move was "a forlorn hope". The priest arrived. If Phyllis Donnelly also followed to the hospital, her presence there went unnoticed by history. Neither in the remaining drama of this night nor in the time of national mourning to come was there any public place for her. From the moment the ambulance leaves the Kurra, she disappears.

King's Hall had come alive. "Glamour was abroad on this evening with women in gleaming satins, rich brocades and filmy tulles," reported *The Age*. "The long white kid gloves, occasional tiaras and graceful feather fans added a note of dignity and formality, heightened by the presence of the many uniforms and orders worn by the men and women." For Cadet Midshipman Malcolm Baird, it was a scene of "majestic gaiety".

Alan Nash was on trumpet in Jim Gussey's band. He remembers playing to an almost empty dance floor for a while. But that was always the way at balls: they only got going after a few hours' drinking. "People, when they get a bit of jump-about in them, get keener." There was lots of booze. "Every variety of drink from champagne to beer flowed freely," said *The Age*. "But for the first few hours of the ball, strict party divisions were adhered to. Liberals and Country Party members kept to the government lobbies and Labor members concentrated in their own Opposition room." Now, party barriers were coming down.

The press gallery, a floor above King's Hall, was still at work. In those days, papers didn't "get to bed" until a little before midnight. So while a few favoured journalists were dressed up and dancing downstairs, the rest of their colleagues were still filing the news of the day – when not nipping down to take a squiz at the celebrations. But at about eleven, a white-faced Don Rodgers appeared with a number of correspondents in evening dress. He rang the gallery bell. "Mr Chifley is gravely ill," he announced. "He is in the Canberra Hospital under oxygen."

But the Labor posse of Evatt, McKenna and Daly had arrived at the hospital to find Chifley was dead. The priest was by his bed. Daly asked if he'd arrived in time. "He said he may have, it was just a question of when life leaves the body." More was hanging on this than Chifley's salvation: unless extreme unction had come in time, the church should not bury its distinguished son with full religious honours. Some newspapers were to fudge the time and place of the death but *The Age* and *The Sydney Morning Herald* reported it with secular clarity: Ben Chifley had died in the ambulance on the way from the Kurrajong before the priest arrived.

Daly rang Elizabeth Chifley in Bathurst. She collapsed. The Labor men then returned to the party. Evatt went straight to his room. "The tears were pouring down Evatt's face," wrote his biographer Kylie Tennant. "Arthur Calwell, leader of the Victorian Labor men, was hardly less affected. Menzies, who came hastening with offers of help, was also genuinely grieved. He had always had a personal regard for Chifley. Now he asked if they thought there should be an announcement. Should the guests be sent home? Yes, they said, the ball should be terminated."

Grief had a peculiar geography that night. Upstairs, journalists had abandoned the party to type, off the top of their heads, obituaries for the locomotive driver who became prime minister and lost office trying to nationalise the banks. John O'Hara, later a veteran Fairfax political correspondent, was one of the young men upstairs: "A hell of a lot of the gallery were in tears." The kitchens heard from the real sleuths on these occasions: the waiters. "We were all upset," recalled Colin Telfer, then a storeman and later a catering manager of parliament. "Mr Chifley was a very kind man. He was always working and coming to the dining room late. I'd heard him say to waitresses, 'Don't worry, dear, just bring me a corned beef sandwich.' They'd rush back to the chef and shout, 'Stop! Heat up blah blah blah for Mr Chifley.' And it would be done."

At 11.29 the ABC put out a news flash that Chifley was dead, played the national anthem and shut down its networks for the night. But in King's Hall the dancing continued. The Beazleys were dancing unawares. So were the Bill Wentworths. As far as Frank Crean was concerned, "It was going along in all the usual gaiety of the occasion." But a very angry Clyde Cameron confronted the Liberal minister Wilfrid Kent Hughes and told him to stop the music. "Kent Hughes said, 'Don't be so bloody silly. That won't bring him back.' I was desperate, broken down and crying. I went over to Menzies and said, 'Ben Chifley's dead and Kent Hughes won't stop the dancing.' Menzies said, 'I just found out myself,' and went straight up to the band wiping tears from his eyes ..."

Australia has a way of not quite delivering great gestures. About 11.50 pm, the prime minister climbed the steps of the platform with awful news to announce. The occasion demanded a tall figure in tails raising his hand to stop the Jim Gussey band in the middle of a modern waltz. What happened was more like life. The musicians were resting for a moment in a bracket. Alan Nash remembers: "Some departmental person told us not to go on, there was going to be an announcement." The room was absolutely hushed. Menzies did not use the microphone. "It is my sorrowful duty to tell you that tonight, during this celebration, Mr Chifley, former prime minister and leader of the Opposition, has died. I do not want to try even to talk about him, because although we were political opponents, he was a great friend of mine and yours, and a fine Australian."

All these years later, Bill Wentworth has only one word for this moment: "Stupefaction. Everyone was stupefied." Evatt had emerged from his room with Fred Daly. Both were crying. Senator Dorothy Tangney stood by the statue of George V, weeping copiously. All over King's Hall, people broke down as Menzies spoke. "But there were no sobs around us," recalled Malcolm Baird. "I wasn't grief-stricken and I didn't look for people weeping. I thought it was another bit of the magic of the night to be there for this. I thought, he sounds just like he did on the films when he announced we were at war."

Menzies continued: "It does not matter about Party politics on an occasion like this. Oddly enough, in Parliament we get to know each other very well and sometimes find that we have the warmest friendship among the people whose politics are not ours.

Mr Chifley served this country magnificently for years, and the sorrow that all of his own people feel is completely shared by myself and by the members of parliament.

I would just like to say that this cruel blow I hope will be softened for Mrs Chifley by the knowledge that there is no Australian who hears this sad news tonight who won't have a tear to shed for the man.

He served his country and undoubtedly accelerated the date of his own passing by the devotion he has shown to the people of his own land and indeed to the peoples of the world."

The great myth of the night Ben Chifley died is that the party came to an immediate halt as the guests streamed, weeping, out into the winter night. In fact, Menzies ordered a compromise: the dancing would stop but eating and drinking could go on. "In the circumstances, there will be no more music. I do suggest that you have supper and that we then leave quietly."

Many did go at once. Most headed for the buffet. Bill Simmons, now a retired air vice-marshal, found himself behind two politicians. "I don't mind if they stop the dancing," one remarked to the other, "so long as they don't stop the drinking." The heavy wooden doors that divided the dining room were open and the buffet, with its tonnage of cold food guarded by ice swans, stretched the length of the room. "No more than a quarter of the guests left," said Colin Telfer. "The rest rushed back and carried on as though nothing had happened." Did they get through the food? "They did." It was well after 1 am before the parliament cleared. Some drunks hung on. "There was this disgraceful aspect," recalls John O'Hara. "Menzies had just won elections on the basis of Chifley being a rank socialist. The younger politicians who didn't understand Chifley kept on drinking and were last seen kicking champagne bottles down the corridors at 5 am."

Thirty hours after the revellers left King's Hall, Chifley's body was lying there in state and the eligible young men were filing past in their uniforms. The body was taken on a gun carriage to the RAAF base and flown home. Now he was dead, old adversaries were gushing about the great man, but O'Hara recalls the priests at the requiem mass that Sunday being very grudging. In Bathurst, the politics of faith were played hard. Elizabeth Chifley didn't make it to the cemetery but the nation's leaders were there, gathered again, this time at a graveside. On the memorial obelisk, paid for by the party, is carved and gilded Ben Chifley's famous last rebuke to his enemies in the Labor ranks: "If an idea is worth fighting for, no matter the penalty, fight for the right, and truth and justice will prevail."

The Sydney Morning Herald, 9 June 2001

John Howard's enterprising father

THE CORNER OF EWART STREET and Wardell Road in Sydney's Dulwich Hill is sacred ground for John Howard and the modern Liberal Party. For nearly thirty years, the prime minister's father, Lyall, ran a service station on this spot, setting an example his son thinks Australia should follow. "I was brought up to believe that about the best thing you could ever do in your life," he said soon after taking office, "was to start up a business with nothing, work your insides out, hope you earned a bit of money, and pass on a bit of it to your kids." His mother's church and his father's service station have come to stand as markers of respectability, honesty and his family's deep roots in the suburban heart of the nation. To be the son of a service-station owner allows John Howard to claim as a qualification for high office that he was and remains an ordinary Australian.

But Howard's father had another life. While he worked his humble Sydney service station, he was also – on paper – a New Guinea planter with a string of estates where two hundred native labourers grew copra in his name. Lyall Howard was a "dummy" for the trading house WR Carpenter and Co. Limited. His own father, ex-digger Walter, was too. The Howard case provoked secret official investigations at the highest levels in Canberra, but the Howards and their powerful backer got away with the scam.

The Treaty of Versailles spelt the end for the German planters of New Guinea. Australia took over the colony, stripped them of their land and sent them packing in the early 1920s. The prime minister, Billy Hughes, promised "New Guinea for the returned serviceman", and ex-diggers were offered very generous terms when 40,000 hectares of plantations went on the market in 1926 and 1927. A hefty catalogue spruiked them as "The

Envy of Planters, The Magnet of Copra Buyers" and quoted Shakespeare to inspire investors down south: "There is a tide in the affairs of men which taken at the flood leads on to fortune."

For Lyall Falconer Howard, the tide was well out. He had fought in France, was gassed at Passchendaele and returned home to work as a mechanic at CSR. The prime minister remembers his father as "a very quiet, very, very lovely bloke". About the time Lyall married the forceful Mona Kell, he lost his job at CSR. As the plantations came on the market, she was about to give birth to their first son, Walter. Yet at this nadir, Lyall Howard tendered to buy four plantations on Karkar, a volcanic island with perfect soil off the coast of Madang. He was awarded two: Kavilo for £9800 and Marangis for £30,600 – in today's currency a total of roughly $4 million. As an ex-digger, he had only to stump up a fifteen per cent deposit and then pay off the rest over twenty years. Every penny of that £6060 deposit – and more – was provided by Carpenters.

Copra went into soap, margarine, cooking oil and even explosives. The market was always volatile and plantations were prey to cyclones and bugs. But until the industry was ruined by American soya beans in the late 1980s, copra brought prosperity to the Pacific and made fortunes for the two Australian companies that dominated the trade: Burns Philp and Carpenters. Both were using dummies: former diggers who bought in their own names but signed management of the businesses over to their backers lock, stock and barrel. Carpenters and Burns Philp could have tendered for these plantations in their own names, but that would mean outlaying twice the deposit and paying the balance back. Using dummies slashed their costs and sabotaged Canberra's policy of favouring old soldiers.

It was a scandal from the start. Canberra fine-tuned the regulations but never took effective action to stamp out what the Commonwealth auditor-general denounced in 1927 as the "dummying evil". His portrait of the typical dummy fitted Lyall Howard to a tee: a returned soldier with few or no assets and no experience of plantation life who may never stir from Australia to visit his holdings. There is a legend still alive in New Guinea that a legless ex-digger found himself the owner of the mighty Bopiri plantation but lived out his days pulling the rope in the Burns Philp lift in Bridge Street, Sydney.

When the third and last tranche of plantations was offered for sale in July 1927, Lyall Howard put up his hand to pay £60,100 for a big place on a remote island near Manus with 150,000 palms on more than a thousand hectares worked by eighty labourers. And Walter – the grandfather of today's prime minister – tendered £25,100 for Enuk spread over a number of sandy little islands near Kavieng, the capital of New Ireland. For the father-and-son team, 1927 was a remarkable year. Here they were, planters on a great scale with estates scattered all round the Bismarck Sea, but their hearts were set on Dulwich Hill. In July that year they took over the Wardell Garage and Service Station at a weekly rental of £4 and began the long slog that was to make them bywords in this country for enterprise and the virtues of honest toil.

Oddly, the Custodian of Expropriated Properties in Rabaul could not be persuaded to take allegations of dummying seriously. By early 1929, the Administrator of New Guinea – the Custodian's great rival in the territory – was fed up with the lack of action and decided to challenge a particularly blatant case. He sent a coded cable to Canberra: "Walter and Lyall Falconer Howard apply consent purchase property valued at £25,000 and £100,000 respectively. Strongly suspect dummies for Carpenter and Coy. Could Investigation Branch enquire into status and financial circumstances these men and report the result urgently?"

The branch – which would one day turn into ASIO – got to work and within a week reported on the financial position of the father – "was chief fitter at the Zoo, Taronga Park" – and the son. The branch thought the garage a well-run little business. "It no doubt provides a living for the proprietors, but could not be regarded as a foundation for such transactions as those mentioned in the passage from the Mandated Territory, and there is no reason to suppose that the private resources of the Howards could make any difference in that regard." The attorney-general John Latham thought it "very difficult" for the Howards to deny dummying. The auditor-general had "no doubt whatever that dummying exists" though he found "the offence is not so open and the pretence is better maintained" than in other schemes he had examined. The auditor-general added that Lyall Howard was applying to have transferred to himself two more plantations financed by Carpenters – Koka and Katu, worth £40,000.

At this point, the government changed and the new Labor attorney-general, Frank Brennan, seems to have decided not to pursue dummies already in place like the motor mechanics of Dulwich Hill. The administrator kept on the case for a few more months, discussing it with the new treasurer, Ted Theodore, but finally – after another confrontation with the custodian – declared himself "satisfied with the bona fides of the Howards". The custodian was to disappear under a cloud soon after and turn up as Carpenters' London representative. But however it happened, the Howards' tropical empire scraped through intact just as the Depression crashed down on copra, Carpenters, New Guinea and the motor trade. An officially approved elaborate sham was now in place from which the family would not shake itself entirely free until the early 1960s.

John Howard declined to be interviewed about his family's adventures in New Guinea, so several questions remain unanswered. His father and grandfather appear to have been paid up front by Carpenters, and the first recorded payment, in June 1927 – about £540 – may have been the seed finance for the Dulwich Hill garage. How they were paid down the track is not clear. Dummies were often paid an annual fee for the use of their names. While it is not certain how the Howards benefited, it is very clear the family remained useful to Carpenters all the way to the end. That these plantations were conducted in the name of a couple of mechanics from Dulwich Hill allowed the trading corporation to cry poor through the Depression, the war and its aftermath. The files are fat with pleas from Carpenters for concessions of one kind or another because their "clients" the Howards could not pay. Rent due to native title holders on Enuk was not paid from 1932 until 1935 while Carpenters brawled with the new custodian for a cheaper lease. The company was adamant that Walter Howard could not pay. The custodian demanded proof: "If he is in such a bad financial position that he cannot pay anything at all, Mr Howard should produce figures showing his revenue and expenditure." Carpenters eventually got the lease it wanted.

After the war, Carpenters decided to abandon a number of unprofitable plantations. In 1950, a rare letter to the custodian in Lyall Howard's own hand backed Carpenters' decision: "I have not the money to carry on and therefore am unable to meet my obligations under the contract." Abandoning the plantations was not easy. Lyall owed £5500 in unpaid instalments for the purchase of Agita, and his father's estate – Walter had died in 1948 – owed a further £2500 for the purchase of Enuk. These debts might have wiped the family out, but after a few months of pursuing the poor Howards of Dulwich Hill, the custodian threw in the towel and the contracts were cancelled in 1951.

By this time, the Howards had "sold" the last of their holdings to Carpenters. But the transfer of Kavilo was never registered, an omission only discovered by a baffled custodian in 1960. Month after month, letters demanding action from Lyall Howard went unanswered by solicitors. Lyall had died of chronic bronchitis in 1955 and only his widow and son John – law graduate and Young Liberal – were left at home in Earlwood. The paperwork for Kavilo's transfer was at last completed in 1962. Then for many years a long silence fell on the story, broken by occasional references in histories and academic papers on the lost plantation world of New Guinea.

Strangely, these plantations never seem to feature in the prime minister's repertoire of stories about the ethos of his family. In February this year, launching a book that celebrates his ten years in office, John Howard once more harked back to the role of the garage in forming his fundamental values. He was myth-making again. "The whole idea of doing something with your life was about personal achievement, and starting a business. That has influenced my attitude, because my father had a garage ... I guess working for yourself, working for private enterprise, and not working for the government, was something I was brought up to believe in." That's one version.

The Sydney Morning Herald, 10 June 2006

Quizzed by the press, an angry prime minister declared he would answer my story. He never did. A planter's widow rang with a late clue to the Howard family's link with the Carpenter empire: Lyall used to service Sir Walter Carpenter's car.

Gorton's last secrets

AS HE DOES EVERY THURSDAY, Sir John Gorton drove down to the Macquarie broadcasting studios in Canberra with half a dozen neatly typed sheets of news commentary. They were his week's work. He arrived in jeans and an old, pale lambswool jumper.

"I didn't see you at Zorba's, Sir John," said the panel operator. He was being breezy. "Gough was there, and Grassby."

"I wasn't asked."

Gorton's face at the microphone is the same patched-up, fractured face that for years was part of the political terrain of the country: the best face in politics since Billy Hughes, the face in the surfboat, the face under the grey top hat, the face in the White House smiling sideways at the Nixons. But age, better than any plastic surgeon, is smoothing it out. The creases are filling, and the bits and pieces of cheek, ear and nose are regrouping for the first time since the war. His hair, a wiry thatch, is now almost white.

He drew the microphone to his mouth.

"I cannot see why women should be regarded as criminals for engaging in prostitution when men who use their services are not." After the headline he paused, and continued ominously, "This is John Gorton. I'll be back in a moment."

He did a professional job. His voice was tough and the scripts snappy.

In the director's office afterwards there were drinks. Gorton had a whisky and ice.

Fred Daly was there, and the two men had a bitch about their tax.

Gorton turned his polished and engaging charm on the only woman in the circle. Taking in his hand the silver-mounted Monaco gambling chip she wore as a pendant, he said, "I'll bet the next time I see you, you'll have spent that." It was a banal remark to make to a hard-faced radio woman, but somehow she was touched.

Gorton is a charmer, a dandy, an old soldier (air force division), the son of an elegant old financier who ended his days, and much of his fortune, on an orange, lemon and grapefruit orchard in the backblocks of Victoria. But not before he gave his son an education in manners at Shore in Sydney, Geelong Grammar outside Melbourne, and Oxford.

The charm of the young Gorton was noted early. A prefect at Shore in the 1920s recalled, "Many a time we thought he was in for a couple on the seat of the pants from a prefect, but he would not only talk the prefect out of it, but end up talking himself into a cup of tea and a biscuit in the prefect's study."

He has remained attached to the apparently straightforward maxims of that GPS education: loyalty, good manners, initiative, leadership. And talking about his life and times, Gorton comes back and back to the twin themes of loyalty and betrayal: the loyalty of the Gorton political machine in the irrigation country along the Murray, the loyalty of the Senate when he trounced Holt in the VIP affair, and the loyalty of his cabinet, even as the party was voting him out of office.

The theme of disloyalty Gorton illustrates with frequent, perhaps obsessive, reference, not just to Malcolm Fraser, but also to Sir William McMahon. It was McMahon, he said, who made the cabinet so hard to work with, who intrigued against him, and then, succeeding him, reversed the policies of Gortonism.

It is now eight years and three prime ministers since the Liberal Party ditched Gorton. He was the man on whom they perfected the technique of the knife – he was, in fact, the first leader they'd deposed since Menzies in the early years of the war.

There are tangible monuments to the Gorton years – ships, buildings, schools, pensions, banks. There is enough there for a fair list of achievement.

But Gorton will be remembered first for the Vietnam War. Holt committed Australia, but it was Gorton who succeeded him and had the country tag along with the Americans like a dog to its master.

"I thought the war could be won if it was fought properly," he said. "I didn't think the Americans were fighting it properly. They didn't seem to realise the sort of war it was.

"They were going in and killing everybody in the villages. They just went in with bullets, shells and everything flying.

"It wasn't an all-out effort. They could have bombed all the irrigation areas in North Vietnam. They could have just overrun it. I expect they were frightened of China. They could have just overrun North Vietnam, but they didn't.

"There was a hell of a lot of corruption there, too, with the Americans. I think Diem was a very good governor of Vietnam – and Madam Nhu was a terribly bad one. She was a shocking woman, as bad as Mrs Soeharto. Just money all the time. Corrupt.

"When Diem was killed, the generals started fighting among themselves, and the people didn't seem to be strongly anti-communist in their fighting. They seemed just to be interested in ripping off American supplies, as far as l could see."

I asked: "Were you able to tell Johnson your doubts about the way the Americans were fighting?"

"No, I didn't tell him," Gorton replied. "I should have, but I didn't."

When Gorton came to make his first trip to Washington, Johnson announced he would not be standing again. The Tet Offensive had already broken him. The Gorton–Johnson meetings were a disaster.

"We had dinner at the White House and Betty (Lady Gorton) was sitting next but one to Johnson and there was some senator in between them. Johnson spent the whole time leaning over to the senator saying, 'You want to have a dam in your state? You go back to your state and get yourself re-elected, because I am not going to see that you get any dam until you get re-elected.' And so on, and so on, and so on.

"Then I was in New York and had an important dinner arranged with Rockefeller. I got a call from Johnson saying, 'Come down to the ranch.' That's a hell of a long way to go, down to Texas. Then I got another message to say, 'I really want you down here.' So we got on Air Force One and flew to Texas.

"Johnson was having a nationwide television coverage in the barn at the ranch, and it became quite obvious that he wanted me there in front of the cameras to show that he had at least one ally in Vietnam and the Americans weren't all alone."

"He was using you?"

"Yes. He handed me a citation for a reserve battalion Royal Australian Regiment and said how fine it was to have Australians there. I had to say.

'Well, we had to be with the Americans,' or something like that. But it was all to get the television coverage."

Back in Australia, Gorton found it difficult to anticipate what was going on in Washington. "The American Embassy had instructions from the State Department. They would come along and say, 'Johnson is going to make a speech' – about something or other. I would say, 'What's going to be in it?' They would tell me that they hadn't got it yet. They would stall until Johnson had made the speech and then come along and tell you what he'd said. But you had heard it all beforehand. It was a stupid way to act."

Things were to improve when Nixon was elected. In Gorton's words, he and Nixon just "clicked". Gorton made two trips to Washington to see the new president, in April and May 1969. The state banquet this time went off more happily.

It was that night that Gorton committed Australia – "wherever there is a joint attempt to improve not only the material but the spiritual standards of life of the peoples of the world" – to go waltzing Matilda with America.

"I think there is a danger of being overwhelmed by American hospitality and making these kinds of commitments, but I don't think I fell into it."

"But were you committing us to another Vietnam War?"

"I don't think it could bring that."

"There was press speculation that you were going to ask Nixon if you could release more details about Pine Gap?"

"I wasn't going to ask him at all. The press might have written about it. I don't even know what Pine Gap is all about. I didn't then. I could have asked but it didn't arise. I didn't ask about it."

When the Gortons arrived back in Australia there was a difficult news conference. But Gorton was able to announce that a hotline would be installed between Canberra and the White House. It was to be used only once.

Gorton had little contact with anti-war opinion. He remembered one occasion. It was to have other connotations later. "The night I got into trouble for taking Willesee ... I have forgotten her name – Geraldine? – to the American Embassy, we were sitting on the couch arguing about the war all the time and she was putting the 'against' arguments to me."

In 1970 Nixon announced he would begin pulling American troops out of South Vietnam. At that point, Gorton said, he knew the war was being lost. Nixon tried to persuade Gorton to keep Australian troops at full strength.

"You haven't got enough to make all that difference," Gorton recalled him saying. "Leave them there." But Gorton decided that one battalion should be withdrawn.

"Was it the time to get out altogether?"

"It probably was, just looking at it militarily. There would have been a hell of a row. The DLP would have turned handsprings, and there were a lot of Liberals who would have said that it was a terrible thing to leave the Americans in the lurch."

"Had you done anything to prepare the Liberals for a change in attitude to the war?"

"No. I probably should have done, but never did."

Gorton held a meeting with McMahon, McEwen and Fraser to confirm they were pulling the battalion out. He then ran the hotline to let Nixon know. It took, he said, ten minutes to get through.

Soon afterwards Gorton ceased to be prime minister. It would have been worse if we hadn't gone in, he said, "but the upshot of the Vietnam War is that the Americans are less likely to come to our aid".

*

The Gortons' house, in Canberra, is rather formal: English furniture, paintings of Indonesia, small chandeliers, some Javanese kites stashed behind the chairs in the dining room; in a bookcase of souvenirs is a signed snap of Gorton and the Queen climbing some stairs. In the hall, beside a Drysdale portrait, is a gold kris studded with semi-precious stones, a gift from Soeharto to Lady Gorton.

Behind the door of a small sitting room is a watercolour in a gold mount of a pretty woman with a baby on her knee. Gorton said, "That is my mother." She was his father's mistress, Alice Sinn.

His father had made his money in South Africa before the Boer War selling American fire engines. He invested in Johannesburg nightclubs, escaped the Siege of Ladysmith and arrived in Australia a rich man. He was married, but separated from his wife, who refused him a divorce.

When Gorton was seven, his mother died in Sydney of TB and he was sent to the North Shore to live with his father's estranged wife, Kathleen. When old enough, he was sent to Shore as a boarder. While there he shared a dormitory with Errol Flynn. Even forty years later Shore boys speculated about Flynn and his sexual equipment, said to be large. "I wasn't much interested," said Gorton. "I don't know." And the matter of Flynn's expulsion? "He just disappeared. We thought he was sleeping with a maid and the housemaster's wife."

After Shore, Gorton went to Geelong Grammar, a less hearty school and socially a notch above Shore.

His father in those years had begun to put his fortune into irrigated orchards. He shared with Alfred Deakin and others the notion that there was untold wealth to be made from the dry lands of northern Victoria. Gorton senior bought a block at Tresco. Then he invested around Kerang. That, said Gorton, was a bummer. But from then on the family was tied to it.

As a cavalier gesture during the Depression, Gorton senior sent his son to Oxford. Gorton met and married his wife there, and returned to Australia with the vague idea of becoming a journalist. He had some connections with the Melbourne *Herald*, but nothing came of it.

In 1936 the Gortons moved up to the orchard. He joined the Country Party, went to war and returned in 1945 with a face smashed up from when his plane came down on an island near Singapore.

At the welcome-home dinner in the Mystic Park hall, Gorton gave the locals a rousing speech about the war: "In the name of the dead and the returned, do not consider this war as a task finished." They asked him to join the local Kerang council.

Gorton became interested in Magnus Cormack's efforts to amalgamate Menzies' new Liberal Party with the Country Party in Victoria.

"He was quite a strange man, Sir Magnus Cormack. He used to like to drive around in vintage Bentleys and have wonderful wines and take you to dinner to the Australian Club and things like that. But it never stopped him from going out and doing political nitty-gritty. He used to like politics very much. He didn't have any money at all but his wife had a lot – she was very rich – and he spent it, I suppose, in politics."

Gorton began to organise for Cormack, switching membership to the Liberal Party. He hit the road, arranging meetings in country halls.

Soon he was given the chance to run for the party in the Victorian Legislative Council elections for Northern Province. "It was a huge area, from Kerang to the sea. I got beaten, but only by 200 votes."

Unexpectedly, Gorton's party machine had shaken the Country Party in its own territory. He was a man to be both rewarded and preferred. He was not afraid to throw his new weight around: at one time he threatened the Liberals that he would take the machine out of the party with him.

The party gave him a place on the 1949 Senate ticket.

His election in 1949 was the last critical one he had to face until he ran as prime minister in 1969. In the Senate, he said, "the base of my support was the state executive of the party. They were my electorate."

Menzies was schooling his candidates at a guesthouse on the Mornington Peninsula. Gorton was called down, and was able to get a good look at the leader for the first time. The weekend was not a complete success: Gorton had the notion they were there for a political seminar. Menzies had them at the guesthouse to be drilled.

John Gorton settled down to a life divided between Canberra sittings, Melbourne meetings and the orchard. "Until I became a minister I was really just running the farm. I'd come to Canberra for the weeks of the session. There were long periods when there was no session, then I would stay on the farm and pack the fruit, I just used to do that."

*

After speaking for a couple of hours, Gorton found he was tired. We went to the kitchen. From a round metal tin near the stove he took a citrus sweet and sucked it: after a lifetime in the grip of the habit, Gorton has given up smoking. "I haven't had a cigarette for a long time now. Well, I have. I have one or two a day." He says he kicked the habit eight months ago, in hospital, having a hernia patched up. "What he doesn't say," said Lady Gorton in a wry drawl, "is that his doctor was going to come in and drag every cigarette out of his hands."

*

Aggressive in the House, friend of far right-wingers like Kent Hughes and Wentworth, tactless in his questioning of Menzies in party meetings – it seemed that Gorton might stay indefinitely on the backbench. But he was rescued by a threat of scandal. In 1957 Gorton's wife was sued by the novelist Jean Campbell, who had been his father's mistress for many years. While at Oxford, Gorton had helped place her first novel with a London publisher. In that time a large number of shares in the Mystic Park orchard were transferred into Jean Campbell's name. At the death of Gorton senior in 1936, Gorton used a signed blank transfer form found among his father's papers to transfer the shares from Jean Campbell to his wife. Claiming not to have discovered this for twenty years, Campbell sued in 1957. There was a Senate election looming.

Gorton went to see Menzies. He explained the Campbell claim and offered to resign if Menzies felt the case would embarrass the government. Menzies asked for time to look at the situation.

"He looked over it and said, 'I think you should stay.' From then on I found his attitude changed."

"Did he give you legal advice at the time?"

"No, he didn't. But he did keep in touch with the case. A man called Hudson was the judge, and he kept in touch with Hudson. I don't suppose he did during the case. Menzies would have methods of keeping in touch."

Menzies was apparently impressed by the demeanour of both Gortons under cross-examination from Keith Aickin QC, now a High Court judge. When Gorton admitted an entry in the company's minute book confirming the transfer of the Campbell shares in January 1937 was fictitious, Aickin hammered the details home. The Gortons argued that Campbell had never held a beneficial interest in the shares and the transfer was done on the verbal instructions of Gorton senior, given before he died.

The judge, commending the bearing of Senator and Mrs Gorton, said the entries in the company minute book were harmless fictions. "In my view," he concluded, "there is no substance whatever in the matters brought out in cross-examination by which it was sought to discredit Mrs Gorton and her husband." That decision was given in late October 1958. Gorton was appointed Minister for the Navy that December.

"The Navy didn't have anything with which to fight at all. It was really a hopeless situation. I really think that I built the modern Navy." Cabinet, he said, instructed him to get rid of the Fleet Air Arm. He didn't do it. He was also told never to use the old aircraft carrier *Sydney*, moored in the mothball fleet off the zoo in Sydney Harbour. "We went and had a look at her. She was full of barnacles and had to be cleaned out. But we just gradually got her out. We said we needed the *Sydney* for operations on the coast with the Army. We made her a bit better, and then said we could send her to New Zealand on combined operations. As a result she was ready for Vietnam when she was wanted. We wouldn't have had any ships to send troops and materials to Vietnam but for the *Sydney*."

In 1963 Menzies made his famous announcement that federal money would be given to private schools for science blocks and libraries. "Menzies hadn't got an idea how to do it," said Gorton. "He didn't know anything about it. He didn't have any plans – none at all. He called me in after the campaign and said, 'I am going to make you Minister for Works, but you are really doing Education for me. Go away and do it.'"

"By 1965 Menzies wasn't quite as much on the ball when you were talking to him. He knew what you were talking about, but just occasionally there seemed to be instances of where you had to repeat yourself." Late that year, Menzies announced he was going to retire. But he was not gone. "Everything built up to push him out. If he was going to go he had to go before the next election."

Gorton disagrees with commentators who say that Harold Holt's arrival as prime minister began a long period of internecine struggle within the Liberal Party over the leadership. He admits there were cabals against Holt but claims they were never serious, and that his only part in them was as a moderator. But Gorton's stunning resolution of the VIP affair struck a blow to Holt's prestige.

"Holt was very nice to meet," said Gorton. "He was a gambler."

"What were his games?"

"The races."

"Big money?"

"Yes, very. He spoke in just the same pitch of voice all the time and you felt he was just talking, just bullshitting on and on. He had weaknesses: he didn't like to fall out with people and then have them dislike him."

In 1967 Holt was on the slide. Allegations were made by the Opposition that political leaders were abusing the privileges of the VIP fleet. The government claimed there were no records of how the planes were used and who travelled on them. The affair wore on for months. Labor's Senate leader, Lionel Murphy, was planning to call the Secretary of the Air Department, Archibald McFarlane, to the bar of the Senate. Gorton rang McFarlane and asked for a final assurance that the records didn't exist. McFarlane told him, on the contrary, that they did. Gorton had him send them to his office. When they were in his office he rang Holt.

"What authority did you have to call on the Secretary for Air to deliver the manifests to you?"

"I don't know that I had any – I suppose he could have refused to deliver them, but he didn't."

"What was Holt's reaction when you told him you were going to table them?"

"On the telephone it was just a sort of eeing and aahing, and then, 'Yes, I suppose you have got to.' Something like that. It was no strong objection. He just seemed surprised."

"Did you give Holt any opportunity to table them himself?"

"No, the motion was coming up in the Senate."

That afternoon Gorton casually threw a pile of manifests onto the table of the Senate. It made his reputation. It was a great blow to Holt's. I asked Gorton, "Why didn't Holt fire you?"

Gorton's face broke into a smile almost of triumph. "Fire me as Leader of the Senate? He would have been asking for trouble. The sort of trouble Fraser got into firing Withers would have been nothing compared with what Holt would have got if he'd tried to fire me. I had the whole of the Senate unanimously behind me, except for Wood and Wright. And not only on this question."

"Where was the VIP affair going when Holt died a few months later?"

"I think it would have just faded away."

"Was Holt in debt when he died?"

"No, I don't think so."

"Have you ever suspected he might have committed suicide?"

"I haven't any suspicions one way or the other."

Holt drowned at Cheviot Beach on 18 December 1967. McEwen headed a short interim government, and warned the Liberals that his party would not serve under McMahon. "It was a very stupid thing to do," said Gorton. "McMahon had no hope of becoming leader." Gorton was elected, ahead of Paul Hasluck, Billy Snedden and Leslie Bury. Very little was known about him: he was thought to be a hawk on Vietnam and a friend of the Formosa lobby; he was known to like good company, good parties and good booze; he had an American wife, three children and an orchard in the backblocks; he was reported to be able to sing three, or even four, verses of "Waltzing Matilda".

*

The Gorton style was immensely popular that first year. The papers carried affectionate reports of his charm and his stumbling. In July, for instance, the Aboriginal debutante ball in Sydney had a big spread in the papers. "I'll never forget it all my life," Pearl Anderson was reported prominently in the *Sun-Herald* as saying. "He came over and clicked his heels in a sort of salute, smiled and said, 'I'll get a dance off you in a moment.' Next thing I knew I was dancing with him – a waltz, I think it was – and I was that nervous I was trembling. But I didn't tread on his toes. He wrote on my ball card, To dear Pearl, with all the luck in the world, thanking her for the dance, John Gorton, Prime Minister of Australia."

Gorton never translated the enormous popularity of 1968 into seats in parliament. He took government, but didn't go on to seize power. He never harnessed the power of the public service; and he made the mistake of trying to assert authority over the proprietors of the Liberal Party in the states – Sir Robert Askin and Sir Henry Bolte.

Gorton is deeply sceptical about power in the Liberal Party. "First of all, you can't do what you want," he said. "You have got to take care of the Country Party and make sure it agrees with what you want to do. You used to have to pay attention to the Democratic Labor Party. Then you have your own members who are getting at you. Then you have your branches. Now you can do things, of course, but you haven't got overriding personal power."

There was power to help friends. One was Rupert Murdoch. "In 1968 he came to me because he was having trouble with the Treasury. He wanted to get money out of Australia to buy the *News of the World* in London. So I said, 'All right,' and he took the money out, bought the *News of the World*, and hasn't looked back since."

Gorton tried out a going-into-smoke style of government. In his first days in power he went into smoke to his old friend Billy Wentworth's estate at Clareville Beach, north of Sydney. He found it a congenial way to work. The press kept his parliamentary office under scrutiny. Later he went into smoke at The Lodge. Here, in secrecy, Gorton conducted the negotiations for fixing the price of Bass Strait crude. "We really did need to keep those oil negotiations quite secret. We got McClennan and ... (a chap from Esso) to come up here in their own plane, get in a car and come to The Lodge for discussions, lunch and more discussions. It was done over several weeks. I think there were only myself and Len Hewitt (head of the Prime Minister's Department) who knew that they were doing it, because if we had let the cabinet know, it wouldn't have been a secret for five seconds."

Some secrets were well kept that year. "Sterling was in pretty grave trouble and the Governor of the Bank of England came out." The British do these things well: they sent with him as his aide a man who'd been at Oxford with Gorton. "They went out through a different gate to get on to the plane in London, and travelled under different names, sort of under an alias. We laid down conditions under which we would guarantee sterling."

From 1968 Gorton had as his staff the abrasive and very young Ainsley Gotto, and Lenox Hewitt (now Sir Lenox and chairman of Qantas). Hewitt had a formidable reputation. He was a public servant who inspired, quite literally, fear in those beneath him. Gorton defended Hewitt absolutely in those days; now he has some doubts. "The only thing about Sir Lenox is that he likes everything to come across his desk. It is too much for one man. I am bound to say that I never did discover he was doing slipshod work, but it was just too much for him."

"It's said Hewitt could get the public service to obey him but not cooperate with him?"

"There might be truth in that," replied Gorton and added, thumping the table in time with his words, "The first thing you need is their obedience. I suppose it is better to have obedience *and* cooperation. But if you just get obedience from them, that is all you want."

The strain of the Gorton style of government – later it focused roughly on the complaint "one-man rule" – wasn't apparent in 1968. He was still immensely popular. He had the chance of going to an election and getting a sweeping personal mandate. But he lost his nerve. The DLP were threatening to switch their preferences because Gorton wanted to bring home the troops from Malaysia and Singapore. "All the DLP cared about really was defence, defence, defence. I remember Santamaria coming to me when I was elected prime minister and saying, 'We don't care what you are doing about the Catholic schools and other things like that. We just want more defence.' They would have gone on and on until they had the whole population in khaki."

A year was to make a great difference. The trouble first appeared in London. Twelve members of the Get Gorton Ad Hoc Committee made their plans in the back bar of the Prince of Wales in Notting Hill Gate. Next morning they turned up at the (wrong) door of the Savoy Hotel to greet

Gorton, in London for the prime ministers' conference. Their main banner declared: Hands off Vietnam. On the back it said: Hands off Liza Minnelli. Gorton saw them: "They came running down the street, puffing and panting as we went into the hotel. I saw the banners. Paul Hasluck was with me and asked who Liza Minnelli was."

It was late in 1968 when Frank Browne's newsletter, *Things I Hear*, carried allegations that Gorton had made a pass at Minnelli in her dressing room at Chequers nightclub in Sydney, and likewise a pass at Geraldine Willesee that night at the American embassy in Canberra. Minnelli was supposed to have given an account of her experiences to *Private Eye*, the London magazine, which was said to have sold the story both to the CIA and a chain of African newspapers. In a chaotic sitting late one night, the allegations were repeated in parliament. Denials of the Minnelli story flooded in from all parties – David McNicol, the CIA, Liza Minnelli's mother-in-law, a couple of African newspapers. It dropped out of sight.

Attention focused on the American embassy incident. Edward St John, throwing away his parliamentary career, attacked Gorton with cold brilliance. The prime minister had gone to the American embassy late at night after a journalist's dinner with some of his staff and a journalist, Geraldine Willesee. That day Johnson had stopped bombing North Vietnam. The time and the company, St John alleged, showed the man not fit to be prime minister. Gorton had said only hello and goodbye to the ambassador: his rudeness was a danger to the alliance.

Gorton denied at the time there was any ill feeling between him and the ambassador leading up to the incident. In fact, they had had a row. "I had ticked him off during the afternoon," said Gorton. It was the same old problem. "Johnson was making a speech on a cessation of the bombing in North Vietnam. The ambassador wouldn't tell me what it was until I heard it on the wireless. I said that I didn't think it was a proper thing to do. The invitation to call at the embassy had come because he wanted to smooth things over."

The Liberal Party fell in behind Gorton, but it was going to be a punishing parliamentary year. His reputation never really recovered. By October, and the election, the year had taken its toll. He was tired. He found it hard to crank himself up for the fight.

There were few new initiatives, but one proved an electoral disaster. Gorton had his Minister for External Affairs, Gordon Freeth, float the idea that Australians should "not get all tangled up in a knot because the Russians have got a ship in the Indian Ocean. That caused enormous traumas, and the DLP turned against us. Freeth could have put in the bit about China and it would have caused more – originally there was a paragraph about China in the speech and I said, 'Freeth, you'd better not put this in.' A group of us were in favour of opening negotiations for recognising China."

The coalition held office but lost fifteen seats. There was an immediate challenge to Gorton's leadership.

*

Brian Fuller of the Canberra RSL Poppy Appeal explained the layout of the lunch to open the 1978 effort: it was to be a buffet for the first time, mostly RSL members, but that was the military attaché from the Indonesian embassy over there, and "the ladies along the wall sell the poppies. We invite them each year to lunch as our way of saying 'Thank you'". Fuller said the committee had thought of inviting a general but settled instead for an invitation to Gorton to launch this year's appeal. "He's slightly controversial," explained Fuller. "He'll speak off the cuff. He always does."

In fact Gorton had found out only an hour before that he was expected to speak. He raged in his kitchen. "Why the hell do they want me to speak? What can I speak about?" Lady Gorton, who was putting away a ten-kilo-gram sack of wholemeal flour at the time, made one or two remarks about the symbolism of the red poppy. Gorton sloped from the room.

Gorton's entry brought back the old days. A group of heavies gathered, the television light shone, the smiles of the RSL men confirmed that Gorton still had that tang of power about him. "The splash of colour on your coat ... the Flanders poppy ... across the fields the poppies grow. Among the crosses row on row ... when you are all dead and I am dead ... there is a tendency to say you can't win a war, but that is nonsense. You can lose a war."

"Well, that is all I have to say," he said. But he went on. It was the rhetoric that dated right back to his days at Shore. He ended by urging "refurbished determination that the nation will be better in the future".

*

Gorton beat off McMahon's challenge for the leadership in late 1969 and then carried through the most extensive cabinet reshuffle for twenty years.

It was risky, but it seemed to be putting Gorton on top of the party – and the government – at last. In fact, Gorton had only a year left in office.

The Seas and Submerged Lands Bill, which he introduced into parliament in early 1970, was the most daring assertion of the Commonwealth's primacy over the states since Federation. It asserted, in law, that Australia was sovereign – not the states. It was contrary to all the shibboleths of the Liberal Party. "We had three or four people who said they would cross the House to vote against it. Finally, we didn't see the point of maybe losing government. Fairbairn, Howson and old Jess were going to cross the floor. They were grabbing at anything that came along."

The bill exacerbated Gorton's running feud with Bolte. It was a feud that dated back years. They had once worked closely together in the early days, setting up the party and electioneering. But they drifted apart. Gorton, rather oddly, dates the drift from "the time of the battle of Dien Bien Phu".

The Melbourne Club was one of the problems. Gorton is a member of the Melbourne Club. He says he doesn't particularly like clubs, but the Melbourne Club was a place to stay on the way from Canberra to the orchard, or later when he was a minister. Bolte and Gorton were both members of the Victorian executive of the party. When these meetings broke for dinner, about half the members would go with Gorton along to the club. Bolte, Victorian premier but not a member, was not invited. "He never went with us," said Gorton. Nor did he return after dinner to the executive meetings. Gorton concedes, "There may have been some animosity in it."

When Gorton ran for prime minister, Bolte commented tartly, "If he gets in, I get out." In fact, the contrary turned out to be the case. Bolte was the prime minister's most formidable political opponent. He wanted new growth taxes for Victoria; Gorton bluntly told him to drop them. He began to campaign quite openly against Gorton. Gorton would not be drawn on Bolte. He just said, "He is a very hard man to understand."

The Seas and Submerged Lands Bill was stalled, but Gorton made headway in other fields that year. In 1970 the Australian Film Development Corporation was set up, the transfer of power in New Guinea began, a battalion was removed from Vietnam, and Gorton, against heavy opposition in his cabinet, set up the Australian Industries Development Corporation. "McEwen came and told me all about it, and I thought the AIDC was a very good idea and we took it to cabinet. We got it through. We had Fraser,

McMahon, Doug Anthony and a whole lot of people opposing us, but we got it through and it has gone on from there."

And there were respites from the cares of office. The Queen was cruising on the north coast of Australia in the Britannia – it was the Captain Cook bicentenary year. The Gortons joined her for three or four days. One morning they anchored off a small island to picnic. "They sent a group of people ashore with flick guns to kill all the insects. They took chairs ashore. Then we all went ashore in the boats. Everyone started chucking everyone else in the water. It was quite fun." Gorton toyed with the idea of throwing in the Queen. He restrained himself. "I didn't think she would like it," he said.

The half-Senate election in late 1970 was a disaster. Whitlam, ridiculing the great convoluted Gorton sentences, set out to make a laughing-stock of the prime minister. The papers were running the same way. The gaucheries that had been so warmly reported two years before had become the raw material of press ridicule. "If there was a way to misrepresent me I think they would try to do it." The coalition lost two senators, and the vote fell to a dangerous thirty-seven per cent.

Gorton had made a particular enemy in Sir Frank Packer when he dropped his protégé McMahon from the Treasury. He met Packer only a few times. "I went round to dinner at Packer's house once. He just seemed to be a bloody bully with a hell of a strong idea of himself. I saw him. I did things for him. He wanted me to get some steel for (his yacht) the *Gretel*. He couldn't get it and wanted me to. It's all right to ring a prime minister on a thing like that. He had a lot of media outlets." When the troubles came over the next few weeks, Packer "rang up other newspapers and said 'Come out and say what a terrible fellow this man is'."

A press story was Gorton's downfall. In March 1971, Alan Ramsey wrote in *The Australian* that Gorton had pledged his loyalty to the army in the dispute it was having over the reduction of civilian aid in Vietnam. The story, which Gorton saw before publication, added that the chief of the general staff had accused the minister, Malcolm Fraser, of disloyalty. Fraser resigned. He, in turn, accused Gorton of disloyalty to him. The story, he said, should have been stopped. "It never occurred to me a minister would resign," said Gorton. "And I wasn't aware, if a minister did, that I would be in trouble."

"Fraser avoided any face-to-face discussion. On Monday he took all the phones off the hook. We rang him and rang him and couldn't get any reply. So Alan Hulme said, 'I'll go around to see what the hell is happening.' He came back and told me that Fraser had all the phones off the hook and had put them under cushions so he couldn't hear anything. It was really extraordinary."

On the Tuesday afternoon, Fraser followed through with an attack on Gorton in parliament. He claimed that Gorton could have stopped the Ramsey story. The party met that night. Before the meeting, Bolte had been on the phone. The Victorian premier later claimed various members of parliament had rung him for advice. Gorton contradicted that: "He approached members. I was told Askin was doing the same thing, but it was really only Bolte. If Bolte hadn't intervened there would have been a majority to say to me, go on the way you are. It wouldn't have been a very good majority but there probably would have been enough."

Gorton voted himself out of office. In a sense it was a gentleman's gesture, a breath of the GPS in the party room. But he had little real choice. The party had tied in their vote of confidence, and four members were willing to cross the floor to bring the government down. "We would have been decimated."

*

On each side of the steep drive at Gorton's house in Narrabundah is a large garden of Australian trees and European flowers and shrubs. Coarse pink bark mulches the soil. Gorton spends a lot of time these days gardening. He likes Canberra and is happy to admit it, but he likes to spend the depth of the Canberra winter in Greece. "I could go to Queensland, but I think it's nicer to go abroad."

He was offered posts after he left the prime ministership. McMahon wanted to send him as high commissioner to London. He turned that down. Whitlam never offered him anything, nor has Fraser. But he wonders what it would be like to be an ambassador: "They have nothing to do. It's cocktail parties all the time and golf." He is still invited to the formal side of politics: the opening of parliament and parliamentary dinners. And last year he accepted a knighthood, assuming it was the Queen's recommendation. He said rather tartly, "Silly of me to think that, I suppose."

After Gorton was thrown out of the government, and then left the party, he was often talked of as a kind of lefty martyr: too much of a socialist to survive. But that doesn't square with the Gorton of today. He believes in business, in conscription, in nuclear power, and in the deep necessity of elites. On that last point no headmaster of Shore or Geelong or any private school could be more eloquent. It might be some balance that he believes marijuana should be legalised.

In the run-up to the 1972 elections he predicted a Labor victory. But his friends campaigned for him – not only in his electorate, but nationally. Jim Killen held a Meet John Gorton rally at the Rocklea Showground in Brisbane. There were sheep-dog trials, a rock band, and the Brisbane Excelsior Brass Band. About 500 people turned up.

"You know," said Gorton one day, "Menzies never said Killen was magnificent."

"What did he say?"

"Nothing." Gorton laughed.

Nothing was quite so typical of Gorton's political career as the way he left it. On the afternoon of 11 November 1975 – his last day in parliament – he abstained in the great confidence vote for Whitlam. He opposed what Fraser and Kerr were doing, but there were the electors of Higgins to think about ...

Then he threw away whatever chance he had of getting a Senate seat by vigorously supporting Whitlam's stand. A vote for Labor, he said, would restore the moral basis of Australian politics. After the elections of 13 December 1975 he was out of parliament.

He is not particularly busy. He did a couple of television commercials – one for Famous Grouse Whisky, another for Kevin Dennis Motors. He is available. His fee, he says, "depends on what the ad is. You could try a thousand, something like that." He spends the mornings preparing his Macquarie Broadcasting commentaries and his weekly newspaper column. "I've had a lot of people come up and say, 'Will you write your memoirs?' But you don't really earn very much out of writing a book, and I can earn a great deal by my broadcasts and my column. Why do a book?"

It is said that Gorton is deeply bitter about those three years as prime minister. I asked if that was true. He seemed stung, but then brushed the question aside. I asked what it had done to him. "It does a lot," he said. "It did to me. It did to me because I wasn't ..." He broke off and came at it from another way. "Menzies didn't care much. He thought what he did was right. I was never quite so sure. Menzies was impervious. I had to cope with dissidence in the party. They were biting at you all the time. I think it took its toll."

The National Times, 30 December 1978

With Charles and Di in the desert

IT LOOKED A PICTURE. FIVE BLACKS were lined up in a kind of cattleyard waiting to meet the Prince and Princess of Wales. Two of the delegation leant on sticks; one wore a maroon dress for the occasion, and their leader held in both hands a plastic bag of gifts. Above them loomed Ayers Rock.

As the girl from the BBC worked the fringes of the small black crowd, a beer gut clad in Northern Territory police overalls led an Alsatian round the cars to sniff for bombs. The royal party was expected in a matter of minutes. Eighty or so photographers, mostly British, stood packed behind the cattleyard rails. Steve Wood of the *Daily Express* ('I broke Prince Andrew and Koo') began to creep across the yard towards the line of blacks. A cop threw him back to the fence.

"Won't you control this man," Wood howled to the tour officials.

"Scum," called a British tourist.

An uproar of baying broke out from the photographers. They turned on the stray desert traveller and from the centre of the pack came a shout: "Then don't buy a newspaper tomorrow and don't buy a magazine." Having dealt with him, they got down to work.

Charles and Diana appeared in a minibus and met the five Pitjantjatjara. The cattleyard was filled with a confusion of curtseying wives, military aides and officials. Charles' hand rested for a moment on a black shoulder and the motor-driven shutters screamed. No one will ever know how many thousands of frames of Kodachrome were shot in the next ten minutes. Charles spoke briefly to his wife (she was wearing flatties, he a safari suit) and they walked a few yards through the sand and began to climb the face of the Rock.

The press swarmed over the railings. The thin black line scattered.

As the couple climbed higher, Douglas Keay of *Woman's Own* (circulation 1.3 million), observing the scene from the roof of a truck, remarked: "Just what we did for Princess Alexandra." He had been here before.

A cheerful lady-in-waiting galumphed up the Rock in her Harrods dress, sticking close to Diana. The protocol of court was being observed even out here, close to sunset, on the face of Uluru. Something very odd is going on …

Ever since these bizarre excursions began they have been justified with rhetoric about *links*. Over the century royal tourists have been promoting links to Empire, to Britain, and for the last few decades the Commonwealth. Now all have been worked through, and with Bob Hawke's vague talk of a republic in the air, Charles and Diana are reduced to promoting that fundamental link with what is politely called the throne but may more simply be identified as themselves.

*

The Gap Motel is a roadhouse set between the railway line and a bend in the Todd River. Last Sunday night in the bar at happy hour, Charles and Diana held the traditional start-of-tour reception for the press.

The British photographers were in a fever of anticipation. They had not had a chance to talk to Diana since they hung about her flat in the days before her engagement. Many had followed her everywhere since. For some she had become their whole life's work. There in the bar at Alice Springs was the man who took the kindergarten shot with the sun through her dress and the hero who photographed her pregnant on the beach in the Bahamas. Most of the squad had been up the mountain in Liechtenstein the day she dug in her edges and refused to pose.

Diana greeted them head-on. Though apparently shy in public, she is direct and unaffected in this sort of situation. The reception was also a first for her, but she handled it with assurance. She is rather jolly and does schoolgirl skips to get to Charles' side. Her teeth are perfect and her fingers extraordinarily long. She does imitations of a snarling bear for children and, once, for the press – when she found them penned up behind glass at the Alice Springs School of the Air.

Close up, she is as beautiful as her photographs. Charles on the other hand is growing ugly in an unspectacular way. His nose is taking over a face from which the fat has been stripped away to reveal a portrait of the young George III. He is balding. He talks like an excellent doctor questioning patients politely, even warmly, but as if to distract them from the examination at hand. Nothing he said can, by convention, be quoted. But we can report that he was interested in Bob Hawke, whom he seems not to have met, and discussed the new prime minister's view that Australia would one day be a republic.

It would not be inaccurate to suggest that the Prince remembers Labour governments in the United Kingdom that also showed a propensity after a time in opposition to want fundamental changes to the system – only to find after a couple of years in office that it worked as it was. Sources very close to Charles believe his opinion on the possibility of Australia one day becoming a republic is that it would be no skin off anyone's nose.

Back at the Oasis Motel, the Brits held a breathless postmortem. James Whittaker of the *Daily Mirror*, who speaks like a suburban major general with deaf daughters to raise, held the floor. "She was just *pleased* to see us. Why –" turning to a colleague – "when she saw you she greeted you like a long-lost friend."

"Well, I've got a baby, of course."

They are as anxious for royal approval, and as unsure of it, as any alderman, any scoutmaster. Some use the royal *"we"* to link themselves and the official party. Many seem to think they are part of the entourage and only, by some obscure accident of logistics, made to stay at separate motels and travel in separate planes. They observe: Charles has no option but to treat the possibility of a republic calmly. The monarchy is safe enough, so long as it does not become an issue, and while Hawke and others believe naively that Australia can somehow drift into a republic.

Monarchies may be silly and at heart demeaning for those who live in them. A few more (Greece, Iran and Cambodia) have disappeared in the last decade. But monarchies are resilient. It takes military disaster or something like a revolution to upset a crown. In Australia, despite 1975, there is not even majority support for the change. The real question facing Labor is not when Australia will by the passage of time turn into a republic, but whether there are those with the will to put together a political consensus powerful enough to get rid of the Crown by amending the constitution.

Experience shows that would require all-party consensus, not only on the fact of change but also on the form of the republic to come. No major political figure has identified himself with that task. All there is to date is the vague commitment to a republic which Labor adopted in its platform in late 1979. Australia's best chance for a republic might be to ride on the coat-tails of a British revolution. If President Benn were established in Downing Street, the Crown in Australia would almost certainly cease to exist. Whit-lam's legislation to make the Queen "Queen of Australia" gave the Crown no local habitation, just a name.

But for the moment all this is speculation. It is a grey area for the few constitutional lawyers who are looking at the mechanics of establishing a republic here. If the Crown were defunct in Britain, Australia would have to decide whether we, too, were free of the monarchy. It raises the bolthole theory, which has been aired once more in the weeks leading up to the royal tour: that if things turn sour in Britain there would be the chance, slim perhaps but not harmed by Charles and Diana touring the country, that Aus-tralia and New Zealand might be their fallback position.

A popular monarch can, as their cousin Constantine of Greece demon-strated, become an ex remarkably quickly. But, again, this is all speculation. Much more to the point is that sources on Charles' staff maintain that he is still as keen as he was on his 1981 tour to become governor-general of Australia.

*

A streak of smoke over Pine Gap was the first sign of the royal approach. On the tarmac the photographers hunkered down for the coming scrum. The man from United Press International had a set of kitchen steps. "You never work without steps, son. You gotta 'av steps." An admiral, a gen-eral and Mick Young took up their positions with wives. Originally no one was to represent the federal government that morning, and Young was a post-Hawke alteration.

They all had their bums to the cameras until the press told them loudly to turn about. They did. Flunkies were disgorged from the plane, and the generator cut. An alert fashion writer caught a glimpse of her hem. The word went down the line: "Green." And then they emerged.

The child came almost unnoticed down the stairs behind them in the arms of a nanny from central casting. William is a squat and, at that hour, rather grumpy baby with gingery hair.

"Do you call that a romper suit?" asked *Woman* magazine, pen at the ready.

"A crawler."

"No, surely a romper suit."

Someone called: "Say da-da."

"Not yet," the father shouted.

Later, *Sunday People* told *The Sun-Herald*: "From the woman's angle, there is a very good story to be done on that romper suit. I'd bet it was bought at Harrods. She does a lot of shopping there. It costs £40."

The cameramen cried, as the baby was toted back up the steps, "Thank you, sir, thank you, thank you." But already they were on the run as the visitors made for the terminal. The charge of journalists obliterated the view of patient locals, who cried, "Goorn, piss off. We waited."

Back at the Oasis, gloom covered the press corps. On the other side of the world, Prince Andrew had taken off his Speedos and stolen the headlines. Was it another case of being in the right spot at the wrong time?

Whitaker dominated the conversation around the Oasis pool. His stories are less exuberant now since he left the *Daily Star* for the *Daily Mirror*, but he remains one of the leading Fleet Street "authorities" on royalty. When American television wants an inside chat on the topic, they interview Whitaker. He and his colleagues caucus to decide precisely what was said, and exactly what the stories are. Whatever might be said about these Fleet Street rags, they keep in step.

It was not long before word got out that Charles and Diana had somehow left the Gap Motel to go swimming. Alice Springs was alive with Thrifty Rent-a-Cars criss-crossing the few streets, camera lenses dangling out the windows, in search of clues. The barmaid at the Oasis, with feigned reluctance, sent crews on hot tips to the far corners of town. Photographer Penny Tweedie overheard on a police radio that the royal party was going swimming at the casino. Abandoning the trip to Ayers Rock, she infiltrated the hotel and hid in a garden shed overlooking the pool where she rigged up some canvas over the windows to avoid detection. Three times she opened the window ready to shoot, and three times the police closed the window without searching inside.

The royal party arrived, but without the royals. They swam and left. A gardener cleaned up and locked the shed door. Tweedie did not emerge until evening. That shot, she told *The National Times*, "would have let me start my film".

The sleuths saw their chance that night when they found Diana lightly sunburnt at the press reception. That was the kernel of what developed from bits and pieces of conversation, exaggeration and invention to become, in the papers of London and Sydney, the story that Diana was burnt raw from the outback sun. But that took a couple of days.

Meanwhile, next morning at the School of the Air, children who sounded on their twenty-five-watt transmitters as if they were questioning Charles and Diana from the far side of the moon produced the first on-the-record quotes about baby William: that he had a toy whale, six teeth and was not crawling yet, though he has "got the right movements". In an ecstasy of professional achievement, grown men and women played over to themselves tapes of these royal scraps. In the months to come forests will fall as the same little details are worked and reworked for consumption on all continents.

This is not the collection of news as we know it generally in journalism. These pictures and quotes are commodities to be traded. The truth about the press obsession with Diana is that their fascination is mixed with hate. They want to break her. The tabloids have her always on the verge of collapse from nerves, the sun, and obsessive dieting. Out here in the desert the reasons became clear enough: she doesn't hand them stories by fluffing her role, she doesn't wilt, and photographing the most photographed woman in the world is surprisingly difficult because her hair falls into her eyes.

*

At Tennant Creek airport a dirt-filmed portrait of Queen Elizabeth as the Wattle Queen of the 1954 royal tour hung over the water cooler. Nearby some ghoul has mounted the shattered block of an aircraft engine as a memorial to the first crash landing in the district. Bush humour.

Here the visiting press began to face the day-to-day reality of royal touring in Australia. The photo call was over and the civic grind had begun. Royalty is invited to this country by Canberra, but once here they are delivered up into the hands of local government, to premiers, mayors and MPs. These men have marginal seats to protect, wives to impress and debts to repay. Royalty does the lot. The process is, for the most part, disguised as inspections. A hospital is inspected royally to thank the nurses for being paid so little. At Tennant Creek, Charles and Diana inspected Karguru Primary

School and met little black children, of whom a squad had been brought in on the Peko-Wallsend bus, now sitting nearby, broken down by the effort. It was very hot.

"It's going to be an absolute scorcher," said Whitaker as he paced the schoolyard in the Fijian straw hat he'd fashioned into a trilby. "Diana will go down like ninepins about midday."

She didn't.

Perhaps it's a dog's life being a royal on tour in Australia, and Charles and Diana are to be admired for getting through their schedule.

The royal program for Tennant Creek read:

11.20 am: See school facilities and attend an assembly of schoolchildren.

12.10 pm: Leave for Eldorado Restaurant.

12.15 pm: Arrive. Attend a buffet luncheon. The Prince of Wales responds to welcome by the mayor.

1.25 pm: Board the RAAF BAC 1-11 Alice Springs.

2.20 pm: Arrive. Farewells.

3.00 pm: Board the RAAF BAC 1-11 for Albury.

6.05 pm: Arrive.

6.20 pm: Leave for Woomargama (59km).

7.00 pm: Arrive.

The National Times, 25 March 1983

Sydney, the irresistible city

THIS UNRULY, CORRUPT AND BEAUTIFUL place is so big now: half a dozen cities in one, sprawling west all the way to the mountains. Big cities are exciting: in the simple mathematics of these things, four million people are much, much better than one. Sydney is these millions of people. The mood of the place is their mood. There is fear, worry and anger here, but this is a city that believes in its bones that the future is good. When pollsters try to measure optimism levels around Australia, Sydney goes off the dial. Not that we care much for comparisons. Sydney laps up flattery, but doesn't really give a damn what other cities think. The rest of Australia lies somewhere over the mountains and we sit here on the edge of the Pacific looking east, but not much further out to sea than the last line of breakers. In Sydney's imagination, this is a city without a hinterland, all of Australia wrapped up in one and a great city of the world.

The truth isn't crucial here: this is how we feel about Sydney.

A great city's sense of itself is fed by rumour and gossip, paintings and novels – surprisingly few good novels of Sydney – by family legends and scraps of history remembered from school, by morning radio and evening television – and by newspapers. For over a century, *The Sydney Morning Herald* has been crucial to Sydney's picture of itself as a respectable but disorderly town, erratically democratic, not quite secular, tolerant but with an undertow of old hatreds. The focus of the picture shifts and changes over time but from the first there's been a sense in this paper and this town that hanging over Sydney has always been a smell of money. Money means optimism and curiosity.

Money has made Sydney the first destination of new ideas, new vices, new fashions, new people and yet more money. Nearly a quarter of the nation lives in Sydney and most immigrants want to settle here – despite the realities they find in Cabramatta and Liverpool. Tourists make Sydney their main port of call and despite these visitors showing an odd taste for opals and Darling Harbour, their presence confirms Sydney's high opinion of itself while feeding the city's coffers. That's a very Sydney arrangement – all the more so because it wasn't meant to happen.

Sydney is a city of mean motives overwhelmed by its own good fortune.

Every town has a reason for being that works like a window into the soul of the place. Sydney is only here because of the harbour. But the British didn't have a clue it existed: Cook sailed right past. The penal settlement of Botany Bay might have been just another abandoned settlement around Australia but for the sheer good fortune of Captain Phillip finding, a few miles up the coast, "one of the finest harbours in the world, in which a thousand ships of the line might ride in perfect security".

We stare at the water from the shore. It's not just a sheet of water – "like silk, like pewter, like blood, like a leopard's skin", wrote Kenneth Slessor – it's a place of hidden towns, neighbourhood wars, deserted beaches, sublime beauty, evil visions, looting and pillage, bribery and sacrifice. It's a territory with its own rules and its own politics where the prevailing weather is greed. Yet the Harbour is the earliest and remains one of the most potent subjects of white art on this continent. You can navigate the harbour by paintings: in through the heads with von Guérard, along the headlands and little beaches of Tom Roberts and Streeton and Margaret Preston, past Conrad Martens' Elizabeth Bay and Lloyd Rees's Opera House then, with Grace Cossington Smith's bridge dead ahead, swing into the bay everyone has photographed and painted since that first awkward effort by William Bradley, "Sydney Cove: Port Jackson 1788".

What was meant to be a dumping house for British convicts flourished through lucky break after lucky break to become a great port, then a great city. Nothing much was planned. The prevailing instincts of government have always been to scrimp and save. In this town, luck has been everything.

The site is so beautiful it shrugs off what would ruin half a dozen cities. The land lies under us with a kind of aboriginal resignation, never accepting the worst it's suffered and never admitting defeat. One of Sydney's great assets is the sense we have that after all that's happened here, we might still get it right. Perhaps that's pitching it too high. Maybe it's just a crazy confidence we share that even after so much has been lost and given away what's left will still be wonderful.

From the moment Phillip dropped anchor, Sydney has been given away, slice by slice. It's probably the oldest continuous tradition of government in New South Wales, from the first plots given to army officers round Sydney Cove to the twenty-four hectares of showground delivered to Rupert Murdoch. Government treats this town like Norman Lindsay's Magic Pudding: however much is taken, there's always a full bowl left: "... of beef and beer: / Onions, bunions, corns and crabs, / Whiskers, wheels and hansom cabs." This is the bedtime story of Sydney's government, and the city is so prodigiously rich it's almost true. Almost.

By the time the *Herald* hit the streets in 1831, Sydney was set in its ways. Phillip's modest town plan had been abandoned by his successors. When irascible Governor Bligh tried to stop army officers building where they liked and fencing off what they wanted, the row hastened his overthrow. Sydney is always said to be marked by its convict origins – it is – but what marks us just as much is the rebellion against Bligh. We know from way back that, when the crunch comes, the powerful of this town – not only the developers – won't worry too much about the law.

Sydney's last chance to be a city to match its harbour was lost with Macquarie. He had plans, but London sent out Commissioner Bigge, that Thatcherite before his time, to stop Macquarie in his tracks. No city squares, no cathedral, no avenues, no viceroy's palace. Meanness triumphed at this crucial point. Sydney was not going to be another imperial city like Dublin or Calcutta: there wasn't the need to dazzle the native population. Redcoats could handle the blacks, and building was left to the merchants.

Not entirely. There were engineers to put in drains and trains, the fire brigade to make sure nothing was built higher than fifty metres in the town, until the AMP at the Quay broke through that ceiling in 1962 and the whole CBD followed. Money won. Money usually does in Sydney. There are rules and norms in the city now, but no absolute ceiling.

And there were rats. *Rattus rattus* brought the bubonic plague to Sydney at the turn of the century, and in its wake the town began to clean itself up. In this city where nearly every planning vision fails before it leaves the drawing board, we developed a modest knack for improvement, planting trees and paving footpaths. Very Sydney. We're still at it with great civic flourish and self-congratulation. Had Macquarie Street been saved from the demolishers it would be one of the great streets – better than anything in New Orleans. Instead the remains were "improved" by Neville Wran for the bicentenary. George Street, the dark and crooked spine of the city, is being "improved" right now for the Olympics.

Not that the grand visions of planners for the last century were much good. The muddle of the town – so hated by this paper – was always richer and more fun than their best intentions. There would be no Paddington by now if the planners had had their way, no Surry Hills, no Woolloomooloo and no Rocks. A very Sydney combination of forces saved them – at least for now. First came pig-headed local politicians: slums breed Labor votes. Then militant Sydney middle classes fought alone or in alliance with communists: the green bans. Then came the money: nowadays suburbs condemned for decades as cesspits of vice and crime are too expensive for governments to muck about with. For the moment, in a few precincts of this city, money is working in the right direction.

The only planners' dream that never dies in Sydney is the vision of a city served by expressways. Nothing has had the impact on this town as cars. For cars we built the Bridge – and who regrets that? Traffic jams on the Bridge gave us North Sydney in the 1960s, and as the traffic jams moved north the car gave us Chatswood in the 1990s and now Hornsby. The same is happening south and west. One side of the city was flattened to build expressways into the heart of the city and now – the lessons of the Western Distributor unlearnt – we're flattening stretches of eastern Sydney to do the same again. In Boston they're putting their old freeways underground. We're told we're too poor.

Not poor: this is one of the richest cities on earth. We're mean. The character of this town is marked everywhere by meanness. Powerlines slung through the air are so mean and so Sydney. And those blocks of flats, built hugger-mugger and mean, right to the edge of the harbour, are so Sydney, standing there brand-new and waiting to be the slums of tomorrow. Meanest of all and most like Sydney is its airport. Hong Kong can find $27 billion to flatten a few islands and build an airport for the future. But Sydney has decided to make do with extensions to the old Mascot polo fields. For everyone but the hundreds of thousands who live under the planes, it's a decision that has the winning Sydney virtue of being cheap.

Fear plays a part in this: it takes some political courage to make big civic gestures in Sydney because the country is always ready to punish a government that does. Paul Keating offered about $200 million to bury the Cahill Expressway, money John Fahey's government couldn't touch once the bush decided Keating's cash might be better spent on drought relief. So Canberra kept the money and Sydney looks like having the Cahill forever. Bob Carr could buy back East Circular Quay tomorrow, but for the fear of the bush's revenge. Already the Olympics are posing problems for Labor because out west they see all this money being spent on Sydney. Even so, Olympic dollars will solve none of the fundamental planning problems. Exasperating.

*

And yet in late October there's a day you can suddenly smell summer coming and forgive the place almost anything. In that burst of heat, houses open themselves again to the air. The suburbs settle into their gardens. Then for a week or so jacarandas – always "really good this year" – flower that astonishing blue against the town's brown brick. Thunderstorms cross the suburbs. Nights are warm. Under the stairs you search for the last of last year's mosquito coils. The water is still cold at the beach, but the sun is already hot. Sydney is back on the sand again, pleased to find how beautiful it still is: beautiful place, beautiful people.

The sea means escape is always in the air in Sydney, always a possibility even though we don't, every hot day, down tools and head for the water. A Sydney year doesn't divide neatly into work and holiday: we can be in the surf any day of the week, and weekends here offer what most of the world calls a holiday. Not that we all go to the beach even on the hottest days. There's work to be done, and four million of us couldn't find space on the sand to spread our towels. The point about Sydney is that the beach is there, always, in our imagination.

Cities are defined by the possibilities they offer. We don't all surf; we don't all spend much time on the harbour; not everyone is noshing their nights away in Sydney's stainless steel cafes. The "What's On" pages in this paper have always been the community noticeboard of Sydney's theatres and galleries. There's a lot happening these days and Sydney is proud of that, but this is a city that's a lot better at knowing what's happening – keeping across the gossip, reading reviews, being really really interested – than actually going. Unless, of course, it's a hit.

Sydney loves winners: horses, shows, writers, painters, football teams, politicians, lovers and crooks. But the long haul of team loyalty isn't for us. When the Swans are on a winning streak we're fans for life – unless they start losing. Sydney is a city of spectators except a few times a year when we play as a city – New Year's Eve and Mardi Gras. What could be more Sydney than a few hundred thousand folk down by the harbour to drink and watch the fireworks? Every week this summer there will be four or five fireworks displays somewhere over Sydney – mostly on the harbour, which, apart from anything else, is rated the best amphitheatre for fireworks in the world. New Year's Eve is now, via television, a world event. The annual bill for crackers in 1997 will be $7 million or $8 million. How we love that Chinese fire.

This city will celebrate almost anything that puts on a good show. Patrick White was not alone in fearing a respectable backlash if homosexuals went round "swinging their handbags" in public. But in the end they won over Sydney by taking off their clothes and marching down Oxford Street. Glitz did the trick. When the police commissioner, the attorney-general and the leader of the Opposition gathered in the VIP room to watch the 1997 parade, it wasn't because millions of pink dollars were being spent out there that night, nor were these dignitaries showing political solidarity. They came for the show. So had 700,000 citizens in the streets – including an unhappy little band of preachers. They are with us always.

Fred Nile once said, "If Jesus wept over Jerusalem, He must be heartbroken over Sydney." On Saturday nights evangelists gather near Hoyts, preaching sin and redemption as they have on street corners every Saturday night since they came ashore with the prisoners. This paper has often allied itself since with those whose mission it was – and is – to deny the town what it's always wanted: pleasure. Even the name of the place is an elegant little time bomb for puritans. "An ugly word, Sydney," wrote Ruth Park. "The city was named for a maggot-headed politician ... Yet the name attests the poetic irony of fate. The convict settlement was to be called Albion, but this never took. Instead we got Sydney, a word which is a corruption of St Denis, in its turn a corruption of the Greek Dionysus. This wild and fatal deity is alive and well in his name city."

Early on, NSW governments reached a worldly accommodation with the preachers. They passed many strange and cruel laws to keep them happy, while knowing that corruption would allow real life to continue more or less unimpeded. No one could say Macquarie Street hadn't tried – but think of the political mayhem if these laws had actually worked! By small acts of courage, NSW governments sometimes face the puritans and clip a few mad provisions out of the Crimes Act, but it's slow going. The touted sophistication of the town in the last few decades was still mediated by the corruption needed to allow dance clubs, gambling, brothels, booze out of hours and sex in arrangements forbidden by the Bible.

The price of keeping puritan Sydney happy has been high: turning – who knows how many? – police, magistrates, judges and politicians into crooks. We're not another Lusaka but corruption deeply affects civil life in Sydney, not least because we've known ever since the army was shipping illegal spirits in from Calcutta that the law enforcers here are entangled with the crooks. The royal commissions we hold to expose this every few years – strongly supported by this paper – are part of a long Sydney tradition. They are as theatrical in their way as the latest David Williamson: great characters, earthy dialogue, tears and laughter, strong moral arguments for improvement and then ... not much changes in the real world.

We've just been through it all again, down to the conventional last scenes on the floor of parliament when the politicians disown the commissioners' hard recommendations and side, instead, with the puritans. Government and Opposition agreed there would be no change to the age of consent, no let-up in the war against drugs, no "shooting galleries" to save addicts' lives. The town rated the James Wood show a fabulous success.

We have a lot to be angry about in this town, but anger dissipates so easily here. It's one of the pleasures – and problems – of the place. Fools in Macquarie Street, crooks in the CIB, goths on the building sites enrage Sydney for a few days at a time, but then comes the weekend: a drink and a film on Friday night, sleep, an hour in the surf, lunch with friends in the backyard with good food, a few jokes and that acid gossip we love in this town. If pain persists, there's always the harbour: symbol of the city's great good fortune, still so beautiful it triumphs over most of the worst that's been inflicted here.

All Sydney feels it owns the harbour. It would be perfectly understandable if families living hard in suburbs on the outer rim of the city resented the privileges of the harbour. But that's not how it works: there's no evidence of animosity. Far outnumbering the backpackers at Circular Quay at weekends are Sydney people in for the day to see their city. It's our Opera House even if we never set foot in it. And along the walkways of the Quay and the Botanic Gardens we exercise a right no Australian questions: to get to the water's edge.

The harbour is more beautiful – but less dramatic – than it's been for a century or more because it's no longer a busy port. Trucks have triumphed over trains in Australia, and trucks find it easier to reach Botany Bay. So the working port has relocated, by supreme irony, to the windswept bay Phillip abandoned a couple of hundred years ago. But in a switch that's very, very Sydney, the harbour is now turning its beauty into cash. It always took a small fortune to own a house with lawns running down to one of the bays east of the Bridge; now huge sums are ventured almost anywhere on the harbour for a decent flat with a view of the water. It's a sort of mania loose in the world.

The GDP of small nations is tied up in harbour real estate. In the last decade, six or so billion dollars have been spent buying and selling along the waterfront streets of Sydney. Even in busts, the market in harbour real estate hardly falters. And the *Herald* prospers on the ads.

The inexorable pressure of money is mounting to put bigger buildings on smaller sites wherever the harbour can be glimpsed. Tourists want hotel rooms with views of what they've flown all this way to see: the harbour. A bit of water is a security prized by Westpac. So the old coal loaders, factories, gas works and docks, decommissioned now, are waiting for apartments to be built in their place. In the name of preserving the heritage, the city is even allowing hundreds of apartments to be built out over the water in old – but virtually rebuilt – wharves in Walsh Bay and Woolloomooloo. This is Sydney pioneering a new kind of real estate, subdividing the sea ...

The shape of the harbour is being decided for the long haul. Those old industrial sites were easy to clear once the factories outlived their purposes. But the blocks of apartments that are now replacing them along the shoreline, each with dozens or even scores of individual owners, will be all but impossible to shift. We've learnt with relief and at times sorrow – in the case of the State Office Block – that office buildings aren't permanent. Even the big ones come and go. Apartment blocks don't: whatever goes up never comes down.

A bad building on the harbour diminishes the whole city. Imagine how we would feel about this city in the late 1990s if Eero Saarinen had not plucked Jørn Utzon's sketch of an opera house out of the discard heap and awarded him the prize. Had we build the Philadelphia-designed squeeze box that came second to Utzon's masterpiece, or the little interlocking British boxes that came third, this city and our sense of this city would have been permanently diminished. Utzon was dismissed for the meanest motives, but even the botched building we got in the end is a triumph – another of those triumphs of good fortune over mean motives that make Sydney.

But for this city and the harbour the winning stroke of luck is that the bush along the northern shore has been occupied all this century by the armed forces of another government: the Commonwealth of Australia. It's been beyond New South Wales's power to give away. Every square inch of the shore in Hong Kong is built over, and that's exciting in its own way; Istanbul, which might claim an even more spectacular site than Sydney, is city to the waterline. Around Manhattan you're lucky to find a tree. What's uniquely beautiful in Sydney is that so much of the harbour's shoreline is almost virgin bush. Behind are suburbs bursting at the seams, over the water is a gleaming city, but setting the scene is this long line of bush. It's the source, in all lights and weather, of qualities in short supply in this town: innocence and serenity.

But the Commonwealth is shedding the land. Middle Head is destined, if the Department of Defence gets its way, to be subdivided – to raise a few millions to fund the needs of the Commonwealth for perhaps a few hours. The fate of this stretch of the harbour now rests in the hands of a South Australian grazier, the Defence Minister Ian McLachlan, whom I suspect has happy memories of childhood back on the property when his nurse would read him Norman Lindsay's The Magic Pudding. Said Barnacle Bill: "You have to be as smart as paint to keep this Puddin' in order. He's that artful, lawyers couldn't manage him ... The more you eats the more you gets. Cut-an'-come-again is his name, an' cut-an'-come-again, is his nature ..."

In a rage a moment ago, I stopped to stare out the window. From the Herald's perch on the twenty-seventh floor I can see to the mountains. The suburbs are softened by hot blue haze. Tonight there should be one of those slow summer sunsets the colour of fire. No sign of the promised thunderstorms. Even the suburbs I spent so many years despising don't seem threatening these days. It looks good. There are still a thousand reasons to rage against Sydney – anywhere we love makes us rage – but no other city here could be so exciting, so funny and alive. Despite everything, this is the place.

The Sydney Morning Herald,
2 December 1997, celebrating 50,000 issues of the paper

Bob Carr holds the fort

BOB CARR IS SCRAPING THE HOLLANDAISE sauce off his smoked salmon. Each slice gets the once-over. At the umpteen-thousandth official dinner of his record-breaking career, the NSW premier is chatting to his left and right – "filling the void", he calls it – but his attention is fixed on the last smears of yellow goo clinging to the salmon.

He's still gaunt after all these years. Except for a pair of old man's jowls, Carr seems hardly touched by time. Sitting on that beanpole figure is the same sad, wry face that was staring out of newspapers and television screens for years even before he became the state's unlikely premier in 1995. And he's still there. Suburbs are rioting on hot summer nights; the mad are sleeping in the streets; the jails are full; water levels are falling inexorably in the dams; hospital queues stretch round the block; commuters wait six deep for trains that never come; and the polls have been grim for months – but Bob Carr is still there. And there's no one trying to elbow him out of his job: no Costello to his Howard, no Brown to his Blair.

At fifty-seven, Carr is already the most senior political leader in office in Australia. Last year high-level efforts were made to draft him to lead Labor into the federal election – he calls this "an alternative universe not explored" – and sometime on Wednesday he beats Neville Wran's record of ten years and seven weeks as the longest-serving NSW premier since Federation. "If I was eating a gourmet sandwich at my desk at *The Bulletin* and a sibyl had entered and said you'll be premier of New South Wales longer than this bloke you're writing about – Neville Wran – I'd have been inclined to dismiss her like the young Claudius who was told he would end up master of Rome."

Carr is only master – if that's the word – of New South Wales, and is working hard at not gloating as the record approaches. Wran's memory is to be honoured. There's to be a certain reluctance about the celebrations. The starting point is that breaking the record means "nothing. It just means nothing … but if I force myself to reflect on it, there's a satisfaction that I delivered for the party and didn't let it down." That's pure Carr. Over the following days he would reveal other sources of satisfaction – frank satisfaction – but his first thought was not for New South Wales and its people, but what his long term at the top has meant for his party. Unique political animal though he is, Carr remains a product and servant of the NSW right-wing Labor machine. A record term for him means another long hold on power for it. What has always mattered in New South Wales is not the record of achievement but the raw fact of being in power.

Carr is a scholar of power as it was wielded by men who held empires together and rescued the world from the Depression. There is something both comic and endearing that a premier of New South Wales should have such intimate working knowledge of how men faced challenges of a scale he will never remotely face. This supremely cautious provincial politician revels in their audacity. Even their lies. He has the maxims of Lincoln, both Roosevelts, Clinton and Macmillan at his fingertips. But his favourite remains Marcus Aurelius. For Carr, the second-century Roman emperor illustrates, for instance, the need to soldier on in politics.

"It is a work in progress. It's always been the case … every day as it was for Marcus Aurelius. Years from now I'll think fondly of the days when you get up and there's a bad poll on your leadership leading the news; and your leadership – in opposition or government – is being questioned. As you leave home you look at Helena and groan and think there's got to be a better job than this; and she says just go and sort them out. You come into parliament and you start dealing with the problems and issues of the day with the staff and the public servants; and you go into the caucus and you give them the homily of the week; and get them ready for parliament; and you do your press conference rebutting the criticism and putting forward the alternative plan; and at question time, with your armour on, you stand up and you belt them away; you come out at 3.30 – blood and flesh spattered everywhere – and you're still holding the fort."

*

Power means a long office high above Phillip Street with views down the harbour and stunning paintings on the walls. He doesn't choose them. That's not his thing. And there are no signs of his predecessors here beyond a couple of caricatures of fat George Reid. The historian premier doesn't dwell on the men who have gone before him or bone up on their maxims. "I feel that I'm part of a pageant of state political leaders. That's not a big deal. No one reflects on them. They sort of fade out of any consciousness around about the time of McKell even for aficionados – with the exception of titanic figures like Lang and Holman and George Reid."

Boilermaker Bill McKell is the only forerunner who counts in Carr's story. He talks passionately of him as the prototype conservative Labor premier who restored a shattered party, held office from 1941 to 1947, became governor-general and then, as an old man with lots of tales to tell, counselled Bob Carr, the young *Bulletin* journalist desperate to get into parliament. "McKell put together the political coalition, the political approach, the political style – better word: the political ethos – that I inherited. That's the cavalcade I'm part of: the Labor Party forged in 1941, updated by Wran. And if I'd failed to get over the line in 1995, if I'd failed to put in the performance in 1991, then that's the tradition I would have let down, I wouldn't have measured up to that."

It's the non-abrasive, cautious, deliberately low-key strategy the Labor machine believes is the way to hold on to power in New South Wales. Carr calls it his step-by-step approach, "taking a step at a time, allowing a notion to grow, exploring our way pragmatically". It means waiting; listening closely to the media – especially the shock jocks of 2GB and 2UE; having the public push rather than the government lead; looking for consensus; keeping surprises to a minimum so that when change comes – if it must – it seems appropriate, not unexpected. Carr's army of critics, not least among his own public servants, blames this timid strategy for so little having been *done* in his record-breaking term at the top. Carr answers as any politician would, with long lists of legislative achievements – always something about national parks – and this rejoinder: "It is something levied against every government and there is no Labor government that has been immune to it."

*

Baffled old ladies hunched over their cards in the bingo room of the Picton Bowling Club reproached the Premier. Carr was on a flying visit to this sleepy town south of Sydney – sleepy and determined to stay that way. Everything had gone to plan at first – the greeting at the door, getting all the names right and then the warm-up speech to the little crowd, praising the new extensions and the dancing two nights a week: "It's a nice modern club." Then disaster struck as he called the bingo. He was in fine voice and very serious. So were the women. "Eleven," he called and there was muttering at the tables and mocking whistles. He might be Premier of New South Wales but he was an amateur here. Carr ploughed on as the room filled with cries of "Legs. Legs. Legs Eleven."

Carr was not in town on the business of New South Wales. He was pursuing the underlying mission of his office: keeping Labor in power. All morning he had in tow the local mayor, Michael Banasik, who is about to put up his hand as the party's candidate for the new seat of Wollondilly. Carr's message at the club, then at a community nursery and a local soccer field, was that his bond with this man could deliver for the district: "He will harass me." The beauty of it, as Carr explained later, was that he could promote the man all morning while "not mentioning the party".

Out here there's no Marcus Aurelius. Instead there are heartwarming anecdotes about the people of New South Wales. They put him in his place. They illuminate him. They get it in a nutshell. Over the next few days every audience he addressed heard about a palliative care nurse at the Prince of Wales Hospital who really loves her patients. Sometimes Carr drops names: "I remember John Dwyer saying, 'Premier ...'" He talks quite unselfconsciously of himself in the third person: "I congratulate you as premier" and "Poor bugger, he had the premier on the phone ..."

With a nickel-plated spade he planted an endangered local species, *Epacris purpurascens*, at the nursery and spoke to a happy band of volunteers about species loss, global warming and the history of bushwalking in New South Wales. At Tahmoor Sportsground a surly group of schoolchildren hear him promise $10,000 towards a bore for "softer and safer playing fields". The turnout is tiny but his hands project his message as if he's talking to an audience of thousands. Carr's hands and fingers fly whenever he's talking, even on the phone. Every time he opens his mouth, it's somehow a public occasion.

By 1 pm he's heading back up the highway, sitting in the front seat of his Holden Caprice eating a bowl of nuts. Driving up the freeway seems a good time to ask what he thinks of his fiefdom. Carr takes it carefully: "New South Wales is the New York of Australia." Pause. "It is jostling interests all intent on more. But the other side of the coin is an essentially good and decent community ... " [very long pause] "that probably does things better than just about any other place in the world." But ask him about the *politics* of the place and he casts all caution aside. Carr's New South Wales is "where argument is endless and the clash of interest groups drives everything; the word solution barely exists; every settlement is only temporary until events again unsettle it. It is a world of constant argument. But you have still got a chance to fight through to get honest compromises and ward off people who want to loot the public treasury. I can smell them coming. I have been premier for ten years, Opposition leader for seven years before that. I know all the interest groups. I know what their wiles are, I know their seductive minds but I know what it leads to. I know what share of the Treasury they've got their eye on."

The premier has a happy knack of being able to read in a car without being sick. A fat file of briefing papers for the afternoon's cabinet lay open on his lap. He dips into them – while ceaselessly monitoring the radio – all the way back to the office. "Cabinet is a marvellous filter because you've got around the table people of diverse backgrounds responding to the prodding of different interest groups, bringing to their ministerial responsibilities different perspectives. One thing I've learnt is the value of cabinet government. When we've got into trouble – our first-term stuff-ups – it's often been as a result of not using the filter of cabinet."

Carr's enemies in the party don't prosper. The factions can still force names on him, but these days Carr largely shapes his ministry. But they are not his friends. Carr remains aloof from them, playing teacher, tutoring them. How much they listen is another matter. One of Carr's key roles in government – and one he seems to relish – is bursting onto the scene to rescue ministers when they stuff up. He agrees. "But it was ever thus." He can screw himself up to sacking them, too. His confrontation with faction heavy Eddie Obeid after the last state election is an event of legend. It's said their exchange could be heard through a concrete floor.

"Any elation is drained from the last days of an election campaign that you know you are going to win – and from election night – because you know what's coming: the distress and the disappointment of colleagues that you are going to have to persuade to stand aside." Paul Keating had told him of the same experience. "He said: 'All the gaiety of our win in '93 was drained from the occasion in those battles about who got into the ministry ... By the time I drove up to Yarralumla for the swearing in, I was just drained by that. But you've got to do it.'" Does much drain him in politics? "You know the Mitterrand quote? The quality most required of the political leader? Indifference. That's too brutal for me, that's too brutal for me. But he was pointing to a truth."

*

A few nights a week, two men can be seen walking the suburban hills of Maroubra. One is the Premier of New South Wales and the other is his bodyguard. "If Helena doesn't want to come, then I go for a walk with the detective and listen to taped lectures. They're produced by The Teaching Company in America and they are university courses. The ones I've got at the moment are a twenty-four-part lecture series on Robert E. Lee and his high command. One is on Chinese dynastic history. I've got a stack of them at home, about a dozen I revisit."

Other leaders say they'll stay around while their parties still want them. Carr's formula is different: "To lead the party in 2007." It's only a couple of years away. He says Helena is keen to stick it out till then – their fifth campaign together at the top. "She likes it. She would resist very strongly any idea of premature departure." Life without politics seems hardly conceivable for Carr. Joining the Labor Party as a kid in the 1960s knitted him together in some fundamental way. "In a sense I could never have been happy before 2 October 1963 – that's an exaggeration – after that I was fulfilled." His party career is more than just an ambition realised. Carr admits "absolutely" that he rates his own worth by the fact of being chosen by his people – his branch, his party and his electorate. "I would rather have been a member of the legislative council of Togoland than editor of *The Times* of London or the world head of Heinz. That's a fever in the blood. But it was sparked by the noblest of adolescent idealism."

Times have been kind to Carr in the ten years since he barely scraped into office in 1995. Australia's prosperity has rolled on uninterrupted while John Howard has flattened the hopes of the radicals inside and outside the Labor Party who once used to harass the Premier to *do* things. Australia is more conservative now, and that suits Carr and the Labor machine just fine.

He won't discuss what bores him but he's eager to confess what's always appealed to him about the job: making decisions. "It's the intellectual stimulus of absorbing streams of different advice and the sometimes untidy discussions around that [cabinet] table, and drawing on your political instincts. And yes, the element of the gamble: backing your judgement and running the risk that you've got it wrong. It's throwing the dice; let the dice fly." Right now the great gamble of the Carr government – to scrimp and save to pay back public debt at the expense of public works – seems not to be paying off. The rating agencies have been over the moon for years but the public is getting fractious. So's Canberra. These days Carr is keen to be photographed anywhere that calls for a hard hat – preferably underground – and his favourite new word is "infrastructure". NSW voters puzzled by this new word should consult the Macquarie Dictionary:

> Noun 1. the basic framework or underlying foundation (as of an organisation or a system). 2. the roads, railways, schools, and other capital equipment which comprise such an underlying system within a country or region ...

By his own rating he is at a rather low ebb now. He talks of having "lived out every variety there is of the political leadership experience ... being an unexpected premier, a somewhat accident-prone premier; to being a premier surrounded by fulfilled Olympic expectations, inaugurating policy successes; a premier then a bit on the defensive mobilising programs for a tilt at a third mandate; now a premier facing disappointments in a few specific areas of public policy and the public anger that arises out of that." Yet he's premier still and on Friday, just about every Labor heavy in Australia is gathering at Sydney's Westin Hotel – plus a thousand diners at $500 each – to celebrate his record-breaking place in the cavalcade of NSW premiers.

The unanswered question is whether any in that pageant actually ran the state. Has New South Wales ever let its leaders be much more than concierges, front men at the door while the shadowy owners upstairs really call the shots? Does Bob Carr, this keen Labor kid from Malabar, really think he runs it? "When over a four-year span I get a raft of tort law reform through; or when with a signature I gazette 100 new national parks between the Bega Valley and Nowra, or mandate design guidelines for everyone who builds apartment blocks; when you determine that the one available extra block of money in your four-year forward projections goes to smaller class sizes rather than to something else – yes I do. Beyond that I live like anyone with the welter of unexpected events, the pressures, scandals and upsets coming out of a clear blue sky."

The Sydney Morning Herald, 21 May 2005

Arts and Artists

Harry Seidler vs
Patrick Cook

ONE SUNDAY A COUPLE OF YEARS AGO *The National Times* carried drawings on the inside back page from the familiar universe of Patrick Cook. The hand of God was striking down cancer victims, a maudlin poet walked his dog by the surf, and a puzzled man was facing a spiked doorknob marked GO AWAY.

Reading the paper that Sunday, 15 August 1982, Harry Seidler was appalled by a fourth drawing on the page captioned HARRY SEIDLER RETIREMENT PARK. He was sickened, outraged, anguished. His barrister and brother-in-law Clive Evatt later described the cartoon thus: "It shows around a very deserted, arid landscape a number of dwelling houses, ugly, box-like, with no roofs on some of them and no doors. A nurse is feeding them meals on wheels. The man there is removing the excrement by his shovel and is putting it into a large drum surrounded by flies and filth ... Far from being a place where the retired can enjoy the autumn years of their life in comfortable and decent surroundings, it is like a prison, worse than Changi jail ..."

Seidler saw the cartoon as an unwarranted attack on his life's work, coming out of the blue, suggesting his architecture was worthless and incompetent and ugly, and that he built inhuman structures, buildings and houses that degrade humanity, which "is the very opposite to that which I have devoted my life ..." Seidler took it that Cook was being quite literal: that he had actually built a house with no roof, no door, able to fit only one inhabitant who had to be fed sandwiches through a slot.

HARRY SEIDLER
RETIREMENT PARK

Was the architect serious, Neil McPhee QC asked last week when this matter got to court. "Certainly," Seidler replied. "The cartoon shows just that." Seidler asked for no apology. But in early September 1982, he and his company sued John Fairfax and Sons Ltd.

Harry Seidler, the foremost exponent of modern architecture in Australia, and according to his counsel virtually a household name, with a reputation unparalleled within Australia and a credit to the country beyond, has not been idle since the cartoon appeared two years ago. The staff at his Milsons Point office overlooking Luna Park and Sydney Harbour grew from about ten to fourteen to handle the commercial work being undertaken by the company. One of the projects in which Seidler was involved was the enormous Grosvenor Place in Sydney, promoted by its builders as perhaps the largest and most expensive office block to be constructed in Australia.

But Seidler had no new commissions for houses, and a month before the case against *The National Times* opened in the Supreme Court, Seidler added to his list of grievances that he had been denied the enjoyment, the challenge and the opportunities for complete self-expression afforded him by designing houses since Patrick Cook's cartoon appeared in these pages. "Somehow," he told the court, "this must be in people's minds."

*

Not since the wartime Archibald case, when William Dobell defended his portrait of Joshua Smith, have the courts seen such an important clash between two artists. And in essence the issue was the same between Cook and Seidler as it was between Dobell and the painters who attacked his work: the question of representation. Portraiture was at stake then, but here it was the future of cartooning in Australia, for on trial was Patrick Cook's style, the elegant drawings by which he aims to say the most with the least, a style that relies on allusion and assumes a reader's informed curiosity about the world.

A good joke is no defence to an accusation of defamation, but the law recognises the right to make honest, even trenchant comment with this technical complication: the comment must be based on material sufficiently identified to the reader.

So at the heart of Seidler's attack was the allegation that Cook's square boxes did not identify his architecture and in particular the buildings on which Cook especially based his opinion: Blues Point Tower (a block of flats on a peninsula in Sydney Harbour), the MLC tower in the city and Seidler's house in the bush in the Sydney suburb of Killara. Cook's boxes were not labelled, Seidler's lawyers argued. And what label there was suggested the architect had built a retirement village. Seidler had never done such a project, and they claimed that error alone vitiated the defence.

Seidler was represented by his brother-in-law Clive Evatt Jnr who, since his return to practice in late 1981, has undertaken a good deal of defamation work, though his old practice was principally in the area of personal injury. His father was the doyen of the Sydney defamation bar, and one of the most colourful figures in the history of Phillip Street. Evatt Jnr was an art dealer in his years away from the law.

He burst through the door of the court the morning the case began carrying a model of one of Seidler's houses. Later trips brought in three or four cardboard boxes of documents, and a bag of books. Behind him sat his client and Mrs Penelope Seidler. One of the Seidler children watched part of the proceedings, as did Mrs Seidler's sister, the president of the Family Court, Justice Elizabeth Evatt.

Opening the case to Justice Miles and the jury of three women and one man, Evatt spoke of "a very serious, a very gross defamation" and called for "a verdict for the plaintiffs in a most substantial amount". He spoke of the colossal circulation of this paper, and argued that "the people who read *The*

National Times count in the community". Of John Fairfax and Sons, publishers of *The National Times*, Evatt said, "They have chucked slime over our (i.e., Seidler's) reputation, a reputation built up over thirty years, hard-won and hard to achieve." Reputation, Evatt mused, "is like crystal glass. Once it is shattered you cannot fix it up again."

A cartoon, he argued, is "the most dangerous, deadly way of defaming. Words are cheap, words are forgotten, but images stick in our mind. They are hard to erase." Evatt cited the Sydney Harbour Bridge, the Opera House, and Botticelli's *Birth of Venus*.

Cook's cartoon, he said, carried three defamatory imputations. First, that Seidler is brutal and antisocial. Second, that he is unaesthetic, with no interest in beauty and good design. Third, that he is incompetent, "that he doesn't put roofs on, or doors".

*

Seidler took the stand. He was a student in Walter Gropius' masterclass at Harvard after the war, and the marks of that time can be seen in Seidler's bow ties and beautiful grey flannel suit, his soft North American accent and, of course, his buildings. He told the court, "Modern architecture, as any other architecture in history, tries to bring into unison the aspirations of the art of the time and the technology of the time and bring these to bear on the social demands of the time."

He came to Australia in 1948 and concentrated on designing houses, some of which won prizes from the Royal Australian Institute of Architects (RAIA) and *The Sydney Morning Herald*. He became in time a life fellow of the institute, and was awarded the OBE. His prizes and honours were all placed before the jury. Seidler began receiving commercial briefs after about ten years in Sydney. In 1961 he completed Blues Point Tower, a very large apartment block on the southern tip of McMahon's Point. He described it to the court as "a fusion of art and technology". The facade with its "simple pattern of the windows and its proportion are paralleled to a painting by Albers who is an internationally renowned painter." Albers was one of Seidler's teachers.

The painting was put before the jury.

From the late 1960s, Seidler concentrated on large office buildings. Australia Square was finished in 1967, and in that year he finished his own house in a bush gully at the back of Killara. From that time Seidler's house design-ing ceased for over a decade. The Killara house won the Sir John Sulman Medal, and was featured in a book of Seidler's work published in Australia, New York and Stuttgart. Seidler provided material for the book.

After the completion of the MLC Tower in Sydney in 1978, Seidler again designed houses: holiday villas at Kooralbyn in Queensland, houses for Commodore Mercen, late of the Royal Australian Navy; Bruce Bland; Jack Hannes, the founder of Hanimex; a Mrs Hannigan; and the house for Dr Basser, the model of which (built by Seidler himself) faced the jury, pool side forward, throughout the trial.

"Have you and the company ever designed any houses or buildings which could be described as insanitary?" asked Evatt.

"Certainly not."

"Or ugly?"

"Certainly not."

"Or which could be described as vertical constructions resembling box-shaped houses without doors, roofs or sewerage or other facilities and with sufficient space for only one occupant who is fed through a small opening and whose excrement is removed manually by a tray?"

"Certainly not."

"Have you had any commissions, either you or your company, for dwell-ing houses or residential houses, since the publication appeared in *The National Times* in August 1982?" asked Evatt.

"No, none."

"Have you had any inquiries for dwelling houses or residences?"

"No, none at all." Indeed, the court was told that neither Seidler nor his company had had as much as a telephone call on the subject.

Cross-examined by Neil McPhee QC for John Fairfax and Sons, Seidler agreed that this was a very strange thing. "Do you want the jury to believe that the reason that you say you have not had one phone call about design-ing a house since August 1982 is because of that one cartoon of Patrick Cook's that was published in *The National Times*? Is that what you want this jury to believe?"

"Yes," Seidler replied.

McPhee, a hard, rather wizened figure, came to the law via the Army. He graduated from Duntroon, served in Korea and was admitted to the Vic-torian Bar in 1960, at the age of thirty-one. For three years in the late 1970s he was a Melbourne city councillor. Earlier this year, during preparation for the Seidler case, he sailed his yacht *Antigua* up to Sydney. He appeared with a local junior barrister, Terry Tobin.

"There are some people who hate modern architecture, are there not?"

"I don't agree with that."

"You never heard any criticism of modern architecture?"

"I have heard criticisms about the environment and the kind of buildings that may be built, but that is not synonymous with modern architecture."

"In recent years there has been a good deal of controversy in architectural circles as to whether modem architecture has been replaced by other movements or styles of architecture, has there not?"

"There is a lot of wordy journalism on the subject. I don't think it has much depth."

"There are those who contend that modern architecture has been replaced by what is called postmodern architecture."

"I don't believe that at all."

"I know you do not agree with it, but there are people who contend that, are there not?"

"There are some, but I would put that in the category of cheap journalism."

McPhee showed Seidler two articles from the RAIA journal *Architecture Australia*: one by the architect and architectural critic for *The Age*, Norman Day, and the other by a Sydney architect and teacher of architecture, Andrew Metcalf. Seidler looked briefly at them and thrust them away. "I haven't read them. I wouldn't read them. I wouldn't be interested in the comments made by those particular authors of those articles."

"Why?" asked McPhee.

"Because they are not worth reading. Not worth taking any note of."

McPhee then produced the reply Seidler had written to the articles, which was published in a subsequent edition of *Architecture Australia*. The letter began, "Receiving the RAIA journal, I find a consistent embarrassment in recent times. It is unfathomable to me how such an obviously amateurish and painfully inept periodical can have the audacity to call itself the official journal of an institute made up of presumably erudite and visually trained professionals. It seems to have reached a climax of intellectual depravity ..."

Seidler admitted that he had read the articles, and that the language of his reply was strong. But he told the court he would "do everything in my power to dissuade people and particularly the young and students whom

I teach from taking notice of that kind of tendency, which is, I am afraid, childish because it is undigested and not a local product. Imported."

Seidler's own capacity to mix it as a controversialist was not at issue here, nor was the quality of postmodern architecture. The letter and the discussion of the new movement was introduced as evidence to counter the suggestion – heavily relied upon in Evatt's opening address – that Cook's criticism had come "out of the blue".

"You have never ever seen any criticism written of your architecture?"

"No, not that I recall."

"Never once?"

"Nothing of any memorable nature."

"Memorable or not, have you any recollection of any adverse criticism of your architecture?"

"Well, there might have been some written by journalists, not by anyone I particularly take note of."

Seidler protested that he found it offensive for McPhee to suggest that Blues Point Tower was "comparable and virtually identical to any structure seen anywhere".

"You don't think you are a bit oversensitive to criticism, do you?"

"You cannot blame me from the way you are questioning me."

"Do you object to criticism of your architectural work?"

"No."

"Adverse criticism?"

"Enlightening criticism I am very happy to listen to."

"Adverse criticism?" asked McPhee again.

"No. From some people I don't, if they know what they are talking about."

"I understood you to say earlier that you are not conscious of any adverse criticism of you ever being made?"

"I am not."

"Does that mean that you do not object to it because there has not been any?"

"Well, if it were to have happened I am not averse to it."

*

Two of Seidler's clients gave evidence on his behalf. The builder, Ron Sevitt, told the court he thought the cartoon showed a complex "dehumanised to the point of being obscene". Under cross-examination, he admitted the drawing had not changed his high opinion of Seidler as an architect.

Jack Hannis, a recent client, had seen the cartoon only a week before the case began. He told Tobin, junior counsel for John Fairfax and Sons, that Seidler is still regarded as the nation's premier architect by those he moves among.

The architect, Peter Myers, read that August 1982 issue of *The National Times* on Bathurst Island in the Timor Sea. He found most disturbing about the cartoon that "it presents the material as fact ... I took it to mean something that actually happened". Tobin asked him, "You understood it to mean that the cartoonist was saying to the public that Harry Seidler has first of all designed a retirement park. Is that right?"

"Yes."

"And in the retirement park he has designed the houses to have no roofs on them?"

"That is correct."

"Did you take any steps to inquire as to whether there had been a retirement park built by Mr Seidler without any roofs on them?"

"Not at the time."

"It would have been a remarkable breakthrough in planning and development of law to have imagined that a retirement park could be designed or built without roofs. Do you agree with that?"

"Let me think of an answer," Myers replied. "I am not here to comment on the merits and demerits of local government acts in planning. It is not a valid question to ask me."

After further questioning Myers admitted he had not actually believed Seidler had built such a park. "It is not a photograph so why make me answer the question?"

Cook's cartoon, he went on to say, showed a "dyspeptic concern about modernities ... it seems so reminiscent of the strictures of people like Goebbels against modern architecture ..." He saw it as a "deliberate and sustained attack upon the reputation and capacity" of Seidler and to have "attributes of a longstanding malcontent in some circles about modern building".

Re-examined by Evatt, Myers accepted the suggestion that the roofs might have been blown off in a storm. "Cyclone Tracy showed that. A whole city of them blew off."

Conrad Nechensky, editor of *Architektur Aktuell*, who had come from

Vienna to appear in the case, was in the box for only a few minutes of confusion (the judge at first thought he was the Australian editor of an Austrian magazine) before his evidence was declared inadmissible. No claim was being litigated of loss to Seidler's reputation in the central European former monarchy.

Penelope Seidler was also examined briefly by her brother. It was a special moment: two Evatts facing each other across the court; two remarkable figures, both tall and long-limbed, speaking in the same accents. She confirmed that Harry Seidler and Associates, of which she is a director, had received no requests, inquiries or commissions for houses since 1982. The cartoon she took as meaning that "Harry Seidler had designed a hideous shocking retirement park".

*

Cook took the stand after lunch on the third day. A student of medieval history at the University of Sydney, he began to contribute cartoons on a freelance basis first to *Nation Review*, now defunct, then to *The Bulletin*. In 1976 he joined *The National Times*. A neat, intense figure, Cook sat in the witness box fixing McPhee with bespectacled eyes.

The defence of comment was only available to Cook if he could convince the jury the cartoon expressed his opinion and that, based upon the facts, that opinion might be held by an honest man. Behind that lay the question of identification: the "ordinary reader" – the law's "reasonable man" with his feet up – had to be able to identify the facts upon which Cook's opinions were based.

"What is a cartoon?" asked McPhee.

"A comment."

He had met Seidler once, at a fundraising function held for the ALP in the architect's Killara home. Cook arrived late in the afternoon. "It was in a very attractive gully with a stream, and to me it seemed it squatted in the gully, like a rather assertive, alien object." He thought the house completely dominated the setting. "It was harsh, it was angular."

Blues Point Tower he had first seen from the ferry taking him to school back in the 1960s. "I think it's hideous. It's a real offence against the harbour ... If you compare it with the Opera House, which is on a point almost equidistant on the other side of the bridge, Blues Point Tower does not,

I think, in any sense complement the harbour so much as seek to dominate it."

"Have you ever been close to the building?" McPhee asked.

"Yes, I have."

"What appearance does it bear?"

"Doesn't get any better."

Cook added that the tower "disfigures the view of the harbour from any
point from where it is visible".

He told the court he was trying to make three points in the cartoon
about Seidler's buildings, "that in my opinion they were ugly, they induced
claustrophobia and that they were fairly severely functional".

"At the time you drew the cartoon, did you have any belief one way or
the other as to whether Mr Seidler had designed or built a retirement park?"

"No. As far as I knew he hadn't."

"Why, then, did you make a cartoon of a retirement park?"

"I was trying to convey the sense that this is where it will all end up."

"This is where what will end up?"

"If you are forced to live and work among buildings of this nature all
your life, then when you are pensioned off, when you are immobile, well,
you are put away; you'll be put away in the same way you are to work in
buildings such as – in a state of mind such as I was trying to convey in the
drawing." That state of mind, Cook told the court, was helplessness and
depression. "If you look at the people in the constructions in the drawings,
they are by no means happy."

Evatt rose to cross-examine. During the preliminary court proceedings
in 1983, the plaintiffs had tried and failed to establish that malice might
have so warped Cook's judgement that it undercut any defence of comment. Mr Justice Hunt had ruled that irrelevant. Now, facing Cook, Evatt
had to try to establish one central contention: that Cook did not actually
hold the views represented in the cartoon. A few kind words about Seidler's
architecture would be a start.

Evatt showed him a picture of the plaza in front of the MLC building,
"You have been to Rome, have you not?"

"Yes."

"I don't know whether you recognise the way the brickwork or cobblestones are arranged on the steps, but do you see any similarity between that
and the Spanish steps in Italy?"

"No, I don't."

Cook conceded Seidler deserved a mark for the open space, and that he, in fact, disliked all high-rise architecture as seen in Sydney. "I hark back to the sandstone buildings in Macquarie Street." Evatt asked, "Would you agree that there are in Sydney many high-rise buildings even uglier than you claim Mr Seidler's buildings are? Worse?"

"There are some uglier, but not as tall."

"Your cartoon could have easily read 'Modern Architecture Retirement Park'."

"No. That wasn't why I did it."

"Wasn't the message that you were expressing in the cartoon this: that you objected to the conformity of modern architecture and you thought persons who lived in, or were, subjected to, modern architecture would end up in boxes like that?"

"Yes, that was one of the points [but] Mr Seidler has been a trendsetter in these buildings, which is why his name is on the cartoon."

Evatt was to come back to that point again and again, but for the next hour or so he concentrated on the question of identification. How could readers know what the cartoon was referring to? And could not readers take the drawing literally, not as comment?

"You haven't put it in brackets: 'It is a state of mind'."

"No. I am hoping people would pick it up ..."

"You would agree that Mr Seidler would have every right to be grossly offended by it, if he took it literally?"

"I don't see how he could."

"But if he did take it literally he could be grossly upset by the cartoon?"

"He would certainly be puzzled."

Evatt took Cook to the other cartoons on that inside back page of the paper. Was not the spiked doorknob, the poet on the beach and the hand of God literal? "Nobody as far as I am aware has actually seen the giant hand of God."

"But the other cartoons are jokes. There is nothing of a joke about Mr Seidler?"

"Humour can be black as well, it is not necessarily uplifting."

"An unkind joke?"

"A rather depressed one. I dealt with my feelings accurately in that cartoon."

Cook had been asked to bring along with him cartoons that represented both cities he disliked and cities of which he approved. These, by Tony Edwards (Ralph the Rhino), Steinberg, Michael Heath and Steadman, were handed to the jury on the morning of the fourth day. They had earlier in the week been given various books about and by Seidler, and books on postmodern architecture in which Seidler had pointed out buildings of which he disapproved.

More hours were spent that morning on the meaning of *literal*, the purpose of allegory and a fresh attempt by Evatt to have Cook concede that the cartoon in question could be taken literally. Cook refused. He refused to concede that it was about modern architecture generally. He refused to concede that the reader would see the cartoon as referring to dwelling houses. The cartoon was based principally on Seidler's Sydney towers.

"Why could you not have drawn a huge, ugly building made of hostile materials, engulfing images underneath?"

"It would have been a different cartoon. This is the one I did."

"I am putting to you that no reader of that cartoon would think you were referring to the MLC, Australia Square or Blues Point Tower."

'They would think that, I would hope so."

"On what basis?"

"On the ground that it has Mr Seidler's name on it."

"A reader in Perth would think that?"

"They are very widely publicised."

"Those three buildings? At the time they were completed? In 1962 for Blues Point Tower?"

"And subsequently. Whenever Mr Seidler appears in the paper, his list of achievements follows him."

Cook was re-examined briefly by McPhee. Asked why he had earlier said that cartoons don't change people's minds, Cook replied dolefully that despite his cartoons of the Fraser government, it survived eight years. "And politicians, for example, when you think you have made a point in criticising their behaviour, will often ask you for the originals. It can be a bit discouraging."

*

McPhee addressed the jury first: "... the right of every citizen in this society to comment on matters of public interest is the very basis of this democratic state ... the law doesn't protect just popular comment or the opinion of the majority. The law says it doesn't matter how cranky, how biased or unpopular a man's opinion is, he is entitled to express it. This case involves very important questions of what comments cartoonists can make ... comment need not be intended to be kind ... you may think it is something of a paradox that in May 1982 Mr Seidler can comment on those articles in *Architecture Australia* and in August 1982 delivers a statement of claim asking for damages after Cook's cartoon ...

"This is not a fight about whether Seidler's architecture is good or not, nor whether readers agree with Cook. At stake is Cook's right to comment." He left the jury with this reflection: the future of cartooning in Australia, a long and vigorous tradition, was in their hands.

Evatt declared Seidler a "knight in shining armour who's come to rescue this city and put in a few plazas. Without Harry Seidler we would indeed live in a concrete jungle ..."

"I can tell you about Utzon. They drove him out of the country, the media and others. Hounded him out of the country. When this Opera House was going up, he was the subject of ridicule and abuse. He left. He was driven out and the inside was furnished by somebody else. That's what this sort of thing can do, members of the jury. Now they come along and call the Opera House a masterpiece. The hypocrisy of it ... Look at some of the other persons who have gone under from abuse. Mozart ended up in a pauper's grave. They didn't even follow the funeral cart. He was lost in the fog. They don't even know where he was buried. They pick on the greats in this country ..."

Evatt attacked the honesty of Cook's defence. He declared it a sham, deliberately concocted by Cook and the newspaper owners to deceive the jury. "They're pretty clever ... a great feat of contortionism and gymnastics that would get us a medal over in Los Angeles next month." Cook's answers reflected a study of the law, he told the jury, and the officers of the company had apparently met to plan their deceit. He declared the defences of comment dishonest and hypocritical.

McPhee called for the jury to be discharged. None of this alleged subterfuge had been put to Cook in the witness box. McPhee said Evatt was alleging "the whole of Cook's evidence from beginning to end was simply perjury". Had his allegations been put to Cook, then the defendants could have called on evidence to rebut the suggestions. "Mr Evatt's address to the jury was an extraordinary departure from the practices of counsel, it had no evidentiary basis and was put on a basis that constituted no part of the conduct of the case."

Mr Justice Miles agreed that Evatt's attack on Cook was put "in an inflammatory way so the jury would be diverted from the true task" but given the trial had gone so long he declined to discharge the jury.

His summing up took the case into its seventh day. At 11.15 last Tuesday the jury retired with a list of questions to answer. They returned after a time and asked if they could deliver a majority verdict. This was at first refused, but after four hours' deliberation they were called back in and, as the law in New South Wales allows, told they could now come to a majority verdict. They retired to the jury room apparently as worried as before.

The speculation in the court was that the jury was split. As the courts around adjourned for the day, barristers wandered in to wait for the verdict. Neither Seidler, his wife, nor Cook were present. McPhee was on his feet pursuing an abstruse point about the need for a "continuing" majority when a knocking was heard from inside the jury room. McPhee had not noticed it, and argued on. Alerted, he sat. The jury re-entered and declared it had a verdict. The questions and answers were read antiphonally across the court.

Seidler and his company had failed to prove the cartoon carried the imputations that they were brutal, antisocial and incompetent. They proved, however, that the cartoon carried the imputation that they lacked aesthetic sensibilities, and this was held to be defamatory. But the jury found the defences of comment established: the ordinary reader would understand the cartoon to be an expression of Cook's opinion, one which an honest man might have held upon the material, and the material itself was proper material for comment. Cook's allusive style was enough to identify the facts. Labels were not required.

Seidler lost. Next morning, Penelope Seidler told radio interviewers that they intended to appeal. They didn't. When this article appeared Mrs Seidler rang to ask why the paper had reported the case. Was this not more evidence of malice? No, I replied: You sued and we won. That's news.

The National Times, 29 July 1984

A mistress with the clippers

THE DOG WAS HOT AND IRRITABLE so I thought perhaps it had to be clipped. I meant to ask last summer but somehow that went by and the animal got through, panting and slobbering a bit. Now I rang the woman I bought it from, for advice. She was German and the voice lashed down the line. Of course it had to be clipped, and why hadn't I come months ago. The dog was two years old. "Didn't you read the chart?"

I explained it seemed so far to come, to the outskirts. "Where do you liff? In Sydney? I have dogs gominck from Canberra, from Newcazle every year."

I reached the kennel a bit after dawn. Late. She was waiting in the garage next to the block: a platform beneath a noose. Laid out on the bench behind her were clippers, poisons, a hammer, drills. John Laws on the radio. She said. "That's not a Airedoyle. That's a golliwog."

The dog's head went in the noose. His collar lay on the floor. She plugged in a set of clippers. "Nummer ten," she murmured as she snapped on the comb. She turned to the dog with clippers whirring and said in a very steady voice, "I am your ex-mozzer. So behave!"

The clippers plunged to the skin. I hadn't expected that. Nor had he. He leapt off the block, choked and was dragged back. "Finished your danz?" The question was rhetorical. To me she said, "Now he knows he can't get anywhere." Nothing like it. He twisted, bucked and howled as she laid his back bare like one of those sad old Labradors with eczema. The sort of dogs you can't touch.

"Good," she remarked. "He's not fat." That was news to me. Under the mad, clotted hair the dog was fit. The scale, she explained, would clear up with frezsh air.

Frankly the dog had never looked right. I found myself confessing this for some reason as he was being stripped in front of me. He stopped growing after the lead business: dramatic fits every Saturday morning (just as the vet closed), which we thought were epileptic, a mark of fine breeding in Airedales. But in fact the pup had eaten ten times the fatal dose of old lead paint left round the house during renovation. But lived. "That I've heard of. Two Airedoyles died in Balmain eating the paint inzide a cupboard." I didn't ask her for details, but the situation haunts me now. "Yours: he's just short."

Also impatient. He took another lunge off the block and gasped for air as he hung there. I jumped to his rescue. She turned on me. "Stand back or you'll get cofvered in hairs."

Now in her stride she became expansive. "Poodle parlours drug the dogs." She didn't have a good word for poodle parlours. "They don't like Airedoyles. They don't underztant the terrier temperament."

The dog's torso was nude. "A bit of eczema on his whiztle." He began to howl as she went for the neck, but she quieted him. "You can't control some of these big ones. Effven he's strong. If they get this high, like a liddle calf, it's too strong for a man." The Americans, apparently, are bringing down the height of Airedales to 23 inches at the shoulder. "Magsimum."

She took a breather. The clippers were too hot to hold. "Doez he bark? Yes? H'ez a good watchdog?" She was very proud. "I'm sure he'd bite." I remembered the story she told when I came to pick up this pup to convince me that Airedales are "good" with cats, breaking their necks (vigorous demonstration) and throwing them out of the yard with "no blood".

The face was terrible. She had a pink rag tied round his jaw and her foot on his tail. "I don't 'urt him. Lightly. Lightly." He hated it. But by now I was mesmerised by the skill of it all. She found nicks in his ears. "Iz he brave?" she asked. I tried to explain about the parks, about living in an Alsatian zone, but she never paused in her cut. "His mouth is *per*vect."

She whispered to the dog, "Daddy will brusch your beard effry night."

I was getting the message on a number of fronts: bowels, exercise, vermin. "He's got fleas so he has worms." I took notes. She took the pen out of my hand and sketched what I have to look for: "On the survace, like cucumber zeedz."

Oddly she drew right-handed, but when she wrote moved the pen to her left. Is this German education? She scissored with her right, trimming the legs like neat jodhpurs. Not like they do in poodle parlours. The legs were difficult. As she worked on the back she warned me when she reached the front he would go crazy. "You think I'm mad?" the question jolted me, but she had the answer herself. "If I don't do it zumbody else will. Now only three legs to go."

The animal, miserable and nude, was looking like an Airedale at last, perhaps with a dash of whippet. "Just in one month his coat will come through beautiful black. Not like a golliwog. If the skin breaks here because he hasn't had his coat off before, then use skin repair."

She trimmed, clipped a little more, buffed, brushed, combed. The comb, a souvenir from America, was good for the odd flick. "I don't hurt him." From the bench she took down a big bottle of hair conditioner and applied it all over. Horrible intimacy. He was finished. Not a nick. I promised to bring him back next October. "He'll look pervect for Chrizmas. Not zat zat matters."

As she slipped the noose from his neck she said, "Now Daddy will pay and you can go home."

Things are difficult at home. The dog has been through an ordeal and expects sympathy, but no one can touch it. A ferret, a dog inside out, a skinned rabbit. There's nothing to pat but his beard. Like someone back from a long stay away he's under scrutiny to see if he's changed. He's easier to discipline. In the park the big girls snicker behind their Alsatians.

But I worry about a dog I saw briefly at the kennels as I was leading mine, pissing with relief, back to the car. This was the dog she was grooming to show at the Royal Easter Show. She said, "He's lost all his hair. I plucked it out."

The National Times, 18 January 1985

Stanley Hawes: an honourable man a long way from Home

I CANNOT FORGIVE STANLEY HAWES for thinking Australia has no history. He was seventy-three, had been living here for thirty years, twenty-five of them as head of the Commonwealth Film Unit – which we now call Film Australia – when he said: 'I've always been amazed by Australia's obsession with its history. It doesn't have any history!' Well, Stanley, we do and you are now part of it. That's why I am here to talk about the life and work of this decent man who is remembered with much affection and gratitude, but who achieved far less than he and this country hoped when he arrived here in 1946, delegate of his master John Grierson, to make a new beginning for documentary in Australia.

I'm not here to blame Hawes for his failures, but to look to the hazards Hawes faced then and we may still face now in making documentary in Australia, a country that allows us to speak the truth and yet forbids us to speak the truth – in a pattern that's subtle, frustrating and in many ways unchanged since the time Hawes arrived. He faced great obstacles to his mission – and he indeed saw it as a mission to establish the Grierson documentary out here – but what emerges from an examination of his life is that the limits set by this country's politicians, bureaucrats, lawyers and commercial filmmakers, the limits set to documentary making also by the odd culture of part-free speech we have in Australia, these limits came to suit Stanley Hawes down to the ground.

There aren't as many men like Hawes in the colonies these days. Once these Englishmen dominated the central institutions of our culture – Charlie

Moses at the ABC, born Lancashire, 1900; Hugh Hunt at the Elizabethan Theatre Trust, born Surrey, 1911; Stanley Hawes at the Commonwealth Film Unit, born London, 1905. We don't sneer at them for being English, nor forget that in those pioneering days their English prestige – perhaps spurious – gave them an authority the locals lacked. But what we must always ask – because these people are still around, many in the ABC – is whether they ever really knew what hit them when they arrived. Could they respond to this deceptive country in which they were given such power and opportunities?

Hawes knew what to do when he landed fresh from the Canadian Film Board: he fought the hostile forces around him to a standstill; defended his patch with a tenacity that amounted to genius; made a handful of his own films and settled down for the twenty-five-year haul in which he supervised the making of about 1100 documentaries. Clearly Hawes loved our landscape, and his commitment to filming Australians at work was sincere – bred in him – but did he know us well enough, this country without a history, to know where to point his cameras? Even at the end of his career, honoured – there was an MBE on his retirement in 1970 – Hawes seems to me to have been as an Englishman, a socialist of sorts, and a disciple of his master John Grierson a long way from Home.

*

The scene is Birmingham, 1931, a meeting of the Birmingham Film Society. Busy at a projector standing at the back of the small room is the society's president, Stanley Hawes, a young council clerk and amateur actor; tonight the members are gathering to see, not for the first time, Viktor Turin's epic of the Trans-Siberian railway, *Turksib*. The film is, of course, silent and black and white. To understand Hawes the filmmaker, we must remember that when he lost his heart to film, they were silent and black and white. In later life he confessed to being depressed by words in films. "Why do we have to listen to so many words?" And he had his doubts about colour. He yearned for the simplicity of the early days. "I think that every great invention in the cinema has taken us further back down the road away from cinema." Stanley Hawes' pure cinema was silent, monochrome and uplifting.

A year passes. In Welwyn Garden City on the outskirts of London, John Grierson has called together the fledgling film societies of Britain. Hawes meets Grierson and his devotion to the man is confirmed. To put it bluntly, Grierson is at Welwyn to organise a distribution network for these films of his he called documentaries, his "creative interpretations of reality". Grierson was establishing "a cinema of social affairs" that deliberately set its face against the sort of films being churned out by the British and American film industry in the Depression. Its subject was nearly always the same: men and women at work – on farms, on herring boats, down coalmines, etc. Its decent purpose was to win respect for the proletariat. The sentimental assumption was that a shift in politics would follow. "Remember," Hawes said, "documentary was born in a quite idealistic period, when all the young people were going to bring a new heaven on earth."

Grierson not only invented the form, but through his peculiar, Presbyterian, relentless charm persuaded the government to pay for it, first through the Empire Marketing Board but soon through the Post Office. Even at this time, Grierson was criticised for the position this left him in: Arthur Calder-Marshall attacked the GPO unit for failing to express discontent among Post Office workers. "Mr Grierson," he wrote, "is not paid to tell the truth but to make more people use the parcel post."

The challenge of making truthful documentary when governments foot the bill is the principal subject of this lecture. How Hawes fared here must wait till I get him to Australia, but it's useful at this point to see how Grierson defined the dangers, and his strategy to overcome them, for here, as in most things, Hawes thought he was following his master. Documentary must push governments towards reform, said Grierson, but they should do so cautiously for at stake is the future of documentary itself. His biographer Forsyth Hardy – also present at Welwyn Garden City on that weekend in 1932 – put it this way:

> It was a tightrope operation. Had his radicalism emerged in the treatment of subjects in a form too extreme for the political party in power the movement would have been toppled. He was later to define his political position as being an inch to the left of whichever party was in office. In other words he accepted his position as a servant of the government but was intent on pushing the administration, as he was later to do more openly in Canada, as far as he could towards reform. He regarded the survival of the movement as of first importance, for the hope and the potential it held.

Soon after meeting Grierson at Welwyn, Hawes threw in his secure job and moved to London with his wife, Jessica – they met in the Birmingham film society – and tried to join Grierson's unit at the Post Office. Grierson knocked him back. But in 1935 Paul Rotha took the young man on as an assistant at Gaumont-British Instructional Films and then transferred him to Strand Films where, with Sir Julian Huxley, Hawes made the short *Monkey into Man*. *The Manchester Guardian* wrote: "*Monkey into Man* traces the social evolution of monkeys ... well directed by Stanley Hawes, this picture is notable for brilliant camera work particularly with regard to gibbons and during a fight among the baboons on Monkey Hill."

(A biographer's work is never done. I'm pleased to have come across this detail even if it is too late. Let me explain: Patrick White provoked a brawl over dinner one night in Melbourne in 1973 – it was actually the night his Nobel was being collected by Sid Nolan in Stockholm. Later the hosts of the dinner wrote apologising for the row and White replied: 'It wasn't nearly as noisy as some in my house, which is sometimes referred to as Monkey Hill.' I never knew what he meant; now I see.)

Hawes made his way to Australia via Canada. The scene is now an old sawmill in Ottawa. Grierson has the Canadian prime minister in the palm of his hand. The Canadian Film Board is protected, independent, well-funded and churning out films on life in the Dominion and the course of the war. Hawes, recruited in 1940, makes his mark in Ottawa not so much as a film-maker but as a trainer of filmmakers. And now, working in Grierson's orbit at last, he was able to watch and model himself on his master.

"He could be very difficult – he expected a great deal from everyone and liked his own way – and I remember that there was a period when we seldom met in his office without pounding the desk at each other. But we all knew that he gave as much as he demanded. We had an enormous affection for him – even when he was most difficult – because we knew that he made it possible for us to do the work we wanted to do ... what perhaps we didn't always realise was the constant battles he fought for us behind the scenes. My wife Jessica used to say that he sometimes had an expression on his face which meant, 'You'll learn, you'll learn.'"

Grierson had already learnt a good deal about Australia for he had spent six weeks here in 1940 advising Menzies' government on mobilising film for national ends. Grierson was bagged unmercifully by the local feature film industry and local exhibitors. They could see no reason to show locally made shorts – particularly on 16 mm rather than 35 mm – when the country was awash with cheap American shorts. (Is this familiar?) Grierson's advice for "showing Australia to Australians and the world" was ignored until Ben Chifley's Labor government came to plan for peace, and established in April 1945 an Australian National Film Board. Hawes was dispatched by Grierson the following year to be its producer-in-chief.

He was forty-one, stocky, laconic and chain-smoking. Canada had not touched his Birmingham drawl; nor did all the years in Australia (I like him for this). He was resented on arrival as an Englishman, but in his favour was the fact that he was not another pensioned-off hack, nor Oxford posh, but an efficient filmmaker. He had kept the habits learnt as a Birmingham clerk: he was neat, a perfectionist and knew the value of mastering detail. Underlying all was Hawes' stubborn pragmatism: whatever happened, whatever terrible reverse, he believed he had to cope. All the effort and occasional humiliation was worthwhile because film was the greatest gift to man.

It's taken me some time to get Stanley Hawes to Australia. I don't apologise. We can't cut to the chase. For the central point I want to make is that by the time Hawes reached this country – with Jessica and their daughters Jane and Barbara – most of the conditions were in place that would determine the scale of Hawes' achievement in Australia: his devotion to the Grierson model, which now atrophied; the hostility of a local film industry, even as it staggered round on its last legs; the instincts of the Canberra bureaucracy, which he had to combat for the next twenty years; and, intangible but important, Australia's tepid commitment to the business of telling the truth about itself.

*

The Canberra dogs went for Hawes and the documentary unit the moment he arrived. Rather than allow the unit the independence the Canadians had given Grierson's team, Canberra handed Hawes and his handful of directors, cameramen and editors over to the Department of Information. There was a sound bureaucratic reason for this: in wartime the department had been the ever vigilant and petty censors of the press. Now it had nothing much to do. So Hawes, who had come out to be producer-in-chief of the Australian Film Board, found himself producer-in-chief of the Film Division of the

Department of Information. "People who ran the Department of Information" – he meant a man called Edmund Bonney – "were so anxious to get rid of me that I decided that I would stay. It was a very slow business against much obstruction to build up the unit." Bonney is another of the lessons we must learn from these years. He was an old journo, a former editor of Melbourne's *The Argus* and one of those print journalists who could never understand what film is about, never grasped that a different language is spoken there. Then as now we must be careful of putting print journalists in positions of authority over filmmakers.

In his first year in Australia Hawes made *School in the Mailbox,* a little film that's now acknowledged as a classic Australian documentary. Out in the bush the children slave away at lessons set back in Sydney by the staff of the correspondence school. Back and forth travel exercise books, reports and texts. The system is depicted with perfect clarity but not what we would now call truth: teachers and pupils are dressed in their best; everyone is eager; there are no problems in sight. Overhead a commentary thunders on about "the future of the children, the country and the world". But the climax of *School in the Mailbox* is a sequence of pure truth: over the wireless a speech training class is being given. The text is "I Love a Sunburnt Country", which the teacher recites line by line in impeccable English English as his pupils stubbornly respond line by line in bush Australian.

School in the Mailbox earned Hawes his spurs, won an Oscar nomination, opened the work of the unit to international festivals and competitions – and pleased his masters. As did his second film, *Flight Plan,* a much less interesting job which does what it can to seem heroic about runways and navigation towers and – this is the subtext – why citizens should be happy to pay taxes to build them all across the continent.

Hawes was making films about Australians at work, the favourite subject of the film unit in its twenty-five years under his leadership: teachers, air traffic controllers, firemen, canecutters, pearl divers, steelworkers, lighthouse keepers, apple pickers, painters, postmen and farmers, farmers, farmers. Chifley's government and the conservatives who took over in 1949 couldn't have enough films of men and women at work developing the nation. The Country Party especially loved these films, and so did Hawes, for rather different reasons. His first love, those early Russian silent films, celebrated the heroism of labour. Now he did so himself in Australia. Though politics had almost died in him, he still held to the notion that film could make society a better place by winning respect for decent working men and women. Grierson at least claimed to stand a little to the left of the governments that paid him. That was not Hawes' view. He was a man of decent principles, sensible at a time of ideological conflict, but nevertheless conservative. His aim was not revolution but respect.

But the ethos of national development that underwrote political approval for Hawes' efforts brought its own freight of caution and censorship. It's no more than a hunch, but a hunch passionately held, that much of the cultural sterility of Australia in the middle decades of this century – from the '30s to the '60s – can be put down to the ethos of national development. Enquiry, challenge, variety, dissent are all distractions from the mighty task of building Australia: one family hard at work, putting aside private visions to dig and pick and write and film for the future. Oddly, the future always has the stamp of government policy.

This ethos has lost its grip on Australia now – but it's very strong in Asia. It would be impertinent of me to discuss here the difficulties under which Asian documentary makers are now working. But it is fascinating to look at the rhetoric of leaders like Singapore's Lee Kuan Yew insisting on the prerogatives of national development. This is Lee in Beijing in 1990:

> Westerners value the freedoms and liberties of the individual. As an Asian of Chinese cultural background, my values are for a government that is honest, effective in protecting its people and allowing opportunities for all to advance themselves in a stable and orderly society where they can live a good life and raise their children to do better than themselves.

That could have been Arthur Calwell speaking in 1945, or Jack McEwen celebrating victory in the elections of 1949.

The shift of government from Labor to Liberal might have destroyed Hawes, but here he showed his genius for survival. Menzies and McEwen had promised to axe what government functions they could when they came to power; it seemed almost certain the film division would be abolished. But Hawes mobilised the support of those government departments for whom the unit had been making films for the past four years. These were good years for the unit – some critics say the best – with Hawes leading a talented group of young directors and experienced cameramen. The bureaucrats liked the product; they wanted more, and they persuaded the new government to keep the filmmakers going.

There was a price for this: the unit's new perch was within the News and Information section of the Department of the Interior, which was all that was left of the old Department of Information. The bitterness among bureaucrats at this downgrading lasted for seventeen ugly years, in which they saw no point in handing successes to the government. It was a long, bitter work to rule in which the film unit survived, but not with any departmental enthusiasm that it prosper.

Hawes survived by stealth: those who dealt with him then say he knew when to keep his head down; he seemed gentle but was tough. He had that essential weapon in any long brawl with the bureaucracy – a great grasp of detail. And he could talk to these people; after all he had been one of them once, a government clerk. Hawes' tenacity, his unshaken belief in the worth of documentary, and the support of the film unit's clients rather than its masters got them through the crises to come. "God, he was tenacious," Dick Mason told me. "He was relentless. He just kept going when others would have folded."

Hawes faced a further difficulty: the unit was split between the Catholics – mostly older cameramen and editors – and the rest, making up most of the younger documentary makers. Hawes was a dedicated atheist. He had an eccentric but absolute list of sequences he would not have in the unit's films: one on that list was the sight of nuns doing anything much at all; another was a pan across a city skyline that showed a church spire. There were others on the list of the forbidden. One I can't fathom was any sequence showing people eating. Perhaps it was bad manners in the world of Hawes' childhood.

The Catholic/non-Catholic split was not only damaging within the unit but presented some political difficulties for Hawes. His north country accent, his atheism, his association with Grierson – who had left Canada after being accused of aiding communism – gave Hawes the aura of a radical man. He was not. Though his loyalties were to Labor, he was one of those cautious, decent men and women who were socialists once and are nothing particular now. Really politics had died in him except, of course, the politics of survival.

More and more the unit was making films for clients – especially the Department of Immigration. Not that Hawes had any burning passion to make particular films of his own. That wasn't the point, his old colleagues say: Stanley loved the business of making films; film was his life, but he didn't have films he wanted to make. Films for the Department of Immigration were not "creative interpretations of reality" so much as propaganda. And the department was very fussy about the details they wanted shown. These films were made to order, and there are distinguished Australian documentary makers who blush still for the lies they turned into films to persuade Europeans to migrate to this ever-sunny land of kookaburras and neat brick homes.

But the vice of that time went deeper than that. Even today we hear protests that we should not make films that show Australia in a bad light to the outside world. Remember the uproar when *Sylvania Waters* hit the screens – and I don't mean Noelene's claim she somehow didn't realise there were cameras there filming her for months. No, I mean the letters to the editor, of which my favourite was the effort of James Thane of Double Bay:

> Sir: on viewing *Sylvania Waters* tonight, one asks oneself how seriously the ABC bears its national responsibility as an organisation funded by taxpayers. Now more than ever, the international image of our country is of utmost importance in selling ourselves in the most attractive manner to tourists, foreign investors ...

Hawes and his documentary unit had the Department of Immigration hovering to stop anything that reflected poorly on Australia as a migrant destination. If, for instance, a film showed drought, it had also to show well-watered plenty. The rule was stated candidly: the unit's documentaries must show a "land of sunshine".

"I had always believed," said Hawes, "in the film which was trying to help society, help understanding, do a functional, educational and informational job." Yet for him film was not a medium of ideas, nor an agent of change or challenge. How is this contradiction resolved? I think this way: that he never knew enough about Australia, this land "without a history", to focus his ambition to do good. His documentaries were cool, generalised, unemotional, impersonal. The narrator alone spoke with authority. The people of Australia were observed at a distance, slightly idealised, innocent. Hawes' Australia was an ethnographic subject, but cautiously ethnographic. The unit's cumbersome old cameras went to remote deserts, down the Murray and up into the New Guinea Highlands – but not to the slums of Surry Hills.

He didn't believe in research: you went out and shot what you saw. He was literal: no set-ups, nothing on the soundtrack that wasn't on the screen. The screen should be as the eye sees life. It was for this reason that Hawes banned the wide-angle lens because he said it distorted reality. He insisted on the use of a particular 35 mm lens because that, he said, showed the world as the world seems through our eyes. Hawes made the mistake of identifying his style with truth. It is a mistake we make over and over again in the documentary industry. Hawes didn't like dramatisations, didn't trust cinema verité – "it lacks any sort of form, and it gets dreadfully dull at times, it just goes on ..." He had no time at all for the brand of "talking heads" documentary which I've had a couple of shots at making. He argued that his way was the Grierson way, but really it was not. Grierson's *Night Mail* – with a script by W.H. Auden and music by Benjamin Britten – would fall outside the rules set down by Stanley Hawes.

All this must, of course, be read in light of Hawes' achievement. The triumph of his career was *The Queen in Australia*. This, as you know, was the first full-length colour film made in Australia by Australians. Hawes was producer and editor, working in London, where the film was flown each day for processing. This is really a film about the Queen, and you can see her tiring: such a fresh wave in Sydney but by the time she reached Launceston, a tired mechanical arm. But it is a wonderful film about Australia too, particularly wonderful for the Australian faces: crowds, officials, children. And there is an ecological disaster tour of the states, deeply truthful of the time: Queensland and its sugarcane; Western Australia, where an ancient tree is felled for the cameras; and Tasmania, the Apple Isle, where Hawes concentrates lovingly on the wall of a hydro-electric dam.

Hawes was a teacher of the craft, an encourager of young people, and the Commonwealth Film Unit was one of the few places you could learn to make film. Hawes believed in equal opportunities for men and women; he believed that women might be directors and sent them out on shoots – for this he had to fight running battles with the Department of Information. Joan Long was one of these women, and in the 1984 Grierson lecture in Melbourne she said:

> Looking back it had elements of the ideal for young trainees. Small units, for one. As a director I had one assistant if I was lucky, quite often none, just me and the cameraman, so I had to pull focus and

carry gear as well as being production manager, continuity, the lot. Directors often cut their own films. I even used to cut my own negatives.

John Morris remembers Hawes as a fierce teacher, a man unable to praise but who could criticise intelligently. He inspired his protégés and then, at some point, they had to fight him. So it always is between protégés and teachers. But Hawes was one of those honourable combatants with whom you could clash and yet maintain respect.

Hawes took the unit to the edge of the bush in Lindfield in 1962. For the first time the filmmakers had a set of buildings designed for their own use. And Hawes put his stamp on this little patch of Canberra: there was a "mahogany row" for him and the executives, corridors for the managers, and somewhere out the back in temporary buildings were the directors. Here things began to come good. We have this odd way in Australia of only funding our cultural institutions properly when they've got a building of their own – like the Opera House and the National Gallery. In Lindfield the unit had more money and more freedom. The worst of the bureaucrats departed and in 1963 Dick Kingsland became Secretary of the Department of the Interior. Kingsland liked film. He told me:

> Stanley was delighted to find in me a friend at court. With skill, restraint and grace he made the most of this opportunity without any act of disloyalty to his immediate chief, a fine performance indeed. The News and Information Bureau recognised that it might be unwise to be obviously beastly to the Commonwealth Film Unit.

But money and freedom had, perhaps, come too late for Hawes. He had been so embattled for so long. The stubbornness was still there, but not the adaptive courage to strike out boldly now the opportunity had come. True, the young filmmakers recruited in the 1950s were now being given the opportunities and seizing them. Documentary was changing and Hawes was not entirely hostile to new possibilities, but there he was at the centre of the unit, an autocratic figure whose favourite word was "sound" – the unit was "sound" and it made "sound" films and he hoped it would stay that way.

A last scene of Hawes at work. An office on mahogany row. A story conference is in progress, for the unit has been asked to make a film about the tourist attractions of Australia. One writer wants to send a typical American family to the Barrier Reef, the other argues for ballet in the parks of Adelaide and a runner jogging across Western Australia. A gloomy Hawes is fielding calls from Canberra, and as he explains the political traps to the eager greenhorns in his office, he works at a chain of paperclips. I don't conjure this scene up from nowhere. It is, of course, the starting point of *From the Tropics to the Snow*, the quirky film Dick Mason and Malcolm Otton made for the unit in 1964. At its centre was Hawes himself and his taste in documentaries. Sure, Hawes objected to their ideas, fought them, imposed on them an English director – Jack Lee – because he said there was no Australian who could direct drama. But the film was made, and when it proved a hit – not least with parliamentarians – Hawes put it on the shortlist of his finest achievements in the *Who's Who*.

Hawes retired from the unit in 1970, was a sensible Chief Commonwealth Censor appointed by Don Chipp and made a last film about retirees called *Challenging Years*. Not long before he died in 1991 he was able, after a Sydney Film Festival screening of some Russian silent classic, to list the sequences missing from the print. I would like to think it was Victor Turin's *Turksib*, first seen in the Birmingham days when it seemed to Hawes that documentary film, the drama of reality, could bring us heaven on this shabby earth.

The Stanley Hawes Lecture at the Sydney Film Festival,

4 December 1993

Lutyens fights the last battle of the Somme

THIS MEMORIAL WAS TO BE one of the first great patriotic projects of the new Federation. On a hilltop in the valley of the Somme where the worst of the killing took place, we staked out our plot. Other hills in this soft landscape of wheatfields and forest were claimed by New Zealand, Canada, Newfoundland, India and Britain. Now that the war to end all wars had been fought and won, the Empire planned to build the very last memorials to war. The British, designed by the architectural genius Sir Edwin Lutyens, was the greatest of these and one of the most peculiar buildings of the twentieth century: a high pile of brick arches, open to the wind, immensely desolate and noble, standing on a rise at Thiepval.

Lutyens, after a bizarre chain of events, was also to design the Australian memorial nearby at Villers-Bretonneux. This was an assignment that put a very original Englishman into the league of Burley Griffin and Jørn Utzon: foreign architectural masters faced with a very Australian refusal to let them get on with their work. The result at Villers-Bretonneux was – like Canberra and the Opera House – another of the botched jobs of our architectural history: fascinating, but so much less than we let it be.

Still, Villers-Bretonneux might have been much worse.

Intense patriotism was the keynote of the competition held in 1925 to find an architect. Even if Lutyens had the time – he was supervising the new Imperial capital in Delhi as well as the graveyards of northern France – he would not have been eligible. Australia wanted an Australian architect, who fought or had a child fighting for the Empire, who would build in Australian stone and plant on that European hill a garden of Australian shrubs and trees. We were willing to spend a fortune on the project: £100,000.

William Lucas, not long back from South Africa – where he explored the Zambesi and designed the Pietermaritzburg post office – had already caused an ugly flurry when he won second place in the competition to design the Melbourne Shrine and appealed twice against the verdict and lost. All this had happened before this combative Christian – an honoured member of the Collins Street Baptist Church – won the Villers-Bretonneux job in 1927.

The great memorials in Northern France are mega-headstones to carry the names of those whose bodies were never found in the morass of the trenches. To carry the names of Australia's 12,000 "missing" Lucas planned a tower, so narrow and high it looked like a lift shaft with its walls stripped away to show four huge columns of polished trachyte holding up a little roof. There, 100 feet (thirty metres) above the battle-fields, Lucas planned an observation platform with figures at each corner representing mercy, truth, righteousness and peace.

The chief of the Imperial War Graves Commission, Sir Fabian Ware, privately deplored the choice. Even the Australian judges were disappointed. Under the rules of the competition they were supposed to send six designs to London for final adjudication. They could find only three to send and Lucas's effort was their last choice. But London gave it the prize.

From the first, Lucas faced the secret hostility of everyone whose support he needed if the memorial was ever to be built. One of these was J.S. Murdoch, chief architect of the Commonwealth: "I am not at all impressed with Lucas' detailed plans of Villers-Bretonneux," he wrote at this time. "I think we will have to make several modifications and anticipate a considerable amount of trouble in dealing with him." He was right. Murdoch, architect of Old Parliament House, was the man who would also, in time, deal with Walter Burley Griffin.

A more formidable opponent was the chief Australian judge, a professional architect and distinguished soldier, General Sir Talbot Hobbs. He had chosen the site for the memorial because here, in the spring of 1918, he was one of the Australian commanders who directed the operation that recaptured Villers-Bretonneux, lost briefly to the Germans in their last push to break the Allied lines. Hobbs privately took credit for the success of this daring manoeuvre, so much was at stake for him in the choice of the site and architect. What's more, he saw himself as an expert on war memorials: his own war memorial in Perth was, by this time, almost built. Hobbs was never going to let go of Villers-Bretonneux.

Lucas exhibited his final drawings for Villers-Bretonneux at the Royal Academy in London. That made news in Australia. Lucas was driving his own publicity machine: he also alerted the Australian press to President Clemenceau of France granting his memorial final approval in April 1929. (Hobbs and the others had hoped the French would force some changes as they had the power to do, but they were disappointed.) And a frustrated Lucas alerted the press in March 1930 to the "temporary" suspension of work on the site because of "the financial position" of the Commonwealth.

Hobbs saw in the Depression a chance to crush Lucas. "Delay," he told the Commonwealth, "gives an opportunity, if I may suggest it, of reconsidering the design." Hobbs had toured the war graves of Egypt and Europe in May 1930 and returned to attack Lucas's proposal as pretentious, expensive and unlikely to be "altogether popular with our people". All that was needed, he said, was a wall to take the 12,000 names and a terrace which "would give a view of practically every battlefield in the Somme country on which Australian soldiers fought".

Australia owned only the crown of the hill. At its foot was a war cemetery for which the great Lutyens was building a very elegant entrance: a pair of classical pavilions on each side of a wide and shallow flight of steps where he placed one of his "great stones" engraved with that awkward line by Kipling: "Their names liveth for evermore." These stone altars were a Lutyens invention that became part of the vocabulary of war memorials everywhere. Cenotaphs were his other invention – even the use of the name was his idea – and his first in Whitehall was the model for cenotaphs around the world.

Lutyens was the obvious choice to take over the work at the top of the hill. He did not refuse. Though by this time the most famous architect in the Empire, Lutyens could always do with more work. And the offer was a little triumph for him: very early on he had agreed to be the London judge of the Villers-Bretonneux competition only to have the Australian government withdraw the offer in favour of his great rival, the cathedral builder Sir Giles Gilbert Scott. Scott chose Lucas. So here was a chance for Lutyens to fix a mistake that need never have been made.

But the Australian put up a colossal fight. Indeed, William Lucas single-handedly fought the last great battle of the Somme. He lobbied the King and two or three prime ministers; he wrote endless letters to editors; he put out a book giving "a vivid idea of the nobility and beauty of the proposed war memorial" and presented copies to everyone who mattered; he persuaded Gilbert Scott that an inquiry should be held; he lobbied the Duke of Gloucester, who was president (perhaps unawares) of the Imperial War Graves Commission, and the commission itself received packet after packet of Lucas's grievances.

Not until June 1935 did Lutyens have the go-ahead from Australia. Then he wrote to Lucas: "I am so sorry this means no Memorial from your hand." His own was sketched in weeks. Though drawings of this are mysteriously absent from archives I've searched in Britain and Australia, Lutyens's description survives: a flight of stairs would lead to a low brick podium walled by stone on three sides. Here the names of the "missing" would be carved and the whole design would focus on "the Australian badge or rising sun" on its rear wall. The one flourish Lutyens intended for this elevated courtyard was a little tower at each corner "in a Greco-Roman order" to match his entrance pavilions already built at the foot of the hill.

Everything suggests that Lutyens conceived here another of his apparently effortless masterpieces. But Talbot Hobbs was not impressed, for over the past couple of years he had changed his mind: a terrace was not enough; there had to be a central observation tower for pilgrims to view the battlefields. Furthermore, he felt it proper that the names of the "missing" should be sheltered under a cloister. Hobbs persuaded the Commonwealth to take the astonishing step of rejecting Lutyens's design. They sent a dull sketch by Hobbs to set the British architect on the right track.

"In the light of the letter from Australia," Lutyens wrote to Sir Fabian Ware at the Imperial War Graves Commission, "it would be well nigh useless to send them a design that does not include a central tower. I am sorry." Over Christmas, he went to work unhappily on a new design with a high tower, not Hobbs's stumpy effort but something tall enough to be seen by visitors arriving at the cemetery entrance below. Everything else in his first version had to be pared away to avoid the "aesthetic mistake" of putting a short tower on a fat hill. There was no money for cloisters, though Hobbs kept trying to find it in Australia. Plans to plant a forest of bluegums were abandoned.

Lutyens's heart seems, by now, to have gone out of it. He had a bright idea for making a big platform on top of the narrow tower by taking the last couple of flights of stairs outside the tower walls so all the floor space would be clear around the "oriented table". Internal ladders to the platform would have achieved much the same result but Lutyens rejected ladders as unsuitable for "petticoated females". The final composition is clever but not – like most of Lutyens's more eccentric work – instantly convincing. Sixty years later you still stare at that odd outbreak of stairs around the neck of the tower and ask: why?

Once the new plans were on their way by air to Australia in January 1936, Ware sent a magisterial telegram in their wake: "Your government may be influenced by knowledge that Lutyens recognised even by critics as greatest architect since Wren. Strongly recommend acceptance without further amendment ... If new design not accepted in order avoid further complications and delays suggest you consider placing whole matter in hands of one man Australia say Hobbs."

Ware's telegram almost did the trick. Not quite. Could Lutyens round off the corners of the projecting staircase? He complied. And when the builders' quotes started coming in, Hobbs's committee wanted cuts. Ware blasted back, "I feel that any mutilation of Sir Edwin Lutyens's design as approved by the Commonwealth is highly undesirable." That, finally, was that. We had to pay a little more money but yet it was a bargain: Lutyens's solution cost a third of Lucas's design.

Poor Lucas. No one was paying much attention anymore as he raged against a memorial that broke all the rules of the original competition and was now "in all fundamental respects non-Australian". He who had lost a son fighting in Macedonia saw his work taken by a man who neither fought nor sent his children to the war. Even the stone was French. No one had ever given him a reason other than cost for his work being abandoned, so why was he never invited to submit a cheaper design? On the advice of a Melbourne QC, Lucas was fruitlessly seeking £5750 for "wrongful dismissal".

The King opened Villers-Bretonneux in July 1938. General Hobbs didn't make the ceremony: he died on the voyage over and his body was shipped home from Colombo. Lucas was not there either and died the following year, remembered for that post office in Pietermaritzburg and his "inspiring" conversations with young architects about "the changing conditions of architectural taste". Lutyens was at the ceremony, a rather jokey civilian figure in all that military pomp. Changing taste was about to consign his reputation to the oblivion of aristocratic memoirs and *Country Life* magazine, from which it only began to recover in the 1970s.

War memorials are not, of course, designed to withstand war. Within two years of the opening ceremony the Blitzkrieg moved across this country. The French (as a plaque pointedly records) "briefly" held the hill. Artillery fire tore holes in the stone lists of dead and brought down part of the tower. The scars of these later battles – still visible on a grey spring morning fifty-five years on – aren't marks of failure but intensify that sense of pointless desolation that hangs over the Somme. All the fine memorials to the war to end all wars failed. So will those for all the wars that follow. All Lutyens could do was build a heap of stone that somehow, in abstract, makes us remember.

The Sydney Morning Herald, 26 April 1997

Hill End: hard country, good painting

EACH OF US COMES TO HILL END in our own way. I went to Shore and the only remotely romantic thing about that school was that underneath an overcoat of 1930s brown brick was Holtermann's old tower and the vague memory of a man who'd found the biggest chunk of gold in the world on the diggings round here. It was a rotten school that offered very little except the notion that, unprepared as we were for life, we, too, might strike it rich.

I think the first time I saw Hill End was on a family expedition when I was at school. And I came here later on some pretentious expedition to the pub when I was at university. God knows what that was about. I was here again last year. And each arrival finds me asking the same question: where's it gone? It's pretty but it's missing. You don't go for a walk around Hill End, you go out walking to *find* Hill End.

I have a theory: this gap between the romance and the reality – between what you expect and what you find out here – is the reason Hill End is still one of this country's great creative landscapes. These days Sirius Cove is just zoo. No one paints there anymore. Heidelberg is being strangled by suburbs and television documentaries on the unusual home life of Sunday Reed. The Hawkesbury is certainly blue, but not the sort of blue anyone would want to swim in, or drink or paint.

But Hill End – home of Drysdale and Friend and all the painters and potters since – keeps coming up with the goods. They come a long way on a bad road; the accommodation is rough; the neighbours are fractious; the soil is poor; the summers are hot; the winters icy – what can they do but hunker down in their imagination and create?

And you can't pick their works as Hillendiana. It's not like Coonawarra shiraz or Illabo lamb: they don't all taste the same. Hill End works on each of its true artists differently. That's a mark of the real thing. What we're celebrating tonight is not a look or a school but a creative place. So can I ask you to raise your glasses, reach for your cheque books and join me in congratulating everyone ...

Opening of *Out of Hill End*, Damien Minton Gallery, Redfern, 10 June 2009

Mr Mitchell's library

A HUNDRED YEARS ISN'T WHAT IT WAS. When I was a boy, my father would point at a house and say, "That's over a hundred years old," as if those years took us back to the beginning of time. But Australia and its institutions are so much older now. Centenaries and bicentenaries come so thick and fast they threaten to debase the currency of celebration. We'll soon be blasting fireworks over the Harbour to mark 250 years since Cook first sighted the East Coast. But even as the numbers blow out so dramatically, no one will begrudge these celebrations to mark one hundred years of the Mitchell, this library of last resort, storehouse of treasures, club of eccentrics and memory of the town.

Waiting for some boxes the other day – those fifteen minutes can seem like forever when you're hungry to start – it struck me I've been using the Mitchell intermittently for nearly half its life. Someone brought me to the reading room of the public library in the '50s when I was still at school and I was bowled over by the faint green light from the ceiling, the vertigo stairs and peculiar smell of linoleum. I was at university before I took a right turn at the map of the world and walked through those swing doors into the crowded, serious, forbidding space of the Mitchell. Two things survive forty years later: the impossible card catalogues and the stern tenderness of the staff.

I was back the other day to track down the details of a little scandal in the theatre world, a story almost forgotten except by those it touched in the late 1970s. We forget so quickly in this town. Amnesia has been a governing principle of Sydney since the earliest days. The Mitchell is the city's office of corrections, the place we come to set the record straight. After a few hours I found the few paragraphs I needed in a misdated edition of a defunct magazine and gave the researcher's inner whoop of triumph. These eureka moments have a thrill it's almost impossible to convey. Grey faces in libraries around the world mask inner lives of considerable emotional volatility. We know the ups and downs. Weeks of tedium are wiped away in a few moments of discovery. Research is pure pleasure.

Like nurses in a ward of the slightly unhinged, the librarians stand at their posts attentive and detached. These are the intermediaries between us and the Mitchell's hidden riches. We can't go where they go, down into the stacks where all the papers lie. Nor can we hope to be as fluent as they are in the old and half-forgotten language of the catalogues. They know what the numbers mean. They know the ways in. We're on our honour with them. At the Library of Congress in Washington, uniformed giants with high-calibre weapons stand by in case of trouble. Security at the Mitchell depends on interrogation and sharp eyes that have seen just about everything in their time. Every time we present a call slip at the counter we're lightly grilled. Then the slips are torn apart with a crisp little rip that says we've passed muster and this transaction is over. Fifteen minutes later brown cardboard boxes appear from below, all ours until we're done.

The Mitchell deserves the rhetoric, brass plaques and civic ceremonies that will mark its centenary. But the best evidence of what we owe this place is found in books. In the biographies I have at home the Mitchell is acknowledged and thanked in Hazel Rowley's *Christina Stead,* David Day's *John Curtin* and *Chifley* ("the ever helpful staff of the magnificent Mitchell Library"), Drusilla Modjeska's *Stravinsky's Lunch,* Brian Matthews' *Louisa,* Manning Clark's *History of Australia* (though not, I note, in volume two), Humphrey McQueen's *Tom Roberts* and even in that most ungrateful historian M.H. Ellis's *Lachlan Macquarie.* A dozen books taken at random prove the point: it is all but impossible to write or read about Australia, the Pacific and the Antarctic without incurring debts of gratitude to the Mitchell.

Libraries are the most personal public institutions. History never forgives those who destroy them and never forgets those who found them. Book burners are execrated; book donors are remembered. History awarded naming rights among many others to Thomas Bodley, Cardinal Mazarin, Andrew Carnegie, Thomas Fisher and David Scott Mitchell.

*

In a handsome house in Darlinghurst, Mitchell camped in rooms stacked high with books. The place was neglected inside and out. "It was pathetic: dust, cobwebs, a musty smell, no real sign of domestic care," wrote Robert Scot Skirving, the doctor attending him in his last weeks. "Furniture, probably valuable; pictures, certainly so; and books and more books and yet more books, everywhere and anyhow." Mitchell had broken off with society and withdrawn into the house on the death of his adored mother. For nearly forty years he ate chops and rarely went out except to buy books. He only ever left Sydney once or twice in his life. He never left Australia. Apart from the scholars he let through the door, Mitchell's only companions at 17 Darlinghurst Road were an Irish housekeeper and an ancient sulphur-crested cockatoo.

He was bidding for books when he was still a child. This passion for books came to him from both sides of his family. He never worked. The money came from Hunter Valley coal. Before his retreat from the world, Mitchell played whist, danced and performed in theatricals at Government House. Comedy and farce were his strength. "A part that could not be identified with his real self he played with gusto," Arthur Jose reported in *The Lone Hand*. "Parts that could, by any possibility, be thought self-revelatory, he shrank from taking." A connoisseur of Shelley, Browning and the Elizabethan dramatists, Mitchell was rather amused by local efforts. Yet even as a young man he began, he told his cousin Rose Scott, to "get all the Australian literature I come across not so much for intrinsic merit which I am unpatriotic enough not to find in them as that I think some day anything like a complete collection of Australian books will be curious."

Yet it was not until the last twenty years of his life that Mitchell abandoned all other collecting to concentrate on accumulating Australiana. Like nearly so much else in his life, the reasons for this remain a mystery. The looming celebrations for the 1888 centenary sparked fresh interest in Australiana among both booksellers and collectors. And Mitchell was in his own way a patriot. "He was proud of his family; he was proud of his state," wrote Jose. "Of Australia and of New South Wales especially as embodied in Sydney, he was a proud and faithful son; and he set himself to collect and treasure every document that threw light on things Australian, as a son might seek out and treasure every scrap of writing that could refer to his dear parents and his famous ancestry."

Mitchell's ambition was to own *everything* in his field. To possess one prized bundle of papers, he would buy another man's whole collection. His deep pockets were known to the trade in London, Amsterdam and Sydney. He had the determination and money to outwit most other collectors of Australiana most of the time. "He haunted the bookshops of all grades," wrote Jose. "He rarely shut his door – otherwise not readily opened – on any man who had material to show. During the last twenty years of the century there were few Mondays which did not see him take a cab to the city ('Three Hours' the cabmen called him, because he was sure to keep them, at least, so long) in search of his new *trouvaille*." And he sleuthed for finds in the society from which he had all but disappeared. "He badgered his friends into selling choice items," recalled the postwar Mitchell librarian G.D. Richardson. "Through his earlier social connections he obtained much that would otherwise not have been offered to him ... and on occasion he obtained choice items from members of old families in straightened circumstances."

Mitchell knew the living underrate the history of their own times. He had no truck with the contemporary wish to hide evidence of convict stains. "The main thing is to get the records," he told H.C.L. Anderson, principal librarian of what was then called the Free Public Library. "We're too near our own past to view it properly, but in a few generations the convict past will take its proper place in the perspective ..." He knew the study of Australia couldn't be divorced from the study of the Pacific and, indeed, Antarctica. Though books were his principal obsession, wanting *everything* in his field meant also hoovering up papers, pictures, medals, erotica, maps, miniatures, letters, charts, broadsides, proclamations and coins until by the end of the century his collection was the biggest of its kind in the world. A witness told the Public Works Committee in 1905: "If Mr Mitchell's library were burnt tonight, the history of Australia could not possibly be written ... because he has the original documents."

His commitment to candour didn't extend to his own affairs. Sketchy reports of his life reveal a man who was shy, reserved, in precarious health and suspicious of the celebrity that would come to attend his name. Such was his mania for privacy that the last image we have of him is a photograph taken at about the age of thirty-five. The library's handsome portrait by Norman Carter was done to honour the great donor eighteen years after his death. The recluse of Darlinghurst Road refused even to pose for a bust which the government of New South Wales wished to commission. Perhaps he had a point: by this late stage he was wizened, fragile and bald.

Mitchell entered his sixties buying on a greater scale than ever before but wondering what on earth would become of his hoard. He had never married. An engagement in his late twenties petered out. Richardson wrote: "He shunned women." At some stage he warned his cousin Rose Scott: "I have already told you, and I now repeat it, that in all probability I shall never ask anyone to share my lot." He was one of the confirmed bachelors the nation has a good deal to be grateful for. Another was Alfred Felton, who bequeathed £2 million to the National Gallery of Victoria. A third was Sir William Dixson, whose name would come to be honoured alongside Mitchell's in establishing the library. Two fortunes – coal and tobacco – bequeathed by two bachelors were at the heart of the project.

It might not have happened. So suspicious was Mitchell of the politicians of New South Wales that for years he was deterred from leaving his collection to the state. He toyed with a huge gift to Sydney University. Jose claims there were times Mitchell "reckoned it wiser to let the library be dispersed after his death by an auction sale, in order to encourage new collectors". The head of the old library took on the task of talking Mitchell round, a task Anderson handled extraordinarily well considering both men disliked and distrusted one another. Business was their link. The library withdrew from the Australiana market, leaving Mitchell a clear run. Within three years, the collector was ready to promise the library his treasures. When news of the gift broke in 1898, the invisible collector of Darlinghurst became a public figure upon whom poured down the thanks of a grateful New South Wales.

But these were terrible times. Drought and bank busts had left Australia in deep depression. The minister responsible for building the new library – "and make provision therein for keeping the collection by itself and making it freely available for students of Australasian history" – was a bush philistine of the old school. Year after year, nothing was done. The donor, his health failing, insisted the building be ready within a year of his death or the gift would fail. A providential change of ministry allowed the project to begin at last. After a good deal of colourful bickering about the site, construction began in April 1906 with Mitchell the Banquo at all ceremonies.

Scot Skirving was summoned to Darlinghurst Road about a year later. Having battled his way past the housekeeper and into a squalid bedroom, he found "a very sick man, probably sick unto death". Mitchell was in the last stage of pernicious anaemia, a then-untreatable condition that prevents the body taking up vitamin B12. He was feeble, tiny and yellow. "I wanted badly to be decent and useful to this interesting and useful man. After some perfectly banal sentences, he looked at me and spoke as follows: 'I have sent for you not because I wish to be treated, for I am done with this world and am indifferent to life. I've merely wished to have someone sign my death certificate, and so cause no trouble.'" The doctor rallied the relatives and "got a nurse or two into that house of piggery, and things were straightened up. The patient was washed and nursed till the end came, I think on 24 July 1907." It's said, but surely this is too good to be true, that very shortly before his death Mitchell secured a prize he had been after for most of his life: a copy of the earliest book of verse published in the colony, Barron Field's *First Fruits of Australian Poetry*.

Mitchell's house, its long-guarded privacy violated, was photographed inside and out before its contents were carted off in damp-proof boxes to the vaults of the Bank of Australasia, where they were stored until the new building was ready. So rushed was the operation that no inventory of the treasures was ever made. The scale of his bequest has been guessed at for the century since. The old claim of 60,000 items was an exaggeration. In preparation for these celebrations roughly 40,000 items have been found in the Mitchell stack bearing some trace of the great collector's bookplate or signature. But we'll never know what he gave. The gift, like the life, has kept its mysteries.

*

"The Mitchell to this day frightens me stiff," Patrick White told a couple of hundred librarians assembled there in 1980. His confession contained, as usual, only enough truth to put us off the track. "In the State Library and the hallowed Mitchell, the frivolous side of my nature finds itself at variance. I can never concentrate. I am really more interested in people than ideas, so my attention continually strays from my book to the faces around me. Perhaps it's all to the good in a novelist, but it sometimes makes me feel an impostor sitting amongst so many serious people ..."

As a White and a writer, the Mitchell was in his blood. He was there at the age of three at the official handover of his uncle's immense stamp collection, clattering over the floors until a librarian called Miss Flower silenced him. "Shhhh! All the poor people are reading." He thought she meant they were sick. "I looked round and couldn't see any signs of sickness in the readers. It rather puzzled me, but she didn't give me time to work it out or ask questions. She led me up to an enormous, yellow-brown globe, and set it spinning to attract my attention. I found it momentarily of far more interest than any sheets of black old stamps or sick readers."

Thirty years later, having published two novels in London and fought with the RAF in Africa, he was back. After posting the manuscript of *The Aunt's Story* to his publisher in New York in January 1947, White spent much of that late summer in the Mitchell researching the novel he planned to write next, a novel about an explorer. He found the letters and journals of Ludwig Leichhardt, the inept and ungrateful visionary who would become the model for the tragic Johann Ulrich Voss. In those months – and again when he returned to the abandoned novel nearly a decade later – White plundered the resources of the library for the details his imagination craved of Sydney in the 1840s and of Leichhardt's expeditions to the interior. His notebooks follow the doomed explorer every step of the way: "23rd: Two mules nearly drowned. Flour & sugar saturated. Spade lost, and portfolio containing insect specimens. 24th: Blacks near Comet River throw up their hands, screamed and ran away. Camped on backwater of river. Rain."

Working in the Mitchell was a democratic business. Great writers, hacks and visionaries, students and law clerks sat side by side under a low ceiling with the fake portrait of Mitchell keeping an eye on their labours. No privileges were extended to the famous. "It felt like scholarly heaven with helpful staff and fast, efficient delivery of material," the novelist Peter Corris recalls of the place in the late '60s. "Manning Clark was there, also Brian Fitzpatrick and others. Later, I met Robert Hughes when he was researching *The Fatal Shore* and I was researching colonial prize fighting. He had the linen jacket and the hat and was very pleasant. There were seductions on the grass (but not consummations) in the Botanic Gardens and the Metropole was the scholars' pub."

Some questions of library practice deserve better attention. Sleep: the struggle to stay awake on long afternoons. Wild enthusiasms: the importance of not inflicting them on library staff. Coffee and tea: how often is too often for the efficient scholar? (In the 1960s a strange little café that sold milkshakes and good pies was put into the roof. It saved exploring Macquarie Street for a feed.) Pencils: when to sharpen? Mood swings: the practical importance of ending the day on a high note. Beautiful people at the next desk: the subtleties of silent courtship.

Tramps rarely broached the defences of the Mitchell, but cold weather saw them gather in strength in the big reading room. So long as they didn't smell or snore, they were allowed to stay. One of these men became, in Patrick White's imagination, the simpleton savant Arthur Brown of Terminus Road, Sarsaparilla. Other writers put the library in their novels. In *Tomorrow and Tomorrow and Tomorrow* Marjorie Barnard and Flora Eldershaw set a gun battle in the reading room. Beset by revolution, fanatic defenders of learning "lay in the galleries and from prepared positions behind ramparts of books sniped at the mob that came in to make a bonfire". But the great novel of the library is *The Solid Mandala*, into which Patrick White pours the sharp observations of twenty years spent working in both the reading room "still smelling of varnish and rubber" and the Mitchell down the corridor.

Arthur's twin was Waldo Brown, White's portrait of a prim librarian who has, as it happens, done a little research on Barron Field. He dreams of writing but never lifts a pen. Waldo is valued by his superiors as "a glutton for continuity" and he, in turn, loves "the hallowed atmosphere of the Mitchell attached – all those brown ladies studying Australiana, and crypto-journalists looking up their articles for the Saturday supplements". A fearful scene occurs when his colleague Miss Glasson points out a tramp who is often there reading the *Bhagavad Gita,* the *Upanishads* and Zen. To Waldo's horror he sees his brother dressed in a heavy overcoat "munching and mumbling" over a copy of *The Brothers Karamazov.* After a whispered altercation about the point of reading Dostoyevsky – Arthur says: "I could be able to help people" – Waldo throws him out of the library. "Arthur did not look back, but walked in his raincoat, over the inlaid floor, through the hall. Nor did the Lithuanian attendant, from some charitable instinct, attempt to arrest the offender, for which Waldo was afterwards thankful."

While he waited for this bleak portrait of the library and its librarians to be published, White was back in the Mitchell researching the social landscape of Sydney in the 1920s and cocaine-sniffing in the postwar theatre world. He was still terrifying library users into the 1970s, this famous and absolutely unapproachable figure, wrapped usually in a raincoat, sitting just *there*. That was in the old Mitchell, where the famous and the obscure worked side by side not so much on a level playing field as a creaking parquet floor.

*

The weight of paper in the building and the Medici tendencies of Neville and Jill Wran provoked the government of New South Wales to build the Macquarie Street wing in the 1980s. This delivered the library's vast reading room to the Mitchell. Like the prisoners in *Fidelio,* its inhabitants clambered out of the darkness into the light. And no sooner were they sorting their pencils than we began to wonder if libraries of paper would be around much longer.

The future may be electronic, but the Mitchell still has to guard the past. Whatever efforts are put into digitising – such an ugly term – old books and papers, the originals must still be preserved. Whatever miraculous ways are found to hunt electronically through old records, we will still need librarians with long memories and sleuthing skills to take us where we want to go. As more and more documents start life in electronic form – so malleable and so dull – we may come to value paper even more highly in the future than we have in the past.

We'll fill in a slip; endure another brisk interrogation; kill fifteen minutes by scanning faces; unpack a box of treasures heavily defended in manila envelopes; and hold in our hands the real thing: the letter, the book, the will, the diary, the sketch. And once in a while – perhaps not by accident – we will come across one of Mitchell's gifts identified by the bookplate he designed not long before his death. Beneath the rather bogus wreaths and helmets and shields is the motto readers, researchers and collectors all live by. It's just one word: eureka.

From *One Hundred: A Tribute to the Mitchell Library*, 2010

MONA: art in the dark

ON THE ASTROTURF ATOP HIS $150 MILLION MUSEUM of Old and New Art, or MONA, David Walsh declined to greet us. One of his minders had announced that "David" was going to say a few words but Walsh, a woolly headed man in a purple t-shirt, muttered "No, I'm not" and the formalities were done. The t-shirt read: "Fuck the art, let's rock'n'roll."

The money is said to come from gambling. The art comes from all over the world. The site is the old Moorilla winery on the Derwent. The crowd was doing what it could to look cool – in command and barely curious – despite having crossed half the country burning with curiosity to see the splendours of Walsh's "subversive adult Disneyland". (His words.)

We were led underground to hear a lecture on "David's" intentions. There is a bit of a cult of "David" on the promontory. "It's David who makes all the final touches – everything ultimately comes down to his say," says Mark Fraser, late of Sotheby's Australia. David disagrees with early press reports that he is obsessed with sex and death. Could we move on from sex and death? Fraser explains it's merely a Darwinian thing. "From the point of view of a Darwinian – and David is a Darwinian – sex and death dominate our lives."

And MONA. Minutes later in the gloom a steward pushes past a trolley with a dead deer on top and unplucked dead birds below. To the left was the columbarium where anyone can turn their ashes into art for a fee of $75,000. The first exhibit is already in place: David's father, Thomas. We are being asked to participate in something uncomfortably private in the dark under high sandstone walls. This isn't Disneyland so much as rich kid

Dick Grayson's Batcave stashed, unexpectedly, with Egyptian mummies, video extravaganzas and the front of a Mack truck.

How Australia – let alone Hobart – will cope with MONA is an open question. Here at last on public display is Chris Ofili's elegant *The Holy Virgin Mary*, with elephant dung, a painting that could not be hung in the National Gallery of Australia in the Howard years. The crowd breezes by, untroubled. Ditto along the long wall of little sculptures entitled *Cunts ... and Other Conversations*.

But steps had been taken to protect the A-list, which did not include, despite local press speculation, David Bowie and Mick Jagger. Curators had cleared away the daily output of *Cloaca Professional*, the million-dollar line of glass artificial stomachs by Belgian Wim Delvoye, which, fed from the Moorilla kitchens above, excrete every day at 3 pm.

Being baffled in MONA is apparently part of the plan. It works. There are no maps, no labels, no chronology. But through a tunnel and round a gloomy bend there, at last, were the stairs. We climbed and found ourselves in daylight. Mount Wellington never looked better.

The Sydney Morning Herald, 22 January 2011

Margaret Tuckson: the widow and the paintings

GREAT ARTISTS IN THIS COUNTRY leave great widows. I don't know if that's true in the rest of the world, but it's the rule in Australia. Wendy Whiteley is still a beginner after twenty-two years' service to Brett. Lyn Williams is going strong after thirty-two years at the helm of Fred's estate. Margaret Tuckson was the senior widow of them all, the doyenne, the great keeper of the flame for Tony Tuckson for forty-one years. She loved that difficult man as a husband and a painter and served him nearly all her life.

Every year after his death a cache of paintings and drawings she had chosen – figurative one year and abstract the next – would come down from Wahroonga to Watters Gallery in Darlinghurst. And Margaret would be there at every opening night doing what she could not to be the centre of attention. She was eager, amused and, of course, pleased while feigning surprise that Tony's work continued to command such attention. Often she would be up there on the wall. I don't mean this unkindly, but she was the least likely life model. Yet it can be said that no other woman of the upper North Shore has had her private parts so brutally exposed as Margaret Tuckson.

She was a child of Warrawee and the Empire, a potter and a scholar of pottery. Her parents were no ordinary British migrants. Her father, O.D. Bisset, was the famous letter-writer to *The Sydney Morning Herald*, perhaps the most published in the history of the paper, lecturing the town for decades on manners, values and politics. The Bissets settled in a huge spread with palms, and a tennis court that Margaret was still rolling with a great iron roller into her late old age. Tony was one of a few stray British airmen her parents invited to her twenty-first birthday. She would say: "He was so handsome when I met him – like a Greek god." They married before the war was over and afterwards studied together at East Sydney Tech.

The North Shore was not entirely hostile to great painters. Margaret Preston put Berowra on the map. Grace Cossington Smith still lived around the corner from the Bissets, endlessly painting her bedroom. But folk up there had trouble coming to grips with abstract expressionism. One day when I was fifteen my mother roared with laughter and said: "You will never guess what Tony is doing now." They had been to the Tucksons for dinner the night before. My mother and Margaret were friends from kinder-garten. "He is pasting his cigarette packets onto his paintings." "Craven A cigarette packets and newspaper" (1962) has just arrived at the National Gallery in Canberra. One of the great gifts in Margaret's will. And it might have been ours, Mother, for thirty guineas.

They mocked Tony's paintings up there but admired Margaret absolutely. She was completely conventional but the freest spirit we knew; absolutely adult but a schoolgirl all her life; a mother like ours tethered to something we only vaguely grasped back then: Tony's huge and hidden talent. We admired her pluck, her zest, her pottery, the old Dodge, tales of her adventures in the Tiwi Islands and New Guinea, the house they built dangerously deep in the Wahroonga bush and her stoicism living with an often difficult man – an artist.

He scared us kids. We never knew how we would find him. Would we get a smile or a cold stare? He had no chat. And what was that beard under his chin all about, a beard that made him look like cartoon sailor? We stayed away. Our parents and all their friends smoked in those days, but Tuckson was the first of them to die. Those packets of Craven A felled him at the age of fifty-two. He died young and had barely begun to exhibit but he left behind the work of a lifetime. Lying in his studio deep in the bush were over 600 paintings and 10,000 works on paper. His widow would devote the rest of her life to protecting, promoting and bringing order to that vast hoard.

Margaret wasn't new to the work. She had been the photographer on their expeditions to Arnhem Land and to Melville Island when Tuckson commissioned the grave posts that are among the treasures of the Art Gallery of New South Wales. Their expedition to Papua New Guinea in 1965 led, in time, to the book she wrote with Patricia May, *The Traditional Pottery of Papua and New Guinea*, which remains the classic work in that field. But after Tuckson's death, all her scholarly instincts were focused on the work heaped in his studio. He had painted to the end and kept everything. Nothing was dated. Only a handful of early works were signed. Nothing had a title. "He didn't believe in giving paintings names at any time," Margaret told James Gleeson in 1979. "I don't think there's a single painting with a name, just a description." She gave them the sparest possible titles, which somehow heighten their mysterious power:

Five White Lines (Vertical) Black Ground

White over Red on Blue

White With Lines (Charcoal) Black Border

She began her inventory – thousands of cards, one per work – as Daniel Thomas prepared for the mighty 1976 memorial exhibition of Tuckson's work at the Art Gallery of New South Wales. Thomas doesn't claim all the credit for setting Margaret on this course. "Remember she was married not just to an artist but a curator. She was well aware of her responsibility. I could only have encouraged her own instincts." Her work on the cards, which she stored in old cardboard shoeboxes, continued for about thirty-five years. For much of that time she was assisted by Richard McMillan, who first made his mark on the Sydney scene as the founding editor of the magazine *Art Network*. Margaret, Richard and his partner – another Watters artist, Jon Plapp – became very close. They were the Tuckson team.

Her eye was superb and she had a vast memory. But she hadn't seen everything as it was painted. To owners of Tucksons keen to know about the works hanging on their walls – is it *of* something? – she would say: "There were so many paintings." Each she measured, named, numbered and photographed. Margaret was not an accomplished photographer. She laid each canvas and every sheet of paper on the floor for the task, and her toes can often be seen at the bottom of the picture. The colour was dodgy and on the cards she would note her own failings with care: "Should have some bits of pink, mauve and blue also."

Dating the work was the great challenge. The very early paintings she could date at a glance: "He did that at tech." Later, a red chair or a Chianti bottle or a bowl remembered from their old house in Gordon was a clue. Paintings of herself clothed and unclothed she could date with confidence.

Anything on newspaper was an easy mark. But beyond that, precise dates proved as elusive for the team as they had for Tuckson himself. "He wasn't able to date with certainty very many of those paintings even for that first exhibition," Margaret told Gleeson. "So we had vague dates, like '58 to '61?" The drawings were particularly hard to date. Tuckson's shifts from one style to the next, one subject to the next, were never steady. "He did some wild leaping forward," recalls Ian Gunn of Watters. "Then he'd pull back."

Margaret was torn: she couldn't bear to part with his work but was keen to see the paintings in other hands. So every year there was a triage: work to be kept by her and by her philosopher son Michael, work to be lent and work to be sold at Watters. "We had a lot of enjoyment together organising the shows," Geoffrey Legge recalls. "She had great perception but she always acted as if the choices were mine." He lobbied her to keep less and sell more. Each year they reached a useful truce. The next year the tussle started all over again.

Margaret saw it as her duty to keep track of the pictures, not only those sold through Watters. "Every time a Tuckson was sold at auction she would ring up and trace the current owner," says Legge. The provenance on the cards would then be updated. But money was almost never recorded. The rocketing prices didn't seem to interest Margaret a bit. She saw it as her duty to keep an eye on Tucksons in public collections. With McMillan in tow she would turn up at galleries to check what they had and see that it was being treated with due care. After a visit to Queensland University she jotted in her notebook: "*Variables* was hanging wrong way so have since sent them a set of the eight slides taken under Tony's instructions …"

Even after twenty years, there was still a pile of pictures in the house. When bushfires tore up the gullies of Wahroonga in 1994, Edmund Capon, then director of the Art Gallery of New South Wales, sent a truck and team of removalists with orders to load every Tuckson on board. Though the house was untouched, Margaret became deeply worried about protecting the work from fire. She built a fireproof store in the garden into which she loaded the pictures every summer, and she distributed hundreds of paintings to her friends. The deal was: they could enjoy them, insure them and when the time came, hand them back.

That seemed a long way off. She was inexhaustible. Her son and her grandchildren lived too far away for her liking but she coped with that. She had her dogs, her friends, her pottery and her writing – and the great, unseen

stockpile of painting. She encouraged scholars, she pushed publishers ̷
galleries, she gave interviews – not something she much enjoyed – a̷
after the deaths of McMillan and Plapp in 2006, she kept working on the
cards. Daniel Thomas believes she only considered the inventory complete
in 2012. By that time a man once regarded as an eccentric curator who did a
bit of painting had come to be seen as the country's leading abstract expres-
sionist. His widow's work was crucial to this transformation. She was not
alone in achieving this, but it would not have happened without her.

Margaret died in 2014 and friends who had warehoused masterpieces
for years were soon staring at empty walls as trucks carried their big
Tucksons to the Art Gallery of New South Wales, the National Gallery of
Victoria, the Art Gallery of South Australian, the Queensland Art Gallery
and the National Gallery in Canberra. After serving Tony's work incompa-
rably in life, she made sure the best of his painting will be public property
forever. Her part in this was deliberately unobtrusive but we who loved her
will check the labels as we stand in the full blaze of Tony's paintings, and
everywhere across Australia we'll see the line: "Gift of Margaret Tuckson",
and we'll murmur, "Thank you."

Eulogy delivered at a celebration of Margaret Tuckson's life on
3 November 2014, and catalogue essay for *Tony Tuckson*,
Art Gallery of New South Wales, 2018

Skin in the Game

Cairns, 1974

MOUNTAINS COVERED IN TROPICAL FOREST surround the bay, the sea stretches away to the islands; bougainvillea, palms and clumps of enormous mango trees dominate the approach to town. But as you leave the airport signs of the May elections remind you where you are. RETURN BYRNE, VOTE DLP says a faded placard beside the road, and at the foot of the tree on which it is nailed a couple of Aboriginal boys of about fourteen are lazing around in the sun sharing a stubby.

This is black country, and the Australian government, even before Whitlam, has been pouring money into the area for Aboriginal relief. It is also Labor country, and the federal seat of Leichhardt has been a stronghold for Labor since the '50s. But in the 1974 elections Bill Fulton, the sitting member, only just scraped back in. As someone said later, "Only the staunchies voted for him." In the south there was talk of a white backlash building up in the area, with whites voting heavily against the Labor Party because of its Aboriginal policy.

Fulton is an old style, genial, no-bulltoss Labor politician: "A lot of Aborigines and Islanders are down here because of the floods. They get a taste of city life and don't want to go back. They can't absorb our way of life and they can't control their drinking."

He talked for some time about the way things were in Cairns between the whites and blacks. "When I was the mayor there was a bloke here worked on the council and bought a block of land at Edge Hill." That's the smart suburb of Cairns. "Well, I had these people on the phone telling me that it couldn't happen and I told them the real estate agent sold him the block, he had a right to, and the black could build a house there."

"Now where he fell down was the septic tank. He had a seven-person tank but in the weekends all his cousins came and there were forty or fifty people in the house. Well, it overflowed. It was only a seven-person tank and it overflowed all round the place and they were urinating everywhere. There were complaints and we had to pump it out. He had to pay for it. I went to see him – he was a bonza bloke – and I said, 'if you're going to have all these people here you have to build the facilities.' He sold the place and moved out."

I asked when this had happened.

"1954, 1955."

"Have things changed since then?"

"No, it's just the same. They're unhygienic. It's not racial prejudice – people think that – but they're unhygienic. He moved out to Bungalow in the end. He couldn't stay at Edge Hill."

Fulton is no crusader for his party's Aboriginal policies – no one remembers him saying much about them in his campaign – and if anything he feels that they leave him exposed to white resentment. The cut in his majority he blames on Country Party propaganda about farm nationalisation but he feels that whites also voted against him because of the government's Aboriginal policy.

"The government is not getting the Aboriginal program over very well. White people up here are hostile because they feel discriminated against. In Mossman (a town forty miles up the coast) there are two families living next door to one another. One's black and one's white. They both work in the mill at the same wage but the black fella gets $80 a week for sending his kids to the high school. It's easy to understand."

Later I tried, with no luck, to find the two families in Mossman – Fulton did not feel "authorised" to give me their names. But they should have been conspicuous enough because that sort of assistance would only be had with about fifteen schoolchildren in the family. The two families of Mossman seem to be an invention and one Fulton could have campaigned against effectively by pointing out that help is there for white families too – if they pass a means test, and with fifteen children, how could they fail?

Most whites in Cairns are, like Fulton, an unselfconscious lot. To them the Aborigines and Islanders who make up some ten per cent of the town are the "coloureds" (polite) or "smokies" (polite for half-caste), "darkies" or "boongs" (both neutral expressions) or occasionally "rock apes" (impolite for any shade of black). While they dislike blacks they do not think of themselves as prejudiced because they feel they have good reasons for their distaste: booze and housing. Darkies can't handle either.

Every morning a group of blacks lines up in the magistrate's court on Abbott Street. The charges might be drunk and disorderly, vagrancy, drinking in the street, or obscene language – the choice available to the police is wide enough to allow a sense of variety in the court – but the offence is nearly always the same. Being drunk. Whites, of course, turn up occasionally but they have to be more than drunk to land in court – at least have a punch-up or disturb the peace.

The morning I saw the court three young blacks were in the dock. They were the only business the magistrate appeared to have that day and the court was adjourned at 10.15. The detective who arrested the three went back to the police station, where I found him in a dark upstairs room that looked out on to a verandah and through a screen of trees to the bay. Another policeman was sitting in the gloom in dark glasses, and between them they gave a performance that seemed somehow on celluloid, with dialogue from an old movie.

Me: I'd like to ask you about the problem of Aboriginal drinking and vagrancy in Cairns.

Detective: Problem? There's no problem. Problem?

Policeman: There's no problem here.

Detective: No sort of problem they don't have anywhere. You name me a spot where they don't have a problem.

Me: Obviously there is a problem with Aborigines and drink in Cairns.

Detective: Just the same as anyone else: they get drunk, we arrest them. Same as a white man.

Me: It's mostly blacks you arrest.

Detective: Same as whites.

Me: Today in court three out of the three drunks were black.

Policeman: So they can't hold their liquor. So what?

(A third policeman enters and I explain again why I am there.)

Third Policeman: No problem, no. It's been going on for fifty years and it's not going to be solved.

Me: Black drinking is a special problem, then?

Third Policeman: Special? No, it's not special. You have it, too, in Sydney. And we get it when blokes come up from Sydney stirring up our blackfellas. We arrest them and they go off on whatever social services the Commonwealth government cares to give them. So they get pissed and we arrest them. That's no problem.

Detective: No, there's no problem.

Policeman: No problem, mate.

Keith Saunders, one of the local National Aboriginal Consultative Committee representatives, took me to see the shell of 7 Nelly Street. "We don't know what happened but there were about forty blacks living here when the coppers marched them out. A couple of people got back in that night, there was a fire and the place burnt down, killing one of them. There are special investigations going on but we haven't heard anything yet."

This was one of the worst houses in town: drinking and fighting went on all through the night, and life for the neighbours must have been, as everyone admits, terrible. At least now it's quiet. "Living this way isn't created by them," Saunders said, "and it's by no way in the wide world what they want. No blacks have been able to rent houses this year and so they all live together. Naturally there are complaints from neighbours to the council. The whole council situation is strictly ratshit."

When the sugar harvest begins and the mills open up along the coast in mid-June there is a job for anyone who wants to work, but in the months before this unemployment is always high – in 1974 the highest for years – and a disproportionate number of those out of work are blacks. To give unemployed blacks work the Australian government funds special local council projects all around the country, and these have made about $150,000 available to the Cairns council in the last two years.

But the money is not there just to keep blacks occupied. The government vetoes council schemes that are not worthwhile, don't teach skills or lead to permanent employment for at least some of the people involved. It's hard to see how the Cairns projects measure up to those standards.

At Edge Hill a gang of thirty-six Aborigines and Islanders under the supervision of a young white overseer are chopping scrub, burning off and planting palms to turn a mangrove backwater into a small lake, which, on the city's 100th birthday next year, will be named "Centenary Lake". With the nearby botanical gardens it will make a nice tourist attraction, an object of some civic pride, and to people like the young overseer it represents "a bloody worthwhile project".

"There was no feeling," said the shire clerk, Mr Trundle, "that the money ought to be more directly spent on Aboriginal projects. From one of the previous grants we did some miles of kerbing and guttering and bitumening in the vicinity of Alluna the Aboriginal hostel." I suggested sewerage projects. "We need $12 million for that. This money would be a drop in the ocean."

"What skills would the men pick up from the work?"

"The nature of the projects is such that it doesn't give them skills. They are using bush hooks and chainsaws out there. But if they are reliable and promising then they will be transferred to the permanent staff of the council."

"How many have been put on permanent work in the last six months?"
"One."

I asked if the council employed blacks on other than menial jobs like the garbage collection and gardening Trundle had mentioned earlier in the conversation.

"We have," the shire clerk replied, "but not at the moment."

The blacks on the Mossman settlement have bought a bus to start a service to town, five miles away. They set up an "integration committee", raised money and, with a grant of about $4000 from Canberra, hoped to get the service underway. But the snag is that a pub owner in Mossman already runs a bus along the route and, because his service is not so hot, the local taxi driver picks up business along there as well. Both have opposed the

Aborigines' plan and the Queensland government has refused the committee a permit to carry passengers in their bus.

But Sid Dunn, the bus driver and owner of the Royal Hotel, is still angry: "They get this grant for $10,000 for this interrogation committee and buy this clapped-out bus from Sydney. Drove it up here without a licence and want to put it on this run. Well, I've got the permit. I saw the state member and he said these bastards can do it. The Commonwealth lets them do any bloody thing they like. But there's nothing in it. They couldn't make a go of it."

I asked if he thought they were capable of running the service if they were allowed. He grinned. "Not a hope. It's like everything they do. It's a bloody wine shop. I bet it's parked down there under the trees with eight or ten darkies drunk in it, plonk bottles lying round everywhere."

The Bulletin, 13 July 1974

The betrayal of the hopes of 1967

FAITH BANDLER WAS SO NERVOUS on the night of the referendum she could barely absorb the figures being posted in the old tally room of the Sydney GPO. "Maybe I was too afraid of being disappointed. I don't know. So I went home. It didn't have an impact on me." Bandler was a young dancer whose Kanaka father had been a forced labourer in the sugar fields. She ran the referendum campaign in New South Wales for the Federal Council for Advancement of Aborigines and Torres Strait Islanders, FCAATSI. She is an old woman now, still full of spark. She remembers it took a friend's remark on the phone a week after the vote to make it all seem real. He said: "There's never been a victory like it, girl."

Nine out of ten Australians voted for the Aboriginal cause. Never had a proposal to patch up the constitution been so enthusiastically embraced. Not before. Not since. Cape York was the most hostile stretch of Australia, where the Georgetown subdivision returned a whopping "no" vote of sixty-three per cent. But across Australia, the "yes" vote spanned all the divisions that mark this country's attitude to Aborigines: men and women voted "yes". So did Labor voters and conservatives. The south-east corner voted "yes" and so did the wide open north. Even as it happened, 1967 turned into myth. The referendum was not about giving blacks citizenship – they'd had that since 1948. Nor did they win the vote in 1967: all Aborigines were able to vote in Federal elections after 1962, and the last state to hold out (Queensland, of course) finally gave way in 1965. Underneath the hype, the voters of 1967 were directing Canberra to take ultimate control of Aboriginal affairs.

Jessie Street had revived the idea ten years before when she came home on a fact-finding mission for the British Anti-Slavery Society. She was an aristocratic radical, a daughter of privilege, a whirlwind in tweed, and the wife – in a complicated way – of New South Wales's chief justice, Sir Kenneth Street. Jessie Street had to be listened to even when she declared there was "apartheid" in Australia. She hectored a number of fragmented bodies into forming what became FCAATSI. Bandler, one of her star recruits, says: "She was like a mother to me and when she found me she felt she'd found a piece of gold."

The FCAATSI leaders were a bunch of remarkable men and women, black and white, burying their political and personal differences in a way the survivors guess would be unimaginable these days. Women were the core of the campaign: the poet Kath Walker, who later took the name Oodgeroo Noonuccal; Street; Bandler; and the scientist Shirley Andrews, who ran the Victorian arm of the council. Don Dunstan was there from the start, and Pastor Doug Nicholls, whom he later made governor of South Australia. The federal parliamentary wing of FCAATSI included Kim Beazley's father, Kim Snr, Gordon Bryant and erratic old W.C. Wentworth. In the McCarthyite Australia of the late 1950s, this mob was respectable. One or two reds were in the ranks but the general tone was civilised. Bandler considered this vital. "They saw me as a respectable person. I can recall Rotary blokes eating out of my hand."

And the campaign they ran was a respectable, old-fashioned affair. There was £6 in the bank when they started, not enough for advertising, no money for anything flash. The strategy was to gather huge petitions demanding Aborigines become a national responsibility. Canberra had the money. Canberra had the nation's reputation at heart. Only Canberra could break the logjam of racial laws in Queensland and Western Australia. Canberra's own record in the Northern Territory wasn't wonderful, but the underlying assumption was that over time Canberra would always give Aborigines the best hearing – an assumption that lasted until the Howard government came to power.

The politics of race changed in the 1960s, taking on a sexy American frisson as John F. Kennedy set about busting segregation at Mississippi University and Martin Luther King told the world his dreams. The violence this let loose was on television for everyone to see, but the solution for American blacks seemed so simple and so close: give them civil rights and the rest will take care of itself. In Australia, the same idea took hold. Shirley Andrews recalls, "We were very much influenced by what was going on in America."

Mythmakers say no one opposed the cause. Wrong. FCAATSI faced an implacable opponent in Bob Menzies for nine years. Street could barge into his office with delegations – she couldn't be kept out – but they got nowhere. Then as now in Australia, prime ministers exert peculiar, perhaps absolute, authority in the politics of race. Menzies had no quarrel with counting "Aboriginal natives" in the census. Coalition strategists had been urging it on him for some time. If Aborigines were included in the official headcount, there would be a couple more House of Representative seats in Queensland and Western Australia and a slightly bigger slice of Commonwealth grants to both those states. But Menzies was absolutely against changing the constitution to give Canberra authority to take over Aboriginal affairs. A power to make special laws for blacks would be "discriminatory", he told parliament. Surely the proper objective of the nation should be to see Aborigines placed "on the same footing as all the rest, with similar duties and similar rights"?

Change came when Menzies bowed out in 1966. Harold Holt was a different man. He axed the White Australia policy, signed the International Convention on the Elimination of All Forms of Racial Discrimination and in early 1967 gave the go-ahead for the referendum. This was Camelot on the Molonglo. It was also the iron law of Australian race politics in action: however irresistible the pressure from below, change comes only from the very top.

But Holt's heart wasn't absolutely in it. Old Billy Wentworth wanted a clear-cut power put into the constitution for "the advancement of the Aboriginal natives of the Commonwealth of Australia". Holt took a more cunning approach. His vehicle was the unpleasant "race" power designed at Federation to deal with Kanaka cane cutters and Afghan camel drivers: a power to make special laws for "the people of any race, other than the Aboriginal race in any state, for whom it is deemed necessary". Holt's device was to chop out those eight words about Aborigines. FCAATSI took what it could get but this lawyer's tactic to give Canberra ultimate responsibility for Aborigines was a betrayal waiting to happen thirty years down the track.

FCAATSI ran a brilliant civil rights campaign. If we make the mistake these days of thinking the fight was to give Aborigines citizenship and the vote, it's because the sustaining myths of 1967 did not grow out of the mechanical changes to the constitution but the spirit and the slogans of the time: Aboriginal Citizenship Rights, End Discrimination, Vote For

Equality, Equal Opportunities for All Australians. The Governor-General Sir William Deane, celebrating the thirtieth anniversary of the referendum, spoke of a campaign that assumed "the dimensions of a national crusade". Shirley Andrews recalls standing outside Melbourne football grounds with people queuing to sign petitions. "It was amazing how easy it was. There was something in the atmosphere."

The public feeling was vague but warm-hearted: a simple sense that something was wrong and a referendum would fix it up. In Brisbane a shy young version of the novelist Rodney Hall found the sympathy for Aborigines overwhelming as he took FCAATSI petitions door to door. Suburban Brisbanites said as they signed, "Poor things," "It's about time" and "We have to give them a fair go." The press thundered in support. Radio was behind the campaign. So was television. One of Bandler's great allies was Channel Seven's agony aunt and beauty expert, Del Cartwright. "She was marvellous. She really was to me. I mean, I didn't go along with all that she was on about but she gave me a wonderful time on television again and again. And also that lovely woman Pat Lovell who made *Picnic at Hanging Rock* would have me whenever I wanted to go on television to talk about the referendum and I'd start talking and I wouldn't be able to stop. I was putting my life into it."

Opponents put up their heads from time to time. A few dinosaurs of the DLP took fright, as always, at the sound of people talking "rights". In the world of these old men, rights still meant reds. Senator Vince Gair dragged himself onto Bill Peach's *This Day Tonight* in its very early days to voice a few last worries. But the DLP had really nothing to worry about. Nor did the hardline states and many hardline opponents among politicians – for the referendum had been betrayed at the very outset. Holt's cabinet papers released only a few years ago show cabinet gave the go-ahead for the vote only on the basis that the administration of Aboriginal affairs would remain with the states. Canberra might win the power but promised not to use it. This is the practical explanation for the civilised tone of the campaign: the enemies of change were aware they didn't need to fight. Canberra had already decided that whatever happened on polling day, it was going to be business as usual in Western Australia and Queensland.

FCAATSI and the public knew nothing of this. Australia went to the polls on May 27 to the tune of rousing editorials and fine political endorsements and nearly everyone voted "yes". Next day was a Sunday. Returning at dawn from a long night in Kath Walker's house drinking tea, Rodney Hall saw Aborigines exploring the city streets. Brisbane was divided then, and blacks were expected to stay south of the river. But on Sunday 28 May they crossed the bridge. "All these people dressed up as if for church, just walking where they had not walked before. They got dressed up and went into town just to assert they could come into town."

Then Holt told the nation he was leaving control of Aboriginal affairs in the hands of the States. Canberra would do some soundings, take some advice, look to the future. Not much more. This was the essential betrayal. FCAATSI hadn't thought so far ahead. "To be quite truthful, here you had this tiny band of people run off their feet and nothing mattered other than to get that referendum carried," says Bandler. "What happened after that we didn't sit down and talk about. We were exhausted." She roars with laughter. "Oh God, we were exhausted."

1967 was the sort of thing we do so well – a magnificent gesture, an expression of goodwill that came without a price tag. White Australia paid nothing: no land, no cash, no privileges. And the vote gave Aborigines nothing immediately: no new rights and no fresh protection. The hopes of white Australia were decent but vague. Underneath them was the bedrock racism that would, in the end, defeat the political ambitions of Whitlam, Fraser, Hawke and Keating. The one prime minister not on this list is Howard: he isn't fighting Australians on race.

This unhappy story has an unhappy epilogue. In 1997, when Labor and the Coalition decided to help Tom and Wendy Chapman build a bridge to their holiday resort on Hindmarsh Island, they passed a law to deny the Ngarrindjeri people the benefit of the Heritage Act. It was the first law a federal parliament had ever passed to the detriment of Aboriginal people. The first ever. But did Canberra have the power?

At the High Court hearing, John Howard's government instructed its QC to argue that 1967 gave Canberra almost unlimited power to make laws against Aborigines. Sure, there was "an expectation" back then that the power would be used for their benefit – but that's not what the words of the constitution were actually changed to say. The slick strategy of lopping words out of the race power meant Aborigines now stand alongside Kanakas and Afghans. The QC conceded – after startled questioning from Justice Michael Kirby – that under this interpretation "there may well be" power in Australia to pass laws like South Africa's Group Area Acts and Germany's anti-Jewish Nuremberg laws.

Shirley Andrews remembers the danger of Holt's approach being discussed by "academic types" during the 1967 campaign but she is sure it was not "in ordinary people's minds" that Canberra should be given a punitive power to keep up its sleeve. Indeed, it is impossible to look at the history of 1967 and pretend that was the case. A Morgan Gallup poll taken a week before the referendum vote showed the greatest number of those polled believed the "chief effect" of a "yes" vote would be "better opportunities" and "improved conditions" for Aborigines. Justice Michael Kirby said: "There was not the slightest hint whatsoever in any of the substantial referendum materials placed before this court that what was proposed to the Australian electors was an amendment to the constitution to empower the parliament to enact laws detrimental to, or discriminatory against, the people of any race, still less the people of the Aboriginal race."

But the drift of the court was against him: what mattered were not the hopes of the Australian people, or the speeches of their leaders, or the mission of FCAATSI and its campaigning women, or the opinion polls or the thundering editorials, or that sense in the air that it was about time Aborigines had a fair go. What mattered were the bare words of the race power as they now stand. The judges are treating Australians as if they've failed a law exam: what you thought you were after wasn't delivered by the words. Tough luck. But that's life in John Howard's Australia, where hard-won constitutional protections are thrown away to help a couple of property developers on the Murray.

The Sydney Morning Herald, 20 May 2000

John Howard,
faith and race

CRUCIAL TO THIS STORY is the man's unshakable sense of himself as civilised and tolerant, sure of the moral foundation of his beliefs. Yet he has shown himself all his career to be uncomfortable with contrary ideas on race. When he is challenged here, he responds as if his integrity is at stake. This matter is deep and personal. What he believes now are mostly Methodist fundamentals – shorn of religious detail – which he absorbed fifty years ago.

Imagine a skinny kid with a quick tongue and a hearing aid. His dad is dead. His mum shelters him from undesirable playmates. The Howards don't mix. They are teetotal, standoffish and proud. At sixteen the boy is already a member of the Earlwood Young Liberals with ambitions to be a politician. It's 1955. Keen as young John's commitment to politics is, his deeper commitment is to his faith. He's a devout adolescent Methodist. The church lies over the road. He spends many summer weeks in the hothouse atmosphere of Methodist youth camps down the coast. Salvation in Christ is his ambition. Methodists earn their own salvation through faith, work, sacrifice and tenacity.

Those who look to Howard's childhood for insight into the mysteries of the man – and behind his apparently dull facade is one of our most mysterious leaders – have usually focused on the colour of his childhood suburb Earlwood, the constant talk of politics in the family, the redoubtable and protective mother, childhood deafness, their pride in prosperity hard-earned in the family service station in difficult years. All mattered. So did the homely snobbery that assured this white Protestant family nowhere near the top of the heap that they were, at any rate, in the right heap. But John Howard was also profoundly marked by Methodism and he has owned to the impact of his faith a thousand times in interviews: "The Methodist Church had a big influence on me and on my attitudes. The non-conformist beliefs remain with me."

The young man's first contact with Aboriginal Australia came through the church. The Methodists had missions in Arnhem Land and in the Pacific colonies of Tonga, Samoa and Fiji. "Missions were very much part of the Methodist Church," says Howard. "It was very much a Christian mission to assist, so it was thought, people towards a better life. The Methodist Church did put a heavy emphasis on that." Methodists pursued the old assimila-tionist ideals of bringing black Australia into the mainstream by teaching Western beliefs and a Western way of life. Howard now sees these views criticised "unfairly" as racist. "It may with the benefit of hindsight be seen as misguided and inappropriate and all those other things," he tells me, "but people at that time acted out of the best of motives."

Racism was not an evil Methodists targeted. "It was not something people were especially conscious of," Howard says. "They didn't think of themselves as racist and because there wasn't a lot of mixing with peo-ple of different races, it was hard to say that people reacted badly." The Methodists were still in the business of taking Aboriginal children from their families. It went on for another decade. Guilt was not on the syllabus. Questions of justice did not arise. Methodist kids weren't taught then that the Aboriginal people were dispossessed of their inheritance or that there might be an obligation on whites somehow to make restitution. "It was not a matter of debate."

But what was mainstream in 1955 came to the boy with the force of religious conviction. The Methodists were about to change, opening them-selves up in the late '60s to wider questions of social justice, especially for Aborigines. Rather appalled by their own record, Methodists were leaders in a renewed public push for redress, justice and respect for Aboriginal rights. But Howard was moving away by then, leaving him, as Sir Alan Walker, the old man of Australian Methodism, judged, "stalled in his old attitudes".

University did not open the young man to other ideas on race. He was not at the Sydney University campus but worked and studied at the law school in Phillip Street. He didn't plunge into university politics and his political world remained the Earlwood Young Libs. He worked for a Jewish solicitor and had many Jewish friends at the law school. They seem crucial in retrospect. These days there's a growing identification in the Jewish community with the situation of Aborigines. Lessons from the Holocaust are being applied. But that was far from so in the late 1950s. The Jewish community was conservative, hardworking, mainstream and successful: a perfect model of assimilation.

Marriage carried John Howard out of the church. The Parkers were a social cut above the Howards, and when Janette married this gawky young solicitor in 1971 she carried him up and away into the Church of England. Her influence on him has been much debated since – particularly, perhaps, in the subtle nuances of race. But intimate friends of the Howards see them as born to support each other: a pair of Young Libs, ambitious, old-fashioned, confidently decent. But the shift to the Church of England was a vital mark of her influence on him: in this town in those years, the spirit of change that was blowing hard through Methodism hardly touched the Anglican parishes of the lower North Shore.

He graduated, he married and for the next fifteen years he pursued his political life without, it seems, giving Aborigines much thought. When Howard was Malcolm Fraser's young Treasurer, Ian Viner was Minister for Aboriginal Affairs. Viner recalls: "Howard showed no interest in land rights or Aboriginal matters." Around the cabinet table, Howard didn't contest the programs of the Fraser government – land rights, the Aboriginal Development Corporation and the first capital fund to compensate for the dispossession of traditional lands. As Treasurer, and without complaint, Howard signed the cheques.

In Opposition, he showed little or no interest in the issue. He very rarely travelled to the outback. Aborigines very rarely, if ever, came into the office. But one of his enthusiasms at this time was South Africa. He hankered to travel there but friends and advisers warned him this would be unwise. He denied being pro-South African but told Mike Steketee in this paper: "I think it is a question of not treating South Africa any worse than other countries which have regimes which to me are even more unacceptable." He cited the Soviet Union and Argentina.

The Liberals had long operated on an understanding that Aboriginal Australia was owed something more than help to come up to scratch on education, jobs, health and housing. There was a sense that amends had also to be made. This had always been contested – in the cities and the bush – and the political response has always been patchy, but making amends for past injustices was a fundamental, more-or-less bipartisan, theme of white politics in Canberra from well before Fraser's time. Then came John Howard – an instinctive politician with no developed ideas on this subject.

When Andrew Peacock walked out in a huff in September 1985, Howard became leader of the Opposition. Rather than fall back on the policies of his party, he turned instead to the plain certainties of his adolescent faith. Not entirely. He wasn't going to force white society on Aborigines as the Methodists once had, but the limits of white obligation were set by the need "to give them opportunities" and "address their current disadvantage". Ten years later Dr Lowitja (Lois) O'Donoghue, then chair of the Aboriginal and Torres Strait Islander Commission (ATSIC), would meet the man and feel, "He was just the missionary type."

*

Among the core lies of One Nation is the claim that debate about race in this country is always smothered by fear and polite caution. It's a sentiment Howard has often endorsed as prime minister. But the truth is that the issue of race – immigrant and Aboriginal – has hardly ever been off the political agenda. The history of the Federation is punctuated by great public and parliamentary debates that saw Canberra ditch White Australia, abandon old assimilationist policies, bring Aborigines under its constitutional wing – with ninety-three per cent support in the referendum of 1967 – and give land rights to traditional owners in the Northern Territory, rights that include the power to veto mining on their land. Justice Woodward in his original commission report called the veto "the reality of land rights".

Even before Howard became leader of the Opposition, brawls over extending land rights to the States had ended a decade's more-or-less bipartisan policies on Aboriginal affairs. Bob Hawke abandoned the plans – it seems with some relief – at the insistence of the West Australian Labor Premier and federal party bagman Brian Burke. This atmosphere of partisan hostility suited the new Leader of the Opposition, an instinctively partisan politician. Not many issues have been rejected in Howard's career as unfit for the party political mill. John Hewson once told the party room that Mabo was one of those issues where they should rise above politics – and Howard treated this as denigrating to politicians.

With land rights dead, Howard turned his attention to the campaign for a treaty or compact between black and white Australia. Howard denounced this as a "cruel trick" on Aborigines. "There is no way the Australian people will ever accept that in some way we are two nations within one – nor should they." Attacking Hawke for supporting the idea, Howard said a compact would "create tensions and antagonisms that could well reduce public sympathy for, and understanding of, the real disadvantage and deprivation which is the lot of so many of our Aboriginal citizens. Whatever may be the history of the past 200 years, the reality of 1987 is that Australia is one nation with one destiny."

His basic "one nation" position hasn't budged since that exchange in the spring of 1987: to give Aborigines advantages over whites, to give them more than "equality", to do more than meet their needs exposes Australia to the danger of deep civil division. Howard takes this to be self-evident. Why? Apparently a country where groups are always jockeying for advantage – wharfies, farmers, poets, Tasmanians, etc – is at risk when Aborigines win advantage. Howard says: "I guess it's just a view I've had all my life about the sort of unity of the Australian people, not a fear that the unity will disappear but a belief that it's such a valuable bond."

The danger lurking here is white resentment and it looks like Howard is the first national leader for decades who breathes defeat when faced with this old problem. He has mounted daring campaigns in his time to change attitudes to industrial and economic reform, but there seems no fight in him when it comes to countering race prejudice. Is he pessimistic about his chances? No, he's optimistic about Australians: "I do not believe the average white Australian is racist."

A few months after attacking the "compact" he turned his sights on plans for an independent ATSIC. "If there is one thing, above everything else, that we in this parliament should regard as our sacred and absolute duty, it is the preservation of the unity of the Australian people. The ATSIC legislation strikes at the heart of the unity of the Australian people." He concluded: "The government will not lift up Aborigines, embrace them, and right their wrongs by signing treaties or creating black parliaments. It will bring upon them more distrust, more hostility and more misunderstanding."

At a stroke he reversed his party's pioneering policy on land rights: "Land rights is fundamentally wrong, because what land rights inevitably leads to is large-scale alienation of enormous sections of Australia to a very few people. I do not accept the doctrine of hereditary guilt. I acknowledge that, in the past, wrongs were done to Aboriginals, but they weren't done by me. They weren't done by my parents. They weren't done by my generation. We are a separate, distinct, Australian nation of which the Aboriginals are a part, an honoured part, a special part, and I am all in favour of giving them special help. They need it. But I am strongly against dividing the country between black and white. I think that is a recipe for disaster."

We'll pass over the slips of fact: his church in his generation was still in the business of taking Aboriginal kids from their families ...

Howard began to be called a racist and didn't like it. "Whenever one disagrees with the minister or the PM one is bashing Aborigines or one is a racist," he complained in the ATSIC debate. "One is not allowed to have a different view. If one does, one lacks compassion for Australia's black citizens. If one disagrees with the minister one does not understand the Aboriginal people. If one disagrees with the Prime Minister's constant professions of moral concern, moral outpourings and moral outrage about the Aboriginal people, in some way one is forgetting the history of this country."

As a kid at Canterbury Boys' High, Howard was a shrewd debater. That was his great skill, almost certainly the skill that set him off on the path to politics. In parliament he has become a truly formidable debater but his great skill fails him when complex moral issues are at stake. It isn't enough, here, to score points. Beating the other side doesn't settle the matter. Deep issues still have to be addressed. But Howard isn't comfortable with reflective exchange about values. His idea of effective argument is a contest about facts across clear party lines. He grapples with the issue of race – an issue that crosses all lines and muddles allegiances across the map – by repeating again and again winning debating formulas.

And he had a number of victories in these years. The first senior black Commonwealth public servant, Charles Perkins, was forced out of the department after prolonged attacks on the administration of his department and the Aboriginal Development Commission. Not everyone on the Liberal side agreed that this campaign had been very useful. "We found numerous examples of petty maladministration," said Michael Wooldridge years later, "but after the 100th time of saying we are attacking the administration of Aboriginal Affairs, all people heard was 'we are attacking Aborigines.'"

But in retrospect the most remarkable gesture of hostility to Aborigines in Howard's first stint as leader of the Opposition came the first day parliament sat in its new palace on the hill. This was the bicentennial year – a year of constant public conflict on race. Hawke proposed that the first resolution in the new House should be a bipartisan parliamentary motion recognising prior Aboriginal occupation of Australia. Howard's Coalition refused.

*

No one paid much attention to the fact that Howard was leading the Coalition down a new path in Aboriginal affairs. This was obscured by internal party brawling, by Labor's capitulation on land rights and by public focus, instead, on Howard's backpedalling on Asian immigration late in the bicentennial year. At heart was the same concern for the survival of Australia as one nation. "It would be in our immediate-term interests, and supportive of social cohesion," he said, "if [Asian immigration] were slowed down a little."

In the uproar that followed, Howard would neither retract nor explain. He insisted he didn't have "a prejudiced bone" in his body. For months the pressure continued from the churches, the press, Labor, migrant groups and the "wet" faction of his own party. Lee Kuan Yew attacked him from Singapore and Malcolm Fraser from Nareen. Somehow it's typical of this whole saga that the uproar Howard's Aboriginal policy might have provoked came instead over multiculturalism and immigration. This was the last straw for his leadership. Trailing Hawke by more than 20 points in the polls, with the "wets" in open revolt and an election coming within months, Howard was dispatched in a party-room putsch on the evening of 9 May 1989. Peacock was leading the Opposition once again and he promised a "fairer" and "more compassionate" country with a return to more-or-less bipartisan policies on Aborigines and immigration.

Politicians in exile, reflecting on their downfall, can use those fallow years to remake themselves as great leaders. That was so for Howard's heroes, Churchill and Menzies. But the six years that passed before Howard was again leader of the Opposition seem to have had little impact on his attitude to the issue that largely precipitated his fall: race. Not quite. He made a number of apologies to the Asian community in 1995. He said:

"I stuffed up on that." Apologies are extremely rare in Howard's career. It's perhaps not irrelevant that by this time his seat of Bennelong had become the territory of a number of Asian communities. Howard didn't altogether quiet their concern.

But more profoundly, defeat had made him bitter towards those who turned against him in the immigration debate. His old staffer Gerard Henderson sees this as the time Howard began complaining about elites and the press, especially the ABC – "Left-liberal by instinct and personal disposition", Howard calls them all. This antipathy was tied up from the start with race, and closed him off to a range of contrary views on race.

Exile made the man more stubborn but didn't seem to leave him any more interested in Aboriginal affairs. Howard's subjects, in and out of office, are the economy and industrial reform. Time and again those who have dealt with him on Aboriginal affairs report that he is not very interested: he isn't particularly hostile, he doesn't hate Aborigines, but he's not comfortable and not interested. "There has never been a sense," says Lowitja O'Donoghue, "that the Prime Minister had any interest in what we said or represented." Rick Farley, once of the National Farmers' Federation and later the Reconciliation Council, has often watched Howard with Aboriginal delegations. "You can see him just sitting there. He honestly doesn't understand where they are coming from. There's no dislike, just a very narrow personal frame of reference."

Power and regaining power always interested Howard. That brings us to Mabo. The Coalition might have been able to make a more generous response to Mabo except that the Liberal Party was embroiled in another leadership brawl. Peacock had long gone from the leadership and John Hewson was hanging on after losing the "unlosable" 1993 election. Howard had tried at that point to regain the leadership and failed. But he was still a contender, and mobilising support in the party for a tough anti-Mabo line against Hewson's initially more accommodating approach.

All the leadership contenders – Howard, Peter Reith and Peter Costello – were economic rationalists, and they bid the party down on Mabo. And as most of the land at stake lay in Western Australia, Hewson had at his heels the same men of the west who'd killed off Hawke's land rights legislation a decade before. The leader needed their votes to fend off challenges. Insecure after the election loss, circled by Howard, Hewson was rolled on Mabo, and the Coalition decided to oppose, absolutely, the native title legislation. When some National senators crossed the floor to amend a few of the bill's most obvious shortcomings – and it appeared the Coalition parties might change tack and try to fix the bill – Howard rallied the troops in the party room to maintain absolute opposition to legislation "rotten to the core".

Howard's instincts don't seem to have been touched by the High Court's decision in Mabo. But overturning terra nullius – the doctrine that Australia wasn't owned by its inhabitants in 1788 – presented a direct challenge to those like him who downplay or deny obligations of justice towards Aborigines. Terra nullius was their friend. Under terra nullius Australia was there for anyone to take and the whites took it. End of story. But the High Court put a lie to that, as law and as history. What whites took, blacks had once owned, and owned absolutely by rights older than the common law.

Howard was a warrior in the history wars. After Mabo these strange skirmishes became more urgent, for they offer the only way out to those denying obligations of justice to black Australia. Their army is commanded by the distinguished Melbourne historian Geoffrey Blainey. For them dispossession happened a long time ago, and the problems must be balanced against the great achievements of this country. The Blainey forces see themselves as optimistic, realistic and patriotic. Ranged against them are troops once commanded by gloomy Manning Clark and now by Henry Reynolds, cataloguing the horrors and illegalities of dispossession from the 1780s on. These armies seem to range across the whole landscape, but what's essentially at stake is that sense of white obligation that gave Aborigines after the 1970s a say – a veto or right to negotiate – over mining on their traditional lands. What starts with history ends with mining.

Howard is a Blainey man. He thinks him the quintessential Australian historian. He and Blainey saw eye to eye on the need to slow down Asian immigration. Howard finds support in Blainey for his own instinct that preservation of national "cohesion" is a fundamental political obligation – as much for our prosperity as our survival. Around the time of Mabo, Blainey began to speak of "black armband" historians who are false to the real Australia by mourning for the country's past. The black armbander, he wrote, "laments … above all the treatment of Aborigines". Howard made that expression his own – and the notion that this was really a contest between optimists and pessimists. The optimists are patriots. "By contrast," Howard said, "the apologists take a basically negative view of Australian history and light upon every great national occasion not to celebrate Australian achievements but to attempt the coercion of us all into a collective act of contrition for the past." Contrition is what young John Howard wasn't taught by the Methodists. Nor did he learn it along the way. Nor has Howard come to respect in others that contrition towards Aborigines that has changed the moral map of this country. Howard's view remains that sympathy to Aborigines is due but contrition is bogus.

Howard has fought the history wars with extraordinary passion. When he regained the leadership of the Opposition in early 1995 – having seen out Hewson and dispatched Alexander Downer – he continued to attack Labor legislation on Aborigines for relying on false interpretations of history and false claims that past injustices entailed present-day obligations. As prime minister he denounced the systematic, insidious and partisan rewriting of history while waging war against the Aboriginal "guilt industry" and republicans. "I profoundly reject ... the black armband view of Australian history. I believe the balance sheet of Australian history is a very generous and benign one. I believe that, like any other nation, we have black marks upon our history but amongst the nations of the world we have a remarkably positive history."

This is history treated as a set of accounts: what matters in the end is the bottom line. According to Howard's calculations, there's no comfort there for those who believe Aborigines are owed other than a fair chance to reach "equality" with whites. He remains so rock-confident of this reading of history that here, too, his impulse is to dismiss contrary views as contrived. He ravels false history up with false guilt and false contrition in the catch-all term of abuse that he has made his own: "political correctness".

In economic debate, Howard is unbudgeable but grapples with his opponents. But when the issue is race his trademark response is to accuse opponents of only pretending to dissent – not all of them all of the time, but so many so often that the characteristic Howard response is to brand his opponents frauds. Aboriginal opposition is self-interested; Labor opposition is partisan; but dissent from the press, his own party, lawyers and the churches is "politically correct". This is not feigned. It's a source of both great frustration and tactical weakness in the man. It leaves him sincerely puzzled by the way black issues play in Australian politics. Locked into the idea that Aborigines deserve decent charity, he's baffled by the continuous demands of what he calls – without embarrassment – "the Aboriginal industry". He directs something like hatred towards the "politically correct" supporters of Aborigines, whom he blames for manipulating the situation for political advantage, using Aborigines, egging them on, exploiting them.

Howard identifies the vice of "political correctness" with the baby-boomer, post-Vietnam generation. He sees the ABC as a particular source of manipulated history, false contrition, bogus sympathy and partisan Labor influence. The ABC doesn't help Aborigines. "I think the apparent obsession with certain indigenous issues does go down very badly in the bush because the feeling is that the interests of the bush are being ignored."

This is the man who found himself in the prime minister's seat when a shock to equal Mabo hit the political system – Wik. In 1992 Mabo said Aborigines might own absolutely what whites had not taken; in December 1996 Wik told white Australia it might have to share some of what was already in its hands. Political challenges don't come tougher.

*

When race became the great issue of his prime ministership, John Howard argued the imperative need for clear public debate. That was not upper-most in his mind when he took the Coalition to the polls in 1996. When the Nationals' Bob Katter complained about "politically correct enviro-Nazis and femo-Nazis and all the rest of these little slanty-eyed ideologues who persecute ordinary average Australians", Howard forced him to apologise. When the candidate for the seat of Ipswich threatened to embarrass the campaign, he forced the Queensland Liberals to disendorse her. As Howard's biographer, David Barnett, remarked: "Whatever the merits of her opinions, there was no room for her in the campaign."

She was in some ways a woman after Howard's own heart. Pauline Hanson complained about privileges for Aborigines. She talked of white resentment in the bush being fanned by unfairly favourable treatment. She said "equality" was due to Aborigines, equality and no more. She complained endlessly of wasted money. Above all she argued the need to preserve "one Australia". Hanson and Howard saw eye to eye on all of this. Only on a couple of crucial points are they at odds. Hanson evidently dislikes Aborigines. He doesn't. She denies Aboriginal need. Howard never does. This was the only point he would correct after that maiden speech of hers. "I don't agree with her when she implies that Aborigines as a group are not disadvantaged; I think they are."

Howard has been accused of a lack of courage towards Hanson. The truth is he has no great quarrel with her – and one of the most distinctive marks of his prime ministership is his determination to be true to himself on race. As leader of the Opposition he had complained often and bitterly of being the brunt of false moralising. As prime minister he would, on race, be honest John. So his first cabinet meeting would decide to put special auditors through ATSIC. Its budget would be cut by more than $400 million. His government would ban the language of shame, past injustice and spiritual needs from the 1966 joint parliamentary declaration on racial tolerance. He would express personal regret for the "stolen children" but refuse absolutely to apologise on behalf of Australia.

He would put before parliament the Hindmarsh Island Bill, the first legislation in the history of the Commonwealth to deprive Aborigines of rights and property already granted. His government would instruct its lawyers, when the legislation came before the High Court, to argue for the widest possible powers to legislate against Aborigines. When talkback went feral he would go on Alan Jones's show and woo the audience by reminding them, "I'm the bloke that's been under constant attack from Aboriginal leaders for being insensitive to their situation … I'm also the prime minister who belonged to the party that voted against the Native Title Act in 1993."

And he would never cease to argue, as he did that day on Jones: "They are Australians like you and me. And when you are dealing with matters that affect the Aboriginal people, like native title, they are entitled to be consulted, they are entitled to be treated decently and ordinarily, like everybody else."

These were the ground rules Howard set for himself in the aftermath of Wik. What we see now in action is a prime minister fashioned all his life to see what he's doing as decent and ordinary, fair and tolerant. There were no Aborigines involved in the Wik negotiations towards the end. What was being done for – and to – them was being done without their say and for their own good. It's the old days all over again. And a man who doesn't trust history isn't going to see that his ten-point plan might be just another step in the dispossession that has never ended.

He has often preached the "sacred duty" of preserving national unity, yet under his leadership we are more deeply divided on race than on any issue since the upheaval of 1975. Howard's whole career is about winning. And he has had the big win he wanted: that black right to negotiate with white miners is gone. He believes we'll calm down now. "The issue will go off, will disappear, not totally but it will largely disappear as a bone of contention." Again, he doesn't trust the history that lies at the heart of the story of Australia. "I tell you what I am. I am the bloke who ultimately wins the last battle, and in political terms that is Churchill."

The Sydney Morning Herald, 4 July 1998

The lingering fear of blacks

NOEL PEARSON SPOKE AND THE ROOM was very, very still. He was not pleading, nor was he bothering much to charm, but a couple of hundred Sydney
lawyers crowded into the Supreme Court were listening to him with something like relief. He was speaking a language they understood. QCs forgot
to fidget. Old Sir Harry Gibbs, last but one chief justice of the High Court,
sat forward in his seat. This was as close as some of these men and women
had ever been to a black Australian.

Pearson's voice is pure North Queensland softened by the Lutheran
cadence of St Peter's College, Brisbane, then ironed out by the years he
spent at Sydney University Law School. Pearson spoke of his time in that
legal factory, where one day he discovered in one of the underground lavatories graffiti that read "True land rights by '88". And underneath in another
hand, "But can fauna own land?" ← |

Experts on the subtleties of racism in this country believe that racism in
its primal form – the notion that Aborigines are a lower order of life, more
another species than another race – has all but died out except in pockets
of far distant Queensland. Pearson spoke of old aunts and uncles at Hope
Vale up on Cape York who not so long ago quizzed a visiting anthropologist
about the "scientific" theory they'd grown up with all their lives: that they
were not entirely human. "How was it regarded these days?"

Well, traces survive in the clever graffiti of a university in the middle
of the city of Sydney. Pearson wasn't moaning about this. He was making
the point that terra nullius sprang from that same notion: an assumption
that the original inhabitants of the continent were not quite human. "We

occupied the land, but we were fauna." Pearson chuckled but the banks of spectators were silent.

We were assembled under the ermined portraits of dead chief justices to open Law Week with an eccentric public discussion about the constitution. Pearson was the only reason for the crowd: a stocky young man, a black from the north still a few formalities short of qualifying as a solicitor. This was not a bad turnout for an articled clerk. He sat there, at ease with his own authority, chuckling away at the little shock he'd delivered this crowd by reminding them how persistent, how close to home white racism is – just over the road at the law school.

Pearson was at the table because he has Mabo and Wik at his back. The law that once bound and excluded blacks is now the ground on which Aboriginal Australia is choosing to fight. Lawyers are winning victories that even sympathetic white politicians have baulked at pursuing. And it's being a black lawyer that brings Pearson face to face with attorneys-general, chief justices, QCs. He would be talking next day to most of them again when he addressed the NSW Law Society. He talks, they listen. They may profoundly disagree with him, but Pearson is bringing white Australia news from the other side in a language it can comprehend.

Mabo is getting hard to talk about: the word is wearing out. But Pearson has a true campaigner's knack of softening up an audience to listen once again to a message they've heard a hundred times before. He concedes that Mabo has produced "impatience, anger, arguments, misgivings" in white Australia, yet he sees the High Court's decision as the best basis we have for reconciliation. "I can see it," he said, holding out his hands, dead level, in the general direction of Sir Harry Gibbs. "I can see it – just down the track."

Poor Dame Leonie Kramer. She too was on the panel to talk about the constitution, but may not have turned her mind to how Mabo and Wik have transformed the oldest debate in this country: the place and rights of those who were here first. She was putting the conservatives' familiar case that a bill of rights might lead to an unfortunate "litigation mentality" in Australia. Pearson had replied in a devastating aside: "I'm rather a fan of litigation myself."

.　　　　　*

"Yes, but she's got something." I first heard that said in my aunt's house on the North Shore. That day Pauline Hanson had made her debut on the

Midday show and half a dozen of my aunt's friends were talking about the woman over their whiskies. These are good people and this was early days for Hanson, but why would none concede the obvious: that she was a racist?

Racism is so subtle that no white Australian can really claim to be untouched by that mix of shame, boredom and fear that has marked white response to black from the start. When we read of terrible things done to Aborigines now and in the past, we try to claim that this was the work of others and in other times. It doesn't work. Public statistics on black disease, imprisonment, literacy and housing are damning in themselves, but it's our unexpected, fugitive responses that really give us whites away.

Did you (like me) jump out of your skin at the sight of the old black man standing in the rain in Peter Weir's *The Last Wave*? It was a fright straight out of childhood. Who taught me about black bogeymen who take little children away? Probably my grandmother. I'm still carrying that baggage and know I'm not alone in that: Weir, a maestro of fear, knew exactly what he was doing when he put that black out in the storm.

The other night a man I've known for years, an artist who works all the time with Aborigines, confessed that as a little boy growing up in the suburbs of Sydney in the early 1960s, he had felt this was really the Aborigines' country and knew that terrible things had been done to them but somehow believed they were dying out. Where all this came from he doesn't know, but it seeped into his life and he realised he felt "secretly grateful" to know they were dying, because "it would be so much easier if they were not around".

Look at the map of Sydney. Despite the policy of the Geographic Names Board to push for Aboriginal names for new suburbs, there are virtually none. The Wahroongas and Killaras of today are called Winston Hills and Chipping Norton. We could be going for a bus tour through the Home Counties. But these names sell and Aboriginal names don't. In the past few years, the board has been able to persuade only a corner of Five Dock to rename itself Wareemba and a bit of Baulkham Hills to be Maroota. For suburbs, that's about that – but there's a chance one of the stations on the new line to Mascot may one day be called Eora. Really, it's too embarrassing to pursue: Eora is the name for the place we now call Sydney.

Remember the moment in the last episode of *Frontline* when Prowsey is fighting Mike Moore's eccentric notion of doing some good on the show with a story on malnutrition in remote Aboriginal Australia? "Yeah, well what can I do?" shouts Prowsey. "That stuff doesn't rate." And it doesn't. There's a rule in commercial television: "Avoid the two As" – that's AIDS and Aborigines. Those shows might win awards, but not big audiences.

The two stories that so far matter most this year – and are yoked together – are Wik and Pauline Hanson. But when *Four Corners* opened the year with a big story on Wik, its ratings more than halved from the twenty per cent of viewers it sees as its regular crowd to about eight per cent. Nevertheless, *Four Corners* went ahead with a show about life on the Redfern "block". That got sixteens. John Budd, executive producer of *Four Corners*, told me: "The strength of the audience surprised me."

There were several conferences to discuss illustrations for this story. There was no question of the commitment of the newspaper to my argument – that it's lingering fear of blacks in Australia that makes sense of so much of what's going on in this country now – but we, too, found ourselves dealing with the old journalists' instinct that black faces turn away white readers. We decided on Neville, the black garden gnome: a kitsch image of Aboriginal Australia, as fake as our worst fears, but still being manufactured somewhere beyond the mountains. Lately, these gnomes have come back into fashion, a bit of chic decoration indoors while surviving here and there behind picket fences in the suburbs where people say of Pauline Hanson, "Yes, but she's got something."

Time is an essential part of Hanson's appeal: the 200 years she puts between us and the guilt revived by Mabo. "I am fed up with being told, 'This is our land.' Well, where the hell do I go? I was born here and so were my parents and children. I will work beside anyone and they will be my equal but I draw the line when told I must pay and continue paying for something that happened over 200 years ago." Exasperation with Mabo and Wik, a sense that we've all gone too far, a feeling that these decisions contradict every expectation of how race works in this country, seem to explain the public blindness to Hanson's racism: this is where the line must be drawn. That has changed the map of race in modern Australia, and the map of politics. Mabo and Wik stand equally behind Noel Pearson, Pauline Hanson and John Howard. It goes much deeper than land. Mabo was the moment when the courts turned face-about: instead of expressing racism through terra nullius, they began modestly to oppose. The law changed sides, but the judges didn't order stolen land to be handed back – as is happening nowadays in New Zealand and South Africa – but said what was left might belong to Aborigines.

Those who found the result impossible, a violation of the proper order of things, were arguing neither from law nor history. Race makes sense of their gut rejection, first of Mabo and then of the court's modest conclusion in Wik that black communities, which have never lost their connection with lands now leased by pastoralists to run cattle, may continue to enjoy access to this land so long as they don't hinder pastoralists in their lawful work.

The hammering the High Court has been getting since for "inventing" new laws is starting to take on the pattern of a racist backlash – supported by most of the governments of the Commonwealth – to decisions that challenge white Australia's sense of its natural place in the system. In the course of this controversy, the difficulties whites now face owning and using land in the bush have been spectacularly exaggerated. Indeed, the challenge of the Wik decision to pastoralists' "certainty" is emerging as one of the great beat-ups in the history of relations between the races in Australia.

The prime minister's ten-point plan – the forced transfer of Aboriginal property rights to pastoralists – could be contemplated calmly only by those unworried by its essentially racial logic, which Howard stood and defended to the Akubras and tweed assembled in Longreach. They wanted the logic pressed to its conclusion: complete extinction of native title rights. Would they – would Howard – want this if whites held those rights? For all the prime minister's wish to locate in the unexamined past our wrongs to Aboriginal Australia, we are planning in the 1990s to take from black to give to white roughly as we always have on this continent. It was always an Australian way – not that most of us want to see it repeated now.

*

Aboriginal paintings were never more in demand than when the Coalition moved into the Parliament House suites just vacated by Paul Keating's defeated ministers. The stores were ransacked for desert master-pieces to hang on the new ministers' walls. This is the art the Howard team wanted to see and be photographed with. Ochre and dots was the new government's look. But the ministers had fought their way there with a campaign slogan, "For All of Us", that whispered the same egalitarian racism that Pauline Hanson was later to preach openly: the idea that minorities (blacks, foreigners, unionists, etc.) were taking too much from government, that it was time for ordinary (white) Australians to be the centre of attention again. And once in power, this was the ministry that made immediate moves against what John Howard called "the Aboriginal industry".

Race has taken its place at the main table. The 1967 referendum wasn't the moment we put all this behind us. Australians are hugely generous when called on to make big gestures that cost nothing – and no referendum has ever been carried with such unanimity as this was to bring black Australians into the Federation. But what followed – land rights, black health, justice for Aborigines – cost white Australia money and a little land. These programs were contested all the way. The politics was tough. Yet for much of the thirty years since the referendum, a decent compact operated in Canberra not to take party political advantage of the persistent racism that both sides of politics know is out there. All their polling tells them this. We're celebrating the anniversary of the referendum with that old compact in tatters. The Howard government boasts this achievement as the end of "political correctness".

Yet, despite the strength of the racial undertow in Australia, we are a better country than the Howard government suggests. More than eighty per cent of us are anxious about levels of racism. As many of us consider the forced removal of children "abhorrent", and more than eighty per cent also expect governments to do everything they can to fix Aboriginal health problems. This account of an essentially sympathetic Australia emerges from national research commissioned last year by the Council for Aboriginal Reconciliation. The polling shows us very concerned about the fate of Indigenous citizens. Even in the bush, sixty-four per cent of us think we should officially recognise Aborigines' prior occupation of the continent and ninety-five per cent of us believe every child should learn "the true history of Australia, including Aboriginal history and culture".

That's mainstream Australia. But for the first time in two decades a prime minister is trying to play to the fringe, to appeal to the recalcitrant fifth of the nation and its persistent racism. Some of the numbers are extraordinary. Nearly ninety per cent of rural Queenslanders consider Aborigines "well looked after" and so do nearly ninety per cent of Territorians living in the bush. Three-quarters of us living across rural Australia believe Aborigines get better benefits than white Australians. Though support for reconciliation runs at more than ninety per cent among the young, it drops away dramatically in the old. Most over sixty-fives are indifferent to the notion and they are also the ones who most believe we should forget the past and get on with our lives.

Having let race out of the bag in which it has been contained (more or less) for the past twenty years, Howard faces the daily more difficult task of keeping the mainstream happy while finessing issues out at the fringe. Noel Pearson calls this "wedge politics" and attacked these "ruthless tactics" in another powerful speech last week – this time delivered at the presentation of the NSW Law Society's media awards. "Whilst elections in the Northern Territory have routinely generated and exploited white paranoia and racism in relation to Aboriginal people and land rights to secure Country Liberal Party victories, I cannot think of an election in which Aboriginal affairs, and particularly questions of Aboriginal privilege and comparative white disadvantage, have featured at all in a national election campaign. It was a big part of the undercurrent of the last campaign – particularly in regional Australia – and in my view it was deliberately so."

It was a rousing speech gently delivered. Pearson ended, as he always does these days, by invoking Mabo as "the foundation of truth" without which a national structure can't endure. "We forsake Mabo and we will be bereft of our one chance at national coherence: an opportunity to come to terms with the past, take its prescriptions in the present and therefore map out the future."

During the ovation that followed, the Sydney QC Rick Burbidge – rather anti the sentiments but very impressed by the speech – leant over to the *Four Corners* reporter Liz Jackson and wondered aloud if Pearson had written it himself. Jackson was shocked: "The speech was so clearly from the heart. It was so personal." The exchange was reported next day in *the Australian Financial Review*. Burbidge has now assured *The Sydney Morning Herald* that he was not sceptical because Pearson is Aboriginal. Burbidge is aware of speakers who speak from drafts and notes prepared by others. He is anxious to make this clear: "I'd have asked it if it was the governor-general making the speech."

The Sydney Morning Herald, 31 May 1997

Founding fathers

I REMEMBER MY GREAT-GRANDMOTHER. She had a crumpled face and faded away when I was too young to notice. She was a blank. Stories weren't told about her. But four years ago, an ancient uncle asked me to find out what I could about Maud. He knew next to nothing. It wasn't long before I found myself staring at a picture of her father in the gold-braided uniform of an officer of the Queensland Native Police. Reg Uhr was a professional killer of Aborigines. Shame hit me like a blow. Then I discovered Reg's brother D'arcy was also in the massacre business. Both were notorious in the 1860s, the bloodiest time on the Queensland frontier. I was embarrassed as well as appalled. I've written about race and politics all my career but never thought to check if my people had blood on their hands. I knew almost at once I had to write the story of the Uhr brothers in the Native Police. What began as an account of the bloody exploits of two men turned into a history of an invasion in which they were foot soldiers. I was drawn into the lives of merchants at both ends of the earth, of the colonial press, wool growers, the church, the law and London's imperial cowardice. I was determined to make no excuses for my family.

The Uhrs were no friends to the blacks. Reg and D'arcy's uncle had been killed by them on the Brisbane River in 1845, the first "gentleman" to die at their hands in Moreton Bay. For years afterwards, blacks were murdered with impunity in the district as "suspected killers of the unfortunate Mr Uhr". The boys' father was a magistrate in Maryborough who issued warrants that sent the Native Police on the infamous invasion of K'gari – Fraser Island – in the last days of 1851 when, according to a local squatter, an unknown number of the island's Butchulla people were forced into the sea "and there kept as long as daylight or life lasted". The dead were not counted. As soon as Reg returned from the King's School in Sydney, his father began to lobby political connections to give him a place in the Native Police.

They were an armed wing of government, loyal, cheap and ruthless. Such forces operated throughout the Empire. In India, South Africa and New Zealand: local Indigenous troopers led by white officers cleared the way for colonists driving their stock deep into black lands. The troopers were recruited far from the territory in which they killed. In the early days, there grew up a certain mystique about the black warriors of the south recruited along the Murray and Murrumbidgee rivers, "in form and gait as fine fellows as would be picked up by a recruiting sergeant in an English county". Men were later trapped, kidnapped and forced into service. Black prisoners in Queensland could serve out their terms as troopers. But in the first years there were many willing recruits – young men in a broken world being offered a place, adventure, women, a few pence a day and a lot of food. "Victims", noted the Wiradjuri scholar Mina Murray, "don't make good choices."

Reg was nineteen when he reported for duty. After a few weeks' training, he was posted with eight black troopers to a camp in grazing country recently seized in the hinterland of Bowen. There he displayed such "zeal and efficiency" that he was promoted swiftly from cadet to officer. In January 1865, he and his men were summoned by Cuthbert "Father" Fetherstonhaugh to avenge the death of two shepherds killed on the Hermitage in central Queensland. As was common on the frontier, Fetherstonhaugh and his stockmen joined Uhr and his troopers in pursuit of the blacks. "Our trip was quite a picnic," Fetherstonhaugh wrote in his memoirs. "We did about ten miles a day, tracking all the time." On the tenth day, they sighted a party of blacks.

> We galloped into them. They were running in all directions. The gins lay down, one was shot by mistake. We shot down two black-fellows and got through them and turned back. A shot from one of our fellows hit my horse in the chest – no harm done. In a few minutes all the blacks, twelve of them, were shot. If one or two tried to fight they had no chance.

Then they rested. "We sat down, and it seemed very cold-blooded that with some of the dead blacks lying close to us, and the gins scowling at us from a little distance off, we ate and enjoyed our pot of tea and our dinner."

Few officers of the Native Police were bushmen. Most found their way into the corps through connections to politicians and colonial officials. The one essential qualification for a commission in the force was social standing. Massacring blacks was work for gentlemen. Squatters complained for years that these men weren't fit for purpose. In 1861 the member for Ipswich provoked gales of laughter attacking them in the Queensland Assembly:

> This corps was looked upon as a refuge for broken-down characters who, after having spent a fortune and ruined their prospects elsewhere, came here with a basketful of testimonials, made friends with somebody in power, and received an appointment in the Native Police.

Every morning in camp, the troopers were up early, fed and drilled. Weapons were cleaned and horses groomed. When Reg appeared, his men sprang to their feet and saluted, addressing him, as they addressed all their officers as *Mamae*, Father. Women lived with the troopers. Many were kidnapped after massacres. There were children about. Recent archaeological digs at campsites across Queensland have turned up countless grog bottles – everyone drank – and children's toys.

The carbines the troopers carried came with a fine colonial pedigree. Originally designed for hunting big game in Africa, they were used by the Cape Mounted Rifles in murderous frontier wars with the Xhosa. Only slightly modified, these clumsy, double-barrelled, muzzle-loaded weapons were issued to the Queensland Native Police. They delivered a fat bullet a long way. Charles Tom, a squatter, suggested in 1864 that the force might use birdshot instead of bullets to disperse the blacks. "This, I believe, would frequently prevent murder from being committed." But the government of Queensland was not interested. Killing was the point. Officers were expected to show "discretion" in both meanings of that slippery word – judgement and secrecy. Their duty was to "disperse" the blacks. An officer at an official inquiry confirmed what that meant: "Firing at them."

Before Queensland separated from New South Wales in 1859, the Native Police had been under some restraint. But afterwards, all restraint disappeared. The Native Police of Queensland were free to kill anytime, anywhere, for any reason. The attorney-general of Queensland let it be known that Aborigines could be killed by the Native Police with nothing to warrant their deaths but the complaints of squatters. Neither proof of some crime nor positive identification of wrongdoers was required. And when the police were out to kill, any black would do. Justice was beside the point. The task was to teach the blacks a lesson.

Queensland was only weeks old when Second Lieutenant John O'Connell Bligh led his men on a slaughter through the streets of Maryborough. From the riverbank, half the town watched as he was rowed in pursuit of a Butchulla man swimming away. Standing in the bow of the boat, Bligh shot him in the head.

Lieutenant Frederick Wheeler cut a swathe through Moreton Bay that began with an unprovoked attack on a sleeping camp at Dugandan, near Ipswich, killing two men and abducting at least one woman for the pleasure of the troopers. He then chased the survivors to Fassifern, a few miles away. Next morning, three of their bodies were found in the scrub. All three had been shot; two had their skulls smashed; all were old men. One of my heroes, Henry Challinor, held an inquest. An Ipswich doctor and magistrate of profound Nonconformist faith, Challinor was no tool of the squatters. He told the attorney-general that the "aboriginals were wantonly and wilfully murdered ... by Lieutenant Wheeler and the detachment of Native Police on that day under his command".

He was ignored.

But so appalled were people by these outrages that the government called a parliamentary inquiry in May 1861. It was expertly hobbled. The terms of reference were vague. Seven squatters on the committee held between them more than 3.5 million acres of the colony. Their shabby report exonerated everyone.

*

D'arcy Uhr was a nasty piece of work from the first. As a kid in Maryborough, he got his kicks stealing guns and game from Aboriginal hunters. He was always able to lie his way out of trouble. D'arcy was a stranger to shame, with a silver tongue. He was twenty when he joined the force in 1865. "Rather young", remarked the *Maryborough Chronicle*, "to have charge of

such a gang, engaged in such fearful work as slaying men without responsibility to any human tribunal." Only months later, he and his troopers joined
the first government expedition to the Gulf of Carpentaria. The plan was
to establish the greatest commercial port in Australia – Melbourne and
Singapore all rolled into one. But Burketown was 30 miles from the sea on
a river choked with sandbanks and prowled by crocodiles. An unidentified
fever was sweeping the place, killing settlers by the dozen.

D'arcy's response was to desert his men to chase horse thieves hundreds of miles south – a long and pointless pursuit he sold to the press as a
heroic colonial adventure. We know so much about D'arcy Uhr because of
his passion for publicity. His contribution to law and order in the shanties
of Burketown was nil. He was a prankster who hung about with the low-
est of the low. Even in the eccentric world of the Native Police, he might
have been sacked for these delinquencies. Instead, he was promoted, for his
cousin's husband, the noted bore Robert Ramsay Mackenzie, had become
premier of Queensland.

In early 1868, D'arcy went to war. Military ranks had given way to police
ranks. He was now a sub-inspector. *The Brisbane Courier* took a close interest in his exploits. When several horses were speared a few miles from
Burketown, "the Native Police, under Sub-inspector Uhr, went out, and,
I am informed, succeeded in shooting upwards of thirty blacks". D'arcy then
took his men east to avenge the death of two shepherds and a drover on
the Flinders River, where, the paper reported, his "success" was complete.

> One mob of 14 he rounded up; another mob of nine, and a last mob
> of eight, he succeeded with his troopers in shooting. In the latter lot
> there was one black who would not die after receiving 18 or 20 bul-
> lets, but a trooper speedily put an end to his existence by smashing
> his skull ... Everybody in the district is delighted with the wholesale
> slaughter dealt out by the native police, and thank Mr Uhr for his
> energy in ridding the district of fifty-nine (59) myalls.

D'arcy's massacre was reported across Australia and up and down the
UK. Most British newspapers deplored the bloodshed under headlines such
as: "Exterminating the Natives in Australia." But the government of Benjamin Disraeli did nothing. British inaction over D'arcy's killings in the Gulf in
1868 was a clue to the future. Whether the Liberals or Tories were in power,

Queensland would no longer be compelled even to make excuses to London for the bloodshed as its frontiers moved north and west. The colony's first governor, George Bowen, celebrated the expansion of the settlement as a triumph of civilisation, "not of war but of peace ... not for this generation only, but for all posterity; not for England only, but for all mankind".

Most officers in the Native Police served for only about half a dozen years. Killing wrecked them. Reg Uhr was one of many who would emerge from the force a drunk. After the Hermitage slaughter, he and his men were posted to the new port of Cardwell near Cairns. "Our black brethren have been keeping quiet lately," reported *The Port Denison Times*. "No doubt they have been kept in awe from the fact of our gallant Sub-Inspector and his 'brave army' having been amongst us, preventing them from 'kicking up a row'." The following year Reg was back in Bowen, where he and his men "dispersed a mob of over two hundred encamped near Euri Creek". No one had died. No stock had been killed. Nothing had been stolen. But the townsfolk were nervous the blacks were "bent on mischief of some sort". The number Reg killed that day was never reported.

Soon after his twenty-fifth birthday, Reginald Charles Heber Uhr was appointed a magistrate, part of a deliberate policy of promoting Native Police to the bench. Sympathetic men were needed in the bush. The last thing the government wanted was magistrates taking a strict view of the law – for no law ever authorised massacres by the Native Police. Reg's appointment troubled *The Gladstone Observer*. With tongue in cheek the paper admitted Reg had "rendered good service to the State in assisting to apprehend criminals, and 'punishing' – that is the correct term, we believe – blacks; but experience of this sort is not the only kind required by a Police Magistrate". Such qualms counted for nothing in the squatter-led colony.

D'arcy's exit from the force the same year was a shambles. Deeply offended when he lost command of the police in the Gulf, D'arcy refused to obey the officer sent north to take charge. At first, his political connections protected him, but he was eventually sacked. As he left, he took brutal revenge on every official he blamed for his humiliation. He kept on killing. He was arrested after an Aboriginal man died at his hands in the hills behind Cloncurry in 1871. But the bush magistrates – who had D'arcy to thank for clearing troublesome blacks from his Gulf run – dropped the charges.

D'arcy earned a place in bush history the following year by pioneering a stock route from the Gulf to the Northern Territory. What the *Australian*

Dictionary of Biography doesn't note in its homage to the great drover is that D'arcy killed along the way. One day on the Cox River, his party stumbled on more than a hundred "beautifully painted" Marra or Alawa men. The drovers had almost certainly disturbed a ceremony, but to white eyes their decoration looked like warpaint. "Mr Uhr was equal to the occasion," wrote one of the party. "Posting his men to the best advantage he made them fire by files at the word of command … With teeth hard set and frowning brows they kept up a continuous rattle of rifle shots, few of their bullets being allowed to speed in vain."

When D'arcy went prospecting on the Palmer River of Cape York in the 1870s and the goldfields of Western Australia in the 1890s, he went on killing. We know so much about these massacres because time and again he sold heroic accounts of his crimes to the press as colonial adventures. And he boasted about them to his friends, who kept diaries and wrote memoirs.

Magistrate Reg died at the end of his tether in Queensland at the age of forty-four. He left three daughters including Maud, my great-grandmother. D'arcy survived for another twenty years as a butcher in the goldmining town of Coolgardie in Western Australia. His death in 1907 was unmourned by the surviving Aboriginal peoples of that district who, having been shot, starved and driven from their lands, were living in camps near the town. In D'arcy's eyes, they had never had it so good.

> Before we came here the natives, who are at present around Coolgardie, had to exist on what? On an occasional lizard and a few grubs, getting just enough to keep them from starving … Now they have more provisions than they can use … As to clothing and house accommodation … It is a well-known and established fact to all Australians that aboriginals always prefer their camp fire to sleeping in any dwelling. It is as natural to them to lie out in the dirt as for us to lie in a bed.

D'arcy almost outlived the Native Police. Despite the rage and disgust the force provoked over sixty years, it was allowed to go quietly out of existence shortly before World War I although one camp survived, at least in name, on the Coen River goldfield on Cape York until 1929. The force survived all its critics because it did its work for Queensland's squatters so well, seizing their acres and protecting their operations from vengeful blacks. We will never know how many were killed at their hands. Scholars working from press reports and the fragmentary records that survive are putting the toll at more than 40,000.

I am not alone. God knows how many descendants are now living of the 442 officers and 927 black troopers of the Native Police. Because I made no secret of what I was writing over the last five years, a few people have told me of their own murdering ancestors. Just a few. Some were squatters. One was a magistrate. The great-great-grandfather of a colleague poisoned dozens of Aborigines on the Clarence River in NSW in the 1840s. She will tell that story one day.

"Must you write this?" my siblings asked me when I began. But by the end, they agreed the story had to be told. One of my sisters added: "But I still hate the fact that our family is involved." She speaks for Australia. The Uhrs are divided. I spent time in Brisbane over the years with a cousin who has researched the frontier wars deeply. He urged me not to focus too much on the fate of the blacks. Australia was always going to be colonised, he said. "To bring 21st-century thinking to the Queensland frontier is a great mistake. We were different then." No. Times change, not people. Greed and cruelty have been with us always. So has decency. Good people condemned the massacres as they happened. Protests never ceased. Murder was a crime on the frontier, just as it is now. Yes, the colonisation of Australia was inevitable. But it didn't have to be so sweeping and cruel.

So many were slaughtered. Kidnapping never ceased. Every acre was taken. Nothing of the continent was set aside for its original inhabitants. None of the huge wealth earned on their lands flowed back to them. Laws counted for nothing. No treaties were made. And when the fighting was done, we set about forgetting that Australia was even conquered.

Books can't change the past, but facing the truth together can change the future. *Killing for Country* is being published as this country is about to decide whether to give Aboriginal Australians a Voice in the country today. At this uncertain moment, I offer a bloody family saga in the hope of us one day reaching the ultimate goal set at Uluru: the coming together after struggle, Makarrata.

Good Weekend Magazine, 29 September 2023

Australia
Under Howard

Australian politics in a nutshell

A HOTEL KITCHEN. Close-up on a plate of lamb. The camera pulls back to show 220 plates of roast stuffed loin. Through the walls comes the roar of a contented crowd. We follow the food into the James Cook ballroom of Sydney's InterContinental Hotel. The camera notes blue dresses, blue balloons, happy red faces. This is election night, 13 March 1993, and John Hewson is about to wipe Paul Keating off the electoral map. Liberal grandees and party workers get stuck into their lamb. Cut to television monitors on the walls. John Elliott, craggy self-styled victim of the National Crime Authority, remarks, "It's not looking good." Intercut between tally room and ballroom. The camera lingers on cold lamb and disbelieving faces. Guests slip away. Keating claims victory for the true believers. In the ballroom women begin to weep, and up the back a distraught Young Liberal shouts, "*Seig Heil. Seig Heil.*" John Hewson has lost the unlosable election.

Five months later the Liberals set out to find new supporters. Out in the marginal seats the party's pollster Mark Textor – who is for good reason the party's polling guru still – discovered an unhappy chunk of Labor voters who didn't like Keating, or Mabo, or the republic, or Asia, or the sort of liberal social goals Australia was drifting towards in the 1980s. They had been buffeted by change under Treasurer Keating and Prime Minister Keating. Many of these disgruntled Labor voters were the survivors and heirs of the DLP, the right-wing, moralising wedge of the party that detached itself in the 1950s Split. Some had drifted early to the Liberals, the rest had never been entirely happy casting a vote for Labor. These unhappy conservatives looked willing to change sides. There were enough of them in enough marginal seats to swing the elections.

As the Liberal teams under Textor were doing their research, Labor teams under Garry Gray were coming to roughly the same conclusions. Labor had an immense problem: the deserters in the marginals were not typical Australians but there were enough of them and they were unhappy enough to tip Labor out of office. Keating didn't listen. While you and I were enjoying the spectacle of a prime minister offering Australia a sense of what a fine place it might become – open to the world, free of the Crown, at peace with Aborigines – the leader's support was seeping away.

The Liberals, on the other hand, acted on their research. They chose John Howard. Since then, he has earned a reputation for having some sixth sense for what the Australian electorate wants. He certainly understands the constituency that was to put him in power. After all, as the son of a service-station owner in Marrickville, he was born into it. And his front bench knew what was going on. About a year out from the elections one of these men spoke to me guardedly about the shift in Australian politics they were trying to engineer on the basis of their polling. It was years before I understood the importance of what he was saying. The Coalition, he said, would offer disgruntled marginal voters what they wanted: reassuring policies about morals, sex, marriage, drugs and violence – in life and in art. One little promise they made along the way was to wage war on porn. It's a promise that's haunted them ever since.

Howard won by a landslide in '96. Australia is a casual, live-and-let-live, secular, modern society. But the key to power in this country is engaging the support of the most conservative, most anxious chunk of the electorate. Gathering these votes calls for great political skill because the big parties have no intention of ditching the economic policies that are actually producing the pain out there. Free-market economics are sacrosanct. So instead, the major parties are appealing to these unhappy electors' prejudices on blacks, Asians, drugs, violence and their general fear that the world is drifting out of control. Each party has its own rhetoric, its own emphasis. There are lines even the Nationals won't cross. But all of them are pitching for the same customers.

From The Macpherson Lecture, Sydney Film Festival, 20 June 1999

Pauline slays Tasmania

"HERE I AM," SHE CALLED, and with a girlish wave Pauline Hanson in little gold shoes stepped onto the stage of Ulverstone's Leven Theatre and
the audience, on the last stop of her Apple Island tour, rose to give her a
standing ovation.

From the evidence of the past few days, ovations are about as far as
their generosity extends. These people are not poor. They were not lines of
unemployed rednecks queueing in the face of the protesters' silent vigil to
get into the hall to hear her. Ulverstone might be the epicentre of suicide,
unemployment and dashed dreams on the "Paradise Coast" of Tasmania,
but Pauline Hanson's folk are doing OK – perhaps not as well as they once
did, but OK – and they are planning to share none of their prosperity with
blacks, Asians or the world. Albert Deverell, a local Aboriginal with a grudge
against ATSIC, is waiting at the microphone. The sight of him had caused
the crowd to hush. He has "Aboriginal flowers" for Pauline – yellow, red and
black cloth roses with plastic drops of dew – but she already has a bouquet
in her hand and a white corsage on her suit. There are kisses and confusion. The crowd doesn't warm to Deverell. "We had tea," he told them. "But
I never got me sweets."

Hanson shines in this assembly. There is no one who looks remotely
like her in the room – pale, precise, immaculately turned out, alert. She
is a hardworking woman who's looked after herself. One of her lines is: "If
there is a little bit of grease still on me, not washed off from the fish shop,
you'll understand." Even from the back row we can see there's not so much
as a speck of lint on that perfectly ironed jungle-green jersey suit. "I've just

sold the shop. March 8 was my last day. Part of my life that's finished. This part has started."

Hanson's face is very familiar from television now – the fine powdered skin, coral lips and dark smudged eyes – but in the flesh there's something uncomfortable about that look: Irish above and Japanese below, Kabuki with red hair. In an odd way, she might be a sister to the student wandering through the Hobart demonstrations the night before dressed as Poona Li Hung, the multiracial lesbian cyborg who, we've been warned by the One Nation Party, may rule Australia in 2050.

"I'm a very strong person," Hanson had said earlier in Launceston. "I'm a very determined person. Don't let the red hair fool you – it's a touch of the Irish." She calls herself "Anglo-Saxon Celtic" or sometimes "Saxon Celtic European" but whatever way she puts it into words, Pauline Hanson is proud to be white, and proud, like Australia, of what she calls her "homogeneity". Those who say she has no policies are flinching from the obvious: that she is a white woman speaking up for old White Australia. She seems to speak most directly from the heart when she says, "I don't want to be Asianised."

We must be frank about this: none of us – the press, her entourage, these people – would be packed into Ulverstone's little theatre on Saturday night if this were a man. Pauline Hanson is the woman who is seen to have had the guts to stand up to the big parties and the forces of "political correct-ness" – to tell the truth. Men respect her for showing courage they know they lack. It's sexy – and so is she. Her Launceston meeting ended in wolf whistles, and Ulverstone would end with shouted offers – "If I didn't think they'd arrest me, I'd kiss yer" – which she returned with a flash of teeth and quickly crinkled eyes.

Though the story of the Bald Archys fell flat in Launceston, she tried it again in Ulverstone. Last month in New South Wales there was a satiric (all nude) portrait competition as part of the Coolac Festival of Fun. A friend rang to tell her to look in the papers one morning, "and there was a picture of me laying on this couch stark naked". Hanson's face lit with fun as she recalled the sight of herself. "And John Howard was washing his hands in a little bowl and the title said, 'John Howard washing his hands of Pauline Hanson.'" She was about the only one laughing, but this lapse of taste – in the town that has the highest penetration of X-rated videos in Tasmania – was immediately forgiven. "So anyway," she said gamely. "Like I said, you have your ups and downs."

Sex is oddly in the air at all these meetings because the organisers are the beaten rump of the Tasmanian anti-gay movement, these days calling themselves the Concerned Voters Association. Hanson's host on the island was Chester Somerville, a chocolate seller from Hobart and for a time president of the Tasmanian National Party before founding the CVA, which, he explained, has no members but "networks" of up to 2500 citizens "depending on the issue". Somerville was a last-ditch stander to keep sodomy a crime on the island. But it's a subject not mentioned at any of the meetings. Nor are guns. "I can see no reason why semi-automatic, conventional firearms should be prohibited," says the Hanson platform. But these days in Tasmania there is the sort of consensus on automatic weapons that Hanson might elsewhere denounce as "political correctness". Every other plank in her platform was discussed, but not this. One of the journalists later quizzed her about guns as she was autographing posters. She offered this: "The government should have control over the gun issue, but now I think it's the criminals who have control."

The preliminaries ground on. Very patiently the Ulverstone crowd was waiting for Chester Somerville to finish with Voltaire. This was a great day for Voltaire: Hanson was citing Voltaire at lunchtime and the prime minister was on the radio all day quoting Voltaire with a brass band in the background. As Sommerville pledged himself and Pauline and the CVA to die for the right of us all to speak our minds, the sound of shouting was coming through the theatre walls. The absolutely silent street vigil of an hour before – with candles burning, in the Tasmanian way – had broken down into noisy confusion and chanting.

But it was nothing to the utter bedlam of Hanson's meeting in the Hobart City Hall a few days before. Somerville was at the microphone calling on Tasmanians to show the world what peaceful people they really are: "This is an opportunity to sell our state ... " But the place was half full of chanting demonstrators, nearly all of them university students: "Pauline Hanson has to go. Hey hey. Ho ho." A stout woman with three Air Force badges on her lapel explained the situation to me. Pointing to the demonstrators, she said: "White Abos bussed in all week from Woop Woop."

Camera crews with their lights flaring, headed through the chaos for the Nazi saluters. There was no fighting, but Somerville was pacing a stage now crowded with plainclothes police. His supporters were hopelessly chanting "We want Pauline" against a roar of "Piss off Pauline". In a brief lull he closed the meeting: "Democracy has been denied." He was personally lia-ble for any damage, he explained to me when I reached the stage. So he pulled the plug.

That was that for Hobart. Hanson called it "anarchy" later at her press conference, but it was just a very rowdy demo of a kind we haven't seen since the Vietnam days. Nor was it, as she said, provoked by the major par-ties. That's Hanson the blamer talking: for every setback there is always someone or something to blame. But what Hanson showed that night is that she's not a rabble-rouser – a cause of rabble, perhaps, but not a rouser.

Next day in Launceston, more chairs had to be found for the lunchtime crowd of about 2000 in the Albert Hall. These people seemed not so dif-ferent from the demonstrators outside, but whiter, much older, and a lot of them, a local journalist said, "have lost guns".

"Can you hear me?" she asks after the second standing ovation subsides. They roar back. But what an odd manner she has: she doesn't work to lift their spirits or muster their enthusiasm. She lays out her complaints and lays them out cold. She isn't exciting. Her voice is as uncomfortable in the flesh as on television. And she doesn't breathe: what often sounds like Hanson on the verge of tears is in fact an unpractised speaker running out of breath.

She loses a syllable in "correctness" and adds one to "Australia". She has a terrifying way of saying "unquote".

But face to face with her people, Hanson at last makes sense of her party's scrappy manifesto. Her essential theme is money, and these purse-proud people respond to the twin prospect of saving money and taking Australia back to some half-forgotten image of itself: white and peaceful where they might again rule the roost. Menzies is the most dropped name, and Hanson is giving Menzies' rhetoric of the "forgotten people" another go: "You are not the forgotten people as far as I am concerned."

Always she is talking about saving money: by cutting aid to blacks, for-eigners, immigrants and single mothers. The cornerstone of the One Nation Party is stopping all immigration at once to make jobs for Australians and save money. Money, money, money. When people say "Pauline has got something", this is what they're essentially responding to: the prospect of money saved and perhaps directed their way.

Race is the chilli in the mix. She denies being a racist: "I am not." And this crowd would deny being racist, too. But she had a great ovation in Launceston every time she brought money and race together. And when she listed the suburbs of Australia – Cabramatta, Surfers Paradise, Richmond, etc. – where "we" now feel foreigners in our own country, the people of this very white town gave her all their attention. When she pledges to get the UN off Australia's back, the applause goes off the meter.

She is strangely uncomfortable in the face of all this. Of course, she likes it but she doesn't surf applause as good speakers do. It dies around her. She's always starting from scratch. Yet she doesn't lose the crowd: there's a kind of protective embrace that keeps her going even when she has the look in her eyes of someone not at all sure of the direction. It's the "poor chook" factor with Pauline Hanson: she's widely seen not to be very bright, but still people listen.

Which gets us to Ulverstone that night. At last all the formalities were done. She was not reading her script now, but speaking a text she knew by heart. This was Pauline Hanson the mother speaking: the mother who had raised children on her own, stood on her own two feet, run a business and found herself in parliament because she was determined to be her own person. "Let me assure you there is no puppet pulling Pauline Hanson's strings. What you see is what you get." This is militant motherhood. And when she attacks special programs of assistance to Aborigines, she attacks them as a mother: "It's like a mother: if you treat one child different from the rest, it creates resentment."

But she was also for this audience a frail woman: surprised to find herself a national figure, much blamed, still getting lost in the corridors of parliament and struggling – but giving herself six years – to learn the "protocol". She was at her most persuasive here: not stumbling through figures on Asianisation or putting a nearly incoherent argument about tax, but presenting this image of her steely frailty.

They gave her three cheers and bought out all the $5 posters of herself wrapped in the flag rather like the Queen in her Garter robes, the great star on her shoulder, staring into the distance. She signed them – with a very big P for Pauline – and I noticed her scarlet fingernails were only plastic. For most of her fans she had only a curt yes or no, but she was a very long time leaving. Then, with a bulky detective at each elbow, and a couple more out front, they ran her through the straggling remains of the mob to her car.

It was a nearly faultless operation. The car was moving before she hit the seat and the rest of the demonstrators arrived to see her tail-lights disappearing into the night. There's more of this to come. As Paul from City Hall said, "She'd better get used to it, it's going to be like this every time."

The Sydney Morning Herald, 12 May 1997

Brian Harradine's lunch

AFTER LUNCH YESTERDAY, the pale senator sat for a moment at his seat, steadying himself perhaps, before walking over to Nick Minchin. From the gallery we couldn't, of course, hear the few words Brian Harradine said before stepping away. Senator Minchin shook his head. Senator Minchin is a man almost devoid of gesture. In all the hours of close debate this week as he defended this immensely complex bill from three-way and sometimes four-way attack from the Greens, Democrats, Labor and Senator Harradine, Senator Minchin hardly ever raised his voice. He struck no poses.

At this point he looked very, very still. He seemed to have another victory almost in the bag. Before lunch Senator Harradine wasn't going to have anything to do with the Opposition's plan to put the bill under the protective umbrella of the *Racial Discrimination Act*. He denounced the idea as "a lawyer's picnic" and told Labor angrily to "face up to the real world".

Senator Harradine left the chamber. Waiting outside the door was one of the invisible senior advisers to the Opposition, John Basten SC. "Senator, you've made a terrible mistake," he said. "This will send the wrong message to all of Australia." Over lunch – a sandwich – the lawyers worked on Senator Harradine. They told him this: the totality of the bill had a much better chance of surviving High Court challenge if it declared itself within the principles of the *Racial Discrimination Act*. Senator Harradine was convinced.

Nothing had changed in his demeanour when he re-entered the Senate. The gruelling work of the past few days hardly seems to have touched him. After delivering the news to Senator Minchin, Senator Harradine sat with Labor's Barney Cooney, a man of Senator Harradine's generation, a barrister who gets to the quick of complex legal issues. Senator Harradine admires him. A weak patch of sunlight fell on the two old men as they spoke. Senator Harradine's big hands were working. They nodded. Senator Harradine returned to his seat to await the moment. "I have been giving this further thought ..."

Ron Castan QC, the hitherto invisible most senior adviser to the government's opponents, was sitting with Senator Harradine's team – John McCarthy QC and Jeff Kildea – at the back of the Senate. Castan was slumped forward in what seemed an attitude of prayer. Harradine took his time. Everyone all week had taken their time. It had meant a long debate – longer spent amending than passing the *Native Title Act* in the first place – but this was parliament working as textbooks said it might. The senators were out to persuade one another, debate was repetitive but lucid – particularly as Senator Harradine drove his colleagues to translate complexity into real English – and the result of nearly every important vote was unknown until it was taken.

Only up in the galleries was parliament not working: hard as it was for everyone else with piles of paper in front of them, it was impossible for the public upstairs to follow the amendments and counter-amendments. But they sat waiting for bursts of rhetoric, or vital votes. Early in the week there was a bit of a showing by graziers. They didn't last long. The Aborigines, of course, were the stayers.

Senator Harradine now laid it out: "Unless we have the act constrained subject to the *Racial Discrimination Act* we may indeed be giving the wrong messages to the whole of Australia and all Australians – not only Indigenous Australians but also those likely to require the provisions of this act to resolve problems in a sensible and orderly fashion." Then came the moment of pure Harradine. With his hands in a gesture of atonement, he said: "I do apologise to the Senate and I indicate now that I am supporting the amendment proposed by the Opposition."

This was a very big loss for the government. Senator Minchin rose, cool as ever. "I don't know what Senator Harradine had for lunch," he said. "I retain my respect for Brian Harradine but he was right before lunch and wrong after lunch." They took the vote. The gallery applauded. Senator Minchin showed nothing. Senator Harradine looked immensely pleased. After that, the vote that sent the bill back to the House of Representatives was an anticlimax – except for the sight of the Nationals' Senator Ron Boswell, weeping.

The Sydney Morning Herald, 6 December 1997

Abbott & Costello vs Ellis

DOGGED BY A HEAVY COLD, cracking lozenges between his teeth, Bob Ellis flew into Canberra yesterday and plunged into the action. At last Banquo was in town. His case got nowhere much as a result but Canberra had a day of circus it won't easily forget. On the footpath outside the ACT Supreme Court, the dishevelled writer argued his innocence to the cameras. In the witness box inside, Bill Hayden was deploring Canberra's rumour mill while giving "wing" – his term – to a few of the best.

The former governor-general spoke of Paul Keating's rumoured affair with a "prominent" woman; his rumoured "predilection for young men"; "stories" about Mrs Keating; and "stories" about Gough Whitlam. All false. And there was the rumour about an MP caught in a Canberra "love nest" with a male diplomat. "If I heard that once I heard it a dozen times and there was never any evidence for it that I could see."

With tabloid panache, Bill Hayden published and deplored in the same breath.

Readers joining us here will need some background: Bob Ellis is the author of a grubby anecdote in his memoir *Goodbye Jerusalem* that has university student Tanya Coleman – now the wife of the federal treasurer, Peter Costello – seducing both young Costello and a young Tony Abbott – sworn in yesterday afternoon as minister for employment services – in order to recruit them to the Liberal cause. This unlikely Mata Hari, the two ministers and Abbott's wife, Margaret, have all now sued Ellis's publisher, the multinational behemoth Random House. The publisher admits the tale is nonsense, has withdrawn and pulped the book, and for some months has been offering cash to the plaintiffs to settle the dispute.

The sums are still not clear, but a letter tendered in evidence yesterday shows the Abbotts last September were asking for $50,000 plus an apology and legal costs. That the Abbotts were a little to one side of Ellis's line of fire suggests the Costellos have been asking much more to settle the action. As late as last week, attempts were being made on both sides to do so. The case appears to have come to court because the parties haven't been able to agree on the money.

Yesterday was get-Ellis day, so it was fitting he'd finally appeared in Canberra. From a seat in the gallery he delivered a number of interjections, sotto and not so sotto voce, as witness after witness got stuck into him. "That's defamatory!" he cried at one point, demonstrating, perhaps, a general failure to grasp the laws of defamation. The one place you can't defame someone is from the witness box.

Laurie Oakes of Channel Nine appeared like a Tongan prince to give evidence for the treasurer's cause. He waved across the court to Ellis, who called: "Bless you, citizen." But Oakes was there like all the rest to try to get into evidence the general proposition that Ellis, for all the beauty of his prose, is a shaky reporter of truth. Oakes was stopped by the judge. So was the ABC journalist David Spicer, who had forced Bob Ellis, on the day of the launch of *Goodbye Jerusalem* last year, to read a long apology for having railed against him in the book – wrongly and with a vivid string of adjectives – for daring to ask a particularly rude question of Bob Carr.

Because Ellis has not been sued and because he's not being called as a witness, the judge refused to allow this exploration of his reputation. Bill Hayden had been called for exactly that task, too, and came up against the same judicial wall. But what a journey it was before he hit the bricks.

The mood was set by an unfortunate incident right at the start. "Call Mr Bill Hayden," said Terry Tobin QC, for the plaintiffs. Out into the foyer went a young court attendant who, alas, had no idea what the former governor-general looked like. He returned. Hayden was only a step behind him as he called: "No appearance, your honour."

For the record, Hayden was wearing a dove-grey suit, a discreet AC in his buttonhole and a look of relaxed determination. The man who might have been king was at the service of Peter Costello, who may yet be king one day. Their common cause was Ellis. Surviving into the page proofs of *Goodbye Jerusalem* was a story about Hayden so terrible – and so entirely untrue – that had it appeared in the published volume this litigation running in Canberra now would have been no more than a rumble of thunder. Luckily for everyone, the error was spotted by the journalist Peter Charlton as he was looking over the page proofs to see if *The Courier-Mail* might like to buy serial rights to *Goodbye Jerusalem*. The error was corrected before publication.

Hayden painted in the witness box an eloquent picture of the power of rumour to harm politicians' public and private lives, expose their children to cruel teasing in the playground and deter men and women from entering public life. "It's as plain as a pikestaff there is no evidence," said the former governor-general of Ellis's allegations against Tanya Costello. "But I believe there are a lot of ordinary punters out there who might believe it."

Before departing the box, Hayden repeatedly urged the court to award substantial damages against Random House. This was not a time to be "soft", he said. The court must be "firm". Bob Ellis growled in his seat, unwrapped another lozenge, threw the paper on the floor and chewed.

For the Canberra press corps, Ellis is an exotic sight, a form of life familiar enough in Sydney but rarely encountered in this city of the predictable media grab. Tired and coughing and sounding a little desperate at times, Ellis stood ringed by press on the footpath outside the court trying two or three times to give his version of events, a version he knows he is never going to be asked to give in the witness box. "Let's do it again," he said after a few blunders, but the cameras kept rolling.

Ellis no longer believes the yarn about the Costellos and Abbotts is true but still asserts his version of how it came to him. But above all, he's arguing that it's trivial. "That university students in the '70s had sex and occasionally talked about politics in bed ... Shock. Horror." Then he slumped up the stairs into court where again, today, his reputation will be fought over with him only a growling spectator.

The Sydney Morning Herald, 22 October 1998

Australia: so British underneath

WE ARE STILL SO BRITISH. This is not generational but structural. Our governments are modelled on Westminster, not Washington. So are our courts. Australian business is clubbish just as it is back Home. Between us we invented trade unions. Together we are alone in the rearguard of democracies opposing constitutional rights, particularly that American notion of free speech. Our indecision over the republic is very British. So is our racism and our suspicion of intellectual life. The novelist Howard Jacobson was not exaggerating much in the latest issue of *Granta* when he wrote: "Everything brutal about Australia is British."

This is hard for locals to face and difficult for travellers to see, even travellers with the fine instincts of Michael Davie. But we all take simil-arities for granted. Differences are so much easier to pick. One difference is incontestable: in the 1990s an Australian prime minister started using a different kind of rhetoric when he spoke about us and Britain. Paul Keating's shift of tone is the starting point of Davie's *Anglo-Australian Attitudes*. "What had he, and others who felt like him, really got against the British?" asks Davie. "Something lay buried, something rarely talked about."

Among other valuable things, Davie's *Anglo-Australian Attitudes* provides fresh evidence of something we find very hard to understand: the impact Keating had in London. They seemed, in a way, to have taken him more seriously than we did. Why? Not because he put his hand on HM's waist – that only dramatised their fears – but because he didn't sound like an

Australian leader. He didn't fawn. They read this as a man bearing a grudge. Hence this intriguing book by a great London journalist reporting what has happened between our two countries before and since he turned up in the late 1970s to edit, and transform, *The Age* in Melbourne.

The reporting is wonderful. Read *Anglo-Australian Attitudes* to discover the origins of the whingeing Pom and the reasons the 1932–33 Bodyline series still causes hostility between our countries. There's a witness's account here of Britain's abandonment of the Commonwealth to enter the Common Market – Davie was on the spot in Canberra when Macmillan's emissaries arrived – and a forensic, funny examination of royal tours and royal bastards in Australia.

Much of this is irritating for an Australian to read in an improving kind of way: you know it's doing you good even as it leaves you a little rattled. Davie sets disturbing British allegations of Australian cowardice at Gallipoli against an account perhaps more convincing than even he realises of British bastardry towards Australia in two world wars.

Of course, he makes mistakes here and there, diagnosing as anti-British all sorts of things that simply aren't. William Charles Wentworth dressed up his greed as patriotism, but his fight with London was really about getting title to the land he had stolen from the blacks. We mocked Menzies' "Britishness" not because we were anti-British but because it was affectation in a Jeparit grocer's son and poor politics in the Australia of the 1960s. And when Ron Tandberg used a top hat in cartoons of John Kerr, this was not a "flicker" of anti-English sentiment: the poor coot wore top hats.

Australians have a perpetual grudge against the British for missing the nuance: they almost get us right, but not quite. And we are constitutionally reluctant to admit that distance, particularly the distance of London, can lend clarity to any view of Australian affairs. Davie knows us well enough to lull us with good jokes and reward us with strange discoveries – for example, Malcolm Fraser's habit of serving ice-cream embedded with dead honey ants – to draw us into an argument we find particularly difficult to deal with: that there's something perverse in our relationship with Britain.

Perverse? Davie cites strange resentments, strange indifference, but above all, strange attachment to Britain. "Looking back now ... the most striking historical fact is Australian reluctance, at every stage, to cut the links with Britain, despite a national reputation for independence of spirit. Separation anxiety," he adds, "affected even the boldest."

That is true and brings us to the republic. Davie is not one of those arch Fleet Street types who mock those Australians who want to break with the Crown. He sees an Australian republic as inevitable. But to my pessimistic mind he rates its chances too highly. The failure of last year's referendum he calls "a moment of hesitation … a classic case of political separation anxiety", but he assumes too easily that time and a bit of courage will see us make the break. Perhaps this is because he looks for remnant British-ness only in the Anglophile upper classes, in clubs and in private schools that recruit British headmasters. (He might have added art galleries that employ British directors.) This is an Australia where *Country Life*, or at least *The Spectator*, can still be found on sitting-room tables. It's fast disappear-ing, but the attitudes of ordinary Australians remain deeply British even if they're expressed in accents that make the British flinch.

The real problem with the republic is that we still revel in romantic British ideas of what a head of state should be: someone with real power, someone to look after us, someone politicians can't kick around – that is, someone oddly like HM herself. We are constitutionally independent and the Queen is powerless here, but rather than accept these dry truths as a way forward to a republic, Australians are entangled in fuzzy old dreams of symbolic leadership that are absolutely British.

The thought of having us hanging round their necks forever horrifies the Brits. A powerful current of astonishment runs through Davie's book that, after all Britain has done to us over the past century or so, we remain so rusted on. He argues that a final break with Britain will allow happy and rational relations to be established at last between our countries. Even that might be a bit optimistic. We would still be family with a family's long his-tory of affection and betrayal, and the grudging resentment of independent offspring that they're not looked after anymore, and the subterranean wish for approval from our parents that never really goes away. Then when we're getting old ourselves we discover we're more like our parents than anyone else on earth. As Larkin wrote in "This Be the Verse":

They fuck you up, your mum and dad,
They may not mean to, but they do …

The Sydney Morning Herald, 26 August 2000

Jones, Laws and cash for comment

MR LAWS WAS NOT ON AIR YESTERDAY. He was talking to one of the smallest audiences since his career began back in Bendigo in 1953, a Legacy kid doing his first "live reads" at the microphone. Time has turned him into a craggy old man with a suntanned face and pale hands, a tight rein on his temper and a very beautiful voice. All day he spoke of long friendships, old loyalties and old habits at the microphone that have turned him into the great man of Australian radio, still having a good time every morning on 2UE entertaining his listeners and giving them a hand. "The other day a little boy lost his teddy bear in a little town in Victoria and we spent the entire three hours finding his teddy bear. And we did by the end of the program."

OK, but those seamless "live reads" – ads read straight to air – are still the man's bread and butter after all these years. Advertisers pay a hefty surcharge to 2UE for John Laws' trademark "sincerity" and deft embellishment of the scripts.

This now leaves him with two problems: first why he takes a separate fee from the advertisers when directives from 2UE's boss John Conde forbids the practice, and second whether these glowing endorsements are part of a wider pattern of trying to conceal from listeners what's from the heart and what's from the wallet on the John Laws show. Laws did not enjoy close questioning on this. "If you could tell me what you are driving at," he pleaded with counsel assisting the inquiry. "Maybe not," Julian Burnside replied. "Cross-examiners," advised Tom Hughes, counsel for 2UE, "don't play show poker."

Laws has no kill button to protect him here, no seven-second delay. At one point he spoke of the thrill of taking callers at random some mornings, "what we affectionately call 'Russian Roulette'. In other words, just hit the button and you don't know what you are going to get; you don't have any idea what the caller is going to talk about." This was roughly the same game – but clearly not as thrilling. Laws's mood shifted from willing, to patient, to miserable as the day passed. But if someone tells you he was a pushover, don't believe them. Under pressure he rakes at his right eye with his index finger and shifts in his seat. His tan faded. But at the end of the day his suit was uncreased and not a hair was out of place. Laws's pride in himself seemed absolutely intact.

But Burnside deftly and relentlessly made him admit that all the problems with "live reads" that 2UE management was complaining about fitted his own practice on his own show. And he admitted it was "possible" that listeners would regard a little differently what was said by a man paid nothing and a man paid, say, $10 million.

Burnside asking about a "surprise" on-air call from Bankers' Association chief Tony Aveling: "By that stage any element of surprise had disappeared?"

Laws: "Yes, maybe I didn't – maybe I didn't have the script of what he wanted – the order of questioning, or something."

*

"We're dealing with two of the highest-profile persons in the land," said John "Brenno" Brennan of 2UE. "Megastars!"

Brennan is an old comfy kind of guy who's been in radio for years, known Lawsie forever, produced Alan Jones and now finds himself the watchdog of compliance at 2UE, responsible for seeing the station's stars obey the broadcasting code. The poor bugger was dying in the box as he tried to explain why he'd never done "a single solitary thing" to investigate the personal deals Laws and Jones had with advertisers. Even where he knew there was a deal in place – like Jones's contract with Optus – Brenno never asked for details. "Jones would find it offensive."

The punters laughed but, head down, Brennan battled on with his explanation for never facing the station's two stars: "I have to keep them psychologically number one when they do their program to make sure that they are hassle-free, and most days they're very, very vulnerable to criticism or questioning." He agreed "all hell would break loose" if he'd questioned Jones about that Optus deal. "And that view guided your conduct in relation to Mr Jones throughout?" asked Julian Burnside QC, counsel assisting the inquiry. Brenno replied, "On that matter, yes."

Jones's last hours in the witness box had given us all some pale indication of what life might have been like for Brennan if he had found the courage to question the broadcaster over the on-air obligations of his deals with Optus, Qantas, Colonial State Bank and four other unnamed "sponsors". Jones had blustered and cried foul as Julian Burnside pressed him over his understanding of what these "sponsors" – known everywhere else in the world as advertisers – expected of him. Jones held to his claim that – notwithstanding being paid huge sums under contracts that clearly stipulate he must plug products and/or refuse to denigrate products – none of this had any impact on what he ever said at any time on air on 2UE. Brennan always believed Jones was that kind of guy, beholden to no one.

Brenno and Lawsie go back forty-four years. How did Brennan explain all the plugs for Qantas? Love. "Lawsie is a great Qantas man." And for the Australian Trucking Association? "He's a great trucking man." Didn't he ever get an inkling that Laws might have a commercial deal with the truckers? "No, he loves the truckies ... I mean, sometimes he even comes in dressed as a truckie. I wish he'd do it most of the time because he returns then to being the great lovable larrikin, and that's how he relates so beautifully to his audience." And Rosemount wines? "Well, I thought he got mostly free wine."

The penny, if such a tiny sum means anything round 2UE, took a long time to drop. When Foxtel complained about Jones plugging Optus on air because he was on Optus's payroll, Brennan ignored the complaint. He explained he got millions of complaints about Laws and Jones. "I think a fellow'd be on a psychiatrist's couch most of the week if he believed every one of them." When *Media Watch* started dropping bombshells, he did "sit up and say hello" but did nothing.

*

Sydney is the city of real-estate miracles. In the 1990s we discovered we could subdivide water. You take old government wharves – at a discount because of "heritage" requirements – and turn them into strata apartments of fabulous value at Woolloomooloo and Walsh Bay. The broadcaster Alan Jones was a player in both these efforts to turn old wharves into gold. Walker Corporation at Woolloomooloo (and elsewhere) is paying him $250,000 a year, and the Walsh Bay consortium is paying him $200,000 a year, to assist and promote their schemes.

Jones reckons the project was "stalled" and about to die when the Walsh Bay consortium hired him to assist with "the development of key media relationships and the general promotion of Walsh Bay". Certainly there were big credibility problems: with the heritage lobby, with disgruntled developers who had lost out and, increasingly, with the public. The very Sydney solution was to bring Jones on board. In late May 1997, after "very negative press reports", Walsh Bay briefed five media personnel including Alan Jones and *The Daily Telegraph* columnist and wit Piers Akerman. Over a couple of meetings, David Mann, a consortium executive, told Jones the project had "copped a lot of flak" and showed him models of the proposal and photographs of the existing wharves. Jones's $200,000 deal is dated 1 June. Mann said he didn't ask the broadcaster to put the Walsh Bay story on air, but to "minimise the negative publicity and impact of that publicity".

"Did he behave as you had hoped he would?" asked Julian Burnside.

"Yes."

"Did he start broadcasting favourable comments about the Walsh Bay redevelopment?"

"Yes."

The day after the deal was done, Jones was on air spruiking. There were no ads for him to "embellish". Walsh Bay had nothing to sell. Jones did a straight editorial. He told his listeners at 8 am this Walsh Bay development was "something which I regret to say I've only just stumbled upon. I mean, this is something that I should have done something about long ago."

That word "stumbled" was to cause Jones some embarrassment. On the one hand he was telling the ABA he didn't need money to spruik for Walsh Bay because he was a long-term advocate of the consortium's plans – "I knew about the redevelopment, I knew about rotting piers" – but here he was on 2UE saying he'd just "stumbled" upon the subject. He explained: he'd gone to see his agent, Harry Miller, the night before on some other matter and to his surprise "stumbled" upon splendid material about Walsh Bay in Miller's flat. Burnside said, "Can I suggest this: that on the chronology of things, what you had just stumbled across was the $200,000 contract and not the development idea?"

"No one can deny that chronology," replied Jones. "I can only argue my mindset and I keep saying – and I've said it and I say it to you with whatever sincerity I can muster, I know how I put a program together and this issue was an issue and I think for the next couple of weeks it was a major issue, and the government had been sending me stuff which I – I'd been reading the stuff in *The Sydney Morning Herald*; I had a very strong view about it."

Meanwhile the Department of Urban Affairs and Planning had come to a rather Solomonical judgement: the eastern half of Walsh Bay precinct would be restored in its original "envelope", but in the western half, one wharf and some shore sheds would be demolished. This was not the green light: new plans for this had still to be submitted by the developers and approved by the Department of Urban Affairs and Planning. Jones, silent on the subject for seven weeks, was immediately back on air praising this "absolutely phenomenal" and "fantastic" proposal. He attacked DUAP for preserving sheds that were "absolute eyesores" and he once more addressed the Premier: "Bob Carr, you and the team have got to decide whether you want this to go ahead or not. It's absolutely essential that government – that's Bob Carr and others – get together and support what is a magnificent restoration project."

The climax to this very Sydney tale came a month later, when the final go-ahead was announced live on the Alan Jones show by the Premier of New South Wales, Bob Carr! Praise tumbled out of Jones; not praise for the premier but praise for the project. Jones asked none of the questions a journalist might be expected to ask: Why haven't tenders been reopened? Why are only Mirvac and Transfield eligible to reap the benefit of the radical new arrangements? How can buildings under a permanent conservation order be demolished? Why is the NSW government kicking in $37 million? "Brilliant!" Jones gushed instead. "Absolutely beautiful!"

*

The last day of the ABA's cash for comment inquiry was a full-dress affair. QCs who had been no more than ghosts in the air turned out to argue for the innocence of the banks and Jones and 2UE. Tom Hughes wore striped pants. Bret Walker affected a long face and a grey demeanour as he insisted on the utter, utter seriousness of the matter at hand. That's usually a sign the clients are in a pickle. Walker complained about jokes. The laughs Julian Burnside QC provoked from the gallery "oppressed" Jones. Indeed, Walker sledged the performance of counsel assisting the inquiry as charming, clever, neat and fit for "a future in broadcasting".

In the battle of trained voices in these proceedings, the nasal baritone of chairman Michael Gordon-Smith was one of the most effective. He kept coming back at Walker: how can Jones continue to insist that his failure to disclose his sponsors' contracts was not misleading? Those contracts are "relevant", Walker admitted, but so are a lot of other things like childhood upbringing, employment by past prime ministers, Jones's sporting career, old opinions, old friendships, old enmities. Contracts are just another relevant fact among many. There isn't time enough in life to reveal all of them all of the time ...

Tom Hughes brought that ramrod figure, that jagged profile, the pants, the AO glinting in the lapel, and the thunder of outrage denouncing the critics of 2UE's executive chairman John Conde: an honourable man working in "always difficult circumstances" who may have had his competence attacked, but never his credibility. But something had happened to Hughes. He was starting to behave like a broadcaster. Perhaps by some strange osmosis after all these weeks of the inquiry they can't be told apart. Here was Hughes doing a "live read" before the ABA, trudging through his script interpolating little asides to give the argument he's paid a fortune to deliver an air of sincerity. This man is a legend at the Bar, but frankly not up to 2UE standards. If Conde has his wits about him, he'll hang on to Laws, shift Jones to Stan Zemanek's slot and hire Burnside for breakfast. Expensive, but it just might work.

The Sydney Morning Herald,
30 October, 12 November, 20 November and 4 December 1999

The Queen makes a comeback

IT ISN'T OVER BY A LONG SHOT. From under their umbrellas on Monday the crowd began to sing, low at first but gathering strength from one another: "God save our gracious Queen ..." To hear that old song again was astonishingly moving. So familiar once, so unfamiliar now: a dull tune with dull words, but still able to bring forgotten emotions and old politics back from the dead. And there was the Queen, a Lazarus in lime green, in Australia again.

The ritual of official welcome on the sodden forecourt of the Opera House underlined the most obvious political truth of the tour: she's a visitor here. Bill Deane took her along the line of grandees standing under rather battered umbrellas, introducing her to the chief justice and the leader of the Opposition and so on. It's the same protocol for any distinguished visitor to our shores. What's done for Clinton and Mandela is done for the Queen. As she shook hands down the reception line the message was clear: she doesn't officially know these men who run "her" country. When the Queen is in Australia she is like any other visiting head of state, except she's ours.

Constitutional riddles were the last thing on the crowd's mind. More people came down to the Opera House to launch Mardi Gras or watch the New Year's fireworks, but the turnout for the Queen in this grey, wet coronation weather was just fine. They sang the old anthem and most of the new, and yelled hurrah and waved the flags handed out by the Monarchists

League: "Free flags, free flags." Guns fired so far offstage they could hardly be heard, and the band played Handel as she walked up and down lines of soldiers. She shook a few hands, took flowers from kids and disappeared down the Man O' War steps to lunch.

The fiction is that monarchy deprives our elected leaders of this sort of ceremonial glory. Nonsense. There was John Howard, without whom none of this would be happening, skittishly happy as he waited for the Queen to arrive, pecking Lady Deane on the cheek and giving Helena Carr a peck, too. There were no cheers for the governor or the governor-general, but there were more than a few for Howard. When the Queen stepped down from the Roller she looked happy enough. The Prime Minister was radiant.

Not so his wife. The values and moods of Janette Howard matter a great deal in this country. For most of his political life, Howard has focused his imagination on the possibilities of economic change. Social policy he's left to his instincts. No one has so influenced those very conservative instincts as this woman. In the presence of royalty, Mrs Howard's face is arresting. It suggests a kind of furious satisfaction. The Queen herself could never risk such a look of triumph.

To see the Queen in the flesh is to be reminded how diffident she is as she goes through the public performance of being our sovereign. She called at the National Institute of Dramatic Art on the Sydney leg of the tour and the administrator, Elizabeth Butcher, looked on the occasion almost as a student exercise. "Royal themes figure a lot in the plays we perform so it was an opportunity for the students to see a real Queen in the flesh." Well, the real thing doesn't command. She has the most famous face in the world but a curious lack of presence. She's polite to politicians, to officials and to children, polite and rather pleased. But she doesn't play to the crowd. There are no big gestures. If those NIDA kids paid close attention, they'll never ham up Shakespeare again.

Nor underestimate the raw pull of royalty. How is it that a country that overwhelmingly wants to ditch the Crown has opened itself to her as it has this week? Kim Beazley was skylarking in the line-up of VIPs at the forecourt welcome on Monday morning, but he was obediently there. And at lunch that day the republican premier of New South Wales, Bob Carr, gave another of his virtuoso speeches of welcome for the visiting great with slabs of Churchill and the Battle of Britain and a grovelling finale:

We have to realise, as the government and people of Britain clearly realise, that change and adjustment to new realities safeguard great institutions. This is the realisation which must guide us all in the continuing debate about Australia's constitutional future. Wherever that may take us in the new century, the second century of our Federation, the fourth oldest in the world after the United States, Canada and Switzerland, we know that we shall have no warmer wellwisher, no one outside Australia more knowledgeable about it and more concerned with Australia's welfare than Your Majesty.

That's quality, but it's still grovel.

Where has all the republican passion gone? In the face of the Queen it evaporates. We are a polite country but there was more than politeness in our response this week: a mess of affection, old loyalties and flattery in the presence of the Crown. We're pretty easy. There were no rallies planned, no calls for a boycott. In the streets there were as many angry Irish as determined republicans. How many? Hardly any. You have to wonder how serious Australia is about constitutional change.

Looking back now, one of the bravest acts in this non-saga was Paul Keating telling the Queen before a barbeque at Balmoral that he wanted to move Australia towards a republic. What she said then she repeated this week: it's up to us. She can hardly say anything different, and saying it again is pretty easy after the shemozzle of the referendum last year won the Crown in Australia an indefinite reprieve.

She spoke, too, this week about Aborigines. At any other time those few anodyne words would be passed over as expressions of simple decency. Not in John Howard's Australia. It was so subtle. Nothing she said about Aboriginal Australia's "legacy of economic and social disadvantage" contradicted the policy of her government in Canberra, but the mere saying of it was a political nudge good for Aborigines and deeply perplexing for those urban republicans grateful for her making even this little stand against the race politics of Australia.

The republican bastions of Mosman and Vaucluse melted ...

The Sydney Morning Herald, 25 March 2000

Australia's Olympic spirit

WE WERE ON OUR BEST BEHAVIOUR. Summer did the decent thing by coming in spring. The men won silver and the women won gold. We had this marvellous party. Medals dried up for a while. The weather turned. Then Cathy Freeman won that race. The sun came out. We blew up a few hundred tonnes of fireworks. Now after some sleep, we've stumbled down to survey the wreckage – and make a few resolutions. I know there are bigger issues to be considered here – the spirit of the nation, the economic wash-up, high hopes for reconciliation and perhaps the last gasp of the cultural cringe – but can I put something on the agenda so it doesn't get lost among these giants?

I speak of "girt" and the embarrassment of being reminded every time we won gold that we live in a nation "girt by sea". When crowds and athletes alike seemed to falter in the anthem, it wasn't because we didn't know the words or we weren't bursting with pride for our country, but because there are silly lines in that anthem. Just plain silly. So we mumble through them and let rip on the chorus. Can't we fix "girt"? If that's impossible, what can we fix in this country in the wake of these triumphant games?

The finishing line is still far out of sight in the last marathon event: arguing What the Olympics Mean for Australia. We can all join in. We don't have to train. No one is lurking with a little red paddle if our heels dance above the track. And until we've exhausted ourselves with post-mortems and resolutions, we can't really say the 27th Games of the Modern Era are over and done with.

Commentators this week split into two packs. The first feels that if we can pull this off, there's no limit to the big things Australia can now do.

Among the frontrunners of the other pack is the prime minister. Nothing flashy. Good over very long distances. His team has burnt off more sprinters than you can name. They're sticking to the long blue line that the triumph of the Sydney Games proves there's nothing much to fix in this wonderful country of ours. They are, to a person, the last defenders of "girt" in the English-speaking world. Proud of it. The natural heirs of those who saw that Melbourne in 1956 did nothing much to transform Australia. They're with us still, on both sides of parliament. It's been easy in the euphoria of the past few weeks in Sydney to imagine all this pride and goodwill will rub off on the politics of this country at once.

That's a dream.

In the next few days, we'll have to tackle the accounts. But for the moment, we're still in post-party euphoria, doing what we can to keep the good times going. Gossiping and remembering, swapping stories about the fools who fled to Bali for the games and those who stayed behind, stand-offish at first, then sucked into the excitement. That's Sydney's story. Once the games worked, Sydney forgot the knockers and the stuff-ups along the way, put out of its mind years of acrimony, hid anything that might get in the way of its brand-new identity as the world's Olympic City. Sydney has this fabulous knack of reinventing itself in this way whenever it wants: with massed fireworks and a good dose of amnesia.

My Olympics brought me some of the great experiences of my life: being in the stands for that Freeman race, a night at the pool when gold rained down on the Australian swimmers, two rounds of *Götterdämmerung* with Elizabeth Connell's Brunnhilde – a woman built superbly for singing or the hammer throw – the pleasure of being part of those immense and absolutely peaceful crowds at Homebush, and the moment the Balarinji red Qantas 747 flew over the Olympic stadium as that fine black singer Deborah Cheetham rehearsed for the opening ceremony under a full moon. At the ceremony itself, a couple of nights later, old Olympic hands among the journalists killed time before the show, talking "Atlanta this" and "Barcelona that" – until that lone horseman rode into the ring. That shut them up. From that moment, we didn't hear another word from those veterans about elsewhere. This was instantly and absolutely Sydney's show.

Before it's forgotten, I want to record the great Mandela rumour. As the athletes were parading into the stadium, a knot of American journalists in the stands were putting the finishing touches to the story that Nelson

Mandela "in a surprise move" had lit Sydney's Olympic flame. We read this stuff over their shoulders. I clambered down to quiz them. "Rumour," they explained. "Persistent rumour." New York had checked with Pretoria and official denials were being disbelieved. A couple of minutes later, a woman in a silver suit gave those Yanks a bit of work to do. That's the way it is at the Olympics. Getting it right is wonderful. Victory is what athletes cross the world for. But the crucial experience that gives the games their excitement is the dashing of high hopes. When the best of the world are competing, nothing is a dead cert. The favourite can go down at any time: ask Ian Thorpe, Susie O'Neill, Marion Jones and Ali Ezzine. And on the faces of the beaten favourites, you can see the true distance between silver and gold.

Running absolutely last at these Olympics was world peace. The Greek idea was to substitute athletics for war during the period of the games. It's not clear how well *ékécheiria* worked in the ancient world. A couple of years ago, our side stopped bombing Iraq for a week or so in honour of the Nagano Winter Games. Last year, the swimmer Daniel Kowalski went to the UN to propose the traditional motion that all hostilities should cease to allow the youth of the world to assemble in Sydney "in the cause of peace". The Koreas marched into the Olympic stadium under the same flag – and won a standing ovation – but in Sri Lanka, the Democratic Republic of Congo, Kashmir, Israel and Indonesia, wars ploughed on as their teams competed in Sydney. Indonesia won gold, silver and bronze.

Some Olympic mysteries were never solved. Why did the crowd give Mexico that great roar at the opening ceremony? Why do Russian swimmers wear thongs to the blocks? (Is there a tinea scare at the pool?) How come so many of the volunteers look like those nice men and women who once worked at DJs? Who won the synchronised swimming? Why do graceless slobs who lift weights bother to shave their armpits? Does no one ever learn that long-distance flash photography at night is a complete waste? How do those male gymnasts bounce on their own genitals without screaming? Can Roy and HG find some other word for "girt"?

The most impressive mystery is the goodwill that losers still show winners on the far side of the line – despite the fortunes made and lost by Olympic victories these days. That bombastic gold medal theme is soon flooding the stands, but for a moment, before the shouting dies away and that music blares, the athletes acknowledge one another's success. It may be through tears and gritted teeth, but they shake hands, they hug and kiss. Among the dozens of lessons we might learn from the Olympics, maybe we should put this one on the list, too: a little civility after ruthless competition.

The Sydney Morning Herald, 7 October 2000

Baying for
border protection

A GOOD RECITAL HALL MAKES applause sound great. Sydney's City Recital Hall is perfectly tuned so an audience can bask in the sound of its own clapping. It took the Liberal Party, professional even in this, to realise what's good for Bach and Boccherini will work to launch an election campaign. The hall offers tight security, no windows for yobbos to bash as they did in Parramatta last time and, despite the empty seats in the gods, great rolling breakers of applause.

For Philip Ruddock, the protector of Australia's borders, this meant a tumult of whistling, stamping and clapping. The needle went right off the dial, not once but twice. The first time he stood and took a bow. The second time he kept modestly in his seat, inclined his head and mouthed "thank you very much" at a beaming John Howard on stage.

Wherever the Tampa tactics lead Australia in the years to come, those of us in the City Recital Hall yesterday will remember the sight and the sound of a white, prosperous audience baying for border protection. They know it's the winning ticket, and John Howard has found it for them. He is a genius of sorts: he looks this country in the face and sees us not as we wish we were, not as we one day might be, but exactly as we are. The political assessment is ruthlessly realistic. Only the language is coy. But who has ever admitted to playing the race card?

"National security," he said, "is about a proper response to terrorism. It's also about having a far-sighted, strong, well-thought-out defence policy. It is also about having an uncompromising view about the fundamental right of this country to protect its borders. It's about this nation saying to the world we are a generous open-hearted people taking more refugees on a per capita basis than any nation except Canada, we have a proud record of welcoming people from 140 different nations. But we will decide who comes to this country and the circumstances in which they come."

As the applause rolled on, Howard gripped each side of the lectern hard, straining upwards a little as if trying to catch the light. He is very good at reading applause. He knows when to smile, when to gesture in triumph and when, as now, to stay resolutely grim.

Still they clapped. All the old premiers of New South Wales brought out for the occasion; the shattered ranks of the Liberal Left, which once rolled Howard for suggesting a faint shadow of the Tampa policy; most of the cabinet; a squad of sitting members and senators; Liberal contenders for hopeless seats that are now suddenly winnable; and the Howard family, wife, children and brothers superbly turned out in the front row.

Up in the second tier, Channel Nine's Laurie Oakes and the ABC's Jim Middleton were standing with their backs to the stage. This looked, at first, like an Aboriginal gesture of disapproval that other journalists weren't brave enough to join. Then it became clear they were waiting to do their pieces to camera when Howard finished. He spoke for over an hour. Howard is not as funny, young and dangerous as his deputy, Peter Costello. He doesn't let himself use laughter. But this was a very effective Howard performance, on song right to the end: "I believe my instincts, my energy, my experience, my successes to date, and my sheer commitment to the land I love best equip me for the job."

There was a standing ovation. He took what bushmen call a dingo's breakfast – a sip of water and a quick look around – then plunged into the applauding crowd. The recital hall rang with a sound very like winning.

The Sydney Morning Herald, 29 October 2001

Beazley's last stand

IN THE HUNTER THEY STILL DO things by the book. On a blustery day at Raymond Terrace, Kim Beazley was piped onto the picnic ground by the United Mine Workers Federation Band. He beamed as he marched behind the kilts and drums into an old, white crowd of CMFEU supporters and their grandchildren. It's a crowd that reminds you a great gut is an old Labor tradition. There are guys here who make Kim Beazley look Olympic fit.

Beazley loves, and is good at, this: the picnic, the band, three cheers, the warm-up speeches from the union heavies, who talk about "workers" and "comrades" without the chic irony of Labor in town. Beazley is affable, approachable, buoyant. And he gives a really fine stump speech, without notes, his black suit flapping in the wind, his words plain, his message clear: "It's time this out-of-touch bunch were gone, time that ordinary Australians had a break, time they had a government on their side."

The wind blew the applause away. Two months ago, this man was coasting to victory. Australia was about to have its second West Australian, Rhodes scholar, conservative Labor prime minister; the second being the protégé of the first, Bob Hawke. He would be the first Labor prime minister since Chifley with solid experience of government before taking the top job; one of the longest-serving ministers in the history of federal Labor; a man so loved by his fractious party that it unanimously elected him deputy prime minister in 1995 and leader of the Opposition in 1996.

Until two months ago, nothing had really gone wrong in Kim Beazley's career. At an early age, he set out to win. He had ambitions rather than causes; he picked as few quarrels as he could with enemies inside and outside the party; he left the party bosses alone and the unions alone; he allied himself with winners. He won every time: a seat, a place on the front bench, leadership of the party. Even his loss to John Howard in 1998 was a victory. No one expected Beazley could come so close. Now he's gambling everything on one more win. "That's right. I mean, this is it for me."

Labor doesn't pretend Beazley is one of its great leaders. They don't speak of him as another Curtin or another Hawke. Beazley is the party's best candidate, and until a couple of months ago he looked a shoo-in to be the party's next prime minister. But on August 27, Beazley woke to learn a Norwegian freighter heading for Australian waters was ignoring orders from Canberra to take 433 rescued asylum seekers back to Indonesia. For the past year Labor strategists have wondered how Howard would try to save himself. One senior strategist close to Beazley saw the key problem for the Coalition as the loss of votes to One Nation. "I came to the conclusion about six months ago that there was no way for Howard to re-embrace One Nation. Therefore he was gone. Even if he managed to put everything else back together, he wouldn't be able to do it, because he didn't have the last couple of per cent he needed to capture Sydney's west, or the NSW Central Coast or North Queensland.

"And I was wrong. It shows you that unpredictable things happen in politics because, even knowing the problem, it never occurred to me that an issue would arise like Tampa, which would allow Howard to waltz around Hanson, claim the constituency for himself; indeed, ignite the rest of relatively civilised Australia to feel a sense of solidarity about this preservation of the borders."

The polls crashed five per cent for Beazley and set the Coalition's primary vote rock-hard. The terrorist attacks on New York and Washington a fortnight later were far less of a problem for the contender: Australia knows Beazley is trained for war. He would be the greatest military enthusiast in the top job since Billy Hughes. But the Tampa crisis made nonsense of all the familiar policy differences between the parties. Howard had put a shaft into the core of this country, and up came race. To those people appalled by the treatment of the Tampa asylum seekers and by the Labor Party then falling in with the government's tactics – pushing off boats, setting up camps on Pacific islands, making life even more miserable for refugees who do make it to Australia – Beazley is discreetly appealing for understanding. The message is: these are terrible times and we have no choice but to do what we are doing. For Labor, what's at stake here is victory. For Australia, of course, something more important is up for grabs.

The night before his expedition to the CMFEU picnic on the Hunter, Beazley and his wife, Susie Annus, met arts leaders in the Bellevue Hotel in Paddington. She is across the lot: film, music and painting. He reads history and biography and collects icons. This meeting would once have been a gala event in a big city theatre, with hoopla and television cameras. But in an age where so much depends on wooing the voters of One Nation (arts policy: no public funding), it's considered wiser for Beazley to meet arts leaders over a few quiet drinks in a civilised pub. He spoke of "bitter angels" gathering over society and the part artists play in making sense of times like these. "Politicians just skate across the surface," he told them, sweeping the air with his index finger. "Following the deeper rhythms of society is what you do." He was on the stump again, and again performing well. Indeed, he was beguiling. Beazley is one of those politicians with the knack of suggesting he's built on a more generous scale than his record might suggest; that inside him there's a big soul biding its time; that victory would see him grow.

Next day over lunch – for Beazley: two Diet Cokes and a caesar salad – he explained those bitter angels were John Howard and the Howard government. "He has a diminished view about the character of Australian society, a very constricted, unambitious view of the capacity of this country internationally. He's been divisive in dealing with working Australians; he's set his face against elements of reconciliation; he's struggled to diminish the emphasis in this country on us being a multicultural society. All these sorts of things, which most Australians live cheerfully with, he has sought to undermine."

So why hasn't Labor been able to stop that? "There's something Paul Keating said once which I think is absolutely true: an election changes a country. A government in many ways decides the character of the society and an opposition doesn't."

This is Beazley's mantra. At the pub the night before he'd said: "In Opposition we are dealt the cards we have to play." It's Beazley's answer to those who say Labor should have fought harder through the Howard years to keep its own image of Australia alive. Labor strategists defend the poll-driven caution of the Beazley Opposition by talking about the "convergence" of modern politics, the imperative to woo One Nation's followers and the vice-like grip of modern economics on a labour party. As the government channelled money to private health funds, cut capital gains tax, censored the internet, baulked at anti-discrimination law reform, ticked funding for rich schools and passed extremely harsh refugee laws, the party's message to doubters was: don't worry, we'll fix it in office. This approach to Opposition was tailor-made for Beazley, but what would be so different in government?

It is clearer now than ever that Labor's tactics depended on making Howard hated. But Beazley was not the man for that job. He has had Howard on the ropes but never landed the knockout blow that announces the arrival of the next big winner in the ring as Gough Whitlam did in Opposition by making mincemeat of Billy McMahon. Of course, Howard is no McMahon. Beazley didn't even try to make his opponent a figure of fun. Beazley has never laid a line on Howard as destructive as the "flip-flopping" accusation over Tampa, with its subtle, insulting allusion to Beazley's bulk. He has never delivered a quip as cruel as Howard's query about Beazley's "ticker". Friends, enemies and the press still talk ticker years later. One of the miners at the CMFEU picnic asked: "Do you reckon he's got the ticker?" The crowd on the riverbank called: "You bet!" They were praising their leader but Howard was setting the terms.

*

Kim Beazley was five when his father returned from the coronation with a new enthusiasm: Moral Rearmament (MRA). Beazley Snr had gone as a delegate of the ALP because, after eight years in Canberra, he was a man with a big future in the party. But this new passion changed the public and private life of the Beazleys. MRA was a Christian cult dedicated to the reform of public life – essentially the defeat of communism through the spread of "absolute moral standards of honesty, purity, unselfishness and love".

Every evening the Beazley children gathered to go over their shortcomings of the day. The rule of the Beazley house was that all conflict must be settled and settled quickly. "You didn't let the sun set on your quarrels. Whatever you might say in terms of an apology or whatever, you may or not mean. But it was done." There are families that raise kids to honour profound differences. "That wasn't our household, that's true. Does that mean I'm a bit more inclined to consensus? It may well be. It may well mean that."

The political life of Beazley Snr was now on the line. He had one of the safest seats in parliament, John Curtin's old stamping ground of Fremantle, but his preselection was always under threat from the sclerotic left machine run by the ALP state secretary, Joe Chamberlain. What saved Beazley Snr and now buttresses his son was the loyalty of the right-wing, conservative Shop Assistants Union. Loyalty is a big issue in the lives of both these men. The Beazleys aren't betrayers. Beazley Jnr has great difficulty firing people, breaking with causes and choosing between loyalties.

In 1954 Beazley Snr led the walkout from the party's Hobart conference that ended in the great Labor Split. He stayed behind in the party, a man of principle whose prospects in the ALP were extremely uncertain. "We were very conscious of my father living on the margin." After nearly thirty years in Opposition, his reward was to be Gough Whitlam's minister for education. "He never complained. He was always grateful for his career, and grateful for his three years as a minister. Lots of people told me, 'If your father had done this' or 'If he hadn't done that ...'" Beazley Jnr recognises this fed his wish to have a political career much more about winning than his father's was: "There is a big difference between us. I've certainly had a much more pragmatic approach to politics than he had, and a much better opportunity. He's more of a loner than I am." There was this urging him on too: Labor lost all the federal elections of his childhood – 1955, 1958, 1961, 1963 and 1966.

After a year in India and Europe evangelising for MRA, young Beazley turned up at the University of Western Australia in 1967 to study history. He immediately joined the university ALP Club. A much underrated qualification for a political career is a love of meetings. Beazley went to them all. By the middle of the year he was elected club treasurer, and while still a teenager was a delegate to the state executive.

There's a lesson for all budding politicians in the university careers of Kim Beazley Jnr, John Howard and Bob Carr. All three put their studies at risk by being tyro politicians and all are remembered for their oddly conservative behaviour on the campus. Howard was thought straitlaced, even for the 1950s. A decade later, John Dawkins's verdict on his fellow student Beazley Jnr was "conservative in every way, really God squad". That's never really left Beazley. He drifted out of MRA but remained strongly attached to his underlying High Anglican faith. After marrying two Catholic women and raising three Catholic daughters, he's long considered crossing to Rome. But as always with the Beazleys, old loyalties are hard to break.

So he worships with the Anglicans, prays and meditates. In his biography of the contender, Peter FitzSimons quotes Beazley's sister Merrilyn Wasson: "He has always had a sense of something beyond himself."

Beazley is a worshipper of causes and people: Christ, MRA, the Labor Party, his father, the US–Australia alliance, military power, Mick Young, Brian Burke for too long, Neville Wran and Bob Hawke. It isn't a question of credulity but a habit of mind. By nature, Beazley is a devoted enthusiast. He's also a pessimist and never gloomier than when things seem to be going right.

After Oxford and his marriage to Mary Paltridge – Labor daughter of Liberal politician Sir Shane – Beazley lectured in history at Murdoch University. The subject closest to his heart was strategic affairs, particularly of the Indian Ocean. Politically, he had taken a bold strategic decision of his own: he set up as a lone political ally in the west of the NSW Right. "They do like to win elections, which is not to be sneered at." Those who believe Beazley has been hiding, all these years, the soul of a radical social reformer should look closely at his allegiances: first to the NSW machine, then to the Shop Assistants Union, the clerks' union and the Irish-Catholic right-wing Labor machine in Western Australia. He is much too substantial a politician to be their creature, but he is their ally.

Out-manoeuvred for his father's safe seat of Fremantle, he won preselection for the marginal Labor seat of Swan. Every prime minister in the past fifty years has built his career on a safe seat. But Beazley found himself until recently with an electorate he could lose at any poll. Once or twice he held it by only a couple of hundred votes. He admits this has made a "huge" difference to his political life. "It does make you more cautious, that is true. It probably makes you a bit more sympathetic. It makes you a bit less willing to experiment with human happiness. They're likely to take the view that if you experiment with their human happiness they might do something about yours."

Not that his real passion in these early years was much of an issue in Swan. Beazley went to parliament in 1980 with a burning ambition to reform the armed forces. Three years later he was a minister in the Hawke government and all his plans fell into place. He was minister for defence for five and a half years before Hawke forced him into civilian portfolios to widen his experience. Hawke's fall was a terrible time of divided loyalties for Beazley. He became deputy prime minister to Keating in 1995, and when Labor was routed in 1996, Beazley was the most senior, most loved and most presentable man left standing.

"It's the worst thing that can happen to you," Carr said. "It happened to me: having to take over the party after one of those monumental defeats. He said to me in that first term as Opposition leader, 'What I did in my political career up till this point I did for myself.' He meant that he got a lot of personal satisfaction out of it. 'What I do now, I'm doing for the party.' He recognised he was in the realm of hard slog. It had been an intellectually challenging, exciting experience to be a senior minister with responsibility for huge policy decisions, but as Opposition leader with a score of seats behind, you're down to earth with a thud: spending your weekends in airport lounges trying to beat up a comment on what a minister said on the Laurie Oakes program. What a vision of hell: to be Opposition leader at the federal level."

*

A glass roof had been thrown over the betting ring at Randwick so 1000 could be fed there at a charity do. In the second week of the campaign there was a Labor fundraiser at Randwick lightly disguised as "A Tribute to Neville Wran". The faithful kicked in $400,000 and the speakers praised Wran, laying it on with a trowel for his miraculous knack of winning elections. It was late when Wran himself rose to speak, old, grey and as good as ever, at the microphone. You have to listen. He can take a sentence anywhere and you must follow every word or risk missing the jokes, the barbs, the twists of his thinking. To say Beazley can't match this at the microphone isn't particularly damning. Few can. And there's menace with the humour. Menace was always part of Wran's attraction, a dangerous sense that he could be a bastard for or against you so you might as well give him your vote. Beazley doesn't have that, either. He projects an absolutely decent sense that he'd be sorry, very sorry, but would understand if you voted for his opponent.

Wran, the great winner, Beazley's backer, the Labor hard man, the speaker who doesn't make a slip at the microphone, very deliberately said this: "The race card has been introduced into this election. It's a card, and an introduction, which we and our children will live to regret. We live in a country in which, despite the smouldering resentment and objections to newcomers, we have handled it all thus far. We have been able to run our country in a sensitive, compassionate and dignified way." That morning, newspapers had carried pictures of children drowned in a refugee boat on their way to Australia. "When I saw those three little girls, something told me Mr Ruddock was wrong. We're not dealing with a problem here, we're dealing with people."

Next day Howard rubbed it in. "If the Labor Party's policy on illegal immigration is, as Mr Beazley claims, the same as ours, then Mr Wran's criticism last night was a criticism of Mr Beazley as well."

Labor was trapped. What followed was pitiful. Trailing around St Mary's Villa Nursing Home in the inner-western Sydney suburb of Concord that morning, Beazley hung grimly to the official Labor line that race was not an issue at the 2001 poll. Anyone wanting to know what Wran was on about should ask him. He promised to keep saying race was not on the election agenda right up to polling day, "because I'll tell you what I think this election is about: a fair society. And I'm going to keep plugging away at that until hell freezes over."

Australians aren't fools. It's already clear to many what is happening here and Labor's refusal to deal with it. The Liberal grandee Malcolm Fraser has added his voice to those pointing at race. John Hewson, the loser in the elections of 1993, described Howard in *the Australian Financial Review* yesterday as a manipulator of prejudice. "At the very least he undoubtedly tapped what is a latent racial prejudice in significant sections of the Australian community."

When the programs each side is offering in this election are so modest and so similar, what matters most this time is the sight of both sides refusing to challenge what is going on here. This election is as much about the damage done along the way as who wins in the end. Beazley is not calling this contest for what it is: there's still a hope he can win. That's what matters for Labor, too.

Curiously, Beazley would have had a better chance of getting away with it were he a less honourable man. All the polls say Labor lost ground by "flip-flopping" the day the *Tampa* was boarded by SAS troops, with the party first offering the government support, then refusing to pass Howard's extraordinary Border Protection Bill. It was the decent thing to do, but a decent man is paying the price. Of course, Beazley and the party then collapsed when they read their pollsters' findings. They passed all the refugee bills Howard put up to parliament in the days that followed. The upshot for Labor was the worst of both worlds: there are now laws on the books that the party had been blocking for years and the public isn't grateful.

On a bus to a bush airport a few days ago, Beazley was relaxed and reflective. It was big-picture time. I asked him whether politicians were born to disappoint.

"Yes," he replied. "Particularly idealists, not that there are many of them about." We reached the airport and he hauled himself out of the bus for perhaps the millionth flight of his life, this time to Adelaide for the next leg of the endless campaign.

"We'll win this one," he said, and paused. "We'll win if they're thinking about domestic issues on polling day. If they're not ... well, we'll have problems."

The Sydney Morning Herald, 3 November 2001

Arne Rinnan, sailor

BY SOME MIRACLE, the Wallenius Wilhelmsen Line managed to keep itself clear of the political storm that broke around the *Tampa*. Yes, that was its ship sitting stubbornly in the waters off Christmas Island, but all through the election the oldest and biggest shipping line in Norway insisted this was just a search and rescue gone wrong. No more. In Oslo the other day Wilhelm Wilhelmsen, owner of the line, revealed he had written to John Howard congratulating him on his re-election and suggesting a case of good Australian red was due for his contribution to the victory. Back in Canberra the prime minister's office is not amused. No letter has been found and no red wine has been dispatched. A spokesman said: "Maybe the letter is on its way by sea."

Wilhelmsen was talking to the press after an Oslo ceremony in which a once obscure employee of the line, Arne Rinnan, was awarded the Order of St Olav, First Class, by King Harald. Norway's king commended Rinnan for the seamanship he had shown, "saving 438 people in distress at sea who would have died without him". The order is not a knighthood as it is understood in Bellevue Hill and Papua New Guinea. When Rinnan returns to Australia on his last voyage with the *Tampa* in May, we won't be calling him Sir Arne. But this was a high honour, a gong that matters.

The world and Canberra disagree about Rinnan. In this season of honours, the *Tampa*'s master has just won second place in Germany's annual media quest to find the "best fellow human being" of the year. New York's mayor, Rudolph Giuliani, with 23.9 per cent of votes, narrowly beat the Norwegian skipper, with 21.8 per cent. A few days after this, the Anders

Wilhelmsen Foundation in Oslo gave him the 2001 Sailor's Prize for show-ing wisdom, charity and firmness in the rescue.

The idea that Australia might have thanked him for his efforts provokes a great roar of laughter from Rinnan, who is in Kongsberg, south of Oslo, about to celebrate Christmas with his family. He is a man who laughs a lot, but this really tickles him. "I haven't heard any word from Mr Howard." No case of red wine will find its way to Arne Rinnan, nor does the Norwegian stand a chance of being mentioned in the New Year's honours list. That doesn't matter a damn. Wherever you stand on the *Tampa* controversy, it's clear no one had such an impact on Australia in 2001 as this bluff, practical man who continues to say, every time he is interviewed: "I have only been rescuing people at sea, and the rest was politics."

Yes, but what politics.

This was not Rinnan's first sea rescue. "We picked up one Cuban between Cuba and Florida one time but he walked off the ship in Miami." It was the mid-1980s; the man was heading for the United States in a rubber dinghy and both the ship and the authorities played the operation by the book. "He just walked off the ship in Miami together with the immigration officer."

Nor was Rinnan a stranger to having a ship seized by the armed forces of a friendly power. "It was American troops. We had some explosives on board and we were going from Italy to Yugoslavia and there was a blockade outside the Adriatic Sea." This was the 1980s again and the early stages of the civil war in Yugoslavia. "That company at that time had not declared that cargo correctly. We were arrested and had to go into Brindisi and clear up the mess. The explosives were cargo for Jedda. It was a big misunderstanding."

But in his long career at sea – he joined the Wilhelmsen Line as a deck-hand when he was a kid – Rinnan had never received a call like the one from the Department of Immigration and Multicultural Affairs (DIMA) that came early on August 27. DIMA was threatening him and his ship with mas-sive financial penalties for people smuggling if he did not turn the *Tampa* around and head to Indonesia with the 400 or so Afghans he had just pulled from a sinking fishing boat. "That was the first time," said Rinnan, laughing grimly. "The first time, yes." From an impeccable source, *The Sydney Morn-ing Herald* now knows the order for the *Tampa* to turn back to Indonesia originated with the secretary to the Prime Minister's Department, Max Moore-Wilton. He was woken about 3 am or 4 am and told the *Tampa* was heading towards Australian waters. He directed those threats be made to

Rinnan and rang personally to alert the Australian head of the Wallenius Wilhelmsen Line, Peter Dexter.

As details continue to emerge about the extraordinary events of that night – and we still need to know a great deal more – it's clear there was an unbridgeable gap from the start between Canberra's objectives and Rinnan's responsibilities. Canberra wanted to send messages to people smugglers and the electorate in those election weeks. But Arne Rinnan was responsible for all those lives on his ship. What made the *Tampa* crisis a defining and shameful episode was Canberra's attitude to those lives. We can argue until the cows come home about the conventions of sea rescue, the evils of people smuggling and Indonesia's responsibilities in the Indian Ocean. What can't be denied is that the master of the *Tampa* believed after threats to his crew and threats of suicides among the Afghans that the lives and safety of some 500 people would best be protected by taking his ship to Christmas Island. That's a decision for the master of a ship to make, but the government of Australia stood in Rinnan's way.

This is not like us.

Some of the honours that have come to Rinnan since are trivial. Some matter. All were given, essentially, for his focus on the lives in his care. All are measures of the regard Australia lost by these events. We didn't, as some people claim, suddenly become a pariah nation on the night of August 26–27. But the verdict of the world has been rough. All nations protect their borders, but at the year's end none has come forward to back Canberra's decision to protect our borders in this way, in these circumstances. Right now, 2001 looks like the year we trashed the brand.

In a matter-of-fact exchange with the *Herald* this week, Rinnan gave fresh details of Australia's attitude to the lives in his care. How many of the asylum seekers were ill is still a matter of controversy. Howard has been at pains to belittle Rinnan's concerns. Rinnan had no medical expertise. His crew treated the ill on advice radioed from the Haukeland Hospital in Bergen, which specialises in rescue emergencies. For days Rinnan implored Australia to send a doctor from Christmas Island. It was to force this issue that he decided, with the backing of the shipping line, to take the *Tampa* into Australian waters.

Rinnan got doctors, but he also got the SAS. When the commanding officer reached the bridge, Rinnan protested: "I've only been asking for medical assistance." Rinnan was warned the responsibility for the welfare of the shipwrecked people rested entirely on his shoulders and he was then threatened: "They say they would not give medical assistance on board before the ship was outside twelve nautical miles." He called the SAS's bluff. "After half an hour or something they started giving them medical assistance."

Rinnan was pleased. "After a couple of days everybody was on their feet again. But they give them lots of vitamins and some strong stuff to get them back to normal life again." He said of an SAS doctor: "He took one hour to examine 438 people, so I really don't know how seriously he had done that. They started treating one lady who was seven to eight months pregnant with stomach troubles and she was on a drip for three days, I think. She was really sick."

As the days passed, Australia continued to insist the *Tampa* take its human cargo to Indonesia. But early on, Canberra knew there was no real hope Indonesia would accept the *Tampa* refugees. Rinnan has told the *Herald* that he, too, knew Indonesia's position as early as the day after the rescue. "We found it out because we had a radio and some news from Norway. We were in daily contact by telephone with the people in the head office in Norway." Again, the core issue here was indifference to the predicament of the people on the *Tampa*. If the ship sailed with the asylum seekers on board, it faced a long voyage to an uncertain port. Rinnan would be confronted once again with all the problems of violence and despair that persuaded him to sail for Christmas Island in the first place. Canberra didn't care.

That's not like us.

Through all this, the Wallenius Wilhelmsen Line conducted a carefully nuanced response to Canberra. There was never a public brawl with the Howard government, nor did the shipping line feed the electoral controversy that ensued. Though the red-hulled ship sitting off Christmas Island was the image of the elections of 2001, the line kept insisting only issues of search and rescue were at stake. It was masterful. Rinnan, the shipping line and his "passengers" all kept clear of the courts. This greatly disappointed the Melbourne lawyers fighting Canberra. A few scribbled words from one of the asylum seekers asking a lawyer for help would have transformed the case. Rinnan stood in the way. "We had only rescued people in distress so we were a little bit afraid of taking part in this as far as I understand from Oslo. That could complicate the whole matter."

But it was the lawyers who negotiated the transfer of the asylum seekers to HMAS *Manoora* for their voyage to Nauru. After eleven dramatic days, the Pacific solution kicked in and the *Tampa* could sail. At the elections a few weeks later Australia overwhelmingly endorsed Canberra's tactics, but not this little corner of Australia. Christmas Island paid tribute to the *Tampa* by farewelling the ship with fireworks. "We were allowed to go into one mile of the coast. Everyone was smiling that night, you see. We brought out some beer and we were using the whistle and turning off and on the lights on deck. We were very pleased to leave."

That's more like us.

Arne Rinnan has been to Australia many times since he came here first as a deckhand in 1960. "I was, as a matter of fact, in *The Fremantle Post*, a big picture of me up the mast spray-painting." But he has seen nothing of the country beyond its harbours. "That is correct. Only seaports." Perhaps in his retirement he will return and get to know the place? Rinnan laughs. "Maybe. No promises."

Sydney Morning Herald, 22 December 2001

Pink Pages

A night out at the Cross

A PARADE OF HOMOSEXUALS CELEBRATING International Gay Solidarity Day in Sydney on the night of Saturday June 24 led to more arrests and violence than has been seen in the city for seven years. On that same day in San Francisco 240,000 people turned out to celebrate. The city funded the march. There were no serious incidents. In Sydney, the march was never more than 2000 strong but ended with fifty-three arrests.

It was a great night. Sydney hasn't seen a mass arrest like that since the Springbok game in July 1971, when 140 people were arrested in the course of an afternoon. From a single demonstration there hasn't been a bigger haul since the September Moratorium in 1970. There are allegations of bashings later at Darlinghurst police station, and when the defendants turned up to court on Monday morning they found a massive deployment of police closing the courts.

The police had their heads that weekend.

The marchers clogged Kings Cross at midnight on a Saturday night, but the police had a couple of opportunities to disperse them before choosing to act in a stretch of the Cross where dispersal was possible. Peter de Waal, one of the marchers, has written to Wran: "My estimation is that it would have taken the marchers fifteen to twenty minutes to pass through Darlinghurst Road and then disperse into William Street, Bayswater Road, King's Cross Road and Victoria Street. The violent operations at Darlinghurst Road by the police and thugs took forty-five to sixty minutes, consequently holding up the traffic twice as long."

It was violent, but it was not the police who were injured. Sergeant

Murray of police public relations checked around the stations for *The National Times*. Police had come from Central, Paddington and Waverley to reinforce the Darlinghurst force. "They've had none off duty," said Murray. "There have been some charges of assault, of course. One constable was bitten by a woman on the thumb."

The men involved came predominantly from No. 3 Division: Darlinghurst police station, about which there is a constant stream of complaints of harassment of homosexuals. That station's beat takes in the area of homosexual nightlife in Sydney. Police continue to photograph and take names and addresses of people they think are homosexual. Many see homosexuals as criminals, and to many of them, that Saturday night march was a march of criminals. This is an antagonism of long standing.

A journalist who has been working the police rounds for years told *The National Times*, "As a personal observation I'd say that if the police were rougher than is normal for NSW coppers, it would be a combination of the category of the marchers and the fact that most of the police would have had a few drinks, it being Saturday night and all."

*

Superintendent Reg Douglas is the policeman whose job it was to supervise marches and demonstrations in Sydney. Despite the fact that a permit had been taken out four days before the parade, he was not informed. He told *The National Times*: "It might have been different if I had." The man who actually supervised the extraordinary police operation on Saturday night was Inspector Ken Miller. He was not available for comment. Douglas said, "The first Miller knew about it was at 10 pm that night when he arrived for night duty. It was sprung on him, so to speak."

The police had half an hour to prepare.

The organisers of the parade – they called it a mardi gras – had picked a route that was too short, and gave the crowd nowhere to go. The organiser who applied for the permit, Lance Gowland, thought the police had agreed that the parade could stop outside the bars of Oxford Street, that singing and dancing would be allowed in the street and in Hyde Park, where the crowd would disperse. The permit did not say this and when the parade moved off from Taylor Square at 10.30 pm the police kept it moving.

About 1000 people moved down Oxford Street. It was more popular than organisers and police had expected. The crowd was euphoric. They chanted, "Out of the bars and into the streets" and "Ho-ho-ho homosexual." A loudspeaker van played music. There were dancers on the van. But the police kept it moving. In only twenty minutes it had reached Hyde Park. The police disconnected the amplifier and drove the truck away. In the confusion two men were arrested. A chant went up, "To the Cross, to the Cross." Without the truck, the organisers had no way of marshalling the crowd. In what followed the police did not use loud hailers themselves to try to direct or disperse it.

At the top of William Street the police had blocked all streets opposite and to the right, but left clear the road to the left. It was the only way the parade could go. The police, in fact, funnelled the marchers into the Cross. It was about 11.30.

The steam had gone out of the parade when it got to the El Alamein Fountain, but wagons were drawing up, and the feeling in the crowd was to disperse and to get out of the Cross. The mardi gras atmosphere had disappeared. Elizabeth Bay Road was blocked by paddy wagons, but the police had cleared traffic from Darlinghurst Road so the parade moved back along its own tracks. It was almost certainly what the police intended.

The front of the parade moved past the only side streets in Darlinghurst Road. One of the marchers said, "Where they halted people, there was nowhere they could disperse. The footpaths were packed on either side. It was like New Year's Eve at the Cross." What followed was clearly designed to make arrests, not to clear the traffic.

"I saw those headlights. I'll never forget those headlights," said a woman at the front of the procession who saw the four paddy wagons bearing down on them, their sirens blaring. Another bystander said, "It seemed that people would be killed by them. It was terrifying." Two more wagons drove through the crowd from the rear and cut off the retreat to the side streets. About 200 people were trapped, and the rest of the procession pressed up behind.

Arrests began after a couple of minutes of general shuffling and confusion. The first was a man who walked between the wagons at the William Street end. He was seized from behind, and a witness said, "People began to protest about that because he hadn't done anything. The protest wasn't terribly heavy, but then the police began to grab people by the hair, feet, tits."

There was a lull for a few seconds after the first two or three arrests. The centre of the road was clear and the marchers were pressed against the footpath crowds. Then someone threw a full yellow plastic garbage can onto the bonnet of one of the wagons and the garbage spilled over the truck. It was the signal for the real business to begin. "Within five minutes it was a battlefield," said one of the marchers. The noise of chanting and shouting was tremendous. Police dragged people from the side of the road towards the wagons. Some of these resisted.

The melee was joined by passers-by, bikies, and apparently some residents of the Cross. All the windows were full. "Everyone in the Cross was watching," said a bystander. There was crying, screaming and panic. One of the parade marshals climbed onto a garbage bin outside Woolworths. "I saw an area of people fighting, wrestling and screaming. I thought something had to be done," he said. He found an officer who he was told was in charge and said, "I want to tell people to disperse, but we haven't got any PA system. Have you got any?" The officer replied, "Don't worry about it. Leave it."

The melee continued for half an hour. Witnesses told *The National Times* they saw a young man thrown into a paddy wagon and allege they saw police repeatedly slamming the wagon door on his legs. More wagons arrived at the William Street end and these were ferrying people to Darlinghurst police station. Fifty had been arrested. A passer-by who watched the vans being driven up Victoria Street has given a barrister a statement that she saw one of the paddy wagons go past at speed in the empty street and then brake suddenly. She heard screams coming from inside the truck.

*

Lawyers, doctors and bail money were fetched to Darlinghurst. A couple had been deputed to bring bail money for the night but one had gone to the opera and the other had forgotten to bring the cash. It hadn't seemed a high priority when the planning was done.

A solicitor, John Terry, was among the first lawyers to arrive at Darlinghurst. He found police blocking the entrance of the station. "I said, 'My name is Terry; I am a solicitor. I wish to see the desk sergeant.' The police constable said, 'Why? You can't come in here.' I said, 'I wish to speak to him about the arrests at Kings Cross tonight. How many people were arrested?' The officer said, 'You can't come past this doorway. If you do you will be trespassing and you will be arrested.'"

Terry named two people he knew to be in the cells. He said, "You can't refuse me access to my client. You know what Driscoll's case says." Another officer replied, "Look, just fuck off, mate. You're not in court now."

Terry and two barristers, Mackrell and Wynn, argued their way in, and after some lengthy obstruction began to interview clients and take instructions.

A doctor had been trying for some time to get into the station. He had heard there was an injured man in the cells. After more than an hour's argument he was allowed in to examine the man. The doctor said, "He had bruises on the head, ribs, stomach, arms and legs. He was in shock. His left lower leg was particularly swollen to about twice its normal size. I suspected a broken fibula." He insisted he be taken to St Vincent's Hospital for X-ray. The injured man was the first out of the station, at 4 am.

A crowd of forty or fifty had followed the wagons to Darlinghurst. There was intermittent chanting and cheering from them. The police made several arrests from this group which witnesses say were conspicuously brutal. Witnesses allege that a girl was tackled by three police, one of whom held her by the hair and pulled her head down sharply onto the footpath several times. This is confirmed by the girl, who told *The National Times* that she then fell unconscious. Witnesses say she was subsequently pulled by arm and her hair into the door of the station.

A loudmouth in the crowd sprang forward and beat his fists on the bonnet of a paddy wagon. A barrister has collected witnesses who say the man was grabbed by four or five police, dragged into the station garage by his hair and had his head, still held by the hair, beaten against the iron gates of the garage and the side mirror of a van. He was then dragged out of sight by his hair.

Inside the station the atmosphere remained tense. The arrested people were being processed with extreme slowness. During this, a witness alleged he saw a woman sitting in a dock, "hit by a policeman very heavily on the left side of the face with a closed fist".

About 4 am the police decided to move the twenty-one women they held in one cell down to Central police station in the city. They were to load them into three paddy wagons. A policeman came to the gates of the station garage where the wagons were drawn up. He had in his hand an iron bar about fifty to sixty centimetres long. A solicitor came up to the officer, introduced himself and asked, "Why have you got that baton? Hasn't there been enough violence for one night? You have a baton. You are not wearing a number and neither are any of the police here."

There were by then about fifteen police around the trucks. The officer said, "You want to watch yourself, or you'll be in too."

When the women drove off, the long process of bailing proceeded. It quickened when the new shift of police came on, and the last prisoners were out of Darlinghurst at 8.30 am. The police had only to fingerprint and release the women at Central. They arrived about 4.30 am. None were released until 7 am and the last was not out until 9.30 am. A barrister there commented, "It seemed designed to delay their release as long as possible."

The police had laid three charges of assault; one of malicious injury (police uniform); five of failure to observe a direction; nine of resisting arrest; four of offensive behaviour; ten of unseemly words; eighteen of hindering police; and nineteen of unlawful procession.

*

Premier and Minister for Police Neville Wran came on Channel ten news on Sunday evening. "These sorts of things happen," he said. "I think it is unfortunate that a couple of police had to receive hospital attention, as well as some of the people involved in the parade or demonstration. I think what should be remembered is this: that those involved in the incident had a pretty good go and they had been given the freedom of the streets since early yesterday morning and I don't suppose that it's unexpected that the police have taken exception to a busy thoroughfare in Kings Cross being completely blocked off at midnight."

Someone had failed to give the premier precise information. And the statement fell into place; it appeared to give the police their heads. What happened the next day seemed a direct consequence: the police closed the Court of Petty Sessions in Liverpool Street to anyone associated with those arrested on Saturday night.

The police have no power to do this. The orders of the magistrates were to keep out demonstrators but to let the general public in. The police kept them all out. For most of that day the business of the Sydney Court of Petty

Sessions appeared to be in the hands of the police.

Superintendent Douglas was in charge of this operation. "You'd appreciate what would have happened if all those people had been let in," he said. The police had taken no similar action a few weeks before, when 152 Greeks and their families fronted the court over the social security scandal. Everyone trying to enter the court was interrogated. People were told, "The courts are closed." Police filled the courthouse door and a double line of police formed an aisle across the forecourt of the building. For a time the police did not allow even the defendants in. They were left standing in the cold drizzle in the forecourt until after 10 am. It meant, among other things, that they were unable to confer with the team of lawyers there to assist them. When finally they filed into the building Superintendent Douglas announced, "The court has been closed."

In Courtroom No. 3, where the defendants were to be processed, lawyers made applications to let the public in. One of the few spectators in the courtroom was a woman of Baltic extraction who had seen the march on Saturday and come to congratulate the police on what they'd done. She had free access all morning.

John Terry told the magistrate Reg Bartley, "I have been trying to prepare cases. I have not been able to find witnesses. This is a major hindrance to me in the preparing of cases." Mr Bartley confirmed that the public and those with business before the court had a right of access. Superintendent Douglas, when told this by Terry, demanded specific orders from the magistrate naming the people needed in court.

Terry consulted Farquhar who said all people with legitimate business were to be admitted. He then returned to Douglas and asked, "What criterion are you using to exclude these people?" Douglas said he didn't have to answer that. "You're acting arbitrarily," Terry replied. 'That's right, arbitrarily," said Douglas. Terry then made an announcement to the crowd: "You are quite within your rights to move through the police lines and into the courthouse in an orderly way." The police allowed no one to budge. Douglas later told *The National Times*, "That solicitor was very close to being charged himself for coercing the people to riot."

A series of violent incidents occurred in the crowd. Some eggs were thrown at the police. Intermittent chanting continued all morning. I saw three women who had climbed over the balustrade on to the courthouse verandah being picked up by their ankles and thrown back into the crowd.

Another woman was thrown down the steps of the courthouse and kicked in midair by a senior policeman.

Solicitor Garth Symonds and barrister David Buchanan conveyed allegations to the magistrate that their clients' bail slips had been ripped from their hands by police as they tried to enter the courthouse. The forms were proof of the essential need of those people to be in the court. The magistrate sent one of the defendants out under escort to identify the policeman who had done it. A constable was brought into the court and his name was taken by the magistrate.

The clerk of Petty Sessions made a few more trips out that afternoon, ferrying Magistrate Bartley's instructions that the police were to allow the public gallery of his court to fill. About 2.45 pm the message appeared to have finally sunk home and the people were allowed in. The demonstration evaporated.

Of all the police incidents that have occurred since Wran's government took office the events of that weekend appear to be the most serious challenge to the administration of the state. It is not just a question of homosexual rights, not only a question of civil liberties and the abuse of police station procedure. Last Monday, for a few hours the police appeared to be contesting the authority of the courts.

The National Times, 8 July 1978

Bigots in the name of Christ

INVESTIGATIONS OF BIGOTRY TAKE US to strange times, strange places and strange corners of the human heart. Tracking the hatred of homosexuality – a commonplace sexual variation as old as the human race – takes us back to the Judea of Abraham's day, to Rome and Alexandria in the early centuries of the church, from whence it's a long, straight, bumpy ride to Botany Bay and, this, its outlying suburb, Canberra, where waiting in the Senate is a bill to protect the jobs of homosexual men and women, a bill fiercely opposed by the churches.

Clever gay biblical scholars try to argue these days that the Bible is neutral about homosexuality. But I agree with the churches. The Good Book plainly disapproves of men having sex with men, and to argue other-wise is as trivial as arguing that the Bible settles the moral issue of homosexuality for all time. There are, I agree, difficulties with Sodom and Gomorrah. Whatever brought fire and brimstone raining down on the cities of the plain wasn't sodomy. The Lord told Abraham he would save Sodom if he could find ten righteous living within its walls. He couldn't. Hence mass slaughter by molten lava. So whatever the vice was – a vice left unspecified in Abraham's conversation with the Lord – the women were clearly involved in it up to their necks.

That's Genesis. But there's no getting round Leviticus. Here traditional Jewish hostility to homosexuality is firmly grounded in the catalogue of sexual and dietary prohibitions dictated by God directly to Moses. These are the rules that set the Jewish nation apart from those tribes around them. They are immensely detailed. They go on for chapters. Dwarfs are forbidden to make offerings to the Lord. It's in this section of the Bible that we learn which of our relatives we can marry and which we can't. It's here the Jehovah's Witnesses find their fatal objection to blood transfusions. And at Leviticus 20:13, God told Moses: "If a man also lie with mankind, as he lieth with a woman, both of them have committed an abomination: they shall surely be put to death; their blood shall be upon them."

Centuries after God issued his orders to Moses, Christians took their distaste for homosexuality into the world of late Imperial Rome. It was, to say the least, unfamiliar there. Rome was never Hollywood's wet dream of an erotic free-for-all. There were rules of decorum, deportment and family life. Some of these touched on homosexuality, but homosexuality was neither forbidden by law nor stigmatised by society. The late John Boswell of Yale, a controversial historian of homophobia, wrote, "Neither the Roman religion nor Roman law recognised homosexual eroticism as *distinct* from – much less inferior to – heterosexual eroticism." Of love poetry written at this time, he said, "It is extremely difficult to convey to modern audiences the absolute indifference of most Latin authors to the question of gender."

The new contempt for homosexuality was one facet of a new idea of the body that Christians brought with them into the pagan world, an idea that transformed the moral universe in which we still live. The Romans saw the body as the sensual, sometimes unruly companion of the spirit. It had to be taught and disciplined, but it also had to be gratified. The spirit looked after the body in a mood of alert but friendly care. But Christianity came out of Judea with the terrible idea that the body was the *enemy* of the soul.

The conquest of death was the revolutionary objective of this new faith, and Christians believed that to conquer death, they must first conquer the body. This would not be so urgent if we left the body behind when we passed to heaven. But body and soul make the journey together. So our flesh must be made a Temple of the Lord here on earth. But how? The Greeks and Romans taught that a measure of sexual abstinence – nothing too extreme – made you *strong*. (They invented the notion that athletes shouldn't have sex before a big race.) But Christians arrived in Rome with the idea that abandoning sex made them *holy*.

Great prophets in many faiths consecrated themselves in this way – usually abandoning sex at an age when sex was abandoning them. Now in the new dispensation of Christ, every believer was a witness and prophet of the Lord, and was drawn to express their openness to the Word by opting for lives of sexual purity. The ideal of chastity and virginity – not unknown, of course, in pagan cults – came in from the fringes to the heart of town.

St Paul, in offering the most famous sex advice of all time – "It is better to marry than to burn" – was making the sensible point at a rather extreme time that celibacy is not for everyone. He praised celibacy highly – "It is good for a man not to touch a woman" – but also recommended a pure sort of Christian sex made holy by lots of rules and denials. One of these denials was homosexuality. And a century or so later another moderate man, Clement of Alexandria, came up with a precise formula to make marriage holy: that sex should be for procreation only. Christ had said nothing of the kind. Not even Paul had taken such a mechanical view of the matter. Clement's idea was essentially pagan – Stoic, in fact – but however foreign, however cruel, however artificial, however unconvincing, the idea took hold at the end of the second century and Western civilisation lurched further down a very odd track.

It took time to work out all the implications of Clement's rule: no contraception, no masturbation (very important, then and now), no sex during lactation or menstruation, no sex for the barren (it would only be pleasure for them), no sex in positions that don't allow conception (anal, oral) and, naturally, no homosexuality.

Just as I think it's idle to pretend the Bible is OK about homosexuality, I think it's wistful to imagine, as some gay scholars do, that the church was never *really* hostile to homosexuality until the modern day. Clearly it was disapproved of and preached against from the earliest times. "Strict codes of sexual discipline were made to bear much of the weight of providing the Christian Church with a distinctive code of behaviour," wrote Peter Brown in his wonderful book *The Body and Society*.

> Sexual prohibitions had always distinguished Jews, in their own eyes at least, from the sinister indeterminacy of the gentiles. These were now asserted with exceptional vigor. Christian marital codes were rendered yet more idiosyncratic by a few novel features, such as the relinquishment of divorce and a growing prejudice against the remarriage of widows and widowers. Above the solid conglomerate of ancient, Jewish notions there now rose the peak of total chastity.

Whatever exotic associations the gesture of continence might have had for the Christians themselves, outsiders could admire it as a form of physical heroism equivalent to the observed capacity for Christians to face down the chill fear of death.

What did seem to take about a millennium to work out was the seriousness of the vice of homosexuality. The Christian emperor Theodosius issued a first edict against homosexuals in 390 AD but his victims were only – if that's the word – prostitutes hauled from the brothels of Rome and burnt to death. Not for another 150 years was homosexuality itself outlawed, by Justinian in Constantinople. The state seems to have been ahead of the church in those early centuries when homosexuality was regarded as only a moderately serious sin like gluttony, or a darker stain like adultery. But these ups and downs offer no comfort on the edge of the twenty-first century because the Western churches' attitude was set in stone by the Third Lateran Council in 1179 and refined – if that's the word – by Thomas Aquinas in the following century.

Homosexual clerics were to be deposed from office and confined in monasteries to do penance. Homosexual laymen should "suffer excommunication and be cast out from the company of the faithful". Excommunication! In turning those rainbow-sashed homosexuals away from communion last Sunday in St Patrick's Cathedral, Archbishop Pell was, 800 years on, acting within the letter and the spirit of that Third Lateran Council: the denial of communion to Christian homosexuals. Though in also refusing communion to their straight – but rainbow-sashed – mothers, Pell may have exceeded Lateran limits.

At the heart of the history of every bigotry is the same moral: it didn't have to turn out this way. Other traditions that might easily have allowed homosexuality the dignity it had in European civilisation before Christ were stifled and crushed. Again, gay revisionist historians try to present this as a series of unfortunate accidents. But it doesn't wash: what's remarkable about Christianity is its persistent focus on issues of sexual purity and its use of homosexuality, right from the start, as a dramatic example of impurity. It comes with the territory.

Doyen of those revisionists is the John Boswell. He has an intriguing theory to explain why in the twelfth century the church laid down its universal rule against the vice of Sodom. Boswell sees it as an aftershock of the decision forty years earlier to enforce absolutely the rule of clerical celibacy. This was a terrible event for heterosexual priests: they were ordered to turn out their wives. Boswell writes, "Contemporaries ... were quick to note that gay priests would be more willing than heterosexual ones to enforce prohibitions against clerical marriage." What followed was a kind of institutional revenge – first against gay monks and priests, later against homosexuals in the society beyond church walls. One rule for all.

The same council that condemned homosexuals set limits to the economic and civil liberty of Jews. Hunting for traitors and heretics became an essential business of both church and state. Sodomy was high on the list of vices said to be enjoyed by the Moors. According to the propaganda of the Crusades, the Moors were rampant sodomites, having their fiendish way with Christian men and boys, bishops and priests. The Holy Land had to be rescued not only from Islam but also from homosexuality. I like to think that the persistent daydreams of the West, in which the Arab world is credited with extraordinary erotic refinement, is a survival of the propaganda that helped launch those bloody and pointless Crusades.

Meanwhile in the modern world, the crusading spirit of Christianity works tirelessly to protect faiths from having to give jobs or offer services to homosexuals. Hence opposition to the Democrats' 1995 Sexuality Discrimination Bill that would offer blanket protection throughout Australia without special exemptions for churches. A Senate enquiry into the bill has drawn submissions from across the country. They're a survey of sorts into the state of homophobia in this outlying territory of Christendom. For those who want to see church homophobia challenged at law, there are wonderfully encouraging things here. The Quakers said: "We don't see the necessity for religious bodies to be exempt from any provisions of the bill." The Anglicans of Western Australia supported them: "Churches and related institutions should not be exempt." The Uniting Church wants no exemptions on the secular side of their work but rather apologetically supports them on the religious side: gay-friendly as the denomination is becoming, it's still deeply divided over the marriage and ordaining of homosexuals.

But for the rest there's an angry mood of surprise and distress that the national parliament would think of such a challenge to church prerogatives. The Catholics and Protestant congregations are demanding to be as free from the working of this new law as they are of old state laws. Some demand Christian exemptions be guaranteed in perpetuity. How? In the prose of the submissions, Genesis and Leviticus figure heavily along with all those familiar dreams of purity and nightmares of disgust that have haunted the church from year one. The stigma must remain to deter "wrong choices"; children are at risk; the family must be protected; new laws will only bring more misery to more people if homosexuals' lives are made easier; and they don't need legislation anyway – they need the love of God through whose mercy they will be reborn as men and women, husbands and wives, mothers and fathers in the perfect image of His Creation.

Bigotry, plain bigotry.

From the third annual Freilich Lecture in Bigotry and Tolerance, Australian National University, 25 May 1999

The Democrats' bill failed.

Conigrave's candour

OVER THE PAST FEW WEEKS I've come to think I'm the only person in the world who didn't know Tim Conigrave. People assume I do because my name has crept onto the cover of *Holding the Man*. I've been embarrassed as Tim's friends "remind" me of episodes I never knew in his life and talk about the outrageously tactless and truthful things he said. But I have decided not to be embarrassed anymore because it strikes me that I know Tim as he's going to be known by everyone now: through this beautiful book.

I read it the first time last year, in manuscript, in a hotel room in Melbourne. The publishers wanted a line for the cover. I told them I was hopelessly busy but if they sent me the pages I'd have a bit of a look. And I found myself that weekend hiding in that room to read Tim's writing in great chunks. I haven't heard of anyone since who has read *Holding the Man* any other way: in great chunks, preferably all at a sitting.

When I finished I rang Nick Enright to tell my old friend straightaway how excited I was – how funny and horny and sad and truthful this book was and how much it had told me about myself. Nick seemed a bit distracted. When I drew breath I asked him what the din was in the background. He said: "It's Tim's wake."

I didn't know he had died. That he had managed against all the odds to write the book and then work on the editing with Nick up to the last moment is all of a piece with the Tim that emerges from *Holding the Man:* a master of the close shave, brave and stubborn and determined to have his say. Did anyone ever shut him up? Death certainly didn't.

Holding the Man isn't the greatest prose around. It is a story worth telling and almost perfectly told. You don't have to be gay to wonder where you will find love – where love will find you – but for Tim and John Caleo to discover each other sitting in the same classroom at Xavier is the sort of blazing good luck we'd hardly believe in a magazine.

I do worry about Xavier. Clearly the school is a hotbed of romance (which is fine) and the priests are often on the side of love (which is a good thing) but there seems little seating discipline in the classrooms. Sometimes John is sitting across from Tim; sometimes he's sitting in the row behind and gently massaging Tim's back. Finally they are side by side:

> Father Bradford was talking about the disturbance of the natural order in *Macbeth*. John and I were rubbing our knees together, caressing each other in long gentle strokes ...

At which point, discipline had entirely broken down. Terrific.

Tim writes beautifully about the small milestones of life. That it's gay life is crucial and at the same time hardly matters. It's life:

> Blue jocks and the first inkling of sex.
> The first wank, which he immediately reports to his mother.
> The first kiss. He writes particularly wonderfully about kissing.
> The first fuck thanks to Father Wallbridge and his retreat at Barwon Heads.
> The awful disappointment of the first GaySoc meeting at
> university.
> The first mirror ball.
> The first adultery.
> The first reconciliation.
> The first symptoms.

This is also a book about dying. The same candour that makes *Holding the Man* an irresistible account of love and partnership makes it also an irresistibly moving account of dying, death and loss.

Tim seems never to have been anything but candid. He couldn't help himself – he opened his mouth and out came the truth. He was an outrageously tactless human being. The only time he seems ever to have been persuaded to shut up in his life was the night of his sister's wedding, just as he was about to announce to his family he was HIV positive. He reports this near catastrophe with the laughter and scorn it deserves.

Tim's candour falls like a bright, soft light over his life and this book. It's that light and his voice that makes us read *Holding the Man* with such greedy impatience. He can admit lust, disloyalty and foolishness; admit the most fugitive and inappropriate longings; admit he's a master of mistiming; and confess his almost shocking curiosity. Yet we are ready for more.

"I wish I could have seen the operation," he writes as he sees John brought back one night from the operating theatre with a new scar that runs from his solar plexus to the back of his ribs. "I would love to know what my boyfriend looked like inside ..." And he can put on paper a moment no one fails to talk about with awe: that last homecoming fuck. In ways we find hard to face, Tim was able to admit he was a human being. We love him for that.

Holding the Man was so good I assumed my line of praise would be one of dozens on the cover. It didn't turn out that way. Even so the publishers wanted it short and snappy. I was told to cut it in half. Now as I launch this book I have a chance to give my verdict in full: "This is a fine, tender and sexy book. Life, it says, is precious and we mustn't waste a day of it."

Launch of *Holding the Man*, Sydney, 15 June 1995

Myths and lessons of Stonewall

WHEN JUDY GARLAND DIED IN LONDON after slurping too much Seconal in June 1969, her body was brought back to New York where 20,000 distraught fans filed through the Frank E. Campbell Funeral Chapel to catch a last glimpse of the fallen diva. It's a fair guess many of those mourners were gay but despite all that's been said since, their grief did not make history.

In the same city on the same hot weekend Garland was buried, a riot broke out when police raided a dive in Greenwich Village called the Stonewall Inn. There's no evidence the two events were linked in any way, yet by now it's hard to think of Stonewall without crediting Garland's angry fans with striking this early blow for gay lib.

Stonewall, whose fortieth anniversary is being celebrated round the world this weekend, has become honoured by the powerful and smothered in legends. A decade ago, that corner of Greenwich Village where police were pelted with garbage and Molotov cocktails was declared a National Historic Landmark. A few weeks ago, President Obama enraged militant Christians by declaring June 2009 the month of Lesbian, Gay, Bisexual and Transgender Pride. "Forty years ago, patrons and supporters of the Stonewall Inn in New York City resisted police harassment that had become all too common for members of the lesbian, gay, bisexual, and transgender community," the president stated. "Out of this resistance, the LGBT rights movement in America was born."

Not really. Stonewall wasn't the first time such violence erupted. The club's patrons were not the frontline troops. This was not the first time political capital had been made of post-raid uproar. Nor was gay liberation born solely out of such violence: Stonewall would not have been what it was if the rights movement had not already been well underway in America and even here in timid Australia.

Don't get me wrong. Stonewall's fortieth birthday is worth celebrating. But the legends are getting in the way of the lessons Stonewall has to teach, lessons about what it takes to achieve sensible and popular reform when police and politicians are hell-bent on standing in its way. Stonewall is about the power of mockery and fun and celebration; about shabby violence and brilliant political invention; about riffraff and the reputable working hand in hand; about the need for supporters of sensible but difficult causes – gay rights, euthanasia, drug reform – to show their faces in daylight. It's about the power of coming out.

The Stonewall Inn on Christopher Street was a trashy firetrap run by the mafia. The windows were boarded up and the walls painted black. The drinks were watered and the toilets overflowed. Dancing was allowed. From the moment it opened in March 1967, Stonewall made a fortune for the mob from blackmail as much as liquor. None of it was ploughed back into the business.

On 28 June 1969, about 200 customers were packed into its two bars when the music stopped and the lights came on at 1.20 am. Tempers were frayed. Raids of gay clubs on Manhattan had been going on for weeks. This was the second at Stonewall in four days. Though the police crusade against homosexuals was more determined than ever in these years, the courts were proving troublesome for the forces of purity. Test cases brought by advocates of gay law reform had established that it was not against the law in New York to serve liquor to homosexuals or let them dance together. But it remained a crime for men to wear women's clothing and vice versa.

Police hadn't come to Stonewall for a mass round-up of homosexuals. They planned to seize only the liquor, Mafia types, bar staff and anyone in breach of the nineteenth-century New York labour law requiring the citizens to wear no less than three articles of clothing appropriate to their sex. The targets of the raid were women in overalls and men in frocks. Defiant drag queens refused to go to the toilets to be "checked out" by the morals squad. Once released into Christopher Street, the club's clientele hung around under a full moon applauding and jeering as police led their prisoners to the paddy wagon. The atmosphere was party until one of the drag queens swung at a cop with her handbag and was clubbed in return. Then a handcuffed lesbian was dragged from the bar kicking, cursing and screaming. She fought all the way to a waiting squad car from which she escaped twice before being driven away. It was this unknown woman who taunted the crowd by calling out: "Why don't you guys do something?"

Loose change was already showering down on police. Now pennies were followed by bottles, bricks and cobblestones. Vastly outnumbered by the swelling crowd, the police retreated into the club and barricaded the doors. The crowd erupted.

Celebratory accounts of Stonewall usually skate over the details of the next hour or so. About 400 people took part in the melee. Most of them were street kids, the scruffiest end of the gay world, who were the shock troops of the confrontation. Everything was being hurled at the bar. All its windows were smashed. Attempts were made to set it alight. An uprooted parking meter was used to batter open the bar's heavy doors. Crude Molotov cocktails were thrown inside and extinguished by the police.

Then the cavalry arrived: two fire engines, a paddy wagon, several patrol cars and two buses filled with members of the heavily armoured Tactical Patrol Force. As the TPF advanced in line abreast, street kids met them with an impromptu high-kicks chorus line. In *Stonewall: The Riots That Sparked the Gay Revolution*, David Carter wrote of witnesses "amazed at the courage of the street kids who dared to mock the TPF to their faces".

The brawling ended sometime after 3 am. The next night a crowd of several thousand gathered outside the reopened bar and blockaded the street. This was, for the time, barely imaginable: a public gathering of men and women identifying themselves as homosexual. They were there because they wanted to be there, and they were angry. It took 300 police two hours to clear the streets.

*

That was Stonewall: sixteen rioters arrested and four police hurt over two nights, with the trashed club reopened at once by a determined Mafia management. Press accounts of the fighting were brief and mocking. It was too soon while the streets were still being swept to cast these events in a romantic light. The respectable forces of gay law reform considered the riots a setback to their agenda. Stonewall was not big news in the outside world but the story quickly reached Australia. *The Sydney Morning Herald* would show haughty disapproval to the gay movement for the next decade or more, but it carried a sympathetic account of the upheaval in Greenwich Village by Lillian Roxon, a very individual Australian journalist based in New York who already saw Stonewall as it was going to be seen.

"Homosexuals, understandably, are anxious to avoid trouble," she wrote.

> Last week the police moved in on a place called the Stonewall, expecting the usual lack of resistance. But revolution is in the air, and what has been confined until now to the ghettos and the universities suddenly happened on nice, quiet, tree-shaded Christopher Street. Instead of the skulking shamefaced deviates they were prepared to encounter at the Stonewall, the police ran slap bang into a mob of terribly angry men.

Though the papers had made fun of blokes in frocks and assaults with beaded bags, Roxon noted: "Those lithe figures in the sequined sheaths and the feather boas also happened to be in very fine physical nick. 'If the queens of America ever get together,' said one redhead, aiming 'her' stiletto with vicious precision, 'it's the end, baby. We've had enough.'"

This was a time of marches in the United States, of huge crowds supporting civil rights and protesting against the Vietnam War. Stonewall was turned into myth by a group of astute gay politicians who worked to commemorate the first anniversary of the riot with a parade of gay men and women through New York in broad daylight. The march stretched fifteen blocks. "It is often assumed that Stonewall is commemorated because of its impact on the movement," wrote sociologists Elizabeth Armstrong and Suzanna Crage a couple of years ago. "In fact, Stonewall made its impact on the gay movement through its commemoration. The first commemoration of Stonewall was gay liberation's biggest and most successful protest event."

*

Stonewall was not an early rallying cry in Australia. The fledgling movement was still taking its cues from England, where a highly respectable, not-necessarily-gay civil liberties movement had won fundamental law reform in 1967. The early gay magazine *Camp Ink* warned Australian campaigners in 1970 *not* to follow the example set in New York. "The influence of Stonewall on the Australian scene in those early years was very indirect," says Ken Davis, a veteran and historian of the movement. "It filtered slowly over here. Back then it took longer for these things to cross the world. What mattered was not so much the riot and its commemoration but the feel of the times. It was about a mood change from homophile reform to a young rebellion-based gay politics."

But it was also about fun. Gary Wotherspoon, another of the historians of the gay movement, sees Stonewall as the moment when "Australian queens began to turn from British to American gay life as the beacon on the hill. Prior to Stonewall all the queens would go to London. From the '70s on, they went to Los Angeles, San Francisco and New York. It was a real turning point. Let me tell you, London in 1970 was boring as shit compared to LA in '73."

Nine years passed before Australians formally commemorated Stonewall but the impulse behind the Sydney march in 1978 had little to do with the riots in New York. Though branded as a Stonewall celebration, it was actually held at the request of Harvey Milk's people in San Francisco who were seeking international support to prevent gay teachers and all teachers sympathetic to the gay movement being expelled from the Californian education system. Though tenuous going into the event, the link with Stonewall was profound by the time the night was over. Just as in New York in 1969, a mighty impetus to change was given by police going too far in pursuit of an old morals agenda at a time when public opinion had undergone a radical shift. In the early morning of June 25, police ambushed the marchers in Kings Cross, beat many, arrested fifty-three and found themselves way out on a limb.

Police violence jolted the reform movement back to life. But change still took time. Indeed, not everything has been achieved. But it's time to begin considering how the lessons of Stonewall – of respectable lobbying holding hands with outrageous bad behaviour in the streets – can be applied to other reforms we've clearly signalled as a society we want to see happen, but that police and politicians continue to thwart. It's a short list of moral issues still policed as gay sex once was, with tough laws and hefty prison sentences – an approach that's never achieved much while destroying lives along the way. We could start with the hardest: decriminalising drugs.

The Sydney Morning Herald, 27 June 2009

A politician in the steam

LET'S NOT PRETEND OTHERWISE: we've all found the David Campbell story gripping. What else has Sydney been talking about since Channel Seven put its grainy footage to air but the sex life and downfall of this ordinary politician? It's an absolutely compelling, five-star yarn. Yet the talkback condemnation of Seven has been brutal. Is that hypocritical? Not at all.

Seven proved nothing on Thursday night but the fact – not entirely secret around Macquarie Street – that the huge-girthed minister was gay. Under the rules the community expects the media to work by, that remains his private business until it affects his public life. Channel Seven has other, old-fashioned ideas that hark back to a time that's all but disappeared in this country when being gay was scandal enough. Seven might note that these days we have gay judges, gay police, gay soldiers and gay politicians. Some are even out. That's public life now in this country.

Campbell was a hypocrite. That's a tragedy for him and his family and sauce for Seven's story. But blowing his cover could only be justified if, once again, his hypocrisy affected his public life. That's the rule. America is laughing this week at a Baptist preacher called George Rekers caught flying home from a ten-day jaunt in Europe with a Florida rent boy. Rekers has been outed, mocked and ruined because he made his career preaching against gays. That's not Campbell.

More is at stake here than the fall of this sad man and the excruciating embarrassment of his family. For years politicians have been hungry to impose on the media a new, punitive regime to protect privacy. Seven has just issued an open invitation for them to take action. The Campbell story could never have been broadcast under the old defamation law, where privacy was protected by humourless judges insisting that even true reports must "relate to matters of public interest". They emphatically didn't mean the entertainment Seven provided with reports of Campbell's visits to Ken's sauna.

But four years ago new uniform defamation laws made truth alone a complete defence. At once, privacy advocates began agitating for new laws to maintain – and dramatically extend – the old protections. The NSW Law Reform Commission recently called for laws to allow people merely "annoyed" by accurate media reports to sue for damages. Such a law would cut deep into the media's capacity to report what goes on in this country. Just how deep, it would take many years and many court cases to discover.

The media has been trying to argue such laws aren't needed: that we don't behave in this country with the gutter instincts of, say, the London tabloids. That stand wasn't helped this time last year when News Limited newspapers declared photographs – probably of a Russian tart – to be Pauline Hanson cavorting in a black negligee. Again: impossible under the old law and possible under the new.

Now Seven has filmed Campbell – and how many other clients? – emerging from a Kensington bathhouse. Is his visit of any public interest? Yes, if Seven can prove his sad, hidden sex life interfered with the exercise of his public life. No proof has so far been provided.

No doubt Seven is scrambling to find any dirt it can on the former minister for transport. Usually you'd wait until you had your evidence before attacking your target. Not this time. As of now, Campbell has been destroyed for one reason alone: being gay.

The Sydney Morning Herald, 22 May 2010

The business model
of the faiths

IF ONLY CHRISTIANS FOUGHT like this for refugees. Imagine if the Coalition's big men of faith threatened to tear down their own government unless it brings home the wretches we've imprisoned in the Pacific. Surely there couldn't be a greater service for Christ? Or what about crossing the floor for the poor, the homeless, for battered wives and illiterate Aboriginal kids? No. What excites these Christian warriors is beating up on gays.

I've watched it all my life. They fought like hell to keep sex between men a crime. As they lost the backing of the public they went about their task more urgently. The rules of heaven were not to be swept aside by opinion polls. Sin had to be punished. Mealy mouthed, they reckoned they didn't want to send us to jail. Oh, heaven forfend! But they demanded the states set an example – a Godly example – by leaving criminal laws just as they were. That meant fourteen years' jail for fucking in New South Wales.

As the numbers drifted away from them the Christian warriors grew, if anything, more determined, better organised and nastier. Again and again, the end of the world was nigh. They fought no-fault divorce law with everything they had. They fought legal recognition of de facto relationships. They attacked anti-discrimination laws and were given extraordinary exemptions from them. And they kept on fighting LGBTI reform until the last state, Tasmania, fell over the line in 1967.

Spectators look on bewildered. Times have changed. This is a secular country. Why these brawls? Surely these bigots know they're on the wrong side of history?

We shouldn't be bewildered. Nothing is inevitable in the imagination of Christian warriors, and no battle is quite as righteous as a battle lost. The

God-given imperative is to fight and keep on fighting. Winning even a little delay is a triumph. So much is at stake. But these days the warriors are a little shy of saying the truth: they're doing Christ's work on earth. The euphemism de jour among the conservative Christians is "saving Western civilisation".

Only a handful of secular warriors are fighting with the army of the faithful. Of course, many Jews and Muslims share their Old Testament disgust. But right now in Australia they are leaving the latest battle in this old, old war to the Christians – yet not many of their leaders or the faithful in the pews.

It's a commonplace of the campaign for equal marriage that it has the support of most Christians in Australia. Catholics are particularly keen. And a Galaxy poll published a few weeks ago also showed their disquiet that crusaders against reform are claiming to represent all Christians in the country.

The bigots have been deserted even by their own followers.

That raises two big questions. First, what's in it for the warriors to keep on fighting? God's word, of course, but also the business of these men is shame. Times change but people don't. Nothing gives conservative faiths such power as preying on human disquiet about sex and pleasure. So they preach against masturbation, adultery, divorce and, of course, homosexuality in all its forms.

There is so much more to Christianity than this. But for bishops of wrath and for hellfire preachers there's no winner like shame. First they work up guilt and then they set their terms for forgiveness. And for half a century, as a great shift occurred in secular thinking on sex, Christian leaders have wanted the state, its laws and its institutions, to keep backing their business model. Think of it as spiritual rent seeking.

The second big question is one for politicians to grapple with. Where are the numbers? When kowtowing to angry bishops isn't even going to win over their congregations, why give them such leverage? Fear is the answer. Tony Abbott stood at the doors of parliament on Wednesday morning and declared in the tones of a desert prophet: "And I say to you if you don't like same-sex marriage, vote no. If you're worried about religious freedom and freedom of speech, vote no … "

That argument resonates with Australians. It scares politicians. We are a secular country. We don't want to worship, but we highly value the freedom of others to worship. This is a decent compact of a tolerant people.

No wonder the battle over equal marriage is represented by opponents of change as a great struggle for freedom. But what freedoms? Archbishops of Sydney will not be forced to marry lesbian couples in their cathedrals. Keen young Pentecostal males – however they might like to let off steam after a hard day's speaking in tongues – won't be forced to marry one another. No preacher will be prosecuted for reminding Australians of God's wrath as set out so vividly in Genesis.

But Abbott and his mates aren't talking freedom. It's time this was said absolutely clearly. Freedoms are something we can all enjoy. These people are talking about the rights of institutions. They want the church to have the power to dictate for all Australians the laws of marriage. That's not a freedom. That's a privilege.

Ireland has stared down the church. Conservative governments in the United Kingdom and New Zealand have ignored religious demands. Germany and most of Europe have turned their backs on furious bishops. Even plucky little Malta said no to the church the other day. But Australians find this so hard. It's as if we feel guilty about the slow collapse of faith on this continent. Perhaps apologetic is a better word. Either way, there's an old habit in this country of politics paying far too much heed to the least attractive demands of Christianity.

We've said no before and we will again. But it takes so much time and such an extraordinary effort. Eventually we will clear a path through the obstructions of abandoned faith and get on with the real life of the country.

The Guardian, 9 August 2017

Modern Warfare

A note on the language

A NEW POLITICAL LANGUAGE BEGAN to be fashioned in America in the 1980s to combat unwelcome fresh ideas about sex, women, guns, human rights and especially race. The fate of Western civilisation was said to be hanging in the balance. This lingo of reaction was hammered out in Washington think tanks and test run in little magazines. Big minds and big money were engaged in the task. The work was wonderfully done. A key purpose of the exercise was to find ways in a disapproving world of continuing to fight for white privilege. Talk of *culture wars*, *elites* and *political correctness* offered cover to politicians as they went about an old familiar task.

Australia lapped it up. An early adopter was the mining industry. The industry's mouthpiece, the Institute of Public Affairs, became quickly fluent in the newspeak. So did News Limited, which became the bridge this American dialect crossed into Australian public life. Decades later, hardly a week – hardly a day – goes by without an opinion piece in *The Australian* deploring *political correctness* and/or the blindness of the *elites*. The language would not have stuck without there being, often enough, a grain of truth in the writing of the harpy columnists. Yes, there are *progressives* who don't give a damn about the people they claim to speak for. And yes, there are *politically correct* politicians afraid of being branded bigots or traitors if they show their true colours. Such horrors have been with us always and the English language has always had ways of dealing with them. The point of the new rhetoric isn't so much argument as abuse. Yet it comes with an attractive plea that we debate race and sex and guns and free speech without abusing one another. "You ought to be able to have sensible discussion on these sorts of things," John Howard told Paul Kelly and Dennis Shan-ahan last year. "But there is a sense in which people are so frightened of being accused of being discriminatory or intolerant that they don't speak the commonsense view."

Evidence of speech silenced is scant. In late February, on the seventh straight day attacking *Q&A* panellist Yassmin Abdel-Magied, *The Austra-lian* published a cartoon by Bill Leak that, not so long ago, would have been considered unthinkable in a national newspaper. Leak has a hipster teacher telling primary-school children: "Out of cultural sensitivity to the beliefs of some of our more devout Muslim pupils we have decided to relax the school rule banning the beheading of infidels." Meanwhile, on the opposite page, Janet Albrechtsen was for the umpteenth time denouncing the anti-insult, anti-intimidation provision of the *Racial Discrimination Act* as "a law that strikes at the heart of Western liberalism". How? Who is it silencing at the *Oz*? Could Bill Leak's abuse have been any more robust? Yet Albrechtsen worked herself up into a fury over the Turnbull government's failure to free Australia from the act:

> It's time to change the party's name to the Illiberal Party. And in that values vacuum you will hear Pauline Hanson's tally-counter clicking fast and furiously as more voters choose One Nation rather than a misleadingly labelled Liberal government that cannot find the polit-ical backbone to defend free speech.

Speakers of newspeak have many enemies in their sights. Some are vir-tual strangers on the Australian political scene. It mattered in America to fashion a vivid new language to attack anyone who might aid abortion or regulate gun ownership. They aren't such urgent causes here, though it's a pleasure to hear One Nation's Malcolm Roberts slip into the lingo to denounce those wishing to punish gun smugglers as "enemies of freedom". Done by the book. But the common enemies are many, and here and abroad two underlying principles are always in play when new rhetoric is deployed: the Left is the enemy of freedom, and race is never about race.

Some key terms:

Assimilation

"Asians," warned Hanson in her maiden speech, "have their own culture and religion, form ghettos and do not assimilate." Not being able to fit in to a new country is a key racist claim through the ages. Once, blood and biology were to blame. That's become unfashionable. Now the fault is said to lie with culture and religion. Asians were bad enough but Muslims are worse. On her return to parliament in 2016 Hanson declared: "Now we are in danger of being swamped by Muslims, who bear a culture and ideology that is incompatible with our own."

Cosmopolitan

Men and women of the world and their shallow ideas. Not really Australian. Backers of *multiculturalism* are by definition *cosmopolitan*. Ditto, rich enthusiasts for a republic like Malcolm Turnbull. Out on the far Right, *cosmopolitans* are blamed for seeking to impose a police state in order to ban guns. Jews are particularly *cosmopolitan*.

Culture war

Ruthless and hilarious skirmishes designed to exhaust the progressive spirit of the nation. The notion is that new ideas on race, sex, religion, freedom, education and so on are a coordinated attack by the enemies of Western values that must be met with full force on all fronts. The metaphor of war conscripts contestants into two armies – Attackers and Defenders – while licensing ferocious combat in the trenches. Reputations are slaughtered. John Howard was the Monash of culture warriors, but these days only his army seems to be in the field. The other got bored and left.

Division

The natural consequence of pampering Aborigines or allowing foreigners into the country who won't assimilate. "This nation is being divided into black and white," Hanson declared in 1996. The threat of Aboriginal partition seems to have receded in Hanson's mind, while the danger of *multiculturalism* is as potent as ever. She has always said: "Abolishing the policy of multiculturalism will save billions of dollars and allow those from ethnic backgrounds to join mainstream Australia, paving the way to a strong, united country." Hence the party name: One Nation.

Elites

Not men who lunch at the Melbourne Club or families that turn up in the *BRW* rich list. Troublesome *elites* live in cities and impose their *progressive* ideas on the *mainstream*. Hanson declared on the day of Trump's victory: "People around the world are saying, 'We've had enough with the major political parties, with the establishment, with the elites.'" Their influence is sinister. They bully. They seize control of universities. The ABC is staffed with *elites*. Hanson's 1997 manifesto used language with a strong whiff of Europe before the war: "Our common oppressors are a class of raceless, placeless, cosmopolitan elites who are exercising almost absolute power over us: like black spiders above the wheels of industry, they are spinning the webs of our destiny."

Equality

"My greatest desire is to see all Australians treat each other as equals," says Hanson. Another key racist concept: that need and not race should decide who gets what. Sometimes expressed: "I am colourblind." Fine in theory. But in Hanson's world it means cheap loans for farmers but no scholarships for black kids. She electrified the nation in her maiden speech by declaring: "I am fed up to the back teeth with the inequalities that are being promoted by the government and paid for by the taxpayer under the assumption that Aboriginals are the most disadvantaged people in Australia."

Free speech

Not about everything. Mainly race. The battleground is section 18C of the *Racial Discrimination Act*, which seeks to put a brake – no fines, no jail time – on speech that might "offend, insult, humiliate or intimidate" people on the basis of their "race, colour or national or ethnic origin". A complex debate continues between those who want the law to stay as it is (nearly everyone); reformists who want to raise the bar by deleting "offend" and "insult"; and abolitionists who claim that being able to humiliate and intimidate Jews and Lebanese is essential to free speech. By driving this debate, News Limited has made 18C the most famous single provision in Australian law. Meanwhile the Murdoch empire campaigns to keep Australia the only country in the Western world without a bill of rights that would, inter alia, guarantee free speech.

Mainstream

Not to be confused with majority. Numbers don't count. The mainstream is white, of Christian background and conservative. Common sense and true Australian values, in such short supply among the *elites*, flourish in the mainstream. *Assimilation* means merging with the mainstream. Care must be taken not to call overwhelmingly popular causes like equal marriage *mainstream*. The word doesn't work like that. Also: while *mainstream* is obviously good, the *mainstream media* is self-evidently bad.

Multiculturalism

The policy of allowing many cultures to survive – or even flourish – in a single country. From the moment she emerged from Marsden's Seafoods, Hanson's primary target has been *multiculturalism*. Over the last twenty years she's found a good word to say from time to time about Muslims and Aboriginals, but not *multiculturalism*. She is the voice of that twelve per cent of Australians who, according to the latest Scanlon survey, disagree that *multiculturalism* has been good for Australia. On her return to parliament in 2016 she declared: "Indiscriminate immigration and aggressive multiculturalism have caused crime to escalate and trust and social cohesion to decline. Too many Australians are afraid to walk alone at night in their neighbourhoods. Too many of us live in fear of terrorism."

Politically correct or PC

A protean term for which new uses are found every day. *PC* began life when American communists in the 1930s criticised the rigid doctrines of Joseph Stalin as "politically correct". Something of that meaning remains after all these years: *PC* is sticking with beliefs that are doctrinaire and out of touch with reality. Hanson has dismissed just about everything she disagrees with as *PC*: special treatment for Aborigines; tenderness to refugees; *multiculturalism* in all its forms; indulging the unemployed; any and all "unworkable socialist engineering doctrines"; and lately a Meat & Livestock Australia advertisement that showed a dozen races gathering for a beach barbeque on Australia Day. "Surely you have all had enough of politically correct stupidity like this," raged Hanson. "It has to stop because it is undermining our Australian culture."

PC also has another meaning: cowardice in debate or ridiculous lengths taken to prevent giving offence. The Urban Dictionary: "Only pathetically weak people that don't have the balls to say what they feel and mean are politically correct pussies." The fundamental charge of harpy columnists: "He doesn't believe what he's saying about blacks/women/refugees/homosexuals/Muslims, he is just being *politically correct*." Cowardice is shackling debate. Oddly, there seems no requirement that the cowardice be proved. It just is.

Progressive

Pejorative. Making it so is a major achievement of the *culture wars*. Useful synonym for *cosmopolitan*, *Left* and *elite*. Progressives sit on both sides of politics. They have no real feeling for the men and women whose interests they claim to have at heart. Progressives are even to blame for the rise of Donald Trump, according to figures like Wayne Swan: "If you're looking for reasons for Trump's victory look no further than the potent combination of powerful vested interests dictating policy and some progressive elites shoving their orthodoxies down working people's throats."

Swamped

Not a fact but a state of mind. Complete this sentence: "Australia is being *swamped* by ..." We're waiting for the new census figures, but the last showed Asians at eight per cent of the population. Muslims numbers are growing but the Australian Bureau of Statistics has them at the moment at only a little over two per cent of the population.

Western Civilisation

Old and fragile, Christian and white. Its oldest continuing institutions are, according to Tony Abbott, the papacy and the crown. Western Civilisation is under continuous attack today from progressive ideas and the long collapse of public morals. Australia has earned a fine reputation in the conservative world as a last redoubt in the struggle to defend Western Civilisation, for example by resisting equal marriage. Supercharging Australia's efforts will be the $25 million Ramsay Centre for Western Civilisation, to be chaired by John Howard. Abbott is on the board. An early task may be to clarify where the Australian Way of Life stands vis-à-vis Western Civilisation. This is not entirely clear. The traditional enemy of Western Civilisation is, of course, Occidental Civilisation.

Quarterly Essay, *The White Queen:*
One Nation and the Politics of Race, March 2017

Manning Clark, Soviet spy

A MASSIVE ATTACK ON THE REPUTATION of the late historian Manning Clark was mounted by the Brisbane *Courier-Mail* on Saturday, but late last night the paper's allegations were looking shaky. Not since the days of the Petrov defection has such a ferocious attack of this kind been seen in an Australian newspaper. *The Courier-Mail* gave the front page and five inside pages to claims that Clark was "indeed a communist" and an "agent of influence" for the Soviet Union during the Cold War and "a spy".

All this rests on one "fact" only: that Clark was covertly awarded the Order of Lenin sometime in the early 1970s. Yet the paper's "most compelling" witness to this told *The Sydney Morning Herald* yesterday, "I wouldn't want to go right out on a swaying plank and destroy a man's reputation for something I'd seen casually at a dinner party." He added that basing allegations of communism and spying on what he'd said was "dirty pool".

The witness is the poet Les Murray. He was rabbiting at the time for the grazier poet David Campbell and called one night in the autumn of 1970 to find Clark having dinner with the Campbells. Pinned to Clark's lapel was a medal: "A biggish coin with a red and yellow ribbon and Lenin looking into the future. It looked like the Order of Lenin."

I asked the poet: "Are you a scholar of Soviet medals?"

"Not really. I went and had a look in a book years later."

"When you were talking to *The Courier-Mail*, did they show you a book of Soviet medals and get you to identify it?"

"No."

"Well, did Manning tell you he'd been awarded the Order of Lenin?"

"That's the part I've been wracking my brains to recall. I won't say he did say it. But he did say it was the real thing." Murray added, "It could have been puckish."

"A joke?"

"Yes. Puckish. We all get puckish from time to time."

Manning's order was an anecdote of Murray's for years. Recently it reached the ears of Peter Kelly, a journalist on *The Courier-Mail*, and it brought to mind an odd incident sometime in the 1970s when the ANU academic Geoffrey Fairbairn told him, in some distress, that he'd seen Clark at the Soviet Embassy wearing "a striking looking gong" which was apparently the Order of Lenin. Kelly took no notes of this exchange. He says he asked Fairbairn how he knew. "Look, I recognised it and it was clear from the conversation. It was no joke." Neither Murray nor Fairbairn appears to have questioned Clark about the gong. Nor does *The Courier-Mail* suggest he ever conceded he had, in fact, been given the Order of Lenin.

The Clark family suggested Manning might have been wearing a medallion awarded when he turned up at a historians' conference in Moscow in the centenary year of Lenin's birth. Mrs Clark told *The Courier-Mail*: "It couldn't possibly be the Order of Lenin. There would have been a lot of hoo-haa."

About 400,000 Orders of Lenin were awarded by the Soviet Union for achievements in art, technology, economics – and politics. *The Courier-Mail* featured snaps of awardees Fidel Castro and Kim Philby. The paper might as easily have published photographs of any number of Soviet poets, or the composer Dmitri Shostakovich. *The Courier-Mail* says what makes the award to Clark sinister is that it was to a foreigner and covert. The paper quotes – at least in early editions of Saturday's paper – a retired KGB officer, Mikhail Lyubimov: "If it is kept secret, then it's got nothing to do with agent of influence; it's got to do with a spy."

The editor, Chris Mitchell, cut that paragraph from subsequent editions. Why? "I pulled it because I wanted to be careful about not making an allegation of spying."

"Why weren't you careful before the first edition?" I asked.

"I was."

The core of the case against Clark, he explained, is that he was "an agent of influence", perhaps unconsciously, for the Soviet Union. Asked how Clark's mission was advanced in the six-volume *A History of Australia*,

Mitchell said: "Words like 'bourgeois' are classic Marxist words and they're all through the histories."

No gong, no story? Mitchell wouldn't agree, but co-author with Kelly, Wayne Smith, did. "If Clark didn't get the Order of Lenin, a very cruel injustice has been done to him."

Les Murray told the *Herald* that if he'd caused any pain to the Clarks, he'd like to apologise.

The Sydney Morning Herald, 26 August 1996

A letter to Chris Mitchell

Mate, I wish we'd spoken before you made an ass of yourself again in your memoirs over the Manning Clark business. We've had our differences over the years but I hate to see you doing this to yourself as you sail off into retirement.

Given the chance, I reckon I could have persuaded you the whole thing – the secret Order of Lenin that never was and the deep mission for the Soviets you never proved – was a cluster, a mighty cluster, and maybe twenty years later was the time to apologise to the old historian's memory.

Instead you've doubled down. It's very you, but not a great move.

When the Soviet archives were finally opened up, you sent researchers in to scour the joint for any evidence that Clark has been awarded, along with about 400,000 others, the Order of Lenin. And you found? Nothing.

Chris, you went on to have a remarkable career. Somehow this spectacular snafu didn't hold you back. You're a genius of sorts: a great newspaper man who ran, at the same time, a political killing machine. You excelled at both.

But on Manning Clark? If we'd had a chance to sit quietly and talk this over I would have whispered in your ear Kerry Packer's famous report from the afterlife: "There's fucking nothing there."

The Guardian, 16 September 2016

Saving the nation
from Salò

SALÒ IS DOOMED. Pier Paolo Pasolini's film has been stalked by the forces of censorship ever since its release in Australia four years ago. Somehow it has survived – playing to smaller and smaller houses around the country – until a neat bit of tit-for-tat politics in Queensland a few weeks ago delivered it back, trussed and bound, to the Office of Film and Literature Classification for banning.

Perhaps 50,000 Australians have now seen *Salò*. "Most of the people who want to see it on a cinema screen have seen it by now," said its distributor, Michael Walsh of Premium Films. "It's an old film." There is only one print in the country. It's sitting idle in a Melbourne basement with no firm forward bookings. "That may change. This censorship thing could excite considerable interest. The phones might start ringing."

The season at the Valley Twin in Brisbane was so poor that *Salò* was about to be pulled on 12 March after only a week when Judy Spence – Queensland Labor shadow minister for women, Aboriginal and Islander affairs and consumer affairs – went to an evening session and emerged after twenty minutes to release next day a statement headed: "Borbidge Must Act on Sex Film That Glorifies Paedophilia."

This was payback. Spence told *The Sydney Morning Herald* she went to the movie "to expose the hypocrisy of this government. Borbidge made such a fuss of it when it came out in 1994, telling Goss that if he cared about Queenslanders he'd have it off the screen that afternoon. And really

I wanted to expose the fact that there is a national government in power and the film was still on and nothing had changed." Denver Beanland, the state's attorney-general, two days later announced he had "moved with all haste and power" to have *Salò* brought back before the Office of Film and Literature Classification. "There is no doubt that *Salò* is a depraved and disgusting film that should never have received an R-rating in the first place. I am a firm believer that most adults are mature enough to decide what they want to watch. However, outright brutality and pedophilia are not acceptable."

Beanland has not seen the film. Nor have I. Nor has the woman who most recently screened the film for some weeks at Sydney's Third Eye Cinema. Nor have cinemagoers in Tasmania and Western Australia. Nor have most of the members of the Senate Committee on Community Standards, which reacted so passionately in 1993 when the Classification Review Board decided unanimously to lift the seventeen-year ban on *Salò*. "It was not a task we relished," said the Board's convener, the film critic and arts bureaucrat Evan Williams. "*Salò* contains scenes of concentrated foulness such as few of us might have imagined, and I doubt if anything would persuade us to watch it again. Yet we reached our decision with surprising ease and a reassuring unanimity ... Based on some notorious writings by the Marquis de Sade, the film depicts the sexual degradation and torture by four high-ranking functionaries – representing the law, the government, the aristocracy and the Church – of a group of teenagers rounded up by the fascist authorities in the last stages of World War II."

He acknowledged that *Salò* went "to the heart of the dilemma facing all censorship bodies in a free society". But he and his colleagues on the Review Board could find "no valid reason" for preventing adult Australians from seeing it. "It is the duty of the censor to protect the young and warn the innocent. It is the task of the artist, at least occasionally, to shock the old and the complacent. There are times when the serious artist will ask us to plumb the depths, to contemplate both heaven and hell. All of us have the right to flinch from doing so, but a mature society will not deny us the choice." So Australia joined Italy, Germany, Sweden, France, Japan, Britain, the United States, the Netherlands, Spain, Israel, Greece and six other countries in allowing Pasolini's film to be shown uncut to adults. Here the film has an R-certificate – restricted to adults eighteen years and over – and a unique ban on its release on video, though pirate copies without subtitles had been circulating illegally here since soon after the film's first release in Italy in 1976.

The uproar at early Australian screenings of *Salò* came with a good dash of comedy. The national premiere at the 1993 Adelaide Film Festival caused church and civic protests and an angry debate in parliament. Mrs Patricia Draper, mother of three young boys, tried to buy all 1200 tickets at that first screening as an investment, she said, in her children's future. "I was prepared to use our mortgage money to buy all the tickets so that no one would be there. Unfortunately, the tickets were all sold out in the first few days."

South Australia then put *Salò* in limbo: to be screened only at film festivals. No theatre has ever been willing to screen the film in Tasmania. Western Australia banned it outright, using old censorship machinery it never gave up after the states joined Canberra in the new national classification code. Queensland did abandon its own film censorship board, for which the Nationals hammered the Goss Labor government when *Salò* had its first sellout season – in the Year of the Family – at the Boomerang Theatre in Annerley. Wayne Goss called it "appalling trash" but the screenings went on.

This was the political embarrassment Judy Spence was avenging.

Goss didn't leave it at that. He promised the Queensland parliament he'd put pressure on Canberra to look at "the composition of the Commonwealth Film Board of Review". That pressure has since been unrelenting – mostly because of *Salò* but also because the board had refused to bow to militant Christian calls to ban Martin Scorsese's *The Last Temptation of Christ*. Indeed, that film was given an M-classification – suitable for fifteen-year-olds – which the board also gave Jonathan Demme's *The Silence of the Lambs*.

These decisions made the board a target of Christian, political and pro-censorship action. But always the focus of discontent was the unbanning of *Salò*. Over the past four years, Pasolini's film has been the most effective weapon conservatives have had to force changes to Australian censorship – changes of mood, regulation and personnel. Senator Julian McGauran called it "a watershed in censorship in this country". McGauran sits with the Independent Brian Harradine and half a dozen other senators on the key Senate Committee on Community Standards, which has used *Salò* as a "window" to examine the whole classification apparatus.

They grilled Evan Williams at public hearings in the winter of 1993 and David Haines, then deputy director of the national Office of Film and

Literature Classification, recalled: "It aged Evan by about ten years in two weeks." Evan Williams' time as convener of the Board of Review was up not long after, but he was not invited (as had been the custom) to sit for a second term. He was replaced by Barbara Biggins, an expert on program standards for children's television.

Few of *Salò*'s opponents in the past few years have actually seen the movie. Harradine is an honourable exception: he told Haines one day as they passed in a Canberra corridor that it was not as bad as he'd expected. So summaries of the film rather than the film itself have been the ground of debate. These range from the clinical to the lurid. Many contain details of an incident with a rat which is not in the film but has wandered in, somehow, from the plot of Brett Easton Ellis's novel *American Psycho*. In these censorship rows, *Salò* was treated by conservatives not as an exception justified by the importance of Pasolini's place in cinema, but as setting a standard for the extreme sexuality and violence that today's "out-of-touch" censors were willing to allow in any R-rated films. In 1994 Keating was persuaded to ban all R-rated films from television, even from pay television. This is almost a worldfirst.

Meanwhile, there were pressures on the Office of Film and Literature Classification to further tighten censorship. This, too, was largely *Salò*-based, and the director of the office, John Dickie, was offering no resistance. Dickie told the Senate committee in 1993 the film was "wallowing in depravity" and by 1995 he was able to reassure senators that "under the new guidelines, *Salò* would be refused", that is, banned. Should it be studied in film schools and shown at film festivals? he was asked. "In my view *Salò* is a refused category film under any circumstances." Since then, during the recent controversy over X-rated videos, the rules were tightened even further.

Counting particularly against *Salò*'s survival are new bans on "unacceptable fetishes" and the use of actors who appear to be under the age of eighteen. It was the young, or seeming-young, actors who particularly offended the Brisbane parliamentarian bent on revenge. Judy Spence came away from the twenty minutes she saw of *Salò* convinced it should be banned. "The actors look like teenagers and behave like teenagers. To me teenagers are still children. Banning the film won't protect children but basically we don't want to encourage people to make films of this kind and use teenagers to make them."

She admitted she didn't know much of the long history of *Salò*, nor had she thought through the repercussions of her protest for film classification in Australia. The first result of her stoush with Borbidge was a rush of publicity that rescued the film's failing season at the Valley Twin. Despite a personal plea by the Queensland premier, the run was extended for a few weeks before the print went down to a rather drab season, now over, at Melbourne's Capitol Theatre.

Last week, advertisements appeared nationwide, announcing the Office of Film and Literature Classification is to reclassify *Salò* on June 25 after considering public submissions. In its way, this is a pioneering effort: provisions allowing the office to take a second look at a film have never been used before. Until now, a classification has stuck with a film for life. But once *Salò* is banned, classifications are likely to become much more fluid, and more frequently challenged. There are more films on the hit list – either to be banned or restricted – including *The Silence of the Lambs* and *The Last Temptation of Christ*.

But the banning of *Salò* will take time. After the Classification Board makes its decision in June, it will be appealed to the Review Board, where only two members survive from the six who released the film in 1993 "with surprising ease and a reassuring unanimity". They are the Sydney psychiatrist Brent Waters and the Melbourne university priest Father Michael Elligate. The other members, apart from the convener, Barbara Biggins of Adelaide, are the television personality Anne Fulwood and the headmaster of Merrimac High in Queensland, William Wilcox. Elligate refused to discuss the merits of *Salò* with the *Herald*. "It's really sub judice now." But he did say: "Most discerning people are happy with the system that saw its release."

Sometime in early August, Premium Films will probably be asked to hand over its print. After that, Australians will have to catch *Salò* on their holidays in Japan, Europe and America. Back home, un-subtitled videos will remain fairly widely available in Italian video stores and the book of the movie, de Sade's *120 Days of Sodom,* will be, as always, a Penguin Classic in bookshops.

The Sydney Morning Herald, 13 May 1997

Salò was banned again. It took a little time for the Howard government to stack the Review Board and finesse the rules, but the deed was done in February 1998. "I'm actually over the moon that the artists have been pulled back into line," said McGauran. "You must remember I'm National Party – artistic merit doesn't mean much to me." Though a DVD with an hour of additional "context" was released in 2010, screening *Salò* all on its own in cinemas remains forbidden in 2018.

What's Left these days?

I'VE BEEN ADDICTED TO NEWSPAPERS most of my life. But I've never read so much, watched so much and listened to so much as I have since joining the *Media Watch* team three years ago. What I have to say about the drift of public debate in John Howard's Australia – the way we argue and what we argue about – comes from this recent immersion in the media after spending twenty-five years moving backwards and forwards between books, broadcasting, editing and writing. I can only offer impressions. These things can't be proved. The conclusions I draw are inevitably personal and coloured by my own politics. But that's the only way any of us can make sense of the country and the times in which we live.

In the summer of 1997 I flew down to interview Brian Harradine. No other interview I have ever done has stuck in my head like this. In those days, Harradine's Senate vote could make or break legislation and the only colour in that remarkably bare office on the Hobart waterfront was a wall of red Senate Hansards. I remember him sitting in the corner like a grasshopper in grey daks and the strange indirection of his conversation. I should go bushwalking, he told me. Head north and get some perspective on things by walking the Blue Tiers. He lost me for a while as he rambled through the forests, deflecting my questions about his life, his politics and his faith. Then we got to Hitler.

I'd come to Hobart because I was hacking away at a story – lonely back then – about the resurrection of religion in secular politics. As the nation's leading backroom Catholic warrior, Harradine was shaping the national debate on drugs, sex, film, overseas aid, new technology and the law, shaping it in strange ways according to Christian doctrine. The fact that he was pursuing the Vatican's agenda in the Australian Senate courtesy of the votes of about 32,000 Tasmanians struck me as an affront to democracy.

"You remember how Hitler came to power?" Harradine didn't give a fig for the maxim that once you start citing Hitler you've lost your argument. "Hitler came to power by popular vote." I'm ashamed to say when I wrote this interview up for *The Sydney Morning Herald*, I made fun of the senator's shaky grasp of late Weimar politics. Any schoolkid knows Hitler never won a free election but it was unfair of me not to acknowledge Harradine's point: that Hitler was popular. Euthanasia had brought us to this point in the interview. I'd brought along a copy of the Hobart Mercury showing 54.3 per cent of Tasmanians wanted euthanasia legalised. That made no difference to Harradine's absolute opposition. He asked: "Should we take account of public opinion polls when we're dealing with fundamental issues such as this?"

What's nagged me ever since is the memory of this strange, unsympathetic man talking life, death and opinion polls. He told me most Australians want the death penalty restored. "Does that make capital punishment right?" But surely we'd all given up on hanging long ago? Later I checked his figures and found he was right. Name a horrible crime – and it doesn't have to be the Bali bombing – and most Australians reckon the guilty should swing. That's a fact, an important fact. But does popular backing make it right? Make it good? Or make any moral difference at all? Harradine hasn't swayed me on condoms, censorship, stem cell research or lesbian motherhood, but I've come to see the question he raised in his bleak office in early 1997 – do we settle big issues of principle according to opinion polls? – as the question of the Howard years.

Harradine's challenge takes people like me places we don't want to go. I work to shape opinion. For a long time I believed that winning over the majority – even if way down the track – was what it was all about. But that's naive. It's also an idea Howard has turned brilliantly against his critics. Of all the gambits used to bully public debate in Howard's Australia, the most effective has been this false model of democracy as a perpetual popularity contest.

That was Tampa. Turning back refugee boats was always going to be popular. Howard wasn't struck by some fresh insight the night he ordered that Norwegian freighter to take – to Indonesia or anywhere – those 400 or so shipwrecked asylum seekers. Australians had wanted that to happen for a long time. Any politician who could read an opinion poll had known since the first boats arrived in the late 1970s there was a big constituency hungry to see them turned away.

So why did it take Canberra so long to take up this sure-fire vote-winner? My guess is that good people in politics and the bureaucracy were simply appalled at the prospect of violating Australia's obligations to vulnerable people, to the refugee conventions, to the UN, to world shipping, to the international rules of sea rescue and to our own Migration Act. John Howard's genius was to understand that whatever impact turning the boats away would have on the way the world saw Australia, none of these violated principles would have much traction at home. They could be swept aside by the overwhelming popularity of taking tough action against boat people.

Howard is a master of this brand of raw democracy. One reason Marian Wilkinson and I wrote *Dark Victory* was to try to come to grips with this. The popularity of Howard's strategy was both a starting point for the project and a theme of the book. Even so, we were routinely accused of not acknowledging the support enjoyed by the blockade and the Pacific Solution. Pointing to the many passages in the book where this is analysed didn't get us far. The point being made by our critics was that raw popularity meant there really wasn't much point grappling with the difficult issues of principle raised by the fate of these people. Popularity was enough.

It gets worse. Both sides of politics – Labor and Coalition – claim that whatever galvanised Australia in the Tampa crisis can't be called racism because it was so pervasive, so popular. Manipulating race for electoral advantage is a hallmark of Howard's government but he insists on the right to cut down native title and turn back boats filled with Muslim refugees without this being named for what it is, "without being accused of prejudice or bigotry, without being knocked off course by ... phoney charges of racism." And the press, itself scared of facing the xenophobia of this country, lets Howard get away with it. It's textbook political correctness: the demand that Australia's pervasive racism be shown democratic respect by leaving it unnamed.

Media proprietors read the same opinion polls as politicians. The same focus groups are telling newspapers what they want to read and political parties who they'll vote for. The popularity of what Howard did in the Tampa crisis explains, in part, the widespread failure of the media to grasp what was really going on here and cover these events the way they deserved.

There were honourable exceptions to this failure – I particularly exempt *The Australian* and the ABC – but to be working inside a newspaper as this shameful episode in the country's history unfolded is to know the power of the media's willed indifference to issues of pure principle when these collide with overwhelming popular support.

This continued long after the 2001 poll. How could there be so little interest in the evidence presented to the Certain Maritime Incident inquiry? So little curiosity about what happened to the sailors and asylum seekers caught up in the naval blockade of the boats? How little protest from the media – virtually none – at finding itself banned from Operation Relex and from Australia's gulag on Nauru? How little curiosity to examine why, after going to such extreme lengths to keep these Afghan and Iraqi refugees out of the country, Australia was forced in mid-2003 to begin bringing them ashore? I can tell you the answer to the last. It's because the rest of the world – apart from New Zealand – told Australia to fuck off. It's a big story with a humiliating payout for the Howard government. It's barely rated a mention in the media.

What is going on here? Blaming it all on media proprietors being too sympathetic to the government is too easy. It's not enough – though true – to argue that Australians don't want to know how the outcome they so welcome has been achieved. The gross failures of reporting since the Tampa have been driven by the knowledge that Canberra's radical course was hugely popular. The media was not the only institution to fail in the face of this popularity. The courts, the bureaucracy, the Opposition and the media were all rattled.

By the time I moved from ABC Radio National to *The Sydney Morning Herald* in 1996, Labor had met the fate it deserved and Howard's people were taunting their critics with the trademark line: "Don't you know Paul Keating lost the election?" Mocking the democratic credentials of journalists in this way worked particularly well in those early years, tipping journalists onto the back foot, undercutting their confidence, introducing a note of apology into public debates. And though Keating is a distant memory in 2004, we still hear from time to time this one-size-fits-all rebuke of Howard's critics: "Don't they know Paul Keating lost the election."

Like nicknames and urban myths, abuse needs a grain of truth to stick. Many critics made the mistake of treating the new government as an aberration, an interruption to the normal course of politics, which would soon resume. They underestimated the new man and the new government. Howard would prove to be the most professional political operator Canberra had seen for forty or fifty years. And he would show himself to be a new kind of prime minister, the first for a long time who came to office with no talk, however vague, of changing Australia for the better. Except for a bit of a hiccup in the McMahon years, every prime minister from Menzies to Keating told us some sort of national self-improvement was in the wind.

In an odd way, this notion let us avoid looking Australia in the face. If we were already heading somewhere else – becoming more open, more tolerant, more reconciled to Indigenous Australians, more attuned to Asia, more in love with the arts, a great independent republic in the south – then we didn't have to bother looking too closely at Australia as it really was. We could wait for change to arrive. But Howard came with a different message. Of course he had plans for economic change but that was just about that. He wasn't planning to take us anywhere. He left us with no choice but to take a long, hard look at Australia as it really is. John Howard is the confrontation with Australia many Australians have been loath to have.

People who keep banging on about issues that mattered under the old government – the republic, reconciliation – are ridiculed as irrelevant, out of touch, members of some self-appointed elite. And if we persist in arguing minority views, we'll be accused of suffering from 'moral vanity'. Brian Harradine has never been troubled by this accusation. Nor should the press be. But this tabloid thuggery has been astonishingly successful in sapping the confidence – and wasting the time – of Howard's critics in the press. You might imagine those dishing out these taunts would remember where they've heard this sort of thing before – demands that the intelligentsia submit to the will of the people. Doesn't it remind them of Eastern Europe before the Wall came down? The same tabloid hacks who – quite rightly – make heroes of Soviet dissenters vilify Howard's critics for failing to see him through the eyes of the people. And they're unembarrassed – perhaps unaware – of the grim echoes of their own abuse.

Another very John Howard idea lurks in the Keating's-been-defeated taunt: the idea that criticism of government is by nature partisan, that critics can never really escape the party divide. This is one detail in a bigger, bleaker picture. Out from Canberra over the last seven years has spread a stultifying image of public life as a contest between government and Opposition. I've never been so aware of loyalty – party loyalty – mattering so much in Australia. A great deal has been written about the impact of this on the public service, on government appointments and the freedom of NGOs to speak their minds. But the notion that press criticism is also inescapably partisan – if you're against us you must be for them – has worked to muffle debate across the media, particularly in the beleaguered ABC.

I'd led a quiet life until I went to *Media Watch*. Then I discovered I was a notorious Lefty. This amused my friends and surprised me. Most of the time, the label was applied as abuse, the counterattack of choice for those we exposed on *Media Watch*. After taking many swings at the *Herald Sun*'s Andrew Bolt over the last couple of years, it was no surprise to read him calling *Media Watch*, "The ABC TV show which left-winger David Marr uses to attack personal and political foes ..."

The old tectonic struggle between Left and Right still shapes public debate in this country – less often as a great contest of values, more often as abuse. Slagging off the Left and its motives has particular – and puzzling – potency. How can this be in a country which again and again shows its indifference to great contests of principle; a country where you have to struggle to remember the last time the Left had decisive influence on national politics?

Four commentators known for wielding the Left word as a weapon, often savagely, are Andrew Bolt, Piers Akerman of *The Daily Telegraph*, Tim Blair of *The Bulletin* and Gerard Henderson of The Sydney Institute. I emailed all four: "I'm trying to pin down what commentators mean by 'Left' these days ... how they identify a Lefty in Australia in 2004." They came to the party.

But the four agreed on only one point: the Left they demonise is anti-- American. Forget Marx and Engels, the core complaint against the Australian Left today is disloyalty to the United States. For most of the four that in turn entails the Left being anti the Iraq war, reluctant to tackle Arab extremists, hostile to Israel and pro–United Nations. On the home front, opposition to private schools is high on the list of Left vices, along with scepticism about Christianity and an indulgent attitude to homosexuals, to boatpeople and to the ABC. But thereafter the lists of the four diverge, often wildly.

For that ancient warrior of Murdoch's tabloids, Piers Akerman, the Left are John Howard's opponents, "opposed to parliamentary prayer, support gay marriage, wish to re-regulate the industrial sector, those who fail to see the Iraq conflict as part of the war on terrorism". Andrew Bolt's Left is a New-Age creature retreating into "tribalism" and inventing their own gods: "Nature gods. Tree spirits. Water sprites. Gaia." His Left is "not just an enemy of humanism, reason and freedom, but of Christianity, too". Those on Tim Blair's Left are chauvinists, republicans and by nature intolerant. Blair's Left:

> opposes commercial media (except Fairfax), wealth that doesn't grow at the same rate for everybody, lack of media diversity (except at the ABC), media deregulation (except censorship), doing anything that makes Australia a terrorist target (except supporting East Timorese independence), liberation of oppressed peoples by any means other than impossible global consensus, inaccurate commentary (except from John Pilger and Michael Moore), scientific advances in agriculture, and an increasingly pleasant, warmer globe. But what is the Left for? Aside from broad, rarely-defined motherhood notions like "democracy", "greater accountability", and "justice", it's hard to tell. A lefty friend supported the return of South Sydney to the NRL; maybe that's it.

What caught my eye in a recent assault on the national broadcaster by Gerard Henderson – this one in late June – was his attack on what he called the "leftist orthodoxy" of the ABC. Here was an image of the Left as a bunch of people bound by an old and accepted creed. Here it is:

1. A belief in the desirability of wide-scale government intervention (funded by taxation) in the domestic economy – in such areas as education, health, welfare and the environment. Along with a corresponding scepticism about private solutions in such areas as education, health, welfare and the environment. In other words, a view that the public sector is good in itself and that the private sector is, at best, a dubious exercise.
2. A belief that governments should not interfere in the realms of private morality – covering such areas as abortion, censorship, same-sex relationships, etc.
3. A scepticism about Western religious beliefs – in particular traditional Christian churches and the emerging fundamentalist Christianity.

4. An unwillingness to support the use of military force abroad – along with a disdain for patriotism at home. An ambiguity towards, or outright opposition to, the Australia–America alliance – along with concern about Israel's role in world affairs.

5. An abiding sense of shame and guilt for the past acts of Western nations in their colonial manifestations – a commitment to reconciliation with native peoples.

6. A belief in the sanctity of international solutions to international problems – comprising a commitment to the United Nations, despite its evident inefficiency and virtual impotency.

7. Opposition to the globalisation process of economic reform – including a resentment of such international organisations as the World Trade Organization, the World Bank and the International Monetary Fund. A preference for international aid over the reform of the political systems and domestic economies of third world nations.

8. A tendency to be alienated from elected mainstream political leaders (whether conservative or social democrat) and a conviction that the modern democratic system is inhabited by politicians who lie by habit.

9. A tradition of moral compromise – leading to a belief that democracies are not much better than dictatorships in the way they operate. In other words, moral equivalence.

Henderson's list gets a bit ragged towards the end. Who beyond a few remnant Stalinists believes these days that democracies and dictatorships are morally much the same? But it's a notion that might spook a few people. On all four lists are ideas capable of sparking fears in the community. But not great fears. They don't come near explaining how effectively denunciation of the Left shapes public debate in Australia these days: rattling the media and sabotaging big public contests of principle this country is so reluctant to face. What is the spectre behind the abuse?

Isn't it really about money? The Left has plans and they're expensive. Isn't this where the fear comes in? That idea drew a blank with my warriors. But I would put my money on money. No one fears these days that the Left is going to break up the estates and nationalise the means of production. But the contest of Left vs Right remains potent because it's still about the public purse vs private purse; wages vs dividends; regulation vs profits; public spending vs tax cuts.

What's worse, the Left challenges the prerogatives of money, and the prerogatives of a government intent on turning Australia into a money-making machine. The problem with "lefty" journalists – particularly at the ABC – is that they don't give money its due. They keep raising issues like equity, lawfulness, candour, dignity – issues that don't have much to do with money or can stand in the way of money-making. It's bias again. The fear that such people might get their hands on the levers is reason enough to demonise the Left – especially now, in these miraculously prosperous times.

The Third *Overland* Public Lecture,
Melbourne, 29 September 2004

A common humanity

I CAN'T REMEMBER WHEN I started reading Robert Manne but I do remember how hostile I was to this gloomy commentator who spent so much time in the 1980s banging on about the evils of communism. And I didn't like the company he kept: the *Quadrant* crowd, old people full of strange rage who already seemed over the hill when I glimpsed them twenty years earlier round the campus of Sydney University.

Then something happened. Manne started to make sense. He was turning his moral intelligence away from the red menace to questions much closer to home – most urgently the question of how we once treated Indigenous Australians and how we must now live with them. By then several things had happened: the Berlin Wall was down, the High Court had decided *Mabo*, and much of the Australian Right had turned venomous and often nakedly racist.

This left Manne in a jam: having to choose between his principles and the company he kept. That he speaks with such authority in Australia today is the direct result of an uncommonly brave decision he took a decade ago to stick to his principles. He lost friends and found his voice. He came to identify where the Right had gone wrong in the long struggle against communism in the Antipodes: "The failure during the Cold War to distinguish those parts of the Left agenda which were foolish or foul from those parts which were founded on a genuine understanding of injustice." With that, Manne walked into the territory he has been exploring ever since.

But not I think as a changed man. Despite the title of his new collection of essays – *Left, Right, Left* – Robert Manne never became a Lefty. God knows what being a Lefty means in this country today, but if you're the sort of Lefty that terrifies the editors of *The Australian* and puts the snarl into Gerard Henderson's prose, you are supposed to be bound by a hidden creed. Even perfectly reasonable beliefs are taken to be code for the dangers that lie beneath. But the key to Manne's career is his intellectual and moral hostility to the idea that *any* ideology has all the answers.

The Manne method is to search for the contradictions. Orwell is his model here. "Orwell's openness to experience is connected to something of which every reader of Orwell is aware, his honesty, or what Orwell himself, with greater precision, called his ability to face unpleasant facts." If Manne were a born-again Lefty, he would argue for the superior scepticism of the Left. He doesn't. When it comes to facing facts, he rates the Left no better than the Right. Perhaps to remind us where he came from, Manne spends a good deal of his time in this collection flailing the Left for the unforgivable sin of apologising for Stalin's Terror in the 1930s and Pol Pot's slaughter in the 1970s. He remarks grimly: "There is no regime too base to be defended."

What Manne wants to do now is get past what he calls, in an essay on Noel Pearson, "the sterility of the present ideological division, between Left and Right". Twenty years of public argument have shown him how often these labels fail to describe deep instincts or strongly held values. After the fall of Saigon, Manne and his then-friends lobbied Malcolm Fraser to allow Vietnamese boat people to settle in Australia. "During the Cold War there had been no group apparently more sensitive to the plight of refugees than the anti-communist intelligentsia," he writes. But in the age of *Tampa*, those people swapped sides. Manne doesn't spare them. "Most of my former political friends supported the Howard policy ... It now became clear that the ocean of anti-communist tears – for refugees from communism – had been shed by ideological opportunists and moral hypocrites." So Manne argues it's time to replace the politics of Left and Right with what he calls "a politics founded upon recognition of a common humanity".

His job – the job of any honest commentator – is to stand in the welter of events, the facts raining down on him, and grasp what is going on. To describe the present takes the skills of a historian and the powers of a clairvoyant. Essential tools are moral discrimination, intelligence, a fine memory and respect for fact. One daunting aspect of the Manne method is his way of gathering and checking facts: he reads. It's an academic's approach, more familiar at La Trobe than in the newsrooms of Melbourne and Sydney. Other newspaper commentators hoard ammunition to fling at their targets, but Manne digs down through layers of documents to make his case – to prove what a wretch Wilfred Burchett really was in the Korean War or compel us to acknowledge that half-caste children really *were* taken from their mothers in a campaign driven – at least in the early decades – by a genocidal expectation that Aboriginal Australia would one day disappear.

Manne stands at a slight distance from those he writes for and those he writes about. It's the indispensable stance of anyone who takes commentary seriously. It means keeping a distance from power. Most of us as we age drift vaguely Right. As time runs out, we grow fearful and lose our early, perhaps sentimental, faith in mankind. We're looking for protection, for the shelter of power. Manne's movement in the opposite direction has a great deal to do with a professional and personal impulse to keep his distance from power. In a recent issue of *The Monthly*, Manne paints a remorseless picture of *The Australian*'s foreign editor Greg Sheridan, who emerged from a "dizzying week" of intimacy with the great in Washington in July 2002 "blinded by American military might" and reduced thereafter to "playing the role of a publicist on America's behalf". It's the portrait of a commentator ruined.

We have our differences. I rate Robert Manne the nation's most rational commentator, yet he has a strange faith in taboo and a hankering to return to a time when taboo kept society's dark forces in check. Manne believes Western civilisation is still dealing with the impact of the anti-puritan revolution of the 1960s. Though he values a good deal of what began back then – the decriminalisation of homosexuality, for instance – he fears where this upheaval may yet land civilisation. He identifies the problem as the weakening of taboo. In "Life and Death on the Slippery Slope", Manne writes: "Our society has been built around certain traditional taboos: that in the past thirty years or so we have passed through a vast cultural revolution, where many of these taboos have been breached at their most vulnerable points."

Respect for taboo contradicts so much of what this man apparently stands for. Taboos demand fear, obedience and silence – not questioning and analysis. Taboo works not by reason but disgust. When Manne starts praising taboo, his moral discrimination and his sense of history are both blunted. And at times – these are the only times – he comes close to losing his temper. The taboos he defends particularly in *Left, Right, Left* are those against euthanasia and pornography. Curiously absent from his discussion of these issues is the human being who – rightly or wrongly – wishes to die and wants to watch porn. It's not that he weighs too lightly the views and wishes of these people. He gives them no weight at all.

In Manne's full-throttled condemnation of porn there's no place for the ordinary folk who consume the stuff in large numbers and don't go about raping and killing as a result. For Manne, porn threatens the moral collapse of society, degrading citizens and stimulating crime. Hence, censorship. In his passionate denunciation of euthanasia, he shows no sympathy for the plight – and the wishes – of those who would rather die rather than endure pain. Why is this nuanced and sympathetic man so absolute here? I sense the answer lies waiting at the bottom of that "slippery slope" on which Manne sees society forever perched. Down there where civilisations collapse is the example of the worst humans have ever done to one another: the Holocaust.

Robert Manne talks of himself as living, thinking and working in its shadow. He is one of a handful of distinguished Jews who have reshaped our understanding of this country by bringing to bear on its history a critique of racism honed by the Holocaust. The intensity of his attachment to the rule of law, to truthfulness in public life and to combating the politics of fear seem to me driven by the example of the Holocaust and a heightened sense of where debauched politics may end.

All this is immensely valuable. But Manne has yet to think through some of the "slippery slope" issues where assertions of personal freedom bring with them old fears of civilisations in collapse, or carry a strong historical whiff of the Holocaust. This is where, in his writing, we find appeals to taboo rather than exposition of principle. Manne writes that allowing doctors to kill under certain exceptional circumstances will "of necessity lead us down a slippery slope into new and unexpected moral territory", and any assumption otherwise "can be shown, with near certainty, to be false". What follows is an expression of deeply felt fear – "why pretend that the distinction between voluntary and non-voluntary euthanasia will hold?" – that falls a long way short of proof.

Holocaust taboo is approached most directly in his condemnation of Helen Darville's *The Hand that Signed the Paper* and, more recently, Christos Tsiolkas's *Dead Europe*. Here the absent person in Mann's argument is the reader who can be trusted to read these books and emerge untainted. Manne and I were on opposite sides in the public dispute over *The Hand that Signed the Paper* nearly ten years ago. Then and now my view is that Darville perpetrated a shabby deception in adopting her Ukrainian guise and her book should never have won the high honours it did – but it was a promising little first novel which I read as condemning Babi Yar and Treblinka. There's never been much room in Manne's argument for people like me who read the book that way. Yet we're here. So why aren't we factored into the discussion?

Manne's magisterial review of *Dead Europe* in the June edition of *The Monthly* provokes the same question. The rhetoric is quieter after a decade: more sorrow and less anger. But there is still this strange absence in his argument of people like me who read Tsiolkas's novel as condemning anti-Semitism rather than endorsing it. For me this book is about the journey of a young man tempted to hate the Jews – he is tempted, he stumbles once or twice, but at the core of his sense of himself is his determination to resist the ugly anti-Semitism he finds everywhere in post–Berlin Wall Europe. Meanwhile, young Isaac is turning into a vampire – a signal, surely, that the plot is not to be taken too literally.

Ultimately, Manne condemns the novel as cheap exploitation of a decent taboo.

> *Dead Europe*, which climaxes in scenes of almost indescribable violence and horror, is nothing if not a transgressive novel. The trouble, however, is that we live in a post-transgressive age in which breaching traditional taboos has almost altogether lost the power to shock. There is, however, one subject that still possesses this power. Since the Holocaust the expression of anti-Semitism has been culturally forbidden … It is a novel where the author has sought to excite himself and his jaded audience by playing, to my mind purposelessly, with the fire of a magical, pre-modern anti-Semitism.

Denigrating Tsiolkas's motives in this way strikes me as deeply unfair. The cheap-shocks argument was used by Manne and many others against Helen Darville. It had more traction then. Manne acknowledges the new Tsiolkas novel is a far more accomplished work, but he levels the same accusation against Tsiolkas. Why? Because in his guts Manne fears novels like this keep anti-Semitism alive. He believes in taboo. The most powerful are those we hardly know are there. Manne simply – and profoundly – regrets that Tsiolkas reminds us of this horror, that he has used as the building blocks of a contemporary novel something all of us wish were buried with the past. Manne acknowledges, of course, that anti-Semitism was not interred with the Holocaust. Yet he regrets its resurrection here – and Tsiolkas's failure to condemn. The worst of it is that the novel is ambiguous: "In my reading *Dead Europe* is neither anti-Semitic nor anti-anti-Semitic." Manne doesn't mean that as praise.

This is a clue to what seems, at first, a strange limitation in Robert Manne. He's a social commentator capable of understanding the finest nuances of argument but he's a bit at sea with fiction. Intellectually he knows he's dealing with something different here: not history, government reports and biographical sketches. He knows fiction works through characters – and that the good, the bad and the ugly must all strut around the little stage of a novel. But when literature deals in taboo, the social commentator in Manne wants the sort of moral clarity that art – even great art – does not always provide. In a revealing aside in his essay "A Case for Censorship", Manne defends *Salò* "Because Pasolini is a genuine artist ... and because in his work the evil is unambiguously condemned ..."

Condemning evil is a good blunt job description for Robert Manne. He doesn't harangue. Somehow he manages, year in and year out, to keep his temper. He is polite. He sets out his reasons with patience. There's evidence on every page of *Left, Right, Left* of his fine ear for language and supple rhetorical skill. His best writing is infused with a kind of sweetness, an understanding of moral and intellectual frailty, an acknowledgement of how contradictory human beings can be. He writes of these essays: "All were written because of my faith in the importance of public argument over values. All express my commitment to the country that provided refuge to my parents and where I was born."

By Manne's reckoning, that country is in bad shape right now. The worst is not Howard, Iraq or children overboard; not greed, porn, racism or the betrayal of refugees; not the gutless Opposition, the debauched conventions of Westminster government or the white lies being told about Australia's black history. The worst is indifference. That's Manne's true opponent. And when he tries to rouse the public from the prosperous coma of our time, the Rotweilers of the Right fight back. That's when the abuse starts, the familiar abuse imported as a job lot from Washington think tanks: elitism, moral vanity, contempt for the will of the people.

Of course, he's undeterred. These days Manne, professor of politics at La Trobe, writes for *The Monthly* long narratives of public scandals that have all but gone out of fashion in Australia's frantic newspapers. Has he at last fixed his place in the political spectrum? Let's hope not. There's time in the next couple of decades for him to shift once more, a bit to the Left and a bit to the Right in his ideological determination to stay free of ideology. Pray Robert Manne doesn't morph into a television pundit. This deeply old-fashioned contemporary commentator is built to write. Words on the page are his weapon. He uses them better than any of us who are trying to make sense of this difficult and beautiful country in the long age of John Howard.

Meanjin volume 64, issue no. 3, 2005

Australia,
land without rights

A MESSAGE TO THE PEOPLE in Federation Square waiting for Oprah Winfrey to arrive surprised to find *me* on the big screen talking about human rights: since coming to Australia the other day Oprah has cuddled koalas and seen Uluru, but nothing about us would surprise her as much as the fact that Australians still don't have the rights Americans have had for the last 200 years. Australians have become a unique species: a people without any national guarantees of free speech or freedom of assembly or of due process. And we seem happy enough to stay that way. It makes us a species worth studying.

For fifty years Labor in opposition has been promising a human rights act once back in power in Canberra. And every new Labor government lets Australia down without much of a fight. Lionel Murphy's bill, for which there had been such high hopes, was allowed to die with the Parliament in 1974. Gareth Evans' bill never made it to parliament. Lionel Bowen's bill was at least debated twenty-five years ago – I think it's probably the last full-scale human rights debate in the national parliament – but like all the others it was allowed to die. Today's Labor attorney-general, Robert McClelland, set Frank Brennan's team off on its national journey of exploration but Kevin Rudd ditched their proposed charter in April without a meeting, without a word of explanation.

This is failure of a particularly interesting order. Elsewhere in the world in those fifty years, Britain, New Zealand and South Africa all signed up to rights regimes. Canada – God bless and preserve her – did it twice. That a charter is on the way in Tasmania, is secure in the ACT, and at least for the time being shelters Victorians is, of course, welcome. Entirely welcome. But it remains a fact that despite all the hopes and campaigns of the last half century, Australians remain uniquely exposed to mistreatment by bureaucrats and government. We want better protection of rights – the polls show us that – but not having them provokes little concern round the kitchen tables of the nation. We muddle through, hoping and trusting. It's the Australian way.

After the latest debacle, campaigners know the human rights bandwagon is going to have to stay under tarps in the garage for quite a while. A few useful ideas proposed by Brennan's team look like seeing the light of day. But an exercise of the Brennan kind, on that scale, can't be repeated for years. My advice – speaking as someone who did nothing useful during that process – is to use the time to make an unflinching appraisal of how these campaigns have been fought and should be fought. It's my view this issue will not gain the traction it needs in this country while the debate remains a polite – if at times heated – series of exchanges between lawyers about laws and models and theories. It is time we were less polite; time to name the enemies of rights and identify their motives. It's time – as George Pell is so fond of saying – to bell the cat.

"No reasonable person can object to the protection of rights," Helen Irving wrote recently in her essay "A Legal Perspective on Bills of Rights". "Those who question the bill of rights agenda are rarely contemptuous of rights ... most are concerned, rather, about the best *means* of protecting rights ..." That has to be questioned sharply. The opponents of bills and charters are tramping the corridors of Canberra and polishing opinion pieces for *The Australian* because they *do* object to the effective protection of rights. That is the point. It is time we said so. This is not a fifty-year contest in Australia about ways and means. This is about outcomes.

Pell throws at rights protection every argument he can muster. He is fighting for the common law; he is fighting for parliament; he is fighting for democracy; he is fighting for what he calls "moral truth". His 2008 *Quadrant* essay "Four Fictions: An Argument Against a Charter of Rights" shows him keenly aware of the fragility of rights protection in today's Australia. He argues: "The asylum seeker issue highlights where the limits of the ethic of the fair-go among the majority can be encountered. I wonder about the consequences for Australian democracy if we were to suffer a major terrorist attack on our own soil ..." And so do I wonder.

But the cardinal has two lists. On the good list are rights he approves: "The rights of Aborigines and Indigenous or racial minorities, women ... homosexuals [so he says], migrants and the poor, the disabled and elderly ..." On the bad list are rights to life, sex and death that don't square with formal, conservative Christian teaching. I might be an exasperated atheist but it looks to me that Pell is willing to see *all* rights exposed to the uncertain protection offered by parliaments and politicians rather than risk "what can happen when a charter of rights is interpreted from the premises of the secular mindset".

Pell is fighting the erosion of the ancient role of bishops and preachers as the sex police of society. This is why a determined group of Christian leaders are the principal opponents of formal rights protection in this country. They in turn enlist conservative politicians on both sides of politics – politicians who agree with them, and politicians who don't have the stamina to stand up to them. As one of the most highly placed human rights observers remarked to me – off the record: "If you could turn church leaders around, you'd turn the debate around. They give credibility to opposition." I know it's hard. I know it goes against the polite grain. But unless human rights advocates are willing to have an open brawl with their most effective opponents the hopes of a national charter – let alone a bill of rights – are doomed.

The human rights movement has deep Christian antecedents which Brigadier Jim Wallace of the Australian Christian Lobby – one of the staunchest opponents of bills and charters of rights – describes so eloquently in his essay "Why Should Christians be Concerned About a Bill of Rights":

> We can see throughout history many Christians taking action to preserve [human rights], whether by ending the slave trade, supporting persecuted believers in other countries, championing civil liberties for negroes in the US, defending the right to life of the unborn, affirming the worth of people with disabilities, or exercising leadership in the early trade union movement.

But the brigadier is dead against letting judges decide rights because that would put at risk his beliefs on life, sex and death, plus – and here he shows his Protestant colours – pleasure.

Wallace deplores the fact that "in America, it has been successfully argued that naked dancing in bars is protected by the outer limits of the

First Amendment because it is a form of sexual expression". Wallace wants a system that will ensure the continued social disapproval of homosexuals – his expression – marriage and adoption only for heterosexuals, and no more naked dancing in bars.

Crucial to the arguments of Christians fighting bills and charters is that they are protecting the mainstream from an unscrupulous moral minority. I love Pell's rhetoric here: "It helps to understand the game that is afoot in the push for a charter of rights to consider the way 'the tyranny of the majority' is used to browbeat majority scepticism about minority agendas." Statements like this are everywhere in the submissions to Brennan, the pages of *The Australian* and the pages, indeed, of *The Age*. Politicians sprout them continuously. Polling doesn't settle great moral questions but as it happens, the mainstream has gone over to the other side. Polls show conservative Christian teaching on contraception, abortion, cloning, chastity, divorce, homosexuality and euthanasia are all now – and have been for some time – minority positions. These Christians haven't even been able to hold the line on gay marriage. While Australia remains divided on the issue, last month's Nielsen poll found fifty-seven per cent support for gay marriage, six per cent undecided, and only thirty-seven per cent backing conservative Christian opposition.

Let's bell this cat: conservative Christians do not want courts protecting rights because the political process is their best hope of defending – and perhaps imposing – beliefs that are becoming increasingly distasteful to the Australian people. It isn't always the way and it isn't always neat but reason works best in the courts while fear still holds sway in politics.

In this glorious week as WikiLeaks delivers a river of truth to the world, I reflect particularly on the rock-solid opposition to bills and charters of rights presented by *The Australian*. It is to my mind astonishing that a newspaper would campaign against rights, particularly the right of free speech. *The Australian* does, led by political correspondent Paul Kelly with a deep and passionate commitment to parliamentary democracy in which he sees no role for lawyers. It does not describe the Australia I know let alone the Australia I want, but it is passionately and sincerely believed.

Over in the United States of America there are calls for Julian Assange, an Australian national, to be hunted down as if he were a terrorist and thrown into prison for the rest of his life. The US government is using its muscle to cut off money to WikiLeaks, to prevent credit card providers having contact with WikiLeaks sites. Washington has bludgeoned Amazon and other sites to stop carrying WikiLeaks. But *The New York Times* goes on publishing because it has the First Amendment on its side. And everybody in America knows that for all the political grandstanding *The New York Times* is free to continue to publish, by my estimation – considering there are 250,000 documents in this pile – for about the next twenty years the truth of the Bush and Obama administrations. And yet there are newspapers here that would prefer to live in the world of lobbying, of influence, of backroom deals rather than the world of rights that can be enforced in public arenas.

In a sense, asking a politician to support a bill or charter of rights is like asking a burglar to endorse burglar alarms. Those politicians who do are to be honoured. Those who don't are caught in an interesting bind. George Brandis claims in his heart to want us all to have the broadest possible ambit of rights. But read his elegant essays, pick your way through the clever contradictions, note those familiar appeals to British habits that are outmoded even in Britain, and you end by knowing in your bones that he is not really committed to rights. He doesn't want to see them guaranteed by courts. He and his party are on the side of lobbying, influence and power. And so are large chunks of the Labor Party. Bob Carr, the man who loves so much about America, American history, and the Democratic Party, loathes the First Amendment that has made America what it is. He wants nothing like it here. Carr is not alone in Labor. The party that has been promising rights and charters forever but no national Labor leader since Bert Evatt has been willing to *fight* for rights, to put skin in the game. He got nowhere.

Since the catastrophe of 1988, we've been told not even to dream of constitutional change in Australia. What an unexceptional list was on offer then. Yet all four proposals – to end gerrymanders, extend trial by jury, confirm freedom of religion and make state governments pay a fair price for properties they acquire – were lost overwhelmingly. That made forty-four failures from fifty-two attempts to change the constitution by referendum. The lesson we are supposed to draw from all of those defeats is that Australians hate change, or at least hate to change the constitution. That's not untrue. But the deeper lesson is that Australians – contrary to our larrikin myths – are people with a deep respect for authority. We are more Canadian than Yankee: more at home with the Canadian notion of "peace, order and good government" than the notion of "life, liberty and the pursuit of happiness" that runs south of the 49th parallel. Americans find it easier to change their constitution not only because of the machinery of the thing but also because they are more used to making up their own minds. We won't move unless our leaders speak as one and tell us to move. This isn't our commitment to the constitution so much as our commitment to authority. In 1988 our political leaders were divided, so those unremarkable proposals went down in flames.

I was disappointed by the Rudd government setting as a ground rule for Frank Brennan's inquiry that constitutional change was out of the question. There would be no Australian bill of rights. The best that could be hoped for was a parliamentary charter. As it turned out this pre-emptive buckle didn't keep out of the contest those furious at the prospect of "unelected" judges deciding our rights by whatever means. They simply ignored the distinction between bills and charters: they kept angry and they carried on.

No one should doubt how hard it is to embed bills of rights in constitutions. History tells us such rock-solid guarantees are rarely given except in the wake of national upheavals we would not wish on this country. Look at the list: the US First Amendment after a war of independence; the Declaration of the Rights of Man after the French Revolution (and that one didn't last); the European Convention on Human Rights after World War II; and South Africa's Bill of Rights after the long nightmare of apartheid.

Australia lost its way over a century ago. Whether we know it or not, advocates of human rights have been picking around ever since in the wreckage of one day in the life of the Australasian Federal Convention in Melbourne in February 1898. It was staggeringly hot. As fires raged through the Grampians and smoke obscured the sun, the best hope of embedding a few rights in the constitution were burnt to a crisp. A bit of history: little fuss had been made at earlier conventions about the idea of incorporating into our constitution the "equal protection of the laws" established in Fourteenth Amendment of the US Constitution after the Civil War. But its enemies were waiting to pounce in Melbourne. It's a strange reflection that the leaders of the contest that day – in whose shadows we still work – were both Australian sons of persecuted peoples. Richard O'Connor, the charming son of an Irish librarian, begged the delegates to put into the constitution they were drafting, "A guarantee for all time for the citizens of the Commonwealth that they shall be treated according to what we recognise to be the principles of justice and equality." But Isaac Isaacs, the brilliant, tedious, dogmatic child of a Polish tailor, couldn't abide the idea proposed.

The delegates camped in the Legislative Assembly of the Melbourne parliament growled and sniped for an hour, broke for lunch and came back – clearly in a foul mood – to shred that rights initiative in less than twenty minutes. First went the notion that: "a state shall not make or enforce any law abridging any privilege or immunity of citizens of the Commonwealth". Then hacked down was: "nor shall a state deprive any person of life, liberty, or property without due process of law". And finally, by twenty-three votes to nineteen the delegates ditched: "or deny to any person within its juris-diction the equal protection of its laws".

According to the great myth that has grown up, this was the point at which an emerging Australia rejected American ways and stuck to its Brit-ish guns, turning its back on the allure of constitutional protection in order to stick with parliaments and the common law. It has been billed ever since as a nation-making moment. Sir Owen Dixon and Sir Robert Menzies sang this song particularly when lecturing Americans on the drawbacks of their own constitution. In his rough, democratic accent, High Court judge Michael McHugh belted out the same refrain in *Australian Capital Televi-sion v Commonwealth*:

> The makers of the constitution ... rejected the United States exam-ple of a bill of rights to protect the people of the Commonwealth against the abuse of governmental power ... because they believed in the efficacy of the two institutions which formed the basis of the constitution of Great Britain and the Australian colonies – repre-sentative government and responsible government ...

But read the transcript of the debates that day in 1898 and you find no such high-flown considerations in the air. No hymns were sung to British ways. Not even the most conservative delegate – stand up if you can after a long lunch Sir George Reid – attacked the theory of allowing courts to set limits to the exercise of government power. This was not a contest in the abstract but the particular. The delegates did not vote against rights but against *these* rights. Why? Because, as Isaacs put it so bluntly, their original object in America was "to protect the blacks", and in Australia they would "protect Chinamen in the same way". The delegates' vote was not about preserving British values down under, but the birth of a white man's Federation.

Sir John Forrest belled that cat during that day's debate: "It is of no use for us to shut our eyes to the fact that there is a great feeling all over Australia against the introduction of coloured persons. It goes without saying that we do not like to talk about it, but still it is so." In fact, as the heat rose the delegates became less and less inhibited. With the point-by-point endorsement of Isaacs, John Cockburn of South Australia spoke with the passion of a planter stripped of his slaves as he condemned the proposed guarantees as vindictive abroad and unnecessary at home:

> They were introduced, as an amendment, simply as a punishment to the Southern States for their attitude during the Civil War … to inflict the grossest outrage which could be inflicted upon the southern planters, by saying: 'You shall not forbid the negro inhabitants to vote. We insist on their being placed on an equal footing in regard to the exercise of the franchise with yourselves.' I do not believe that this amendment was ever legally carried … it was simply forced on a recalcitrant people as a punishment for the part they took in the Civil War. We are not going to have a civil war here over a racial question.

One way of gauging the astonishingly racist temper of the discussion that day is to note that no delegates even mentioned Aborigines. The guarantees they were shredding would have given citizenship, the vote and the equal protection of the law to Aborigines in perpetuity. But this didn't even rate a mention either as a reason for or against the proposal. Aborigines were not in the delegates' minds. It was all about the Chinese. Isaacs had the US case law at his fingertips. The Supreme Court in *Yick Wo v. Hopkins* had called on the "equal protection" provisions of the Fourteenth Amendment to strike down a San Francisco city ordinance designed to put out of business all the Chinese laundries in the city. Isaacs did not object to the validity of that ordinance being decided by the Supreme Court of the United States. His target was not an unelected judiciary. He was not singing anthems in praise of the common law. He just didn't want protection extended to the Chinese in Australia.

What's the point of this excursion into history? To bell yet another cat. History shows the rejection of constitutional rights is not in the DNA of this nation. What is, alas, in our DNA is a reluctance to extend rights to "coloured persons". And it is of no use us shutting our eyes to that fact. In 1898, not for the last time, we chose between race and rights, and the price we have all paid for that choice has been high. The politics of rights protection continues to be – and I seek the polite word – *complicated* by the fact that those who most obviously need protection these days aren't named McClelland or Evans or Murphy or Ruddock but Haneef, Al-Kateb and Ul-Haque.

Isaacs lived a very long time: long enough to be our first native-born governor-general; long enough to watch the anti-German panic that swept Australia in World War I; long enough to watch civilised Germany descend into the Holocaust, and to witness Australia's appalling response in the late 1930s to Jewish refugees who wished to come here. Indeed, he lived long enough to see Auschwitz emptied. I wonder if at any time in his late life he reflected on O'Connor's wise words on 8 February 1898 about the role the law might play in protecting us all – not minorities, but all – from the madness that sweeps nations from time to time. O'Connor said:

> We are making a constitution to endure, practically speaking, for all time. We do not know when some wave of popular feeling may lead a majority in the parliament of a state to commit an injustice by passing a law that would deprive citizens of life, liberty, or property without due process of law. If no state does anything of the kind there will be no harm in this provision, but it is only right that this protection should be given to every citizen of the Commonwealth.

It wasn't. It still hasn't. And we still need it.

The Tenth Human Rights Oration,
Victorian Equal Opportunity and Human Rights Commission,
Federation Square, 10 December 2010

Andrew Bolt bites the dust

FREEDOM OF SPEECH IS NOT AT STAKE HERE. Judge Mordecai Bromberg is not telling the media what we can say or where we can poke our noses. He's attacking lousy journalism. He's saying that if Andrew Bolt of the *Herald Sun* wants to accuse people of appalling motives, he should start by getting his facts right.

Bolt was wrong. Spectacularly wrong. In two famous columns in 2009 he took a swipe at "political" or "professional" or "official" Aborigines who could pass for white but chose to identify as black for personal or political gain, to win prizes and places reserved for real, black Aborigines and to borrow "other people's glories". But Bolt's lawyers had to concede even before this case began in the Federal Court that nine of these named "white Aborigines" had identified as black from childhood. All nine came to court to say they didn't choose this down the track but were raised as Aborigines. Their evidence was not contested by Bolt or his paper.

So as we say in the trade: no story.

Yet Bolt went at it with mockery, derision and sarcasm. They are Judge Bromberg's words. He added: "I accept that the language utilised in the newspaper articles was inflammatory and provocative." Here's Bolt on Larissa Behrendt:

> She's won many positions and honours as an Aborigine, including the David Unaipon Award for Indigenous Writers, and is often interviewed demanding special rights for 'my people'. But which people are 'yours', exactly, *mein liebchen*? And isn't it bizarre to demand

laws to give you more rights as a white Aborigine than your own white dad?

Among the problems here are that Behrendt's father was a black Australian, not a white German. And like all the others, Behrendt was raised black. Judge Bromberg wrote: "She denies Mr Bolt's suggestion that she chose to be Aboriginal and says that she never had a choice, she has always been Aboriginal and has 'identified as Aboriginal since before I can remember'." Bolt didn't contest her evidence.

The nine chose not to sue. They did not want damages but a public correction and a promise not to print such stuff again. So they brought an action under the *Racial Discrimination Act*, which has embedded in it a strong freedom-of-speech defence: insulting or humiliating people because of their race or colour is not unlawful when it is done "reasonably and in good faith" in pursuit of a matter of public interest.

The act left Bolt with the task of making a list of convincing denials to explain his mistakes, language and motives. Denials are one of Bolt's great talents: with a smile on his face and his hand on his heart he is happy to claim the purest motives even in the unhappiest circumstances. Usually it works like a charm. Not with Judge Bromberg. Brushed aside was Bolt's claim that he was not writing about race at all. The judge found: "Race, colour and ethnicity were vital elements of the message and therefore a motivating reason for conveying the message, even if the message is to be characterised as ultimately about choice of racial identity."

Also brushed aside was the claim that any offence was unintended. "Mr Bolt is an experienced journalist," said Judge Bromberg. "He has high-level communication skills. His writing displays a capacity to cleverly craft language to intimate a message. I consider it highly unlikely that in carefully crafting the words utilised by him in the newspaper articles, he did not have an understanding of the meaning likely to be conveyed by those words to the ordinary, reasonable reader."

Rather tartly, the judge said the more reliable guide to Bolt's motives came not from his evidence but his writings. The judge seemed not too impressed. "Having observed Mr Bolt, I formed the view that he was prone to after-the-fact rationalisations of his conduct."

Nor was the judge bowled over by Bolt's efforts as a reporter. He taxed Bolt with errors in the genealogy of the nine – some of them "gross errors" – and in describing their upbringing always at white hands. "Mr Bolt presented evidence of having undertaken some online research about the individuals," he said. "But it was not evidence upon which I could be satisfied that a diligent attempt had been made to make reasonable inquiries."

But Judge Bromberg was perhaps most scathing about Bolt's failure to acknowledge that any of the nine had been raised black. "In my view, Mr Bolt was intent on arguing a case," said the judge. "He sought to do so persuasively. It would have been highly inconvenient to the case for which Mr Bolt was arguing for him to have set out facts demonstrating that the individuals whom he wrote about had been raised with an Aboriginal identity and enculturated as Aboriginal people.

"Those facts would have substantially undermined both the assertion that the individuals had made a choice to identify as Aboriginal and that they were not sufficiently Aboriginal to be genuinely so identifying. The way in which the newspaper articles emphasised the non-Aboriginal ancestry of each person serves to confirm my view. That view is further confirmed by factual errors made which served to belittle the Aboriginal connection of a number of the individuals dealt with, in circumstances where Mr Bolt failed to provide a satisfactory explanation for the error in question."

So Bolt and the *Herald Sun* and *The Weekly Times* went down.

Outside the court, Bolt declared this "a terrible day for free speech". Not according to the judge: "The intrusion into freedom of expression is of no greater magnitude than that which would have been imposed by the law of defamation if the conduct in question and its impact upon the reputations of many of the identified individuals had been tested against its compliance with that law." Perhaps the *Herald Sun* and its star journalist should be thankful they're not facing nine separate defamation trials. An appeal is expected – so is some spectacular rhetoric from the now martyred Andrew Bolt.

The Sydney Morning Herald, 29 September 2011

The fright of our lives

WE ARE IN A PANIC AGAIN. This golden country, so prosperous, so intelligent, so safe and orderly, is afraid of refugees arriving in fishing boats. This is the great Australian fear, one that never really goes away. Hearts are hardened. Terrible things are done in the name of protecting the nation. It is not the first wave of boats and won't be the last, but the politics are more rancorous than ever.

Panic has been with us from the start. It is so Australian. Panic over the Chinese was the midwife of federation, and we have been swept by waves of panic ever since. What were they all about? It's a mark of panics that once they die down they seem, looking back, unconvincing and even comic.

The past fifteen years have seen Australia in states of exaggerated alarm over native title, Muslim preachers, Muslim rapists, drugs, terrorists foreign and homegrown, demonstrators in the streets and pictures of naked children on gallery walls. But we end the decade as we began, in a full-scale panic over refugees coming here – as they reach countries all over the world – uninvited in little boats.

When I was reporting the mad uproar over Bill Henson's photographs a couple of years ago, it came to me I've been writing about panics all my career: how they are whipped up, do their worst and disappear, leaving only wreckage behind.

Perhaps I'm alert to the subject because I'm gay. When I was growing up, preachers, police, politicians and the press were keeping panic alive about people like me. It has left me despising panic merchants, particularly those Tory fear-mongers who represent themselves as guardians of decency. The politicians I most admire are those who hold their nerve in the face of irrational fear on the rampage.

I've come to believe that the fundamental contest in Australian politics is not so much between Right and Left as panic and calm. This is an issue that goes deeper than division between the parties. It's about the willingness of Australia's leaders to beat up on the nation's fears.

They coarsen politics. They narrow our sympathies. They make careers for themselves in this good-hearted country by making us afraid. These panic attacks can be exhilarating in their own way, but they leave behind damaged people and a damaged country.

I was a kid journalist in 1975. My heart was with Whitlam even as I watched his government fall to pieces. His defeat was inevitable but his opponents wanted him out at once. To that end, a mighty panic was beaten up in the press, in parliament and at the big end of town. By October 1975, a deeply conservative paper such as *The Sydney Morning Herald* was unashamedly calling on its front page for the overthrow of a government. Two lessons were there to be learnt about the politics of panic: how willing conservative politicians in this country are to toy with disorder, and how popular that can be. Whitlam's dismissal by the governor-general was endorsed overwhelmingly at the ballot box. But who except a few monarchists and Liberal hacks are left willing to defend 1975?

Panics can't be whipped up out of nothing. They must have something at their heart that really matters. Panics are reasonable fears twisted out of all recognition. A decent face has to be put on the passions aroused. Appearances count. Language matters.

Skilled panic merchants find ways of suggesting, however vaguely, that the survival of the nation is at stake – not always the integrity of its territory but its heart, its health, its spirit, its way of life. The argument always is that desperate times require tough laws and strong leadership. Panic is a rallying cry for power.

The fall of the Berlin Wall was a low moment for old panic-mongers. Communism had been a great gift to panic in this country, keeping the right people in power for a long, long time. There was much to fear in and after World War II from communist espionage, treason and industrial mayhem. But fear of the red menace was kept alive in this country long after the party was spent.

Energetic attempts in the Howard years to ignite fears about the agenda of the Left – particularly of Lefties entrenched in the "taxpayer-funded" ABC, universities and museums – failed to excite the public. The red menace was utterly exhausted. In the end, communism even betrayed its detractors.

Race took its place. The discovery of native title by the High Court in 1992 let loose across the country wild fears and old hatreds that had not died down when the judges delivered a second shock in 1996: first Mabo and then Wik. Pauline Hanson surfed both waves of panic to a series of political victories that briefly turned her One Nation Party into a third force in national politics.

John Howard dealt in the same panics, implacably opposed to Mabo and determined to cut Wik to the core. By the time Australia calmed down over native title in the late 1990s, the prime minister was more firmly entrenched in power than ever and the redhead from Ipswich was a spent force. When it came to playing the panic game, one was a professional and the other an amateur.

Australians aren't much impressed by great abstractions such as justice and liberty. We are an orderly, practical people. We trust our politicians. We expect them to look after us. When they call for fresh powers to meet fresh dangers we nearly always agree to their demands. The warnings of lawyers and the civil liberties brigade don't have much traction.

September 11 2001, and the London bombings in 2005, provoked Howard to introduce – and Labor to support – a radical regime of secret detention without charge or trial; house arrest and control orders without charge; detention of witnesses for questioning; covert surveillance of non-suspects; blocking the access of lawyers to evidence; criminalising anti-war protest and extending the reach of already shadowy sedition laws.

Yet using those laws can be dangerous for their backers. Injustices we can't grasp in the abstract are clear enough to Australians in practice. We didn't need any convincing that the jailing of the Gold Coast doctor Mohamed Haneef was very wrong indeed. It helped unseat a police commissioner and was another blow to the already ragged reputation of the prime minister.

In the face of panic, the courts in this country have a mixed record. When the mob is restless and the shock jocks are howling for action, judges are supposed to stay aloof, focus on the facts and be guided by principle alone. But judges aren't immune from irrational fears. The noise of the mob too often reaches the courtroom.

For a long time, the High Court gave its seal of approval to the cruel and unusual measures Australia put in place to punish and deter refugees arriving in this country by boat. After the court signed off on mandatory detention in the early 1990s, a parallel prison system for refugees grew up in this country. Had the judges brought calm to this issue then, governments of all stripes would be looking back now with profound gratitude.

But the mood of the court has shifted. Late in 2010, with fears of the boats running high, the court came to the unanimous conclusion that everyone detained in the system had to be treated fairly and according to law. In August 2011, the court made a decision as radical and as simple: any asylum seekers we send away to another country for processing must have the same rights up there they would have had down here. This might have been a moment for taking stock, for calming down. Instead the court's decision provoked political uproar, with the opposition driving and the government driven by this defining panic.

The fears of the most fearful Australians cannot be ignored in a democracy. They must be decently addressed. But what gives Australian politics its particular flavour is the willingness of Labor and the Coalition to indulge fears they haven't the courage or the will to contest. These come and go. Old fears recycled work their magic over and over again. We don't seem to learn. Yet most Australians are not fearful. According to the polls we are on the whole optimistic, open and accepting. Even so, at every election since the mid-1990s – Kevin Rudd's victory in 2007 being the only exception – the mandate of the fearful has decided who governs Australia.

Radio, television and newspapers are so often the friends of panic. There's a cynical old saying that the purpose of tabloid journalism is to maintain a perpetual state of false alarm. My years at *Media Watch* were largely spent investigating those alarms and becoming, in the process, enthralled by the leading panic merchants of the media: Piers Akerman, young Andrew Bolt and the indestructible Alan Jones. There is another old adage about tabloids: that their purpose is to persuade the working class to vote Tory. I once put this to Bob Carr. He replied, "I think it is incontrovertible."

Politicians who deal in panic wear out their welcome. The grubby business of terrifying the electorate over and over again takes its toll. Howard was the most professional politician I expect to see at work in my lifetime, and nothing was more professional than his manipulation of Australia's fears. But a decade of this left him rather shopworn. So many scares had come and gone, failing to deliver on their bleak promises. His last days in office caught the disenchantment perfectly. Sydney was locked down for a gathering of world leaders – and into this great security panic drove a team of comedians in Arab dress. Howard looked foolish. Australia laughed all the way to the polls. Panic can't take a joke.

Under other parties and different leaders we soldier on, the same country we've always been: a wonderful place but gullible at times. We trust our leaders but that trust is not always repaid. As Australia grows inexorably more prosperous and progressive and relaxed, the forces of reaction have to work a little harder to frighten us from time to time – just enough to make it difficult to imagine how much better life might be if we were ruled more often than not by good sense, order and calm.

From *Panic*, 2011

Chris Kenny fucks one dog ...

THE ABC HAS CAPITULATED TO CHRIS KENNY. Apologies have been offered and cash will be paid to the News Limited journalist. The Chaser boys are forbidden to mock the ABC's grovelling. News Limited and the national broadcaster's many enemies in government ranks are enjoying a sweet victory.

A brief scene in an almost empty courtroom in Sydney on Friday was the last episode in this nine-month brawl over a lame joke. The ABC's lawyers expressed sorrow at the distress the Chaser skit caused Kenny and his family, a skit that was "triggered by criticism of the ABC" that "falls short of the quality demanded by the ABC's audiences". Kenny also spoke through his lawyers. He assured the court that protecting his reputation was only one reason he sued the ABC. "The second – counter-intuitively to some people perhaps – was in defence of free speech."

As an associate editor of *The Australian* with a perch on Sky Television, Kenny has a loud voice to reply to the Chaser's taunts. Instead he sued. Late on Friday, he told *The Guardian*: "To the extent that I am remembered for this, I'll be remembered as the journalist called a dog fucker who stood up for his rights."

What a jury would have made of the Kenny skit we will never know. The last big name to take a joke to a jury was Harry Seidler thirty years ago. At stake was a brilliant, abusive cartoon by Patrick Cook. The architect lost and made a fool of himself. But Seidler didn't have what Kenny has: the brass-band backing of News Limited and the endorsement of a prime minister.

The Hamster Decides episode five, broadcast a few days after Abbott's election victory, was all mockery. The Chaser team mocked the new prime minister, the defeated Kevin Rudd, Cory Bernardi, Kerry O'Brien, Peter Hartcher of the Fairfax press, the ABC, Nine and Seven. Craig Emerson "sang". Hapless candidate Jaymes Diaz mocked himself. Phillip Adams and I starred in a grainy black-and-white newsreel of chardonnay socialists fleeing Abbott's Australia.

Ten minutes into this melee Chas Licciardello gave the "boring pundit" Chris Kenny a serve: "I enjoyed the way he took almost an hour after Tony Abbott's victory speech before he started demanding cuts to the ABC." And there was Kenny on the screen with urgent advice for the new government: "They need to actually start to question the $1.1 billion they throw to the ABC for instance ..." Andrew Hansen agreed: "They've just got to cut ABC funding. This is a network that broadcasts images of Chris Kenny strangling a dog while having sex with it." There were better jokes and better laughs that night but the studio audience let out a happy roar when Kenny's face appeared crudely pasted on a man with his pants down mounting a Labradoodle. A sign said: "Chris 'Dog Fucker' Kenny". Licciardello declared the image disgusting. "Very childish," added Hansen. "I mean, they have got to be cut, they've got to be cut."

The Chaser saw it as a joke against the ABC as much as Kenny, a self-defeating joke about an outfit so wasteful and silly it would lash out like this against one of its most relentless critics. Licciardello explained to *The Guardian*: "It was meant to be about poking the bear in the most over-the-top, ill-advised way."

The ABC lawyers had cleared the skit. The show was watched by 1,323,000 people. The ABC received only one complaint. It wasn't from Kenny. Licciardello had assured the team there would be no trouble from him. He knew Kenny as a thick-skinned pro with a robust sense of humour.

The dog joke has form. After an Indonesian paper depicted Howard and the foreign minister Alexander Downer in 2006 as humping dingoes – their crime was to give forty-two West Papuan independence campaigners temporary protection visas – *The Australian* retaliated with a cartoon of President Yudhoyono as a dog having sex with an unhappy Papuan. John Howard was unfazed by the Indonesian effort: "I've been in this game a long time. If I got offended by cartoons – golly heavens above, give us a break." President Yudhoyono shrugged off Bill Leak's reply. "It's in poor taste," said his spokesman. "Sometimes the media ... both in Indonesia and other countries, resort to poor taste, which actually demonstrates the level of their quality."

The Guardian asked *The Australian*'s editor-in-chief Chris Mitchell if he ever apologised for the Leak and what he saw as the difference between that cartoon and the image of Kenny and the dog. He replied: "Bill's cartoon was in response to one published about Alex Downer on page one of the tabloids in Indonesia."

The furore over those 2006 cartoons quickly faded. But they featured the prime minister of Australia and the president of Indonesia. The Chaser had mocked Chris Kenny.

For a few days Licciardello's assessment of Kenny seemed justified. He responded the morning after the broadcast as a hardboiled journalist might after being roughed up by a bunch of comedians: he joked back. "Betrayed by @ChasLicc," he tweeted. "Heartbroken. Chas, I've left your dog suit on the porch." On Sky the next night, Kenny was hurt but still managed to laugh: "They have had their fun with me," he said. "I take their point: I will never criticise the ABC again. They have now silenced me. I am only joking, of course. I'll keep criticising the ABC and it will be fun to see what they do next. What can they do next? They have defamed me. They have shown me up a dog. What will they do next, next time I criticise the ABC? We'll see. Keep watching."

His son Liam swiftly contradicted his claim that the Kenny children would be hurt to find the skit on the net. "Kenny is a staunchly neo-conservative, anti-progress, anti-worker defender of the status quo," the son wrote on *Junkee*. "He is an unrelenting apologist for the Liberal party. He was one of Alexander Downer's senior advisers at the time of the Iraq War ... and it's a jokey picture of a bestial embrace that I should be afraid of discovering online?" Kenny senior tweeted: "I am proud of my children, love them deeply, and encourage them to think for themselves."

But the News Limited journalist's mood darkened. He wanted someone from the ABC to ring. "I was astonished that there was no response from the ABC to reach out and say they had gone too far," he told *The Guardian*. He had watched the show with his young, pregnant wife. "It's not just about you but whoever you're sharing your bed with. I saw it as a horrible slur on her as well as me."

Kenny had allies. The shock jocks were marshalling behind him. Complaints began arriving at the ABC in bulk: 188 in all. Andrew Bolt wrote a column not intended to be funny that began: "I am nervous. I saw what the ABC did last week to a friend who called for balance ..." Though Bolt has campaigned hard for his right to offend, insult, humiliate and intimidate light-skinned Aboriginal people, he now weighed in on Kenny's behalf: "Yes, the graphic was clearly fake. But the issue is that it was obscene, humiliating and viciously abusive."

When *Media Watch* condemned the skit, the Chaser team offered a picture of its host Paul Barry mounting a pig. Same legs and backyard; different animal. "Of course I am not going to sue," said the *Media Watch* host as he put the picture to air. "But what would happen if Chris Kenny decided to do so?"

The lawyers' letter came three days later. Whatever has since been said about Kenny wanting no more than an apology, let this be clear: he was asking for money on day one – for an apology, removal of the picture from the ABC website and payment of "an amount in compensation for the damage caused". The figure he would put on his hurt and pain was $95,000.

News Limited was hammering Mark Scott and the ABC. The themes were familiar: an organisation out of control, politically biased and wasteful. Scott's critics were provoked rather than mollified by his admission that he personally found the Chaser skit tasteless and undergraduate. But Scott continued to defend its broadcast. "It was over the top," he told *The Age*. "However, our editorial policy is to give very broad licence around comedy and satire, and properly so."

A few weeks after the broadcast, the ABC's audience and consumer affairs division dismissed the complaints against the show. Though "likely to offend" the skit was deemed legitimate satire with "a clear editorial purpose and was ultimately considered to be justified in the context". That decision was then appealed to the Australian Communications and Media Authority, ACMA.

By this time, three teams of lawyers were investigating the old intractable question: how do jokes work? Why we laugh is a mystery that's never likely to be solved. But why jokes offend is much easier to decide: in life and at law jokes most often come unstuck when they can be taken literally. From start to finish, Kenny's solicitor, the leading Sydney defamation specialist Patrick George, claimed the Chaser boys were suggesting Kenny *actually* had sex with animals and was the sort of lowlife who engaged in bestiality of a most perverted kind.

The ABC's lawyers were absolutely confident no jury would believe that. The image was obviously fake, a clumsy digital mock-up that could not to be taken literally, especially in the context of a satirical show. They saw the skit being, at worst, on the margins of defamation. Though they believed a judge would let it through to a jury, they saw a number of strong defences available to the ABC: comment, contextual truth and qualified privilege.

When the broadcaster refused to retract, apologise or pay, Kenny decided, "Bugger them, I am going to fight this." He does not deny he had News Limited's financial backing to take the ABC to court. "I don't want to go into that," he said. "I could not have asked my employers – both at News and Sky – to be more supportive of me."

Journalists can sue for defamation. There is no rule of the trade that says they can't defend their reputations in court. Though rare, it happens. When it does, journalists tend to look for some big reason to overcome their commitment to the freest possible speech. Kenny claimed – not as a joke any longer – that the ABC was out to silence its critics.

Not that he let up. Since the Chaser skit went to air Kenny has continued to attack the ABC with all his familiar energy. On his list have been salaries paid to ABC executives and presenters; Barrie Cassidy's appointment as (unpaid) chair of the Old Parliament House museum; and the deplorable collaboration with *The Guardian* to report the Yudhoyono phone taps which, he said, showed none of the maturity required by "an organisation with the charter obligations and public funding of the ABC". Kenny has continued to belittle the ABC's coverage of climate change, accuse the national broadcaster of being out of touch with taxpayers and lately claimed the ABC is dividing the nation by promoting "a progressive or green left world view that sets it against mainstream Australia".

So they haven't silenced him? "No. But this sort of extreme ridicule can only have a chilling effect. We should be able to have full and robust debate without retaliation of this kind." You would say the same about critics of News Limited? "Of course."

A few days before Christmas, ACMA gave the ABC the thumbs down. The broadcasting regulator had come to a preliminary finding that "the high level of offence" given by the skit "was disproportionate to the satirical purposed advanced ... and therefore its inclusion was not editorially justified". The ABC insisted, in reply, on its right to make shows for particular audiences: "We know from the feedback we receive from our audience that viewers falling outside the target audience can find programs like *The Hamster Wheel, Ja'mie Private School Girl* or *The Elegant Gentleman's Guide to Knife Fighting* baffling, shocking and deeply offensive. But the response from target audiences is strikingly different ..."

The regulator was still reconsidering its verdict when *Kenny v the ABC* reached the NSW Supreme Court in March this year. The opening round of a defamation case sees a judge sitting alone deciding what claims can later be put to a jury. Justice Robert Beech-Jones clearly loathed the skit, which he condemned as "a massive exercise in ridicule". But he dealt Kenny's case a perhaps fatal blow. The picture of the reporter and the Labradoodle could not, he decided, be taken literally. "The reasonable viewer, in my view, could not possibly have considered that such a lightweight show as this would be the forum for exposing actual instances of bestiality."

That left Kenny only able to claim the Chaser boys had shown him to be, in the words of the judge, "a contemptible person". The right jury and a powerful barrister could bring that home for Kenny. But the verdict would depend largely on how he withstood a wideranging – and inevitably hostile – cross-examination about the ins and outs of his long career. Kenny appealed. His lawyers clearly regarded it as vital that he be able to stand before a jury and say: *The Hamster Decides* showed him literally having sex with – and strangling – dogs. Both sides appeared to understand that without that Kenny's chances of success were slim.

But politics were coming to matter far more than the law. Kenny and News Limited had a remarkable ally. In the aftermath of Beech-Jones's decision, Tony Abbott had intervened, giving his view of a yet-to-be-decided court case and, at the same time, delivering an unveiled threat to Mark Scott and the ABC. "Government money should be spent sensibly," the prime minister told Ben Fordham of Sydney radio station 2GB. "And defending the indefensible is not a very good way to spend government money. And next time the ABC comes to the government looking for more money, this is the kind of thing that we would want to ask them questions about."

Abbott's threats worked. Left to choose between defending satire or the budget of the ABC, Scott went with the budget. A few days after the prime minister's comments, Kenny had a call from Scott, who gave the journalist a long and expansive apology that was followed up in writing and published widely by News Limited papers and elsewhere. The case had travelled into uncharted territory. Scott's apology was delivered without any quid pro quo. Normally apologies are not made until a settlement is thrashed out between the parties. That hadn't happened. The ABC had lost no legal advantage by making the apology, but it was now politically impossible to fight Kenny in court.

The Chaser team marked the apology by posting a fresh buggery joke online: this time Scott was shown mounting an enormous hamster. He didn't threaten to sue. "He did exactly the right thing," remarked the Chaser's Julian Morrow. "He showed he was above it. Perhaps we should have used a hamster all along."

News Limited celebrated with editorials and triumphant commentary. This was a big victory in their long campaign against the ABC and its managing director. An editorial in *The Australian* deplored how long it had taken to get to this point. "But ABC managing director Mark Scott's apology to *The Australian*'s Chris Kenny is welcome. Mr Scott finally bowed to public pressure and decency." Miranda Devine pulled out all stops in *The Daily Telegraph*: "This wasn't mere satire, this was demanding silence with obscene menaces. This was Scott giving the green light to vicious Chaser executive producer Julian Morrow, thirty-nine, and anyone else at the ABC to defame and vilify critics of the taxpayer-funded media outfit. This was a terminally weak leader outsourcing defence of his organisation to bovver boys, like Putin is outsourcing his Ukraine invasion to bikers and military 'tourists'."

The fight had now come down to money. With the apology made, the ABC proposed the case be dropped with each side paying its own costs. Kenny wouldn't have it. "They dug in and spat in my face," he told *The Guardian*. "They are so belligerent I'm disappointed it didn't end up in court." But it didn't. Two months of negotiations led to another version of Scott's apology being broadcast on ABC1 before the latest episode of *Jonah from Tonga,* a couple of dismissive tweets from the Chasers – attacked in a fresh editorial in *The Australian* – and then Friday's little ceremony in the NSW Supreme Court.

We asked *The Australian*'s editor-in-chief Chris Mitchell: "How does your support for Kenny square with your call for overhauling the *Racial Discrimination Act*? Why do light-skinned Aborigines have to suck it up in the name of free speech when they are offended, insulted, humiliated etc, but when Kenny is offended, etc. he has a right to an apology and damages?"

Mitchell replied: "Silly question. Our point on 18C is precisely that other remedies – the defamation law for instance – exist."

Kenny is happy enough with the outcome. He says he doesn't regret suing even though "the last thing you want to do is appear wounded and show they've hit the mark". From sources, *The Guardian* understands a cheque for $35,000 is on the way. "I'll take my wife to dinner," said Kenny.

The Chaser team cannot speak freely about the outcome. They are not parties to the settlement but have promised not to "detract" from the ABC's apology. They have not had to apologise themselves, but they have given up any dream of fighting on. As far as they are concerned it's over. Asked what the lesson of the case is, Morrow paused for a moment and ventured: "That the culture war hasn't got beyond a joke."

The Guardian, 7 June 2014

Howard's End

The old Voltairean

THOUGH SAIGON IS NOW THE communist metropolis of Ho Chi Minh City, the best hotels cluster where they always have, around Lam Son Square. There in the Park Hyatt John Howard faced the Australian press in November last year. The event was low-key: no podium, no flags and little time. These were the last hours of the prime minister's first visit to Vietnam and his motorcade was about to leave for the airport. Howard had called the press together to plug nuclear power and farewell Ian Thorpe from the pool. He was relaxed. A week of hobnobbing with the leaders of APEC had climaxed late the night before in a restaurant where the Bushes and the Howards feasted alone on crabs and lotus-seed soup. The president paid.

David Speers from Sky News caught the Prime Minister's eye. "Just before you leave Vietnam, can I ask you, do you think the Vietnam War was a mistake?"

Someone had asked at last. From the moment Howard arrived in Vietnam, he had been lavishing praise on the communist regime. He spoke of the Vietnamese as people after his own heart with "entrepreneurial flair and spirit", committed to "the role of small and medium-sized enterprises". He imagined a future in which Australia and Vietnam were "forever linked in the fastest-growing area of the world economy". One night at an Asialink dinner, he made a vague allusion to the war: "Australia's relations with Vietnam have, of course, gone through a number of iterations." It's an awkward word for ten years of combat.

Once the Howards and their entourage travelled south from the APEC meetings in Hanoi, the war was everywhere. They lit incense at a cemetery for the war dead of Vietnam at Go Cat. They drove in convoy to the rubber plantation at Long Tan where eighteen Australians died in a single night of fighting forty years ago. John Howard laid a wreath and expressed a few regrets: not for the 500 Australians, the one and a half million Vietnamese military and the two million civilians who died in the war. To a handful of Australian veterans gathered at the white cross that marks the battlefield, Howard acknowledged the shabby treatment soldiers had back home when they returned from the fighting. "We won't make that mistake again."

Speers woke next morning thinking it odd that no one in the press pack had asked Howard – simply and directly – what he thought of the war. "He had been telling us a lot during the week about the success of Vietnam and the great opportunities it afforded for Australian business," he told me. "But the question of the war hadn't been raised." This seemed particularly odd because of the obvious parallels with Iraq. "I must confess it didn't strike me until the day we were leaving that, hang on a minute, does he still think that fighting the Vietnam War was the right thing to do when the rest of the world has moved on?"

Howard took his time answering Speers' question. He was thinking it out carefully as he spoke.

> I supported our involvement at the time and I don't intend to recant that. I believe that in public life you are accountable for the decisions that you take. I mean, I didn't hold any position of authority then, but I supported the reasons for Australia's involvement and nothing has altered my view that – at the time, on the assessments that were made then – I took that view properly. And I don't intend to indulge this preoccupation that many have in recanting everything that they supported when they were in positions of authority.

Journalists glanced at one another. Was he bagging Malcolm Fraser? Or perhaps Robert McNamara, the former US secretary of defense who now says the Vietnam War was "wrong, terribly wrong"? Howard wasn't naming names. His point was that conceding the truth isn't his style.

> I think in public life you take a position and I think particularly of the positions I've taken in the time I've been prime minister. I have to live with the consequences of those both now and into the future.

And if I ever develop reservations, well, I hope I would have the grace to keep them to myself ... You take a position and you've got to live by that and be judged by that – and that's my position.

At the heart of democracy is a contest of conversations. The tone of a democracy is set by the dialogue between a nation and its leaders. For the last decade, Australia has had a prime minister who thinks it beneath him to admit mistakes. Speers could hardly believe his ears: "He was virtually saying, even if I think I'm wrong, I'm not going to tell you." In one of the few press commentaries on this extraordinary moment, my colleague Peter Hartcher wrote of Howard putting himself "beyond political resolve into a realm of almost superhuman recalcitrance".

Debate ploughs on in Australia. Hansard is fatter than ever. The prime minister is always at the microphone. But after being belittled for most of his political career, Howard came to power determined public debate would be conducted on his terms. They are subtle, bizarre and at times brutal. This essay is about those terms and why Australians put up with them. Since 1996, Howard has cowed his critics, muffled the press, intimidated the ABC, gagged scientists, silenced non-government organisations, neutered Canberra's mandarins, curtailed parliamentary scrutiny, censored the arts, banned books, criminalised protest and prosecuted whistleblowers.

This is not as Howard advertised himself on arrival. Then he spoke proudly of his party's tradition of defending individual liberty and the rule of law. He still does. He painted his victory as a repudiation of "stultifying political correctness" that left Australians able "to speak a little more freely and a little more openly about what they feel". The ravings of Pauline Hanson he represented as a triumph of free speech over stifling orthodoxy. And after Aboriginal protesters burnt the flag on Australia Day last year, he rejected calls for their prosecution. "Much in all as I despise what they did, I do not believe that it should be a criminal offence," he told Neil Mitchell of radio station 3AW in Melbourne. "I do hold to the old Voltairean principle that I disagree with what he says but I will defend to the death his right to say it, and I see that kind of thing as just an expression, however offensive to the majority of the community, an expression of political opinion."

The Old Voltairean has fallen a bit short. He leads a government notably uncomfortable with freewheeling debate. "Uncomfortable" is too kind a description: the dislike is profound. For a decade now, public debate has been bullied and starved as if this were an ordinary function of government. It's important not to exaggerate the result. Suppression is not systematic. There are no gulags for dissidents under Howard. We reserve them for refugees. The occasional victories liberty wins in Canberra are illuminating. There are limits. But Howard's government has been the most unscrupulous corrupter of public debate in Australia since the Cold War's worst days back in the 1950s.

We haven't been hoodwinked. Each step along the way has been reported – perhaps not as thoroughly and passionately as it should have been, but we're not dealing in dark secrets here. We've known what's going on. If we cared, we didn't care enough to stop it. Boredom, indifference and fear have played a part in this. So does something about ourselves we rarely face: Australians trust authority. Not love, perhaps, but trust. It's bred in the bone. We call ourselves larrikins, but we leave our leaders to get on with it. Even the leaders we mock.

We've watched Howard spin, block, prevaricate, sidestep, confound and just keep talking come what may through any crisis. Words grind out of him unstoppably. He has a genius for ambiguity we've almost come to applaud, and most of the time he keeps himself just this side of deceit. But he also lies without shame. Howard invented the breakable or non-core promise – the first was to maintain ABC funding – five years before those children weren't thrown overboard. The truth is we've known he was a liar from the start – though we didn't know, until he said so in Ho Chi Minh City, that he sees denying the obvious as a virtue, as the act of a graceful leader. Howard can admit error, but it is extremely rare. Apologies are almost unknown. More than any law, any failure of the Opposition, or any individual act of bastardry over the last decade, what's done most to gag democracy in this country is the sense that debating John Howard is futile.

One response has been to turn away and wait for him to disappear in the belief that Australia will once again be what we remember it was: free, open, principled, fearless, fair. It wasn't. Most of what troubles us now about the state of public discourse began under Labor. Many of us complaining now did not complain loudly enough back then as Paul Keating bullied the press, the public service and the parliament. But Howard has come to dominate the country in ways Keating never could. To the task of projecting his voice across Australia, he brought all the ruthless professionalism that marks his government. Perhaps the man has now exhausted his welcome,

but even when the Howard years are long gone, we will be left confronting the damage done and the difficult question of how we let this happen.

Quarterly Essay, *His Master's Voice:*
The Corruption of Public Debate Under Howard, May 2007

Wheat and chaff

Witness One

Dead silence leaves no traces.

When students of the greatest international scandal to touch Australia in living memory leaf through the transcripts of the oil-for-food inquiry, they will find nothing to show the deep hush that fell as the Australian Wheat Board's Michael Long struggled to answer a simple question: was the UN deceived?

This was the tenth time John Agius SC, counsel assisting the inquiry, had asked the question. He was chasing a grubby plan hatched by AWB in 2003 to secretly "load up" wheat bills so that UN-held cash could be used to repay, on Iraq's behalf, an old debt the regime once owed BHP. The two men locked eyes across the room. Nothing happened for a long time.

Long broke first. "If it turns out, in hindsight, that the commission or the UN believe that they have been deceived, so be it." Agius had one last go and got this impossible reply through gritted teeth: "I don't believe the UN has been deceived."

Long had returned for his second day in the box as burly and surly as before. This is not a man who needs to be loved. His exchanges with the commissioner, Terry Cole QC, drew gasps from the crowd. Again and again Cole urged Long to listen carefully and answer directly.

"I am doing the best I can, Mr Commissioner."

"I think you can do better."

"Thank you for your vote of confidence."

These AWB executives don't like answering questions. To be fair to them, it may be the first time they've really had to find words for what's been going on inside the wheat trade all these years. Long said it was only last year in Jordan that he discovered the trucking company AWB had paid hundreds of millions over the years to move Australia's wheat in Iraq was (a) half-owned by the Iraqi government, and (b) had no trucks. Yet when he returned to headquarters, he found his colleagues didn't want to talk about it. "People weren't inquisitive."

He sank as the day went on but had moments of passion. There was an outburst about weapons of mass destruction being "absolutely discredited" as a reason for going to war. It's fair to guess Long wasn't pro the invasion. And faced with documents discovered in Baghdad that show, ship by ship, how the money AWB paid its "trucking" company was funnelled to the Iraqi Ministry of Finance, he confessed: "I now fully understand that it was a clever ruse by the Iraqi government to enact an elaborate scheme of deception."

We nearly rose in applause.

Witness Two

Leave a tractor out in the weather too long and it's damn hard to start. So it is with Trevor Flugge's recollection. The Cole people tried jumper leads. No luck. They primed the carburettor, but after coughing once or twice the engine died. Tomorrow they'll have to strip the block.

Flugge was a disappointment from the start yesterday. First he disappointed the large contingent of cameras waiting in Market Street by turning up in a shirt and tie with no visible side-arms. Then he disappointed the packed room of the Cole inquiry where, until about 3.45 pm, there was some lingering expectation that the former chairman of AWB would talk. That hope died swiftly as counsel assisting the inquiry, John Agius SC, began to quiz him about the early days of the kickback story.

Up on the screens around the room flashed half a dozen documents showing that the key issue on a trip Flugge led to Baghdad in October 1999 was bedding down the new "trucking fees" to be paid on 700,000 tonnes of wheat heading for Iraq. But the very little Flugge could remember about those days in Baghdad included none of those details. He did recall a technical seminar and lunch afterwards, but not being briefed for the journey; nor ever discussing "trucking fees" on the trip; nor being at the crucial meeting with Iraqi officials that two of his colleagues have given unequivocal evidence he attended.

Other witnesses have grovelled as their memories failed them. Flugge chuckled. In a man-to-man kind of way he told Agius he'd been working with his lawyers for weeks to try to jog his memory. No luck. "If a trip report can be shown that this is what we did, this is what we were briefed on, then so be it. My recollection doesn't take me there." With light scorn Agius replied: "I appreciate you will admit it if you see it in writing."

Flugge let the laughter brush over him. He's a compact man with more hair than most senior AWB executives. He doesn't have the weather-beaten face of the wheat farmer he's been most of his life, but he has the voice: a nasal drawl that must be all but impossible to stop in the boondocks or at board meetings. Sentences come out of the man like road trains. Yet his memory fails him.

In March 2000, Austrade's Alistair Nicholas called Flugge and several of his colleagues to Washington to discuss Canadian complaints that AWB was paying kickbacks to the Iraqis. This meeting was to spark urgent inquiries with the United Nations and provoke very careful denials by AWB channelled through the Department of Foreign Affairs and Trade – but the chairman of AWB could remember nothing at all about the occasion that might help Terence Cole's inquiries. His mantra was a bushman's complaint about the picky ways of the city: "Aw, Mr Agius, with respect."

Witness Three

Tom Harley slipped into the witness box like a grey schoolboy taking his seat in class. Neat and willing, he took the oath in an accent best described as Melbourne Oxbridge, each syllable distinct: "I swear by almighty God ..."

After all this time spent grilling AWB executives, weeks after the inquiry's terms of reference were widened to encompass the shabby Tigris affair, BHP's time at the Cole inquiry had finally come. Alas, these Big Australian executives proved not to have memories to match. Harley, a legendary backroom operator at BHP and in the Liberal Party, handed over one of the fattest statements to date, but he answered the first question put to him in the box with those old, familiar words: "I don't recall." His problem is this: he was around in the mid-1990s when BHP sent a shipload of wheat to Iraq to try to curry favour with Saddam's regime. The new Howard government regarded any attempt to sell the wheat on credit as sanctions-busting. So $5 million worth of grain went off disguised as a gift.

While Harley needs to convince the Cole inquiry he never noticed the ceaseless manoeuvring that followed to have the deal badged as a sale – "I always thought it was intended to be a gift" – Phil Aiken, the heavyset BHP Billiton boss who followed him in the witness box, has to convince the commissioner of the opposite: that he never knew this was anything but a commercial deal. Hopeless, but commercial.

So two men from the same company, on the same afternoon, represented by the same lawyers, before the same inquiry, find their reputations in the commercial world now depend on Terence Cole believing they've been sincerely, absolutely and in complete ignorance, at odds with each other over this deal for a decade.

Alice hardly watched anything stranger underground.

Witness Four

John Howard is a roughhouse debater of immense skill. On street corners, in the pit of the House, under television lights, they don't come sharper. But the Cole inquiry treated him with velvet gloves. More than thirty witnesses have faced the same levelling question from counsel assisting the inquiry: "May we have your full name for the record?" It's only a little thing, but yesterday John Agius SC spared the prime minister this formal humiliation. He asked: "Your full name is John Winston Howard?" It was.

Howard never surprises. He's always himself. He wore his reasonable face in the box, and as he admitted his deep ignorance of the scandal – for which he blames no one, not even himself – he gestured with those big, old hands of his.

Agius worked him very, very gently. There were jokes and chuckles from the commissioner, Terence Cole QC. The failings of the prime minister were revealed, but only in sketch. Agius pulled back from the forensic exploration that makes him such a formidable advocate. Instead of growling, he purred.

In another age I watched Bob Hawke in hand-to-hand combat with teams of QCs before the Hope royal commission. The brawling went on for days. Hawke had given that commission terms of reference wide enough to investigate the "reasonableness" of what he had done. Howard's terms of reference allowed him only to be examined on his knowledge of AWB's kickbacks. He came to the box heavily self-protected.

Before the prime minister arrived and the sniffer dogs were still doing their thing, there was an atmosphere of Speech Day in the room. Here we were, at the end of a very long term, gathered to listen to a VIP before all disappearing on holidays. Suits were darker. Bags were packed. Farewells were being made.

The press was caucusing on Cole. What's his verdict going to be? Things certainly look grim for AWB. On Tuesday, Cole poured scorn on the suggestion that the company might have told the truth years ago, if only the government had asked the right questions. Everything was denied almost to the end, he said. "Not just general denials, specific denials."

Agius leapt to his feet to reel off a list of crucial documents AWB withheld from the United Nations' Volcker inquiry as late as last year. "I'm certainly not going to sit here and hear misrepresentations put as submissions. AWB was denying that it had done anything wrong right up until at least October of 2005." The frustration of months spent clawing documents out of AWB erupted into the room. The deep reach of the inquiry is due almost solely to this man's talent for snaring documents. Even in the last few weeks, Agius has been hauling in more. But not without a fight. AWB will be in the Federal Court in ten days trying to withhold one last batch.

Cole has clearly marked AWB as the deceiver. But was the government deceived? That's the question that brought two ministers and a prime minister to the inquiry this week, eager to prove they were duped. Howard told Cole: "The culpability of AWB did not really enter my mind until 2005."

Apparently that impossible claim makes sense once we understand how haphazard things are in the prime minister's office. It has been a big week for poor office procedure. Cables and intelligence reports touching on the AWB scandal reached ministers' staffs but never – or hardly ever – reached ministers. Howard said it's all about the riding instructions he gives his advisers: "'Well, you've got to exercise your own judgement, I can't possibly read everything, and clearly I want things brought to my attention which are, in your judgement, important and are relevant to issues in front of the government at the time.' But it was no more formal than that. It can't be."

Only game Terry Forrest QC put up his hand to cross-examine the prime minister. His clients had spent six days under relentless examination in the box. Cole wouldn't even grant him six minutes with Howard. Instead he turned to the box and brought the whole show to an end after forty-eight minutes: "Thank you, Prime Minister. You are excused."

The Sydney Morning Herald,
2 February, 28 February, 10 March, 2 and 14 April 2006

The upshot was so Australian. Traders in the United States caught rorting the United Nations Oil-for-Food Programme went to prison and paid millions in fines and restitution. Not here. Cole concluded AWB had knowingly paid by far the biggest kickbacks of any company in the world to Saddam Hussein's regime – US$225 million – but no Australians were prosecuted. After years of hand-to-hand combat in the courts, three AWB executives were ordered to pay modest civil penalties. One was Trevor Flugge, whose total ignorance stood him in good stead to the very end. In 2017 the Victorian Supreme Court merely chastised him for failing to do what a chairman should have done – ask a few questions – ordered him to pay $50,000 and banned him from managing a company for five years. That was that.

Kingaroy farewells Joh

AS THE HOUR OF JOH'S FUNERAL APPROACHED, the scene outside the town hall looked like the Logies gone west. As the very old, the once great and the half remembered made their way along the concrete carpet, press crews swooped for quick interviews. The chooks had gathered to be fed by Joh one last time.

The day was cool and grey, with a strong smell of roasting peanuts drifting over Kingaroy. The 15,000 predicted by the *South Burnett Times* had not turned out. A couple of thousand was more the number. There was no need for the traffic barriers in the end, but then Sir Joh Bjelke-Petersen was famous for taking no chances where crowd control was concerned. Lines of mourners in wide hats and dark suits had queued since early morning for the few public seats: country couples in their seventies and eighties, the women big, fit and set for a few more decades, their husbands sunburnt shells.

Waiting at the front of the queue were the demolishing Deen brothers – Ray, George, Happy, Louie and Fazal – who all those years ago did away with the Bellevue Hotel on Joh's instructions. Their motto: "All we leave behind are the memories."

The Anthonys – father Doug and son Larry – led the Nationals grandees into the hall. Ex-Nat Bob Katter turned up in a big fawn hat. Earlier in the week he had threatened violence if sat near his old party colleagues. And the Liberals were there in dark suits. Queensland MP and Joh-for-Canberra backer Peter Slipper was asked: "How do you think they'll be handling the corruption question in there?" He snapped back, "I think that's just an entirely inappropriate question. The country is saying farewell to a giant today."

Kingaroy's few flags were at half-mast and everywhere in town are signs farewelling one of their own. As a mark of respect the hotel beside the town hall had shut the drive-through bottle shop. Outside the high school was a sign: "Vale Sir Joh". On the walls of Anderssons Fruit Market: "Chicken thighs $2.99 2KG. Goodbye Sir Joh the only 'real' politician we've ever had."

Inside the town hall was a scene of patient calm. Crowded onto the stage were a large choir and a few sticks of church furniture. John Howard entered looking old, flustered and very alone. Then something entirely unexpected happened. The Bjelke-Petersen family came forward in small squads to pay respects to the coffin and this big political show turned into a funeral. In silence filled only with the hum of the speaker system, Flo came forward on her son John's arm, her face old and blank, to bow her head over her husband's body.

So how did they deal with the corruption question? Not at all. The state funeral was always going to be a difficult exercise in remembering and forgetting the Joh they honoured in Kingaroy yesterday was the Joh of dams, roads, bridges and railway lines; the Joh who electrified the tracks and opened up the coal mines; the Joh who, as Peter Beattie said, "was never defeated by the Labor Party and never thrown out by the people of Queensland". Heads nodded all over the hall. The Labor premier was hitting the note perfectly. This was one of the great skilful speeches of his career. All week he had been explaining his part in this show: "My mother taught me respect, courtesy and good manners." But that's not the half of it. Beattie has been in the market for Joh's people all along. So many are his people now.

They're John Howard's, too, but the prime minister – in a speech about as drab as it gets for him – made his political pitch nakedly clear. He dwelt on the close bonds between him and Joh on industrial relations. Struggling to lift his game, Howard quoted Sir Christopher Wren – "If you want my memorial, look around you" – then looked around the vast plain barn of the Kingaroy town hall and let the matter drop.

You could feel the live TV ratings falling away. Perhaps viewers hung on for Kamahl AM, who slipped onto the stage in a silver suit to sing the Lord's Prayer. It was terrible, really terrible. He put it down to a bad case of flu. The service moved on. I won't easily forget the sound of a thousand farmers and their wives in the town hall reciting the creed in a low, confident roar.

By the time three Lutheran pastors and the deputy prime minister John Anderson assured us of Joh's deep Christian faith – "Joh knew what it meant to be happy in Jesus," said the Reverend Ken Schmidt – one last unanswered question hung in the air: how come his faith failed him so spectacularly in public life? But all is not lost for the man the church called Johannes. His coffin left the town hall to the assurances of the preachers that he was on his way to eternal life.

On the steps, the official guests in medals and uniforms and big hats and awkward frocks froze like a huge class photograph. It was the picture of the day but it seems not to have been taken. Across that empty forecourt, the prime minister approached the widow of his nemesis. She towered over him. He went for the kiss. She grimaced and pulled away. Those pictures were never printed.

The great white hearse pulled away for a victory lap of the town. I followed around the corner but there was no one there to honour its passing except schoolchildren mustered one deep along the street. They looked completely baffled and missing their lessons.

In Kingaroy that day much was made of Joh's catchphrase, "Don't you worry about that." But another great Johism was more to the point as the cortege finally disappeared down the road to Bethany: "Just you wait and see." By now old Joh is finding out.

The Sydney Morning Herald, 4 May 2005

Shock jocks on the beaches

BY THURSDAY ALAN JONES WAS SCREAMING like a race caller whose horse was coming home. "I'm the person that's led this charge here. Nobody wanted to know about North Cronulla, now it's gathered to this." The riot was three days away and Sydney's top-rating breakfast host had heaps of anonymous emails to whip his 2GB listeners on. "Alan, it's not just a few Middle Eastern bastards at the weekend, it's thousands. Cronulla is a very long beach and it's been taken over by this scum. It's not a few causing trouble, it's all of them."

Sunday's trouble was brewing all week on talkback, especially on 2GB, where Jones mate Steve Price was dead keen for a demo at the beach: "A rally, a street march, call it what you will. A show of force." Meanwhile, Jones was assuring his audience he "understood" why that famous text message went out and he read it right through again on air: "Come to Cronulla this weekend to take revenge. This Sunday every Aussie in the shire get down to North Cronulla to support the Leb and wog bashing day ..."

Daily he cautioned his listeners not to take the law into their own hands, but he warmed to those who had exactly that on their minds. On Thursday Charlie rang to suggest all junior footballers in the shire gather on the beach to support the lifesavers. "Good stuff, good stuff," said Jones. "I tell you who we want to encourage, Charlie, all the Pacific Island people because, you want to know something, they don't take any nonsense. They are proud to be here – all those Samoans and Fijians. They love being here. And they say 'Uh huh, uh huh. You step out of line, look out.' And of course, cowards always run, don't they."

When John called on Tuesday to recommend vigilante action – "If the police can't do the job, the next tier is us" – Jones did not dissent. "Yeah. Good on you, John." And when he offered a maxim his father had picked up in the war – "Shoot one, the rest will run" – Jones roared with laughter. "No, you don't play Queensberry's rules. Good on you, John."

Pity poor Berta – "not of a Middle Eastern family" – who reported hearing "really derogatory remarks" aimed at Middle Eastern people on Cronulla beach. Jones cut her off: "Let's not get too carried away, Berta. We don't have Anglo-Saxon kids out there raping women in western Sydney."

Yesterday 2GB broadcasters claimed two-thirds of calls to the station supported "what happened" on Sunday. But Alan Jones is not around to deal with the aftermath. He's having a well-earned holiday.

The Sydney Morning Herald, 13 December 2005

When his favourite broadcaster, Alan Jones, was nailed in April this year by the Australian Communications and Media Authority for making statements "likely to encourage violence or brutality" in the lead-up to the Cronulla riots, the Prime Minister leapt to his defence. "I don't think he is a person who encourages prejudice in the Australian community, not for one moment," Howard said. "But he is a person who articulates what a lot of people think."

The Sydney Morning Herald, 23 November 2007

Slapstick and the veep

WANTED, TO PROTECT THE LEADERS of the world when they meet in Sydney in September: police who can see a joke. In a scathing decision yesterday that drew on the Village People, Popeye and *The Pirates of Penzance*, the Sydney magistrate David Heilpern had to point out to senior police from the APEC squad that the Tranny Cops arrested during a demonstration outside Dick Cheney's hotel in The Rocks in February were joking. "Australia has a long history of street theatre as part of demonstrations stretching back to the Sisters of Perpetual Indulgence and the Vietnam Moratorium," explained the magistrate. And street theatre provided a "reasonable excuse" for wearing fake police uniforms. "Part of protest has always been challenging figures of authority."

He dismissed all charges.

Sarah Harrison and Anika Vinson turned up to the Cheney demonstration wearing dark blue overalls embroidered with the motto "Cop it sweet!" Though their costumes may have passed muster at first glance, Senior Sergeant Ian Franke, of APEC Security Command, admitted he could tell their moustaches, sideburns and goatees were ink from five metres away.

The sergeant's meticulous descriptions of the Tranny Cop routines drew laughter from the crowded court. "Ms Harrison placed her thumbs inside her belt and rocked back and forth in a heel-toe manner," he said, wiggling a little to make the point. Defence counsel John Berwick asked if he had ever seen the Tarantara scene from *The Pirates of Penzance*. He had not.

Trouble began for the Tranny Cops when first a silver and then a black Mercedes drove to the edge of the demonstration wanting to get through.

At this point, according to the prosecution, the two women impersonated police within the meaning of the *NSW Crimes Act* by "exercising the function of directing vehicular traffic". But the case against Ms Vinson failed almost at once when the magistrate discovered she'd done nothing with the cars. Her performance at the demonstration showed no intention of deceiving anyone, he said. "The only conclusion I can draw is that she was engaged in conduct for satirical purposes."

Ms Harrison entered the witness box to demonstrate how she walked over to the first Mercedes – like Popeye, observed the magistrate – and spoke to the "very irritable" driver. A few minutes later, she at least locked eyes with the driver of the second Mercedes. Both drove away, she claimed, without any direction from her.

And no one stepped forward in court to contradict her. Why? Because neither Sergeant Franke nor any of his colleagues from APEC Security Command, nor any of the hundred or so police present at the demonstration thought to note the numberplates of the cars. Struggling to find the right word to describe his response to this, the magistrate rejected "amazement" in favour of "surprise".

Reassured by everyone in the court that the Village People did, indeed, include a policeman, the magistrate declared there's "a Village People–style defence" for demonstrators and dismissed the final charges. Police still aren't laughing.

The Sydney Morning Herald, 11 July 2007

Haneef's week
in the watch house

MOHAMED HANEEF WAS ABOUT TO board Singapore Airlines flight 246 when two police entered the departure lounge of Brisbane International Airport. "You are under arrest for providing support to a terrorist organisation," said Detective Sergeant Adam Simms. The doctor was interviewed first at the airport and then, after midnight, at the Wharf Street headquarters of the Australian Federal Police.

The long arm of the law had reached Haneef from Glasgow where, forty-seven hours before, his cousin Kafeel Ahmed had driven a burning Jeep Cherokee packed with petrol and gas canisters into the airport terminal. Earlier, two cars packed with explosives had been found in London. British police had arrested both Kafeel and his brother Sabeel, a doctor at a hospital near Liverpool. The really sexy detail linking the Brisbane doctor to the Glasgow explosion was a mobile phone with a SIM card in his name found – it was said – in the wreckage of the Jeep at the airport. That was until yesterday morning when the ABC's AM revealed police actually seized the phone from Sabeel Ahmed hundreds of kilometres and many hours away from the explosion in a little town outside Liverpool. But that was a glitch for the future.

On that first night in Brisbane, Haneef was not panicking. He insisted he didn't need a lawyer and would stick to that for the next three days, saying he could straighten the matter out. But he was tired. Sometime before Haneef was brought a bed at 3 am, he told his interviewers he had been trying to ring British police that afternoon to clear up the matter of the SIM card. His calls weren't returned.

Haneef had slept only a few hours when police woke him. Were this an ordinary criminal matter, he would be charged or released at about this point. But police were using for the first time the nation's new anti-terrorism machinery that would allow the prisoner to be questioned for a total of twenty-four hours over an indeterminate number of days without any charges being laid. At the request of police, a magistrate might extend the stay behind bars indefinitely.

By the time Simms and federal agent Neil Thompson turned on the tape machines for the long interrogation ahead, the police had Haneef's phone and financial records from Australia and Britain. While the prisoner was eating breakfast, police had raided his Southport flat, turning up notebooks and diaries. They had yet to strip down Haneef's computer, but they weren't starting cold. They had evidence of a number of social and financial contacts between the detained man and his accused cousins. Yet by the end of that day, they had not unmasked a terrorist. Haneef emerged from the questioning a nerdy guy with fractured English who has done little in the past decade but study. And whatever else he may have been doing along the way, he had performed to perfection the classic role of the good Indian son – becoming a doctor, supporting his mother, seeing his sister married and marrying well himself. He told the police: "I am the sole carer for my family."

He was eighteen when his father, a teacher, died in 1997. With a little money and a scholarship, the son entered medical school in Bangalore. The family lived in an ugly lower-middle-class Muslim quarter of concrete flats. Old neighbours still speak highly of a wholesome and studious boy. His aim was to become a physician, an ambition that took him to England in March 2004. Money was tight. Police seized from his Southport flat an old diary in which he had meticulously noted the sums he borrowed from Indian doctors to stay afloat in England: £180 here, £200 there. He lived in a boarding house run by Mufeed, an Indian charity that looks after newly arrived trainee doctors and dentists. Police would later say that Haneef told them his second cousins Kafeel and Sabeel also lived with him in these Bentley Road digs. He had not.

Those cousins were the only family he had in England. He spent four or five days with Kafeel at Cambridge that first summer. Something is a bit odd here: Haneef says he was "a bit low", having failed an exam, but the Royal College of Physicians has no record of him failing. Kafeel also lent his cousin money: £300 he didn't want back. He said: "Just give it to any of the poor people in India." That first year in England Haneef spent observing and studying. From July 2004 to April 2005 he did unpaid work as a locum registrar at Halton hospital, just outside Liverpool. In May he passed the first round of his physician's exams. It was a life-changing success.

What followed was so Indian. Haneef returned home to bask in his achievement. Now with the prospects of a good job in Britain, he found a wife. Firdous Arshiya came from a family way up the ladder from Haneef's. They lived in a beautiful house in a beautiful suburb of Bangalore. They were modern Muslims. They read. They travelled. Their engagement was announced in July. Then Haneef returned alone to Britain to begin work at the Royal Liverpool Hospital.

His alliance with this family did not come cheap. From his brother-in-law-to-be he borrowed £3000 for the wedding. Here was a source of rich misunderstanding for police who would later be trawling through Haneef's financial records: his brother-in-law is Dr Siddique Ahmed and his second cousin is Dr Sabeel Ahmed. Both figure in records as "S. Ahmed". It could be so confusing.

The wedding took place in Bangalore in November 2005. Haneef told police this was the last time he met Kafeel. The newlyweds returned to Liverpool and moved into a flat in Pembroke Place near the hospital. Haneef got himself a mobile phone with a one-year plan. By December he was making his first repayment to "S. Ahmed": a heavy £550. He was also supporting his family – or that is Haneef's explanation for a transaction that makes sense to Indians but puzzled Australian investigators. He paid £960 into Kafeel's English bank account in October 2005 on the understanding that his cousin – who was still out in India – would pay the same sum to Haneef's family. The doctor's explanation to the police reads: "He had made arrangements to pay … in India to my family."

Meanwhile, Kafeel's brother, Sabeel, had turned up in England. Sabeel had been a year or so behind his cousin at medical college in Bangalore. Now he took a job at Halton and often came up to Liverpool to see Haneef and his wife. "He used to visit us," Haneef told the police, "as a family friend on the weekends." The following spring, Sabeel drove the hire car that took a family party on a tour of Scotland. The passengers were Haneef and his wife, her parents and her brother. They visited Glasgow, prayed at the mosque, but slept that night in a motorway hotel. Oddly, police didn't ask Haneef if they toured the airport.

With his one-year contract at Liverpool drawing to a close in the summer of 2006, Haneef answered an advertisement in the *British Medical*

Journal and was accepted for a post at the Gold Coast Hospital, in Southport, Queensland. He and his wife prepared for the journey to Australia via Bangalore. Haneef left all his "excess baggage" with Sabeel. As well as dumping books, an overcoat and a picture he'd been given of Mecca's holy shrines, Haneef gave Sabeel's address to his bank – and gave his cousin an 02 SIM card. "There were some free minutes left on the mobile phone. So he said: 'I would like to use that.'" Haneef understood Sabeel would take over the plan and make the phone his own.

*

Haneef's first interrogation at Wharf Street went from 11 am until about 7.30 pm with breaks for meals and prayers. The tone was mostly polite. The prisoner was willing. He refused only to give his views on the situation in Iraq and Afghanistan. "I don't like to comment." The two police officers didn't press the point.

Haneef denied ever touching a rifle, ever having any training in firearms, explosives or logistics, or ever being part of a terrorist organisation. He denied any knowledge of the Glasgow attack and the London car bombs. He denied knowing his cousins' friends or their politics. He denied raising money for political causes and denied taking part in anything that could be considered jihad. "Every drop of blood is human," he said. "And I feel for every human being." The police probed his religious beliefs. Was he Sunni or Shia? "I'm basically a Muslim, that's all." Had he had formal religious training? "No." Where did he pray? Sometimes in a hospital prayer room. Sometimes at the Liverpool mosque and later at the Gold Coast mosque. "I try to go at least once a day."

Much of the questioning involved the financial transactions that bound this young doctor to his family: repayments of his wedding loan, repayments of a small loan to finance his sister's wedding and monthly payments to his family in Bangalore. In Australia he was sending up to $3000 a month from his $70,000 a year salary back home to his family. At every turn, this is a very Indian story.

Haneef began work at the Gold Coast Hospital last September and lived with his wife in a one-bedroom flat in Pohlman Street, Southport. Firdous became pregnant soon after the move and returned to Bangalore in March. "We didn't have enough support here," said Haneef. "We thought it would be better for her to be there with the parents." Their daughter, Haniya, was born by emergency caesarean on June 26. That day Sabeel "chatted" with his cousin on Yahoo, offering his congratulations on the birth. That was their last contact. A couple of days later the mother and child were back in hospital. The baby had jaundice. Haneef would later claim he was prevented from flying home at this point because there was no cover for him at the hospital.

Here the story lurches into horror.

Late on the afternoon of Friday June 29, news broke in Australia that a car had been found in London stacked with explosive material. Over the next two days a second car was found in London and then the flaming Jeep was driven into the Glasgow airport terminal. By Sunday morning on the Gold Coast, Haneef's two cousins had been arrested: a badly burnt Kafeel in Glasgow, and Sabeel working at his hospital in Halton. Sabeel's mother rang Haneef from Bangalore that morning. British police had rung her looking for him. She said: "There was something wrong with your mobile phone. Someone was misusing the thing." She gave Haneef the number of Tony Webster, one of the British investigators. He left it for a day before ringing.

That Sunday, Haneef got a week's leave from the hospital and rang his father-in-law in Bangalore asking him to arrange and pay for a ticket home. By this time he knew Sabeel was in custody. He says his father-in-law reassured him: "Come here and we'll have support here for you." Haneef was booked to fly late the following night. Sometime on the Monday, Haneef left his Honda Jazz, some jewellery and a laptop with Dr Mohammed Asif Ali, a colleague at the hospital. (This would lead to Ali being detained and questioned under new counterterrorism powers, for the federal police suspected Haneef was acting "to conceal evidence". Dr Ali was released after twenty-four hours, having been vilified as an associate of terrorists. This innocent bystander faces five years in prison if he reveals what happened to him in custody.)

That same busy Monday afternoon, Haneef tried four times to ring Webster's number. Police knew the precise details: three goes between 3.08 and 3.29 pm and another at 4.32 pm. Haneef said: "I didn't get any response to that number." No mention of this attempt to cooperate with the British police was made in the dossier that later convinced Minister for Immigration Kevin Andrews to cancel Haneef's visa on character grounds.

The Joint Counter Terrorism Team arrested Haneef that night waiting for his flight. Why was he leaving on a one-way ticket, asked police?

"I going to get a ticket on my own, with my money when I come back," Haneef replied. The interviewing officer later gave a Brisbane bail court an affidavit that stated Dr Haneef "had no explanation as to why he did not have a return ticket".

Before the tapes were turned off on that long first day's interrogation, Haneef told police: "I haven't done any of the crimes. Just want to let you know. And I don't want to spoil my name and my profession. That's the main thing. And I've been a professionalist until now and I haven't been involved in any kind of extra activities, what sort of activities which you were discussing earlier. And I just want to live in life as a professionalist in the medical profession. That's what I want."

*

On the afternoon of Thursday July 5, a hard-bitten Brisbane criminal lawyer named Peter Russo had a call from the Brisbane watch house to say there was someone in the cells needing a lawyer. "It's not an unusual request," Russo told *The Sydney Morning Herald*. "I've been called to the watch house more times than I care to remember." But this wasn't a drunk or a petty crim needing help. It was the man now being billed in the press as the nation's most famous terrorist prisoner.

Haneef had spent the best part of two days and two nights since his interrogation waiting in a double cell with a small five-metre by seven-metre yard attached. He had access to magazines but no daily papers. He had made only one phone call, to the Indian consulate, to send a message to his family he would not be arriving on the flight as expected. He had not been questioned again. Each time the police returned to the magistrate to ask permission to hold him longer, Haneef was offered the right to be represented by a lawyer. He had kept saying no until the Thursday afternoon. So Russo appeared. They spent less than an hour together. Haneef's instructions were simple: "I want to go home."

The secretive nature of the proceedings was quickly apparent when the hearing began at 7 pm. Russo was not allowed to hear the police evidence. The magistrate's decision was made in Russo's absence. All he could do was put on record his client had been cooperating. The magistrate decided the prisoner could be held for another ninety-six hours. Russo's appearance marked a turning point in the case. That night Haneef briefed him and the next day Russo rang round the Brisbane bar and engaged Stephen Keim, SC. Their strategy was to force the government to provide information to explain why it wished to continue to hold Haneef without charge. Keim told ABC *Lateline*: "I went before the magistrate, they handed up the secret information to the magistrate. I said: 'Hey, that's not natural justice. I've got a right to make submissions, I've got a right to know generally what your case is.'"

Huge police resources were being thrown at the Haneef matter. Police were stripping Haneef's computer. "I am told it is the equivalent of reading 31,000 pages of paper to look at the amount of material that actually has to be analysed that has been retrieved through the exercising of search warrants," said the attorney-general, Philip Ruddock. And the story was a continuing bushfire in the press, with a steady series of leaks suggesting Haneef was a darker figure than the government could ever reveal.

On July 13, police decided to use the last hours of questioning allowed them to conduct a second full-scale interrogation. Russo was present, his nasty cough turning into flu. The questioning went all through the night. "Geography was not one of my better subjects at school," Detective Sergeant Simms admitted to the prisoner in the sixth hour of the interrogation. "Bangalore, where's that in relation to Pakistan?"

As good a reason as any for the AFP being so furious at the release of the transcript of this interrogation is the embarrassment the force will endure as the ignorance of the interrogators is displayed page after page. For ten days detectives on three continents had been gathering whatever evidence they could about the Gold Coast doctor, but Detective Simms had not opened an atlas. He did not know where Liverpool was from London. The name Mysore meant nothing to him. It seems he'd never heard of Urdu. The ways of Skype were new to him: "I'm a bit of a dinosaur when it comes to this sort of thing." His grasp of doctors' career paths was shaky. He had no clue what Muslims do during Ramadan. "OK," he said when Haneef explained. "Excuse my ignorance, yeah."

Simms emerges as a decent man from the 378-page transcript. He dealt with Haneef politely, hour after hour, as the interrogation went on through the night. But Simms ignorance of Islam is bewildering. This was, after all, the man to whom the federal police had delegated the task of discovering whether Australia was holding a dangerous fanatic in league with Islamists who had just tried to detonate car bombs in London and Glasgow.

The interrogation continued with breaks roughly every hour until just before dawn. Several times during the night, the police read Haneef his rights. Almost as often Simms reminded the prisoner what this was all about: "Let's not forget, Mohamed, the reason you are sitting here and the reason you've been in police custody is because of this issue with this SIM card. Now, it's causing you a lot of grief. We need to be clear as to what is happening with this SIM card." But police knew by this time that the card Haneef had left with his cousin Sabeel Ahmed in Liverpool a year earlier was not a bomb component, had played no part in the terrorist attacks and was not found at the scene of either the London or Glasgow crimes. The SIM card still sat where it had for a year: in Sabeel's Nokia.

Police must also have known that Sabeel was not one of the bomb plotters. He was in custody in Britain because he had failed to alert police to an email received from his brother Kafeel as the bomber was heading north to Glasgow. Received but not read. *The Guardian* (UK) would report that Sabeel did not open his brother's email until ninety minutes after Kafeel drove his Jeep Cherokee crammed with gas canisters into the airport terminal. Sabeel first heard of Kafeel's plans as his brother lay in a critical condition in a Glasgow hospital with burns to most of his body. He had only a few weeks to live.

All through the night at the Brisbane watch house, the detectives crisscrossed the record of Haneef's time in Britain, his travels, his colleagues, his career and the sums of money – mostly small – that flowed in and out of his bank accounts. But always the questioning returned to the SIM card and his cousins. What emerged was a much clearer picture of the intimacy between Haneef and Sabeel. Both were enmeshed in a family of cousins. Keeping in contact was obligatory and expensive. They used Yahoo chat rooms, Skype and mobile phones. Haneef said of Sabeel: "He is talk a lot on the phone, always on the phone." The SIM card he left with his cousin – along with a winter overcoat, duvet, sheets, crockery, a food processor, a framed picture of Mecca and a pile of books – had 100 or 200 minutes of credit left. Sabeel never transferred the card into his own name. Though he had been paying the monthly fees after August 2006, police believed Kafeel had paid the last bill in June. Haneef expressed surprise. "Dr Sabeel wanted it for his use. He said he just wanted to make normal calls to India and friends."

About 3 am, having apparently thrown everything they had at Haneef, the police turned to the suspicious circumstances of his rushed attempts to depart Brisbane on the night of Monday July 2. These were crowded hours and Haneef's answers has to be judged against the timeline of events in Britain, Brisbane and Bangalore.

Kafeel drove his jeep into Glasgow on Saturday June 30. Over the next couple of days reports of several arrests in Britain flashed round the world. But for the moment, the names were not released. Also on the Saturday, Haneef's newborn child had been readmitted to hospital with jaundice. Haneef was uncharacteristically hazy about the exact date. He thought it was Saturday. He says everyone was ringing everyone through this crisis and on Sunday he began to think he should get over to Bangalore. Back at work on Monday, he called HR to ask about family leave, but says he had had no time to do more than inquire that morning because he was very busy at the hospital. Then about 2.30 pm, his colleague, neighbour and friend Mohammed Asif Ali brought him a message: there had been some "misuse" of his old SIM card, Sabeel was in custody and Sabeel's mother wanted to talk to him.

Dr Ali had been brought into the loop because Haneef's brother had been trying without success to reach him all morning. Haneef went home and made several rapid calls: to his brother in Bangalore, then to pin down a week's leave from the hospital, and then to his father-in-law Ashfaq Ahmed to ask for a one-way ticket home. Haneef says he was waiting for his next pay and had only about $100 in his bank account. All his spare cash had, as usual, been sent home to support his family. He would buy the ticket back to Australia himself. Email confirmation for a flight that night came through within about an hour.

Simms asked Haneef: "Was the decision to go and take leave made because you found out about this telephone issue?" He replied: "No. Not about that at all." Later he would concede in the interrogation: "This was the second reason probably why I would have gone."

Sabeel's mother now rang and gave Haneef the number of a London detective who wanted to speak to him. She did not tell Haneef why his cousin had been taken into custody. He rang the detective's number several times, but could not get through. Late in the afternoon he returned to the hospital and found Dr Ali in the emergency department. He gave him spare keys to his flat and his new Honda Jazz. He also told his colleague he had been trying without success to call the London detective. Dr Ali lent him an international calling card to try again. That did not work either. Back home again he had one more favour to ask of his friend: to collect from the flat for safekeeping his laptop and his wife's jewellery. What jewellery, Simms asked. "Some bangles and some necklaces and things." Why not take them home to his wife? "She had enough with her," replied Haneef. "I mean, obviously we were going to come back."

By early evening he was waiting for the airport transfer van and exchanging messages in Urdu with his brother Shuaib on Yahoo chat. These were later downloaded by police from Haneef's computer. Somehow, Shuaib knew that one of the arrested doctors in Britain – still days away from being publicly named – was their cousin Sabeel. "Watch BBC.com," says Shuaib, and they both paused to glance through the latest report on the failed bombings. Later Kevin Andrews would say that federal police suspected this internet exchange "may be evidence of Haneef's awareness of the conspiracy to plan and prepare the acts of terrorism in London and Glasgow". But it was not Haneef but Shuaib who made the connection. And the translation being used by Australia's frontline forces in the fight against terrorism was simply gibberish. This did not deter the police in the closing minutes of their interrogation. Haneef had the original Urdu in front of him, but federal agent Thompson brushed aside his protests: "We can go back through it then I'll ask your version."

That never happened. The interrogation ended without fanfare at 4.42 am. The police called a break and never came back. Instead, they conferred in a nearby room with Ramzi Jabbour, manager of domestic counterterrorism for the federal police. Then, about 5 am, the flu-riddled Russo was told his client was to be charged with intentionally providing a SIM card "to a terrorist organisation consisting of a group of persons including Sabeel Ahmed and Kafeel Ahmed, being reckless as to whether the organisation was a terrorist organisation".

*

Once charged, Haneef found himself back in the traditional criminal system and Russo immediately applied for bail. The *Herald* understands the magistrate, Jacqui Payne, queried the logic of anyone giving a SIM card to terrorists: surely its discovery would immediately implicate them in the crimes? Barristers for the Crown argued the phone was intended to be obliterated in the fire that destroyed the Cherokee Jeep at Glasgow airport. Payne was not impressed. Having considered her decision over the weekend, she granted Haneef bail. She noted there was no evidence of a direct link between him and the group blamed for Britain's recent failed terrorist plot, nor evidence that Haneef had intentionally provided his SIM card to a terrorist organisation. She observed Haneef was a doctor with no criminal record and a good employment history. She set bail at $10,000 and under stringent reporting conditions, and ordered his release.

But his release was immediately quashed by the minister for immigration. In a move that set off a depth charge in the legal profession, Andrews cancelled Haneef's work visa on "character" grounds, claiming to "reasonably suspect Dr Haneef has had an association with persons involved in criminal conduct, namely terrorism". That power is designed to detain for deportation convicted non-citizens. It has apparently never been used in the past to detain non-citizens pending court proceedings. The president of Liberty Victoria, Julian Burnside QC, declared this "a serious misuse of power". The president of the Australian Bar Association, Stephen Estcourt QC, called Andrews' move "a threat to the rule of law". The Gold Coast doctor was driven away from the watch house, shoeless in a prison smock, hunched over on the floor of a paddy wagon.

That same morning, the transcript of Haneef's first interrogation was published in *The Australian*. The prime minister and the attorney-general were outraged. And with the case against the prisoner beginning to look rather thin, news broke that the SIM card – the single vivid detail that linked Haneef to these crimes on the other side of the world – was not in the burning Jeep at Glasgow but in the possession of his cousin Sabeel, who has not been charged in Britain as a terrorist. The government held firm. Police commissioner Mick Keelty urged lawyers and journalists to stop commenting on the case. Kevin Andrews spoke darkly of a secret dossier of evidence against Haneef. But after less than a fortnight, the Commonwealth director of public prosecutions, Damian Bugg QC, dropped the charges. An investigation is now proceeding into how they came to be laid in the first place.

Dr Haneef has left for home pursued by the Australian press.

The Sydney Morning Herald and *The Age*,
21 July 2007 and *The Sydney Morning Herald*, 25 August 2007

The Federal Court declared Andrews had no grounds to cancel Dr Haneef's visa. He was free to return to Australia at any time. An inquiry by retired Supreme Court judge John Clarke QC confirmed the doctor had been wrongly charged and wrongly detained. The AFP banged on for a time about possible links to Al Qaeda but after spending over $8 million on the case declared Dr Haneef innocent. The Commonwealth apologised. Mick Keelty made an early exit from the force. Haneef was paid substantial compensation, reported *by The Times of India* to be as much as $1 million. But by stroke after stroke of good fortune, Kevin Andrews' ignorance protected his ministerial prospects in the next Coalition government. As I reported over a year down the track:

> Courage was the word Kevin Andrews plucked from nowhere to describe his handling of the Haneef matter. "The Australian people expected me to act," said the former minister for immigration this week. "I had the courage to do so." Did he mean ingenuity? How but by the most ingenious devices could Andrews have remained, as he claims, entirely ignorant of ASIO's cheerful view of Mohamed Haneef until ASIO's submission to the Clarke inquiry was shown to the world in July? He told *The Age*: "The first I knew of it was when I saw their submission."

Those thirteen months of ignorance rank with some of the great blackouts of the Howard era: the five or so years Alexander Downer spent out of the loop as wheat scams to the tune of $300 million crossed the desks of his Department of Foreign Affairs and Trade; the year the whole cabinet remained convinced Iraq bristled with weapons of mass destruction; and the iconic month no one got around to telling the prime minister that kids weren't thrown overboard.

Recall the problem Andrews faced in July last year: Haneef's arrest was a God-given pre-election terrorism scare that would deflate like a used party balloon if the vilified doctor was allowed to go back to work at the Gold Coast Hospital. As Andrews prepared to cancel Haneef's visa on "character" grounds, ASIO kept reporting all around Canberra the doctor was clean.

Andrews says only the "general tenor" ever reached him though ASIO officials were briefing officers of his department almost daily. As Haneef was entering his tenth day of detention without charge in the Brisbane watch house, ASIO put its verdict in writing. Surely that got to Andrews? No. Clarke reports the assessment was delivered to the acting secretary of the Department of Immigration and Citizenship but "Mr Correll did not circulate the report to anyone else in DIAC or to the minister". How close it came. There must have been days the minister's cuffs almost brushed the file.

Did he know not to ask? Is there some wink or nod, some Masonic hand-shake that tells a minister not to go there? A thumbs-down from the spooks was all Andrews needed to cancel Haneef's visa and, though he had his law-yers searching in the dimmest recesses of the legislation for help, he never picked up the phone to get ASIO's verdict.

Hours after a Brisbane magistrate granted Haneef bail, Andrews had the rare privilege of attending a meeting of the national security committee of cabinet. ASIO was there. ASIO delivered its unchanged verdict: Haneef was clean. An impeccable source tells me Andrews was in the room at the time. Not so, according to the then minister. He told Clarke he only arrived in time to hear the police commissioner, Mick Keelty, give a briefing on con-tinued police suspicions about the Indian doctor.

Immediately after the NSCC dispersed, Andrews cancelled the visa and Haneef stayed behind bars for another fortnight. It's a neat trick we can pull in Australia: imprisonment by ministerial decree ...

The Sydney Morning Herald, 27 December 2008

Farewell to a fine old bastard

FOR A MAN WHO WAS ABSOLUTELY right so often, Alan Ramsey could be magnificently wrong. Not weasel wrong in the political fashion he so deplored, but no wiggle room, chin out, out on the high wire without a net, entirely wrong. "Latham?" he asked on the morning of the 2004 poll. "I think he can get there."

Ramsey was rough on himself; he ran risks; and every time he came a cropper he picked his battered body up again and was back on the field the next Saturday laying into the players, the ref, the crowd, the press, the linesman – everyone in sight down to the kid with the oranges at half time.

This week is the last time Ramsey stakes out his familiar territory in the middle of the Saturday *Sydney Morning Herald*. After twenty-one years, four prime ministers, eight federal elections and God knows how many hundreds of thousands of furious words, he's hanging up his columnist's hat. Bad temper is hard to sustain over a couple of decades. Week in week out, rage isn't particularly attractive. We're schooled in this trade to be suave and pretend detachment. Not Ramsey. And his readers loved his rage – just as his subjects had little choice but to respect it – because Ramsey was one of the few in the Canberra press gallery who wrote from his heart. So he was right passionately, wrong passionately and patronised at times by his hardboiled colleagues for taking a stand in their shifting world. He was a moralist – still is of course and will be to his dying day – and as an unflinching moralist he did the work over the last decade that mattered most to his readers: seeing

John Howard for exactly who he was.

The old prime minister was not among the walking dead who came to Ramsey's farewell dinner at Old Parliament House a few weeks ago. Someone, it seemed, had wandered into Madame Tussauds – go with me on this – and offered the waxworks one last outing on the hill. Andrew Peacock was there looking trim, suspiciously trim. Bill Hayden had misplaced his equerry. Tony Eggleton represented the Pleistocene. Keating picked the eyes out of the room. Max Walsh had taken time out from a financial crash more appalling than any of the disasters he's spent his life so frequently predicting. And Ramsey was king of them all for the night: subjects, sources, victims and colleagues. The breadth of his friendships on display was astonishing. One of the silliest men in parliament, Bill Heffernan, was in the same room as one of the sanest, John Faulkner. They had nothing to say to each other then, but each has spoken eloquently over the years through Ramsey.

In an age addicted to the grab, Ramsey never lost faith in the speech. His head was full of Hansard. Yes, he quoted in slabs, but through great speeches he brought parliament and its arcane drama alive. And he did what commentators rarely do: he allowed his subjects their own voice. Not infrequently, they had the privilege of speaking from the grave. As time went on, Ramsey lived with legions of the dead in his imagination. Perhaps because he had explored the territory too often himself, the border between this life and the next became rather hazy for Ramsey. He honoured the known and the unknown dead in his columns. History was alive in his analysis. One of Ramsey's signature lines was: "Nothing changes."

So the fact that he was out the back working frantically on his own speech that night – even while the video tribute was playing – surprised none of his many editors in the room. Ramsey is a chronic late filer. He is loved by his colleagues for this alone: that he is the worst of us, the one that's always last to file. If once or twice in the last couple of decades you didn't hear the satisfying thump of *The Sydney Morning Herald* on your doormat early on Saturday morning, talk of paper breaks at the Chullora printing plant were only ever a cover. Ramsey was to blame.

I never thought he got native title. Somehow refugees didn't engage his heart. These were quirks loyal readers like me bore for the satisfaction of finding Ramsey next week, say, spewing lava over the Howard government for its servility to Washington and neglect of the Guantanamo prisoner David Hicks. Every election was Howard's last in Ramsey's mind. Then came 2007, and on the morning of the poll his readers found him at his scornful and triumphant best. Celebration calls for a slab of his own words. There is no one now, and no one coming along, who can write like this:

> The end of the line. Remember that heading in the *Herald* a few weeks back, after one of the opinion polls bumped up the government's lousy standing a point or two? "Lazarus stirs", it said optimistically of John Howard. Wrong. It was just the flies moving.
>
> Yesterday, in the nation's parliament, with hardly a politician to be seen anywhere, we got some election realism. Three rows of recycling bins, whacking big green ones with yellow lids. More than 300 of them.
>
> Where? In the basement corridor of the ministerial wing. The bins seemed a more apt commentary than all the desperate, last-minute Coalition windbaggery going on around the nation on what is about to descend on the prime minister after thirty-three years in public life and almost twelve years remaking Australia in his own miserable, disfigured image. They arrived two days ago and whoever they're for, forty-eight hours before a single vote is cast today, you felt somebody, somewhere, finally got it right.
>
> The end of the line.

It's said all political careers end unhappily. That's where journalists enjoy a distinct advantage over their raw material. Ramsey is not defeated. He's going simply because it's time. He will be missed.

The Sydney Morning Herald, 20 December 2008

The Writing Trade

Demidenko: history, horror and fairytales

WE BURIED HELEN DEMIDENKO THIS WEEK. Around the crowded grave came whoops of triumph, laughter and rage for the passing of this strange child who somehow packed a full life into her very few years. Helen Demidenko was conceived at Queensland University sometime in 1992 and came to final grief yesterday with her apology. An immigrant of fantasy. Now that her bona fides are impossible to defend, the attack has redoubled on the book. The argument has a powerful, deceptive simplicity: the woman is a disgrace, *The Hand that Signed the Paper* is a disgrace and to like it is disgraceful. No, that word is too gentle: the core humanity of those who have admired the book is being casually questioned as if such matters were up for grabs in literary debate.

The fighting was tough before Demidenko's death and burial. Now, as a raucous wake continues, the fighting turns nasty. The literary community is being directed to hang its head in shame. The publishers are under pressure to withdraw the book from bookshops. It's *Satanic Verses* time. The row is not essentially about the quality of the writing – though there is controversy there – but about the right of fiction to deal in this way with the Holocaust. Indeed, it is about the liberties of fiction. These things as they affect our very different experience of that great moral catastrophe are very hard to put into words. But we must try.

The point, said Guy Rundle in *The Age* the other day, is that Demidenko – or Helen D., as I shall call her from this point – "wantonly used the pain and suffering of millions to turn herself into a literary star. Anyone with basic decency should be able to see that this is an immoral act." This puzzles me. Patrick White created Mordecai Himmelfarb in *Riders in the Chariot*,

397

a scholar who survived the camps only to be crucified in Australia. This great synthesis of imagination and research earned White praise, prizes and money. Every six months a cheque comes into the estate. Is this indecent? Should the cash be returned, not only by White but by the many thousands of authors who have written by now about the Holocaust, its causes and victims? The key, surely, is the decency with which Holocaust material is handled. We don't differ on this: ultimately it is a matter of decency.

I saw the manuscript about a month before Helen D. won the Vogel because the publishers wanted me to present the prize on the night. I was so impressed I rang at once to accept the chore. And there she was at the dinner, like a blonde awkward pony, reaching into and shying away from the light. For a time I felt a fool about the lecture I delivered from the microphone that night. I forget my exact words now and don't have a copy of the speech. Wish I did. But my warning was that in doing what a novelist must, make evil live and breathe, give it a human face, she would be accused of endorsing it. Such accusations – such confusions – are as old as fiction and the more terrible the events the more often the accusations are made.

And here was this young girl dealing with the Holocaust in a narrative that had for me the clarity of a folk tale: so cool, written almost without rage, yet so vivid it left me enraged as I read her depictions of rape, looting, humiliation and slaughter. These she showed; there was no voice to tell me they were terrible; she made me feel the evil of those years. The great risk she took – not unprecedented but daring and dangerous – was to tell the tale through the eyes of the perpetrators of the Holocaust. The brothers Vitaly and Evheny Kovalenko are workhorses at Treblinka. Mordecai Himmelfarb might have been, but for his miraculous escape, one of their victims.

Nothing happened after the Vogel. The anger came after the judges of the Miles Franklin Award, led by Dame Leonie Kramer – an apparently fearless but, this week, silent woman – awarded the novel the ultimate Australian accolade. In the months that followed, the book continued to win enthusiasts, but as it went on to win further prizes and gather further critical praise, its detractors declared it anti-Semitic. At stake now is the power of that declaration. Put simply, I don't agree. I remember thinking when these attacks began that if *The Hand that Signed the Paper* had an anti-Semitic purpose, it hadn't worked on me.

Cut to Thredbo. The snow was great this year – best I can remember since I was a kid – and the week was the more fascinating because the film producer Bob Weiss was there and we spent many hours discussing *The Hand that Signed the Paper*. In these civilised arguments, my reading of the book as an anti-anti-Semitic work didn't count for anything much at all: Bob thinks it's terrible and that that should settle the matter for both of us. Over and over again I found myself saying: "But it didn't read like that to me." So?

Then came the sudden death last weekend of the Demidenko identity and the anger this provoked in all of us who have had a strong response – either way – to the novel. When has such bad faith been shown to readers in this country before? Her bad faith doesn't lie so much in the fake identity – cf. Baron Corvo, Nino Culotta, Waverly, Brent of Bin Bin – but in the unforgivable lies she told to defend the text. She'd recited these fantasies to, and been believed by, us all – critics, journalists, publishers and Gerard Henderson – until she was exposed by David Bentley of *The Courier-Mail*. The passions this has roused! On my answering machine the other day was the voice of an old woman who hasn't contacted me for ten or more years, a musician who lost friends and family in the slaughters of the 1930s and 1940s. "David, ring me. I want to talk to you about that pathological liar who won the Miles Franklin."

Many of my colleagues, unable for some reason to get through to Leonie Kramer – not gone limp, surely? – asked me if I thought the book could survive the farce of Helen D.'s unmasking. I was confident at first that the text was unaffected but I was quickly dissatisfied with that answer. I'd absorbed the fantasy of Helen D.'s Ukrainian family before I read the manuscript and I know that part of my excitement then was my sense that this text had some authenticity as a kind of oral history: that, despite the disclaimers up the front, this was a risky exploration of her own family's guilt. Now I knew this was nonsense. I had to read *The Hand that Signed the Paper* again, hold a private wake in the week of Demidenko's burial.

The pages were full of surprises. I had forgotten how clearly Helen D. signals her disapproval through the narrator Fiona Kovalenko, the Brisbane University student who declares her uncle a war criminal on page two and accuses him of doing "unspeakable things" on page five, by which point she has also fingered her own father for taking part in the Holocaust, and finds the evidence – photographs – in his bedside table on page six. "My father. My father."

I had been told so often that no Jews are given names in the text – this is said to be evidence of the book's anti-Semitic intent – that I was quite surprised to rediscover Judit, wife of the local commissar, who is given a name, a history, a character and a voice. The book described her rape and death in a way that evokes in me horror and despair. I can't believe Helen D. didn't mean me to have this response.

I found no apologia for rape and death and looting and violence, no apologia for the slaughter of Babi Yar. The violence described is by communist officials against Ukrainians, by Ukrainians against Jews, by Nazi troops against Jews and Ukrainians. At every turn, Jews are victims of brutal pogroms. *The Hand that Signed the Paper* makes me feel rage and pity for their fate. And I can't believe Helen D. didn't mean me to feel this.

This is a book about people who don't like Jews. They think and say unspeakable things about them. They take part in their slaughter and scratch together justifications for themselves as evil people do. The great charge brought against *The Hand that Signed the Paper* is that it endorses overtly or covertly those cheap, inadequate, ahistorical "reasons" with which the peasants comforted themselves in their hate. Perhaps the worst of these "reasons" for revenge was the equation of Bolshevik with Jew, in the aftermath of the famine and purges of 1930–33. This is classic anti-Jewish propaganda repeated often by the narrating voices in the novel. Perhaps the core question in the Demidenko row is how we are to read this leitmotif, this identification of Bolshevik with Jew. Is this the thesis of the book, as so many are now arguing so passionately? Or is it the thesis of murderous bastards brought to life in its pages, men who slaughtered the Jews?

Fiction is always throwing up this problem. What is special here – and the source of all the vilification of the past few days – is a feeling that the Holocaust is too terrible to be dealt with in ways that call on this age-old ambiguity of fiction. It isn't decent. The tricks of fiction are too dangerous, we're being told, they might be misunderstood. Really? But by whom? Who is at risk of finding false comfort here? I write history; I love fiction; I believe there's no subject fiction can't find a way of addressing. This book found a way for me and – to name just a few of the newspaper critics – for Andrew Riemer, Miriam Cosic, Susan Mitchell, Vic Alhadeff of The *Australian Jewish News*, Margaret Jones, Peter Pierce, George Papaellinas, Marion Halligan, Frank Devine and Michael Jacobson.

What decent response can we make to those who read this book quite the other way? We should listen, consider, but not betray our own reading. I know many who have been through the maw must approach *The Hand that Signed the Paper* in quite a different mood to me. I know that where I find clarity and imaginative power in this text, others find lost opportunities for condemnation and a reluctance to tackle complex issues of history. I am moved by the simplicity of the figures on this Ukrainian landscape but I can see others might find this cardboard and think that Helen D. trivialises the psychopathology of these butchers.

For me, an understanding of evil requires us to remember that evil is committed by men and women. Others, of course, think it's too like a compliment to accord the perpetrators of the Holocaust the status of human beings. Let's engage in debate without these terrible smears and vilifications. We can all be patient, listen to the many more arguments to come, read the many books on the subject that have yet to be written. After all, what we are dealing with here is one of the defining horrors of the human race.

The Sydney Morning Herald, 26 August 1995

McNeil's life sentence

BENEATH THE STATE, in what was once a little newsreel theatre, an unknown company is reviving what's now an almost unknown play, Jim McNeil's *How Does Your Garden Grow*. It's a prison play from twenty years ago when it seemed Australian jails, in those bad times, were hothouses of writing. Poets and playwrights are working behind bars still, but none of them now has the clout of the names that emerged then: Bob Adamson, Bobby Merrit and, most of all, McNeil.

What a beguiling, dangerous, cocky mess of a man he was. One of Jim's many lovers told me the other day she remembers the look he had "of a cornered animal". That was McNeil, sunk in a chair, sweating and restless, sucking on cigarettes and beer: cornered perhaps, but not defenceless. Jim could talk. He was one of the funniest, canniest men I've ever met. The writing was impressive, but what drew us to him – "and was the secret of his success with women" – was the stories and the talk.

After last week's opening night, some of the old campaigners stood about in the upstairs bar of the State remembering Jim in his prison days and the wild, sad years of freedom that followed. We were thinking the best of him. How could we not after seeing his neglected little masterpiece on the stage again? We were remembering and mourning him in what's become a ritual: retelling the stories Jim told, stories we once thought would feed a writer's long career.

The stories started with the nuns and leaving school to roll Yanks in St Kilda during the war. He was a bad kid on the waterfront in Freddie Harrison's gang. "He ruined my life," Jim once said of Harrison. "But I was sorry when they blew his head off."

That was McNeil to the press, to be counted on for a downbeat one-liner. To us, he boasted of killing Harrison himself, along with seventeen or so others. Maybe. But these were the stories Jim told after a couple of dozen cans, a crumpled wreck on a sofa, all cigarettes and bravado, letting us know how nasty he was. The criminal career was long and inept. McNeil was extraordinarily funny about this. The main problem was the bottle of spirits he needed before every armed robbery and, though he claimed turning over a dozen Melbourne TABs and never being caught, there were enough catches to keep him in prison almost continuously from sixteen until forty-two. But not quite continuously: he married and in short bouts of freedom had six kids. "Whatever I did, I always staggered home to the wife and kids."

When we met him, he was in Parramatta Gaol doing seventeen years for shooting a cop in a paddock by the Hawkesbury River. Again there was a mass of funny, beguiling stories about this disaster: crossing the border with his wife and kids after holding up a pub in Preston, running out of cash in the Blue Mountains, getting up his courage with a bottle of Bacardi outside the ES&A bank in Windsor until a policeman came tapping on the window of the car asking for his licence. Jim had never had a licence in his life. There was a chase and a shootout that left the cop wounded in the leg but both men miraculously alive.

Smart-arse law students like me were invited out to Parramatta Gaol in the late 1960s to debate prisoners in the Resurgents Society. We thought we were seeing Life, perhaps even contributing to Rehabilitation; they were getting a break from boredom and enjoying a fortnightly supply of quality cigarettes. Jim McNeil was a bad debater but had the sharpest, most attractive mind. To try to force some Salvos to grasp the reality of prison, he'd written a little dialogue he called *The Last Cuppa*, and it was performed one day for the Resurgents. Jim had never been to the theatre in his life, but this was a play and it worked. Jim was a natural.

Within a couple of years his one-act plays, *The Chocolate Frog* and *The Old Familiar Juice*, had been performed all over Australia and he knew he could write his way out of prison. The key to his escape was a group of young lawyers gathered by Robyn Potter, a determined woman who's now a bureaucrat in Queensland. I was a bit player in this group. Also working for Jim's release were theatre directors, writers and critics, of whom Katharine

Brisbane was both the most influential and one of the few who stuck this story out to the end.

Jim was transferred to Bathurst in the months before the riot and, in isolation from the Resurgents network, wrote his first – and really his only – full-length play, *How Does Your Garden Grow*. It's about a man like Jim facing parole, putting behind him the domesticity of prison to re-enter the world outside the walls. The language seems very gentle these days – probably because the text had to be passed for circulation by prison authorities – but what the play has to say about sex, domesticity and the power people hold over one another is as strong now as it seemed twenty-something years ago.

Katharine Brisbane's verdict then was that the new play placed Jim "among the top three playwrights in this country". And this was a verdict delivered in the boom years of Australian theatre, when David Williamson, Alex Buzo and Stephen Sewell were firing and anything seemed possible on the Australian stage. For Brisbane and those who'd seen his earlier plays, what mattered even more at this point was what McNeil would write once he was free. Waiting for him when he got out was a hefty Australia Council grant.

But, said his sister, Nancy, "You've never seen him drunk."

We did on his first night out of prison and just about every day and night in those first grim and exhilarating weeks of freedom. He was living with me and Jennie Delisle in our little house in Balmain and nothing in my life, to that time, seemed as sinister as the pffff of a beer can being opened down in the kitchen at about 5.30 every morning.

Life and art were very entangled then. Rehearsals for the play had begun at the Nimrod Theatre. The plot of *How Does Your Garden Grow* involves the transfer of "Brenda" – George in the yards – from Mick, who is about to be released, to Sam, who has a long sentence still to run. This is not homosexual romance, but a domestic arrangement behind bars. "Brenda" is cellmate, lover and servant to two straight men. Jim looked over the boy playing "Brenda" and plumped for the woman playing the wife. It's not much of a role, but Robyn Nevin, great artist as she is, made something of it. Before the Melbourne season of the play had opened, she and McNeil were married.

The revival of the play the other night – shamefully it's the first down-town revival in twenty years – brought back one of the minor bizarre incidents of those first weeks of Jim's freedom. I'd delivered him to the home of Ron and Annie Robertson Swann – he the sculptor and she a devotee then and now of Stanislavski's acting method. Annie was particularly revved up about the method at the time and when I suggested it was mostly nonsense she threw me out of the house. Jim said later: "You got what you deserved."

It's Annie Swann who is to be thanked for this revival of *How Does Your Garden Grow*. I suspect, like most of us, she feels a sense of there being unfinished business with Jim. It's not a great production but it is an illuminating act of devotion to his memory. In his little body of work, Jim created a unique comedy of tedium that makes great demands on directors and actors. Rhythm and nuance are everything. Daniel Roberts as Sam, Doug Scroope as the sweeper and Gerard Sont as "Brenda" catch that rhythm and together come close to recreating the world we blind do-gooders glimpsed in those Resurgents days.

Once he was free, Jim didn't need to write. Talk was enough, fascinating talk, talk and booze. There was one more play, *Jack*, which he finished with the help of a bottle of whisky, but it was no patch on *How Does Your Garden Grow*. A few more years followed of drink and bad temper that burnt away his talent and wore out his welcome in this world. But not quite. Jim never lost the affection even of those who could never bear to see him again. Katharine Brisbane found him derelict in Melbourne and brought him back to Sydney, where he died still telling fascinating stories on 16 May 1982. He was forty-seven. A few days after getting out of prison he said: "I'm the greatest playwright in Australia, but it hasn't happened yet." It might have and didn't. That's the pity.

The Sydney Morning Herald, 2 July 1996

I had written him a letter ...

WE'LL HAVE NO FUNERAL TALK TONIGHT about the death of the letter. The letter lives. The post box on the corner is proof enough. We all write letters. Of course, we regret the letters we never get round to writing – but that's no evidence that letters are dying. We regret the diaries we never began, the novels unwritten, the great idea we once had for a film we never got round to jotting down on paper. To regret is human, and every educated human being regrets not putting more down in writing.

Too often – perhaps this is an Australian thing – we let the moment slip and have to come up with a good excuse before making start on a letter. Elegant excuses will do. Convincing excuses are best. The challenge of formulating excuses leads, inevitably, to further delay. Among other wonderful things, this book is an inventory of excuses.

The lost address is the most common excuse through the ages. There's also rushing around and Charles Kean's "one thing and another". That's my favourite. In a letter of stupendous self-pity, advising all and sundry never to emigrate to this country, Henry Parkes gets close to formulating a national style of excuse, "I was unwilling to sadden your hearts with a tale of misery." Though, of course, there's quite a lot of that in this book: it's an unwillingness very frequently overcome.

But the great Australian excuse for not writing sooner is, of course, the heat: in 1882 Margaret Nihill would have sent a letter "long ago but the heat made me very weak". Mary Gilmore nearly a century later tells Daniel Thomas she's been "too much knocked about by the heat to get at this fully till now ..." I would argue the great Australian contribution to the art of the letter is the heat excuse.

Which is why we should celebrate Jessie Miller tonight. Imagine the scene: the heat on the Darling Downs is intense, there's a drought, the war is on, fifty people have been for lunch – and none of this deterred her from writing. There was also a plague of beetles:

> My Dears, I promised to let you have an account of Grace's wedding so here goes, I will do my best but the insects tonight, as every night are driving us mad. I have a large basin of water beside the lamp and have caught hundreds but there are hundreds more.

And here there's a dash on the page: "A break occurred here, a beetle flew into my ear and for a while things were hectic as the family rushed round trying to get it out and it continued to sting and flutter. No more writing that night. Now Sunday morning and will have another go at it."

She did. She wrote all Sunday – the frocks, the gifts, the rituals – and still hadn't finished. Monday night came and she was still at it. She was utterly determined. With night came the beetles but, she writes, "I have both ears filled with cotton wool to continue my story." That's why Jessie Miller deserves an honour: the Jessie Miller prize for perseverance in letter writing: a certificate and a bag of cotton balls to be awarded annually and in perpetuity; judges: Brenda Niall and John Thompson.

This is not a book for the faint-hearted. More swiftly than all but the greatest short-story writers, these letter writers take us into their hearts and the heart of their troubles. I was shaken by things I discovered in this book. It's a volume of laughter and shock, one of those rare books that leave you often pausing for breath. Be prepared for deaths, weddings, lynch mobs, suicide, lucky escapes, grief, fabulous good fortune, murder – and bloodcurdling snobbery.

Ignore the advice of that reviewer the other day who said this was a book to dip into. Do as I did – read it from beginning to end. Don't miss a word. Watch the country change. Watch the language change. Watch us shake free of the suffocating intonation of polite speech of the last century and be grateful all over again for what the twentieth century has done for English.

Be reminded that so much that matters in our history happened by letter – Barwick to Kerr, and Kerr to Whitlam. But our history turned on more than these letters of state: take Ethel Malley to Max Harris. Poor Max

Harris! However much we admire the ferocious trickery behind the Malley poems, that great hoax turned on Ethel's letters and their gorgeous, seductive flatness. "Dear Sir, When I was going through my brother's things after his death, I found some poetry he had written ..." Faultlessly plain, absolutely vicious.

John and Brenda made the decision to use whole letters only. I gutted Patrick White's letters to give him a chance to write his own life in his own words. For this collection they were right to take the worthier, more formal approach. It means we get these letters real. Even great letters may hit the mark only once or twice. You can read a flat few paragraphs wondering what's this one here for – then comes the zing, the perfect phrase, that gives that letter greatness. Then it will drift off. Even the greatest letters usually end with details about the chooks, the garden, the children. But that's letters.

Usually when we talk about the value of letters we talk about raw information, contemporary opinion and that sort of thing. But this collection reminds us that what matters most is voice. Great letters, great voice. This is a book of voices. John White: "I want to come back to Wannon." Mawson's fiancée, Francisca Delprat: "Come home at a nice time of day." Hugh McCrae: "I WANT to die."

Hugh McCrae is one of the discoveries I made reading this book. I knew about McCrae but hadn't known how wonderful his letters are. And the other discovery was Cynthia Nolan – what a *blazing* letter from Hydra. What a voice. In all the years I spent wondering why this difficult woman was so admired and loved by her friends – I never really had a clue until I read this letter. Her letters have to be published too.

This is not a review. If it were I would have to say boring things about how well the book covers just about every genre – except, I think, letters of demand ("Unless by the 12th inst. you pay 12,000 pounds ..."). There are even suicide notes, splendid suicide notes, and the editors have a bleak, probably Australian, fascination with notes written in the shadow of the gallows.

But the glory of this book is the love letters – letters of courtship, letters written in the limitless hope of early marriage and letters marking the death of a spouse – including a never-explained death by traffic accident in Venice. They're letters that remind us how much gratitude counts in love and in love letters: the gratitude of men rescued by their spouse from lives of waste and uselessness. These are the most moving love letters: those that say love marks the moment at which real life begins.

The letters here catalogue great change in this country. Up the front of the book are harrowing accounts of the massacre of Aborigines. Down the back is a letter by Banduk Marika asking the Northern Territory government to cough up $120,000 towards the cost of the sublime house Glen Murcutt designed for her in Arnhem Land. But what makes this book so wonderful is the way it captures what never changes, then and now, here and there in letters that are living fragments of birth, love and death. This is not just another anthology, not just a collection of good letters. Brenda Niall and John Thompson have given us a book that reminds us what it's like to be alive.

Launch of *The Oxford Book of Australian Letters*,
edited by Brenda Niall and John Thompson, 14 October 1998

Farewell, dark spirit

SASHA LOVED A CRISIS. Friends rallied. He was the centre of attention again. Whatever the scrape – betrayal, eviction, injury, neglect or poverty – someone always came to his rescue. But the latest crisis got a little out of hand and Sasha hasn't been around to enjoy the fuss.

After years of drinking, this impish writer and troublemaker died of liver failure at St Vincent's Hospital early on the morning of 30 August. As he drifted towards death, old friends and lovers hung about in the corridors trying to piece together the story of his life. It wasn't easy. Each of us knew only fragments.

Alexander (Sasha) Pavlovich Soldatow was born near Stuttgart to Russian parents washed up in Germany after the war. The boy was two when they reached Melbourne in 1949. Raised by a suffocating troika of mother and aunts, he was playing the piano in the Box Hill Town Hall at six. The piano became another of the many things Sasha could do but rarely did, like making love to women or holding down a job.

When he fled Melbourne and his family for the freedom of Sydney in the early 1970s, he announced he was a writer and plunged into the politics of the Push, the only gay man in that hard-drinking hetero crowd of radicals. He played a brave part in the stoushes of those years with rotten cops and corrupt developers.

To fall in with Sasha at this time was a life-shaking experience. He marched and drank under the banner of liberty. Behind him he trailed the notion that he was a spirit from another place – that his ideals, his taste, his thirst and his often-gloomy soul were essentially Russian. He had things to teach and he was not to be contradicted. The deal he offered was this: place yourself in my hands, and I will set you free.

Meanwhile, he was a dab hand at finding people to look after him. He lived in Margaret Fink's fine Woollahra mansion for years. She said, "He handled poverty rather well, until the end." He did it all on nothing in those early years – good lunches, good travel, good company and endless time for writing. Back then it was poetry, stories and gossip for pamphlets and a little magazine he roneoed himself called *The Only Sensible News*. Sasha was a highly principled gossip. He would insist: "It has to be true."

His other career – for which there remains a discriminating fan base – was as Russian subtitler at SBS, where he immersed himself for most of the 1980s in flagon red and the great classic films of Soviet cinema. When SBS tried to sack him – he always claimed it was for gossiping – the union had him reinstated. Thereafter, he didn't bother to turn up to work. He argued: "They can't get rid of me now." But they did.

He craved literary recognition but he was nearly forty before Penguin published a volume of short stories and portraits called *Private – Do Not Open*. "Soldatow is one to watch," was this paper's verdict. "He writes like no one else in Australia at the moment." But he spent the next few years slaving over an edition of the work of Fink's old flame, the poet Harry Hooton. This appeared in 1990 but was never destined to sell.

Frustrated by this failure to make his mark, he sued the Australia Council, claiming he represented "all those authors who have been set outside the cabal of chosen writers which distributes the taxpayers' money each year". He liked the notoriety and fuss, but his efforts yielded little. He was given a few residencies here and there, including three months as writer in residence at Sydney's Long Bay jail. He told the press he trusted murderers: "You don't have to have 15,000 dinners with them. You get straight to the heart of the matter quickly."

The heart of the matter for Sasha was always Russia, and in 1991 he embarked on the great adventure – and perhaps the great disaster – of his life. His attempt to live as a Russian in Moscow failed after a few months and he retreated to the luxury of Monica Attard's ABC apartment. Long, smoky nights with drunken intellectuals followed. Then in midwinter he slipped on the ice, shattered his leg and, after grim weeks in a Soviet hospital, was shipped to Australia an invalid.

This was the beginning of the long slide – he was now addicted to Valium and drinking heavily – but the next few years were his best as a writer. After *Mayakovsky in Bondi* appeared in 1993, he was midwife to Christos Tsiolkas's fine first novel *Loaded*, which enjoyed the instant celebrity that evaded Sasha all his life. His last book was an odd mutual biography the two men wrote together called *Jump Cuts*.

Old friends were dropping away. There were still flashes of the carefree naughty boy, the dangerous charmer of his heyday, but Sasha was becoming hard work even for the most loyal. After a doomed attempt to live in the bush, he retreated to Melbourne, where he ended up in a room at Percy's hotel in Carlton above a bar where intellectual conversation of a kind was available night and day. Friends rallied and brought him back to Sydney. For a year or so he lived in Cremorne, talking a lot but writing nothing, turning into a little old babushka. He still loved a good lunch.

His last stop was a housing commission flat in Waterloo, where Bruce Pulsford, the guardian angel of his last twenty years, found Sasha collapsed and took him after the usual arguments to St Vincent's. He died five days later.

Sasha Soldatow is survived by countless people whose lives he changed; by great jokes and unforgettable conversations; by books published and unpublished; by the carefully catalogued memorabilia now in the Mitchell Library; by his mother and stepsiblings. He asked for a literary prize to be established in his memory to honour writers who haven't had the recognition they deserve. His last publication will be the words he ordered for his tombstone: "I See."

The Sydney Morning Herald, 9 September 2006

Last train to Venice

NO ONE ON RADIO LOOKS LIKE THEIR VOICE. But what face could fit the silver voice of Robert Dessaix? For years he led Australia across the high ground of new writing – writing from everywhere, about almost anything – on Radio National's Books and Writing. Now he is a writer himself and the show is behind him, but one of the great pleasures of reading Dessaix is hearing the voice again in every line he writes. The eager, teasing, lucid, worldly, at times rather cross voice of a book man who has read on our behalf God knows how many thousands of the things but never doubts the magic black type works on a white page.

A couple of years ago he found he was ill with, perhaps, not long to live. Since then he has been searching for a voice to say "certain difficult things" and the result, published this week, is *Night Letters*, part novel and part memoir, a meditation on the most complex and simplest of all subjects: how we should live.

Dessaix was once a Russian scholar. The daring and humour of this book is Russian. So is its relish in tackling big moral questions Anglo-Saxons are usually too embarrassed to address. Russian, too, is the tetchy pedantry of the man who is supposed to have edited the letters, Professor Igor Miasmov. That's miasma in English: the breath of death. It's a very Dessaix joke, black and literate. "When I started writing I felt it was all a bit earnest, a bit self-regarding, and I thought, there is another me in there who is very sceptical about all this sort of thing – about the philosophising, about the mysticism. I thought, I will make this me an official editor and let him have his say in footnotes." His face creased with smiles as he revealed his tactics.

"It's a wonderful way of taking two positions at once."

It's the face, by the way, of an extraordinarily bright kid with big eyes, a bony forehead and generous lips. Most faces change a little to fit the times, but in the years I've known Robert Dessaix, his has been just as it is now: immediately interesting, absolutely his own. *Night Letters* is absolutely his too. Who but Dessaix could have written these twenty letters from Venice telling fairytales of courtesans and erotic amulets ("a sad mishmash of Orientalist stereotyping," comments Miasmov), tracing Casanova's search for bliss ("a spiritual figure") and Marco Polo's strange way of disappearing into his own narrative ("his self is always in the past or in the future, there is no now")? They take us on expeditions to Switzerland's abandoned Theosophist colony of Monte Verità and the gorgeous gardens of the Isole di Brissago. These may have failed as paradises, but Dessaix locates hell on earth after a terrible journey from Lugarno via Bologna to the lip of the pit itself: midnight on the whores' beat at Vicenza station.

Among questions he addresses between heaven and hell: why an ordered society requires adultery; the shortcomings of happiness ("terribly suburban – I would say very American") and the advantages of bliss ("it involves wisdom"); the dreadful ugliness of modern Italy; the virtue of never putting your life in order ("the more loose ends the better"); the sacred nature of heresy and the true pleasures of travel. All these brilliant excursions lead us back and back to a single question: how should we use our ration of time?

The letter writer is someone we know only as R. "He is a dilettante in the way ninety-five per cent of educated people are," said Dessaix. "We know a bit about painting, we know a bit about music, we've read a few books. R's just started reading Dante; he's read his Thomas Mann, no doubt; he's read some Laurence Sterne and probably keeps up with a bit of modern literature. What else can one do?

"But he is governed by love. He loves certain things and follows them up and then branches off, as he reads, into some other area he's glimpsed in the background and falls in love with that. Miasmov, who thinks he's got everything straight, is much more a specialist, much more a modern intellectual. Like most of our intellectuals, what he doesn't know doesn't bother him."

Why, I wondered, when time has become so precious, has Dessaix spent these past months writing? "It depends how mystical you want to be about it. I wrote this book as part of what I call 'riding'. I feel that most of us most of the time when faced with adversity are expected either to fight it manfully or to flee, either to lie down and be killed by it, or run in a cowardly fashion away from it. But I'm saying I think there are other possibilities, and one is to leap onto the beast that is stalking you and ride it. And this book is about riding, about saying, 'OK, you're pursuing me with lethal intent, I'm neither going to run from you nor lie down, I'm going to jump on your back and make something beautiful out of it.'"

This is his third book. For Oxford University Press he edited an anthology of gay and lesbian writing in 1993, and the next year published his memoir, *A Mother's Disgrace*, an entirely unmawkish tale of illegitimate birth, adoption and eccentric upbringing in Sydney, of his life as a student in Moscow and teacher of Russian in Canberra, of his marriage and divorce, the search for a partner and the late discovery of his mother. *A Mother's Disgrace* proved Robert Dessaix more than a radio voice: the critic had become writer.

I wondered if he regretted, now, not being a writer sooner. "No, I don't regret. I would reject the discourse of regret. If I regret anything it would be that I lived inside ideologies for too long and thought that that was the right thing to do. And it was the right thing to do at the time, but I don't think you can live inside an ideology and write imaginatively at the same time.

"I was also mentally a teacher for most of my life – and is that something to regret? I don't know. I like to think I was a good teacher. But I don't think you can be an imaginative writer and a teacher at the same time. And I still find this hard to get out of my head. You'll notice I had to make one of my main characters a teacher, Dr Heinrich Eschenbaum."

The mysterious Eschenbaum gets out and does what Thomas Mann's Aschenbach only dreamt of doing as he faced death in Venice eighty years before. Today's Eschenbaum comes south every spring to live for a fortnight and then goes back north, a bit battered by Venetian thugs, to recuperate in theory. Was this, I wondered, a pattern in Dessaix's life? "I don't think," he replied after a considered pause, "I don't think I live a double life any more. I don't think I have for some years, not in any important way. There are things about myself I suppose I don't want discussed in public, but in general I think I live a fairly integrated life and I don't have to go south or north to take a rest from my everyday official self any more. And when I try it, I don't know quite what to do with myself. In the sort of society

Eschenbaum lives in, the only thing of nature that's left is sexuality and appetite – food. He basically goes to Venice from Münster to experience nature through sexuality and food."

"You're very tough on Italian food."

"I've never admired Italian food. I've always thought it was humbug."

"Italian food in Italy or – "

"In Australia in particular, and in Italy it's the tourist food that most of us can afford. Real Italian food is hard to come by on a tourist budget and simply hard to find. Peasant food has never charmed me."

Night Letters reads as a meditation on the need to be – simply be. But Eschenbaum admits he's only able to be in the back room of a sex club where all is simply touch and feel and appetite in the dark. Was that, I asked, the cross Eschenbaum has to bear or a lesson for us all? "That's the cross he bears as an urban European at the end of the twentieth century. It's true when you say the lesson of the book is really to be, and if that's where you need to start, start there. Start with your sensuality. But I don't think that that's where it should end. I think you can be in an almost infinite number of ways, but I'm not condemning Eschenbaum's way either. We all have to start somewhere and the place to start may be walking the dog, or gardening, or reading novels, or going to the movies. It can be anything but it's all about paying attention to what is happening now."

"Now?"

"Now is the important point. It's a word that occurs hundreds of times in the book. We have to try to break out of the way of looking at life as a linear series of events, always imagining for the future or remembering for the past – and try to deepen what you've got now. It's a book about experiencing rather than always projecting and remembering."

We had been talking for some time. I asked Dessaix if he wanted a break, perhaps to eat lunch. The new dog was underfoot, a big affectionate mess of ridgeback and mutt. The garden was dripping wet after a morning of cold Melbourne rain. Somewhere in the house Dessaix's partner, Peter Timms, editor of *Art Monthly*, was working on the next issue. It feels like a house where a lot gets done. Dessaix was for going on. "I realise how much of my life I have spent not looking, not seeing. My mind has been full of abstractions, full of projections, full of intellectualisations and I haven't actually looked at what's in front of my eyes. When you become very aware of mortality, suddenly you want to see very, very acutely now. And not necessarily even to analyse. You want to see – and hear and smell to some extent – but particularly to see. And colours become terribly important."

"Why have you got it in for yellow?"

He laughed. "That would be a Russian thing. A prostitute is said in Russian to have a yellow ticket. That is her permission slip to work as a prostitute. A madhouse is called a yellow house. Yellow is associated particularly in a symbolist way with unhealthy, disordered appetite. Colour-coding fills the book, particularly the colour-coding of Dante. Colour is very, very important in seeing."

R encounters a splendid woman on a Swiss train who tells him he must see the little islands of Brissago "before you die". What do we mean by that odd expression, I wondered? "Well, it's a funny thing we all say. I started to think about this phrase after the diagnosis, of course. There is something wrong with it, you realise, because you're not going to see it after you die – so what do people mean? They mean in order to have a complete life, in order for your story to be a really good, rich, full story it should include this element. That's what they mean. And this is precisely what I'm trying to get away from because, for many people threatened with death soon, the possibility of adding to their curriculum vitae actually isn't there. They are not going to be able to go to Venice, they're not going to be able to see Kilimanjaro."

"But many do. Many who get the diagnosis embark as quickly as they can on the trip of their life, to see the things they've always wanted to see."

"First-class, I notice. I do approve of the first-class bit; you may as well do it in comfort. That's right. I think it's a push we should reject in some way."

"Why?"

"Because I think you're ignoring what's already here in order to tick things off. I don't think there is anything wrong with going to Kilimanjaro if that's really what you want to do. Do it. But I don't think you should believe that this is going to make your life more worth having been lived. What makes your life worth having been lived is something you can make happen in the next five minutes."

"And in Melbourne?"

"If you put your mind to it."

Night Letters challenges us to talk bluntly about death but I found myself putting off the questions. Death is one thing, his death is another. Finally

I cranked up the courage to ask why being given the news that death was not far off should have the effect it had on his life. After all, we all know we're going to die.

Dessaix doesn't search for words – the words are always there – but there was a pause at this point. "When this sort of thing happens it's like growing old very, very suddenly. It's like suddenly finding you're in your seventies and you realise that the point of being established – when you'd promised yourself you'd consider questions like the whys of everything and how you should have lived – that point actually never comes. It's a kind of blandishment that life always holds out but you are never settled like that. Your grandparents aren't. Nobody is. The moment is now. So you're going to have to face mortality now.

"I haven't ever named the disease in this book. This is not because I lack any kind of barefacedness – I think I can be as barefaced as anybody else – it's because I think what really interests people is the question of mortality, not this disease or that disease. And if they've taken time to read this book then they will perhaps pause, at least while reading, and think about it now. Not in twenty, thirty or forty years time. So this book is a meditation on that question and some people will see some directions in it, some people will be absolutely unconvinced. That's alright."

The book is also a mighty attack on Europe and a defence of Australia – a country, Dessaix says, that R realises he has not loved enough. Saturated with the riches of Europe, R decides to come home, where, "allowing for a multitude of exceptions, people are a little kinder to one another. Love, passion, creativity, intelligence, knowledge – all terribly important, of course. By comparison, kindness (like hope) seems a trifle dull, a very second-rate, suburban sort of virtue, I suppose. Well, I think it's undervalued. I don't want to live without it."

"Are you afraid of hope?" I asked.

There was a Dessaix pause. "Partly. It's let me down in the past, it's let all of us down in the past, so I'm leery of it. But I can't help having it. What I think I've learnt over the last two years is to hope not for salvation from this disease or that accident – mortality will get me after all whether through this route or another: it will get all of us – it's to try to change the object of my hope. And at some sort of level, although I'm excited as anyone would be that this may not be the one that gets me, I do honestly think I have learnt to hope for something else: for this circle of time I'm living in at the moment to be wonderful. It seems to be working.

"It sounds as if I'm avoiding the question and being airy-fairy but it doesn't feel like that. I just feel that to focus on hope that this disease will be taken care of too strongly – though you can't help being excited – would be to unlearn the lesson I've learnt and I don't want to unlearn it, because the basic problem is the same whatever happens and that is: how do you not waste time, given mortality?"

But I pressed the point. Had recent good news of medical breakthroughs from the Vancouver AIDS conference, I asked, changed his sense of the possibilities of life for him? "I'm not thinking too far ahead. What it makes me feel is a kind of joy that a nightmare is beginning to dissipate for millions of people, including me." And another pause. "I notice I'm more interested in the news in the past three weeks, world news, a bit more interested in politics, I'm more likely than I was a few weeks ago to feel cross about things I wouldn't have bothered being cross about a few weeks ago, to engage with things that are obviously temporary things."

"And that worries you a bit?"

"A bit, because I learnt really good lessons. I don't want to unlearn that and I would particularly hope that the gay community doesn't unlearn what it's learnt over the last ten years and simply say to itself, well, that's all right then, let's start being what we were." He laughed. "I've been thinking more of what I would like to do with the house we've bought in the country. If I'm going to live there for some time I think I would like to have more say in what colours we paint the walls."

The Sydney Morning Herald and *The Age*, 3 August 1996

Staying out of the picture

I'M ON THE SIDE OF INVISIBLE BIOGRAPHERS. I don't give a damn about their happy thoughts as they tread in the footsteps of their subjects. Spare me their personal reflections on the Strait of Gibraltar. I'm not interested in their research triumphs. I want the life, not the homework. And I don't need to be chaperoned. I am an adult. After reading biographies for fifty years or more, I can safely be left alone – indeed, I long to be left alone – in the company of ruthless cardinals, Labor prime ministers and crusty Nobel laureates.

My partner dreads me bringing biographies to bed. Novels don't come between us. Histories provoke no interpersonal stress. But when I have a life in my hands I drive him mad lying there laying down the law. "For Christ's sake," I mutter. "You can't do that." And a few pages later: "That's not the way to do it." His light goes out, but I keep going, page after page, all the way to the end, muttering, "You can't, oh no, no, that's completely impossible."

I know biographies come in all shapes and sizes. I agree with the great English biographer Frances Spalding that biography is "a hybrid and fluid genre, always spilling out of neat packages and persistently reshaping its enquiry as the questions that interest each generation change". But in forty years of writing biographies – some big, some little – I've worked up a few rules for myself. I know they are personal. I know I've broken them once or twice when it's seemed necessary. But they are my way of working. There are three that matter.

One: biographers must command the lives they write. They must make sense of them. Telling is not enough. The paintings, the sex, the parties and the voice must be clear on the page, but the point of any biography of Brett Whiteley is to explain how he took a road that ended in a motel room in Thirroul.

Two: we must not rob time of its mystery. Narrative is the most flexible beast. We can start a story anywhere and jump in the most surprising directions. But in biography, as in life, we must always be moving into an unknown future.

Three: biographers should stay out of sight. Artists who hover at their exhibitions get in the way of the work. Playwrights don't wander onstage. Directors are never in shot. And while there are exceptions, glorious exceptions, biographers should leave their readers alone to read.

I'm not shy. I'm not saying I've kept myself at all times out of my writing. I'm not reluctant to use what old subs at Fairfax call the vertical pronoun. I came into the trade in the 1970s, when something called the New Journalism was all the rage. Tom Wolfe and Hunter S. Thompson were showing us what could be done by writing directly about their own responses to the predicaments they were reporting. This could get out of hand. Bright beginners like me could think the most interesting thing about a story was their own response to it. That had to be beaten out of us, and those old subs were there to do it. But the vivid and intelligent reporting in *Rolling Stone* and *Esquire* renewed reporting in Australia, first in *Nation Review* and *The National Times* and later in the big city broadsheets.

I am a product of that time, but it never crossed my mind to make myself a player in my first biography. It was 1977. My subject – perhaps target – was Garfield Barwick, the tin-pot chief justice who gave his imprimatur to the coup of 1975. He received me cordially in his old chambers in Taylor Square a couple of years later, didn't, on reflection, much like me, and made certain over the next three years that none of his friends spoke to me.

I had a good look at his face and wrote what I saw. But we had no personal relationship. That wasn't the case with Patrick White. Ours was complicated. At first wary, he came to trust me. I was never blind to how appalling he might be but I came to love him. He was the wisest man I have ever known well. But I *never* saw myself as a player in his story. I witnessed heart-stopping crises at Martin Road. They are all in the book but I made a promise to myself that I would remain invisible. Of course I'm everywhere in the biography, everywhere as a biographer must be. My judgement is at play in every corner of the text, I wrote the words, it's my book but David

Marr, awkward, stumbling, occasionally charming, is nowhere in its pages, pulling focus from Patrick White.

My determination to stay out of sight was also, I have to admit, a question of manners. To write someone's life is one thing, but to elbow your way into it seemed then – and now – discourteous as well as misleading. However much I had come to like Patrick, our relationship was essentially professional. I was not one of his class or circle. I was not there as a colleague or as a member of the family. I had work to do.

These days, my editors would be urging me to put myself at the foot of the stairs as that terrified bundle was carried down to the ambulance. They would want me to weave into Patrick's life the story of me chasing after him around the world with vignettes of people I met and places I visited.

Don't get me wrong. They are good stories, and I have told them often *after* publication. I went to strange corners of the world and met fascinating people. I had triumphs in libraries from Wellington to Austin, Texas. I tracked down a grandfather who was Patrick's lover in Cambridge. And there was a night on the trail that still haunts me after all these years when I stumbled on a Nubian wedding in a back street in Alexandria.

But those stories would not have done the book much good.

Our Man Elsewhere, the recent – and in many ways splendid – biography of Alan Moorehead by Thornton McCamish, is written to the new template of the biographer on a quest. Early on in the book he bares his soul about discovering, in his late twenties, "a writer who would forever be indispensable to my imaginative sense of the past". A few pages later, admiring the faded splendour of Moorehead's favourite hotel in Cairo, it seems to McCamish that the man himself appears:

> I could almost see him drawing back the accordion grill of the elevator car, releasing a gust of big-band mood music, and stepping out neat and alert, tie tightly knotted, folded cap tucked under the epaulette. I could see him dropping into a club chair *right there*, ready to set out on his brilliant career. Right *there*.

McCamish is such an assured writer and shows such supple judgement of his subject that none of his personal reflections or the many pages he devotes to his search for Moorehead are in the least bit necessary. I'm being harsh, I know, but I don't care that the biographer is standing in a bar or on a street corner or on a hill where Moorehead once stood. I want everything he saw and everything he learnt absorbed into the text. I don't care if this or that excites him. His task is to excite me, not about Thornton McCamish but about Alan Moorehead.

I blame the new template on television. The model is David Attenborough in the jungle, Brian Cox on the edge of the universe and Bob Hughes down among the cubists. They are miraculously good at their task – eloquent, personable guides to the complexities of the universe. They are men on a quest. They give abstract subjects a human face. But lives aren't abstract. Biography is an act of re-creation. The only life that matters is the life of the subject.

Quest biographies raise two fundamental difficulties. First, research is boring for everyone except the researcher. Biographers find it thrilling or they couldn't be in the game. I have had some of the most exciting days of my life in libraries. But the thrills of research are personal and hard-won: moments of triumph after long stretches of boredom. You have to be there, you have to endure. It's a long haul between discoveries. Kind writers save their readers from their homework.

Quest biographies also muck around with time. All biography is time travel. Taking readers to another time is hard. It doesn't help to be shuffling between then and now, between the life and the quest. If you want to take readers to Cairo in the 1940s, it's best to inhabit that time, not move back and forth between Moorehead and McCamish, between the go-getting war correspondent and the fan who turns up in Egypt seventy years later driven by the thrill of the chase.

Even as I lay down the law, I must acknowledge great exceptions. The greatest of these is surely *The Quest for Corvo*, A.J.A Symons' life of the writer, pimp and religious nut Frederick Rolfe, who wrote the Edwardian fantasy *Hadrian the Seventh*. I think of it every time a pope dies because the novel is built on the notion that anyone – any man – on earth can be called on to be pope. He doesn't have to be a cardinal or even a priest or perhaps even a Christian. Rolfe, or Baron Corvo as he styled himself, taught me this. Every time a pope dies, I wait for the knock on the door.

Symons' 1934 book is, as critics have pointed out for years, biography as detective story. It's an endless delight as Symons tracks through the delusions of this paranoid would-be priest to reveal that apart from his strange capacity to write there was almost nothing there. Rolfe wasn't a priest or an aristocrat. He made his living at one point hiring gondolier prostitutes for Englishmen visiting Venice. *The Quest for Corvo* is both the first and best of quest biographies, which, I willingly admit, have at least this purpose for which they are perfectly suited: writing the life of a fraud.

So what do I do with James Boswell? Don't he and his life of Samuel Johnson make nonsense of my plea for the invisible biographer? No. I'm not demanding an absolute ban. I'm arguing that we should stay out of the way unless our presence serves some purpose. Boswell had a purpose when he wrote one of the great double acts of literature. But Boswell earned the right to be Boswell.

I read his life of Johnson when I was twenty-four years old and working in the bar of a ski hotel in Austria. I'd brought it as my winter book. There was a lot going on around me. Over Christmas this rather spartan hotel was an outpost of the Austrian aristocracy. The place belonged to Ribbentrop's former private secretary, who had returned with his family from the Argentine only a few years earlier. This did not deter his clientele. One family was so grand that the governess looking after their children was a Habsburg. There was a lot going on around me that winter, and what did I do? I read Boswell's *Life of Johnson*. And the other day I picked it up again and was reminded how compelling it is. I took it to bed, chortling.

Boswell tells us he's writing for the curious. It's a key word. In the late eighteenth century it had a scientific flavour. Boswell sits among the great writers of his time but he was also one of the greats of the Scottish Enlightenment, those pragmatic philosophers and economists and scientists who were bringing fresh eyes and sharp intelligence to the task of finding how the world really worked.

Boswell's world was Samuel Johnson. He gathered the evidence and threw it all in, unconcerned that it might show himself as much as his subject in a bad light. Boswell was immune to embarrassment. His account of his first meeting with the great writer is a scene all the more wonderful for him allowing himself to cut such an abject figure.

Boswell had been trying for ages to engineer a meeting with the writer. A list of people – and he lists them – had failed to deliver on promises to introduce him. Then one day Boswell bumps into Johnson in a bookshop and accosts him with a light sally about Scotland. Johnson slashes him down. He tries another sally and Johnson once again crushes him. All this Boswell recounts in embarrassing detail.

Despite losing these exchanges so comprehensively, he felt he might now call on Johnson. How can you not trust a man who humiliates himself in his own text and then turns his eye on the subject of his devotion and writes this?

> He received me very courteously; but, it must be confessed, that his apartment, and furniture, and morning dress, were sufficiently uncouth. His brown suit of cloths looked very rusty; he had on a little old, shrivelled unpowdered wig, which was too small for his head; his shirt-neck and knees of his breeches were loose; his black worsted stockings ill drawn up; and he had a pair of unbuckled shoes by way of slippers. But all these slovenly particularities were forgotten the moment that he began to talk.

And for the next twenty years Boswell wrote down all their talk. That's what I mean when I say Boswell earned the right to be Boswell. He built a biography on scientific lines, gathering every document he could and recording a couple of decades of conversation. They quarrel, they quip, they test one another, they fall out, they make up. He was an indispensable part of that to-and-fro. And from these exchanges emerge an often-comic picture of Boswell and a portrait of Johnson that remains after 225 years an unequalled masterpiece.

So my advice to biographers determined to clamber onto the stage and play with their subjects in the limelight is do the work, put in the years, entangle your lives with your subjects', and then you have earned the right to walk the stage together. But even so, you will be marked down as a show-off unless you deal with yourself as ruthlessly as Boswell did with himself.

I know there are no fixed rules. I know I'm arguing questions of taste. I'm a grumpy old guy who hasn't found in twenty years another big life worth writing. I write little lives these days, of priests and politicians. Sometimes I have to be there in the text, for the power of the Quarterly Essay so often lies in face-to-face encounters. But I read big biographies with an impatient eye for biographers who demand we pay attention to them. Frankly, we are rather tedious people. Where should we stand? In the shadows – in the shadows manipulating everything, leaving readers with the illusion that they are alone in the company of Wittgenstein or Lyndon Johnson or Randolph Stow. The potency of biography is its compelling intimacy. That is why we read biography with such passion – compelling intimacy with people far more interesting than us.

The Seymour Biography Lecture,
National Library of Australia, 15 September 2016;
revised for *The Monthly*, December 2016

The wisdom of Malouf

FOR THE PAST YEAR KNOPF has been publishing elegant collections of David Malouf's essays, reviews, speeches, prefaces and, now, libretti. You strain to tell one volume from another. The covers are absurdly sober and nothing is made of that famous face. Malouf's fine schnoz is tucked out of sight. The message of these handsome books is plain: what matters are the words.

Malouf has been quietly insisting for forty years that we pay attention, reconsider, discriminate and learn. He was once a teacher and he has the voice of a teacher still: purposeful, a little lofty, unafraid to be abstruse when the subject demands, a master of the art of winning our attention.

His manners are perfect. He never raises his voice. Though he argues hard for lightness and play in art ("Comedy seems to me to be the greatest of all forms of drama"), Malouf is the most serious writer at work in this country. He can grow a little testy when he sees us indulging the national tendency to laugh things off. He is never facetious.

Serious attention is given in these thousand pages to antibiotics, the invention of landscape, fairy tales, birds, public buildings, Hollywood discovered in childhood ("Half of my life is spent in an American dream made up of Judy Garland and Mickey Rooney musicals"), space in the Australian imagination, the Ringstrasse, carnival and its prerogatives, Glenn Murcutt's houses, duets, Christina Stead in great age, and the brand of English imported by the First Fleet.

That's a short, short list. The treasures are endless. Every few pages there are lines that call for a standing ovation. ("It is one of the conditions of genius that the world he is born into has already prepared a place for him; the time and the place are always right.") Some of these pieces are more lucid than others, more persuasive. None is less than wise.

The first of the Knopf volumes, *A First Place*, appeared in March last year, just before Malouf's eightieth birthday. It is a sublime meditation on this country in all of its illuminating contradictions. Several months later came *The Writing Life*, critical essays from Ovid to Patrick White. *Being There* appeared this year with libretti for *Voss* and *Mer de Glace*, a "free version" of Euripides' *Hippolytus*, and essays on theatre, opera, film, painting and architecture.

All three read as memoir. Again and again Malouf returns to his childhood on the south side of the Brisbane River and the ambition that made his name at the age of forty-one with his first novel, *Johnno*: to give "fictional life, against all expectation, including that of my narrator, to what had always seemed to me, in my literary way, to be the most unliterary place in the universe, the Brisbane I had grown up in".

Is there an educated Australian who doesn't have some grasp of David Malouf's childhood? His father's people were Lebanese. His grandfather spoke only Arabic. A bank crash brought his mother's English Jewish folk down in the world and out to Australia. Boxing was the connection between the families. Young David grew up in a house on stilts, and the first world he explored was the hot, dark place under its floor. "It's a sinister place and dangerous but you are also liberated down there from the conventions. It's where children go to sulk ..."

Malouf has a lot to say about the dark. It is where we test our fears and find ourselves. As a little boy at the pictures every Saturday afternoon he learnt to look more closely at himself and the world: "There in the dark ... we were off the hook; no one was watching. *We* were watching." And all our lives, when music and theatre work as they should, we can shake off our civilised selves and "go back to some darker and more primitive condition of human existence".

One of Malouf's great subjects is the hold the past always has on us. His curiously bracing message is that there's little new that matters under the sun. We are what we have always been; what moves us has always moved us; we're writing now what we have always written. The first essay in the first of these volumes begins: "One of the oldest stories we tell is the story about leaving home ..."

Malouf casts a sceptical eye over proud claims to be unique. Australia's identity as a settler society? No. Aren't all societies at some point settler societies? Britain, he notes, is particularly keen to keep alive in its national narrative invasion by Anglos, Saxons and Jutes. "It is worth noting that the Romans too presented themselves in this way, not as natives of Latium but as invaders and settlers, immigrants from Troy."

Greece and Rome are the natural benchmarks of the man. Ovid is as alive to him as Patrick White. Homer is a contemporary source. The gods are still around, perhaps even in the hills of Brisbane and certainly everywhere in great art. Christianity seems hardly to engage his imagination. Ditto Judaism. This absence, in someone so steeped in the culture of the West, is extraordinary – and once again bracing. On the evidence presented, Malouf is pagan.

The gaps in the pattern leave this man, who has written so much about his life, rather a mystery. Politics is also absent from these essays. Power seems hardly to interest him. And he has little to say about sex. It is entirely his choice to make, but Malouf is the least confessional of gay men. He doesn't apologise and doesn't explain. He leaves sex to fiction.

Malouf poses a big question in *Being There*: why does art delight us? What do we find in paintings, plays, poems, novels, dance and music that brings us such pleasure? "What is the nature of our satisfaction? What is the ground of that capacity for simple delight in us on which so much complexity can be built?"

He finds the answer in the body, in its heartbeat and breath. "All music," he writes, "takes us back to the body." So does all performance, from opera to acrobatics. So do writing and painting. All have the same knack of stripping away our preoccupations and leaving us more aware than ever of what Malouf calls "the presentness of things – that enlivening sense of our own being, in space, in time, in the world, that is the real pleasure of art".

We break free. "Our spirit soars." At times we glimpse other worlds more "real" than our own and we are taken again into those "dark places in ourselves" where we may find "something energising, uplifting, healing". Great art, it would seem, lands us back where he began on sweltering mornings under the floorboards at 12 Edmondstone Street.

Malouf's passion for opera is almost as old as his love of the movies. He has seen all of both. He was briefly, and with great distinction, an opera critic for *The National Times* in what was not quite the heyday of the since-deceased Fairfax weekly. He served for years on the board of Opera Australia. And in the late 1970s he was commissioned to write the libretto and Richard Meale the music for one of the two or three finest operas yet to come out of this country, *Voss*.

Patrick White's novel is an epic exploration of Australia. Malouf had been tracking across the same territory most of his life. White sent a visionary manic into the desert. Malouf brought to bear a unique, cosmopolitan intelligence on the puzzles of this country. His setpiece 1998 Boyer Lectures and mighty 2003 Quarterly Essay, *Made in England*, are both republished in *A First Place*.

The spirit of that inquiry, if not the gorgeous detail, was already there in the spare poetry of the *Voss* libretto. Those of us who were there will never forget the opening night at the Adelaide Festival in 1986. So many voices were contending on the stage, White's and Meale's and Malouf's. But in the last moments it seemed Malouf was speaking directly to his country. When will Australia realise its future, a man asks at the foot of the memorial to the dead explorer. "Now. Now," comes the reply. "Every moment that we live, and breathe, and love and suffer. Now. Now ... And what we do not know the air will tell us, the air will tell us."

The great ovation that night seemed to mix wonder with relief. Malouf was delivering a welcome message: that this country does not have to be invented. The great enterprise is already underway and has been, perhaps, forever. We must pay it serious attention – and three volumes of occasional writing is serious attention – but it is already happening. And what we don't yet know about ourselves and this place, we will learn in time. The air will tell us.

The Monthly, May 2015

Patrick White:
the final chapter

WE GATHERED EARLY IN THE MORNING. Barbara Mobbs had the ashes in a smart paper shopping bag. Manoly Lascaris hadn't wanted his scattered with Patrick White's in the park in front of the house but in "the sea around Sydney". There was talk of a yacht to take them out past the Heads but in the end Mobbs, the shrewd guardian of White's career and estate, decided we would do the deed from some "very Greek rocks" at Clovelly. At about 7 am, eight of us struck off across the park. All those Manoly had charmed and intrigued in his long life had come down to these few: the loyal literary executor, three nurses, the biographer and a handful of Manoly's "young friends". Kerry Walker, wearing a heavy coat and dark glasses, carried a bowl of white daisies. We came out on the lip of a cliff to find bare rocks below us. Mobbs said, "The tide is out."

We climbed down and after some hesitation found a spot where waves were washing through a rock pool. A couple of fishermen had lines in the surf not far off. One of the young friends wanted to read a love poem by Cavafy and said a few words about Manoly meeting the poet in Cairo, an old man in a yellow suit with teeth stained from cigarettes. I said, "He told me it was Alexandria." One of the nurses added, "They met in the bank." As it happens, both Lascaris and White were rather sniffy about Cavafy, preferring the verse of his fellow Greek George Seferis. We stood stiffly at the edge of the rock pool as the lines were read about two men fucking in a café through "half-opened clothes". It was terrible but no one flinched.

I held the plastic box while the poetry reader worked away at the lid with a knife. It popped open. We all looked in, as if we'd see something telling or unexpected there. I handed the box to Mobbs. She demurred briefly, then went to the edge and scattered a handful of ashes that fell straight to the bottom. The water was only a foot or so deep. We all took a turn and there was soon a carpet of white on the floor of the pool. The flowers – hibiscus as well as daisies – did what the ash was supposed to do and drifted away very beautifully. We stood about in the sun for a bit and then drove to a café in Bronte for breakfast. Grizzled men were coming up from the beach and beautiful Cavafy boys climbed out of delivery vans. We swapped Manoly stories. He was a great storyteller and a great source of stories. Over coffee Mobbs recalled remarking to him at some point in his long widowhood in Centennial Park: "You have had a big life and now you have a small life." And he replied, "Both are equally satisfactory."

Lascaris's death freed her to pull off perhaps the greatest surprise in this country's literary history. In mid-2006 she offered the National Library of Australia a stockpile of White's letters, notebooks and manuscripts. Outside a very small circle, their existence was entirely unknown. The library was both amazed and abashed. On display at that moment in a travelling exhibition of its treasures was a gruff 1977 letter from White to the library's director: "I can't let you have my papers because I don't keep any. My manuscripts are destroyed as soon as the book is published and I put very little into notebooks, don't keep my friends' letters as I urge them not to keep mine, and anything unfinished when I die is to be burnt."

Mobbs was directed to do just that in White's will but found she "couldn't burn them in a blue fit". By the time of his death, she had been working for him in one capacity or another for seventeen years. He dedicated his last novel, *The Memoirs of Many in One* in 1986, to the woman he called 'The Flying Nun'. Though the will was emphatic, she believed that had he really wanted this evidence of his long literary life to disappear, he would have burnt the papers himself. White and Lascaris spent days destroying letters and manuscripts before moving from the outskirts of Sydney to Centennial Park in the 1960s. Had White wanted to stage another conflagration before his death he only had to ask Mobbs for a hand. Many times he showed her the notebooks, letters and manuscripts crammed into his desk but, she said, "He never told me to get the matches."

The survival of thirty-two boxes of White's papers was revealed with immense hoopla. 'Patrick White's return from the pit,' read the banner head-line in *The Sydney Morning Herald*. For the first time in many years, White was back on the front pages of the papers. But here was something curious: while the press, fans and scholars dived on the biographical material – the notebooks and letters – we shied away from the manuscripts. It says a great deal about the sinking reputation of the most prodigious literary imagina-tion in the history of this nation that we were all more curious about the life than the writing. After being displayed for a few triumphal weeks, the three manuscripts were returned to the library's strongroom all but unexamined.

I've now read them from beginning to end, the first person to do so, it seems, since White put them away in his desk. I already knew a good deal about two of them. "Dolly Formosa and the Happy Few" is a fragment of a novella about an ageing actress. "The Binoculars and Helen Nell" is a great fat novel of about 160,000 words about the many remarkable lives of a cocky farmer's daughter. Both projects were begun and abandoned in the late '60s. Letters White wrote at the time discuss their plots, their progress and his reasons for putting them aside. Having them to read is a wonderful experience, but they don't give any radical, fresh insight into White and his work.

The third is a different kettle of fish. When I was writing White's biog-raphy, I came across brief references to a novel begun and put aside in 1981. I gave the project the code name "Novel Y" in my research notes and its fate rates a bare mention in my book. But here is the manuscript, and hav-ing read it I realise "The Hanging Garden" was a masterpiece in the making and its abandonment after 50,000 words was a watershed in White's life and a loss, a damn shame, for Australian writing.

*

Mobbs works in a glass eyrie over Double Bay. Beneath her lies White ter-ritory: the big houses of the Sydney rich he knew all his life. It's not her world but she keeps a sharp lookout. She's abrupt and funny. Her clients are a shortlist of the best: David Malouf, Helen Garner and Kate Grenville. No one who has dealt with her is fooled by her pose as a plain country girl who somehow strayed into the business of books. Mobbs hoarded White's papers all those years, then released them knowing exactly what she was doing: keeping her client alive in the country's imagination.

How much further she can now go with the papers is a matter for careful consideration. Many collections reach the National Library under embargoes that shield them from the public for years, often decades. That's not the case with White's papers. Anyone can read them now. Mobbs has allowed the precious notebooks in which he jotted ideas for over forty years to be digitised and uploaded, any day now, to the internet. But I'd come to see her to plant a seed: the possible publication of "The Hanging Garden". She quizzes me. She will have to go back to the manuscript. One thing we share: we can both read White's handwriting. But the logistics are difficult. The abandoned writings are considered too fragile to photocopy and too precious to post on the net. Mobbs is sceptical but does not stop the idea in its tracks. She says: "Fifty thousand words is a good length."

White's last bestseller appeared twenty-five years ago at the end of an amazing final run that began with the Nobel Prize in 1973, included the mighty *Twyborn Affair* and climaxed in 1981 with the book that sold more than any other in his career, *Flaws in the Glass*. Even before his death a decade later, his reputation had begun its long, slow – but not uninterrupted – slide. These days, students and customers shy away from his novels. Alphabetical order doesn't help. He's found in bookshops on the bottom shelves. We buy him on our hands and knees.

Backlists were once the great asset of established publishing houses. No longer, says Mobbs. "Too much frontlist." Promotion goes to the new, the latest, the candidates for this year's prizes. That's business. But somewhere along the track, for reasons that go deeper than publishers' neglect, we stopped buying the distinguished writers of our own recent past. White was one of three Australians of his generation with big literary reputations at home and abroad. None sells strongly now. Nielsen BookScan, that pitiless surveyor of the trade, tells me that last year White's thirteen titles in print sold only 2728 copies. Shirley Hazzard did better: her eight sold 4270 copies. Christina Stead's seven sold 199. That's not a misprint.

Publishers are fighting back by culling their backlists and repackaging the best titles as 'classics'. *Riders in the Chariot* and *The Twyborn Affair* are already Vintage Classics. *The Aunt's Story*, *The Tree of Man*, *The Solid Mandala* and *A Fringe of Leaves* are all about to join the Vintage Classics list either here or in London. Yet for a few dollars at a second-hand bookshop or online, all but the rarest editions of White's books can be bought in sturdy and elegant hardback. That's how those who love his writing tend to own his work, so we can return whenever we like to his strangely familiar universe without bindings breaking and pages falling like leaves.

Mobbs is a realist. She acknowledges the slump in White's reputation. She argues it happens to all great writers when they die. At least for a time. She blames today's waning enthusiasm on shifting taste in language. "Read," she says, opening a new American novel and one of White's books at random. It's true no one writes quite like White anymore. But fans of Cormac McCarthy and Annie Proulx know there's an enduring taste for contemporary baroque. Indeed, Proulx is a big White fan and says his novels are among the few she keeps on her shelves. For the 1994 American edition of White's letters, Proulx volunteered the judgement that White was "indisputably one of this century's greatest writers".

I suspect the problem runs deeper than the difficulties of his prose. More than we care to admit, we want novels to offer at least the hope of happiness. White's fiction campaigns against false hopes of happiness and the perils of seeking it in sex, power and possessions. Such ascetic restraint is truly out of fashion these days, for the "march of material ugliness" he denounced almost from the moment he returned to Australia after World War II has all but overwhelmed us. We're calling for a truce in the pleasure wars, but White is still fighting, still absolute. For him, intense happiness is to be found in marriage, work, integrity, even purity. For those who feel no connection with this, Patrick White seems a grumpy dinosaur, a monster of reproach.

Though book sales are slack, the enthusiasm for mining White's work remains undiminished. Translations and film rights are always in negotiation. Mobbs has on her desk the latest draft of a screenplay for *The Eye of the Storm* – it's thrilling – plus options for *The Aunt's Story* and *A Fringe of Leaves*. Opera Victoria is looking at doing something with *The Cockatoos*. The Italians are translating *A Woman's Hand*. Random House is preparing fresh jackets for the reprints. The plays are firmly in the national repertoire. One of the ironies of the afterlife of Patrick White is that he earns as much or more these days in the theatre – which so many saw as his downfall – as he does from his novels.

The plays are fixed in the terrain of Australian theatre. They are career markers for actors and directors who continue to bring these extraordinary, often wayward creations to life. The director Jim Sharman remade his reputation with White's work, and Robyn Nevin's fearsome Miss Docker in his production of *The Cheery Soul* has been praised for thirty years. Neil Armfield cut his teeth on White. Lately Benedict Andrews has confirmed his ranking as the best of a new generation of directors with his *Season at Sarsaparilla*, seen in Sydney and Melbourne. Pamela Rabe has done nothing finer in her career than her Nola Boyle in that production, and Peter Carroll so perfectly inhabited Girlie Pogson it seemed as if White had written every line just for him.

GIRLIE: It's peaceful enough in Mildred Street. Nowadays, at least. Remember all those dogs? How disgraceful! I'll never forget. Anyway, it's finished.

PIPPY: But it's gunna begin again.

CLIVE AND GIRLIE *(together)*: When?

PIPPY: In six months time.

GIRLIE *(almost crying)*: But it shouldn't be allowed!

Sitting in the dark at the final night of the *Season* in Melbourne, in February, it struck me how much we missed White in the Howard years. Not for the fireworks, even apoplexy, they would have provoked in the old Cassandra, but for his understanding of the man. John Howard and Girlie Pogson might be from the same family. White knew people like him in his bones. Everywhere in his work are small-town figures who talk about duty to hide their narrowness. Howard appealed to something in Australians that White knew, feared and fought all his life: our yearning for small comfort and respectability.

As it happens, Howard was intrigued by White. Now that it's no longer a name to drop, I can report that in his early days in office, Howard praised my biography once or twice. I took advantage of this to win one interview – subject: the influence of Howard's old-fashioned Methodist upbringing on his attitude to Aborigines – after which he never spoke to me again. But he stuck rather generously to his guns and put the biography on a 2002 shortlist of books which had "made an impact" on him over the years. Whether he ever read any of White's novels is unknown. If not, he has the time now.

*

White wrote his first drafts in unbound bundles of foolscap: twelve sheets folded in two, with the outer sheet used as a cover. Each bundle holds about 11,000 words. They tell us not much about his creative chemistry. All the hard work was done in his head, not on the page. He scratches out paragraphs here and there, but essentially the prose rolls out in a long, clean ribbon. Characters, scenes and dialogue emerge fully formed. Question marks appear occasionally in the hand-ruled margins to indicate facts that needed checking. White had a horror of anachronism. Preparing to write the first of the abandoned works in October 1965, he sought out a psychiatrist at Sydney's Callan Park to advise him on cocaine addiction. The ageing actress Miss Dolores (Dolly) Formoza was to sustain herself on a gruelling Arts Council tour in the bush by snorting cocaine. White was not confident he had what he wanted. "I expect in the end," he wrote to the critic and poet Geoffrey Dutton, "I shall have to go gingerly hand in hand with my intuition and my own schizoid nature."

Dolly's one-woman show is only a moderate success. At every town, it seems, amateur playwrights thrust scripts into her hands: "Miss Formosa, I have written a play." Though able to draw on her own resources on stage, she tucks into her "powder boxes" to endure the civic receptions. "She was riddled by now with destruction. Her nostrils eaten by it." After a terrible scene at the Bullivants', in Snape – he a dentist, she a star of the Brolga Players in her youth – all the best homes along the tour are closed to her. She couldn't be happier, hunkered down each night in rough country pubs. By Mungindribble the old girl is clearly losing it, wandering about the bush collecting silver bark, sticks and stones.

There the novella stops mid-page. "The whole thing smells a bit of carpentry and bookmaking," White told Dutton, and confessed he found it difficult to write about theatre and theatricals in ways that didn't "lose touch with the ground in developing their abnormalities". After only a couple of months' work, White put the one and a half bundles of about 16,000 words away in his desk, where they lay for nearly twenty years until becoming the basis for *The Memoirs of Many in One*. Cocaine was no longer the issue. "It's about premature senility," White wrote. "No. No. It is a *very* funny subject." Now it is Alex Xenophon Demirjian Gray of Alexandria and Sydney who is – at least in her mind – on an Arts Council mission in the outback performing her Dolly Formosa monologues, and wreaking revenge on thick actors, pretentious directors, small-town worthies and hostile critics until the crew dumps her in the streets of Ochtermochty and she retreats to Sydney. The writing is exactly where White, by then, wanted it to be: out of touch with the ground.

Only weeks after stashing "Dolly Formosa" in his desk, White settled down at the start of 1966 to write a novel he'd had in his mind for some time. Later, as he was struggling to keep "The Binoculars and Helen Nell" alive, he would wonder if it had simply been too long in his imagination. After fourteen hard months and 160,000 words, he gave up. "I think I have been indulging in too many fantasies," he told Dutton. "It is an overblown mass, of too much flesh, and not enough bone."

That the first half of this manuscript has never until now seen the light of day is hard to mourn. Helen Nell lies comatose in the Blair Athol Rest and Convalescent Home waiting to have her "gross watermelon of a figure" pumped out. The patients are delusional and the staff are feuding. It's a difficult start but the novel is soon out in the fresh air of her childhood on the western plains of New South Wales, from where she – and the writing – drift to Sydney, onto the musical stage and then into marriage with a bloke who comes back from World War I a broken man. Though Helen Nell is entirely passive as she drifts into these unchosen lives, she shows surprising enterprise in fleeing them once their possibilities are exhausted.

Things look up for Nell and the novel at the 80,000-word mark, when she lands a job in the Taylours' opulent Villa Borghese on Sydney Harbour some time in the 1920s. "I have cooked for a Spanish ambassador," she explains. "He didn't complain." At last she is in command: of the fractious servants fighting a religious war backstairs; the teenage children whom she beds; and brittle Mrs Taylour, whose social ambitions are imperilled by her husband's hobby of robbing their friends' houses after dark. Once, before disaster strikes, Nell goes along for the ride. The Villa Borghese sequence is in fact a novella of nearly 40,000 words written at full throttle. It's good. Very good. The climax is one of those comic extravaganzas into which White poured all his pent-up love and fury for the glamour of the Sydney rich. A stiff dinner party on a thundery night ends in a triumph for the cook and ruin for the Taylours as the host is led away in handcuffs at dawn.

White was battling domestic difficulties as he wrote, for he had invited his niece to live with them at the house on Centennial Park and it was not going well. He began to complain that she did not show initiative, spent too long washing her hair, would not pursue the openings he found for her, was making too many calls to London to a man who was, to White's dismay, divorced. He was writing, much of the time, in a rage of disappointment. The troubles of the niece and the novel fed one another. But once Helen Nell left the Taylours, things went more smoothly. "The flow has set in, perhaps because I have got amongst the whores," he told Dutton. "It is always easy to write about prostitutes."

Though cooks of genius were, surely, still in demand in the Depression, Helen Nell is working the streets of Darlinghurst. Why? "I'm hard up, and I like men." Nell abandons booze and makeup. She wears only black. "They were afraid of the black whore. They heard her shoes arriving on the beat. They loved her too." She offers her clients succour, not lust. Luckily for White, they tend to be born storytellers. This life also ends in a rout – a wild party of grog and flagellation thrown for corrupt local coppers – into which walks a mysterious stranger who turns Nell the black whore into Hélèn, his distinguished mistress. "It has always been my ambition to do a good job," she says. "In whatever profession I've found myself stuck in."

White was halfway through the fifteenth folder of foolscap when he put the manuscript away. But not for ever. Helen Nell trailing round Vaucluse with a society burglar would emerge a year later in the story and then the film *The Night the Prowler*. But the spirit of the book – its tone, its setting and the shifting identities of its hero on a long journey towards bedrock integrity – prefigures *The Twyborn Affair* a decade later. There is even a first draft of Eddie Twyborn's iconic homecoming on a stinking day in Fremantle. Hélèn leaves the same ship and wanders into the same café, to find herself interrogated by its owner: "'Where you come from – eh?' he asked in his Greek Australian. 'From Europe – now,' she said, 'originally from here.'" In time, that answer would be pared down to Eddie Twyborn's two perfect words: "From here."

*

After nearly ten years working on White, I needed a complete break. I refused invitations. I left seminars to academics. The last stop of my White career was a book tour of New Zealand that ended in a Timaru bookshop in 1994. Around a trestle table of dips and glasses were a scant four or five customers. So we abandoned the shop and all went out to dinner. It was a wonderful night. White loved to read newspaper reports of murders and rated New Zealand's among the best. By the kind of chance he might have taken to be part of God's great design, I was eating with a bunch of criminal lawyers with tales of inept clients: "I mean, he'd worked on a farm all his life. He should have known he first had to slake the body with lime ..."

I didn't rush down to look when White's letters poured into the National Library over the next decade, with little tributaries feeding into Sydney's Mitchell and Melbourne's La Trobe. I'd seen most of the material and a 644-page biography didn't need any fresh detail. But the Mobbs consignment to Canberra in 2006 broke my resolve. I was down there in a flash, working quietly with the librarians before the big public announcement, laughing and gnashing my teeth that the old bastard had kept so much from me. Up to a point, I understood what he was about. Happy to let me dig around in the entrails of his life, he was determined to keep me from trawling through this intimate evidence of his *work*. Apart from anything, he knew I would get lost in there for years. He was impatient to see the biography before he died. Over the last six months, as I was labouring away, the phone would ring and it would be Patrick: "When are you going to finish that *fucking* book?"

The revelations in Mobbs' boxes were followed by a handful of collections I had never seen. Some were no more than a few scant letters. Then White's old friend the artist and set designer Desmond Digby sent the National Library his own stack of boxes. For years the two men had a "good old yell and shout" on the phone every day before breakfast. For a time in the late '70s and early '80s Digby made notes of these exchanges. Often the little index cards simply record where White was that morning on the Richter scale: "Furious!!" "Big Explosion."

Over time he pursued the failings of the critic Maria Prerauer – "Furious with silly bitch" – and the historian Manning Clark: "Fury at Manning going to Yarralumla. For days he was hysterical on phone." Odd snippets of information emerge: "Jimmy Sharman 'actually nearly' got Patrick White to Meatloaf!!" And there is this eye-opener from an early morning session after White had seen a production of Racine's *Britannicus* in Sydney in 1982: "Met David Marr whom has hated since when he was editor of *The National Times* during *Big Toys* – praised Kate Fitzpatrick and not him!! Quite liked him though because of his Barwick book – though obviously lots of mistakes in it. *Britannicus* not very good ..."

Though nothing in the new troves of White papers make me want to rip the biography apart, there are things I deeply regret not having seen when I was working on the *Life*. I wish the critic Jim Waites had dug out for me in time a postcard of that immense relic of the 1890s hanging in the Art Gallery of New South Wales: Edward Poynter's *The Visit of the Queen of Sheba to King Solomon*. White wrote to Waites, "One of the big springboards of my fantasy life as a child." I would have opened a chapter with little Paddy standing in front of that vast romantic canvas – perhaps clutching the hand of his nurse, Lizzie – and dreaming the first of the stories that paintings would inspire in him all his life.

And, yes, I regret not having the seven notebooks that begin when, just down from Cambridge in the mid-'30s, White sketches his first literary ideas: a handful of plays and then the unmistakable bare bones of *The Aunt's Story*. The notebooks establish that the third of White's novels to be published was, in fact, the first conceived – the fundamental novel, the true starting point of his career. His mentor and lover Roy de Maistre was its first inspiration but its hero morphs – in White's second, wartime notebook – into one of his great creations, Theodora Goodman, the aunt of the novel: "this difficult stranger in shapeless clothes".

Jumbled and haphazard though they are, the notebooks are filled with biographical gold: scraps of diary, poems, reflections, lists of characters (121 for *The Vivisector*), the first pages of at least six novels in early draft, reams of detailed research for *Voss* ("Sydney hospital was known as Sydney Infirmary till 1881"), timelines, fashion notes and fragments of conversations overheard in the street. White did let me have a typescript of one gorgeous chunk of the notebooks: a diary he kept during his time with the RAF in the Sudan. Now I've found bits and pieces of diary from his later posting in Alexandria during which, at afternoon tea in the Quartier Grec in July 1941, he met Manoly Lascaris. Of the meeting and the man there is no mention but afterwards – or so it seems – he wrote a couple of lines I might have used as an epigraph for the *Life*, a claim that love can teach a writer everything: "In a deeply felt personal relationship, it is possible to experience emotionally all that one never has, and perhaps never will experience in life. This is the answer to people who say to the novelist: how did you know about something you haven't experienced yourself?"

That White had lived on dividends not royalties was always known, but among his papers are the figures that prove the point: in the last six months of his life he earned $7000 from royalties, but his share portfolio at the time of his death was valued at $2 million. Again, corroboration of his lifelong passion for theatre was hardly needed, but the National Library now has piles of old programs he collected over many decades on several continents. His letters and Digby's index cards are a running commentary on theatre from Broadway to Belvoir, from before Laurence Olivier to past Jim Sharman. I confess I find nothing quite as dead and gone as the unseen shows of the past, but even here there is gold for historians.

White's business was fiction, but he was also a great reporter of life in this country. Whatever fate awaits his novels and plays, his thousands of letters are already a national resource for those writing about Australia in the second half of the twentieth century. Who can beat him for the just phrase, the great anecdote, the telling portrait? Just one – but my favourite – is his 1961 sketch of Stravinsky:

> He was quite different from what I expected – which was something tall, cold and cerebral. In reality he is a dear old thing, but very old, tiny and arthritic. His wife is a kind of St Bernard; one imagines her carrying him about the house in her teeth … Stravinsky and I sat together at dinner. He told me: "I am a professional drunkard. All the time I drink whisky, whisky, whisky!" I must say he held it very well. During dessert he passed me shelled walnuts on the palm of his very soft hand. Lots of rings.

The old cliché is only partly right: history is not only written by conquerors, but by spectators of genius.

*

1980 ended badly for White. Malcolm Fraser's third election victory left him depressed and raging. For a few weeks in December he feared he was dying of lung cancer. And presenting the finished typescript of *Flaws in the Glass* to Lascaris on New Year's Day provoked what I now suspect was one of their greatest brawls. Lascaris was shattered by White's portraits of his family and appalled by the prospect of strangers reading a frank – though chaste – account of their long marriage. The storm had been building for months. One of the Desmond Digby cards in September records: "M. obviously

wants it altered – could see it not being published. THINGS SO BAD –
BOTH of them Drink!! – and that only happens after disastrous ROWS."

A New Year obligation White took seriously was to catch up with his
correspondence. In a swag of letters written in early January, he spoke of
a new novel "churning" in his head. No more details were given: no plot,
no cast and no title. It remained both unseen and unidentified, but we now
know it was "The Hanging Garden". White was working on it in January but
within a couple of months his despair with politics tempted him to make
a rare appearance on television. He was inundated afterwards with letters
of support, all of which had to be answered. In early April he told his old
agent, Juliet O'Hea, "The novel I had started has suffered as a result of all
this and continued arguments over *Flaws in the Glass* and proof correcting,
if we get as far as that, will drive the novel further into the ground. I hope
to get back to it eventually."

The garden of the title is the private kingdom of two children brought
to a house on Neutral Bay to shelter from the war. In the branches of the
darkest fig, which "seems to be hanging above the water, floating without support from the precipice", they build a tree house where they form
an extraordinary, not quite sexual bond. Both are about thirteen. Gilbert's
mother has died in the Blitz. His father is in the army somewhere in India.
Eirene is the daughter of an Australian mother and a Greek communist
father who has died, presumed executed, in prison. The survival of both
children is at stake: not their physical existence, which is safe from the carnage on the far side of the world, but the survival of the fine possibilities of
each in the strange and demanding society of wartime Sydney.

The prose is assured, unhurried and absolutely disciplined. White is
everywhere and absent, as only the greatest novelists can be. Everything
is seen and felt through his characters. These children and their guardians,
their friends and tormentors, live in a precisely realised world. Old Mrs
Bulpit, who owns the rambling house above the harbour, is a familiar prim
figure in White's work but there are fresh characters everywhere in "The
Hanging Garden", and a tenderness and rigour that mark this as the work
of an old, wise novelist who still has large ambitions and knows exactly
what he's doing.

Mrs Bulpit dies and the children are separated. Gilbert is lost to a fresh
guardian on the far side of the bridge. Eirene, already orphaned after her
mother's death in Egypt, is thrown into the dangerous household of her

aunt Ally Lockhart, a sunburnt smoker with a cold blue stare who prowls the streets of Sydney in a dilapidated Chev. Her garden is of vegetables, bound by a paling fence. Her husband is a sexual predator: "One of these people who know what they want." When the war in Europe ends, Eirene waits nervously to be called home to Greece: "And Gil to London? To the bomb craters, and his mother's coffin, and his friend Nigel Brown's ghost. Gil himself a ghost haunting the garden on the precipice in Cameron Street, as you are haunting this mouldy backyard. Twin ghosts in the one haunting."

This first, self-contained third of a novel White imagined would run to 150,000 words ends in the Lockharts' kitchen on VE Day, with Eirene asking the question we can guess "The Hanging Garden" was going to answer: "Is this where we belong then?"

White showed no sign of being dissatisfied with what he had written in the winter of 1981, but by early summer the following year he was talking about the project in the past tense. He told his London publisher: "I doubt I shall ever get back to a normal writing life." He was coming to doubt he could say what he wanted to say in big novels. Indeed, he wondered if there were even readers for them. "Today people can hardly bring themselves to read a story let alone a novel," he told his translator Jean Lambert. "They have been rotted by television." White knew where he wanted to go with the new novel – "It is all in my head" – but his enthusiasm was fading. "I feel such things don't matter in the face of nuclear war, and that I can resist that more effectively through plays and public appearances."

In October he launched People for Nuclear Disarmament with a rousing speech in Melbourne which he counted a great success. His rhetoric caused exactly the kind of stir he wanted to provoke. Less welcome were the raging controversies that broke in England and Australia that month with the publication of *Flaws in the Glass*. It was front-page news. Out of the blue, Sidney Nolan discovered he had an implacable enemy and replied in kind. The various rows would go on for years. White might have returned to "The Hanging Garden" in early 1982, but by this time he had been lured away by the siren song of the theatre. For that year's Adelaide Festival, Jim Sharman had commissioned a new play, *Signal Driver,* which White dedicated to its young director, Neil Armfield. White wrote to an old friend in America: "I find this reviving to be with all these intelligent and enthusiastic young people but it also leads to a lot of cooking. I doubt I shall write another novel ..."

A few weeks ago, sitting with the papers all around me in the National Library, I sent a message to Armfield: "I have made a great PW discovery: 50,000 words of a fine novel set on the North Shore, abandoned to write *Signal Driver*. I blame you." He replied: "O fuck."

*

There were no more big novels, but speeches, plays and shorter prose works. He was a pro and kept writing almost to the end. Though he complained when I questioned him about his rich childhood, my curiosity seems to have provoked him to write *Three Uneasy Pieces*, published hurriedly in late 1987 before his self-imposed boycott of the bicentennial year. In one of those pieces, the story of schoolchildren playing on the northern shore of the harbour is a faint ghost of "The Hanging Garden". Very faint. White did write one piece for 1988: a private prayer the National Library's curators found tucked into the back of a pocket diary: "May I be guided in the coming year in my efforts to unite people, through the written and the spoken word, that we may abandon despair and apathy for a fresh belief in spiritual progress and universal peace."

White was failing. His asthma came with a number of nasty complications, and X-rays of his lungs were a familiar, though anonymous, sight to generations of Sydney medical students. Back in the '50s, White was one of the first Australians to be given lifesaving Prednisone and its "hangovers" afflicted him for over thirty years. In his 1990 pocket diary – his last – he recorded in shaky block letters the days he was taking the drug. The word tolls through his final weeks: PRED, PRED, PRED, PRED.

We had a deal that after his *Life* went to the publishers, he could see the text for the purpose of identifying errors. Nothing more. He didn't want and didn't have a veto. So in July of that year, he made me sit with him as he read the manuscript through again, slowly, page by page, complaining and laughing – always at his own jokes. He loved in particular reading what he'd written in the letters he'd begged everyone to destroy. On some of the sticky issues he finally acknowledged the truth, even admitting one morning that despite all the abuse he had heaped on his mother over the years, his life was the realisation of her ambition for him: to be a writer. I counted this a late victory in a long tussle. He identified a couple of dozen errors of fact and corrected spelling mistakes in several languages but did not ask me to cut or change a line.

But Lascaris was humiliated to find a stranger in the text. In the diary I was keeping at the time, I wrote:

August 3: A terrible storm this morning and when I arrived at Martin Road, signs of a bad storm inside. ... PW had read ahead a little last night. He said, "I keep crying as I read this." "This chapter?" "No all the time, and when my friend is over there reading I have to hold the book up so he can't see." M has nearly finished. Jill [Bailey, his nurse] later told me M is rather in the gun for taking so long about it ...

We stopped at the end of chapter 16. The storm had cleared and M walked down to the gate with me. "I am finding it very moving, sometimes painful – and surprising." I asked what had surprised him. "I did not know of the existence of Spud Johnson. And Patrick wrote to him for years after we met."

Johnson was a poet in Santa Fe. He and White were lovers briefly in the early '40s and corresponded only until 1945, when White wrote from Athens laying out his plans for settling down after the war with Lascaris. White had told me nothing about Spud. I found their letters after making just-in-case enquiries of that great literary goldmine, the Harry Ransom Center at the University of Texas. White was impressed. Lascaris was not. After reading the manuscript, he became convinced White's rages in the early years back in Australia were designed to drive him away and have Spud Johnson take his place. He could not be comforted about this.

"You know I don't care what people *think*," White had announced when I first handed him the book. Once we'd finished with the corrections he declared he was looking forward, more than anything, to the great gnashing of teeth he expected in a year's time, on its publication. But he didn't make it. A mild bout of pleurisy in August triggered yet another bronchial collapse. When I returned after a couple of weeks in Cape York, he was very frail.

September 10: I found Patrick sitting in his chair when I arrived at 11. He had had to come down for the X-ray and decided to stay down to see me. He was pleased with himself, bright, not really curious at all about the trip. My attempts to give an account of the time he interrupted with the ordinary bulletins of grim news: Gwen Moore had had a number of small strokes; Desmond Digby had been down to see him and was "enormous". He told me Josie the night nurse, whom he had approved at once, had nursed Gulbenkian for six years in Cannes.

We gossiped for about an hour. He refused the glass of orange juice Jill brought and asked for his usual stout. He only sipped this. M returned and more, much more forcibly than usual, took charge of the conversation. We talked about Arabs and the Middle East, some Jordanian neighbours etc. Then M said to PW are you tired? Do you want to go up? And I saw that he was in fact exhausted. He said he did, and that he had no appetite after the eggflip and the stout. Perhaps he would have some cauliflower later.

M on one side and Jill on the other helped him to his feet. "Get your balance," said Jill, "and then we'll take a run at it." He grunted. They walked him very slowly to the foot of the stairs. He took the handrail and Jill helped him climb. She said, "We'll take a few steps and rest." M came back into the sitting room, his hands up in a gesture of resignation. "I think he's had it."

PW is resisting the night nurse saying there isn't the money for her, that he doesn't want her. "He's got millions," I said. "You know he's always been rich and mean. He's that type. You know he lies about money."

"Patrick is not a liar – but he does lie about money. Though once I asked him and he said, 'There is money. There is money!' I must talk to one of the trustees I know, but I cannot ring him from here because Patrick picks up the phone and listens."

A few days later: PW was in the chair by his bed. I had a cup of tea with him. He was bright but not strong. We talked for about an hour. There was a Bible on the shelf behind the bed – I'm sure I'd seen it there before – and I asked if he ever read it. Sometimes, he said. Now it was mostly cookbooks, and there were several of these in the stack along with Shūsaku Endō's *Scandal* that Jim Sharman was introducing people to. He said he missed Zoe [Caldwell, the actress].

September 27: Patrick was lying under a sheet. His teeth were out. He smiled, drawing his mouth into an O. "How are you?" "Not my best." For weeks his lungs have sounded as if there's bitumen there, but now as if they're full of water. An awful bubbling. He was breathing hard through his mouth. To M he said something only roughly coherent about a sick woman. "I don't know any sick woman," M replied softly and precisely. Patrick has lost a lot of weight, and his skin is grey, but he doesn't seem angry and distressed as he has been. Just exhausted. His hands lay outside the sheet, palms down, still, almost formal …

I said I'd go and see him in a couple of days. "We have lots more work to do." He didn't move, looked calm, but his eyes were struggling and imploring. I waved from the door and he lifted his hand.

M and I had a beer on the terrace. Again, a beautiful spring day. Azaleas and wisteria out. The air smells wonderful. The dogs in the houses behind were baying. It sounded like a great pack of distressed animals, but died away. M had a basket with dog biscuits sorted neatly. Milly was on one side of his chair, Eureka on the other. He fed them a biscuit each, into their mouths, until they were finished. We drank warm beer. M only chills beer if there's a "scorcher".

He does not think Patrick will get his strength back. "He is just a skeleton with skin stretched over him." Last night he was alert, demanding and called for a coddled egg. Neither M nor Jill had ever coddled an egg, so there was confusion while they researched. All that was good. But this morning he only wanted a little ice cream and now for lunch some apple. He is exhausted and in great discomfort … I said he had always held onto life stubbornly. "Yes, and one wants him to continue while he still welcomes life." Patrick refuses to go to hospital. "He is adamant." The doctor wants to be able to put a drip into his arm. I asked how M felt about hospital. "I won't countermand Patrick. If he doesn't want to go back there, then he must stay here." He said, "I have reached the point where one way or another I want him to rest."

There have been night nurses for a week now. Tonight it's a man, their first man. His name is David. M worries about cooking for the nurses. Jill says this is the first house where she's been properly fed – usually they leave out a white loaf and some sliced Devon. "You must feed the nurses. You must feed servants properly. If they have good food and good clothes then they will not leave you. It is a principle." M says this half-joking, but with absolute conviction …

"We have been together for fifty years." He laughed. "I would not wish that on anyone. What causes him pain hurts me, we are so ..." He knotted his fingers together and said nothing. I said he was the stronger of the two. "I know I am the strong one, and knew that he was weak who thought himself strong. He used to tell me I was weak – weak for not shouting at people and calling them bastards. That shouting was not strength but temper. I was not weak, but strong." He says this feebly and softly. Part of him, it seems, is wondering what will be left of him when Patrick dies.

September 28: He was supported by about six pillows and was eating what looked like mashed banana. A very clean, ragged tea towel was folded on his chest like a bib ... He asked about the book and I said the next step was fixing American page numbers for the endnotes and I would need those books he'd said he would lend me. "Not now, this place is in chaos." "No, not now." "But it will delay the book?" "No, there's tonnes of time."

September 30: The phone woke me at 5.45. It was the nurse to say Patrick had died at 5.20. I spoke to M for a few minutes. He asked me to ring some people ... I asked if Patrick had been comfortable at the end. M paused: "We will talk about that later." ...

The immediate crisis was that M didn't have the will, and didn't know what Patrick's instructions were about his body, the press etc. Dying in the middle of the long weekend meant two days before they could find out. A call had gone through to one of the managers of the Perpetual Trustee and the crowd in the kitchen – Jill, Elizabeth Riddell and Barbara Mobbs – were waiting for the call back. M took the call and I could hear him agreeing he would wait until Tuesday. I asked M for the phone. The trustees have a system of putting the special requests of their "will clients" on microfiche. This has now been checked. It indicated there were special requests, but there were too many of them to fit on the fiche. We would have to wait until the vault could be opened on Tuesday because the men with the keys were out of town on holiday. I pointed out that M was distressed, that Patrick and his family had been with the trustees for generations and that an effort might be made, that if the keys could be located I would drive and pick them up wherever they were. Terry Struck said he would ring back … [He did.] Patrick's instructions were: no ceremony, no speeches, nothing to be said to the press for a week from the time of death, the body to be cremated by the undertaker and the ashes scattered on the lake by Barbara …

M and I took the dogs into the park … We walked through the scrubby country between the house and Anzac Parade. This is the lake where the ashes will be scattered. On the Martin Road shore is a clump of melaleuca. A garden seat is there, and while Patrick was still able to go walking in the park he would come down to this seat and rest. One arm of the lake is full of lilies. Along the shore is a scurf of plastic cups, plastic bags. "We will have to do it very early in the morning," said M, "because there are rules against pollution."

October 4: Barbara rang that night. She'd gone to Martin Road at 5, and they drove down to the gap in the railings. The party was M, Milly and Barbara. She asked M to do the scattering.

"But the will said you must do it."

"That was just Patrick wanting to save you from it. I'll say the prayers and you do it."

She led them to a spot in front of the seat that seemed the cleanest, and she kicked aside some beer cans. There was a mist rising on the water. "It looked like Ireland." As M began to pour the ashes into the lake a couple of ducks swam over to investigate. Barbara prayed: "Eternal rest grant to Patrick … O Lord … and may he rest … Amen."

M said: "I think that's it." He crossed himself three times. "Barbara, I think we've done the heroic deed."

*

I was aware by this time that Manoly was rewriting the death scene to his own specifications. His version was elaborate, touching and untrue. I faced a difficult problem as I drafted the dozen extra paragraphs that would now end the biography. If I wrote about White's death with White's absolute attention to the truth, I would expose Lascaris's innocent lies. I flinched. He would have enough to cope with when the book came out, so I decided to save him from this last embarrassment. I wrote: "At about 9 Lascaris went to sleep in his room across the landing. He was exhausted. At 5 the next morning he heard a disturbance and went in to help. White stopped breathing a few minutes later ..."

I came to regret the decision. In a rather unhappy review of the biography, a protégé of White's, the poet Robert Gray, accused me of stinting on White's death. He was right, but the version he gave in the *Times Literary Supplement* was wrong. It was pure Manoly:

> The nurse came and woke him towards morning: "You had better come now," he was told. White lay very still, sunken into his bed, but when Lascaris came near, opened his eyes and looked at him. He held out his hand, and the two men, who had been together for fifty years, shook hands. Then Patrick died, without speaking.

Not exactly. White was a great believer in coincidences: "They always revive my faith in divine order." He did not want his life to end in a last coincidence, dying as his mother had in her lavish London flat in 1963, sitting on her commode. White later dispatched the heroine of *The Eye of the Storm* in just the same way: "Mrs Hunter had slipped sideways on her throne while still hooked to the mahogany rails. One buttock, though withered, was made to shine like ivory where the rose brocade was rucked up. The eyes were mooning out through the mask ..."

With iron determination, White set the terms of his own death in his attic room. He would have no oxygen, no drips, no last trips to hospital and no commode by the bed. Early on the morning of 30 September, the nurse was helping him to the lavatory when he had either a stroke or a heart attack on the landing and died at once. Lascaris and the nurse carried White back to his bed. Lascaris told me: "The nurse was very strong and picked him up under the shoulders and I was to take his legs to carry him back to the bed, but because of my bad back I couldn't. But then I knelt down and slowly straightened up and we carried him back to the bed."

And that is what I should have written.

Athens now seemed Lascaris's natural destination, if only for a few months to shake off the misery of life and death in Martin Road. We were entirely wrong. Though he lived a great deal in the past and carried with him the exotic baggage of a family claiming descent from Byzantine emperors, Lascaris had come to see himself as Australian, and to see it as his duty to live for as long as he possibly could by the old, inflexible timetable he and White had established. These were the routines that made the work – their work – possible and he was their keeper. Lascaris did accept a few immediate changes: a housekeeper was engaged and a dozen of us chipped in to buy a television set. He was delighted. The ABC news was immediately embedded in the schedule.

Late on the morning White's ashes were scattered, the trustees came to read the will, a document that was to become a source of bitter complaint. Lascaris would tell old friends and strangers alike: "Patrick left me nothing." Over time, this story found its way into books, the press and documentaries: the final martyrdom of Manoly Lascaris at the hands of Patrick White. No amount of trying could convince Lascaris he was being unfair. The will was an old-fashioned grazier's will: everything to the widow for life and then on to the heirs. While he lived, Lascaris would have the house plus all White's royalties and all the income from his share portfolio. At his death, the capital would then be split between four of White's favourite causes: the Smith Family, the Art Gallery of New South Wales, the Aboriginal Education Council of New South Wales and NAISDA, the Aboriginal and Islander dance college. Lascaris didn't get the capital, but for the rest of his life he would live as he deserved: on some scale. As his health deteriorated, the housekeeper was joined by a band of nurses and carers. No expense was spared, but he continued to complain that White had left him penniless.

When the biography appeared, a year after White's death, Lascaris once again found his sex life and the foibles of his family paraded before the world. That had to be borne because White had demanded it. Lascaris did not attend any of the celebrations surrounding the publication. Nor did he turn out for the first nights of White's plays in the years that followed. He said, "I will be gawped at as a curiosity." Yet he shyly enjoyed his celebrity. His portrait was painted in 1995 but did not win a place in the annual Sydney ritual of the Archibald Prize. The attention of White's fans sometimes alarmed him. A party of Koreans appeared on the lawn one morning after *The Tree of Man* was published in Seoul. "They are swarming up the path like possums," he told Mobbs on the telephone. "They are banging on the windows." Perhaps a little late in life, he gave one or two interviews to radio and television. He was still saying, "Patrick left me nothing." He refused to travel. In the thirteen years he lived after White's death, he rarely travelled further than Double Bay. What mattered to him now were the dogs, the garden, books, his Orthodox faith – he prayed every day while resisting the overtures of the local archbishop – and the company of the small band of friends who continued to call for afternoon tea. He remained a bewitching storyteller.

Parkinson's disease began to take its toll. He no longer walked the surviving Jack Russell. He shrank. Unable to manage the stairs, he slept in one of the dark little bedrooms near the kitchen. At night the nurses heard him calling for mercy in his sleep. He told many friends he wished to die. In September 2001 the trustees decided the house had to be painted inside and out. Lascaris was taken to a private hospital where he became bewildered, fell and was rushed back with a gash on his nose to a pristine house stripped of its pictures. The house was soon reassembled but Lascaris never really recovered.

Much of the time now, his mind was in Egypt. "My uncle Mario gave me this house," he said over tea one afternoon. We corrected him. "This is a Greco-Alexandrian house," he persisted. "There are many rooms." Later, as we made to leave, he said, "When I next have a holiday I will go to Egypt."

A last coincidence was waiting. When it was time for Lascaris to move to a nursing home, he was taken to Lulworth, the old mansion at the back of Kings Cross which was Patrick's childhood home before becoming a hospital after the war. The shades of so many of White's characters hung around the house. Aunt Theo gazed across the water to Darling Point. Laura Trevelyan waited here for the explorer Johann Ulrich Voss to call. Hurtle Duffield played under the bunya pine on the drive. Now the cast was joined by the original of all the dark, wise, muscular Greeks of the novels. Manoly died at Lulworth on 13 November 2003, at the age of ninety-one, oblivious to the closing of a great circle that had come to embrace Scone and Smyrna, Sydney and Alexandria, the Whites and the Lascaris.

The Monthly, April 2008

Table for Two

Table for Two

And Rudd came among us ...

HUNDREDS OF US WERE TRAPPED for two and a half hours without interval in a rowdy piece of community theatre called *Waiting for Kevin*. Everyone was shouting. No one could be heard. Beautiful young party workers – children the last time power changed hands in Canberra – posed in Kevin07 t-shirts. Cameras flashed like firecrackers. Up on the big screens Kerry O'Brien was tolling through the count like an old priest saying mass. No one was listening. A little after 7 pm Queensland time, the premier, Anna Bligh, appeared from the party's headquarters upstairs and walked through the melee confiding to those in her path: "Kevin Rudd is the prime minister of Australia."

But there was no sign of Kevin. As the scythe of democracy cut across Australia, the decibels kept rising in that long room under Brisbane's Suncorp Stadium. The rough dignity of John Howard's concession speech was met with catcalls and booing. Only the sight of Maxine McKew hushed the crowd for a few moments at a time. Her battle for the seat of Bennelong was the nearest the night had to a cliffhanger. She won, she lost and she seemed to be winning again. Over her left shoulder could be glimpsed the old party strategist Bob Hogg, struggling to hide his triumph as his partner trounced the man who had dominated Australian politics for a dozen years.

Men with wires in their ears appeared from nowhere, generic rock-and-roll pumped out of the speakers and Rudd was among us. The room responded with a mighty roar as he and his family climbed onto the platform: "Kevin. Kevin. Kevin." Thérèse Rein was ecstatic. The pride of the children in the face of this ovation was heart-stopping. Then Rudd killed the party.

"OK, guys," he said, holding up his hands like a slightly weary teacher to shush the rowdy enthusiasm. "A short time ago, Mr Howard called me to offer his congratulations …" Such courtesies are obligatory, of course, but Rudd went on and on about the virtues of his fallen opponent. The revellers waited him out: waited to burst back into life; waited for the moment when Rudd's face would break into a smile of triumph; waited for him to lead the celebrations. That never happened. The rhetoric was leaden:

> Today Australia has looked to the future. Today the Australian peo-
> ple have decided that we as a nation will move forward to plan for
> the future, to prepare for the future, to embrace the future and
> together, as Australians, to unite and write a new page in our nation's
> history to make this great country of ours, Australia, even greater.

He seemed neither to welcome nor need acclaim. He wasn't basking in the verdict of the ballot box or the delight of his audience. God knows what emotions were coursing through him on the platform – vindication, relief or perhaps exhaustion, after having fought his way towards this moment for at least twenty years – but he was losing the crowd. Rein could tell: her face fell as he ploughed on.

> Tomorrow, and I say this to the team, we roll up our sleeves, we're
> ready for hard work. We're ready for the long haul. You can have a
> strong cup of tea if you want in the meantime; even an Iced VoVo
> on the way through, for the celebrations should stop there. We have
> a job of work to do. It's time, friends, for us, together as a nation, to
> bind together to write this new page in our great nation's history.
> I thank the nation.

The klieg lights went out. The cameras packed up. The screens fell silent. That was about it for the party. Sober revellers wandered out into a warm Brisbane night. The peculiarities of the event were passed off as a joke: that's Kevin! But at victory celebrations across the nation there were those who, however jubilant to see the back of Howard, asked themselves: what have we here?

Quarterly Essay, *Power Trip: The Political Journey of Kevin Rudd*, May 2010

2020

Part one: hope

My heart sank when I got home the other night to find a fat dossier from Morris Iemma in the mail. He has about a thousand things he wants me to keep in mind while I am pursuing the "unique opportunity to guide Australia's future" at 2020.

So much to remember. So many to represent. Their wish lists have been arriving for a fortnight and I hope I'm up to the task. Authors expect me to speak up for authors. Gays for gays. Refugee advocates for refugees. Republicans for the republic. A man in Pyrmont with ideas for improving "sub-federal fiscal governance" hopes I'll promote an Australian Interstate Fiscal Commission to examine "ex-ante and ex-post the full impact of Commonwealth monetary and fiscal policy on the states and localities". Vince, I can only promise to try.

Monarchists are whingeing they're underrepresented. I can do nothing for them. Their ranks may be thinning but we'll show them the sympathy actors traditionally show at matinees – knowing that for many tottering in on their Zimmer frames, this will be their last public outing. Brisbane trans activist Linda Petrie emailed that no one has been chosen to speak for the nation's "roughly 15,000 plus transgender citizens". So she's asked if I'll "try and squeeze a word in".

I'm feeling stretched thin.

The Melbourne intellectual Andrew Bolt has spotted a gerrymander within the gerrymander: a deliberate overrepresentation of current and former ABC employees among the "1000 Leftists, rent-seekers, courtiers, string-pullers, patsies and token tame conservatives" going to Canberra. In a recent *Herald Sun* column, Bolt lists me among these ABC types intending to tell the PM "nice stories".

Candour demands I reveal that the indefatigable Glenys Stradijot of Friends of the ABC (Vic) sent me an email with attachments the minute the 1000 were named in the press. "Pls find attached FABC submissions for a few areas for Summit. Am sending to you our submissions in hope you will consider raising the ABC in context of what you might say about the role of media ..."

Meshed in conflict, I've resolved to represent no employer I've ever had, not the Sydney Water Board or Mrs Pickett or Allen, Allen and Hemsley or even the mysterious Reinhard Spitzy of the Club Hotel, Hinterthal am Hochkönig. (Google if curious.)

From South Africa came an email urging me to remember how "God miraculously saved and delivered us as a nation ... Let us rise up on wings as eagles as the people we were intended to be, a light unto the gentiles." This may have been a mistake.

If only Iemma's chunky dossier were too. It's the state plan repackaged so we can have at our fingertips "what the NSW government is doing to contribute to the Summit topic areas". The gobbledegook is terrifying: "Communitybuilders.nsw is an interactive clearing house where the users contribute to its content and ongoing development by publishing their stories and tips to the site ..."

But what killed any ambition to represent New South Wales is Iemma's spruiking for the state's wretched FOI regime. "Since its introduction in 1989, the Freedom of Information Act has contributed significantly to the openness and accountability of government. The act continues to perform that function, and its operation is continually subject to scrutiny and review ..."

Having exhausted all the sexual, political and professional possibilities still flowing in as I write – an eloquent plea has just arrived from community legal centres to bear in mind Australia's poor record implementing the International Covenant on Economic, Social and Cultural Rights – I've decided as a last resort I might as well represent myself. After all, we're only in Canberra for a yak ...

Part two: reality

Extensive soundings among delegates confirm I was not the only one who suddenly realised on Saturday morning as I was singing "Advance Australia Fair" that among the urgent tasks we face as a nation is ditching this wretched anthem. Dud tune. Dud words. Dud song.

But that was not an idea 2020 shook out of the tree and no doubt the professional facilitators were relieved. They had enough to deal with. And if you thought the ideas summit produced mostly fuzzy expressions of good intentions, understand that was a job well done by teams of facilitators who fought for two days to order, abstract and distil our ideas. "Mush," declared Jack Waterford of *The Canberra Times* as he read their attempt to boil down the first day's work of our "Open Government and the Media" substream – sorry about the language – of the governance stream. He demanded to know: "What's happened to all our ideas?"

Pity the poor facilitators who copped us: lawyers, journalists, a discreetly attentive Sir William Deane (abstaining on the republic) and Allan Fels pushing the case for absolute media deregulation in the presence of Seven's Kerry Stokes. "We're here to come up with new ideas," murmured Stokes, "not debate your old ACCC reports."

Time was short. Speeches were many. Though we assembled soon after breakfast on Saturday, it was 11.05 before the first participant participated: Professor Helen Irving calling for a convention to "completely reconsider the appropriateness of the constitution in the twenty-first century". Within minutes our bright ideas collided with the needs of the facilitators. We have to build a house, we were told, and out came the butcher's paper. Ideas make up the foundations – scratch, scratch with a marker pen – the walls are our themes, and the roof is our ambitions.

So, we were asked, did we think "making the constitution say what it means and mean what it says" an idea, a theme or an ambition? At that point, we knew we were in trouble. And as we struggled with these vital distinctions, the facilitators hit us with another: "the articulation of a theme" which is not quite an idea and not really an ambition.

A day of house building reduced many of us in many streams to teeth-grinding frustration. None of this made it to the big screens in the Great Hall of the People that evening. Up there it was all "amazing", "fantastic" and – the buzz word of 2020 – a wonderful "challenge". I don't want to hear these words again for a while: discourse, engagement, connection, centrality, model, accommodate and opportunities. Perhaps the prime minister might avoid a few he wore out at the microphone this weekend: benchmark, benchmark, each and every one, overarching and benchmark.

Don't get me wrong. These two days rootling around in the national too-hard basket were a great thing. Ideas were found. We had to fight for their preservation, but the summit sent out a message that this is a country still willing to have a go at getting the fundamentals right. It was worth a trip to Canberra to hear how the rhetoric has shifted and the faces changed. These are the early days of the post-Howard era, but it's already possible to grow a little nostalgic for elite bashing. All gone.

And it was worth the drive down to the national capital just to hear John Hartigan, the chief executive of News Limited, telling the governance stream he chaired: "We're sick and tired of vituperative combat that passes for political discourse in this country."

Less encouraging was hearing time and again that the young leaders of tomorrow can't pronounce the name of their own country. What's going to happen to the place if the tongue roll on the "l" goes missing?

More troubling is the return of a cringing question that disappeared in the Howard years. "What does the world think of us?" was the theme of a one-hour Sky News broadcast for which the thousand delegates were co-opted – though time was short and getting shorter – as a Sunday morning studio audience.

We could have used that hour as we fought to rescue our ideas from the mush. We had them on the whiteboard but then they disappeared again. The prefab house was taken apart and never reconstructed. Youngsters from think tanks commanded the microphone. Hardened senators held their heads in their hands.

The republic was lost, it seemed to me as the guillotine was about to fall. So I made a heroic last-ditch stand in its defence. After all, we had voted 98 for with only Sir William abstaining and Senator George Brandis opposing. But it was always safe and sound, just on another sheet of paper.

So all the streams fed paper into the great maw of 2020 and after lunch all our good intentions emerged in the Great Hall digested, homogenised, wrapped in conference-speak and welcomed by Kevin Rudd. One of the dozen overarching points the prime minister made was spot on: "It's just the beginning."

The Sydney Morning Herald, 19 and 21 April 2008

The Henson panic

OVER BREAKFAST MANY OF THE POLITICIANS, police, journalists, government officials, and radio and television producers who would be driving the story later that day glanced at Devine's column in *The Sydney Morning Herald* and did nothing about it:

> Opening tonight at the elegant Roslyn Oxley9 Gallery in the heart of Paddington is an exhibition of photographs by Bill Henson, featuring naked twelve and thirteen-year-olds. The invitation to the exhibition features a large photo of a girl, the light shining on her hair, eyes downcast, dark shadows on her sombre, beautiful face, and the budding breasts of puberty on full display, her hand casually covering her crotch ...

That invitation has few friends. I have yet to meet anyone who told me they opened the envelope with wholehearted pleasure. Even those who loved Henson's naked junkies in the 1980s, and didn't flinch from the gawky adolescents he photographed in the 1990s partying by night in piles of wrecked cars, were unnerved by the beautiful image of that child. The response of many was: "Here's trouble." The gallery received half a dozen complaints by email and telephone after sending out the usual 3500 invitations. One client asked to be removed from the mailing list. Many of the rest binned the card and waited as eagerly as always for the day.

On the gallery wall or inside a catalogue it might not have provoked the same response. But the invitation was promoting the exhibition. The image was intended to sell. The unease so many felt had a peculiar source. The most powerful taboos operate without most of us suspecting they are at work. We discover them only when they are broken. Without breasts or with full breasts this image would have caused far less fuss. Perhaps it would have passed unremarked. But these are budding breasts, rarely seen and almost never celebrated. In our culture, budding breasts are extraordinarily private. Taboo isn't sacrosanct, but Henson had broken a taboo.

He chose that image for the invitation with "no thought at all for what if, and who and other things". He heard no warning bells. The image had come after working with his twelve-year-old model N for some months. Of all the images in the exhibition he thought this was the most interesting and most alive. "I can speak about how fantastic images are, without it being at all egotistical on my part. It's not about that. It's as though the pictures make themselves. Obviously they don't, but it feels like that. You have this strange feeling that it's so good that it almost has nothing to do with you. You are along for the ride."

Roslyn Oxley had qualms. "Bill doesn't work off the cuff. He does drawings, he writes about exactly what he's going to do when he photographs a model – so it's not a chance, not left to snap snap snap away. He orchestrates it down to the last tee. I knew that he really wanted to get that sort of image. As he was talking about it, over the last year or whatever, I was always a bit worried about it. I thought 'Bill, aren't you going a bit far?'" But when the time came, Oxley kept her worries to herself. Usually Henson gives her two or three choices for the invitation. Not this time: "As far as he was concerned, that was the image. So fine."

Henson is notoriously fussy about every detail of his exhibitions, especially the hanging and lighting of his huge – 127 by 180cm – prints. He had brought forty-one works from Melbourne. Half were sombre shots of imperial Rome, sarcophagi, dark forests and twilit cloudscapes. The other half were nudes: a couple of studies of the head and back of a thirteen-year-old boy; one of an unknown girl of unknown age; and all the rest were images of N, pensive and alone in the dark. Her nipples are visible in nine of these pictures; her vagina is lost in heavy shadow in two. One of these two was the picture from the invitation, *Untitled # 30*. Oxley's verdict: "It's one of Bill's most restrained exhibitions we've had ever."

The hang had begun a day early – and the first customers had been coming through the gallery door since Tuesday – because Henson had to fly to

Melbourne the day before the opening to join the actor Geoffrey Rush and the director Fred Schepisi in launching the National Gallery of Victoria's appeal to raise an endowment fund of $150 million to mark its 150th birthday. Thursday morning saw him back in the gallery on Soudan Lane at the bottom of Paddington. Beyond a little fussing, there wasn't much left to do. The ABC was quietly filming the exhibition for the inevitable new documentary on the photographer. About midday, after some delay, the new Hensons went up on the gallery website.

He had answered his last questions from the press. There had not been much fuss that week. It was a low-key opening, something for the connoisseurs. Josephine Tovey of *The Sydney Morning Herald* had asked him a couple of days earlier why he worked with kids of that age.

> It's the most effective vehicle for expressing ideas about humanity and vulnerability and our sense of ourselves living inside our bodies, the breathtaking moment to moment existence as you're walking down a street and feel a cool change come through, feel the weather on our bodies and the way we feel about being in the world. All of this is focused more effectively through this age group, so it's the age group I work with.

Devine's column might have sunk without trace but for Darren of Engadine who, at about 1.30 pm, emailed Chris Smith of Sydney radio station 2GB: "Chris I saw an article by Miranda Devine in today's *Herald* where she mentions that the Roslyn Art Gallery in Paddington has a display of photographs of naked twelve and thirteen year old girls. I'm looking at their website. They are displaying the images there as well. Surely this cannot be legal?"

Smith's producer Phil Sylvester sensed a great afternoon's radio and began hunting urgently for someone to come on air to explain the difference between art and pornography. That he failed says something about the complexities of this story, but he swears he was not out to get Henson. "I was getting fodder for a radio talkback show. It's one of the great topics: what is art and what is porn? And here it was again."

But the story was richer than that. It could break in any number of ways. There were kids, artists, rich customers and the delicious possibilities for chasing deceit in the art world. Art fraud stories have a strange power to convulse the Australian media. We pride ourselves on having a democratic nose for picking charlatan artists. It goes way back. Ern Malley the fake poet is part of our folklore; Bill Dobell accused of passing off caricatures as portraits still lingers in the popular imagination; Helen Darville's fake Ukrainian inheritance is a live scandal fifteen years after the publication of *The Hand that Signed the Paper*. Now 2GB was presented with a chance to portray the nation's most honoured photographer as another in a long tradition of fakes: the photographer as pornographer. But these operations don't take fire unless there is some issue in the mix – however confused and buried – that really matters. Here it was plain: children and their protection.

Sylvester had no help from the Classification Board, which rates films, DVDs and the internet. Nor could the Attorney-General's Department in Canberra lend a hand. His boss at the microphone couldn't wait any longer. A few minutes before the 2 pm news, Smith told his listeners: "I've got a copy of exactly what Darren is referring to and what Miranda Devine wrote about today. I don't think I've seen anything more disgusting. How the people at the Roslyn Art Gallery in Paddington think this somehow comes under the category of art defies logic. It is disgraceful. It is disgusting. It is pornographic. It is woeful." There followed the sound of paper being scrunched and flung in a bin. "I can't even look at it."

Back in the 1990s Smith was caught forging a signature in order to spring a prisoner he wanted to interview for Channel Nine's *A Current Affair*. *Media Watch* nabbed him and the courts gave him a two-year suspended sentence. Nine took him back but he was soon in trouble again. Drunk at a farewell party in the station's boardroom in October 1998 he gave a couple of women the good news that he had a very big penis and opened his pants. He was sacked. After a stint in China he returned to join 2GB where his particular line in moral indignation earned him a huge audience.

His producer next turned for help to Tony Ritchie, former head of news at Channel Nine and now media adviser to the NSW commissioner of police, Andrew Scipione. Could Ritchie find someone in the force to come on air and talk about art and porn? By another of the blind accidents that make sense of this story, Deputy Police Commissioner Nick Kaldas was sitting with Ritchie as he opened Sylvester's email and clicked on the link to the gallery's website. "That better go to the Child Protection and Sex Crime Squad," said this policeman. The whole transaction took only minutes. Ritchie was sending the link through to the squad about the time Smith came back on air to hammer the story again first up.

"Here's a suggestion for you," Smith began. "Either read Miranda Devine's column in the *Herald*; try and Google this and have a look on the website, though I wouldn't advise it because you might puke; or even better, phone the Roslyn Art Gallery in Paddington and give them what for. If they think that kids in a state of undress is somehow art, it's got me beat. I know I've said that before because I don't have a great appreciation for anything artistic, because I'm a little bit of an artistic moron, but in this case it is just off. It's sickening. So give them a call and tell them what for, especially if you know a little bit about what they're showing and I'm not going to put it on the website or anything like that because it's just off." The phones began to ring at the gallery a few minutes later. The staff had never heard such intense anger on the line. "You're all pornographers," callers screamed. "We're going to burn the gallery down."

Barry O'Farrell, leader of the Opposition in New South Wales, was the first politician to seize on the story. His office was monitoring 2GB. After checking the gallery website, O'Farrell's press secretary, Brad Burden, contacted the state political editor of *The Daily Telegraph*, Simon Benson, suggesting he put aside the usual reluctance to follow up a column in the *Sydney Morning Herald* and pursue the Henson business. The quid pro quo for O'Farrell was a chance to grandstand about child protection in the pages of the highest-selling paper in the city. "Sexualisation of children under the guise of art is totally unacceptable ..."

Of all the politicians who would denounce Henson over the next twenty-four hours, O'Farrell was the most familiar with his work. He had been among the 115,000 Australians who saw the huge Henson retrospective staged at the Art Gallery of New South Wales and the National Gallery of Victoria in 2005. He made no protest at the time and now can't remember the walls of naked adolescents in that show, photographs far more confronting than anything waiting to be seen at the Roslyn Oxley9 Gallery. "My memory of it was more about buildings and more mainstream images."

The Telegraph ran with the story. Clare Masters rang the premier's office for comment at about 3 pm. Iemma was in China. His staff asked the office of the police minister, David Campbell, what's the story, is there an issue here, what are the rules? After passing swiftly through several hands, those queries landed on the desk of Assistant Commissioner Catherine Burn, commander of the Central Metropolitan Region. Knowing nothing of the gathering Henson storm until this point, she contacted Superintendent

Allan Sicard of Rose Bay, whose patch covers the gallery in Soudan Lane. Sicard had already had calls about the exhibition. Burn placed him in charge of the operation.

The clock was against them. In three hours time an influential bunch of citizens would be gathering at the city's most prestigious contemporary art gallery to look at these pictures. Emotions were running high in several pockets of the force. They didn't know and didn't particularly care who this photographer was. He had no history in their eyes. What they saw on the gallery website looked like porn to them. No one had heard of them before lunch, but now inquiries were coming in from the premier's office, the commissioner's office, the Sex Crime Squad and the public. According to police, three people who had actually been to the gallery would lay formal complaints about the pictures in these hours. A visit to the lane by Sicard's men was inevitable. A police source says: "Everyone knew it was not going to be a pretty scene."

Radio producers were talking to television producers. Newsrooms were monitoring 2GB. Journalists were already gathering in the lane and more were on their way the moment the police were mentioned. Slipping out at 3 pm to have her hair washed – an old opening day ritual – Oxley found herself facing Robert Ovadia and a Channel Seven news crew. "I nearly died." Would she let Henson put her own daughter "on public display", asked the reporter? "She's been in some of his shots," replied Oxley and drove away.

In the middle of the afternoon, three senior officers of the Classification Board, working in their loft office in Sydney's Surry Hills, downloaded the Henson images and concluded, swiftly, that there was nothing much here to worry about. The role of the board is to classify films, DVDs, images from the internet and publications – including exhibitions – and pin on them the familiar warning labels: G, PG, MA, R, X and RC. These professionals, exposed to appalling material from day to day, could see at a glance that Henson's pictures of children would neither be rated X (porn) nor RC (refused classification; that is, banned). If the images ever reached them – and it was by no means certain they would – then they would have the task of declaring the gale blowing outside was a storm in a teacup. But for the moment they could only watch and wait.

Soudan Lane ends at a cliff face. Even empty, it feels claustrophobic. When Oxley returned with her hair washed about 4 pm, the lane was packed with press. She slipped inside to find the staff dazed. The phones were still ringing nonstop with wild abuse and pleas for interviews intermingled. At least they now knew where it was all coming from: one of Henson's fans had rung to wish the gallery luck for the opening and alert them to the attacks on 2GB.

Henson was finding the atmosphere in the gallery really weird. "A few clients of Ros's had been through, people were coming in and putting stickers on things. The National Gallery of Victoria had reserved two; the NSW Art Gallery had reserved two, so that was just ticking along a bit." He went out onto the terrace and was shocked to see the crowd of journalists and cameras gathering in the lane. The sight of Henson ducking back inside would look particularly furtive on television news that night. Last preparations were being made for the opening. "People were still answering phones, cleaning up, bringing drinks and at a certain point I said 'do you think we should call the police?' After I made that suggestion – it was mine I think – within five minutes, ten minutes, these two guys walked upstairs."

The police officers from Rose Bay were low-key. They seemed only really concerned about crowd control. Oxley says: "We were relieved." After making a few calls, the two were joined by their commanding officer at the station, Superintendent Sicard. "We do have a bit of a problem," he told the Oxleys. "I think we need to wander off and look at the gallery."

Out in the lane, Channel Ten's reporter crossed live to the five o'clock news. The story jumped to television. Even more press now headed for Soudan Lane. At roughly the same time on the other side of town, Iemma's staff received their instructions from China: they were to draft a statement strongly disapproving of the pictures and the girl's parents for putting a child in such a situation. The finished words were given to Clare Masters for publication next morning in the *Telegraph* but the gist – at least – of the premier's views was also sent through to the police. Though he could not direct them, Iemma could let them know what was on his mind.

Sicard and his men still seemed most worried about security. "I'm really concerned about potential damage to the work," said the superintendent when he finished his tour of the exhibition. Henson was too. The prints weren't behind glass. One nick with a Stanley knife and they'd be ruined. They were particularly precious because he had finally run out of printing paper hoarded over the years as factories closed around the world. Henson was bravely facing a digital future and these were just about his last analogue prints. He was fearful for the work but told police: "I'm more worried about the people in here." Sicard's worries about the pictures themselves were also on the table by this point. The superintendent asked the Oxleys to suspend the exhibition "to allow enquiries of legality of photos". The Oxleys took their lead from Henson. He didn't put up a fight. "I said 'right, that's it, let's shut it.'"

At about 8 pm the Oxleys led the way up the fire escape to waiting cars, leaving the lights blazing behind them, tubs of ice melting, the phones still ringing, the website crashing, and baffled Henson fans beating their way up Soudan Lane against the tide of dispersing journalists only to find, instead of the familiar open foyer with the name of that night's artist spotlit on its bare white walls, a roller door locked to the ground.

The Henson Case, 2008, and *Panic*, 2013

Rudd declared the photographs "absolutely revolting". Police carted them away. Across Australia they swooped on public galleries look-ing for criminal Hensons. The photographer went to ground. For a fortnight the media storm continued unabated, one of the great press panics of my lifetime. Then it all fell apart. The Office of Film and Literature Classification rated the exhibition G – free to be viewed by all ages – and the NSW Director of Public Prosecutions declined to prosecute. The pictures were returned and the exhibi-tion reopened.

A chill in the death zone

AS YOU CLIMB TOWARDS KINGLAKE, the desolation is absolute. Gates open onto nothing. The earth is cooked. Across the hills there is no sign of green. In the distance, mocking all this destruction, are postcard- pretty views of Melbourne's skyscrapers. And to make it even more bizarre, it's cold.

Valleys are burning not far away. The smell is evil. A horse lies on its side like a fallen bronze. There are carcasses of kangaroos everywhere. Some cattle pick away among them. Someone has been through delivering hay. On a gatepost is a sign we see once or twice: "Family all fine."

As we near the summit, the damage seems at first less extreme. Stands of trees are untouched. The stock of the sawmill is only lightly singed. An orchard is in fine shape though a line of pines along its fence is still smouldering. But we turn a corner and there are the houses, one after another, reduced to ash, a few chimneys and sheets of iron turned to paper by the heat.

The citizens – we hear that word a lot – of Kinglake are meeting. Maybe 150 of them are crowded round to hear what help is available and what help is coming. There is cash for those who need it, says a woman from the Department of Human Resources. There are no tents, says a guy from the army. The little row of shops nearby has turned into an open-air market with a difference: everything is free.

"We lost our house," says Penelope Forde, watching her young sons eat fat meat pies. Insured? "Thank God."

Neighbours embrace in the street passing on good and bad news. "Half the shed is gone." They tell us about the noise of the fire. Like a freight train,

472

they say. Like a 747. "It's a noise I will carry with me all my life," said Darren Webb-Johnson. His parents' house is only standing because, at 5 am on Sunday, he investigated a niggling sound that turned out to be spot fires in the roof. He and his father, Neville, got to work with buckets. His mother, Gloria, ran for help. The sitting room is in ruins but the house is intact.

Around them, ruins. "In that one over there a woman survived by climbing into a wombat hole," says Peter Beales, a local councillor. "A lady died in that one with her children and grandchildren." There is nothing to mark the houses of the dead. They are all alike. All shells.

In a garden where everything is charred and melted, the owner finds a spade and flourishes it as if he'd won a prize. In that little Armageddon of his yard, a wooden table sits there absolutely untouched. "Fire is completely random," says Beales. The great surprise of this one was speed. These people weren't careless. Beales was one of many who tell us Kinglake was listening all day to the ABC and the bushfire scanners. But then it was there. "They didn't even have time to get in their cars. It just went bang."

We were tourists in Hades and these wonderful people spoke to us, told their stories, were patient with the cameras and the microphones. Some have barely slept in forty hours. They've been promised the press will stay away now for a few days to let them get on with the unexpected lives they face after fire ripped through their paradise.

As we drove down – pausing for electricity crews and gangs tearing burnt trees from the sides of the road – a woman was at work in a neat little vegetable garden beside an untouched house. The paddocks all round were burnt black. And she still has that beautiful view all the way to Melbourne.

The Sydney Morning Herald, 12 February 2009

Time on Christmas Island

IN A TIN SHED ON PHOSPHATE HILL, a brisk woman from the Department of Immigration and Citizenship sits facing a slight kid of seventeen. Though Ali Jaffari knows something of what is coming, he is battling nerves. His face is grey. One leg is trembling. His father, Sharif, sits quietly beside him, his head bowed. An air conditioner thunders in the background. Both men keep an eye on the envelopes the DIAC officer has on the table: brown envelopes that hold the answer to the rest of their lives.

The Jaffaris are Hazaras from Afghanistan, a people long persecuted as Shia Muslims in a country overwhelmingly Sunni. Sharif was still a boy when he fled the country to grow up in the large Hazara community in Iran. At some point, he moved to Pakistan and raised a family in Quetta. But as interfaith violence intensified in Pakistan over the last year, the city became dangerous. Sharif talks of more than sixty Hazaras murdered in the city. The Jaffaris narrowly escaped death. "Two persons came by motorcycle. They stopped. They fired on us and they escaped." It was time to leave. "There were rumours Australia accepted refugees and it's a safe and secure country. So therefore we decided to come to Australia. That was our plan."

Their arrival on Christmas Island in early May, along with another 185 refugees collected by HMAS *Tobruk*, provoked fresh denunciations by the Opposition of Labor's "soft" response to boat people. "There cannot be any serious argument about it now," said Malcolm Turnbull. "It has failed to stop the dreadful business of people smuggling." Hate was back in the air. The press noted the biggest spike in "unauthorised boat arrivals" since the heyday of the Pacific Solution in 2001. The island was said to be reaching bursting point. As always, Christmas Islanders gathered to watch the refugees brought ashore. It's a spectacle that predates the *Tampa* affair by a decade. But things have changed: the islanders were no longer held back by police barricades, and there were no guards in riot gear on the barges.

Flying Fish Cove lies under cliffs covered by dark forests. Jurassic birds wheel overhead. The dusty hulk of the phosphate loader waits for ships. Along the shore are barracks, warehouses and a little mosque. This was not where the Jaffaris expected to find themselves. That all boat people heading for Australia are now held on Christmas Island came as a complete surprise. "No one told us." They hadn't heard of attempts by Labor and Coalition governments over nearly two decades to deter people like them from coming here by boat. The messages had fallen on deaf ears. The Jaffaris paid a smuggler to bring them to this country because, where they come from, Australia has a vague reputation for decency.

As Ali was only seventeen, father and son were not taken to the high-security immigration detention centre at North West Point but to the old Construction Camp on Phosphate Hill above the town. The immigration minister, Chris Evans, says Labor converted the facilities here to give children and families a "community environment". It's a grim fib. A high fence was torn down, but what's left is a cluster of tin boxes and concrete walkways surrounded by gravel. Workers building roads in the bush sleep in dongas like these and are well paid for their discomfort. But on Phosphate Hill families sit behind closed doors day after day with air conditioners working away. There is little privacy. Heavy rain turns the camp into a mosquito-ridden swamp. Although the guards have gone from the gates, no one is free to leave without an escort. "It's not a community," said an islander who knows the place intimately. "It's a shithole."

Under John Howard, boat people were held in detention for years as a harsh warning to those who might follow in their wake. Labor has dramatically sped things up. The Jaffaris have waited only two months and twelve days for this encounter in the rec room with the woman from DIAC.

Her news is all good and delivered swiftly: "The paperwork has gone very quickly and I'm pleased to let you know that the minister has granted you a protection visa." Ali sags a little and thanks her quietly. The father nods. In real life, victories aren't marked by shouts and high fives, but relief that mimics exhaustion. She slips documents from the envelopes for them to sign. Ali asks that word be sent to a friend he made on the boat who is being held at North West Point. Ali wants to say goodbye. "I only know his name as Said." Promises are made. (And kept.) There follows a last, bizarre interrogation. It's so pointless it's almost insulting, yet it's proof the Jaffaris have now achieved the privileged status of ordinary travellers.

"Are you," asks the woman from DIAC, "carrying goods that may be prohibited or subject to restriction such as medicines, steroids, firearms, weapons of any kind?" Ali and his father confer. "No, we don't have any." Nor do they have $10,000 or its equivalent in foreign currency. Nor any dried, fresh, preserved, cooked or uncooked food. The translator labours away and the woman from DIAC crosses each box in their entry cards. Tomorrow they will be driven to one of the most fickle airports in the world, where a plane will be waiting to take them 2600 kilometres to Perth. The scene is not quite finished. The air conditioner is turned off and in the silence that fills the shed, Ali thanks those who have looked after them on the island. "We can't consider them as human beings," he says, "but better than human beings, like angels. We are very pleased being treated well and feeling safe and secure here. It can't be described by words."

*

Christmas Island is not a sunny atoll but a gloomy mountain sticking out of the Indian Ocean. It appears from the air black, cloud-smothered, defended by cliffs and ringed by surf. It's tiny and a long way away. The sea is everywhere. It sets the moods of the place, brings the cloud and nights of thundering rain. It's a tough stretch of ocean ending in the poor harbour of Flying Fish Cove. A navy boat has been hovering off the coast for days waiting to intercept little boats making their way down from Indonesia. It's an island for waiting: waiting for something to come along, waiting for the supply ship, waiting for friends to visit, waiting for the weather to clear, waiting to get away.

Seven hundred detainees, housed in town, up in the Construction Camp and out in the forest detention centre, are waiting for news of hearings and applications and visas. Driving around trying to make sense of this baffling place on my first afternoon, I find the oval on Phosphate Hill just as it is getting dark. Gnarled frangipanis guard the gates. Lichen grows on the goal posts. Eighteen young men are playing soccer, the jungle behind them a hazy shadow in the mist. They are waiting, killing time in their own way. Clouds sweep across the field and the men disappear, lost except for their shouting.

This rock was given to Australia in the great dispersal of the Empire fifty years ago. Jakarta is the nearest big city. Buddhism is the main religion. Most of the island is locked away in a national park. The tiny population is sixty per cent Chinese, twenty-five per cent Malay and the rest European. They live in little suburbs scattered over the cliffs above Flying Fish Cove: below Drumsite come Poon Saan ("half way") and Silver City, with the offices and big houses of the Settlement running along the waterline. All told, the permanent population is less than 1500. Christmas Island is so tiny it's not so much a territory as a parish of Australia.

What to do with the place has intrigued Canberra for decades. One inquiry is barely finished before the next begins. Reports pile up while life goes on. Big visions disappear in the tropic heat. A casino used by Tommy Suharto and his mates to wash their loot collapsed a decade ago. The satellite launching pad never got anywhere. Phosphate mining has kept the place in work since the 1890s but perhaps for not much longer. For years the mine has been threatening to close down in four or five years' time. It wants another 256 hectares of forest to strip and mine. Peter Garrett's decision will shape the economic fate of the island. Meanwhile, the place has been handed another future: as a prison for refugees.

At the Australian National University in July last year, Chris Evans laid out Labor's new regime for handling boat people. Much of the tough Howard architecture would remain: excision, military interception and mandatory detention. But now detention would be brief: only as long as it took to carry out health, identity and security checks. After that, asylum seekers would be released into the community while waiting to see if Australia would take them as refugees. The process would take months instead of years. But it was to happen a very long way away: "Those unauthorised arrivals," said Evans, "will be processed on Christmas Island."

Evans treads gently. Rudd laid down Labor's policy on boat people early in his time as leader of the Opposition. Nauru would be closed, but all processing of boat people would continue way offshore. "If people are on the high seas and then indicate that they are going to seek asylum in Australia ... then they should be taken to Christmas Island for processing," said Rudd. "That's our policy." Howard had held some boat people on the island, but Rudd would use the island as a prison for them all. Evans' number-one reason for the enormous effort that's since been put into this operation is unambiguous: "It was an election commitment."

*

The weather on the island is brutal. It wipes inscriptions from graves. Television sets last a couple of years. Duco warps and shreds like skin with strange diseases. Buildings rot. All that's left of the old CI Club, one of the great institutions of the island, is falling apart in the trees behind Flying Fish Cove. Here in March 2002, the Minister for Territories, Wilson Tuckey, called a meeting that's seen as a turning point by the islanders. He told them: "You're going to get a new detention centre and I'm not here to argue."

The new island prison didn't have to be so big but it did need to be more secure after the riots at Baxter, Woomera and Villawood. At this point, Howard might have reassessed the policy of deliberate long detention that had incubated the riots. Instead it was decided that security at North West Point would be increased dramatically. The project would involve building new roads, a new port and a big recreation hall back at Phosphate Hill. As usual, when it came to saving Australia from boat people, money was no object. When Baulderstone Hornibrook won the tender and took a closer look at the plans, the budget rose swiftly from $276 million to $336 million and kept rising for another three years. Canberra was discovering all over again that the high symbolic value of Christmas Island comes at a mighty cost. Everything out there – except the tax-free booze, cigarettes and second-hand luxury cars from Singapore – is grossly expensive.

The site was a nightmare. There were limestone pinnacles and "covered caves" that threatened the project with collapse. And then there was the weather. Rick Scott-Murphy of the department of Finance and Administration told a Senate estimates hearing: "In the period since we have been constructing it we have suffered a near pass with a cyclone, we have had a tsunami and we have had a 6.4 Richter-scale seismic event." The Minister for Human Services Ian Campbell piped up: "Building the runway in Antarctica was a lot easier than this, seriously. And cheaper." The completion date kept being pushed back. This out-of-date, over-engineered, hugely expensive building – perhaps *the* building of the Howard era – was still not finished when the Howard government went to its grave.

*

"Basically, my kids have no fathers," says Jennie Collins, a freckle-faced teacher of fierce determination and indeterminate years. A tattoo on one ankle suggests Miss Jennie has seen a bit of life. Today she's teaching eighteen Hazara boys polite English. They are slight kids dressed in the school uniform of the island: black shorts, t-shirts and runners. A few may be in their early twenties but most are about seventeen, the age at which the Taliban begins to take a predatory interest in them, the age when they flee. "Whole villages have clubbed together to get these boys out. Some have mothers and siblings, maybe in camps in Pakistan, but they don't have fathers."

She asks each boy in turn what he would like to be if, *inshallah*, he reaches Australia. It seems we have, heading our way, three would-be mechanics, two doctors, a poultry farmer, four tailors – already qualified – an engineer, a teacher, an artist, a cook, a software programmer, a social worker and "the top richest man in the world". One kid says he wants to join the Navy. "Who remembers the Navy rescuing them from their boats?" asks Miss Jennie. "Are they good people?" The boys roar, "Yes!"

They came in five boats. One, with sixty people aboard, was ten days at sea. Another, with seventy-two aboard, was at sea for eight days and leaked all the way. "There was a hole in the bottom. They don't have a water pump to take the water out. They were doing it with a bucket and our hands." They were all seeing the sea for the first time. None could swim. All seem to have travelled via Kuala Lumpur airport, the refugee gateway to Australia. They came the rest of the way by boat. "It is really, really unbelievable that we are alive," says one older detainee, AR. "Unfortunately we lost our way. There is only that much food not to die. That much. There was that much water not to die. The ship was not working. Big waves. The ship was not good. Blue sky and blue water. You can see nothing. It is just like to see a death from your eyes. A big sea. Ocean." Another of the kids adds: "On the way we saw sharks, whales, dolphins, everything."

Now Miss Jennie is teaching them to say sorry. Out of the hubbub as they practise on each other come "no probs" and "no worries, mate". When do you apologise, she asks each in turn. "When you are late, miss," one replies. Another says: "When you break someone's heart."

*

Crabs edge across a muddy road cut through the forest. Phosphate trucks thunder by. You have to know where you're heading out here because the prison, although it's the biggest building on the island, isn't marked on maps. The road swings round and there it is: sprawling like a vast factory behind high wire fences. The fences are remarkable. The first apparently stops the crabs frying on the second, which is about four metres of mesh topped by half a dozen single strands of wire, the whole thing being, as they say in the prison trade, 'energised'. Inside that is a perimeter road equipped with microwave probes that are capable, according to plans leaked to *Crikey* in 2007, of detecting the slightest movement. Inside that is yet another fence – quite friendly, merely man-high – before the buildings fill the landscape to the horizon.

It cost $400 million in the end. A jail this size can be built in New South Wales for roughly a tenth of that sum. The cost doesn't stop with the building. A senior executive of G4S, the company that until this month ran all Australia's detention centres, told me labour costs double on Christmas Island. DIAC foots the bill, of course, and this includes daily food and accommodation allowances of $190 per worker. That's a lot to pay before spending a cent on wages. Oxfam estimates it costs $1600 per day more to hold someone on Christmas Island than the mainland. The budget for reassuring Australians is bottomless.

A fortnight before I found myself at these gates, Graeme Innes of the Australian Human Rights Commission had been here inspecting the facilities. The commission is scathing about both the prison and the Christmas Island operation. Innes told me: "We come from the position that people should not be detained on Christmas Island. First because it is so remote and the cost of everything out there is so huge. But second because in a small community of 1000 residents there are not the resources to sustain the refugees. But this government is stuck with a $400-million resource that they've got to use. They are making the best of it, but it is still a prison."

It wouldn't take much to cut the fences down, but Evans isn't planning renovations. "One, it's brand new, so one's not likely to be spending a lot of money on redesigning the centre, given we've just invested $400 million in building it. Secondly, I looked at some possible adjustments to the place and the costs were prohibitive." At both Phosphate Hill and North West

Point, Evans is trying to implement Labor's immigration values inside John Howard's grim facilities. It's a most uncomfortable mix.

Entry to the IDC took all the security checks you would expect of a serious prison. Inside the yard there was something disturbingly modish about the tropical plantings and corrugated iron. It has the feel of a deranged holiday camp. The whole place is iron, steel and glass. It won't burn, rot or rust. On a stretch of grass worn almost to death, a 25-a-side soccer match between Sri Lanka and Afghanistan is playing itself out. Soon the game will end and both the gym and what they call the "internet café" will close. The 569 single men in the place will then trail back to their yards – where the furniture is bolted to the floor – for a headcount and the evening meal. Keeping an eye on them are 247 cameras.

The polite detainee I'm visiting won't be helped by me discussing his case. But he's been here for over four months, one of the hard cases beginning to queue up on the island. Hazaras and Tamils are moving through at roughly the speed promised by Labor: in and out of the system within three months. But Iraqis and Singhalese, with more fragile claims to refugee protection, are facing longer detention as their cases are decided. This man is waiting to hear how he went at an Independent Merits Review held a couple of weeks earlier. It was his second and last chance. Had he reached the mainland he might have taken his case all the way through the courts. But out here on "excised" Christmas Island his only appeal was to a "non-statutory" hearing in the training room of the Christmas Island Shire Council. Though gloomy about the outcome, he was not without hope. He is taught English for an hour each week. He can find nothing to read in Farsi. He kills time smoking and sleeping.

*

Four interpreters stand like a UN delegation at the counter of the Rockfall Café examining the menu. It's a familiar document. These rather scholarly men have been on the island four weeks and the food is getting them down. There's not much choice. It's expensive. Except for the odd catch of wahoo, everything fresh is flown in. That explains the coolite boxes on nearly every trolley queued for my flight at Perth airport. The cargo manifest of the plane listed, among other things, 108 kilos of sausages. No one starves out here, but feeding the hundreds who have come to deal with the detainees is straining the island's resources to breaking point. Distance makes everything more difficult. "Christmas Island goes against the laws of economics," one local observed. "In the face of demand it contracts."

Islanders complain about expensive food and lost peace of mind; their daughters sitting at school with Hazara boys of unknown age; the hospital stretched to the limit; the dentist overwhelmed; DIAC making it up as it goes along and the tourist industry "shattered" for want of rooms, restaurants and cars to rent. On a hot Thursday night, in a garden behind the mosque, I had dinner with Zainal Majid and a few of his friends. Zainal is a senior executive with the mine and president of the Islamic Council. I'd wondered why the council was not batting for the detainees. After all, so many of the boat people are Muslim. But here's the wrinkle: they are Shia and the island is Sunni. Majid defends the presence of the detainees but does not see himself as their spokesman. An offer of help was made by the mosque some time ago but not repeated. The detainees are welcome to pray there, he says. "But they don't come."

*

Perhaps because they know how bad the figures might be, refugee advocates were cheered by a Newspoll in April that showed support and opposition for the government's handling of asylum seekers evenly balanced. But a closer reading of the numbers shows how fragile the situation is: a third of those polled hadn't made up their minds. The Opposition hasn't gained much traction bashing boat people over the last few months, but it's far from clear how the nation might yet jump. Evans says he doesn't pore over the polls. "I find those things too depressing."

Labor is not contesting the nation's old fears. No party has actually campaigned on behalf of boat people since Malcolm Fraser went on the stump in the late 1970s to try to calm the panic that broke out when the first Vietnamese boats reached Australia. Labor has instead mounted this extraordinary performance out in the Indian Ocean: doing at a distance what might be done at home in order to comfort Australians with the idea that we alone decide who comes to this country. And until they prove themselves out on this rock, these strangers won't be let loose in the streets of Melbourne and Sydney. No other country goes through such an elaborate rigmarole. But Christmas Island *is* Australia. Refugees who make it so far have nowhere to come, in the end, but the mainland. They could come here from the start.

The terrace of the Lucky Ho café was alive with rumours on my last night that more boats were on the way. A policeman's wife had told her hairdresser, who told her daughter, who told the other kids at school, who told the teachers eating wahoo in special sauce at the next table, that 150 refugees would arrive in Flying Fish Cove in the morning. It proved to be rubbish, but such rumours can't be wrong for long out here. The boats will keep coming and, until we're willing to face our fears, we will continue to deal with them out here in a way that's essentially theatre: an expensive, deeply satisfying, national farce.

The Monthly, September 2009

Build on the rock and not upon the sand ...

AS CATASTROPHES GO, the great Bellevue Hill landslip was extremely civilised. The only reported casualties are two cars, a lamppost and a tree. The horse trough on Victoria Road survived in situ. By nightfall a twenty-tonne excavator was down in Cooper Park shifting sand of tennis court quality.

Woollahra Council and Sydney Water are already at each other's throats and lawyers are queuing outside, hungry for work. But an architect with a fashionable practice in the eastern suburbs had a word to *The Sydney Morning Herald* about the deeper cause of the problem: sand.

"You never hit rock in Bellevue Hill," he confessed on condition of anonymity. His houses dot the margins of Cooper Park. All are built on sand. The mansions of half Sydney's rich sit on ancient sand hills. It's a biblical situation.

Yet when the edge of Victoria Road slipped out of sight on Thursday night, God was forgiving. No houses were swept into the park. Nor was the TAB. Even St Stephen's Anglican Church, home of the anti-gay firebrand the Rev Richard Lane, survived prim and intact.

Sydney was being reminded of a lesson the residents of Los Angeles and Lima know by heart: that the land under our feet can give way at any moment. And if no one is killed, we find it immensely satisfying. That it happens in a nice suburb adds to the fun. Nothing had amused Sydney so much in years as that block of flats that nearly sank into the Lane Cove Tunnel in 2005. The pet budgerigar rescued by a robot was the talk of the town.

Yesterday Paul Stradbrook, nineteen, surveyed the huge, wet rift where the side of Victoria Road used to be and declared: "It's a bloody disaster, it's fantastic." He and his father were in the last car through on Thursday night. "We moved some stuff into our house and we came out and you could hear the pipes [gushing] and then one of the cops started screaming 'Get back! Get back!'"

Jill Johnson, who lives on Victoria Road, met the last pedestrian to get clear before the collapse. "He had been pushing two children in a stroller and then he heard this shocking noise and he said he turned around and watched as the whole section he just walked along gave way."

Like most of the great hole stories, the Bellevue Hill landslide involves warnings ignored. Soon after water began dribbling into the park last Tuesday, locals began ringing both the council and Sydney Water. Nothing happened. By 6 pm on Thursday, it was gushing. By 7 pm the spring had turned into a waterfall. The hill gave way soon after. Water and electricity failed across the suburb. Ruptured gas pipes roared until shut down at 4 am.

It may get very messy now, but Bellevue Hill had one of its rare exciting nights.

The Sydney Morning Herald, 30 May 2009

On the beach with Rudd

THE LAND IS GREEN, THE SEA IS BLUE. Coal ships are strung along the horizon. But on this brief hop from Townsville to Mackay only the security guards are gazing out the window. Everyone else on the prime minister's plane has his or her head stuck in a ringbinder. Rudd's toy-town version of America's mighty *Air Force One* is a neat jet emblazoned with the familiar but incongruous word *Royal*. As a concession to the needs, or perhaps the addictions, of his staff, mobile phones are only turned off at the very last minute, almost as the plane is leaving the ground. These young men and women look oddly naked without phones to their ears. And they *are* young: in their twenties and early thirties. The work never stops. There is no chiacking. Serving the prime minister may offer them profound satisfaction, but you don't read it on their faces. They make a sombre band.

Rudd was up north handing out large licks of money to hospitals a week or so before his showdown with the premiers in April. His daily routine was this: give early morning radio interviews by phone, visit hospital, give news conference, disappear with staff to attend to matters of state, emerge for coffee or sandwich with local newspaper editors, then fly to next town. Cameras and press trail after him. Everywhere he goes, citizens ask to have their photographs taken with him. Usually one of the security guards takes the snap. Whatever dark techniques they have been taught to protect Rudd's life remain, thank God, a secret. What we did see everywhere on display in North Queensland was their skill with cameras: digital, disposable, SLR and phone.

"They can't be *too* sick," an administrator at the Townsville Hospital confided. Patients the prime minister visits have to be up for the ride, presentable and not at death's door. After all, the footage is destined for the evening news. Yet finding four television cameras, half a dozen local journalists, two or three hospital administrators and Kevin Rudd at your bedside is an alarming experience. He asks chipper questions about the disease/condition/operation being endured. He's personable. Not insincere. Then he launches into a little stump speech: "We're here to deliver ... seventy million bucks. It's a big investment but I think it's worth it ... It's not just here – we're rolling it out across the country ..."

Half an hour later we're in the air. Trim air-force stewards, their hair in neat buns, serve chicken and avocado baguettes with a refreshing glass of water. Rudd wanders out of his room for a cake cutting: one of his staff is leaving after a couple of years on the trail. The celebrations are modest. Rudd is pale, precise and a little puffy. His hair is ghost grey and his eyes are sharp. Standing in the cabin eating a tiny slice of chocolate cake, he has the slightly distracted air of someone who has woken from an afternoon nap. We fall into conversation: about his school days and his time as the right-hand man to Wayne Goss. Did I realise, he asks, that we'd just flown over Mundingburra?

That was the seat in Townsville's suburbs that brought Goss down, a sad end to an extraordinary era. Goss had broken the Nationals' grip on Queensland, come to power with such high hopes and won a second big victory at the polls before his government was carried off on a tide of disappointment, antagonism and weariness. Rudd was at Goss's side almost to the end. There are veterans of the administration who claim Rudd must take a share of the blame for the Goss collapse. They are not without admiration for Rudd's achievements but remember him as an arsehole, mechanical, cold, a cunt, unbelievably arrogant and an absolute prick to deal with. Watch out, they say, history is repeating itself. What happened in Brisbane then is happening in Canberra now.

What had gone wrong back then? The Right swore Goss had done too much, the Left too little. The Right blamed change fatigue. The Left argued the Goss crowd – and Rudd in particular – had disappointed the high hopes of those who swept Labor to power. Rudd says he has no regrets for the control he exercised, the time he took, the enemies he made, the bureaucrats he frustrated, the staffers he exhausted. He told me: "I know of nobody who's ever occupied a position – either being the chief of staff or a head of a central agency in the public service, state or federal, in this jurisdiction or abroad – who doesn't have those sorts of criticisms levelled at them." That's leadership. Wreckage is to be expected. People are upset when their advice is rejected, their performance criticised, their career hopes thwarted. There are no lessons for his later life in Canberra to be drawn from these criticisms. "They are structural to any person who occupies those positions. I say that, by the way, with no sort of idealistic view of any sort of perfection of my role in times past."

Though Rudd sloughs off criticism of his bureaucratic style, he is extremely sensitive to accusations that the policies he was driving were without heart. But his mantra always was: evidence-based policy. And how good were his political instincts? Nil, according to one colleague from the Goss years: "He has a computer-like mind that can analyse all 12,000 policy options, but he chooses by comparing and contrasting, by elimination. Not by instinct." He remains in awe of the way Rudd taught himself to be a formidable bureaucrat but puzzles over his lack of *feel*. "Does that instinct come from liking and trusting people?" he wonders. "He doesn't have that."

The manager of this waterfront pub in Mackay has put on a few jewels and stationed herself in the foyer to miss none of the fun. Prime ministers and their staff are not her usual line of work. "We serve the miners," she explains. The place is frantic. Aides come and go, sometimes in running gear but always on their phones. Out on the terrace where things will turn ugly later, Rudd holds court with the usual suspects: the mayor, the editor of the local paper and the Labor candidate. Mackay needs a big new road to get coal trucks to the wharf. The price is high. Alister Jordan takes notes. Waiting patiently to shuttle Rudd's people around the town is a taxi driver who has, at his own expense, packed an esky of ice-cold mineral water for his passengers. He says: "I've been Labor all my life."

At sundown Rudd suggests a walk and we set out in bare feet along the weed-strewn beach. Security guards walk at a distance fore and aft. A passing straggler calls out: "You are the best prime minister ever." The clichés of the day drop away. He talks about himself as a child with great affection but oddly, as if that kid in Eumundi was someone else entirely. The memory of Ashgrove is still blazing away. He was a sick kid then, he says, but he is someone who has grown stronger as he grows older. By this time he was puffing a little as we slogged along the sand. That Rudd is still a puritan is beyond doubt, but he's not the prig who preached in Burgmann College. Prime Minister Rudd isn't touting the virtues of Calvin's Geneva.

He laughs to hear some think he is a creationist. Not true. Once or twice he shies away from questions, declaring he's just not a reflective person. I don't believe him: I sense no one is more curious about the mysteries of Rudd than Rudd himself.

People come out of the dark to shake his hand. He grabs young kids with obvious delight. Perhaps the happiest version of himself is Rudd the father. Rudd the leader is a loner: it's been a lonely business all along and gets lonelier the higher he climbs. "I think it's just inevitable. Ultimately you have to make calls. And that is an individual and solitary business." But he wouldn't have it any other way. In the months I spent writing this essay I came across no one who had enjoyed working closely with him. The bitterness of some is shocking. He claims not to have reflected much on the unhappiness he's left in his wake. Some exchanges might have been handled better, he says. But that's life and leadership.

There is no force field around him. As we ate dinner, people dropped by the table to chat. "I'm Kevin," he says. They know. Years ago, when he was first presenting himself to the public as a human being, he was asked to name his favourite book, film and composer. The list has hardly changed since 2003. *The Brothers Karamazov* now trumps *Crime and Punishment*, *Babette's Feast* beats *Dr Strangelove* – though his eyes light up at the memory and his right hand half-rises in a Nazi salute – and Mozart is now the master, not Beethoven: "Over Easter I listened to the Requiem again and it's just sublime." The painters he most admires are the Pre-Raphaelites. "They saw poverty for what it was and had, you know, certain Christian overtones." I struggle to remember something from my childhood: the knock at the door? "Yes, *The Light of the World*." And out pours the history of Holman Hunt's image of Christ standing with a lantern in his hand knocking at an overgrown doorway: one of the great recruiting posters of Christendom.

Almost as he is leaving the table he asks me the argument of this essay. It's a man-to-man question, so I tell him. I'm pursuing the contradictions of his life: the farmer's kid who runs away to China, the politician unloved by his own caucus who turns out to be such a potent electoral asset; a decent man with decent political ambitions who leaves so much wreckage in his wake; a great orator who can be a bore; a man with modest policy ambitions but a strong drive for power. And I'm wondering if his government will go the way of Goss's.

I don't notice his face changing at first, but by the time I finish giving this bare-bones account I realise Rudd is furious. I have hurt him and he is angry. What follows is a dressing-down which registers about a 5.4 on his Richter scale. He doesn't scream and bang the table as he does behind closed doors. We're in the open. The voice is low. He is perfectly composed. From the distance of the next table it would be hard to tell how furious the prime minister is. Indeed, some boys come over in the middle of it all to ask to have their picture taken with him. "Later," he says politely and returns to his work. More revealing than anything he told me in those twenty minutes is the transformation of the man. In his anger Rudd becomes astonishingly eloquent. This is the most vivid version of himself I've ever encountered. At last he was speaking from the heart, an angry heart.

Face to face, it's so clear. This man is driven by old anger. It's the juice in the machine. But it's hidden by a public face – a diplomat's face – that is hard to read. Who is Kevin Rudd? He is the man you glimpse when the anger vents. Volcanoes breaking through the ice were in the news as I wrote, but Icelandic images are far too theatrical for Rudd. He is not ice and fire, but a stoked furnace. There is heat there to drive him for a lifetime.

He finishes, leans over the table, shakes my hand and strides inside, walking straight past the boys waiting so patiently for their photograph. An aide rushes after him. He will not come back out onto the terrace. The boys have to go in to him. A flash bursts inside and the prime minister disappears.

Quarterly Essay, *Power Trip:*
The Political Journey of Kevin Rudd, May 2010

Eloquence or else

IMAGINE THE SCENE AT THE MUSEUM of Contemporary Art in Sydney in late January this year. It was a hot Sunday afternoon. The harbour glittered, blue and inviting. Inside, a crowd of distinguished – or as best we could do in Sydney – people, standing shoulder to shoulder on the hard marble floors of the museum with very rapidly emptying glasses in their hands listening to Kevin Rudd deliver a speech in honour of Australia Day.

Was it a stirring account of our nation's past and glorious future? No. Was it a thoughtful analysis of the Australian character? Only very briefly and in passing. Was it a witty reflection on the nature of anniversaries and celebration? Not at all. Carefully numbering each step as he went, our late PM addressed the challenges Australia faces, the strategic options available and the measures that must be taken. Of these, the measure Rudd saw counting most and the one on which he spent most time was building things. His government, he informed this crowd of notables, was providing a "123 per cent increase in transport infrastructure; $1.5 billion for the Hunter Expressway; $600 million for the Kempsey Bypass; $1.8 billion upgrading the rail networks in the freight system of this state ..."

I regret the departure of Rudd. I swear my Quarterly Essay on Kevin had nothing to do with it. I've reproached very much my friend Annabel Crabb for messaging me in England a fortnight into Julia Gillard's reign: "Come home and kill again." And the succession has not solved the problem that began when the mandate of the outer suburbs passed from Keating to Howard, and from Howard to Rudd. It's the deficit we never address: the eloquence deficit. It is now fourteen long years since we have had a national leader who could crack a joke, illuminate an argument, or move us profoundly.

We are Australians. We are a tolerant people. We are passive. We put up with the vagaries – especially the tedium – of our leaders. Of course, there have been moments. Rudd's Apology counts among the greatest speeches ever delivered in this country. But alas, most of what he went on to say afterwards was so ordinary it brought us back to the long-tolerated status quo: Howard droning on for a decade; Beazley waffling; Crean whining; Latham snarling; and Rudd, well, Rudd a decent man disappearing month by month in a fog of words. His Australia Day address this year was another of his – and I wish I had heard this expression while I was writing my Quarterly Essay – "information dumps".

Rudd was so longwinded he risked becoming the Castro of the South Pacific. With him gone, I judged it safe to return home and arrived last Saturday in time to hear Gillard – fresh from Yarralumla – proclaim twenty-two times in a single speech and eighteen times in the questions that followed that she will keep Australia "moving forward".

Not since the heady days of John Howard's "incentivation" has so much abuse been heaped so immediately on a political slogan. We whose business is words felt the shock particularly personally: could she – a woman of intelligence and cunning, the prime minister of a not particularly backward nation – really be saying this over and over again? "A lump of dead meat", dour old Don Watson called it. "A lump of dead meat ripped straight from the corporate world." He was speaking for us and perhaps millions of Australians when he accused Gillard of treating voters like imbeciles.

Savage commentary back in 1987, savage and immediate, drove "incentivation" into the ground. Howard, a brave man, cut and ran. The word never passed his lips on the hustings. But the abuse of the last week has not deterred Gillard. She is made of sterner – or is it deafer – stuff. I regret to report that today she called her big speech announcing a "citizens assembly" – of all things – to advise on dealing with CO_2 emissions: "Moving forward together on climate change". "Climate change," she began, "is a pivotal issue for Australia. It is fundamental to the question I have put to our people. The question about whether our country moves forward or back."

Is there a writer in this room who would have written that? Is there an editor in this room who would have allowed that to stand? What is it with our leaders and their problem with words?

It pains me further to report that Gillard was not done with the cliché of the month. Having used it in the title, she deployed it in the opening; she scattered it here and there in the body of her speech; and she came back to it, home happy to the cliché at the very end. "If we face up to this challenge, if we work carefully and methodically, and if we give support to Australians to make the changes that are necessary, then I am confident that we can" – let's say it with her – "move forward together."

On a point of balance: Tony, you have to choose. WorkChoices once killed can be buried or it can be cremated. We don't do both. Not bury *and* scatter. Bury *or* scatter. What you really have in mind, I think, going on the rhythm of your sentence, is "hung, drawn and quartered", though I suspect you don't feel as strongly about the evils of WorkChoices as that. You don't think it deserves the most horrible form of execution our culture has yet to devise. What about a compromise, Tony, a compromise that would make dramatic sense: "stake driven through the heart". That would please me enormously: buried at the crossroad with a stake through the heart.

Further on the question of balance: Bob Brown. Darling man. Bob Brown speaks for the trees. If trees could talk they would talk like Bob Brown. When he opens his mouth he is at one with his subject.

Those of us whose business is words have to face the fact that words are failing our politicians. Why? What can we do about it? Gillard is reported as eloquent, persuasive and witty in private. I've seen her tear Abbott apart in Question Time with gorgeously honed abuse. So why does she stand and deliver speeches of terrifying banality? Why can't she talk like an intelligent, living human being? Where has wit gone? Where is nuance? Where is the detail of real life that convinces us out in the audience that she is part of – and understands – our world? What the hell has gone wrong with rhetoric in this country?

Strangely, pollsters never ask: who do you like listening to? Which leader, Gillard or Abbott, can best be trusted with the English language? Would you change your vote if the other side could make you laugh?

Of course, everything is the media's fault, and this is the media's fault too. John Curtin all those years ago could stand on a street corner and woo the crowd unafraid that every word would be picked over by the press, hungry to fill the twenty-four-hour news cycle. Press scrutiny – that great virtue – can be in certain moods an invitation to vice. In honour of Rudd, I will number the vices one, two and three.

Vice number one: we in the press search for inconsistency like sniffer dogs sniffing out salami in the hand luggage of arrivals from Europe. We search for the tiniest inconsistency. Inconsistency is a story. Inconsistency can be a split in the party. Inconsistency can be a U-turn. Inconsistency can be a falling out. Inconsistency can be evidence of a feud. Actually it's usually only a slight inconsistency, but hard pressed you can put an inconsistency story on page one of the paper. You can put it fairly high in a news bulletin. Inconsistency is news.

Vice number two – a more serious vice. We have in this country, as there is in Europe and America, a commentariat ready to pounce on ambiguity, a commentariat that claims the right to hold against politicians what they *might* mean even when it's perfectly clear it's not what they mean. Ambiguity is an invitation to misrepresentation. I'm not going to name names, Piers and Miranda. Nothing will pass my mouth to suggest I have any particular person in mind, Andrew. The misrepresentation of ambiguity is their meat and drink.

Vice number three: plucking out sound bites and making hay with them, perhaps on Fox News. You may have read this morning the story of the high-ranking black American public servant who was fired because of a sound bite the White House feared might make trouble on Fox News, a sound bite in which she confessed to showing a degree of prejudice as a young black woman towards a white farmer. So she was sacked. Once the context was looked at, it was realised she was admitting error, showing what she had learnt from it and indeed had become great friends with the farmer as a result. The farmer came forward to say so. The public servant has not been reinstated. The whole squalid exercise was simply because of the fear that Fox News – but it could have been any other news broadcast – might do the president damage.

Modern political leaders have to armour-plate their rhetoric, so they say absolutely nothing new unless they mean to say something new, to be unambiguous in what they say, and to make what they say safely quotable at any given length. Whether it is paragraph, sentence, clause or phrase, everything must be safely quotable.

How curious it is that the hungry twenty-four-hour news cycle actually broadcasts so little. A whole speech? Forget it. A chunk of a speech? Very, very unlikely. Sound bites. Twenty-four hours of sound bites. Not argument but sound bites. I am hoping the ABC can do better.

So what can we – whose business is words – do about this? I do not have life enough left, or hope enough, to think of changing the media's ways. It is easier to tax BHP or put a price on carbon than to break the habits of News, and Ten, and Sky and Fairfax, and, alas, the ABC.

We could, of course, write as citizens to our politicians in the crispest possible terms: if you continue to bore me and insult me and infuriate me – particularly if you say anything about "moving forward" once more – I will vote for the other side. Make it clear that rhetoric is a vote-changing issue in a literate world.

But I also think it's time that we, whose business is words, took advantage of the hunger for eloquence out there, and formed a political party of our own. Not counting on money power or people power but word power. Let's put this as a basic proposition to the political class of this nation: if you can't handle a sentence you can't run the country. Let's tell Julia and Tony, Kevin and Bob, we ain't going forward, we ain't going back, we ain't going anywhere until you talk to us like human beings.

We have a lot to do this weekend. Tomorrow alone we are solving population policy, grief, survival, cities and global warming. But in the spare time that we have, in the time we talk to one another, we should draft what might be called the Cooroy Declaration, asserting the need for eloquence in public life in this country. I don't know how the declaration would end, but I've had an inspiration for the opening: "In the beginning was the word ..."

Reality Bites Literary Festival, Cooroy, 23 July 2010

MacKillop makes good

LET ME WHISPER THIS from the back of the crowd gathering for the celebrations in Rome: miracles don't happen. Fine as metaphor, rubbish as fact. Say what you like about the qualities of Mother Mary MacKillop, she's not out there somewhere doing magic tricks for the living. Two cancer remissions – one of the blood and one of the lungs – were happy outcomes for the women known only as X and Kathleen Evans, but uncertain proof that the laws of nature can be suspended by relics and prayer. What about a real demonstration of Mary's clout in heaven: keeping the tundra frozen perhaps, reviving the thylacine, or bringing good government to New South Wales?

Rome would ignore them all. Only medical miracles count these days. Pioneering service and/or a messy death once qualified saints to be saints. Even carrying the infant Christ across a river earned St Christopher honours only stripped from him last century. Now all saints must cure. How does heaven keep track as the rules chop and change down here below? As late as 1983, John Paul II was finessing the rules to speed through the Congregation for the Causes of Saints battalions of the blessed. Until then, three miracles were needed. Since then, only two.

The two saints whose feast day falls today would get nowhere even under these relaxed rules: Callixtus I, a third-century Pope killed by a rioting mob, and Justus of Lyon, an early bishop who ended his days as a monk in the deserts of Egypt. Not a single cure between them. Nothing for acne. Nothing for shingles.

Praying for miracles may be worse than a waste of time. Harvard Professor Herbert Benson organised three churches in 2006 to pray in quite precise terms for 1800 coronary artery bypass patients to have "success-ful surgery with a quick, healthy recovery and no complications". By fine margins, those unprayed for fared best. Explanations for this differ. Maybe knowing divine reinforcements are on the way tempts patients to neglect their medication. Richard Dawkins thinks prayer brings not comfort but anxiety: "It seems more probable that those patients who knew they were being prayed for suffered additional stress in consequence: 'performance anxiety', as the experimenters put it." The lesson is: don't pray for your loved ones if you want them to live.

With the bells ringing for MacKillop on every television channel and her face in brown hijab staring from the pages of every newspaper in the land, we miracle sceptics know we are in a minority. Doubt is not mainstream. We know this not by divine reproach but by the findings of last year's faith survey, conducted for the *Sydney Morning Herald* by Nielsen polls. It told us only thirty-eight per cent of Australians believe in hell and only fifty-three per cent in life after death. An even fifty-six per cent believe in heaven but a solid sixty-three per cent in miracles.

We are outnumbered but we know that among our silent minority of riff-raff are citizens of distinction. Over scones and cream on the prime min-ister's plane during the election, I asked if she thought the dead MacKillop can work miracles for us on earth. "I do not," Julia Gillard replied. "Not being a person of faith, I don't believe in miracles, no." But she does believe in saints. How this works has yet to be explained. Perhaps it's a folksy mean-ing of "saint" like Joe Hockey's folksy meaning of "audit".

At the big Mary MacKillop fundraising dinner in August, in the presence of Cardinal George Pell, a sorority of Josephites and Tim Fischer, the Aus-tralian ambassador to the Holy See, our atheist prime minister, sang a hymn to Mary of the Overflow: "This is a saint who rides horseback for days under the searing Australian sun, just to visit a few isolated sisters, who has grit under her fingernails and sweat on her brow? On October 17, Australians of all faiths and backgrounds will therefore have great cause to celebrate the life and legacy of this great Australian pioneer and as we will soon be able to say, this great Australian saint."

Perhaps it's what we've needed all along to become the nation we've never quite felt we are: a saint. A Navy and a Federation aren't enough. A couple of world wars and a sheaf of Nobel Prizes don't quite do the trick. Courtesy of the Pope we now have a special friend in heaven: Australia's

George, our own Joan of Arc, our Wenceslas. After Sunday we will wait for news of hospital queues disappearing and prayers to St Mary leaving nurses with nothing to do. From the church and the cash-strapped governments of Australia will come the one message: pray and keep praying.

The Sydney Morning Herald, 14 October 2010

If at first

DON'T TRUST ANYONE WHO TELLS YOU it was exciting. It was a sad, sad day. The outcome was inevitable. Wreckage is everywhere. A cloud of gloom hangs over the parliament, not least because, after this bloody diversion, it's back to business as usual. Everyone was themselves. One K Rudd (OKR) surged out of the party room after his defeat with a great smile fixed to his face and managed to hold it there for the next couple of hours as he faced first the media and then the parliament.

His followers looked shattered as they walked the green carpet. Chris Bowen had the same stricken face he had the day the High Court destroyed the Malaysia plan. The member for McMahon's reward for backing the wrong horse will no doubt be to wake up in the morning still the minister for immigration.

OKR observed the formalities. We gathered in the party room for him to thank the world for the "great things" achieved in his brief career as foreign affairs minister. As a plus we heard about Australia's contribution to "seed productivity" in Somalia.

On that unhappy stage were all the family OKR could muster. At least that poor kid who stood behind him as he struggled through his resignation speech in 2010 was spared another ordeal. His father explained he was "in the tender care of the Chinese government at Peking University". The jokes were agony. The rhetoric was huge: paths walked, journeys taken, no grudges and no malice. The smile never faltered.

"We will now take our leave," he declared and a mob of photographers scattered the chairs as they walked backwards before him to the door.

Julia Gillard is looking shakier in victory than OKR does in defeat. She is saying good things about him now. She is even saying them in parliament. But OKR paid little attention as he sat in an inconspicuous seat nattering to one of his backers. He was still smiling. There was no sign yet of the basilisk face that glowered across the chamber after his defeat in 2010. So the attention of the parliament drifted back to the main players: to Tony Abbott and the prime minister at each other again, as shrill and tedious as ever.

An odd mix of numerology and psychiatry is being practised in the corridors of parliament to try to answer the big unanswered question: what do thirty-one votes mean to a man of OKR's peculiar disposition? Does that number kill or keep alive his ambitions? Don't trust anyone who says they know. For Abbott the number is the makings of a great new mantra that he rolled out all afternoon: "A third of caucus and a quarter of cabinet." We're going to hear it for the next couple of years: this is the headcount of those who knew their cause was lost but cast their vote against Gillard anyway.

The Sydney Morning Herald, 28 February 2012

Pell's nod

HE IS A BIG OLD MAN. He steps down from the altar carefully, watching his feet. In that huge bulk is at least one new hip and a pacemaker. His heart isn't the best. He leans a little on his crook. Most men of his age would be out of their game by now but, pushing seventy-two, George Pell remains eligible for the highest offices in his church. The Vatican is a gerontocracy and he is still a contender. On the nineteenth Sunday of the year, St Mary's Cathedral is respectably full. These are Pell's people: devout, not grand, some ancient skinny figures in tweed, one or two big hats and many prosperous Vietnamese families. Overhead loom several hundred thousand tonnes of Sydney sandstone, and on this bright morning a power station somewhere up the Hunter is working hard to keep the place lit. The choir is magnificent. It must cost a fortune in conductors and scholarships for schoolboys, but as Pell says, casting a backward glance to his two frugal predecessors: "I am spending for three." Would but that Pell had saved on sculpture. He loves religious statues. The new stuff in St Mary's is heavy and white. Pell is exercising the prerogative of an ecclesiastical prince: art, music and ceremony.

But the tide is going out. How grim it must be for Pell to have spent his whole career watching it recede. He does not chide himself for emptying the pews. Correction is necessary. The pruned tree will grow with renewed vigour. It just hasn't happened yet. Preaching the hard things of Christ makes him a hero on the right flank of the church – in Opus Dei and the Neocatechumenal Way – but all his years as bishop haven't reconciled parish Catholics to his brand of Catholicism. They aren't angry these days. Anger was common when I began writing about Pell over a decade ago, but he's become predictable. Nothing much about him surprises Catholics any-more. They endure Pell. They say: he's Roman and that's the Roman way. Tom Keneally sees it as something deeper than that:

> He has a holding-the-line temperament. Think of those Communists who held on through everything. Some left after the famine or Hungary or Czechoslovakia. Others stayed whatever happened. It's the same in the church: people holding on no matter what. Pell is one of these, a man with a holding-the-line mentality ...

Pell hasn't won over the bishops. Though he has appointed a number, they have still never elected him president of the Australian Bishops Conference. That post once came with the red hat, but not so for Pell.

"A Kyrie" by Orlande de Lassus rolls down the nave as Pell sits in state. He has a heavy cold and clouds of incense set him coughing. Even so, this is as it is meant to be: a mighty sight. Pell on his throne exudes the authority he so often disavows. "I am not the Catholic prime minister of Australia," he assured the Victorian inquiry. "I am not the general manager of Australia ... my authority is limited to my archdiocese." Modesty does not become him. He is not all-powerful but there is no other church figure in this country with anything like his authority and reach. He can call Rome to his aid. He chooses bishops. Through schools, colleges, universities and hospitals he exerts influence way beyond the narrow boundaries of Sydney. He has unique leverage over religious orders, having been given a say in the fate of their valuable properties, now almost empty of monks and nuns. He keeps going for years until he gets his way. He bullies but he can also charm. His sudden acts of generosity can be disarming. Opposition to Pell is possible if kept private, but career-threatening if it spills over into the public arena. He does not hesitate to rebuke big figures in the church who cross him. He writes slashing letters. The wounds he inflicts are deep. When he puts people down, they don't get up again.

Everything that makes him a formidable figure inside the church gives him clout in the secular world. He is good with people of power. They see him as one of them. He is one of the survivors of the Movement still holding to their faith in B.A. Santamaria in the church, trade unions, the opinion pages of *The Australian* and soon, it would seem, The Lodge. He and Tony Abbott have been close for a long time. Abbott is at times embarrassingly sycophantic.

What a strange turn Australian politics has taken: forty years after the DLP collapsed under the weight of its own irrelevance, the Movement will have one man in the Curia and another in Canberra. Pell is about to live the dream of every prince of the church: to be spiritual adviser to a national leader.

The Gospel is read and the cardinal climbs the stairs to deliver his homily. Pell's translation of the mass is being used across the English-speaking world, but words fail him in the pulpit this morning. He can't preach. Reading Pell's sermons and newspaper columns, I was struck by how little they reveal of the man. Despite flashes here and there, his words are so shallow, so impersonal. Spiritual insight is sparse. He is intelligent, has led an extraordinary life and pursued big ambitions. Yet when he speaks there is so little there. The Gospel this morning includes Christ's difficult direction: "Sell your possessions and give to those in need." For a cardinal standing in full rig beneath the spotlights of an immense cathedral, these are challenging words. But he just rambles. At one point, reflecting on popular enthusiasm for the new pope's devotion to the poor, he remarks: "Oddly enough, those clamouring for a more valid expression of poverty are often loudest in their attacks on celibacy – although surely someone who appreciates poverty (and the essential principle behind it) should be deeply sensitive to the value of celibacy."

Celibacy again. What hymns of praise this church has sung to not having sex. No sex is sacred. No sex is an offering to Christ. No sex proves our first love is to God and not one another. No sex releases energy and spirit for the service of man. No sex leaves the heart undivided. No sex makes each priest another Christ called to spiritual paternity through the sacraments. No sex means a life full of friendships. Monks brought Europe out of the Dark Ages by not having sex. Not having sex remains the distinguishing mark of holiness in a deeply sceptical world:

> The sacrifice of celibacy is still the best sign to people generally
> that a man is not a priest out of self-interest, while it also remains
> a potent witness to the reality of life after death where Christ has
> explained there will be no sexual intercourse.

What a relief. No struggle in heaven.

Bach, that great ecumenical spirit, thunders through the cathedral as priests, choir and liturgical extras with banners flying begin slow a procession to the west door. Pell is bringing up the rear. What a strangely ordinary man. His world is the church. People are shadowy. He has the consolations of friendship, music and a good cellar. And he has what inspired him from the start: a place at the highest levels of his church and a voice in the nation. He has power. His mitred head nods politely as he passes.

Quarterly Essay, *The Prince: Faith, Abuse and George Pell*, September 2013

Jobs for the blameless

I HESITATE TO SAY THIS but the prime minister is living in sin. I don't give a damn. Nor do most Australians. But that sort of thing bothers religious leaders. So much that Labor's Human Rights and Anti-Discrimination Bill will renew their authority to bar anyone in Julia Gillard's shoes from a job in any of their schools, hospitals and charities, even those they run with public money. It's a curious spectacle, a prime minister legislating against herself.

Should she wish to work some day as, say, a cleaner in an Anglican hostel, she could solve the problem by marrying. But the woman who will be shepherding the legislation through the Senate really hasn't a hope. The new law will back any faith-based organisation that refuses to hire Penny Wong if having a lesbian on the payroll injures "the religious sensitivities of adherents of that religion".

This is not a summer spoof. Nor is it a distant symbolic issue like gay marriage. This is here and now. The bill is before a Senate inquiry. At present it will leave unprotected a long list of ordinary Australians working or wanting to work with some of the country's biggest employers. Most conservative faiths have most of the following on their lists of the sackable: gays and lesbians, single mothers, adulterers – yes, even adulterers! – bisexuals, transsexuals, the intersex and unmarried couples like Gillard and Tim Mathieson. Zealots call this a necessary exercise of their faith. Only school funding is as heavily defended by bishops, orthodox rabbis and imams as the "freedom" to punish these sinners in the workplace. Struggles over this are subterranean, largely unreported and almost always successful.

The issue spooks politicians. They know even the faithful don't enthusiastically back their leaders on this one. But grappling with bishops and rabbis complaining about threats to religious liberty is about the most unwanted contest that a government can imagine. Plucky little Tasmania stripped religious bodies of the "freedom" to sack sinners from schools, hospitals and charities more than a decade ago and there are no reports from the far side of Bass Strait that their Christian mission has suffered.

Britain tried to do much the same in 2010 and was denounced by Pope Benedict – he claimed the Labour plan "violates natural law" – and wound back by Anglican bishops in the House of Lords. But under British law discrimination was already forbidden when religious bodies were spending public money. Secular function, secular rules.

Not here. Labor has given up on all this without a fight. Other countries and other Australian states have sweated over legal formulae to balance the demands of the faiths and the needs of the vulnerable. But Labor's bill offers the religious open slather. It's a bigots' charter.

Some faiths, denominations and dioceses want nothing to do with these privileges. The Anglican Bishop of Gippsland, John McIntyre, remarked a few years ago when they were being debated in Victoria: "How bizarre that the followers of Jesus Christ would oppose, and ask for exemptions from, a legal instrument that has at its heart a declaration of the dignity and value of every human life and the basic rights of every person."

But that's not how Labor sees it in Canberra. As early as Kevin Rudd's time, religious leaders were reassured they would lose none of their privileges when the Commonwealth tidied up its old anti-discrimination regime and brought gender identity, sexual orientation and same-sex relationships under Canberra's protection for the first time. Labor is insisting on one tiny concession: the faiths will have to accept same-sex couples in retirement villages and nursing homes that have Commonwealth funding. But those same homes and villages will still be able to refuse to employ gays and lesbians to look after them.

It's absurd but it works. The faiths know they have thousands of lesbians, gays, single mothers and the rest on their payroll and know they can't do without them. Catholic and Anglican leaders know that any serious attempt to purge them from their hospitals, schools and charities would see the parishes rise up in revolt. But services can be denied to them, applications rebuffed, promotions blocked and individuals picked off. And because these men and women can be sacked at any time simply for being who they are, they have little to nil job security.

So deals are done by the vulnerable that vary from faith to faith, diocese to diocese and employer to employer to stay on the payrolls. They are expected to shut up, be discreet and hide who they are. The zealots of the faiths see this as God's work, to be done, it seems, with the aid and blessing of the Gillard government.

The Sydney Morning Herald, 14 January 2013

A few sleeps to victory

THIS IS WHAT VICTORY LOOKS LIKE: an exhausted man cuddling puppies and inspecting a guitar factory. There are no more votes to be mopped up. Tony Abbott is going through the motions. As a backdrop for the last press conference of the campaign, he brought the cameras to Melbourne's Box Hill, to Maton Guitars – "handmade for the world stage".

Politicians come here. In the hall of fame that is the Maton foyer there's a snap of John Howard with Lee Kernaghan. It's not a meeting of minds. Joe Hockey finds a poster of The Seekers. "Look, Tony, your favourite band." Hockey plays kid brother. He looks fresh but admits to exhaustion. What does victory feel like? "Climbing Kilimanjaro." The same thing day after day: a long, hard slog to the summit.

Abbott is in the factory talking politics with guitar-makers over the roar of the sanding machines. It's hardly likely Abbott PM will miss the factory visits he has made his trademark. How many hundred has he done denouncing the carbon tax? Today he's not hands-on. They don't let him near the guitars.

His eyes are exhausted. His shoes need a polish. He's so tired he seems to be listening to his own voice as the lines come out of his mouth. He spares us nothing: the waste will end; the boats will stop; the carbon tax will be scrapped. He's word perfect. But for a moment he drops the script. "The great thing about successful prime ministers is that at every stage of their public life they have grown into the role." At the back of his head since he was a schoolboy he has had the idea that power when it comes will transform him.

"If you look at people like John Howard; if you look at people like Bob Hawke – they certainly grew throughout their public life as Opposition leader, as prime minister. Whatever faults and mistakes the pair of them might have made, by the time they were in the prime of their life as prime minister they were different, almost ennobled figures from those they had been quite a few years earlier. That's what high office does. It's a burden but it also does act to bring the best out of the better people who have got those jobs."

What makes next week, let alone next year, so peculiarly hard to predict, is this romantic notion that a better person will emerge once he gets there: a Tony Abbott that resolves the old contradictions between the principled Catholic and the ruthless populist who has got him where he will be tonight. Unlikely as Australians might find the prospect, he sees nobility on offer.

At the Pedigree Pal guide-dog breeding centre on the banks of the Yarra in Kew, Abbott is not welcomed as Opposition leader. Those are the smiles, the turnout of the board plus all staff and a contingent of volunteers, that greet a prime minister. All that's missing is the little flag on the car. "These are all from the one litter, Janice?" asks Abbott, cuddling an eight-week-old labrador pup for the cameras. There is a smell of dog piss in the air. No pups disgrace themselves in the arms of the politicians.

We fly to Richmond, west of Sydney. They are back-burning in the Blue Mountains and a smoky sunset is beginning. On the military tarmac the press contingents pass one another. We're heading for drinks at Panthers Leagues Club. They are off to Brisbane to watch defeat. Slowly through the haze comes Kevin Rudd's car, flag flying and soldiers saluting. The etiquette will be faultless to the end. But the man who clawed his way back to the front seat ten weeks ago has only a few hours left.

The Guardian, 6 September 2013

Back in
Safe Hands

Tony Abbott: freedom rider

IN TODAY'S AUSTRALIA, A YOUNG WOMAN faces jail because word got out that one of Tony Abbott's daughters was given a $60,000 "scholarship" to study at the Whitehouse Institute of Design. This scholarship was never advertised. Students at the college in Sydney had no idea such largesse was available. Disclosure of Frances Abbott's win provoked a two-month investigation by the New South Wales police and a charge of accessing restricted data without authorisation. Penalty: imprisonment for a maximum of two years.

How different it was all those years ago when young Tony won his Rhodes. Now that's a scholarship. The win wasn't a secret. No one faced jail when the news broke. But the young man and the prime minister have this in common: a most uncertain respect for free speech. Abbott made his name at the University of Sydney as one of Bob Santamaria's acolytes working to silence student unions by starving them of funds. The day the Rhodes was announced, in November 1980, he told *The Sydney Morning Herald* that John Kerr, Malcolm Fraser and the uranium industry (he backed them all) were not "legitimate concerns" of student unions. "In my view, vast amounts of student money are being spent on extreme causes."

Abbott never seemed the sort of man who would go out on a limb for liberty. Yet one morning in August 2012 he walked into the Amora Hotel in Sydney and pledged to take up arms in the Freedom Wars. "We are the freedom party," he told an exuberant crowd gathered by the Institute of Public Affairs:

We stand for the freedoms which Australians have a right to expect and which governments have a duty to uphold. We stand for freedom and will be freedom's bulwark against the encroachments of an unworthy and dishonourable government.

No Coalition leader has ever talked freedom as Abbott did that morning. The passion, the rhetoric and the undertakings he gave were new in the politics of this country. He might have been an American on the stump. Angels sang and trumpets sounded. He was promising to do more than stop the boats, axe the tax and end the waste. As prime minister, he would restore our lost freedoms. A new Abbott had appeared from nowhere to join the others who jostle for our attention. Politics Abbott is the one who rules them all. Values Abbott has his commitment to faith and a unique political past. Intellectual Abbott can turn out opinion pieces on anything from reshaping the Federation to the future of marriage. But here on the stage of this big city hotel was Freedom Abbott:

Without free speech, free debate is impossible and, without free debate, the democratic process cannot work properly nor can misgovernment and corruption be fully exposed. Freedom of speech is part of the compact between citizen and society on which democratic government rests. A threat to citizens' freedom of speech is more than an error of political judgement. It reveals a fundamental misunderstanding of the give and take between government and citizen on which a peaceful and harmonious society is based.

Two years later, I sit here writing Freedom Abbott's obituary. I'll honour the biographical form with the story of his rise from nowhere, the hopes he raised in his brief life, his impact on the politics of the nation, and his sudden death in August, in the same week the cops charged the supposed Whitehouse whistleblower. They were rough days for liberty. By the time the prime minister abandoned his crusade to gut the Racial Discrimination Act, promised new powers to ASIO and prepared to store our metadata for the use of intelligence agencies, Freedom Abbott was on the slab.

*

Abbott could always *talk* freedom. It was a topic fit for think tanks: civilised, big-picture, fundamental but tame. He always saw the dangers. They went back to Genesis: "In the Garden of Eden, Adam and Eve could do almost as they pleased. But freedom turned out to have its limits and its abuses, as this foundational story makes only too clear." Cynics might argue the church had to be fought tooth and nail for liberal democracy to emerge. But Abbott has always said we have Christianity to thank for freedom and "the presumption of innocence, universal suffrage, limited government, and religious, cultural and political pluralism". Among today's great defenders of "freedom under law" he lists the Crown and the papacy.

He never thought freedom owed much to the Left. Tom Paine is not among his heroes. No revolution, not even the French, is given credit for liberty's rise. Nor are unions, the labour movement and Marx. He is polite to Americans: he acknowledges the overthrow of George III matters to them, though he's sure it means nothing to us. His praise stops short of the First Amendment. He doesn't gush about the Universal Declaration of Human Rights.

For the past few centuries, freedom has spoken English. True, there were one or two upheavals along the way, but Abbott has always seen peaceful England setting the standard for liberty's rise. He doesn't turn to the great legal theorists to make this point. He quotes Tennyson's lines about

> A land of settled government,
> A land of just and old renown,
> Where Freedom slowly broadens down
> From precedent to precedent.

This is his go-to quote when he talks freedom. He finds these lines pithy and beautiful. He loves to quote them when he's talking liberty to American think tanks. Sometimes he rolls on to the next verse, condemning another England where

> ... banded unions persecute
> Opinions, and induce a time
> When single thought is civil crime,
> And individual freedom mute.

An Oxford man is expected to dish out this sort of stuff. But an Oxford man might also have a closer look at what Tennyson is writing here: a Tory attack on the *Great Reform Act* of 1832 and the political division its passing provoked. His favourite quote on freedom is, in fact, an attack on one of the key, hard-fought victories against aristocratic power in Britain. Perhaps Abbott has no idea of this. Perhaps he's just smitten by the poetry. What's certain is his affection for the idea that liberty evolves naturally over time, dropping gently from the heavens. This is not freedom made by great upheavals or witnessed in declarations. There is nothing hard and fast about it. More than anything, it's a matter of instinct. You know it when you *feel* it.

Abbott was always worried about the need to keep a brake on freedom. It's the lesson of Adam and Eve, the teaching of his faith, and the fear that drove Santamaria's crusade all those years ago in the universities of Australia. The Santa crowd saw themselves as campaigning for order in a world where too much freedom might mean curtains for civilisation. Abbott has grown since then as a man and a politician, but in 2002, as a young minister in Howard's government, troubled by divorce and drugs, he was still lashing out at

> a highly contagious mutant strain of liberalism that can't work out when one person's freedom stops and another's starts, and which feels constrained by the ideal of freedom from discouraging (let alone preventing) self-indulgent, counter-productive and destructive behaviour. The liberal state carries within it the seeds of its own destruction if it is just liberal, if it cannot coerce or even criticise the misuse of freedom.

Abbott believed in a liberty of rules with freedom restrained and protected by the state. He doesn't celebrate free spirits except, rather touchingly, those who ride bikes: "The bike is a freedom machine." And he finds repugnant the idea of having a bill of rights to guarantee our liberties. He is not alone there on either side of the House of Representatives. Politicians look after themselves. Their instincts are finely honed. As Abbott told Laurie Oakes one night in 2008: "The problem with a bill of rights is that it takes power off the elected politicians."

Freedom Abbott was still a few years away. Politics Abbott played a part in his unexpected birth. From the United States, Australian conservatives had imported the strategy of branding their opponents – "liberals" there and "the Left" here – as enemies of freedom. This works better in the United States, where there's a big constituency for the notion that controlling guns, taxing carbon and giving medicine to the poor are a frontal attack on freedom in a nation whose defining purpose is the pursuit of freedom. Here, we hanker as much for fairness as we do liberty. We don't fear government. We're not happy about paying tax but we don't see it as a fundamental assault on freedom.

But Australian commentators took up the drumbeat of Fox News, and Liberal Party leaders began, shyly at first, to present themselves as evangelists for liberty facing the hostility of the Left. "The Left has embraced a new authoritarianism," Brandis declared in April this year, in a ripping interview with the libertarian Brendan O'Neill for the website *Spiked*. "Having abandoned the attempt to control the commanding heights of the economy, they now want to control the commanding heights of opinion, and that is even more dangerous." Brandis invokes the ghosts of Stalin and Pol Pot to press home his attack on the Left. Those with a taste for personal abuse more developed than mine might call this line of argument insane. I call it surprising.

"How can it be," Brandis asked a crowd at the Centre for Independent Studies in August last year, "that at the end of a century that saw the embrace by the authoritarian Left of murder on an industrial scale as a political and ideological method, how can it be that we, on our side of politics, abandoned human rights as a cause to the Left?" His message was: "We have to re-embrace the human rights debate. We have to remind people that we in the Liberal Party are the party of human rights."

More than anything, the Left is charged with smothering dissident voices in the debate over global warming. They treat sceptics with disrespect. Laugh at Lord Monckton. Reserve ABC science shows for scientists. Fail to give dissenters an honoured place on the platform. The exercise of judgement – scientific and editorial – in the debate is condemned as the bullying, authoritarian, anti–free speech behaviour of the Left. When Abbott jumped the ditch in late 2009 to join the sceptics, this became part of his thinking. So too did the American notion that small government equals freedom. He had dismissed the idea earlier that year in his memoir, *Battlelines*, but it began to shape his rhetoric. Replying to Rudd's budget in 2010, the new leader of the Opposition declared: "The Coalition wants lower taxes, smaller government and greater freedom."

And the leap to the sceptics drew him closer to Andrew Bolt. Abbott came to comfort the shattered columnist a few days after the Federal Court's mortifying judgement in the class action brought by nine Aboriginal applicants Bolt had attacked baselessly in the *Herald Sun*. Bolt told John van Tiggelen of *Good Weekend* that his "very influential" guest had "dropped in to urge him to keep going on all fronts. The impromptu dinner guest told him and his wife that his TV show, merely by existing, gave heart to a good many people." Abbott did not defend Bolt's journalism: "The article for which Andrew Bolt was prosecuted under this legislation was almost certainly not his finest." But Abbott called for the gutting of section 18C of the *Racial Discrimination Act*, which penalises speech likely to "offend, insult, intimidate or humiliate" on grounds of race. The court had found that Bolt ticked all four boxes. Free speech advocates, long worried that the act set the bar too low, were calling for "offend" and "insult" to be pruned from the section. Julia Gillard's government was hammered by Abbott for defending 18C as it stood.

Freedom Abbott was conceived in the Culture Wars. He quoted Edmund Burke and John Stuart Mill, and even Voltaire, but his passion for freedom wasn't a thing of abstract philosophy. Abbott was about to do what he did so well as leader of the Opposition: blast the government with whatever was to hand.

Something else was in the air in the days immediately before Freedom Abbott's birth. *The Australian* had received a fresh cache of documents about Bruce Wilson, the crooked former Australian Workers Union official who was once Julia Gillard's lover. Earlier attempts to smear her with Wilson's crimes had damaged Gillard badly. But she fought back hard and saw Bolt silenced, Glenn Milne dumped by *The Australian* and shock jock Michael Smith ousted from Sydney radio station 2UE. Now after a year's lull, the story had returned. It was gold for Abbott, but, inside and outside the government, News Limited was being accused of a vicious beat-up. *The Australian* on Saturday 4 August 2012 had the story everywhere: on page one, "Cops Wanted Gillard's Ex Charged"; on page two: "Coalition Wants Alleged Bagman Investigated"; on page twenty-three, Cut and Paste: "Fifty Shades of Nay, or How the Real Dr No of Politics Keeps Labor from Getting Tied Up"; and on the same page an editorial: "AWU Scandal Questions Linger".

Two days later, Freedom Abbott materialised in the ballroom of the Amora Hotel, electrifying a crowd of 300. His rhetoric was wonderful.

Again and again, he was stopped by applause. He was so forgiving about the press. No journalist could fail to be pleased by his promise to protect speech that wasn't always accurate and wasn't always fair: "The price of free speech ... is that offence will be given, facts will be misrepresented, and sometimes lies will be told. Truth, after all, only emerges from such a process. But thanks to free speech, error can be exposed, corruption revealed, arrogance deflated, mistakes corrected, the right upheld and truth flaunted in the face of power." Then his focus narrowed:

> This is not a government that argues its case. Mostly, it simply howls down its critics using the megaphone of incumbency ... Late last year, Communications Minister Stephen Conroy accused the Sydney *Daily Telegraph* of a deliberate campaign to "bring the government down". The prime minister had a screaming match with former News Limited boss John Hartigan over an article about her prior-to-entering-parliament dealings with a union official ... The prime minister personally insisted that News Limited in Australia had "questions to answer" in the wake of the UK phone-hacking scandal even though she was not able to specify what these might be. It seems obvious that her real concern was not Fleet Street–style illegality but News Limited's coverage of her government and its various broken promises, new taxes and botched program.

News Limited was facing a distant threat on another flank. The former Federal Court judge Ray Finkelstein had delivered his report on media regulation. Controversy had been raging for months. All the proprietors were furious, but at the Amora Hotel Abbott leapt only to the defence of News Limited, claiming Finkelstein's proposed News Media Council "looks like an attempt to warn off News Limited from pursuing anti-government stories".

Freedom Abbott drew his first breaths speaking the language of a News Limited executive. Hardly anyone noticed at the time. Abbott's commitment to fight the Freedom Wars made the headlines. He nominated Brandis as his consigliore in the Coalition campaign for liberty. An agenda of sorts emerged: 18C would be slashed, anti-discrimination laws wound back and a "freedom audit" conducted of all Commonwealth laws to identify those that violated traditional rights and freedoms. Asked if he had what it took to achieve these reforms, Brandis replied: "I was born for it."

Abbott's calls for fresh candour and vigour in public debate were pitch perfect. The week before polling day he told *The Australian*:

> Any suggestion you can have free speech as long as it doesn't hurt people's feelings is ridiculous. If we are going to be a robust democracy, if we are going to be a strong civil society, if we are going to maintain that great spirit of inquiry, which is the spark that has made our civilisation so strong, then we've got to allow people to say things that are unsayable in polite company. We've got to allow people to think things that are unthinkable in polite company and take their chances in open debate.

Australians frustrated by Canberra's old indifference to liberty could cast their vote on 7 September 2013 with reason to hope. Even on the Left there were signs of goodwill. Think tanks were cautiously delighted. But on victory night, something odd happened. I was there at the Four Seasons Hotel in Sydney in a throng of excited Liberals, drooling lobbyists and exhausted journalists. Flanked by his wife and daughters, the new prime minister declared Australia open for business. All the old mantras about boats and waste and carbon tax had a run, but there wasn't a word about liberty. Freedom Abbott didn't show.

*

The swearing in of a cabinet was once a silent show except for the muttering of oaths. Now there are speeches. In the drawing room of Yarralumla with his cabinet duly sworn, Tony Abbott faced Quentin Bryce. He told Her Excellency: "We hope to be judged by what we have done rather than by what we have said we would do." Fair enough.

10 October 2013: The state and territory attorneys-general meet in Sydney without discussing shield laws. The issue was on the agenda. With the change of government it vanished. It hasn't appeared since. Efforts begun under Gillard to introduce uniform national laws to give effective protection to journalists and their sources have ceased.

25 October: Scott Morrison first utters the phrase "on water operations" to justify the unprecedented secrecy that surrounds the Abbott government's blockade of refugee boats. Morrison whittles away the few rights and freedoms left to those caught up in Operation Sovereign Borders.

2 December: Brandis authorises an ASIO raid on the Canberra office of Bernard Collaery, the lawyer representing East Timor in its dispute with Australia over the Timor Sea Treaty. In March this year, the International Court of Justice at The Hague orders Australia to seal the material seized and keep it from all officials involved in the dispute. The order is binding.

3 December: Abbott rages against the ABC and the "left-wing" *Guardian* for together reporting that Australian spy agencies had targeted the phones of Indonesian president Susilo Bambang Yudhoyono and his wife. "The ABC seemed to delight in broadcasting allegations by a traitor," he later told Ray Hadley of the Sydney radio station 2GB. "This gentleman Snowden, or this individual Snowden, who has betrayed his country and in the process has badly, badly damaged other countries that are friends of the United States, and of course the ABC, didn't just report what he said, they took the lead in advertising what he said."

11 December: Brandis announces terms of reference for the Australian Law Reform Commission's audit of Commonwealth laws that compromise freedom. The terms' focus is not individual liberty but "commercial and corporate regulation; environmental regulation; and workplace relations". Free speech barely makes the list. Brandis tells the *Australian Financial Review* he is most perturbed by the "reversal of the onus of proof, the creation of strict liability offences, the removal of lawyer–client privilege and removal of rights against self-incrimination". It reads like a list of everything tax evaders loathe about the law.

17 December: Brandis appoints the policy director of the IPA, Tim Wilson, to the Australian Human Rights Commission. Wilson's mission is to restore balance to a body which the attorney-general believes "has become increasingly narrow and selective in its view of human rights" under Labor. This is code for the culture-war complaint that the Left is manipulating anti-discrimination laws to impose its moral agenda on a reluctant society. The Bolt case is a particular focus of the fear that protecting blacks, poofs, foreigners and cripples from discrimination is stripping the rest of us of our freedom.

29 January 2014: Abbott blasts the ABC for reporting claims that Australian military personnel have punished asylum seekers by burning their hands. "I think it dismays Australians when the national broadcaster appears to take everyone's side but our own," says the prime minister. "You shouldn't leap to be critical of your own country." News Limited joins the attack. The

ABC falters. Its managing director, Mark Scott, apologises for imprecise wording in the original report, but three days later, Fairfax's man in Indonesia, Michael Bachelard, finds asylum seeker Yousif Ibrahim Fasher: "He says he has no doubt that what he saw at close quarters on about January 3 was three people's hands being deliberately held to a hot exhaust pipe by Australian naval personnel to punish them for protesting, and to deter others from doing one simple thing: going to the toilet too often."

6 March: Abbott threatens to cut the ABC's budget if it doesn't cave in to Chris Kenny. The Chaser team had crudely photoshopped the head of the News Limited pundit onto a man with his pants down mounting a labradoodle. Kenny sued for $90,000. Missing in action is Abbott's defence of lively debate where "offence will be given, facts will be misrepresented". He tells 2GB's Ben Fordham the ABC should settle the case or else: "Government money should be spent sensibly and defending the indefensible is not a very good way to spend government money. Next time the ABC comes to the government looking for more money, this is the kind of thing that we would want to ask questions about." The ABC buckles. Kenny gets an apology and cash.

13 March: Brandis decrees artists who refuse private sponsorship on political grounds may be stripped of public funding. Troubled by Transfield's links to offshore detention centres, a handful of artists had pressured the company to withdraw sponsorship from the Sydney Biennale. Brandis asks: "If the Sydney Biennale doesn't need Transfield's money, why should they be asking for ours?" He directs the Australia Council to find a formula for deciding when public funding will be withdrawn because private sponsorship has been "unreasonably" rejected. He does not rule out compelling arts organisations to take tobacco money. Months later, the council is still labouring over the words. However it's done, Brandis wants artists to know they will pay a price for embarrassing the government. This threatens direct political intervention for the first time in the allocation of Australia Council funds.

24 March: Brandis tells Senator Nova Peris: "People do have a right to be bigots, you know." The next day, he releases draft legislation to gut sections 18C and 18D of the *Racial Discrimination Act*. Abbott backs him. The proposal – drafted by Brandis himself – would allow almost unrestrained racist abuse in the name of freedom. Ethnic community leaders lobby for the act to be left as it is. Polls swiftly show nine out of ten Australians disapprove of the changes. Three-quarters of the 4100 submissions received by Brandis' department are hostile. The department blocks their release.

23 May: Morrison strips the Refugee Council of Australia of half a million dollars allocated in the budget only ten days before. The minister explains: "It's not my view, or the government's view, that taxpayer funding should be there for what is effectively an advocacy group." The CEO of the council, Paul Power, calls the cuts petty and vindictive. "This in many ways illustrates the state of the relationship between the non-government sector – particularly organisations working on asylum issues – and the government at the moment."

1 July: Community legal centres across Australia are also forbidden to use Commonwealth money for advocacy or to campaign for law reform. During the Labor years, funding for NGOs had come with the guarantee that they were free "to enter into public debate or criticism of the Commonwealth, its agencies, employees, servants or agents". Under Abbott, the guarantee disappears. So do many sources of independent advice. The budgets of the National Aboriginal and Torres Strait Islander Legal Service, the Environmental Defender's Offices and the National Congress of Australia's First Peoples are slashed. Axed are the Social Inclusion Board, the National Housing Supply Council, the National Policy Commission on Indigenous Housing, the National Children and Family Roundtable, the Advisory Panel on Positive Ageing, and the committee of independent medicos advising the refugee detention network, the Immigration Health Advisory Group.

16 July: Brandis threatens laws to double the sentence for reporting "special intelligence operations" by ASIO. Whistleblowers would not be protected, and journalists would not even need to know the operations were "special" to find themselves in prison for up to a decade. No public interest defence would be available. The shadow attorney-general, Mark Dreyfus, says: "We will not tolerate legislation which exposes journalists to criminal sanction for doing their important work, work that is vital to upholding the public's right to know."

4 August: Twenty-two-year-old student Freya Newman, a former part-time librarian at the Whitehouse Institute of Design, is charged with unauthorised access to restricted data following reports of Frances Abbott's scholarship, after complaints to the police by the institute. The chair of the institute is Liberal Party donor and friend of the prime minister Les Taylor.

5 August: Abbott announces the metadata of all Australians is to be kept by internet service providers for two years and made available to ASIO and police. That trawl will, of course, include the metadata of whistleblowers and journalists. He abandons at the same time his two-year crusade to amend the *Racial Discrimination Act*. Both moves he justifies in the light of terrorist outrages by Australian nationals in Syria. "When it comes to counterterrorism, everyone needs to be part of 'Team Australia'," he says, "and I have to say that the government's proposals to change 18C of the *Racial Discrimination Act* have become a complication in that respect. I don't want to do anything that puts our national unity at risk at this time, and so those proposals are now off the table."

Muslims were furious. Every ethnic community in Australia had put up their hand to protest, but Abbott had used the Muslims to cover his retreat. Tabloid pundits rammed the message home. It didn't help that depraved clowns with Australian passports were cutting off heads for the caliphate. Bolt blamed the Jews, the Muslims and, most of all, politicians who caved in to Muslim constituents:

> Pardon? We must placate Muslim Australians by restricting our freedom to say something critical of their culture, for example, extremists being so prone to jihad? Of course other ethnic and religious groups – not least Jews – also fought to save these restrictions. But make no mistake: muzzling Australians is now seen as necessary to please migrant communities ... politicians are now so desperate for these blocs of ethnic votes that they sacrifice Australian values to accommodate imported ones.

*

Freedom Abbott had outlived his purpose. He was useful in Opposition. That's when phony contests like the Culture Wars can wreak havoc on your opponents. But to keep the banner of freedom flying in office was always going to be hard. No Australian government has ever managed the feat. And Abbott is proving no political pioneer. Nothing done in his first year advances the cause he championed in Opposition. His rhetoric has proved threadbare. Poor old Values Abbott died on budget night when an ordinary Liberal Party agenda was served up to the nation. A couple of months later,

Freedom Abbott followed him to the grave.

The IPA marked the burial with a brutal full-page ad in *The Australian*. "Freedom of speech is an essential foundation of democracy," said Abbott across the top of the page. Across the bottom the IPA replied: "We agree, Prime Minister. That's why we will fight to repeal section 18C of the *Racial Discrimination Act*. Even if you won't." John Roskam, the executive director of the IPA, spoke of a party base betrayed and Australians left "sad, angry, disappointed and worried" by Abbott.

The death wrecked Tim Wilson's Free Speech 2014 symposium. Gathered in Sydney that week by the new human rights commissioner were figures from the Left, Right and Centre, a peace council of the factions called to explore the great prospects for liberty under an Abbott government. But the day was a wake, with the same coffee and smoked salmon that come with a funeral – and the same gloom. The attorney-general, George Brandis, found another funeral to go to at the last minute. It wasn't brave, but what could he have said to us?

Wilson, left with no agenda, announced he was setting off on a "Rights and Responsibilities" tour of the nation to hear what we have on our minds. He will likely discover nothing new. Our worries don't change much with time: the fate of the ABC under Coalition governments; the expanding reach of intelligence agencies; heavy-handed film censorship; feeble protection for whistleblowers and journalists; punitive laws against demonstrators; attacks on freedom of association; and the old bugbear of defamation. Nothing stifles public debate in this country as much as the fear of being sued for defamation. But a smart guy like Wilson knows even before he sets out that the Human Rights Commission can't fix much on that list. Almost all our worries are matters of state law. In July, the retiring disability discrimination commissioner, Graeme Innes, told the National Press Club: "The best way, frankly, for the attorney to provide the commission with the greater capacity to deal with the freedoms he talks about would be to put forward legislation for a charter of rights."

And Abbott? Abandoning his freedom crusade has left him a diminished figure: not a pioneer of liberty in anyone's eyes, just a blowhard on the campaign trail. The promises of freedom join all the other broken promises. Under Abbott no laws limiting freedom have changed for the better. Movement has all been the other way. The Coalition is running on instinct. We are back where we were under Howard. Freedom counts for little in political contest in this country. The only Abbott that matters, Politics Abbott, soldiers on. He has not lost his faith in himself. Astride the grave of Freedom Abbott in early August, as he ramped up ASIO's powers and ditched his libertarian ambitions for 18C, he was still declaring: "I'm a passionate supporter of free speech."

The John Button Lecture, July 2014, and The Monthly, September 2014

Freya Newman pleaded guilty to accessing restricted data. The prosecution urged she be jailed. The magistrate released her on a two-year good behaviour bond: "I accept that Ms Newman was motivated by a sense of injustice rather than a desire for personal notoriety, greed or any desire to embarrass the student."

Slamming the door

THE BIG NEWS FOR SCOTT MORRISON and his military sidekick, Lieutenant General Angus Campbell, at Friday's Operation Sovereign Borders press briefing was the arrival of the monsoon.

The two would say nothing about reports that Indonesia is emptying its refugee camps; nothing about the Australian Navy apparently withdrawing from waters north of Christmas Island; and little about yet another series of damning reports from the United Nations High Commissioner for Refugees. The dozen or so journalists who had managed to scramble to the press conference were treated instead to grim warnings from both about the hazards of the monsoon and a little slideshow of boats with useful captions: "A crowded vessel listing in large swells."

You doubt Campbell will look back on this operation with pride. As Morrison blathered on about the failings of Labor, the general stood resolutely still. He licked his lips. He sniffed. He held what seemed a steady focus on the exit sign above our heads. Then his turn came and he had nothing to say that Morrison could not have said. Nothing. He announced this week's modest arrival figures – "nine illegal maritime arrivals and two crew from one suspect illegal entry vessel" – and the dangers of the looming monsoon. He refused to say anything about military operations or other "on-water matters".

Campbell's function at these encounters is to give military authority to a political determination to keep the operation against the boats as secret as possible. Poor bastard: he's a stage prop.

Half an hour's notice was given of the city and time of Friday's press conference. That's how Morrison operates: everything except the day of the week is a mystery until the last minute. Were we at war with Indonesia the drama and secrecy might make sense. Journalists assume Morrison is simply trying to shelter from the Canberra press gallery and the heavyweights of television current affairs. "That's rubbish," he declared when *The Guardian* raised the point. That there was even less notice than usual this time he put down to the rush of events: "There is quite a lot on today."

Morrison is more polite than he was in the early weeks of Operation Sovereign Borders. Complaints of arrogance appear to have been heeded. Perhaps he is also growing more secure in the business of stonewalling. Indeed, he's almost soothing. Colourlessness is becoming his camouflage. Morrison is as grey as Philip Ruddock, his great predecessor in the cruel business of stopping the boats.

He projected at the microphone in that flag-draped room a weary understanding that the press will keep on asking these questions until they get the message and, maybe, find something else to write about. His blocking is dogged rather than clever: in these "sensitive times" he will not give "details of operations" or "comment" or "speculate" on reports or say anything that will not "assist" the success of this "very challenging process". So he says virtually nothing.

The Guardian asked Morrison once again to identify the law refugees are supposed to be breaking by coming to Australia by boat. If they are here illegally, why no prosecutions? Morrison hazarded a guess that it was section 4 of the Migration Act. No, minister, that sets out the general objectives of Australia's visa regime and doesn't use the tainted language of illegality.

He was generous with his time. He usually rations his dealings with the press to thirty minutes a week. But he gave us a few minutes more before disappearing down the glass shafts of the snazzy new building in Sydney to which federal politicians have recently removed themselves. Next week it will all not happen again. This might be a government which, according to the attorney-general, George Brandis, has freedom of speech at its heart. But the right to know, it seems, is something else.

The Guardian, 29 November 2013

Faction man

THEY FOUND GREG WILTON DEAD in his car at 9 am on a remote road in the bush. The Commodore was running. Its lights were on. After a terrible couple of months, the Labor member for Isaacs had killed himself. His marriage collapsed when he was sprung having an affair in Canberra. Weeks later, he was disturbed in another stretch of Victorian bush with his kids in the car, rigging a hose to the exhaust. Police were considering charges. It was all over the papers. He checked himself into a psychiatric hospital in Geelong, but left to live with his sister. She insists the last straw was an article in the *Herald Sun* reporting the manoeuvres already underway in his faction to dump him: "And the last words that Greg said ... were about his so-called mates in the ALP desperately trying to take his job off him." Wilton drove alone into the Yarra Ranges, found a spot on the Tea Tree Track and reconnected the hose. This time it worked.

After a day of tearful condolence speeches in Canberra celebrating Wilton's knockabout virtues and the perils of public life, factional warfare erupted in Victoria. They do politics differently there. Wars are fought in the name of peace. Explosives are packed under the foundations of the Labor Party in the name of stability. They call the wreckage left after these brawls rejuvenation. The wonder is that Victoria delivers any Labor talent to Canberra and remains, decade after decade, a stronghold of the party. Long before Wilton's death in the winter of 2000, the factions had ceased fighting over policy. All that was at stake in the conflicts that had shaken the party for over a decade were places in parliament. In no other party and no other state has so much political blood been spilt for half a metre of leather.

Unexpected preselection contests are the most vicious. The conflict is swift and brutal. In caucus, Stephen Conroy was blamed for planting the *Herald Sun* story to promote the candidate he, Shorten and Feeney wanted for Isaacs. Conroy denied the charge. "How low can these animals go?" Mark Latham wrote in his diary the day of Wilton's funeral. "Hounding a bloke already in deep shit."

Bill Shorten didn't invent the system. He mastered it. In the early years of the new century he came to learn everything he needed to know about courtship and betrayal, deals and numbers, to make him a power in the factions. If he were ever to become Labor leader, he had to turn the machinery to his advantage. The war in the Right that began over Isaacs would see the factions in Victoria splinter; put the careers of Steve Bracks and Kim Beazley into play; distract Labor in two federal campaigns; and end with Shorten's translation to Canberra. It was tough. He suffered at this time some of the few setbacks of his career. But these were the years in which he consolidated his authority in Victoria and the party beyond. The player became the master of the factions. He still is.

A little history: first there was the Split and then the Intervention. "It was the beginning of a golden age for Labor in Victoria," recalls Race Mathews, now retired to his books in a house by the Yarra. "Those were good years to be in the party if you were serious about politics. Victoria leaned more left than the rest of Australia, but the Left had no hegemony. It was a very lively and interesting party where the grassroots mattered, where there were spirited debates in the branches and party conferences." But the new rules that came with Whitlam's intervention in 1970 had a downside: "The formation of the factions."

Officially there were three in Victoria: Labor Unity on the Right, the Independents in the middle and the old trade union push rebranded the Socialist Left. The labels are confusing: Labor Unity was a byword for bitter division, and the Socialist Left had abandoned socialism and its old dream of bringing down capitalism. Those dreams had lingered into the 1980s, when Hawke compelled Labor in Victoria to allow the return of the big unions that departed with the Split. Their arrival at the 1985 state conference of the party at Coburg Town Hall, with the president of the Musicians Union up in the gallery playing the last post on his clarinet, was a magnificent occasion: "As right-wing delegates arrived at the conference they were met by screaming abuse, jostled, punched and pelted with tomatoes. The brawling continued into the conference hall with some delegates scuffling on the floor and tomatoes being hurled across the room ... scuffles, screaming and tomato throwing continued as party officials struggled to maintain order."

That was the year young Bill Shorten joined the party. With rank-and-file membership falling away, the manoeuvres of the factions were becoming more urgent. Rules introduced to bring democracy to the party were being gamed expertly by both sides. Branch stacking was rife through the Labor suburbs. The Svengali of the Right was portly senator Robert Ray, whose chief lieutenant was Stephen Conroy. Andrew Clark wrote of Conroy in the Australian *Financial Review*: "He quickly honed the skills required in the brutal world of factional politics: recruiting new faction-friendly members in key branches, cutting deals across factional lines, flattering waverers, shoring up allies and intimidating enemies."

The bonding of Conroy and Shorten in the 1990s had shifted the plates under Victorian politics. Together with David Feeney, by this time state secretary of the party, and Richard Marles, who had become ACTU assistant secretary, the men formed a new subfaction called the ShortCons. It has had – and continues to have – a big impact on national politics. In the late 1990s, this band of brothers set about winning a cut of the spoils in Victoria at the expense of the smooth old warrior who ran Labor Unity for years. The struggle between Greg Sword and the ShortCons broke into open warfare when a candidate had to be found to replace poor Greg Wilton in Isaacs.

Sword was boss of the National Union of Workers. He was the great pioneer of fundraising from employers. The NUW was cashed up and well organised. It had clout. "They were the industrial pack leaders," says Shorten. That was until he came along. The rivalry of the leaders was intense. Some speak of hatred between them. According to the press at the time, when Sword found the ShortCons pushing their own candidate for Isaacs, he threatened to have Feeney sacked. Sword is said to have told Conroy: "If the NUW is going to be fucked over, if there is going to be a war between us, then David will be the first casualty."

The ShortCons blinked. They agreed to back Sword's candidate. But so public had this stoush become that the national executive of the party intervened and Isaacs was given to a local woman with no factional backing, Ann Corcoran. Hers was to be a short career in Canberra.

Power in Victoria meant finding allies on the other side of the aisle. Unlikely alliances were key to the mastery of the factions. Shorten was courting the "new militants" of the union movement, led by a rabble-rouser called Craig Johnston, whose specialty was leading raiding parties of bala-clava-clad unionists through factories and offices. In Bendigo one of these "run-throughs" saw the tires of every car in the factory carpark slashed. At Skilled Engineering in Box Hill in the winter of 2001, Johnston's AMWU (Australian Manufacturing Workers Union) mob broke through the front door with a crowbar, smashed computers, tore pictures from the walls, let off fire extinguishers and terrified the staff. With national elections only months away, Labor leader Kim Beazley was deeply embarrassed by this outbreak of union thuggery.

But when the law threatened, Shorten went into bat for Johnston, join-ing delegations to plead on his behalf to Bracks and the ACTU secretary, Greg Combet. They were ignored. At an ACTU event in June, Shorten manoeuvred Johnston and a group of "new militants" into a photograph with Beazley. He and Combet were furious, fearing the photo-graph would be used as a bargaining chip to compel their support for Johnston, who was charged, a couple of days later, with riot, affray, criminal damage and aggra-vated burglary. At this, Shorten backed off, apologised to Beazley and lent his support to calls for a new code of conduct on picket lines. He declared: "We recognise unions need to be strong and militant at times and vigor-ous on picket lines but not violent and not unlawful." *The Age* mocked the idea of a code. What might it say? "How about simply: 'Keep the peace?'"

Sword, determined to block what seemed Shorten's inevitable rise to the state presidency of the party in June 2002, pulled off a daring factional play. He took the NUW out of Labor Unity and into a pact with the Social-ist Left. Driven by little more than Sword's hatred of the ShortCons, this "modernisation alliance" gave the Left mastery over the Victorian party for the first time in a decade. Vengeance was in the air: Feeney was sacked as state secretary; Marles lost preselection for the seat of Corio; and Shorten lost the race for the state presidency. For the first and one of the last times in his rise to power, Bill Shorten hit a wall. His rivals derided him as "Bye Bye Bill". A union insider calling himself Delia Delegate observed in *Crikey*: "His flag is barely still flying, riddled with bullet-holes and mud and blood. His friends say he regrets ever running for President, suspecting that his overreaching may have triggered the whole split of the Right."

In Canberra, which for Victorian purposes might be called the outside world, Beazley had been toppled after his crushing defeat in the *Tampa* election. Simon Crean failed to inspire excitement as leader of the Opposition. In December 2003, Shorten backed the transition to Mark Latham. "When I first became leader, Ludwig and Little Billy Shorten pledged AWU support for me," Latham wrote in his diary six months later. "But you can't trust them as far as you can kick them." Nevertheless, Latham was guest of honour at the 2004 annual AWU shindig at Crown Casino and sat on Shorten's left. Latham was surprised to find the union leader urging him to support the free trade agreement being negotiated by the Howard government:

> I said that I thought both he and his union were against it, to which he responded, "That's just for the members. We need to say that sort of thing when they reckon their jobs are under threat. I want it to go through. The US Alliance is too important to do otherwise. Politically, you have no choice." Great, the two faces of Little Billy Shorten: Public Shorten against the FTA, Private Billy in favour of it. Is this why he's being groomed for one of the top slots in the corporation? Political courage is not his long suit. Not a bad night otherwise.

After Labor's next beating in October 2004, Shorten published a hard critique of Latham's policies and campaign. It was a bold move. By this time, he had been elected to the party's national executive. Even so, he had no official imprimatur to launch this attack. From one defeat to the next, his message had not changed: "Labor's task now is to move to the centre ..." A few weeks later, in January 2005, Latham was gone and Shorten took a leading role in restoring Beazley to the party leadership.

Victoria was again in turmoil, but this time Shorten was riding triumphantly above the confusion. He had pulled off the greatest factional coup of his career. It had taken time, patience and perseverance, but the impact on Labor would be profound. First, Sword fell. The old leader had made the mistake of surrounding himself with young people of talent and ambition while maintaining an iron grip on the union. His protégés came for him in early 2004. Over lunch in a North Melbourne bistro they told Sword his was "a magnificent achievement", but it was time to go. He did so with great dignity. The man who took his place as Victorian secretary of the NUW was a Young Labor sparring partner of Shorten's, Martin Pakula. Public assurances were given that the NUW's "modernisation alliance" with the Left was there to stay. But Shorten and the hirsute Pakula began to talk. They talked all year. In late November, Pakula brought the NUW back into Labor Unity. They called the new alliance Renewal. The deal was done in writing: a peace treaty between warring unions that restored the old order in Victorian Labor and handed power to the ShortCons.

For these faction warriors, this was a career-defining achievement. Renewal controlled about fifty-six per cent of the numbers in the Victorian branch. The state conference in May 2005 was as vitriolic as anyone could remember as the Left confronted the reality of Shorten's pact with Pakula. There was a Christmas tree of preselection deals all the way down to little local councils on the fringes of Melbourne. Six members of federal parliament – three of them Opposition frontbenchers – were to be ousted simultaneously. Shorten was promised Maribyrnong.

The party machine is not entirely blind to talent. It can't be. The factions don't guarantee the best people win seats – far from it – but the machine knows talent is survival. Among the time-servers, the burnt-out hacks and the sons of Labor fathers sorted into the parliaments of the nation, there has to be some talent or the party will never see power. As Melbourne was distracted by the Commonwealth Games in early 2006, a new Labor team of promise was selected for Canberra. The Renewal pact took some knocks. Three of the six designated victims managed to survive. But what Shorten was promised, he secured. Shorten emerged triumphant.

Quarterly Essay, *Faction Man: Bill Shorten's Path to Power*, September 2015

Behind closed doors
in St Kilda

RABBI YITZCHOK GRONER DIED JUST IN TIME. He was a dominating figure in Melbourne's Jewish world, a mountain of a man with inexhaustible energy, deep religious learning and a stare that stopped grown men in their tracks. As the Melbourne emissary of the Chabad-Lubavitch leader Rabbi Menachem Mendel Schneerson, Groner's authority was absolute. He spent fifty years building the Yeshivah sect into a wealthy, powerful and very private community of several hundred families living around a busy synagogue and thriving schools at a campus on Hotham Street, East St Kilda.

Yeshivah is ultra Orthodox: fundamentalist, intellectual and charismatic. God created the world in six days. Families are big. Sex is never discussed. Modesty is everything. Men and women mark their days with prayer and ritual. Instead of dying in the face of the modern world, old-fashioned, rule-bound Chabad-Lubavitch Judaism flourished.

Groner died in the winter of 2008, but his power didn't die with him. To question his authority – indeed his saintliness – after his death was considered a particularly grave sin among the Chabad. Protecting his memory were the rabbis he had trained and sent out into the wider Jewish world, and the interlocking mesh of Chabad families that seemed to make everyone at Yeshivah the son-in-law, nephew or sister of everyone else.

A couple of months after Groner's death, news broke that David Kramer had been sentenced to seven years in prison in St Louis, Missouri, for molesting children at a youth camp where he was supposed to be teaching "hot topics for Jewish teens". The story died in Australia for the time being, but from this point, a number of Chabad leaders, teachers and parents knew an appalling scandal threatened Yeshivah. Kramer had taught at the Yeshivah primary school in late 1989. The young American rabbi was immediately popular and immediately began molesting children. The number of his victims is not known – perhaps dozens – including two of the sons of Zephaniah Waks.

So begins a story that would see the torment of Chabad rabbis streamed live to the world as the Royal Commission into Institutional Responses to Child Sexual Abuse probed the city's secretive and powerful Yeshivah community. Orthodox Judaism has never been exposed to such public scrutiny. The cast is Jewish, yet the bones of this story are familiar to anyone who has followed the scandal of child abuse in Christian schools and parishes. This story is about the dangers in any faith of blind obedience to holy men.

Waks was a most unwise man to cross. The Waks name is all through this story. Tenacity runs in the family. Half measures aren't in their DNA. Their sense of right and wrong is strong and personal. As the father of seventeen children, Zephaniah Waks had more than proved his dedication to Chabad. But in the end those children would mean more to him than any obligations to the sect.

Waks discovered the abuse in 1992. He says he complained to the principal of the Yeshivah school, Rabbi Abraham Glick. Within hours, Waks learnt that Kramer had admitted the abuse. When he wasn't fired, Waks says, he confronted Glick again, only to be told: "There is a danger of self-harm. So we can't fire him." Glick doesn't deny learning about Kramer at this point, but can't recall discussing the teacher's fate with Waks. He told the royal commission: "I think he had that conversation or a similar conversation most probably with someone else."

Waks was outraged by the failure to act. He didn't call the police because at this time he had no doubt that doing so "would be in breach of the Jewish principle of *mesirah*". This ancient rule, still alive among the followers of many faiths including Judaism, threatens believers with expulsion if they take crimes within the faith to the civil authorities. Waks called a meeting of parents hoping to pressure the school to sack Kramer. Hours before it was due to begin, he was told Kramer had been dismissed. What he did not discover until years later was that Groner had given Kramer an air ticket to Israel, on condition he leave Australia immediately.

Another threat was looming at Yeshivah in those weeks. Police had discovered another paedophile active on the campus, a man whose abuse of Chabad children Groner appears to have known about for nearly a decade.

David Cyprys had been to school at St Kilda and never left. He hung around Yeshivah in various guises: as a helper at youth camps, security guard, locksmith and martial arts instructor. He had keys to the ritual bath, the *mikveh*, where he abused boys. He abused them in one-on-one kung fu lessons. He abused them at youth camps. He raped them at his house.

The earliest known complaint about Cyprys was in 1984. One victim and the father of another complained to the head of Chabad Youth. The father also confronted Groner, who promised to look after the matter and assured him his son was so young he wouldn't need counselling. Years later the father would give evidence that from that time he didn't hear another word from Groner. Complaints about Cyprys kept coming. In 1986 Groner told a thirty-year-old mother whose son was being abused: "Oh, no, I thought we cured him." She trusted the rabbi's assurances that all would now be well. A long time later she discovered the abuse of her son continued for another two years.

At the start of the summer holidays in late 1990, a scholarship boy with ambitions to be a rabbi arrived at St Kilda from interstate. He was fifteen and very vulnerable. His mother was dying of leukaemia. There was no father in his life. This lonely kid, known at the royal commission as AVR, welcomed attention from Cyprys. "I thought he was a really cool guy," he said. "He seemed genuinely interested in me."

Cyprys repeatedly abused the boy for nine months. Found crying one day in the playground, AVR was taken home by a kindly family. His mother flew immediately to Melbourne. The boy told her something of the abuse but couldn't mention the rapes. "She was quite sick and I thought that would push her over the edge." She rang Groner. AVR remembers them seeing the headmaster, Glick, next day and also telling him about Cyprys. But Glick would assure the royal commission he had no memory of the boy at the school at all; no memory of this exchange with him and his mother; and no knowledge of the allegations against Cyprys for something like a decade.

AVR was expelled from the school that day. "They did not want me there any more," he told the commission. "They did not offer to help me or provide me with any counselling. From the time of the disclosure, no one associated with Yeshivah would speak to us or help us. Even our family members would not help us and we had a lot of trouble getting back to the airport and getting home." AVR and his mother went to the police. The case was looming over the St Kilda community as Kramer was given his air ticket to Israel.

Cyprys was charged only with indecent assault, for the boy was still unable to talk about the rapes. Cyprys pleaded guilty in September 1992 and was fined $1,500. No conviction was recorded. Newspapers carried no reports of the case. Cyprys returned to his old stamping ground and his old ways.

*

In 1996, Zephaniah Waks was appalled to discover another of his sons had been abused. Back from Israel for his sister's wedding, Manny Waks had heard about Operation Paradox, the hotline for abuse victims run each year by Victoria police. In the history of combating abuse in many institutions and many faiths, Operation Paradox was to play an honoured role.

Manny told his father he had been abused for many years at Yeshivah, first by the son of a senior Chabad rabbi and then by Cyprys. He believes the abuse ruined his childhood. It was known in the playground, and he was mocked for being gay. He became wild and alienated from his schooling and his family. By the time of his Bar Mitzvah he had come to loathe the Chabad way of life. "I was lost," he told the commission, "in the only world I knew."

The police were called. Cyprys denied everything.

With the pluck so typical of his family, Manny confronted Groner in the street and told him of his abuse. "The conversation was a brief one," he told the royal commission. "It seemed clear to me that Rabbi Groner was aware of the circumstances so there was very little I had to say. He said that Yeshivah was dealing with Cyprys and that I should not do anything of my own accord."

Having finished his military service in Israel, Manny brought his wife home with him to Melbourne in 2000. They lived apart from the Chabad community but visits to his parents' house for Sabbath took him past the Yeshivah centre, where it infuriated him to see Cyprys still on duty as a security officer. "I recall many occasions when our eyes met while I was walking past," he told the commission. "He seemed to deliberately smirk at me. Often he fixed his eyes on me and continued to smirk until I was forced to look away. To me his facial expression said: 'We both know what I did, and I got away with it.'"

Once again, the young man confronted Groner. "How can you have this person here providing him access to children when you know what you know?" he asked the rabbi. In his evidence to the commission, Waks recalled Groner pleading with him not to pursue the matter. "He said that he was taking care of it; Cyprys was getting professional help and, according to these professionals, was making improvements. My final question to Rabbi Groner was: 'Can you assure me that Cyprys is not currently reoffending or that he will not reoffend in the future?' To which Rabbi Groner responded: 'No'. At this point I said I had to go, and I left."

How many complaints Groner received about Cyprys will never be known. The last the commission examined was particularly heartbreaking. It came from the mother who first complained to the rabbi in 1986. Her son, now thirty, had just told her his abuse continued for years after her meeting with Groner. "You promised me you would take care of the matter and you didn't and my son is suicidal," she told the rabbi on the phone in 2002. According to the evidence she gave at the royal commission, Groner asked if her son was planning to go police. "I said: 'Probably.' And Rabbi Groner then said: 'Well, what do you need me for?' And I think we both hung up. I don't recall who hung up first."

Her son did go to the police, but his allegations were vague. He was coming down from years of heavy marijuana use and was, by his own account, all over the shop. The police case against Cyprys wasn't closed but by 2003 it seemed to be getting nowhere. That was the year Yeshivah says it cut its formal links with Cyprys. His security licence would say he was still employed there for many years, but Yeshivah says his services were terminated in 2003, not because of allegations of abuse, but late bills, illegible invoices and high prices. He was not shunned in the Orthodox community. On the contrary: he remained on the board of the Elwood synagogue and in 2006 became a director of the Council of Orthodox Synagogues of Victoria.

Groner was, by this time, very old but his immense authority in the Chabad community was unchallenged. He had determined that his successor would be his son-in-law, Zvi Telsner. When Groner died in 2008, honoured in the secular and religious press, Telsner inherited the post of chief rabbi.

He could not be sacked or directed or disciplined. He was in charge because Groner had put him there. His authority depended on the continued and unquestioned dedication of the sect to the memory of a man whose achievement would be questioned over the following years in the most mortifying way.

Not that Telsner, even today, has any doubts about the fundamental goodness of Rabbi Yitzchok Groner. "His sensitivity to every child was something which cannot be described," he told the royal commission. "His whole life was taking care of children. Anyone who could think that he would want to harm any child in my estimation would be not only erroneous but just not acceptable, totally."

*

With David Kramer due to be released from his St Louis prison in 2012, someone in Melbourne kept reminding the police about Yeshivah's role in spiriting this paedophile out of the country years before. For the first time, Victorian police began investigating Kramer and turned to Yeshivah for help. The school provided police with names and addresses of students at the school in Kramer's time, and in the middle of June 2011, Telsner put a brief notice up on the wall of the synagogue urging parents to cooperate with the investigation.

The Chabad community was in an uncomfortable position. Only months before, the Orthodox rabbis of Victoria had made it clear that the old prohibition of *mesirah* did not apply to child abuse. Jews were not only free to take allegations of abuse to the police but the Rabbinical Council of Victoria declared that as a matter of Jewish law it was "obligatory to make such reports". Events would prove the Chabad community deeply divided over this fresh development. Some simply could not accept the right of the secular world to interfere in the affairs of the community. Others saw it was impossible to keep the police out but had little appetite for helping them. Widely felt in this private world was a loathing for the public exposure that investigation might bring.

For a time it was not known in the community that one of their own was helping the police. AVB finished his schooling in St Kilda, but had grown up in the sister Yeshivah community in Bondi. There as a boy in the 1980s he was abused by Daniel "Gug" Hayman, a major donor to that community. But AVB had also been abused by a youth leader who brought a party of Yeshivah students up from Melbourne: David Cyprys.

AVB was puzzled by the list of students Yeshivah had given the police. "My name and address, my brothers' names and addresses, and the names and addresses of many of my friends and classmates was not on it." So he emailed his contacts within the Melbourne Chabad community, urging them to encourage and support victims who might be willing to speak to the police. Retribution was swift. The day after the email went out, Telsner delivered a fiery sermon reminding his congregation of the false spies who condemned the people of Israel to wander forty years in the wilderness.

A few days later, Manny Waks was shocked to read in *The Age* a story that began: "Police are trying to breach a wall of secrecy at a private boys school in St Kilda East over allegations of sex crimes by a former teacher who is now in jail in the United States." The paper's education editor, Jewel Topsfield, wrote of a community afraid to speak. One former student told her: "If you are labelled an informer it gives the family a bad name and makes it hard for children to get married … the issue is not just about the sexual abuse investigation, it is about the culture that enables it."

Waks had his life back under control. At the age of thirty-five he was married, working in Canberra and a vice-president of the Executive Council of Australian Jewry. He rang Topsfield. He knew this could be very difficult for his family. But he felt he had no choice but to take a leadership role in bringing this impasse to an end. He detailed Groner's failures to act. He identified himself as a victim.

This blew the lid off the story and Chabad's response was everything Waks feared. Zephaniah was attacked in the street. He and his father were denounced around the world in blogs and on Facebook. The terrible accusation *moser* – betrayer – was levelled against them. Documents that emerged at the royal commission suggest the accusation was also being made in email exchanges between rabbis and at meetings of the Yeshivah centre's committee of management. Zephaniah begged the Chabad leadership for help. He supported his son. He wanted a statement from them that neither Manny nor his family was to be blamed for him going public. "I am sick of being smeared, along with my family," he wrote. "I attribute a lot of the problem to Yeshivah's inaction, or worse, in this matter."

No protection was offered.

Zephaniah sat in the synagogue as Telsner delivered another slashing sermon. "Who gave you permission to talk to anyone, which rabbi gave you permission?" Telsner asked. It was a week after Manny's revelations in *The Age*. Victims must go to the police, said the rabbi, but the congregation must cease spreading *loshen horah* – false rumours – that Yeshivah and his father-in-law Groner had failed to act. Accusations, he said, should first be brought to him, the rabbi. Telsner named no names, but Zephaniah Waks had no doubt the rabbi was attacking his son. He and his wife, supported by a few friends, walked out of the synagogue. He then made notes of what he had just heard Telsner preaching: "The rabbis have the power to excommunicate people when they disobey the rabbis … the worst sin is besmirching the name of Rabbi Groner." And: "In the last few weeks, people have argued about who I meant in my sermons. Now I am saying clearly: if you think it refers to you, it does. Don't think it means someone else …"

Honours previously shown to Zephaniah in the synagogue were withdrawn. He and the rabbi would sit there side by side for years, but Telsner never said anything that might reassure Waks that he and his family were not the target of that attack. "We had a very, shall we say, cool relationship," the rabbi told the royal commission. "Therefore I didn't think that actually speaking to him would clear up matters."

As the shunning intensified, AVB and the Waks father and son made futile appeals to a number of Jewish organisations for support. Years later, senior Orthodox rabbis would say what AVB and Manny Waks had done was correct, even admirable. But at the time, none spoke out on their behalf. There was no one to condemn *loshen horah* when the targets were victims of abuse who had defied Chabad's old code of silence.

Cyprys was charged a mere seven weeks after Waks went to *The Age*. He faced sixteen counts of indecent assault and thirteen counts of gross indecency involving twelve victims. AVB was there in court. He was seen talking to the police. The attacks on him in Chabad blogs redoubled. He was accused of lying, of inventing his abuse, of welcoming his abuse, of setting out to destroy the Yeshivah community. There were calls for his wife to be burnt as a witch. "I was gut wrenched," he told the royal commission. His boss was told. He feared losing his job. He heard that Cyprys's lawyer at the bail hearing, Alex Lewenberg, was complaining about the help he was giving police. AVB rang the man and an authorised recording was made of a conversation in which Lewenberg accused AVB of being a *moser*.

"I am not exactly delighted," said the lawyer, "that another Yid would assist police against an accused no matter whatever he is accused of. That is the reason why I was very disappointed, because there is a tradition, if not a religious requirement, that you do not assist against Abraham."

The charge list against Cyprys kept growing. He was eventually committed for trial on forty-one charges – including rape – committed between 1982 and 1991. The magistrate took the opportunity to say the claim by the school's headmaster, Rabbi Glick, that he had not known sexual abuse was occurring in his school in the 1980s was "unfathomable". Cyprys was found guilty of rape and subsequently pleaded guilty to twelve further charges and was sentenced to eight years' imprisonment. Manny Waks was granted permission by the court to identify himself as a victim.

The Australian Jewish News carried a full page ad demanding Glick be stood down by Yeshivah. It didn't happen. On advice from senior counsel, Yeshivah issued a very carefully worded apology: "We understand and appreciate that there are victims who feel aggrieved and we sincerely and unreservedly apologise for any historical wrongs that may have occurred." That's as far as they were willing to go at that point: "May have occurred ..."

Kramer was extradited from the United States and pleaded guilty in July 2013 to molesting four boys at Yeshivah back in the early 1990s. He was sentenced to eighteen months in prison. His own lawyer accused the school of covering up these crimes and helping his client flee the country. Yeshivah issued an unreserved apology but the parents of one of Kramer's American victims were not impressed. They told the Melbourne *Herald Sun*: "We arrive at the inescapable conclusion that the blood of our child ... rests upon the head of those complicit in Kramer's escape from justice. We call upon the Yeshivah centre to do the right thing: not by offering hollow, meaningless platitudes of 'we're sorry', but to take concrete action by releasing from its employ all who were responsible for Kramer's escape from justice."

*

The witness stand of a royal commission is a cruel place for men of any faith. Cardinals and preachers are not used to being held to account. In their world, facts don't necessarily matter. Belief is everything. Up against the law, compelled to answer, they find themselves trapped in daylight. Over ten long days of hearings in Melbourne, rabbi after rabbi apologised for the failings of the Chabad-Lubavitcher communities of St Kilda and Bondi. Some did so bluntly. Some only when they were cornered by tough questioning.

Rabbi Meir Shlomo Kluwgant made smooth headway in the witness stand until almost the end. The most senior rabbi in Australia said all the right things. His downfall came when he was read a message he had sent while watching online as Zephaniah Waks gave evidence a few days earlier. "Zephaniah is killing us," he messaged the editor of *The Australian Jewish*

News. "Zephaniah is attacking Chabad. He is a lunatic on the fringe, guilty of neglect of his own children. Where was he when all this was happening?"

Kluwgant resigned three days later as president of the Organisation of Rabbis of Australasia. He is also no longer chaplain to the Victorian police.

Rabbi Yosef Feldman made such a hash of his appearance in the witness box that he resigned next day as a director of Yeshivah Sydney.

Feldman's mother, Pnina, emailed Manny Waks last October: "Why do you keep highlighting Yeshiva?! ... You need counselling! I haven't met a person yet with one nice word to say about you. Most people consider you a lowlife – not because of any molestation, which wasn't your fault, but because of your malicious blame game, which is unjust, unwarranted, unde-served and wicked." She was not called to the commission to give evidence.

This week, Rabbi Glick resigned from his positions at Yeshivah College. He told *The Age* he felt the victims would want him to break all his links with his old school. "That's where the abuse took place and it was under my leadership. I haven't taken this lightly."

But Zvi Telsner is still the spiritual leader of Melbourne's Chabad com-munity in St Kilda despite calls from many quarters in the Jewish community that he resign. To the end, he manfully claimed those famous sermons were not attacks on AVB and Manny Waks. It was all a misapprehension. Yes, he could have corrected that any time in the past three years in a heart-beat. No, he didn't. For that failure and for any pain it caused, he wished to apologise.

Counsel assisting the royal commission, Maria Gerace, finished her withering examination of Telsner with a long question: "Rabbi, if the evi-dence of Zephaniah Waks and AVB is accepted in relation to the shunning, even if you didn't do the shunning but you stood by whilst it was occurring, do you accept that you were complicit in the process of shunning that was undertaken by other members of your community?"

Telsner replied: "I do."

AVB remains, despite everything, a member of Telsner's St Kilda com-munity. He holds to his faith. He will not be budged.

Alex Lewenberg is practising law in Melbourne. The legal services commissioner, Michael McGarvie, will not comment on any disciplinary proceedings a lawyer may or may not be facing. He told *The Guardian*: "It is impermissible for lawyers to intimidate witnesses. That goes to the heart of the justice system and the role a lawyer plays as an officer of the court."

Zephaniah Waks has broken with Chabad, trimmed his beard and put the St Kilda family home on the market. But how many Melbourne families need a house with thirteen bedrooms and six kitchens? The target market is Yeshivah, directly over the road. They aren't buying. Zephaniah and his wife are dividing their time between Israel and Australia, living outside the sect that was their shelter, their world, for most of their lives.

Once the hearings were done, Manny Waks flew to his new home in France. "If it was up to my wife," he told the commissioners as he fought his tears, "we would have left a long time ago." Before he flew out he met, at their invitation, five of Rabbi Groner's children who wished to apologise to him for the abuse and the cover-ups in their father's time at Yeshivah and for the intimidation the victims have suffered since. That last meeting capped a fortnight of remarkable victories that have left Waks feeling profoundly vindicated. But he does not believe the saga is over. He is calling for the complete renewal of the leadership of Yeshivah in St Kilda and Bondi – starting with Telsner: "For the pain and suffering he has caused to so many people over the years he must resign. He has brought the entire Jewish community into disrepute."

And Waks is still waiting for an apology from the peak Jewish bodies that did not stand up for him and the other victims. "They must apologise not just for the abuse, not just for the cover-ups. They left us out to dry."

The Guardian, 19 February 2015

Alex Lewenberg was found guilty of professional misconduct and banned from practice for fifteen months. Acting president of the Victorian Civil and Administrative Tribunal, Judge Pamela Jenkins, said she had no confidence Lewenberg had any insight into his conduct, or remorse for it.

Meir Kluwgant was appointed principal of Adass Israel school in Melbourne. After a month's uproar, he resigned. Meanwhile, the whistleblower at *The Australian Jewish News* who alerted victims to the rabbi's attack on Zephaniah Waks ("He is a lunatic on the fringe") was made redundant by the paper.

Zvi Telsner officially stepped down as senior rabbi at Yeshiva in September 2015. Manny Waks tweeted: "Finally. The news we have all been waiting for." But evidence given to the royal commission indicated he remained on full salary for at least a further eighteen months. He still has an office at Yeshiva. The community still looks to him for spiritual guidance.

Not far to fall

TONY ABBOTT IS FADING FAST. Within days of his fall he's looking like a prime minister we once had a long time ago. The drama of his execution this week was muted by the lingering disbelief that he was ever there. His government has slipped easily into the past. He is gone and barely missed.

"The beauty of being leader is you are freer to be yourself," he remarked five years ago after becoming leader of the Opposition. But that self proved, in the end, not made for the politics of today. Abbott was a brawling politician of great skill but he was also – and fatally – still in many ways the Cold War kid who rode out with Bob Santamaria's forces in the late 1970s to confront the zeitgeist and save Western civilisation.

Along the way, Abbott would abandon nearly every policy Santa stood for but he never lost the old man's fear of the future and the belief that his God-given mission was to save us from enemies we don't even realise are there. In Abbott's political imagination danger lurks everywhere. Whether it's the death cult abroad or the ABC at home, there is always more at stake than meets the eye. Ruin is at hand. Combat is imperative. Hyperbole is the order of the day. In the end, that didn't wash with Australia.

Abbott used to talk of himself as a mutt chasing a car. What happens, he used to wonder, when the dog catches the vehicle? The answer when he became prime minister turned out to be: not much.

It's not that he didn't have ideas. Opinion pieces were his strength in his early career as a journalist. Even as minister for health – and he was a good minister – he liked to lock himself away for days at a time to write newspaper pieces in which he threw around big, bold ideas. But missing from these tens of thousands of words was much about strategy. Abbott does not have the profoundly professional imagination of John Howard, whose mind focused instinctively on the task of getting where he wanted to go.

Without his superb talent for political conflict, he would never have brought his party in from Opposition. True, he wrecked the joint to get there, but the victory of 2013 can never be taken away from him. That's when his troubles began. He found he had little to carry him forward when he came to power except his instinct for brawling. There was no strategy. Persuasion was at a minimum. He picked fights everywhere. Like the worst of World War I generals, he led his government straight at the machine guns.

In Opposition he had built up a great political asset: trust in his word. That he was caught out so often ducking and weaving didn't matter. Abbott convinced Australia that he was the truth teller and his opponent, Julia Gillard, the liar. This political gold was squandered in his first budget. From that strategic error, Abbott never really recovered. That the budget picked so many fights he couldn't win only compounded a fundamental miscalculation that reduced Abbott to the ranks of ordinary politicians.

His devotion to the Crown was comic yet it didn't bring him undone – though even his supporters regard his knighting of Prince Philip as one of the silliest political gestures in living memory. Nor was it a bar to his survival that Abbott was a John Paul II brand of Catholic warrior. His defence of marriage as an honourable estate fit only for hetero-sexuals was one of the few times in his career Abbott tried to force his religious beliefs on the nation. These old loyalties gave a sepia wash to his leadership but were not the cause of his downfall. Abbott was only Santa-lite but in the end he failed in the same way Santamaria failed half a century ago: we didn't buy his vision of a nation in peril. We don't see ourselves that way.

He is a unique man. His was a unique failure. And he was true to himself all the way out. In his last appearance in the prime minister's courtyard he lectured the media in grandiose terms: "Refuse to connive at dishonour by acting as the assassin's knife." He sees himself as he always has: surrounded, indeed white-anted, by enemies. By that point, of course, he wasn't entirely wrong.

He leaves behind a band of ultra-conservatives distraught at his fall. For a time they had a champion. It seemed under Abbott they might yet fend off the future. They imagined an Australia free of everything from wind turbines to lesbian offspring. But this has all been plucked away from them.

The leaders of this band are Eric Abetz, Cory Bernardi and Kevin Andrews, the man who scored a remarkable thirty votes in the contest for deputy leader early this week. They are for Malcolm Turnbull to deal with now.

Whatever else happens this will be the defining task of Turnbull's time as prime minister. He spoke of changing the discourse on economics. But he must know the discourse has to change across the board. The bounce he enjoyed in the polls this week has been modest. He's on notice that Australia wants much more than the leadership to change.

The Guardian, 18 September 2015

Torture in the Pacific

NAURU IS AUSTRALIA'S WORK. We own this despair. These thousands of reports from within the refugee prison that have come to *The Guardian* reek of misery. There is no narrative here. It's the same, numbingly the same, day after day.

Tolling through the Nauru files are the words "I want to die". Nauru is on perpetual deathwatch. In the face of daily threats of suicide and self-harm, the guards struggle as amateur psychologists and social workers become connoisseurs of despair.

Suicide occupies so much of the prisoners' imagination. They threaten death as escape or simply in the hope of being treated decently. In the crushing tedium of the camp, swallowing a handful of screws or slashing their wrists offers prisoners a break in routine. Death is something to do.

"I will walk into the ocean with my daughter," warns a desperate mother. A social worker assesses the risk of death as major. But Wilson Security knows better. A scribble by the prison administration downgrades the risk to minor.

Day after day the forms record the cries of people Australia has deliberately brought to the brink:

"I just don't care."

"I do not want to be alive any more."

"I will kill myself."

"I will not stay here. I will be dead."

"I will do what I want to do."

"Enough is enough."

"I don't care any more."

"One more week until I die."

"I cannot control my thoughts."

"My head is full of crazy."

"I need poison so I can kill myself."

"I want to die. I want to die."

The prisoners threaten death by hanging, jumping, swallowing razor blades, slitting wrists, cutting throats, overdosing, refusing medication and walking into the sea. At any time a cohort of prisoners toys with death by refusing to eat.

There are no surprises for our officials here. Australia has been a long time in this business. We know what endless, hopeless detention does: it sends people mad. We put a lot of resources into the task of trying to keep them alive. It's costed into the Pacific solution.

Parking refugees on distant islands worked last time to keep their predicament hidden. But secrets are so much harder to keep these days than they were in John Howard's time. An incident report from January last year records a prisoner threatening to "report to Save the Children, to immigration, *Guardian*, ABC". Canberra's passion for secrecy has always been contradictory. Surely the more the world knows of the fate of refugees in these island camps, the more the deterrent power of holding them there?

But secrecy has its purpose. It helps hold the political consensus together. The truth is terrible. The regime of official secrecy allows us – even when so much is known – not to face the facts. It's a service for the squeamish.

Two years ago Peter Young, the detention system's former chief psychiatrist, told *The Guardian* that in his professional view the department of immigration was deliberately inflicting suffering on prisoners. The purpose was to force them to return home. His verdict was measured and devastating: "If we take the definition of torture to be the deliberate harming of people in order to coerce them into a desired outcome, I think it does fulfil that definition."

Since then there has been revelation after revelation of degrading conditions, bashings, rapes and sexual assaults on Manus and Nauru. Yet the politics of detention have not shifted. A man burns himself alive; a woman survives horrifically scarred; and the political settings haven't budged.

The Guardian is now publishing the largest cache of material ever to be leaked from within the detention network. These are the Panama papers of

Australia's refugee gulag. Here is the raw evidence of torture deliberately inflicted. Lives come apart in stupefying boredom. Prisoners keen for the children, sisters and parents Australia has taken from them. One of the great themes of these reports is the grief of separation.

Bored kids push the rules. Parents vent. Security guards pull brawling children apart on the football pitch, in the rec room, the gym, the school bus and the patch of crushed coral that serves as a volleyball court. Fights stopped one day break out the next. No one is surprised. But the reports are also full of apologies, courtly apologies by children and their parents for tempers lost, for threats made, for allowing their despair to show. "I am sorry," one woman says. "I am a hundred times sorry."

Their children are growing up in a contradictory little world of total surveillance and endless vulnerability. They are touched, ogled and threatened. Courtesy of Australia they are enjoying a dystopian coming of age in broken families trapped in a makeshift prison on a sweltering island. Release into the tiny community of Nauru has its own terrors. An incident report in early 2015 records a Nauruan guard telling an asylum seeker child: "Once you get a positive RSD [refugee status determination] I will kill you in Nauru."

Australians are not brutal people. This is not like us. One of the great questions that hovers over this system is how we can allow it to go on – how we can know so much about our prisons on Manus and Nauru yet manage not to face the facts of the Pacific Solution. Put simply: we think the horrors are worth it. First because both sides of politics tell us that only by detaining refugees out there will the boats stop coming here. And second, we're assured there is somewhere in the world ready to take our prisoners off our hands.

Those are both lies. The boats are stopped because they are turned back. They are still setting out from Sri Lanka, Vietnam, India and Indonesia, hoping to ferry asylum seekers to Australia. In June, both the prime minister and the minister for immigration, Peter Dutton, boasted they'd turned back their twenty-eighth boat. If the smugglers' customers knew about the prisons on Manus and Nauru – widely and expensively advertised by Australia – they were not deterred from risking an expensive voyage by fear of ending up there. Australian Border Force and the Navy stopped them reaching Australia. Turnbacks have their own horrors and present diplomatic dangers for this country, but there is no doubt they work – just as they did last time under John Howard.

The second lie is worse: that some country will take the prisoners on Manus and Nauru off our hands. The hunt for the "regional solution" for resettlement is up there with search for Lasseter's lost reef. Papua New Guinea and Nauru offer, at best, a temporary and dangerous existence outside the wire. The Cambodian solution was a stupendously expensive flop. New Zealand's offer was snubbed: too close to Australia for Canberra's liking.

Last time it was called "burden sharing" and ended – as it will again – with hundreds of refugee prisoners brought ashore to Australia because they have nowhere else in the world to go. The maths was brutal for Canberra's grandstanding politicians: some hundreds of prisoners gave up and returned to Iraq and Afghanistan; a cohort was forced to return, some to their deaths; a handful were reunited with their families in Canada and Scandinavia; New Zealand took more than 500 (verboten this time); and all the rest reached their original destination: Australia.

We lived with that because we had to. The last men and women to leave Manus and Nauru were damaged souls. We did that to them. They are now getting on with their lives in Brisbane and Ballarat and the outskirts of Adelaide.

Now would be the time – in the aftermath of an election campaign in which the boats barely featured – for Canberra to start bringing its prisoners quietly ashore. The problem is, the promises made to keep every last one of them out of this country are so much more extreme than last time.

What's new is the river of information flowing here about life in the island prisons. At some point – closer now that *The Guardian* has this cache of incident reports – Australians will know too much to be able to keep shying away from the facts. The truth is in the detail. We are trying to break these people. They are resisting.

The reports reveal little yearning for the countries we are trying to force them back to. Homesickness is not a theme. Even after being trapped on Nauru for years, they see themselves on a forward journey. There is nothing to suggest history won't repeat itself here. They will land. The only question is: how much will we make them suffer before we accept the inevitable? Despite all that's been done to them and all that their treatment at our hands tells us about Australia, they still want to live here. It's a humbling verdict.

The Guardian, 10 August 2016

Rome, a hard beast to wrangle

WHEN I GREW UP ON THE sheltered Protestant North Shore of Sydney it was a given that when push came to shove the Catholic Church would obey Rome rather than the law. This was a time when the election of a Catholic president of the United States was widely considered impossible or at the least dangerous. Where would JFK's loyalties lie in a crisis, to Washington or Rome? I worked to get that fear out of my system because I saw it as religious bigotry. Australia shed it too. So did the Western world. JFK turned out to be the poster boy for Catholic leader-ship, a man of undivided loyalties to his country.

But when I began reporting the Royal Commission into Institutional Responses to Child Sexual Abuse I could see evidence everywhere in the squalid history of the church's part in the abuse of children – evidence from around the world – that the only law that really counted here was the law of Rome. Across the world the church hid paedophile priests and snubbed their victims. Whether in Buenos Aires or Berlin or Ballarat, the story was absolutely the same. There were no whistleblowers. It was a faultless, international operation to defy criminal laws in the interests of the church.

Tens of thousands of questions have been asked in the last five years before the royal commission: brusque and discursive, technical and folksy, kind and absolutely lethal. Two great questions mattered. To victims: what happened? And to institutions: why didn't you just pick up the phone and call the cops?

Shame, embarrassment and cowardice are, in a sense, the easy answers. Archbishop Mark Coleridge of Brisbane, one of the big men of the Catholic Church in this country, pointed to a deeper truth: "It was that sense of the church doing its own thing, being a law and a world unto itself." This was brave. "In many ways, the Catholic Church in Australia has been profoundly embedded, but paradoxically, on the other hand, the Catholic Church in Australia has at times looked the other way, been a law unto itself, and seen that it does things its own way: 'We'll look after the problem ourselves.' Well, we didn't ..."

The political challenge that must be faced across the country now the commission has finished its work is how to grapple with Rome – an old, shrewd and complicated institution that has never quite abandoned its role as a world power. Rome has never issued an unambiguous directive to priests and members of religious orders who become aware of child abuse in their ranks to call the police. Coleridge cited lots of talk but no "structured discussions" on the point. Canon lawyers assembled by the chief royal commissioner, Peter McClellan, debated the issue for hours. Leo XIII seemed to say something quite promising but in the end they couldn't turn up a clear direction from the church to report priestly abusers to the state. McClellan thought the discussion extraordinary. How can church law be so opaque? "Maybe I'm just an ordinary common lawyer, but we normally say things in simple words." The canon lawyers balked. McClellan suggested Rome might adopt a plain formula: "Obey civil law."

What emerged from the evidence of church lawyers, theologians and a slew of bishops about the workings of Rome in Australia was the blueprint of an organisation perfectly suited to eluding control. Coleridge made rather a joke of it: "When I hear people talk about the monolithic Catholic Church, I think to myself, which are we in? It's like herding cats ... " Here is the gist of their evidence.

First, the church is a monarchy. "I'm not so naive to think that the monarchy is going to fall," Tom Doyle told the commissioners. "There has never been a monarchy that we know of that has voluntarily given up its system in favour of democracy." Doyle is one of the heroes of this saga. As a young priest working in the early 1980s in the papal ambassador's office in Washington, he saw what was looming. In Louisiana, juries were beginning to award victims huge damages. Police were beginning to pay attention. The press was waking up to a great scandal. Louisiana was news around the world. Doyle warned American bishops a catastrophe was looming. He was ignored. The church hunkered down. Doyle's rise through the ranks never happened. Monarchies resist change.

Second, the church is a foreign power. In 2014 it used its status as a little state to deny vital documents to the commission. The refusal was not blanket. Rome's obstinacy came hedged about with respectful rhetoric. But when it mattered the church said no. McClellan got the message: "Our experience is that documents generated in Rome in relation to a perpetrating priest won't be available to civil authorities in the state where the priest lives. That's what it amounts to."

Third, the church really doesn't exist. It's everywhere but nowhere. It has no more legal form in Australia than a gathering of book clubs. All those dioceses and orders with their immense property holdings are mere unincorporated associations. Among other things: they can't be sued.

Fourth, no one here can issue orders to every corner of the Australian church. There's a local bishops conference with considerable authority. But all decisions that really matter are referred to Rome. And bishops have no authority over the orders that run schools and hospitals. Between priests and brothers is a great divide. And the orders have been found to be sheltering appalling numbers of paedophiles. "It's my experience that many of these orders are laws unto their own," Dr Michelle Mulvihill, a psychologist working within the church on issues of child abuse for the last twenty years, told the commission. "They're their own people and they will do whatsoever they want. There's like a licence to do whatever. I think it's very fraught and it's very dangerous for the Australian community."

Fifth, the fiction in this monarchy is the lack of downward control. Coleridge explained: "A priest is not an employee of mine. It is a bit like the government appointing a judge. The government appoints the judge, but once she or he is appointed, she or he has a quality of independence that is quite unusual. So I appoint priests, but not as employees ... It's not unlike bishops and the Pope, I hasten to add. The Pope, in the end, formally appoints me, but I'm not his branch manager. Once I am appointed bishop, I'm conceded a great deal, perhaps an excessive amount, of independence."

Its contradictions are its strength. Here is an ancient machine capable of great good yet built to defend its worst with astonishing tenacity. And it's a monarchy that claims to have anarchy at its heart but ruthlessly exercises internal power. An institution of deep charitable purpose with walls to defend its wealth against all comers. In short: a hard beast to wrangle.

Cardinal George Pell lost his cool the afternoon the royal commission was announced. He was by turns weary and defiant. Under interrogation by journalists he complained about the media: "Because there's a press campaign focused largely on us it does not mean we are largely the principal culprit." Four years later the commission rolled out the figures that proved the cardinal wrong. It was not designed this way but the evidence determined that this would turn out to be, at heart, an inquiry into the Catholic Church.

The commission picked over the failings of the Scouts, the YMCA, the Salvation Army, children's homes for Aboriginal kids, the notorious Parramatta Training School for Girls, Swimming Australia, the ultra-Orthodox Jewish Yeshiva sect, a Yoga ashram, the Jehovah's Witnesses, performing arts centres, the military and a number of the most expensive private schools in the nation. But its principal focus became the failings of the Catholic Church. There is no arguing with the figures. Most survivors attending the 8000 private sessions with commissioners reported abuse in faith-based institutions. Two-thirds of those were abused in Catholic institutions. With cool precision, Gail Furness SC, counsel assisting the commission, ran through the numbers: "Between January 1980 and February 2015, 4444 people alleged incidents of child sexual abuse made to ninety-three Catholic Church authorities. These claims related to over 1000 separate institutions."

Francis Sullivan, the chief executive of the Truth, Justice and Healing Council, the body representing the church before the commission, was aghast. He had expected maybe a hundred paedophiles would be turned up in Catholic parishes and schools. The figure was nearly 2000. "If this was to have occurred in any other institution," he told the commission, "it is hard to imagine that it could continue to operate."

The hearings were the public face of the commission, the interrogation of men of such exalted rank they'd clearly forgotten what it was like to be asked questions – let alone be compelled to answer them. The double act of Furness and McClellan was beautiful to watch. She would hack her way through the undergrowth and take an axe to the tree she was after. But if it stubbornly refused to fall, McClellan would give it a nudge, such a gentle little nudge, and bring it crashing down. Men of faith were made to deal in facts. Fragile survivors were led gently through appalling revelations of abuse. Memories failed. Lies were told blind. All this was streamed to the world. In New York and Israel, members of the Yeshiva sect watched as their leaders faced public interrogation. Unprecedented, too, was the grilling of leaders of another secretive sect, the Jehovah's Witnesses, and 22,000 viewers followed that contest live.

But the ratings winner in all the years of hearings turned out to be Case Study 28: Catholic Church authorities in Ballarat. It's no surprise. In the public imagination, Ballarat was the epicentre of neglect, abuse and the outrageous protection of the notorious paedophile Father Gerald Ridsdale. Fifty-four thousand viewers watched as these horrors were brought to light.

Behind the scenes the staff of hundreds were gathering, sorting and analysing documents. From the moment the commission got underway, orders for discovery – as they are known – went out to the faiths, to schools, to sporting groups and insurance companies. The demand: search your archives, empty your desks, clean out the cupboards, open the safes and give us your documents. Documents poured in for four years. They were not only evidence of what happened but of what the faiths knew. They mapped in extraordinary detail the scale and patterns of abuse in this country. But they also measured the extraordinary capacity of schools and churches and orphanages to keep their terrible secrets.

How secrets were kept – and how pitifully easy it was to keep them – turned out to be one of the key lessons of the commission. It was easy to overlook, as we sat in the hearing room, aghast at the latest revelations, that somehow, only the other day, these were deep secrets.

So we come back to the equivocal position of the Catholic Church and its particular methods of keeping secrets – to make sure no one broke ranks for all those years in Buenos Aires, Berlin and Ballarat. Francis Sullivan, chief executive of the church's Truth Justice and Healing Council, says secrecy is simply in the DNA of the church. "Bishops and religious leaders embrace their diocese or religious order in familial terms. It's intimate and therefore they approach strife, difficulty and conflict by circling the wagons. They keep the family mess to the family. I think it's instinctive. And that's what I mean by culture, like DNA."

That's not an explanation that satisfies lawyer critics of the church. They look to Rome. Kieran Tapsell, a former seminarian and acting judge of the New South Wales district court, has written in depth – and gave evidence to the commission – about obligations of secrecy imposed by Rome through canon law. Angels dance on pins. Canon lawyers cite vague Latin texts back and forth but none dispute that whatever the instincts of the church might be, tough rules of "pontifical secrecy" were laid down by Rome in 1922 – a rule so secret it may hardly have been known by the church in Australia – and again in 1974. Both forbade in almost all circumstances victims, witnesses and church officials going to the police. Offenders faced excommunication. The question that concerned McClellan was whether those rules still bind Catholics.

Clearly they have been wound back. Under pressure from bishops in Ireland and the United States facing prosecution for failing to report paedophiles, the Vatican gave a dispensation for them to go to the authorities. There would be no martyrdoms. That dispensation was extended in 2010 to the religious in all countries where reporting is mandated by law. But the default setting of the Vatican, according to evidence before McClellan, remains secrecy. "I don't think there is any doubt that if there were no civil laws requiring reporting, then the pontifical secret still applies," says Tapsell. "In Western Australia and Queensland, for example, just to take two, bishops are under an obligation *not* to report, under canon law, to the police."

Sullivan points to the Towards Healing protocol of the Australian church as proof that things are not as bad here as they might seem. "In places like Australia or the United States – in Western countries where the rule of law is respected – it's a no-brainer," he says. "All of us should go to the police without condition." But on close reading the 2016 protocol is still not an unequivocal direction to pick up the phone and dial 000. It's hedged about with conditions. If the law demands it, obey the law. But where the law doesn't mandate reporting and the victim is reluctant to go to the police, church personnel are merely advised they should – not *shall* – give the authorities particulars of the abuse stripped of any "details that could lead to the identification of the complainant".

Australian bishops can't even agree if the sacred seal of the confessional forbids them telling authorities what they learn, not from paedophiles seeking absolution but from their victims. The rapist priest is safe, but is he also saved from the revelations of his victims in confession? Some think so. Some don't. McClellan suggested the bishops ask Rome to adjudicate. They declined.

Politicians may look back on the last few years as the easy time in this saga. With the presentation of the commission's final report this week, responsibility for dealing with the wreckage of the past and protecting children in the future now passes back to them. Every government in the country backed the commission. Now all those governments must consider its recommendations. Some will call for money – a great deal of money – and others for courage. It might be thought that after the shame visited on them during commission hearings and brutal verdicts in commission reports, the political influence of the faiths must be spent. That's not the case. Now the equal marriage debate has died away, the commission's recommendations present the next battleground as this country grapples with defining a new balance between church and state. As always, the cards are stacked against change.

The Guardian, 13 December 2017

High crimes and misdemeanours

ON HIS LAST DAY OF FREEDOM George Pell drew a crowd. The world knew where to come and the courtroom was packed. As always, the first on the scene were the Catholic women who turn out to every inquiry and trial to bear witness to the lives destroyed and the children lost. They are the implacable wounded. Carmel Rafferty was waiting for the doors to open. She was sacked years ago for trying to save her pupils at Doveton Primary from crazed Father Peter Searson. With her was Judy Courtin, who has shepherded a little army of victims through the courts. And by their side, a cup of coffee in her hand, was Chrissie Foster, the mother of two daughters raped by Father Kevin O'Donnell. The cops used to say of O'Donnell: "He was a two-a-day man."

As we settled in the court there was an end-of-term feeling in the air. Break-up and the holidays were only hours away. Journalists took what seats they could find. Sitting quietly up the front was Detective Chris Reed, the Victorian policeman who had pursued Pell for years and seen a jury convict him of abusing two boys one morning in the sacristy of St Patrick's Cathedral. Reed's work was done. Two artists arrived with paper and pencils. Photographs are forbidden in court. Somehow, they would bring the business of justice undone. But the ancient art of the sketcher is still honoured by the law. For weeks, they had had the best view of Pell's face. Today, as he entered the dock, it was clamped shut. The cardinal hadn't dressed for prison. He wore the same clerical collar and black bib he always wore, under a cotton jacket which in another setting – on, say, the Amalfi Coast – would be the rig of a great cleric on holiday. Not today.

The jury having spoken, the only question left to decide was how long a man who once bestrode the Catholic world would be living behind bars. "I appear on behalf of the cardinal," said Robert Richter. It was hardly news. He cuts a Hogwarts figure: fuzzy, old fashioned and lethal. Richter's task was to deal in grim hypotheticals. He had to debate the appropriate sentence his client should serve for offences never admitted. Pell was not, he suggested, acting as an archbishop when he put his penis in the boys' mouths. Mass was over. "The only differential of power is that he is an adult – for reasons inexplicable – with an urge to do what he did," Richter continued. "He is not abusing his position as archbishop, but he is abusing his position ... as a grown man." Judge Peter Kidd squirmed, snapped his glasses off and on, leant forward, leant back, put his chin on his fist and kept saying, one way or another: "You've lost me, Mr Richter." It got worse. If Pell had in fact done what he did, said the barrister, he exerted "no force greater than was required to achieve penetration".

The gallery was polite. Only occasionally were there gasps and laughter.

Kidd reserved his decision. But Pell's time was up. At 3.10 pm Kidd said: "Take him away, please." The cardinal picked up his stick, nodded to the guards fore and aft and walked through a plain door at the end of the dock into the underworld. The judge made his own exit, his robes gathered around him and a look like death on his face. Helicopters could be heard hovering overhead loaded with cameramen hoping for a shot of Pell departing in a prison van.

We will see him again when the appeal begins, the grounds already being argued on the front pages of the papers. By then Pell will be in one of the prisons where Victoria houses paedophiles. He will know so many of the faces, so many priests and brothers who have done what he continues to deny having done himself. What reunions there will be. For the first time since they shared the St Alipius presbytery at Ballarat in the 1970s, George Pell will be back under the same roof as the worst of the worst paedophiles. He and that monster Gerald Ridsdale will have so much to catch up on.

The Guardian, 27 February 2019

New lawyers argued Pell's case
before the Victorian Court of Appeal

Rule number two on these occasions is not to trust the look in their eyes. Judges are masters of disguise. Smiles can be the kiss of death. But by the end of the first day of George Pell's appeal it was clear the bench was listening to the case being argued on his behalf by Bret Walker SC with more than respect. Walker spoke quietly. His task was not to sweep the judges away with a stirring narrative of innocence. That's for television. In real life – if that's what the proceedings of a court of appeal can be called – the job of a great advocate is to pick apart the prosecution's case, to unravel their knitting.

Which brings us to rule number one: it's impossible for the public to follow what's happening in any detail because we are never shown the documents piled on carts behind the bar table and lined up like a mobile library behind the judges. "Can I draw your attention to an incident in table L which I can amalgamate with table M?" Walker asked the judges. They grabbed folders, found tabs and opened wide. We're left to follow as best we can.

That Pell would appeal his conviction was inevitable. That's how the law operates – not because Pell is a great man but because verdicts in sex cases of this kind are always difficult. There were no witnesses, no corroborating evidence. This was a classic he said/he said. Unlike the army of Pell's defenders, Walker was not arguing the crime was impossible. Close to impossible might set Pell free. But how close? The English language was ransacked by Walker to define that sliver of doubt: barely possible, extremely improbable, inherently improbable, so unlikely as to make it barely possible, not realistically possible and so on and on.

He did not neglect the nitty-gritty of Pell's case: the West Door alibi – that the cardinal was farewelling the faithful on the steps of the cathedral at the time he was accused of raping choir boys in the sacristy. There was the Crown's confusion of robes worn by an archbishop when "presiding" with those worn when merely "officiating" at mass. And Pell's accuser was birched twenty-two years down the track for failing to recall that school holidays fell between him having a penis forced into his mouth in December and his genitals grabbed as Pell processed down a corridor in February.

The performance of Walker's opponent, Christopher Boyce SC, was woeful. At times he was reduced to silence. At times the judges had to jog him back onto his path. But he did enjoy a little victory by persuading the judges that it's not impossible for an archbishop in chasuble, alb and cincture to take out his penis. The proof? The ability, by bunching up the robes, to go to the toilet, in Boyce's words, "standing up as a man". He invited their honours to try on the set of robes provided. They seemed keen on the idea. It would make a remarkable picture.

The Guardian, 5 June 2019

The Court of Appeal decides

George Pell has withered in the weeks since his appeal. He was ashen as he entered the box. The verdict was swiftly delivered. There were little gasps in the room. Pell displayed once more his Olympian detachment. Don't believe reports that he flinched. His lips pursed a little as he stared at the judges. That's all.

What now for Pell's defenders? Their faith in this man is depthless, proof against any evidence that might be brought to bear against him. Many of Pell's supporters stood outside the court after the verdict looking shellshocked in the sunlight. This was not as they – or indeed so many in the court – imagined things would turn out. Once more, helicopters hovered over the streets.

Let's hope Pell finds some sort of peace while Rome decides what to do with the most senior man in its ranks ever to be imprisoned for crimes that have stained the reputation of the church around the world.

The Guardian, 21 August 2019

Waiting for the High Court

The word at the Melbourne bar is that George Pell will walk free. The barristers haven't had an early warning. They're only talking among themselves. Historic child sex assaults make difficult cases. They test the criminal law. Those who have followed this prosecution as it has made its slow and dramatic way to the High Court must face the possibility that the cardinal is about to be acquitted.

Lawyers don't doubt Pell's accuser is convincing. This the public can't judge, for he gave all his evidence *in camera*. We know, of course, that his accusations convinced the police and prosecution authorities in Victoria, a jury and two out of three judges of the Court of Appeal. Even Pell's lawyers agree he is convincing – indeed, the lynchpin of Walker's case is that Pell's accuser was so convincing that everyone downplayed the evidence of twenty church witnesses in the cardinal's favour. In lawyer-speak: "Belief in a 'compelling' complainant does not, *ipso facto*, equate to the elimination of reasonable doubt."

Is it poor form to pray for an acquittal? Perhaps. But how many hours, I wonder, has Pell spent in his cell contemplating his decision not to give evidence at his trial? It's his right, of course, but how evasive he must have looked to those jurors: this mighty figure sitting there stumm, not denying the accusations, not exposing himself to questioning, while his accuser gave compelling evidence that he had, indeed, been raped.

The Guardian, 10 March 2020

Release

This is a mighty triumph not just for George Pell, who is breathing free air for the first time in a year, and his backers who invested millions in his defence, but for the narrative of prejudice the church has spun all the years since the Melbourne police came for the cardinal in Rome. The beleaguered church. The misunderstood church. The church under attack by secularists. The church pursued by abuse victims, police and journalists with axes to grind. The unanimity of the High Court's decision is crushing for Pell's prosecutors and, of course, for the young man who brought this complaint to the police nearly five years ago. From the start the contest was simple: who was to be believed here? The police, the prosecution authorities in Victoria, a jury and two judges of the Court of Appeal realised it was hard for Pell to have raped that boy, but decided it was possible.

The judges of the High Court do not accuse him of being a liar or a fantasist. They do not find his evidence contained discrepancies or displayed inadequacies "of such a character as to require the jury to have entertained a doubt as to guilt". Their doubts arose elsewhere. As has been the practice of the High Court lately, the judges dug right down into the evidence. More than a hundred paragraphs of their judgement are spent reconstructing the rituals of the cathedral – of doors opened and closed, of robes and processions. The judges did what the jury and judges below did not: trust the evidence of Pell's master of ceremonies, Monsignor Charles Portelli, that Pell could not have abused those children for he never left the cardinal's side that morning, following him from the steps of the cathedral to the sacristy where he helped him unrobe.

Tolling through their honours' judgement is the word "unchallenged". Pell's acquittal relies almost entirely on the failure of the prosecution to challenge – let alone destroy – the evidence of the old cathedral officials, particularly Portelli. The prosecution found gaps but never tore down the fence protecting Pell.

He is free and has offered Christian forgiveness to his tormentors. He can leave it now to his supporters to rage on his behalf. It is going to be a mighty storm. Category Five. Next comes the verdict of the Royal Commission into Institutional Responses to Child Sexual Abuse, kept under wraps so as not to poison the minds of jurors in the criminal trials he faced in Melbourne.

The Guardian, 7 April 2020

The commission's verdict

This is the portrait of a deceitful man. The findings against Pell have stayed hidden for years – a buried ordnance, exploding only now. It's now clear that no senior figure in any church emerged from the commission as damaged as George Pell. Again and again, the commissioners find that Pell failed to protect children from paedophile and violent priests. His excuses are dissected forensically and rejected one by one. Key claims in the cardinal's evidence are condemned as implausible, inconceivable, untenable and unacceptable.

Mighty ecclesiastical careers aren't often made by men who don't know what's going on around them. But that was how Pell pitched himself to the commission: a priest who didn't gossip and didn't keep his ear to the ground, and a bishop who didn't ask hard questions. He never knew, he was too distracted, he was kept out of the loop, he was deceived by officials, even bishops, while – he was forced to admit – priests and brothers around him in Ballarat and Melbourne were abusing children.

On his own evidence, he was found to have known enough about the mad priest Peter Searson to see that he had to be removed from his parish. He knew enough about the brutally abusive Brother Edward Dowlan at St Patrick's College in Ballarat to have, in the words of the report, "ensured that the matter was properly treated". He didn't, and Dowlan went on abusing Christian Brothers students for more than twenty years before being jailed for dozens of offences against boys. But above all, the commissioners found – in direct contradiction to Pell's evidence – that he must have known that Father Gerald Ridsdale was being moved from parish to parish for abusing children.

Though the priest's crimes were common knowledge in a number of parishes and were known to the bishop as well as to most of the "consultors" on parish appointments with whom Pell sat in the 1970s, the cardinal claimed he'd heard nothing of the scuttlebutt about Fr Ridsdale. But the commission found: "It is inconceivable that the consultors did not know by this time, given the usual practice and the general knowledge in the community." Yet they simply moved him on, and Ridsdale would abuse children on an extraordinary scale for another fifteen years. Pell walked him to court when he first faced charges in Melbourne. He's been convicted for hundreds of child sex offences. He will die in jail.

For those who have been following the Pell saga for years, the royal commission's findings are unsurprising. The cardinal's failures have been canvassed in the parishes and the press, in documentaries and over years in the witness box of the commission. His denials were always wretched. Now the commission has said so officially. This man did not do what he might to protect children. He was not straight with the royal commission. He has been acquitted of terrible crimes by the High Court but the verdict of the commission on his conduct is ghastly.

How, I wonder, will his cheer squad cope with the commission's findings? What dark plots will be hinted at here? What collusion between lawyers and journalists will be discovered to explain this grim result? Is the ABC about to cop it all over again? Maybe, just maybe, his spruikers will now recognise that Pell is a human being, a pretty ordinary human being, who has fallen from grace and must now live with his reputation. Pity isn't called for.

The Guardian, 7 May 2020

Malcolm on the Western Front

THOSE DAMN FRENCH NEVER COULD BE TRUSTED. The opening of the Monash Centre at Villers-Bretonneux was supposed to mark a century of amity between our two peoples yet the French prime minister, Édouard Philippe, delivered a speech that blew Malcolm Turnbull's to smithereens.

A lot of words have been shed on the Western Front. This is a place of blood and poetry. A national leader opening a new museum commemorating these battles has to have something to say.

Let's not be cruel. Turnbull's effort would have passed muster back home. Nuts-and-bolts stuff. A useful explanation of General Ludendorff's tactics in the 1918 March offensive. Family connections. Many deaths. No household untouched. We must never forget, etc. Applause. Then the Frenchman went to the microphone with, it would seem, aggression in his heart and literature in his kitbag, launching himself into the crowd with a line from Erich Maria Remarque's *All Quiet on the Western Front*: "He is entirely alone now with his little life of nineteen years, and cries because it leaves him." Then he seized the high ground:

"Coming here, seeing this centre and tower, looking at the names of the 11,000 Australians who died for France and for freedom, I could not help thinking of the terrible loneliness which these thousands of young Australians must have felt as their young lives were cut short in a foreign country. A foreign country. A faraway country. A cold country whose earth had neither the colour nor texture of their native bush. A faraway, foreign country which they defended, inch by inch, in Fromelles in the Nord region, in Bullecourt in Pas-de-Calais and of course here, in Villers-Bretonneux. As if it were their own country."

"And it is their own country. 'The earth is more important to the soldier than to anybody else,' continues Erich Maria Remarque, 'the earth is his only friend, his brother, his mother. He groans out his terror and screams into its silence and safety.' For many young Australians, this earth was their final safe place. For many of them, this earth was the final confidante of a thought or a word intended for a loved one from the other side of the world."

Somehow he wove in Francois I and the Chevalier Bayard with the hell of the trenches: "The mud, the rats, the lice, the gas, the shellfire, the fallen comrades." Men and women near me were crying.

We were gathered on a hill not far from Villers-Bretonneux to celebrate $100 million spent on a high-tech temple to the memory of General Sir John Monash on the centenary of his victories in this stretch of France. "Meticulous, wise and dogged," Philippe called him and ventured the unthinkable at this time and in this place: Monash might have had peers. "This Australian engineer, with his unerring instinct, came to be hailed as one of the best Allied tacticians, on par with France's Estienne and Britain's Fuller."

The old general himself would have been furious: this event was nineteen minutes late getting underway. He knew that's no way to win battles. There was much kissing up the front of the great plastic shed they'd built beside the old war memorial as we waited for the seats to fill. The band played "Pack Up Your Troubles". Canberra sent a handful of ministers and ex-ministers and men with emu feathers in their hats. Tony Abbott was present in a sombre suit. The town provided a mayor with tricoleur sash and akubra, a man clearly built for these occasions. The Monash family was there. Ditto the family of General Pompey Elliott.

Not on the list were men and women I'd seen in the centre in the last few days, old Australians with questions to ask, who come to France with a sheet of paper in their hands showing the face of a great uncle or a grandfather, the dates of birth and death much too close together. No. This was an official occasion.

The leaders arrived at last. David Hudson played the didge. There were speeches and anthems and more tears when the kids from the local school sang "Waltzing Matilda": "... under the shade of a kooo-li-bar tree ..." And the leaders unveiled a brass plaque. Turnbull whipped out his glasses, gave the fineprint a quick once-over, registered his approval and together the two prime ministers left the stage. Only champagne remained to be opened.

The business of remembering is taken seriously up here, not least because the valley of the Somme looks the most peaceful landscape on earth. In late April the country is covered in sheets of early wheat and canola in flower and patches of pale ploughed land waiting to be sown. Memorials are the only evidence of war. The big towers of Britain, Canada and Australia cut the skyline. In the fields are walled cemeteries with formal gardens, pale headstones and perfectly clipped lawns. A century's gardening is keeping the memory of war alive.

But hardly anyone comes to the Australian memorial built in the 1930s by the great British architect Sir Edwin Lutyens. That's the harsh truth the new centre is trying to reverse. Outside Anzac Day only a couple of hundred people wander each week up this hill near Villers-Bretonneux. Canberra is hoping $100 million will turn that into a couple of thousand. It's big money for a modest outcome.

There's such irony here. One of the leading architects of the twentieth century had his great plans slashed by Canberra in the Depression. Now a team of Australian architects led by Joe Agius and Tim Williams were handed all the money in the world to build in the shadow of Lutyens' effort. The architects call theirs an "almost an anti-building" but while it hunkers down, it's hardly self-effacing. It's elegant, big and muscular. How much they spent is still a closely held secret. Officials are coy. But the shell cost nearly $30 million and a large part of the rest of the budget went on the exhibition it houses.

This is not a museum. It's what they call in the trade these days an experience. If you want to explain slavery and civil rights in America or the battles on the Western front, this is what you do. Walls light up. Old photographs fade into freshly filmed live action. Actors struggle and die. Orchestras play. Howitzers blaze away. Gas seeps through the floor. A few glass cases hold mementos of battles fought round here. There are guns and badges and rusted weapons, some dug up on the site. My grandfather Jack's war diaries are beautifully preserved here, one held together with a safety pin as it has been for a century.

But the Monash Centre is not for scholars. This is entertainment, cutting edge and thrilling in its way, but entertainment. Crowds will no doubt come. Tour operators are already rejigging their itineraries to fit an hour or so for their customers in this dazzling maze. But war buffs should stay out in the battlefields. Devotees of the great general will learn nothing new about their hero here. True, war isn't glorified. But there's hardly a breath of politics in the exhibition. It's all battles and no scandal.

That's by design. That Australia was being torn apart by conscription campaigns isn't explored. That old Keith Murdoch tried to have Monash sacked as an uppity Jew goes unmentioned. Dud generals who slaughtered their men hardly get a guernsey. Addressed only by implication is the great question of what this war was really all about.

But it's getting late. In an hour or so the first figures will appear on the hill for what's expected to be the biggest Anzac Day dawn service ever. Sniffer dogs are running through the press centre. French soldiers with heavy weapons are patrolling the grounds. The rain is holding off.

There is an Australian headstone that one or two may see as they leave in daylight or glimpse for a few seconds projected on the underground walls of the centre. It's the grave of twenty-four-year-old Private W.L. Rae on which his parents paid to have inscribed: Another life lost hearts broken for what.

*

At the Last Post we dug out our ponchos. First the bugler and then the padre brought down the rain. Our discomfort was complete. Only one umbrella rose above the congregation at the dawn service at Villers-Bretonneux. It sheltered the Prince of Wales.

That's royalty. The rules for everyone else were terribly strict. We handed in our umbrellas in at the gate. But not HRH and, edging in for a little shelter, were Malcolm Turnbull on one side and Édouard Philippe on the other. And, as the rain fell, there rose from the ground the absolutely authentic stench of blood and bone.

Dawn services are indestructible. We know what they are about: speeches, music and wreaths. And suffering together in the open is so much part of it all: showing we, too, can endure even if only a cold, wet morning in northern France. As they say in the theatre world: it's a long sit.

The Prince of Wales had appeared like a ghost out of the shadows at 4.45 am. He has grown old waiting and looks more than ever like his Mountbatten cousins. He performs his chores with perfect goodwill but his face has the look of a man a little distracted, perhaps by matters of state. Everyone with an iPhone knew sunup was still two hours away.

What a great director could do with that time in such a setting and with such a purpose. Trim the speeches. Coordinate them so we don't get three or four descriptions of the battle that – in Australian eyes – turned the war around. And can we, please, do something on solemn occasions like this about the petty rules of politeness? How many times must Turnbull be announced at the microphone as "the Hon" and "MP"? Give us a break: he's simply "the prime minister, Malcolm Turnbull".

He was enjoying himself. There's a particularly mischievous grin he has and a way of rocking on his toes that signalled he was having the time of his life chatting to HRH and HE the PM of the French republic. Perhaps moments like these make being prime minister bearable for Turnbull. Up to his elbows in the grubby brawls of his party he can take heart that soon enough there will be another guard of honour to inspect and another chance to chat man to man with the leader of a nation two or three times our size.

They are his people.

What brings the crowd here? Patriotism and celebration but perhaps also to wonder whether any of this, in the end, will do the trick. Hardly anyone in this crowd would have been alive the last time Europe mobilised against itself. But can these ceremonies, these monuments and museums, save us from another war?

"Please remain in your seats," ordered Major General Mark Kelly AO DSC as hundreds of wreaths were laid in the rain. This commemoration went on and on as every name of every family and organisation was carefully announced and yet more flowers were brought forward. But up in the stands the ranks began to break. It was perhaps the worst insurrection in these parts since the British 5th Army broke in the face of Ludendorff's advance. "Remain in your seats," begged the general but the crowd had made up its mind.

The sun was up and the rain was coming down again. It was time for breakfast, time to find somewhere dry and warm. Leaving the official party in the lurch, the crowd headed for the buses, reclaiming their umbrellas on the way.

The Guardian, 25 April 2018

Falling in love again

FOR A MOMENT MY EXHILARATION was mixed with rage. The crowd in Prince Alfred Park was cheering. The place had gone off. Applause was rolling across the country. Even in the newsroom of The Australian there was whooping when the news came through – yes: 61.6 per cent.

But I was furious, too. How could we have been put through this wretched exercise? Why has politics in this country been for so long in the grip of preachers and moralising politicians obsessed with doom, sin and sex? They long ago lost the numbers but they never lost their clout. Whatever mayhem they provoke over the next weeks, equal marriage will become law. And when that's done and dusted they may, at last, lose their power to make change so hard in this country.

This is shaping as a double victory. The doomsayers have their constituency, one that cannot be ignored. But today's result said once again and emphatically, they don't speak for Australia.

But for a couple of grim days in September when *The Guardian* Essential poll suddenly slid away, the victory for yes was never in doubt. Even so we've been anxiously talking numbers for months. How high could the yes vote be? Might it reach the seventies? Could we live with something in the fifties? The result loomed as a verdict on Australia. It would put a figure on our commitment to fairness and good sense, to our freedom from old bigotry and even where we stand in the twenty-first century. But this morning it suddenly felt personal. I had a nasty sense of waiting for my exam results. I haven't felt that for more than forty years. This was a national verdict about my lot, too. That fed my anger.

But we passed: the nation gave itself not quite a credit but a good sound pass. And we – the country and its LGBTI community – will never feel the same about ourselves again. Just look at the scoreboard. Those figures are better than they seem. They have to be read against an old truth: Australians are easy to scare. The fear of where changes might lead is so strong here that it defeats nearly every attempt to fix our rackety constitution. It sets its problems in stone. That was the fear the no case tried to mobilise with its claptrap about religious freedom.

It looks as though it worked, to some extent. The $10 to $15 million spent by the no case seems to have knocked two to three per cent off the vote. No doubt they reckon it was money well spent. But it was not enough to defeat a nation determined to settle this matter for ourselves, not one way or another but with an emphatic yes. This was our vote, our verdict. It's not a gift from above. Canberra stood aside. We did it for ourselves when the politicians lost their nerve.

I've fallen in love with my country all over again.

For old men like me this is another step on a once-unimaginable journey. Sex was a crime when I made my first stumbling entry into the gay world. Even when those crimes were wiped from the books, so much complicated shame was left to be negotiated. The business of coming out was endless. The smothering respectability of official Australia back then came back to sex. It was all about sex.

But censorship collapsed. The press relaxed. Queers began to be accepted in public life. The obvious became unremarkable. Australia became a better place. We could put our energies where they mattered. Today's result is fresh proof we live in a wonderfully muddled, lively society that happily accepts all sorts of confusion and contradiction. We're real, relaxed and alive.

We're not busting to be pure. That's the mission of the reactionaries who are with us always, and always obsessed with sex. I've listened to the likes of Lyle Shelton and Eric Abetz for forty years, and all they ever bang on about is sex. Their grim message is always the same: change the sex rules and the roof falls in. The roof is up there still, secure as ever, yet that's all they're preaching now.

I'm not surprised they waited until the voting was over before letting us see their draft legislation. God's work can call for sly measures. They knew the bill wasn't a vote winner. They didn't want its outrageous demands debated when that might affect the nation's verdict. So they waited, hoping that in the end equal marriage will be decided where the preachers and ultra-conservatives have had such success in the past: in the corridors of parliament. They demanded equal marriage be decided by the people but they didn't trust the people. Plain bad faith.

And on the issue of pious bakers for one last time: not even the craziest Christians claim it's a sin to bake a cake, or drive a limo or rent stack-away chairs with white satin covers to a couple of poofters getting married. We're not talking damnation here, just discomfort. And for that they want to collapse the anti-discrimination laws of the nation.

How do we treat the losers? With the understanding they don't extend to the rest of us. And while they furiously lament the result, we should remember another old truth about Australia: change is fought hard here but when it comes we settle down with it quickly. In a few months, we will be faintly puzzled that same-sex marriage was the subject of such prolonged, expensive and painful contest. It has been a terrible time for many in the LGBTI community – young and old – in the last few months. But it has been this too: a fresh time for coming out.

What a parade Australia has seen of citizens making the most politically effective argument of all: I'm one too. And then most of the rest of the country took a ballot paper to a letterbox to make it clear that's just fine by them.

I'm off to celebrate a big day in a wonderful, at times perplexing, country. My country more than ever. Here's a last truth about this place we demonstrated today: we always come good in the end.

The Guardian, 15 November 2017

Once is enough

I AM, OF COURSE, COCK-A-HOOP about the *Marriage Amendment Act*. Couldn't be happier. Wept on television. How good it was to see the last division in parliament that afternoon – the yes side of the House as packed as the Royal Easter Show and on the other side four lonely figures voting no. After all these months of ugly blather let's never forget that sight: the forces we are up against can be counted on one hand with a thumb to spare.

By late that night my man and I had been offered a cake, a venue and a DJ for our wedding. But we're holding back. We have no plans. I'm not proud of the reason for this. It's not just the embarrassing prospect of Sebastian and me kitted out in matching tuxedos, with matching carnations and matching flowers. I'm terrified of the ceremony itself.

You see: I've been married, and that midwinter day in Queensland in 1975 remains the most troubling day of my life by a long, long way; the day I came face to face – not before time and not without chemical assistance – with the Inescapable Truth.

I was a bit embarrassed by the whole thing so the wedding was a small affair: just a few family and a few friends at a weatherboard church in Montville, which in those days was still a pretty village on a high ridge behind the Sunshine Coast.

It was not one of those Australian weddings where the best man is in love with the groom. Not by a long shot. But who has not heard stories of what goes on between grooms and best men on their last nights together in bush motels? Who has not noticed sidelong glances at the altar as best men and grooms wait for the intrusive arrival of the bride? Not for us. I was standing there in an old tweed jacket at St Mary's Montville to set things straight.

Everything went perfectly: the ceremony, the photographs, lunch – a delicious spread – and then at about 3 o'clock our families disappeared, leaving Jennie and me and half a dozen friends on the verandah of what real estate agents these days call "a Queenslander" to enjoy the distant view, the afternoon sun and the wedding presents.

My wife of a few hours had an old schoolfriend from Firbank who turned hippie and was living with a man in the Dandenongs. They had come to the wedding not with Georg Jensen spoons but a little something for the bridal couple to while away the afternoon. "This is clearlight," she said, handing us little shards of gelatin. "It's just a taste. Just a taste." A few of us washed them down with warm champagne.

LSD was starting to seem old-fashioned by this time. We knew about the music, the t-shirts, the catastrophes. But what we didn't know about at this point – and would not learn for decades – were efforts by the CIA to use LSD as a truth drug. The aim? To break commie prisoners as a red tide threatened to sweep down through Asia. But after many years of scientific investigation the CIA abandoned Project MKUltra. I quote an internal report:

> By disrupting defensive patterns, LSD may sometimes be helpful in interrogation, but even under the best conditions it will elicit an output contaminated by deception, fantasy, garbled speech, etc. No such magic brew as the popular notion of a truth serum exists ...

All I can say to the CIA at this distance is: you didn't ask me.

Like marriage, the drug was a first time for me. How perfect that name clearlight seemed when, after a little, the sun paused to illuminate the landscape spread far below us, to stroke the little towns and farms, the remnant patches of forest and the distant ocean with a soft yet intense light – a quality of light I'd never noticed in my life, certainly never on the many occasions I'd looked down on the Sunshine Coast from the heights of Montville.

I have an urge – an unfortunate urge – to point out beauty to anyone in my vicinity. It's a compulsion I can't fight. I feel the need to place at the service of others my remarkable eye for beautiful landscapes, beautiful books, beautiful people, beautiful *everything* ...

"Look at Nambour," I said. And there was gentle, knowing laughter along the verandah. Not yet celebrated as the birthplace of Kevin Rudd, the sugar refinery belching smoke into the late afternoon air, Nambour did seem at that moment ravishingly beautiful in the distance.

And then came the moment of truth. I had been married not five hours and with perfect clarity – yes, chemically assisted clarity – I knew what I had done was wrong. The wedding was a mistake. A life mistake. Yet I felt absolutely calm, almost relieved, as the certainty of my blunder settled on me.

In my research for this speech – for I was determined it would be more than confessional – I came across the words of an American psychoanalyst called Sidney Cohen, an early LSD researcher and mate of Aldous Huxley. He captured exactly my mood late on my wedding day: "The problems and strivings, the worries and frustrations of everyday life vanished," he wrote. "In their place was a majestic, sunlit, heavenly inner quietude." Exactly. And a heap of trouble.

The only drug I recommend to anyone these days is Panadol. I could never endorse LSD, not after all I've read and all that happened on that Montville afternoon over forty years ago. I didn't have terrifying hallucinations. I didn't see the world ending in a rain of toads. I didn't jump out a window. I faced the truth that I was queer. It would have come, of course. Inevitably. But did it have to come on my wedding day?

Twenty years later I met the man who has been my partner ever since. We backed the campaign for equal marriage. And once it was all settled, all done and dusted, our friends assumed we would marry. For a few hours it seemed like the right idea. I would ask my straight best man to be best man again. I would insist on gifts.

But then I thought of the last time and hesitated. Jennie has died. That old Queenslander was demolished years ago to make way for a shopping centre. Nambour remains down there in the valley as ugly as ever. Even as the public gallery in the House of Representatives burst into song after the final vote on the bill I thought of Nambour. It just popped into my head: Nambour as a warning.

My man isn't keen to wed. "We've had our ceremony," he said and he was right. A couple of years after we met, we were on the dance floor at

Mardi Gras. Who spoke first we can't now remember. But in the face of that congregation of thousands and with the perfect sobriety that comes at about 3 am on such nights, we agreed: "We're married."

Queerstories, Sydney, 19 January 2018

Notes on editing

This is a collection of journalism, speeches and essays. I've chosen to republish almost nothing from my books. Many pieces here have been trimmed. To one or two I've taken an axe. I've untied a few knots in the prose and corrected slips here and there. Newspaper pars have become book paragraphs. Otherwise I've aimed to keep these pieces as much as possible as they were when published in *The Bulletin*, *The National Times*, *The Sydney Morning Herald*, *Overland*, *The Monthly* and as Quarterly Essays. Chris Feik edited this book with the determination and impeccable taste he has brought to all the work we have done together over the last decade. He was assisted by Dion Kagan, a young man with laser eyes. Thanks to my old friend Patrick Cook for permission to reproduce his brilliantly combative cartoon "Harry Seidler Retirement Park", to Text for permission to republish a section of *The Henson Case*, and to Allen & Unwin for permission to republish "Shame and Forgiveness", the opening chapter of *The High Price of Heaven*, a few paragraphs from Barwick and "Afterlife", my chapter in Susan Wyndham's beautiful collection *My Mother, My Father*.